THE COURAGE
TO ACT

THE COURAGE TO ACT

A MEMOIR OF A CRISIS AND ITS AFTERMATH

BEN S. BERNANKE

W. W. NORTON & COMPANY

Independent Publishers Since 1923

NEW YORK | LONDON

For information about permission to reproduce selections from this book, write to
Permissions, W. W. Norton & Company, Inc., 500 Fifth Avenue, New York, NY 10110

For information about special discounts for bulk purchases, please contact
W. W. Norton Special Sales at specialsales@wwnorton.com or 800-233-4830

Manufacturing by RR Donnelley Westford
Book design by Chris Welch
Production manager: Devon Zahn

ISBN 978-0-393-24721-3

W. W. Norton & Company, Inc.
500 Fifth Avenue, New York, N.Y. 10110
www.wwnorton.com

W. W. Norton & Company Ltd.
Castle House, 75/76 Wells Street, London W1T 3QT

1 2 3 4 5 6 7 8 9 0

CONTENTS

PART III. AFTERMATH

AUTHOR'S NOTE

In all crises, there are those who act and those who fear to act. The Federal Reserve, born of the now little-known Panic of 1907, failed its first major test in the 1930s. Its leaders and the leaders of other central banks around the world remained passive in the face of ruinous deflation and financial collapse. The result was a global Great Depression, breadlines, and 25 percent unemployment in the United States, and the rise of fascist dictatorships abroad. Seventy-five years later, the Federal Reserve—the institution that I have dedicated the better part of my adult life to studying and serving—confronted similar challenges in the crisis of 2007–2009 and its aftermath. This time, we acted.

The title of this book was inspired by my colleagues at the Federal Reserve, policymakers and staff alike. When the economic well-being of their nation demanded a strong and creative response, they mustered the moral courage to do what was necessary, often in the face of bitter criticism and condemnation. We were joined in the fight by others in government—the leaders and staff of the Treasury Department under two administrations deserve special note—as well as many of our counterparts at central banks and finance ministries around the world. I am grateful to all of them and proud to have been part of the global effort to contain the most dangerous economic crisis of our time.

I am most grateful, however, to my wife, Anna, the love of my life, for suggesting the book's title—and for so much more, as will become clear.

I Can Still Stop This . . .

I t was 8:00 p.m. Tuesday, September 16, 2008. I was exhausted, mentally and emotionally drained, but I could not sit. Through the windows of my office in the Federal Reserve's Eccles Building, I could see the lights of the traffic on Constitution Avenue and the shadowy outlines of American elms lining the National Mall. Dozens of staff members remained at work, but the corridor immediately outside my door was hushed and empty. Michelle Smith, the head of our communications office and my chief of staff, sat quietly, the only other person in the room. She was waiting for me to say something.

FOUR HOURS EARLIER, Treasury secretary Hank Paulson and I had sat side by side in tan leather armchairs in the windowless Roosevelt Room of the White House, steps from the Oval Office. A portrait of Teddy Roosevelt as Rough Rider on a rearing horse hung above a fireplace. Facing Hank and me across the room's polished wood table sat the current occupant of the White House, a somber George W. Bush, with Vice President Dick Cheney at his side. The president's advisers, Hank's senior aides, and representatives of other financial regulatory agencies filled the remaining dozen seats around the table.

Usually, the president liked to keep things light at meetings, by opening with a wisecrack or good-naturedly teasing a close adviser. Not that afternoon. He asked bluntly, "How did we get to this point?"

The question was rhetorical. We had been fighting an out-of-control financial crisis for more than a year. In March, the Fed had lent

$30 billion to help JPMorgan Chase save the Wall Street investment bank Bear Stearns from failure. In early September, the Bush administration had taken over Fannie Mae and Freddie Mac to prevent the collapse of the two companies responsible for financing roughly half of all residential mortgages in the United States. And just the day before, at 1:45 a.m., Lehman Brothers—the nation's fourth-largest investment bank—had filed for bankruptcy, following a frantic and ultimately futile search for a merger partner led by Hank and New York Fed president Tim Geithner.

Now I found myself explaining to the president why the Federal Reserve was planning to lend $85 billion to American International Group (AIG), the world's largest insurance company. The company had gambled recklessly, using exotic financial instruments to insure securities backed by subprime mortgages. Now that those mortgages were going bad at record rates, the financial firms that had bought the insurance, together with other AIG counterparties, were demanding payment. Without the cash, AIG would go bankrupt within days, perhaps hours. We weren't motivated by any desire to help AIG, its employees, or its shareholders, I told the president. Rather, we didn't think that the financial system—and, more importantly, the economy—could withstand its bankruptcy.

Reacting to the Lehman failure, markets already were in the grip of a full-blown panic of an intensity not seen since the Depression. The Dow Jones industrial average had plunged 504 points on Monday—its steepest one-day point decline since September 17, 2001—the first day of trading after the September 11 terrorist attacks, and the selling wave had spread to markets worldwide. As confidence in financial institutions disappeared, interest rates on loans between banks had shot skyward. Ominously, we were receiving reports of both large and small investors pulling their cash out of money market mutual funds after a large fund suffered losses stemming from Lehman's collapse.

Everyone in the room knew that rescuing AIG would be terrible politics in a presidential election year. Just two weeks earlier, the president's own party had declared flatly in its 2008 convention platform, "We do not support government bailouts of private institutions." The Federal Reserve's proposed intervention would violate the basic principle that companies should be subject to the discipline of the market and that the government should not shield them from the consequences of their mistakes. Still, I knew that, as chaotic as financial conditions were now, they could become unimaginably worse if AIG defaulted—with unknowable but assuredly catastrophic consequences for the U.S. and global economies.

With more than $1 trillion in assets, AIG was more than 50 percent larger than Lehman. It operated in more than 130 countries and had more than 74 million individual and corporate customers worldwide. It provided commercial insurance to 180,000 small businesses and other corporate entities employing 106 million people—two-thirds of American workers. Its insurance products protected municipalities, pension funds, and participants in 401(k) retirement plans. AIG's collapse could well trigger the failures of yet more financial giants, both in the United States and abroad.

The president, grim-faced, listened carefully. Paulson had warned him earlier in the day that action on AIG might be necessary, and he knew that our options were severely limited. No private investors were interested in buying or lending to AIG. The administration had no money and no authority to rescue it. But the Fed could lend to AIG to keep it afloat if the company's many subsidiaries retained enough value to serve as collateral for the loan.

Bush responded as he had consistently during the financial crisis, by reiterating his trust in Hank's and my judgment. He said that we should do what was necessary, and that he would do what he could to provide political cover. I was grateful for his confidence, and for his willingness to do the right thing regardless of the likely political consequences for himself and his party. Having the president's support was crucial. At the same time, essentially, the president was telling Paulson and me that the fate of the U.S. and global economies was in our hands.

OUR NEXT MEETING, at half past six that evening at the Capitol, had been even tougher. Hank and I gathered with congressional leaders in a cramped conference room. House Speaker Nancy Pelosi wasn't able to attend the hastily arranged gathering, but Senate majority leader Harry Reid and House minority leader John Boehner were there, along with Senate Banking Committee chairman Chris Dodd, House Financial Services Committee chairman Barney Frank, and several others.

Hank and I again explained AIG's situation and our proposed response. We were besieged with questions. The lawmakers asked about the Fed's authority to lend to an insurance company. Normally, the Fed is empowered to lend only to banks and savings institutions. I explained a Depression-era provision of the Federal Reserve Act— Section 13(3)—that gave us authority in "unusual and exigent circumstances" to lend to any individual, partnership, or corporation. The lawmakers wanted to understand the consequences of letting AIG fail and how the loan would be paid back. We answered as best we could. Yes, we believed this step was necessary. No, we could make no guarantees.

As the questions began to die down, I looked over and saw Senator Reid wearily rubbing his face with both hands. Finally he spoke. "Mr. Chairman. Mr. Secretary," he said. "I thank you for coming here tonight to tell us about this and to answer our questions. It was helpful. You have heard some comments and reactions. But don't mistake anything anyone has said here as constituting congressional approval of this action. I want to be completely clear. This is your decision and your responsibility."

I RETURNED TO my office. Tim Geithner, who had negotiated the bailout deal, called with the news that AIG's board had agreed to our proposed terms. The terms were tough, for good reason. We didn't want to reward failure or to provide other companies with an incentive to take the types of risks that had brought AIG to the brink. We would charge a high interest rate on the loan and take an ownership stake in the company of nearly 80 percent, so taxpayers could benefit if the rescue worked. The Federal Reserve's own Board had approved the deal earlier that day. All we needed to do now was put out the press release.

But I needed a few moments to think about it all. I believed we were doing the right thing. I believed we had no other reasonable choice. But I also knew that sometimes the decision-making process acquires a momentum of its own. It was important to be sure.

Without doubt, the risks we would be taking were huge. Though $85 billion was an enormous sum, much more was at stake than money. If AIG failed even with the loan, the financial panic would intensify, and market confidence in the Fed's ability to control the crisis could be destroyed. Moreover, the future of the Fed itself could be at risk. Senator Reid had made clear that Congress would accept no responsibility. The president would defend us, but in a few months he would be out of office. If we failed, an angry Congress might eviscerate the Fed. I did not want to be remembered as the person whose decisions had led to the Fed's destruction.

I can still stop this, I thought, as I looked out at Constitution Avenue. The loan required unanimous Board approval, so all I would have to do would be to change my own vote. I said as much to Michelle and added, "We haven't announced anything."

If we acted, nobody would thank us. But if we did not act, who would? Making politically unpopular decisions for the long-run benefit of the country is the reason the Fed exists as a politically independent central bank. It was created for precisely this purpose: to do what must be done—what others cannot or will not do.

Michelle interrupted my thoughts. "We have to put something out," she said softly.

"Okay," I said. "It's got to be done. Let's look at the press release one last time."

It began, "For release at 9:00 p.m. EDT: The Federal Reserve Board on Tuesday, with the full support of the Treasury Department, authorized the Federal Reserve Bank of New York to lend up to $85 billion to the American International Group . . . "

PART I

PRELUDE

CHAPTER 1

Main Street

The morning of September 1, 2006, was drizzly and unseasonably cool. Our three-vehicle caravan pulled out of the horseshoe-shaped driveway of the Abingdon Manor, a bed-and-breakfast in Latta, South Carolina. The manor, a 104-year-old mansion built in the Greek Revival style, is a ten-minute drive south of my hometown—Dillon, South Carolina. Stuffed with antique furniture, fine linens, and chintz curtains, the old house evoked the tastes of affluent Carolinians of earlier generations. After a speech in Greenville, on the western side of the state—where the preacher delivering the benediction had asked God to aid me in my task of making the nation's monetary policy—I had spent the previous evening at the manor, dining and visiting with friends and family.

We pulled onto Highway 301 and headed toward Dillon. A local police car led the way. I sat in the backseat of the second vehicle, on the passenger side, as always. In front of me, next to the driver, sat Bob Agnew, the veteran agent in charge of the security detail. Dave Skidmore, a Federal Reserve media relations officer, sat to my left. Two more Federal Reserve security agents followed in the vehicle behind us.

At the polite but firm request of the security team, I had not driven a car in seven months. Bob and the agents of the Protective Services Unit were unfailingly friendly and courteous but always insistent on enforcing security protocols. They had been my constant companions since February 1, 2006, the day I was sworn in as the chairman of the Board of Governors of the Federal Reserve System. My predecessor,

Alan Greenspan, had described life in the security bubble aptly. It was, he had told me, like being under house arrest with the nicest jailers you could imagine. The agents—as well as cable television camera crews—would shadow my every step that day in Dillon. As a boy, I had roamed the town unaccompanied, pedaling my bicycle from home to the library or to my family's pharmacy at 200 West Main Street.

We were headed to 200 West Main that morning. The space was now occupied by Kintyre House, a casual restaurant with an exposed-brick wall and polished wood floors. Instead of stocking the magazine rack or guiding a customer to the shampoo as I would have forty years earlier, I would breakfast with twenty or so Dillon notables—mostly elected officials and business owners. We filled our plates from a buffet offering fruit, grits, eggs Benedict with prime rib, and challah French toast. I wasn't sure whether the challah was an allusion to my Jewish background, but, more importantly, I was glad to see that the breakfast attendees included both whites and African Americans. In the Dillon of my childhood, segregation was pervasive, with separate public restrooms and water fountains. The town's black citizens would not have been able to eat in this restaurant at all, much less as part of a group of local leaders. Todd Davis, the mayor of Dillon, and Johnny Braddy, a town councilman who had played trumpet opposite my alto sax in the school band, joined the breakfast.

It was the first event of Ben Bernanke Day in Dillon, which would culminate in a ceremony on the front lawn of the ninety-five-year-old red brick Dillon County Court House, a block from the restaurant. I received the key to the city from Mayor Davis and the Order of the Palmetto, South Carolina's highest civilian award, from Governor Mark Sanford. (Darius Rucker, lead singer and rhythm guitarist for the rock band Hootie & the Blowfish, had been a previous recipient.) I knew this award-giving was premature. I hadn't been in the job long enough to point to any real accomplishments. But to see so many classmates, neighbors, and former teachers sitting on folding chairs on the front lawn of the Court House was touching nonetheless.

I had not been to Dillon in nearly a decade—not since my parents, Philip and Edna, had retired and moved to Charlotte, North Carolina, where my mother had grown up and where my younger brother, Seth, now lived with his own family. As a teenager, I could hardly wait to leave Dillon. But as I grew older, and especially after entering the Washington policy world, my thoughts often returned to my hometown. It was where I had learned about hard work, responsibility, and respect for others. When you work in an ornate government building, poring over faceless statistics and making grand plans, it can be too easy to forget where you came from. This day was a reminder. After the brief ceremony, I shook hands for an hour, desperately trying to put names to faces.

DILLON, WITH A POPULATION of about 6,500, lies just west of the Little Pee Dee River, which meanders through the farms, pine forests, and swampland of northeastern South Carolina. Established in 1888, Dillon is the seat of a county of the same name. The nearest town of any size, Florence, with a population of less than 40,000, is about twenty-five miles away. For much of my childhood, we had to drive to Florence to see a doctor other than the local general practitioner, or even to see a movie.

Both the town and the county were named after James W. Dillon, a local merchant, banker, and cotton broker who headed a citizens' drive to bring a railroad line to the area. Completed the same year as Dillon's founding, the railroad opened the isolated area to the wider world. Amtrak's Palmetto passenger train, traveling between New York City and Savannah, Georgia, still stops in Dillon twice a day. But now a visitor is more likely to arrive via Interstate 95. Dillon's chief claim to fame today is South of the Border, a sprawling Mexican-themed tourist attraction just south of the state line. Wedding chapels and fireworks stores stand along the highway, strategically located to take advantage of South Carolina's more lax regulations.

By providing a shipping point for cotton and tobacco and later textiles, Dillon's railroad depot brought, for a while, a measure of prosperity. But by the time of my visit in 2006, Dillon had fallen on hard times. Tobacco, the area's most important cash crop, had mostly vanished after Congress dismantled federal price supports. The textile industry—facing increasing competition from imports—was disappearing as well. Public services reflected a shrinking tax base. A few years after my visit, in 2009, eighth-grade student Ty'Sheoma Bethea drew national attention to Dillon by writing to members of Congress pleading for help for her dilapidated school—a school I had attended forty years earlier.*

HARD TIMES HAD originally propelled my family toward, not away from, Dillon. My grandfather, Jonas Bernanke, ran a series of pharmacies in New York City during the Great Depression, without much success. In 1941, at the age of fifty, he spotted a for-sale ad for a drugstore in Dillon and decided to start over. He moved south with his wife and three sons, including my father, the middle son.

Jonas, a broad-shouldered cigar smoker with a deep voice and a stern manner, projected Hemingwayesque machismo and self-confidence. He named the drugstore Jay Bee Drug Co., a play on his initials. Like all four of my grandparents, he was an immigrant. He was born in Boryslaw in what is now western Ukraine but was then part of the Austro-Hungarian Empire. Drafted into the army of Emperor Franz Josef I during World War I, he served as a corporal, although his stories always made it sound as if he were an officer. Sent to the Eastern Front, he was captured by the Russians. At war's end he somehow made his way from a prison camp in Siberia, near Vladivostok, to Shanghai,

---

* Her plea succeeded. President Barack Obama invited her to sit with First Lady Michelle Obama during his February 2009 address to Congress requesting economic stimulus funding. A new school, financed mostly by federal loans to be repaid by a county sales tax increase, opened in September 2012. However, a few months later, Ty'Sheoma had to leave Dillon temporarily when her mother lost her welding job at a local factory and moved to suburban Atlanta.

and from there back to Europe via a steamship to Marseilles. In 1921, Jonas decided to try his luck in America. He and my grandmother, Pauline, known as Lina, steamed from Hamburg, Germany, to Ellis Island with 957 other passengers aboard the SS *Mount Clinton*. They arrived on June 30. Jonas was thirty. Lina was twenty-five and pregnant with her first child, my Uncle Fred. The ship's manifest noted that they were steerage class passengers and that each was bringing $25 into the country.

Lina was remarkable in her own right. Born in Zamość, Poland, near the border with Ukraine, she had earned a medical degree in 1920 at the prestigious University of Vienna. After arriving in New York, she launched a small medical practice among Jewish immigrants on the East Side, while Jonas studied pharmacology at Fordham University. But Jonas's decision to move the family south ended Lina's medical career, since South Carolina did not recognize her European credentials. I recall Lina as extremely intelligent, with refined European tastes. She was unhappy in Dillon, doubtless feeling out of place in the Bible Belt culture of the rural South of the 1940s and 1950s. Her marriage to Jonas, who could be volatile, was (as best as I could tell at my young age) often stormy. She raised her boys, and then in later life—especially after Jonas died, in 1970, of a heart attack—occupied herself with reading and painting. Like many assimilated European Jews, neither she nor Jonas had much use for traditional religious practice, although they occasionally attended services in Dillon's small synagogue.

In their lack of interest in religious observance, Lina and Jonas contrasted strongly with my mother's parents, Herschel and Masia Friedman (Americanized as Harold and Marcia). Herschel and Masia were orthodox Jews who kept a kosher home and strictly observed the Sabbath. They immigrated to the United States from Lithuania around the outbreak of World War I and had lived in Portland, Maine, and Norwich, Connecticut (where my mother was born in 1931), before moving to Charlotte, North Carolina—a two-and-a-half-hour drive from Dillon. Today Charlotte is a major banking center surrounded by affluent suburbs, but when my grandparents lived there it was sleepy and a bit down-at-the-heels. My first extended visit to their home came when I was three years old, when my parents took my infant sister, Nan, who was born with a heart defect, to Johns Hopkins Hospital in Baltimore for treatment. The treatment was unsuccessful, and Nan died at age three months. I spent a week with the Friedmans every summer until Masia's death in 1967, when I was thirteen. Afterward, Herschel moved to Dillon and lived at our house. He died at age ninety-four or ninety-five. He wasn't sure of his age himself; his parents manipulated their records to keep him out of military service.

Herschel was a kosher butcher, a Hebrew teacher, and the *baal koreh* (professional Torah reader) at Temple Israel, an old Charlotte congregation affiliated with the Conservative movement, which balanced acceptance of modernity with traditional observance. A Talmudic scholar, Herschel, besides his accented English, spoke multiple European languages and was fluent in Hebrew, Yiddish, and Aramaic. During summer visits, he taught me to play chess and to read and translate biblical Hebrew. He taught me to read and interpret some portions of the Talmud as well, but I didn't have the patience for its complexities. To reinforce Herschel's lessons, Masia would have me "teach" her Hebrew that she knew perfectly well.

In contrast to Lina, Masia was warm and outgoing—everything a boy could want in a grandmother. On pleasant summer evenings in Charlotte I would sit and talk with her for hours on the front porch. I trace my lifelong interest in the Great Depression to her stories of life in Norwich during the early 1930s. The family was proud they could buy new shoes for their children every year, thanks to Herschel's job in a furniture store. Other children had to go to school in worn-out shoes or, according to my grandmother, even bare feet. When I asked her why their parents didn't buy them new shoes, she said their fathers had lost their jobs when the shoe factories closed. "Why did the factories close?" I asked. She replied, "Because nobody had the money to buy shoes." Even a small boy could see the paradox, and I would spend much of my professional career trying to better understand why deep economic depressions occur.

Grandma Masia cooked in the traditional Eastern European Jewish style. She made matzo ball soup from scratch, brisket, and tzimmes (a sweet stew of carrots and yams). On May 23, 1958 the *Charlotte Observer* featured her recipe for blintzes. I was quoted in the article as asking, "Grandma, why don't you teach my mommy to make blintzes?" I was four and a half years old, and it was my first recorded statement to the media. But it was not the last time that I would come to regret making an unguarded comment to a journalist.

My father was fourteen when his family moved to Dillon from New York City. He must have found the move disorienting, but we never spoke of it. In many ways he was the opposite of his imperious, barrel-chested father: physically slight (I doubt he ever weighed more than 125 pounds), shy, and gentle. He graduated from high school in Dillon and served in the navy during the last year of World War II. Except for a brief stint on a destroyer, he came no closer to the action than Reno, Nevada, where he was assigned to manage the post exchange. My father enjoyed the irony of having spent his navy career in the Nevada desert.

Philip met my mother, Edna, after the war, while pursuing a master's degree in drama at the University of North Carolina at Chapel Hill. She was a student at the Women's College of the University of North Carolina, now the University of North Carolina at Greensboro. He fell in love with her, but I think he also fell in love with the warmth of her religious family. He longed for community and a sense of belonging that had been absent from the austere atmosphere of his own home. My parents were married in Charlotte on June 15, 1952.

In our home, my mother preserved the traditions of her own parents, making sure that we observed the Jewish holidays and keeping a kosher kitchen in Dillon. Our meat was frozen and shipped by bus from Charlotte. My father was not strictly observant; for instance, he worked in the drugstore on Saturday, the Jewish Sabbath. But he embraced Jewish culture. He would sit in his chair in the evening, with a yarmulke on his bald head, reading books on Jewish philosophy and history. And, taking a break from work on Saturday, he enjoyed leading the family in singing the traditional blessings after lunch. While my father relished those lengthy blessings, my siblings and I raced to see how quickly we could complete them. We sounded like those disclaimers at the end of drug commercials.

While my father, like his mother, was a devotee of the arts and philosophy, my mother was, though intelligent, not particularly intellectual. She was hard-headed, pragmatic, a stickler for appearances—and a worrier. She worried how I was doing in kindergarten and sent my father to check on me. When I left home to attend Harvard University, she worried about whether I had the clothes and social skills to fit in. She must have had in mind the Harvard of the 1950s rather than the Harvard of torn blue jeans and protest rallies that I experienced in the early 1970s. And, in 2014, as I prepared to leave the Federal Reserve, she worried whether at age sixty I would be able to drive myself safely after an eight-year absence behind the wheel. (So far, so good.)

She and Philip, newly married, moved to North Augusta, South Carolina, where my father worked as the manager and stage director of a community theater. My parents were living there when I was born, on December 13, 1953, on the other side of the Savannah River, in Augusta, Georgia. They named me Ben Shalom—son of peace, in Hebrew. With a wife and child to support, my father realized he would need to earn more money. He returned to Dillon to work for his father at the drugstore. His brother Mortimer—two years younger—was already working there.

My father learned pharmacology on the job and later passed the state licensing exam. Over time his theater days became a source of nostalgia, and whenever we went to the movies he would comment on various aspects of the direction and acting. Unlike his mother, however, who felt that her ambitions had been thwarted, he didn't seem embittered. He believed that he was doing what he needed to do, and he worked diligently to be the best pharmacist he could be, studying up on new treatments, medications, and vitamins. In a town with few doctors, he was known as "Doctor Phil"—and my uncle as "Doctor Mort." My father thought of himself more as a health-care provider than as a shopkeeper and, a half century before the CVS pharmacy chain stopped selling tobacco, Jay Bee Drugs did not sell cigarettes. He worked six days a week, often seven if emergency prescriptions needed to be filled on a Sunday. Typically I did not see him for dinner.

My mother, after spending an unsatisfying year teaching the fourth grade in Dillon, left to be a homemaker and worked half-time as the pharmacy's bookkeeper. As a small boy, I was often left in the care of Lennie Mae Bethea, a black woman my parents employed to clean and cook. (She must have been one of the few black women in South Carolina well versed in the rules of keeping a kosher kitchen.) Although my parents always treated Lennie Mae respectfully, I was aware of the social distinctions between us, probably in part because Lennie Mae herself was so aware of those distinctions. As a child, I once innocently referred to her as our maid. "I ain't nobody's maid," she told me. "I'm the housekeeper." Lennie Mae worked for my parents until well after I left home for college. When she was no longer able to work, my parents (as I would learn later) provided her with a pension.

After the loss of my infant sister, my parents had two more children: Seth, five years younger than me, and Sharon, two years younger than Seth. Given the age differences, I didn't spend a lot of time with my siblings, except when pressed into service as a babysitter. Today Seth is a worker's compensation lawyer and Sharon is an administrator at a music conservatory in Boston. As adults, we and our spouses visit often and sometimes vacation together.

THE DILLON OF our childhood looked like many other southern towns. It still does today. A commercial district of one- and two-story brick-front buildings stretched for a half-dozen blocks along Main

Street. During the 1960s, a mule-drawn wagon could still occasionally be spotted among the cars and trucks. Further east, Main Street narrowed and became leafy and residential, with some fine old homes. One housed the Dunbar Library, a favorite childhood haunt. Once a gracious two-story home, the library held a musty collection of mostly donated books. On Saturdays I would bike there and ride home with three or four books in my basket.

Our family home at 703 East Jefferson Street, a three-bedroom brick ranch, was situated in a middle-class neighborhood, five blocks north of the larger and older homes along Main Street. My father had bought the house from his father at about the time I was entering first grade, and we moved from a smaller house a half-mile away. All of our neighbors were white. Much of Dillon's substantial black population lived on the outskirts of town, along State Highway 57. Their houses were modest—some were mobile homes—and the streets unpaved. I didn't have occasion to visit that neighborhood until, as a teenager, I sometimes gave Lennie Mae a ride home.

I attended East Elementary School through the sixth grade. It was close enough that I could sometimes walk home for lunch. From seventh to eleventh grade I took the bus across town to Dillon High, a few blocks from downtown and Jay Bee Drugs. During those years, I often walked to the drugstore after school. I'd do a little work but mostly I had the run of the place. I'd hang around and eat a candy bar, then catch a ride home with Moses, a black man with one arm who was employed by my father to deliver prescriptions. During the summers, my father paid me 25 cents an hour to work half days. I started out sweeping up, stocking shelves, and unpacking magazines. Eventually I was entrusted to work the cash register.

My academic career began auspiciously. I spent only two weeks in the first grade and, after it became clear that I already could read and add and subtract, was moved to second grade. I remember seeing a book on my parents' shelves, with a title something like *Your Gifted Child*. I was six. I knew perfectly well what it was about.

At the age of eleven, I won the state spelling bee and a chance to compete in the National Spelling Bee at the Mayflower Hotel in Washington, D.C. I wanted to win because the winner would be introduced from the audience on the *Ed Sullivan Show*. I finished a disappointing twenty-sixth out of seventy contestants, adding an "i" to the first syllable of the word "edelweiss," the name of an alpine flower. I had not seen the film *The Sound of Music*, which featured a song about edelweiss. By then, Dillon's only movie theater, where as a younger boy I had paid a quarter to watch double features, had closed.

As a fourth and fifth grader, I favored young adult novels, often about sports, and, in my early teens, science fiction. As I grew older I read more widely. Teachers gave me books and articles to read on my own. My high school didn't offer calculus, for instance, and I prepared for college math by working through the introduction to calculus in the Schaum's Outline Series. I never read the business pages of the newspaper; I couldn't relate to the stories.

I had many teachers whom I remember gratefully. In the fourth grade, I began taking saxophone lessons from the dedicated and indefatigable Helen Culp. She led a band—a marching band or concert band, according to the season—that gave me a low-pressure way to participate in the school community. Because of the band I was able to march at halftime during high school football games on Friday nights rather than attend the service at the synagogue.

Bill Ellis, a soft-spoken physics instructor, stoked my interest in science. As a high school junior, I won a prize for achieving the highest score in the state on the Scholastic Aptitude Test, and when asked to designate my favorite teacher, I named Mr. Ellis. My prize was a seventeen-day bus trip through something like eleven European countries—my first time out of the country.

John Fowler, my English teacher in high school, encouraged me to write. During my junior year, he submitted seven of my poems to a competition run by the University of South Carolina. When they were published in a collection called *The Roving Pen*, I began to imagine myself as a writer. My father had paid me a penny a line as a young boy to write stories. Perhaps already understanding economic incentives, I wrote the stories in a large hand. Later, I drafted two-thirds of a young adult novel about black and white kids forming friendships on a high school basketball team. I submitted it to a publisher and received a kind, encouraging rejection letter.

The theme of my unfinished novel reflected what I was about to experience in my own life. Through the eleventh grade, the schools I attended were for white children only, with only a few exceptions. But in 1970, Dillon opened a new, fully integrated high school, where I spent my senior year. For the first time in my life, I had black friends my own age. I quit Miss Culp's band to make time to edit and take photos for the class yearbook, was the valedictorian of the class of 1971, the new school's first, and was also voted most likely to succeed. I felt more part of school that year than I ever had. The new school and integration jumbled social relationships and broke up cliques.

My modest social successes of senior year were new for me. Although I had gotten along well with most of my classmates, I was bookish and shy and often on my own. One of my best friends in my early teens was Nathan Goldman, also Jewish. We shared common interests in both baseball and math. During summer evenings, we'd spend hours immersed in Strat-O-Matic baseball, a board game played with three dice and a card to represent each player. I had played Little League baseball for one season, mostly as a benchwarmer, but I often stayed up late listening to Los Angeles Dodgers games on my father's shortwave radio. I rooted for the Dodgers because their star pitcher, Sandy Koufax, was Jewish. I learned all the statistics of every Dodger player and lived and died with the fate of the team, especially when they played the despised San Francisco Giants. Sometimes, impatient for the late scores, I would call a friend at the local radio station and ask him to find out how the Dodgers had done.

Strat-O-Matic was designed to replicate the play-by-play action of real baseball and, through the course of a "season," would produce statistics not much different from real baseball statistics. It was one of my first experiences of thinking in terms of probability and statistics. Eventually, Nathan and I wanted something more sophisticated than the commercial board game. So we replicated, as best we could, the baseball dice game featured in a novel I had read at around age fourteen—*The Universal Baseball Association, Inc., J. Henry Waugh, Prop.*, by Robert Coover. The book is densely philosophical (its theme is the relationship between God and morality), but at the time I was most interested in the baseball game it described. That the main character in the story, the inventor of the game, was driven insane by his obsession with it somehow escaped my notice.

I got my bookishness and introversion from my parents. The extroverts in the family were Uncle Mort and my brother, Seth. We didn't travel much as a family, except for a week at Myrtle Beach, South Carolina, every summer—and even then, in the evening we'd all gather in silence in the family room, each with his or her nose in a book. My parents' social life, such as it was, centered on the small synagogue in town, Ohav Shalom, meaning lover of peace.

A synagogue plunked in the middle of a small southern town isn't quite the oddity it seems. Jews have lived in the region since before the Revolution, often making their living as merchants. In South Carolina, Jews had established a presence in the port city of Charleston by the early 1700s; they arrived in the Pee Dee region in the late 1800s, along with the railroad, opening stores in Dillon and nearby towns.

Temple Ohav Shalom, which, like Grandpa and Grandma Friedman's temple in Charlotte, was affiliated with the Conservative movement, was built in 1942. It was sustained on a shoestring budget by the work of a few families, including my own and Uncle Mort's.* We conducted our own services, occasionally borrowing a rabbi from nearby Florence. For the High Holidays each fall, we invited a student rabbi from the Jewish Theological Seminary in New York. Since my mother

---

* As the next generation moved away, however, the synagogue could not be sustained. The seven remaining members of Ohav Shalom, including Uncle Mort, agreed to close and sell it in 1993. Most of the proceeds went to Florence's Temple Beth Israel.

kept our home kosher, it generally fell to us to host him (always a him in those days). Thanks to Grandpa Friedman's Hebrew lessons I was able to lead services by the time I was eleven and I was well prepared for my bar mitzvah at age thirteen.

Around the time of my bar mitzvah, I began to question religion. I would argue with my father about the conflicts between religion and science, for example, sometimes getting under his skin. The subject got mixed up in teenage rebellion. But I wasn't much of a rebel, really, except for the long hair I sported as a high school junior and senior. My parents tried to expose me to Jewish life beyond Dillon, and I cooperated grudgingly. I spent some time at Jewish summer camps but disliked them intensely, not so much because they were Jewish but because I didn't like the mild regimentation of camp life. At thirteen, I spent six weeks at Camp Ramah in New York, where, in theory, campers spoke only Hebrew (nobody actually did). I spent most of my time in the library studying baseball box scores. I had a better experience when, at fourteen, I participated in a six-week United Synagogue Youth bus tour around the country. I not only got my first opportunity to see some of the rest of the country outside the South, I attended my first Major League Baseball game, in St. Louis.

In Dillon, Jews were a small minority but not often the object of prejudice. The white community reserved that role largely for blacks. Still, I knew I was different. As a boy in elementary school I was asked on several occasions by other children, quite innocently, I believe, if I had horns. (The belief that Jews have horns apparently derives from a mistranslation from Hebrew of a verse in Exodus, compounded by a Michelangelo sculpture that portrays Moses with horns.) As I grew older, I became aware that many of my peers, evangelical Christians, believed as a matter of doctrine—if they thought about it—that I was condemned to eternal damnation.

My family fit uneasily into the social fabric of Dillon, in a limbo somewhere between Christian whites and blacks. When I was very young, I didn't think much about racism and segregation. They were just part of my environment, seemingly normal, not something to be questioned. As I grew older, I became more aware of the inequities. I was exposed to what passed for progressive thinking at a few meetings of a Jewish youth group in Florence, where we heard presentations on race, prejudice, and anti-Semitism. So I took note that, when black teens began driving to the park near my house to play basketball, the city removed the hoops, making it impossible for anyone to use the court. And I was shocked when a high school friend, someone I thought of as a "nice kid," expressed satisfaction at the assassination of Martin Luther King in April 1968.

My parents never sat me down and explained the evil of racism in so many words. But I saw how they behaved. Jay Bee Drugs welcomed everyone in Dillon, white and black. (Even my overbearing grandfather Jonas, who seemed to hold everyone in equal contempt, served both blacks and whites at the soda fountain—unusual in the 1940s and 1950s.) My father and uncle offered advice, and credit, to everybody regardless of color, and they hired and promoted employees on the same basis. They believed that anyone who worked hard to feed his or her family, no matter how humble the work, deserved respect. Doctor Phil and Doctor Mort would sometimes have quiet talks with customers who had run up large bills, but they did not press those who clearly could not afford to repay.

On my visits back to Dillon as Fed chairman, it seemed to me that racial attitudes had improved immensely. The town leaders I met were both white and black. I sensed a spirit of mutual trust and cooperation. They shared the common goal of making Dillon a better place to live. Of course, people (and society) change slowly, and I am sure the attitudes of the past have not been washed away. But the direction of change was unmistakable.

THE GOOD RELATIONSHIPS my father developed with several generations of black families in Dillon benefited me in an unexpected way. Ken Manning, the accomplished son of a prominent black family whose members included an attorney and a local basketball star, took an interest in me. Ken had attended high school in Connecticut as part of a special program and had gone to Harvard for undergraduate studies. He was a graduate student at Harvard when I was finishing high school and would ultimately earn a doctoral degree there and go on to a long and distinguished career as a professor of the history of science at the Massachusetts Institute of Technology (MIT). Awakened to the opportunities afforded by education, Ken took it upon himself to convince me—and my parents—that I, too, should leave Dillon to go to Harvard.

Today one would expect middle-class parents to be eager to send their child to an elite college, but going to Harvard, or even leaving the Carolinas, was outside my parents' concept of what was feasible. The assumption was that I would go to a college nearer home. But during his visits to Dillon, Ken visited our home and talked earnestly to me and then to my parents. He stressed the importance of making the most of my academic talents and being exposed to the wider world. Ultimately, his boundless self-confidence and infectious laugh were hard to resist. I applied to Harvard, and several other Ivy League schools for good measure, while my parents nervously reviewed their savings in light of the $4,600 it would cost to attend Harvard my freshman year. One day after school the phone rang. The caller said he was from the Harvard admissions office. I had been admitted. Some of my classmates knew I had applied, so I assumed it was a practical joke and asked who it really was. It took a while for the caller to convince me the offer was genuine.

After I graduated from Dillon High, my parents strongly suggested I get a job to help pay Harvard's tuition. I walked the six blocks from our home to St. Eugene Hospital (now McLeod Medical Center), where construction was under way on a new building, and applied for work as a manual laborer. They hired me at $1.75 an hour even though I was five foot eight and weighed about 140 pounds. I came home after the first day covered in cement dust, too tired to eat. All I could do was sip water. I fell asleep in my chair. I remember helping to carry Sheetrock and, at first, sometimes having difficulty keeping up my end. Once I lost control of a wheelbarrow of fresh cement and dumped it in the wrong place. But over the summer I became much stronger and better able to pull my weight.

As a seventeen-year-old middle-class, Ivy League–bound son of a pharmacist, I didn't have a lot in common with my co-workers at the construction site. Most were older and either black or rural white. They called me Abercrombie. I got along with them pretty well, though, despite some initial hazing. When I was standing on the roof of the two-story building, near the edge, a daredevil co-worker with an unsubtle sense of humor unexpectedly grabbed me from behind, pushing but then holding on as I lost my balance. After a while, I was entrusted with jobs that took a bit more skill, including applying a layer of concrete to the walls underneath the eaves. Two of the crew members engaged in that task, African American brothers, had plans to start their own construction business. They tried to persuade me to join them as an apprentice. It was good money, they said, and in a few years I could be running my own crew.

THE SUMMER ENDED. My parents drove me to Florence. There I boarded a twin-propeller puddle jumper to Charlotte, where I would change planes for Boston. I arrived at the historic center of campus, Harvard Yard, not long before midnight, a suitcase in each hand. I took it all in. The Yard was filled with students—horsing around, calling to each other—and music. I put my suitcases down and, looking around at the looming facades, considered how unprepared I was for the changes I was about to face.

After a while I made my way to my dormitory suite on the fifth floor of Weld Hall, John F. Kennedy's dormitory a generation before me. I threw my suitcases on the lower level of the bunk bed I would be sharing, then sat down heavily on the floor, exhausted and overwhelmed. Students I didn't know were wandering in and out of the suite, calling to their friends. There were speakers in the window, blaring Jimi Hendrix into the Yard, and a couple of nickel bags of marijuana on the floor. "Don't you want to lock the door or something?" I asked my new roommates. "Don't worry," they said. Moments later, a uniformed police officer stood at the open door and looked down at me. I thought, "I have only been at Harvard for twenty minutes and now I am about to be expelled, probably arrested."

"Is that your stereo?" the officer asked. I noticed that he was a Harvard University policeman, not a member of the Cambridge police department. "Turn it down and take the speakers out of the window," he said. I said I would. Then he left.

I was a long way from Dillon.

CHAPTER 2

In the Groves of Academe

I felt more at home in Cambridge than I ever had in Dillon. Here, nothing seemed more important than ideas. I couldn't believe the range of topics listed in Harvard's thick course guide, from Sanskrit to biochemistry to medieval art. For the first semester, I picked math, physics, a creative writing seminar, Japanese history and culture, and a graduate course on Jewish history. I was curious about Asia, of which I knew little, and hoped the Jewish history course would offer me a new perspective on my heritage.

My suitemates on the top floor of Weld Hall included a football player, a Vietnam vet (whom we called "Sarge"), and a math prodigy. We were all a little nervous about how we would do in classes and whether we would fit in. A couple of my new friends and I enjoyed paging through a student "facebook," hoping to identify pretty freshman girls.* I got to know Cambridge, spent hours browsing in bookstores, went to cafés featuring folksingers and movie theaters showing Bogart and Bacall, and stayed up late playing bridge.

I was excited when classes began, but I did not at first appreciate how academically disadvantaged I was—especially compared with classmates from elite prep schools like Andover and Exeter and top-flight public schools like Bronx Science. I didn't have the background that my classmates had, especially in math and physics, and

---

* Three decades later, Harvard's facebook would inspire student Mark Zuckerberg to create the online social network of the same name.

I didn't know how to study. My wake-up call came when the grades were handed out for my first midterm exam in physics. The exam had started at 9:00 a.m. I had attended classes conscientiously but hadn't done much work outside of class. Not a problem, I thought. I got up early, around 7:30 a.m., so I could hit the books for forty-five minutes before taking the test—more study time than I had ever allotted for an exam in high school. Naturally, I flunked. The grades in my other courses were better but I did not distinguish myself.

I was saved by Harvard's quirky academic calendar. Fall classes ended before Christmas, but final exams were not given until mid-January. Between the holidays and exams was a stretch of several weeks, called the reading period, during which students were expected to complete term papers and study for finals. So when the holidays came, I packed up my textbooks and boarded a bus toward Dillon, worried and depressed. Once home, I slept, ate, and studied, and then, back at Harvard, studied more. As a result, I did well on the physics final, earning a B for the course, with grade inflation probably the moral equivalent of about a D-plus. I also received a B in Japanese history but As in the other courses. I was determined to improve.

Ken Manning, the person most responsible for my arrival in Cambridge, looked in on me from time to time, taking me to dinner to find out how I was doing. He was close to a Jewish family in suburban Brookline and invited me to High Holiday services—but he was more interested in the services at that point than I was. I would always be proud of my heritage but I would never return to being traditionally observant.

Harvard during my first year was still a center of protest against the Vietnam War. Two years before I arrived, in 1969, members of the Students for a Democratic Society took over University Hall, one of the oldest buildings on campus. Police with billy clubs and Mace ended the occupation. The protests were still going on when I arrived in 1971. One protest included days of round-the-clock drumming in Harvard Yard. At seventeen, with a small-town background, I was not political and more than a little naïve. I viewed the war protests with sociological detachment, as part of my education. Still, I was relieved when, in February 1972, toward the end of my freshman year, I drew a lottery number (335) that made it unlikely I would be drafted. As it turned out, it didn't matter. By 1973 the war was winding down and the draft had ended.

When school ended for the summer, I returned home to Dillon and waited tables at South of the Border. Alan Schafer, a member of one of Dillon County's few Jewish families, had established South of the Border as a beer stand in 1949. He took advantage of the fact that the neighboring North Carolina county restricted sales of alcohol. Over the decades, it grew into a square-mile complex with a motel and campground, a sombrero-shaped restaurant, an amusement park, a reptile lagoon, and shops selling fireworks, beach supplies, and souvenirs that were Yiddish-themed, mildly risqué, or both. Its billboards, once stretching as far north as Philadelphia and as far south as Daytona Beach, Florida, made use of politically incorrect images of South of the Border mascot Pedro and corny humor ("Don't Miss Pedro's Wedding Suite; It's Heir-Conditioned") to lure snowbirds from the Northeast.

While the entire enterprise seemed out of place in rural South Carolina, the Border provided hundreds of jobs to area residents. Few locals ate there; it was too expensive. Waiting tables was hard work, though far less grueling than construction. With tips, I made a lot more than I ever could have earned hauling Sheetrock. The job drew me out of my shyness. You had to talk to people if you wanted good tips. I discovered that southerners are friendlier than northerners (Yankees, we called them) but northerners tip better. I would work two summers there, driving my grandfather Herschel's 1964 Plymouth Valiant to and from the complex, and wearing a serape while on duty. My co-workers were a mix of fellow students, a few local teachers picking up extra money during the summer, and South of the Border veterans, mostly middle-aged women who waited tables year-round.

Race relations were still tense in Dillon in the early 1970s, but restaurants had been desegregated, and South of the Border had long
served all races. Near the end of one ten-hour shift, the hostess seated
a black couple in a section next to mine. The hostess apparently did not
realize that the waitress covering that section had clocked out. I should
have waited on them, but it was late and I, too, wanted to go home. So I
ignored them. They sat about twenty minutes. Finally, the man slapped
his menu on the table and the couple got up and left. During their
lifetimes they doubtless had been refused service elsewhere because
of their race; in all likelihood they assumed this time that it had happened again. Their race had nothing to do with it, but they didn't know
that. I still think about that moment with great regret. I wish I could
apologize to them.

I returned to school for my sophomore year and to a new dorm—
Winthrop House, my home for the rest of my stay at Harvard. Despite
my summer earnings, money was tight. A roommate and I made extra
cash by running a small grill in Winthrop's basement. We tossed burg-
ers and made milkshakes. The grill had a black-and-white TV, usually
tuned to a Bruins or Celtics game. Boston, then as now, was a great
sports town. Bobby Orr played for the Bruins, Dave Cowens and John
Havlicek for the Celtics, and Carl Yastrzemski for the Red Sox. We
went to games as often as we could, and for many years I would be a
die-hard Sox fan.

When I entered college, I had thought about majoring in math,
but it quickly became clear that I had neither the talent nor the preparation to compete with Harvard's best math students. In truth, my
problem was that I was interested in everything. In my mind, I cycled
from math to physics to history as possible majors. I had enjoyed the
creative writing course I had taken freshman year, as well as a Shake-
speare course I took as a sophomore, so I briefly considered becoming
an English major.

In the fall of my sophomore year, I made a last-minute decision
to take Ec 10, introductory economics, taught by the prominent con-

servative economist Martin Feldstein. Feldstein lectured to hundreds of students in a huge auditorium, and much of the real teaching took place in small sections led by graduate students or junior faculty. My section leader was Lee Jones, now a professor at Boston University. Jones was interested in the economies of developing countries, and he helped me see economics as an intellectually challenging subject that also might improve the lives of millions of people. I also liked that economics offered a way for me to combine my interests in both math and history. That spring I declared economics as my major.

After two years at Harvard, I had only taken the introductory course in economics. To catch up, I registered for four economics courses in the fall of my junior year. One of them, econometrics and statistical analysis, was taught by a senior professor, Dale Jorgenson, who would become my mentor. He was brilliant, with a cool temperament paired with a clipped way of speaking. And he was very good to me. He employed me as a research assistant for the next two summers, and he liberally dispensed career advice. Under his tutelage, I learned how to program a computer with punch cards and to build mathematical models of the economy.

At the time, the focus of much of Jorgenson's work was the economics of energy—an especially important topic during the 1970s, when sharp increases in the price of oil were inflicting both inflation and recession on the U.S. economy. My work with him was the basis of my senior thesis, in which I explored how government energy policies affected the performance of the overall economy. My undergraduate research also led to my first professional publication, written jointly with Jorgenson. We analyzed the effects of government-imposed natural gas price ceilings, concluding that they inhibited the development of new supplies of gas and thus were counterproductive. Jorgenson was invited to testify to Congress on the subject and he took me along.

My senior thesis was named 1975's best undergraduate economics thesis at Harvard and, despite the rough start my first semester, I graduated summa cum laude and Phi Beta Kappa. I also won a National

Science Foundation fellowship, which meant that the NSF would pay my tuition and expenses for the first three years of graduate school, wherever I chose to go. I set my sights on the Massachusetts Institute of Technology, whose PhD program in economics was widely viewed as the best in the world. I worried that Jorgenson would be upset if I chose MIT over Harvard but he said, "You need to go to the best place."

MIT, THOUGH NOT much more than a mile and a subway stop away, was very different from Harvard. Harvard reveled in its long history and its traditions. As far as I could see, MIT happily dispensed with such sentiments. Science and engineering dominated the culture and the curriculum, and students had little time for softer subjects. (Later, as a graduate teaching assistant, I taught a highly mathematical economics course to MIT undergraduates. When I asked a few students what led them to take the course, they informed me that it satisfied MIT's undergraduate humanities requirement.) As the joke about the MIT-Harvard divide went: A popular grocery store is situated about halfway between the two schools. A sign in front of the store advertised, "5 Cans of Soup for $1." A student walks in and asks, "How much for 10 cans?" The clerk replies, "Are you from Harvard and can't count or from MIT and can't read?"

MIT's economics program was housed in the Sloan School of Management, at the far eastern end of the campus, between Kendall Square and the Charles River. Today Kendall Square is filled with tech firms, upscale condos, and gourmet restaurants, but then it was a collection of rundown warehouses and other unimpressive structures. The gustatory scene was a greasy diner.

The existence of a top-notch economics program at an engineering school was a bit of an accident. The critical moment came in 1940, when a young Paul Samuelson—not yet having completed his doctorate—agreed to move to MIT from Harvard. Samuelson, who would go on to win the Nobel Prize and write the most influential economics textbook in history, had done foundational work as a graduate student in the application of sophisticated mathematical methods to economics. Samuelson's mathematical approach did not sit well with the old guard at Harvard—some residual anti-Semitism may also have been at play—and he left for MIT. He was followed by another future Nobelist, the growth theorist Robert Solow, in 1949. It was a time when mathematical and statistical methods were gaining greater prominence in economics, and MIT was the perfect place for a blossoming of quantitative approaches. When I arrived there in 1975, mathematical methods were well entrenched, but economics was in ferment over a new set of controversies, between Keynesian and New Classical economics.

Keynesianism, which Samuelson and Solow espoused, is based on the ideas of the famed British economist John Maynard Keynes. Keynes, in his search for a cure for the Great Depression, sought to develop a general explanation of economic booms and busts. His writings were often obscure, and historians of economic thought continue to debate "what Keynes really meant." But, at least as interpreted by his most influential followers, Keynesian analysis depends importantly on the notion that wages and at least some prices are "sticky"—that is, they do not adjust rapidly enough to always ensure full employment and full utilization of the capital stock (factories and equipment). In Keynesian theory, an unexpected decline in demand—say, a fall in business investment in new equipment or a reduction in government spending—can lead to increased unemployment, as companies, facing lower sales, reduce production and lay off workers.

Keynesians see stretches of unusually high unemployment, like the Great Depression, as a waste of resources that timely government action can ameliorate. In particular, Keynesians see fiscal stimulus (tax cuts or spending increases) and monetary stimulus (lower interest rates) as ways of restoring normal demand for goods and services and, consequently, ensuring full employment of labor and full utilization of the capital stock. They argue that fiscal and monetary policy should be used actively to fight recessions and unemployment.

Spurred by the advocacy of Samuelson, Solow, and other prominent economists, Keynesian ideas gained many adherents in the
1950s and 1960s. President Kennedy gave a Keynesian rationale when
he proposed a major tax cut, ultimately passed in 1964 under Lyn-
don Johnson, that was widely credited with kicking off the economic
boom of the 1960s. In 1971, President Nixon declared, "I am now a
Keynesian in economics." However, at the time I entered graduate
school, Keynesianism had fallen into some disrepute, at least among
academics. In part, the decline in Keynesianism's popularity in academia reflected the economy's poor performance in the 1970s, especially the sharp increase in inflation, which was blamed on excessive
government spending—for the Vietnam War and for President Johnson's Great Society programs—and monetary policy that was too easy
(interest rates kept too low for too long). Many economists also questioned Keynesianism's theoretical foundations. Why, for example,
are wages and prices sticky, as Keynesian models require, rather than
freely adjusting in response to supply and demand pressures? Keynesian models of the time did not have good explanations.

In response to the dissatisfaction, a group of economists led by
Robert Lucas of the University of Chicago, Thomas Sargent at the
University of Minnesota, and Edward Prescott, also of Minnesota,
all also future Nobelists, developed New Classical macroeconomics. Essentially, Lucas and his colleagues revived, in modernized and
mathematical forms, Adam Smith's classical "invisible hand" view of
self-adjusting markets—the idea that free markets produce socially
desirable outcomes even though each buyer and seller acts purely
out of selfish motives. They dropped the Keynesian notion of sticky
wages and prices, assuming instead that markets are always in supply-
demand balance, except perhaps in the very short run. If that's the
case, then recessions do not reflect a significant waste of resources,
as Keynesians believe. Rather, they are periods when the economy is
adjusting in a more or less optimal fashion to changes such as a slowdown in productivity growth.

In contrast to Keynesianism, New Classical economics took a dim view of both the need for and the effectiveness of government intervention in the economy. In particular, if wages and prices adjust rapidly to balance supply and demand, then monetary policy has at best only short-lived effects on output and employment.

New Classical economics was highly influential when I was in graduate school, in part because of its methodological innovations. However, many economists, while agreeing that traditional Keynesianism had shortcomings, were uncomfortable with the conclusions of New Classical economics, particularly the implication that monetary policy could have only fleeting effects on employment or output. This implication looked even less plausible during the early 1980s, when the Fed under Chairman Paul Volcker raised interest rates to very high levels in an effort to cool the economy and thus bring down inflation. Although Volcker's policies conquered inflation, they also produced a deep and sustained recession—a direct contradiction of New Classical economics, which says that should not happen.

Some researchers worked to incorporate the insights and technical advances of the New Classical school into a modernized Keynesianism. At MIT, they included Stanley Fischer, a young professor originally from Northern Rhodesia. Their work in melding New Classical and Keynesian ideas would lead to the so-called New Keynesian synthesis that undergirds the thinking of most mainstream economists today. Critically, New Keynesians, using new models and approaches, rehabilitated the view that sticky wages and prices can result in markets being out of supply-demand balance for a sustained period. They accordingly returned to the original Keynesian characterization of recessions as wasteful and restored roles for fiscal and monetary policies to help keep the economy close to full employment.

As a graduate student and a newcomer to these controversies, I was neither devotedly pro- nor anti-Keynesian. I wanted to see where my own intellectual journey would take me. Over time, I have become convinced that New Keynesian ideas, leavened with insights from other schools of thought, including elements of the New Classical approaches, provide the best framework for practical policymaking.

It was Stan Fischer who, near the end of my first year at MIT, most influenced the course of my studies. After taking his first-year class in macroeconomics and monetary policy, I went to talk to him about the possibility of focusing on those areas. Stan suggested some books, including *A Monetary History of the United States, 1867–1960*, by Milton Friedman and Anna Schwartz, published in 1963. He told me that the 860-page tome would either excite me or put me to sleep, and that I should draw the correct inference from my reaction.

I found the book fascinating. After having spent my first year in graduate school mostly absorbing mathematical methods, I particularly liked Friedman and Schwartz's largely historical approach. They looked at U.S. history over almost a century to try to understand how monetary policy affects the economy. In particular, they documented how three episodes of money-supply contraction by the Federal Reserve—one before the 1929 stock market crash and two in the early years of the Depression—had helped make the Depression as terrible as it was. After reading Friedman and Schwartz, I knew what I wanted to do. Throughout my academic career I would focus on macroeconomic and monetary issues.

MY LIFE CHANGED in another big way during those years. I met Anna Friedmann in October 1977, at the start of my third year at MIT, just as I was beginning work on my thesis. She was a senior, majoring in chemistry and minoring in Spanish at Wellesley College, fourteen miles west of MIT. We were set up on a blind date by Mike Smith, a roommate at Harvard and later my best man. Mike got the idea to introduce us from the young woman he was dating at the time, Nicole Ahronee, who lived on Anna's dorm floor. Nicole and Anna cooked a spaghetti dinner for Mike and me at Wellesley's center for international students. Dinner was followed by a game of Ping-Pong. As Anna would recall later, "Nicole thought I was very nerdy and she thought

Ben was really nerdy, so she thought we should meet." And, it helped that Anna was as warm and outgoing as I was shy and inward looking.

Anna and I had similar family backgrounds—we were both of Eastern European Jewish descent—but grew up under very different circumstances. Her parents, Otto and Lenka Friedmann, were Holocaust survivors. In 1943, recently married, they were living in Split, Yugoslavia, on the Adriatic Coast of what is now Croatia. Following the German occupation of Yugoslavia and the creation of a pro-Nazi Croatian puppet state, they had been making plans to leave, along with Otto's parents, his brother, and Lenka's mother. Someone banged on their front door in the middle of the night. Germans and their Croatian allies were rounding up Jews. They ran out the back door with nothing but the clothes on their back. With the assistance of Serbian partisans, they made their way north, walking over the Alps and into Italy. Otto's parents, his brother, and Lenka's mother didn't make it. They died in the Jasenovac concentration camp, run by the fascist Croatian regime.

Otto and Lenka settled first in Bari, a coastal city in southern Italy, where Anna's brother, Victor, was born in 1944. After the war, the family moved to Grottaferrata, a little town on the outskirts of Rome, where Anna was born in 1956. Following a crackdown by the Italian authorities on illegal immigrants, they immigrated to the United States while Anna was still a baby. The Friedmanns settled in Denver, where they had relatives.

Neither of Anna's parents graduated from high school. Nevertheless, education was paramount in the Friedmann household. Victor would graduate from Harvard, earn a master's degree at MIT, and become a petroleum engineer. Anna would attend Wellesley on a full scholarship, but only after Victor assured her parents that it was a top-flight school even though it admitted only girls. She majored in chemistry for her parents, but her true love was Latin American literature. She would introduce me to the writings of Gabriel García Márquez and Jorge Luis Borges.

I proposed to Anna two months after our blind date. We were

married on May 29, 1978, at Temple Israel in Boston, three days after Anna's graduation. We honeymooned in Italy, visiting the Friedmanns' home in Grottaferrata and meeting people Anna's parents and brother had known when they lived there.

Our first home together was a small, roach-infested apartment in a six-story tan-and-brown brick apartment three blocks from Harvard Square. My National Science Foundation grant had run out, and we lived on my teaching assistant stipend and what Anna earned working as a receptionist in an optometrist's office in Harvard Square. For entertainment, we budgeted $5 a week to play pinball together at a place across the street from our apartment.

As I worked to complete my thesis, I applied for teaching positions and was offered assistant professorships at Harvard, Stanford, and Princeton, among others. Anna, meanwhile, was accepted into several master's programs in Spanish literature. We agreed on Stanford.

During the summer before my job and Anna's program began, Anna and I shared a house near the Stanford campus with a graduate school friend, Jeremy Bulow. To help pay the rent, we invited Mark Gertler, an acquaintance of Jeremy's, to join us. Mark had earned his doctorate at Stanford a year earlier and had arranged to spend the summer there working on his research. Mark and I both were excited about beginning our careers and we found that we had many common interests. We talked for hours. It was the start of a long and fruitful collaboration and friendship.

My first challenge at Stanford was teaching. My position was in the Graduate School of Business rather than the economics department. At twenty-five, I was younger than many of the students, who had returned to school after several years spent working. They were skeptical of my youth and inexperience, probably rightly so. Often they were paying their own way and were looking for a good return on their tuition dollars. I had been trained largely in theoretical economics but I quickly learned to tie my lectures to things the students ultimately wanted to do. I asked them, for example, to analyze the economic policies of emerging-market countries and to think through the implications for investing or starting a business in those countries. The experience helped me approach economics in a more applied way. And I found that I was good at explaining things.

AFTER READING FRIEDMAN and Schwartz at MIT, I had become a Great Depression buff in the way that other people are Civil War buffs, reading not only about the economics of the period but about the politics, sociology, and history as well. But the essential question—the Holy Grail of macroeconomics, I would call it—was why the Depression happened, and why it was so long and deep. (It was basically the same question I had asked my grandmother as a boy in Charlotte.) Before Friedman and Schwartz, the prevailing view—based on John Kenneth Galbraith's 1954 book *The Great Crash, 1929*—was that the Depression was triggered by the speculative excesses of the 1920s and the ensuing stock market crash. Friedman and Schwartz showed that the collapse of the money supply in the early 1930s, rather than the Great Crash, was the more important cause of the Depression. The sharp decline in the money supply hurt the economy primarily by inducing a severe deflation (falling wages and prices). Prices in the United States fell by nearly 10 percent per year in 1931 and 1932. This violent deflation in turn led households and firms to postpone purchases and capital investments in anticipation of lower prices later, depressing demand and output. Moreover, the international gold standard, which created a monetary link among countries tied to gold, spread America's deflation and depression abroad.

Friedman and Schwartz's perspective was eye-opening, but I wondered whether the collapse of the money supply and the ensuing deflation, as severe as it was, could by itself explain the depth and length of the Depression. Unemployment in the United States soared to 25 percent in 1933, from less than 5 percent before the 1929 crash. It did not fall below 10 percent until the eve of the U.S. entry into World War II, even though the deflation occurred mostly prior to 1933. It seemed to me that the lack of credit after the collapse of the banking system had to have played a significant role in the slump as well. More than 9,700 of the nation's 25,000 banks failed between 1929 and 1933.

The notion that the failure of more than a third of the nation's banks in a five-year span would impede credit flows and damage the economy seems unremarkable today, but my first paper on the subject was greeted with skepticism at conferences and seminars. Many economists at the time saw the financial system as a "veil"—basically an accounting system that kept track of who owned what, not something that had significant independent effects on the economy. Surely, they argued, if a company's bank goes out of business the company will find financing somewhere else.

But, in reality, finding alternative financing may not be so easy. The collapse of a bank, resulting in the effective destruction of its accumulated experience, information, and network of relationships, can be very costly for the communities and businesses it serves. Multiply that damage by more than 9,700 bank failures and you can readily understand why the disruption of credit helps explain the severity of the Depression. It took some time to publish my paper, but finally, in June 1983, it appeared as the lead article in the *American Economic Review*, the profession's most prestigious journal.

A later paper, which I wrote with Princeton historian Harold James, supported my interpretation of the Depression in an international context. We looked at the experience of twenty-two countries during the Depression and found, basically, that two factors dictated the severity of the economic downturn in each country. The first was the length of time the country stuck with the gold standard. (Countries that abandoned gold earlier were able to allow their money supplies to grow and thereby escape deflation.) That finding was in keeping with Friedman and Schwartz's emphasis on the money supply. The second factor was the severity of the country's banking crisis, consistent with my view of the importance of credit as well as money.

Through much of the 1980s and 1990s, Gertler and I (later joined by one of his students, Simon Gilchrist, now of Boston University) worked on analyzing how problems in the financial system can exacerbate economic downturns. We identified a phenomenon we called "the financial accelerator." The basic idea is that recessions tend to gum up the flow of credit, which in turn makes the recession worse. During a recession, banks lend more cautiously as their losses mount, while borrowers become less creditworthy as their finances deteriorate. More cautious banks and less creditworthy borrowers mean that credit flows less freely, impeding household purchases and business investments. These declines in spending exacerbate the recession.

More generally, our work underscored the importance of a healthy financial system for the economy. For example, it implied that recessions are worse when households and businesses start with high debt levels, as falling income and profits make it more difficult for borrowers to pay their existing debts or to borrow more. Likewise, if a country's banking system is in bad shape at the outset of a recession, the downturn will likely be worse. In extreme cases like the Depression, a banking collapse can help create a prolonged economic slump.

The financial accelerator theory also helps explain why deflation is so harmful, in addition to the tendency of households and firms to defer purchases. If wages and prices are falling, or even if they are growing at unexpectedly slow rates, borrowers' incomes may not grow quickly enough to allow them to keep up with their loan payments. Borrowers under pressure to make loan payments will naturally reduce other types of spending, and their weaker financial conditions will make it harder for them to obtain additional credit. The deflation of the 1930s led to widespread bankruptcies and defaults, gravely worsening an already bad situation.

My reading and research impressed on me some enduring lessons of the Depression for central bankers and other policymakers. First, in periods of recession, deflation, or both, monetary policy should be forcefully deployed to restore full employment and normal levels of inflation. Second, policymakers must act decisively to preserve financial stability and normal flows of credit.

A more general lesson from the Depression is that policymakers confronted with extraordinary circumstances must be prepared to think outside the box, defying orthodoxy if necessary. Franklin Roosevelt, who took office in 1933, exemplified this by experimenting boldly in the face of an apparently intractable slump. Some of his experiments failed, such as the National Industrial Recovery Act of 1933, which tried to stop price declines by reducing competition in industry. But others proved crucial for recovery. Most notably, FDR defied the orthodoxy of his time by abandoning the gold standard in a series of steps in 1933. With the money supply no longer constrained by the amount of gold held by the government, deflation stopped almost immediately. Roosevelt also quelled the raging financial crisis by temporarily shutting down the nation's banks (a bank holiday), permitting only those judged sound to reopen, and by pushing legislation establishing federal deposit insurance. These measures brought intense criticism from orthodox economists and conservative business leaders. And they were indeed experiments. But, collectively, they worked.

AS MY SIXTH YEAR at Stanford approached, I began to think about my career options. Junior faculty generally either were awarded lifetime tenure after six years or moved on. The administration had let me know that my prospects were good. But on a visit to Stanford, Hugo Sonnenschein, an economist who was then provost at Princeton, urged me to consider joining Princeton's faculty instead. Alan Blinder, the best-known macroeconomist at Princeton, called as well. At Stanford, I had been promoted from assistant professor to associate professor without tenure in 1983. Now both Stanford and Princeton were offering me full professorships at age thirty-one.

Professionally, I liked both places, but Anna much preferred Princeton. Six years earlier, we had both been eager for a change from the Cambridge and Wellesley scene, and for the chance to live in California. Our son, Joel, had been born in December 1982, and Anna saw the leafy environs of Princeton as more conducive to family life. I was fine with the choice.

And so, in 1985, we moved across the country to Rocky Hill, New Jersey, a historic village of about seven hundred people four miles north of the Princeton campus. We bought a two-story colonial with a big yard and delighted in the view of an apple tree, a fig tree, and a huge rhododendron from the screened-in porch. It seemed as if all of the families on the block had children. They roamed from yard to yard. Our daughter, Alyssa, was born in June 1986. David and Christina Romer, junior economic faculty members at Princeton, lived a block from us and also were expecting.

After six years in Rocky Hill we moved to a larger house in Montgomery Township, about eight miles north of campus. We weren't alone. Families with children were pouring into the township, which was fast changing from a farming area into an exurb of New York City. The township's schools, which also served Rocky Hill, would soon be overwhelmed by rising enrollments. Anna and I were both educators (by then she was teaching Spanish at the private Princeton Day School), and we both strongly believed all children deserved a quality education. Our own kids attended public schools. Anna, who was more plugged into the network of local parents than I was, persuaded me to run for the school board—or as she would put it later, "I made him run."

I was elected, twice, and served six grueling years. A constant battle raged between the newcomers to the township, like us, who wanted more and better schools, and the longtime residents, who worried about the cost. I observed more than once that two of the things people cared most about were the welfare of their children and minimizing their taxes, and here was a case where these values directly conflicted. In 2000, my last year on the board, I provided the tie-breaking fifth vote in favor of asking voters to approve a bond issue that would raise property taxes to pay for new schools. Five years later, a brand-new high school opened its doors. By then, Anna and I had moved to Washington, and both Joel and Alyssa were in college.

MY RESEARCH INTERESTS continued to evolve at Princeton, influenced by new colleagues and by ideas percolating in the profession. I was beginning to focus more on monetary policy—how it works, how to measure whether policy is tight or easy, how to estimate the effects on the economy of a change in policy. My interest in monetary policy led me to accept various advisory roles with three regional Federal Reserve Banks (in Boston, Philadelphia, and New York) and to make visits and presentations at the Board of Governors—the Federal Reserve's headquarters—in Washington.

I knew that the process of making monetary policy could itself be quite complex. In most central banks around the world, policy decisions are made by committees, whose members must analyze a wide range of economic information. And it's not enough for committee members to agree on a policy: The policy decisions and their rationales must also be clearly communicated, including to the legislature (typically, the body responsible for overseeing the central bank) and to participants in financial markets (because the effects of monetary policy decisions depend crucially on how interest rates and asset prices respond). Policymaking is more likely to be consistent and communication effective when both are underpinned by a coherent intellectual framework. I found myself becoming increasingly interested in the policy frameworks that central banks use, and in how those frameworks might be improved. In 1992, jointly with Frederic "Rick" Mishkin of Columbia University, I completed a series of case studies of the frameworks used by six major central banks. Mishkin and I had overlapped in graduate school and found that we had similar interests, including a fascination with financial crises and the Great Depression. Rick was brash, with strong opinions, and sometimes outrageously funny, in contrast with the calm and understated Mark Gertler.

One especially promising framework for making monetary policy, inflation targeting, was still very new when Mishkin and I began work-ing together. Simply put, an inflation-targeting central bank publicly commits to achieving a particular inflation rate, say 2 percent, over a particular time horizon, say one to two years.

A central bank can't achieve low and stable inflation by mere declara-tion, of course. It has to back its words with actions by adjusting mone-tary policy—usually by raising or lowering a benchmark interest rate—as needed to hit the inflation target over its stated time horizon. If a central bank can't do what it says it will do, having an official target won't help much. Nevertheless, announcing an inflation target instills discipline and accountability, because it forces policymakers either to hit their target or to offer a credible explanation for why they missed. Indeed, frequent pub-lic communication—both prospective, about the central bank's goals and plans for achieving them, and retrospective, about past performance—is a key element of most inflation-targeting strategies. New Zealand's cen-tral bank was the pioneer of inflation targeting, starting in 1990. Canada followed in 1991, and then Great Britain, Sweden, Australia, Chile, Israel, and others. Ultimately, several dozen countries, both advanced and emerging-market economies, would adopt the approach.

In follow-up work in 1997, Mishkin and I looked at the experience of the early adopters and asked whether the United States could benefit from inflation targeting. The question was controversial because the Federal Reserve had long valued its discretion to respond flexibly to economic developments without the constraint of an announced tar-get. As critics of inflation targeting pointed out, under the chairman-ships of Paul Volcker and Alan Greenspan, the Federal Reserve had employed its discretion to good effect, bringing inflation down from a peak of 13.5 percent in 1980 to around 2 percent by the late 1990s.

Mishkin and I nevertheless argued that inflation targeting would improve U.S. monetary policy. For one, setting a permanent inflation target would create an institutional commitment to continuing the Volcker and Greenspan policies that had lowered and stabilized infla-tion, while producing two long economic expansions during the 1980s and 1990s. Just as important, from our perspective, the increased transparency that accompanies inflation targeting would, by shaping market expectations of the path of future interest rates, help the Fed to better achieve its objectives. In contrast, less transparent policies would keep markets guessing unnecessarily.

In other papers, I argued that inflation targeting helped not only countries with high inflation but also those, such as Japan, with the opposite problem of deflation. Japan in the 1990s had experienced a "lost decade" (which eventually became two lost decades) of alternating subpar growth and outright economic contraction. The country had plenty of problems, including slow population growth and an aging workforce, inefficiencies in agriculture and the service sector, and troubled banks. Nevertheless, it seemed to me that the deflation that followed the collapse of Japanese stock and real estate markets in the early 1990s surely was a major reason that Japan went from being one of the most dynamic economies in the world to being perhaps the most sluggish advanced economy.

In a 1999 paper, I suggested that inflation targeting not only could have helped prevent Japan from tipping into deflation (by inducing the Bank of Japan, Japan's central bank, to react more quickly to falling inflation), it was also part of the cure for getting out of deflation. By then, the Bank of Japan had moved short-term interest rates down to zero and had pledged to keep rates at zero "until deflationary concerns subside." With prices still falling, Japan needed even easier monetary policy, but its policymakers repeatedly asserted that because interest rates cannot be lower than zero, they had done all they could. I disagreed. First, I suggested, instead of continuing to hold out the vague promise about deflationary concerns subsiding, the Bank of Japan should try to shift the public's inflation expectations by setting an explicit target for inflation.* Second, I noted that, even with the

---

*   In my paper I suggested a temporary inflation target of 3 to 4 percent. I suggested the higher rate because years of deflation had resulted in a level of prices much lower than

short-term interest rate at zero, Japan had other tools to stimulate the economy, such as buying large quantities of financial assets—a suggestion also made by Milton Friedman.

My diagnosis of the Japanese situation was right, I think. Indeed, the Bank of Japan would adopt my suggestions some fourteen years later. However, the tone of my remarks was sometimes harsh. At a conference in Boston in January 2000, I had started by asking whether Japanese officials were suffering from "self-induced paralysis," accused them of having "hidden behind minor institutional or technical difficulties in order to avoid taking action," criticized them for "confused or inconsistent" responses to helpful suggestions from academics such as myself, and concluded by blaming them for an unwillingness to experiment. "Perhaps it's time for some Rooseveltian resolve in Japan," I pontificated. Years later, having endured withering, motive-impugning criticism from politicians, editorial pages, and even fellow economists, I found myself wishing I had dialed back my earlier rhetoric. In 2011, in response to a question from a Japanese newspaper correspondent, I confessed, "I'm a little bit more sympathetic to central bankers now than I was ten years ago."

IN 1996, I WAS asked to serve as chairman of the Princeton economics department, a position I would hold for six years. Being chair carried prestige and some ability to set the department agenda, but not much in the way of actual authority. Important matters were decided by consensus of the faculty, with considerable input from the university administration. I joked later that I was responsible for major policy decisions, such as whether to serve doughnuts or bagels at the department coffee hour. Faculty hiring and tenure decisions generated the

---

borrowers had expected when they took out longer-term loans, implying much higher debt burdens than borrowers had anticipated. Higher than normal inflation for a while would offset the effects of protracted deflation. What was key to my argument, however, was not the numerical value of the target but that a specific target be announced.

most heat. Professors often pushed for colleagues they believed shared their own views or who would strengthen their subfield within the department. I quickly learned that trying to resolve disputes by fiat didn't work in a crowd of strong-minded people with high regard for themselves. I had to consult, and listen, and listen some more. Once people had an opportunity to express their concerns they would often be satisfied, if not happy.

As my time as department chair wound down, I was looking forward to shedding administrative duties and spending more time on professional pursuits and writing. I had recently taken on two positions that would give me greater scope to influence the course of research in monetary economics. In 2000, I was named director of the monetary economics program at the National Bureau of Economic Research (a nonprofit organization headquartered in Cambridge, Massachusetts), and a year later I was selected to be editor of the *American Economic Review*. I had started writing a book about the Depression that I hoped would appeal to a broad audience. I had 120 pages and a title, *Age of Delusion: How Politicians and Central Bankers Created the Great Depression*.

Early in 2002, a phone rang outside my office in the economics department. It was Glenn Hubbard, a Columbia University professor on leave and serving as chairman of President Bush's Council of Economic Advisers. "Will you take the call?" a secretary asked.

CHAPTER 3

Governor

G lenn asked a simple question: Would I be interested in coming to Washington to talk with the president about possibly serving on the Federal Reserve Board?

It was not a question that I had anticipated. I had studied monetary policy and the Federal Reserve for years, but mostly from the outside. Frankly, I had never expected to be part of the institution and contributing to policy decisions.

I thought about Glenn's offer and discussed it with Anna. It was a big decision for both of us. For me, professionally, it would mean several years away from research and teaching just as I was finishing up my time as department chairman. And it might mean stepping down as editor of the *American Economic Review* only a year after taking the position. Going to Washington would also entail family sacrifices. It wouldn't be fair to ask Anna and Alyssa to move with me—Alyssa was still in high school—so I would have to live in D.C. and commute to New Jersey on weekends. Joel, at nineteen, was attending Simon's Rock College in Great Barrington, Massachusetts.

But a stint at the Federal Reserve Board would allow me to see the process of policymaking from inside one of the country's most powerful institutions. I was interested in all of the work of the Board, including the regulation and supervision of banks. The big attraction, however, was the chance to be involved in U.S. monetary policy. I had studied monetary economics and monetary history my entire professional career. What good was economics as a discipline, I asked myself, if it's not used to improve policymaking and thereby make people better off? The nation was still recovering from the shock of the 9/11 attacks—our next-door neighbor, a good friend, had died in the World Trade Center—and I knew that many people were going to be called on to serve the country. Public service at the Federal Reserve was hardly on par with what soldiers and first responders endure, but at least I could hope to contribute. With Anna's assent, I called Glenn back and told him that I was interested.

I HAD READ extensively about the history and function of the Federal Reserve in the course of my research. It represented the fourth attempt by the United States to create a central bank, depending on how you count. Before the ratification of the Constitution, the congressionally chartered but privately owned Bank of North America (1782–1791) served as a de facto central bank. It was followed by the First Bank of the United States (1791–1811), initiated by Treasury secretary Alexander Hamilton over the bitter opposition of Secretary of State Thomas Jefferson and James Madison. Its twenty-year charter lapsed amid pervasive popular distrust of financiers and big banks. Next came the Second Bank of the United States (1816–1836). Congress voted to extend the charter of the Second Bank, but President Andrew Jackson—the exemplar of populist antagonism to the bank—vetoed the extension in 1832, and Congress did not try again.

Despite not having a central bank, the United States established a national currency—the greenback—in 1862, eventually replacing a system in which private state-chartered banks issued their own currency. And in 1873, the country returned to the gold standard, which had been suspended during the Civil War. Still, the absence of a central bank in the United States after 1836 had serious drawbacks. Most obviously, the country had no public institution that could respond to the recurring bank runs and financial panics that buffeted the economy, including major panics in 1837, 1857, 1873, 1893, and 1907, as well as many minor episodes.

Indeed, the final and ultimately successful attempt at creating a central bank, led by President Woodrow Wilson in 1913, was motivated by the Panic of 1907. Beginning in October 1907, runs by depositors in New York City, and the failure of a large financial firm called the Knickerbocker Trust, contributed to a sharp decline in stock prices and a significant recession. In the absence of a central bank, a private consortium led by the legendary financier J. Pierpont Morgan worked to end the panic, extending loans to institutions experiencing runs, examining their books, and reassuring the public. That a private citizen could act where the government could not was an embarrassment. In response, Congress in 1908 created a National Monetary Commission to study whether and how a central bank could be established for the United States. Legislative proposals appeared before Wilson took office.

As financial experts understood well at the time, central banks can help end financial panics by lending cash to banks that are threatened by depositor runs, taking the banks' loans and other assets as collateral. The classic prescription for central banks facing a panic was provided in 1873 by Walter Bagehot, the British journalist, economist, and longtime editor of the *Economist* magazine, in his short book *Lombard Street: A Description of the Money Market*. To calm a panic, Bagehot advised central banks to lend freely at a high interest rate, against good collateral, a principle now known as Bagehot's dictum.

In a panic, depositors and other providers of short-term funding withdraw out of fear that the institution will fail and they will lose their money. Even a bank that is solvent under normal conditions can rarely survive a sustained run. Its cash reserves are quickly exhausted, and its remaining assets, including its loans, cannot be sold quickly, except at depressed prices. Thus, a run that begins because depositors and other providers of funds fear a bank may fail risks becoming a self-fulfilling prophecy. By lending freely against good collateral during a panic—that is, by serving as a "lender of last resort"—a central bank can replace the withdrawn funding, avoiding the forced sale of assets at fire-sale prices and the collapse of otherwise solvent institutions. Once depositors and other short-term lenders are convinced that their money is safe, the panic ends, and borrowing banks repay the central bank with interest. The Bank of England, the world's preeminent central bank at the time Bagehot was writing, served successfully as lender of last resort throughout most of the nineteenth century, avoiding the regular bank panics that plagued the United States.

The United States needed a central bank to achieve its full potential as a global economic and financial power. But finding political support to do so remained challenging. To blunt opposition from midwestern farmers and others who feared that a central bank would serve eastern financial interests at their expense, President Wilson, together with Senator Carter Glass of Virginia and others, proposed creating a central bank that would be a truly national institution—responsive to national interests, not only the interests of financiers. To achieve that goal, Wilson and Glass supported an unusual structure. Rather than a single institution located in Washington or New York, the new central bank would be a *federal* system (hence the proposed name, Federal Reserve), with eight to twelve semiautonomous Reserve Banks located in cities across the nation. Each Reserve Bank would be responsible for a district of the country. Ultimately, twelve Reserve Banks would be chartered.*

As with earlier central banks in the United States and many central banks abroad, the Reserve Banks would, technically, be private institutions, albeit with a public purpose. Each would have its own president and a board of directors made up of private citizens, including commercial bankers, drawn from its district. Each of the Reserve Banks would be allowed some latitude to make decisions based on local

---

* The Reserve Banks today are in the same cities as they were when the Federal Reserve was created: Boston, New York, Philadelphia, Cleveland, Richmond, Atlanta, Chicago, St. Louis, Minneapolis, Kansas City, Dallas, and San Francisco. The Reserve Banks also have branches in twenty-four cities within their districts.

conditions, including setting the interest rate at which it was willing to lend to commercial banks in its district. As Wilson observed, "We have purposely scattered the regional reserve banks and shall be intensely disappointed if they do not exercise a very large measure of independence." The responsibility for oversight of the Reserve Banks and the System as a whole would be vested in the Federal Reserve Board, made up of political appointees based in Washington. The original Board included two administration officials ex officio: the secretary of the treasury and the comptroller of the currency (the Office of the Comptroller of the Currency, or OCC, is the regulator of nationally chartered banks). Congress accepted the plan, approving the Federal Reserve Act in 1913, and the Federal Reserve System began operations the following year—although not in time to stop another major panic, in 1914.

The innovative design of the Federal Reserve created a nationally representative and politically more sustainable institution. But it also created a complex system without strong central oversight or clear lines of authority. For a time, the appropriately named Benjamin Strong, the head of the Federal Reserve Bank of New York, provided effective leadership. (As a rising young star in the financial world, Strong had been a protégé of J.P. Morgan and had helped Morgan end the Panic of 1907.) But no one of equal stature stepped up after Strong's death in 1928. The Fed proved far too passive during the Depression. It was ineffective in its role of lender of last resort, failing to stop the runs that forced thousands of small banks to close, and it allowed the money supply to collapse, the error emphasized by Friedman and Schwartz. Reforms under Franklin Roosevelt subsequently strengthened the authority of the Federal Reserve Board in relation to the Reserve Banks. These reforms also increased the Fed's independence from the executive branch by removing the treasury secretary and the comptroller of the currency from the Board.

Today, the Board consists of seven members, appointed by the president and confirmed by the Senate to staggered fourteen-year terms. A new term opens every other year, and new members can be appointed to open seats at any time. For example, I was being considered for a seat whose term had less than two years to run. To stay longer (which I did not expect), I would have to be renominated by the president and reconfirmed by the Senate. The Board also has a chair and a vice chair, members who are nominated and confirmed to those leadership positions for renewable four-year terms.* Alan Greenspan, the chairman when I received Glenn Hubbard's call, had served since 1987. The long, overlapping terms of members were intended to give the Board greater independence from political pressure, although this effect is diluted in practice because Board members almost never serve full terms.

To improve the performance of monetary policy, the Roosevelt reforms also created a new body, the Federal Open Market Committee (FOMC), as a successor to earlier internal committees. The FOMC would oversee the Fed's buying and selling of government securities, the primary tool through which the Fed determined short-term interest rates and influenced the money supply. Since then, participants in FOMC meetings have included nineteen people—the seven Board members and the twelve Reserve Bank presidents. The chairman of the Fed's Board is also, by tradition, the chairman of the FOMC. Although nineteen policymakers participate in FOMC meetings, only twelve have a vote at any given meeting: seven Board members, the president of the Federal Reserve Bank of New York, and four of the other eleven Reserve Bank presidents, with the votes rotating annually among the eleven. This convoluted design gives regionally appointed Reserve Bank presidents a voice in monetary policy decisions while also granting a majority to the politically appointed members of the Board.

In 1977, Congress set explicit objectives for monetary policy. It directed the Fed to pursue both "maximum employment" and "price

---

* The Dodd-Frank Wall Street Reform and Consumer Protection Act of 2010 created a second vice chair position, for supervision. As of early 2015, it had not been filled.

stability." These two objectives constitute the Federal Reserve's so-called dual mandate.* The dual mandate both ensures the democratic accountability of the Fed's unelected technocrats and forms the cornerstone of the institution's independence. The Fed cannot choose its own monetary policy goals, which are set by law. But, within a framework of congressional oversight, the FOMC decides how best to achieve the objectives the law lays out. As one tool of congressional oversight, the 1977 law required the Board to provide semiannual testimony about its objectives for the economy. The Humphrey-Hawkins Act of 1978, named after its sponsors, Senator Hubert Humphrey of Minnesota and Representative Augustus Hawkins of California, expanded this oversight by requiring the Fed chairman to testify twice a year (usually in February and July) before the Senate and the House to report on the state of the economy and the FOMC's efforts to meet its dual mandate. These hearings have been known ever since as the Humphrey-Hawkins hearings.

Besides making monetary policy, the Federal Reserve also has responsibility for regulating parts of the financial system, including banks. It shares this role with other federal agencies, including the Office of the Comptroller of the Currency and the Federal Deposit Insurance Corporation (FDIC), as well as with state regulators. The Board in Washington—not the FOMC or the Reserve Bank presidents—is vested with the Fed's regulatory powers, including the authority to write rules that implement laws passed by Congress. The Reserve Banks are in turn responsible for supervising banks in their districts, applying the policies set in Washington.

While the authorities for monetary policy and financial regulation are clear, the governance of the Federal Reserve System remains com-

---

* Actually, the law specifies a third objective for monetary policy—low long-term interest rates. Because long-term interest rates tend to be low when inflation is low and expected to remain low, this third part of the mandate is seen as being subsumed by the goal of price stability and does not often figure in FOMC decisions.

plex. The Reserve Banks continue to have boards of private citizens who advise the banks on operational matters and tell the president of the bank their views on the economy. They do not, however, weigh in on banking supervision and regulation. These boards do help choose the Reserve Bank's president—a rare example of a small group of private citizens helping to choose an official who wields government power. Ultimately, though, the Board in Washington has authority over the Reserve Banks; it must approve the appointment of presidents as well as the banks' budgets.

MY APPOINTMENT WITH President Bush was just after lunch. I did not want to risk travel delays, so I took the train the evening before. Following instructions, I reported thirty minutes before my appointment to a side entrance of the White House. The administration did not want journalists to spot me. At the scheduled time, I found myself in the Oval Office, feeling a little overwhelmed. I had never been in the White House or met a president.

The president welcomed me cordially and said he had heard good things about me. He dutifully asked a few questions that obviously had been prepared by a junior economic adviser with an Econ 101 textbook at hand. I remember explaining how I would respond to a hypothetical change in the inflation rate. With that chore over, the president relaxed and asked me about myself, my background, my family. Finally, he inquired whether I had any political experience.

"Well, sir," I said, "it won't count for much in this office, but I have served two terms as an elected member of the Montgomery Township, New Jersey, Board of Education."

He laughed. "That counts for a lot in this office," he said. "Being on a board of education is thankless but it's important service." That exchange seemed to seal the deal. I met with others in the White House, including Bush's friend and adviser Clay Johnson and Josh Bolten, the White House deputy chief of staff. A few days later, I heard from Glenn that the president had enjoyed the meeting and intended to nominate me after all the necessary preliminaries had been completed. I agreed to accept the nomination if offered.

The preliminaries, it turned out, were not simple. Background checks took months. They included what seemed like endless paperwork to document where I had lived, whom I had associated with, where I had worked, where I had traveled, and how I had managed my finances since leaving college. I was interviewed by the White House personnel department and twice by FBI agents, who wanted to know if I had ever conspired to overthrow the government of the United States. Has anyone ever answered yes?

The vetting complete, the White House announced on May 8, 2002, that President Bush would nominate me. The process moved over to the Senate Committee on Banking, Housing, and Urban Affairs, the body with jurisdiction over nominees to the Fed. Fed staff prepped me for my as yet unscheduled confirmation hearing, and I spent hours with thick binders that detailed the Fed's responsibilities and positions on various issues. I was warned not to comment in public on policy issues or to speak to the press. My nomination wasn't controversial, and the goal was to keep it that way. My hearing before the Banking Committee, on July 30, lasted not quite an hour. The committee approved my nomination, and then, on July 31, the full Senate did so, without dissent. After it was all over, an advocacy group devoted to speeding up Senate confirmations sent me a T-shirt that read: "I survived the presidential appointee confirmation process." In reality, my confirmation had been reasonably smooth.

Along with me, the Senate also confirmed Donald Kohn to a seat on the Board. Easygoing, thoughtful, and without ego, Don was a Federal Reserve System veteran. After receiving his PhD at the University of Michigan, he had begun his Fed career in 1970 at the Kansas City Federal Reserve Bank before moving, after five years, to join the staff in Washington. Over the years Don worked his way up to become the head of the Board's Division of Monetary Affairs (a position created for him) and a close adviser to Chairman Greenspan. Don and his wife, Gail, were fitness buffs, with Gail an ardent rower and Don a hiker and bicyclist. Some reporters speculated that Don would serve as Greenspan's proxy and would clash with me on issues like inflation targeting, of which Greenspan was a known skeptic. But in fact Don and I worked closely together and I trusted his judgment.

Don and I were sworn in by Chairman Greenspan on August 5, 2002. I won Greenspan's coin toss, was sworn in first, and thus would remain forever senior to Don for official purposes, despite his thirty-plus years of experience at the Fed to my none. With Don's and my arrival, the Board was at full strength, with all seven seats filled.

Once confirmed, I began to get to know the other Board members. Roger Ferguson, the vice chairman and an appointee of President Bill Clinton, and only the third African American to serve on the Board, had grown up in a working-class neighborhood in Washington. Quiet and unassuming but with a puckish sense of humor, Roger had earned undergraduate, law, and doctoral degrees from Harvard. He was working at the New York law firm Davis Polk when he met his wife, Annette Nazareth, who would go on to serve as a commissioner at the Securities and Exchange Commission.

The job of the vice chairman can involve a good bit of administration—helping to oversee the Reserve Banks, for example. Roger did that well. He also played an avuncular role, checking on me periodically to be sure that I was settling in. The critical moment of Roger's career at the Fed had come on September 11, 2001. When the planes crashed into the World Trade Center and the Pentagon, Roger was the only Board member in Washington. Under his direction, the Federal Reserve issued a statement affirming that it was "open and operating" and stood ready to serve as a lender of last resort if needed. He and a staff group set up a bank of telephones in a conference room near the boardroom and worked tirelessly to keep critical components of the financial system functioning. Roger could see the smoke rising from the Pentagon through the windows of his office. The Board's quick response helped protect the economy by minimizing disruptions to the systems for making payments and transferring securities—the little-known but critically important plumbing of the financial system.

Two other Board members, Susan Bies and Mark Olson, had been bankers. Like me, both were Bush appointees. Sue, who had a doctorate in economics from Northwestern, had been in charge of risk management at First Tennessee, a regional bank. Mark had had a varied career that included being CEO of a small bank in Minnesota, working as a congressional staff member, and serving as a partner in the accounting firm Ernst & Young. In 1986, at age forty-three, he had been elected president of the American Bankers Association. Sue welcomed me in her warm and outgoing way, Mark in his understated Minnesota style.

Board member Edward (Ned) Gramlich, a lanky, white-haired former economics professor and dean from the University of Michigan, also made me feel at home. Ned had served briefly as a staff economist at the Board during the late 1960s and also as acting director of the Congressional Budget Office. He was appointed to the Board by President Clinton in 1997. Ned's work as an academic economist covered a wide range of mostly microeconomic issues, and at the Board he tackled a diverse set of tasks, including serving as part-time chairman of the Air Transportation Stabilization Board, created by Congress after the 9/11 attacks to assist the airline industry. Ned also led the Fed's efforts in community development and consumer protection.

After the welcomes, Don and I were sworn in a second time—in a formal ceremony in the two-story atrium of the Board's headquarters (named for Marriner Eccles, Fed chairman from 1934 to 1948). The formal ceremony was legally redundant, but it was a nice event for our relatives and for the staff. Anna, Joel, Alyssa, and my parents all attended. I was amused and touched to see my small-town pharmacist father, brows furrowed in concentration, in earnest conversation with the renowned Greenspan.

In most countries, the head of the central bank is called the governor of the bank. At the Federal Reserve, the head of the central bank is the chairman, and members of the Board have the title of governor.

(Since the Roosevelt-era reforms, its formal name has been the Board of Governors of the Federal Reserve System.) So I could now officially claim the appellation "Governor Bernanke." Once, a clerk at an airline ticket counter would ask me what state I was the governor of.

The formalities over, I settled into my new job and life as a long-range commuter. I rented a one-bedroom apartment in Georgetown, and most weekends drove my metallic blue 1998 Chrysler Sebring convertible the 186 miles each way to our home near Princeton. After brief discussions with Greenspan and Cary Williams, the Board's ethics officer, I also kept, at least for the time being, the (unpaid) editorship of the *American Economic Review*.

On weekdays, I attended Board meetings and briefings, met with visitors, and traveled, including visits to Reserve Banks. On my first trip, Sue Bies and I went to Brownsville, Texas, to see the Dallas Reserve Bank's community development efforts there. Yet I was feeling far from overworked. I talked to Roger Ferguson about it. Roger explained that it often took new governors time to find their niche, to determine the issues that mattered most to them.

To find my niche I had to contend with the Board's committee system. Much of the work of the Board, outside of monetary policy, is done by committees of two or three governors, who then make recommendations to the Board as a whole. Seniority matters when it comes to assignments, which are made by the vice chairman in consultation with the chairman. I would have been interested in becoming more involved in bank supervision. But Roger headed that committee and the two bankers, Sue and Mark, completed it. I could have volunteered for more administrative jobs, but I had done similar work as department chair at Princeton and I wanted to be involved in policy. I ended up on the Committee on Payments, Clearing, and Settlement (which dealt with the plumbing of the financial system) and on the Committee on Consumer and Community Affairs (which handled consumer protection and community development), chaired by Ned Gramlich and with Sue as the other member. I also had administrative oversight of economic research—a natural fit. In that position, I would help found a new journal, the *International Journal of Central Banking*, dedicated to publishing policy-relevant research from around the world.

But I had come to Washington to be involved in monetary policy. Realistically, I knew that Chairman Greenspan—the "eight-hundred-pound gorilla" of the Federal Reserve, as Roger once called him—would have a predominant influence on the direction of interest rates. That didn't seem unreasonable to me. After all, by the time I joined, Alan had sat in the chairman's seat for fifteen years, and his decisions had earned him the sobriquet "the Maestro." I could at best influence meeting-to-meeting rate decisions on the margin, I assumed. And in fact, I was less interested in each individual decision than in the broader framework in which policy was made. In that respect, it seemed to me, the Federal Reserve was behind the times.

Traditionally, monetary policy decisions had been shrouded in the so-called mystique of central banking—an approach that led the journalist William Greider to title his 1989 book about the Volcker Fed *Secrets of the Temple: How the Federal Reserve Runs the Country*. In a similar vein, Montagu Norman, the iconic governor of the Bank of England in the 1920s, 1930s, and early 1940s, purportedly expressed his philosophy in the motto "Never explain, never excuse." Various arguments have been advanced in favor of maintaining secrecy in monetary policymaking, but it seemed to me that one of the main reasons was the same one that keeps hot dog manufacturers from offering factory tours—it detracts from the appeal of the product if the public knows how it is made.

Secrecy cuts two ways. It can make central bankers seem more all-knowing and increase their short-term flexibility, but it can also confuse the public, wrong-foot markets, and fuel conspiracy theories. And, in a world of greater transparency and accountability throughout the public and private sectors, secretive policymaking at the Fed was beginning to feel anachronistic. I also believed that, on net, secrecy reduced the effectiveness of monetary policy. As Rick Mishkin and I had argued in our work on inflation targeting, monetary policy works better when the central bank communicates clearly with markets and the public.

I attended my first meeting of the Federal Open Market Committee on August 13, 2002, a little more than a week after my swearing-in. (The FOMC conducts eight scheduled meetings each year.) Over the weekend before, I studied the voluminous background materials prepared by the staff. There was the Greenbook, named for its green construction-paper cover, with data and analysis of both the domestic and international economies, as well as the staff economic forecast. The Bluebook reviewed financial market developments and compared the likely effects of alternative choices for monetary policy. Various staff memoranda and other documents added to the pile of paper. The staff's forecasts, like those of private-sector forecasters, were as much art as science. They drew on a range of economic models developed over many years. But staff economists added substantial professional judgment to the mix, including their assessment of influences hard to capture in the standard data, like severe weather, possible changes in government tax or spending policies, and geopolitical developments.

The accuracy of both central bank and private-sector forecasters has been extensively studied and the results are not impressive. Unfortunately, beyond a quarter or two, the course of the economy is extremely hard to forecast. That said, careful projections are essential for coherent monetary policymaking, just as business plans and war strategies are important in their spheres.

Greenspan was known for his economic forecasting skills, having run a successful consulting firm, Townsend-Greenspan & Co., before his time in government. He put less weight on computer-simulated models and instead practiced an idiosyncratic, bottom-up style of forecasting. He regularly reviewed hundreds of small pieces of information. In my own thinking, I tended to emphasize developments in broader economic indicators—the forest rather than the trees—but I appreciated that the chairman's approach could sometimes yield interesting insights that more standard analyses might miss.

On the morning of the meeting, breakfast was served in the top floor of the 1970s-era Martin Building, behind the Depression-era Eccles Building. (William McChesney Martin served as Fed chairman from 1951 to 1970.) I joined the breakfast to meet and talk with the Reserve Bank presidents. I knew some of them from my days as an academic and Federal Reserve hanger-on. FOMC members mixed amiably, with little tendency to form cliques based on their policy views. It wasn't like a high school cafeteria. The hawks (shorthand for policymakers who tended to worry more about inflation) did not sit at a different table than the doves (policymakers who tended to worry more about growth and employment).

Ten or fifteen minutes before the start of the meeting, participants began to filter toward their assigned places at the mahogany and black granite table in the Eccles Building's boardroom. The boardroom is high-ceilinged and elegant, fifty-six feet long, with high draped windows facing Constitution Avenue. On one wall, a large map of the United States shows the borders of the twelve Reserve Bank districts.

Besides policymakers, four or five staff members with speaking parts also sit at the table. The head of the Open Market Trading Desk at the New York Fed, which manages the Fed's purchases and sales of securities (which are done in the "open market") and maintains frequent contact with market players, would typically begin the meeting by summarizing key financial developments. When I joined, the desk chief was Dino Kos. The directors of the Board's Division of Research and Statistics (Dave Stockton) and its Division of International Finance (Karen Johnson), or their top deputies, would follow with presentations on the staff's U.S. and international economic forecasts. Later in the meeting, the director of the Division of Monetary Affairs (Vincent Reinhart, heir to the position created for Don Kohn) would present the policy options as explained in the Bluebook. Collectively, the three Board division directors wielded considerable influence. My Princeton colleague Alan Blinder, who served as Board vice chairman in the mid-1990s, nicknamed them "the barons."

Greenspan's chair, still empty at a few minutes before the start of the meeting, was at the midway point of the twenty-seven-by-eleven-foot two-ton oval table, facing the main entry to the room. To the chairman's right sat the president of the New York Fed—by tradition also the vice chairman of the FOMC—Bill McDonough. A former banker from Chicago, McDonough had been the New York Fed president since 1993. Ferguson, the Board vice chairman, sat on Greenspan's left. The two most junior members, Kohn and I, were squeezed into corners of the table, out of the chairman's line of sight. About thirty-five staff members from the Board and the Reserve Banks took their seats around the room.

At precisely 9:00 a.m., a door next to the fireplace opened, and Chairman Greenspan emerged from his office and strode to his seat. The room quieted. Greenspan sat and organized his papers. In one sentence, he welcomed me and Don, then called for the staff presentations.

Greenspan had met with me over breakfast before my first meeting to make sure that I understood how FOMC meetings were organized. First on the agenda were the staff briefings on financial markets and the economic outlook, followed by questions from the nineteen Board members and Reserve Bank presidents. The "economic go-round" came afterward. Each of the participants spoke for four or five minutes about the economic outlook. The Reserve Bank presidents typically reported first on developments in their own district, then turned to their views of the national economy. Governors usually spoke later, followed by the vice chairman (McDonough) and, finally, Greenspan. At one time, the nineteen presentations had been at least partly extemporaneous. Unfortunately for the quality and spontaneity of the discussion (although good for transparency), the FOMC, in response to demands by Representative Henry González, then-head of the House Financial Services Committee, had agreed in 1994 to release full meeting transcripts after five years. Since then, most participants had taken to reading prepared statements.

I WAS JOINING the Committee at a complex moment for the economy. The country was in the early stages of recovery from a recession (a period of economic contraction) that had lasted only eight months, from March to November 2001. (Once output begins to increase again, the economy is said to be in recovery and the recession over, even if the jobs and output lost have not been fully regained.) Recessions can be triggered by many causes, or combinations of causes. The 2001 recession had followed the collapse of the dot-com bubble and a sharp decline in the overall stock market; in the middle of it, the economy received a further blow from the 9/11 attacks.

The FOMC had reacted quickly to the downturn. Through the course of 2001, it slashed its policy instrument—the target for the federal funds rate—from 6-1/2 percent to 1-3/4 percent, quite a rapid response by historical standards. The federal funds rate is a private-sector interest rate—specifically, the rate that banks charge each other for overnight loans. Although the federal funds rate is a private rate, the Federal Reserve was able to control it indirectly by affecting the supply of funds available to banks. More precisely, the Fed managed the funds rate by affecting the quantity of bank reserves.

Bank reserves are funds that commercial banks hold at the Fed, much like the checking accounts that individuals have at banks. A bank can use its reserve account at the Fed for making or receiving payments from other banks, as well as a place to hold extra cash. Banks are also legally required to hold a minimum level of reserves.

The Fed was able to affect the quantity of bank reserves in the system, and thereby the federal funds rate, by buying or selling securities. When the Fed sells securities, for example, it gets paid by deducting their price from the reserve account of the purchaser's bank. The Fed's securities sales consequently drain reserves from the banking system. With fewer reserves available, banks are more eager to borrow from other banks, which puts upward pressure on the federal funds rate, the interest rate that banks pay on those borrowings. Similarly, to push down the federal funds rate, the Fed would buy securities, thereby adding to reserves in the banking system and reducing the need of banks to borrow from each other.

At that time, moving the federal funds rate up or down was the FOMC's principal means of influencing the economy, and the level of the funds rate was the primary indicator of policy. If the FOMC determined that economic activity needed a boost, it would cut the rate. A cut tended to push down other interest rates—from the rates on auto loans to mortgages to corporate bonds—and thus promoted borrowing and spending. As Keynesian theory predicts, so long as the economy had unused capacity, increased spending causes firms to raise production and hire more workers. If the economy had little or no unused capacity, however, increased demand might push prices and wages higher—that is, boost inflation. If the Committee believed that the economy was "running hot," with output above sustainable levels, it could raise the federal funds rate, leading to increases in interest rates across the board and slowing economic growth and inflation.

Raising rates wasn't a serious option in August 2002. The rapid rate-cutting campaign of 2001 had no doubt contributed to the relative brevity of the recession. However, the recovery that followed had been tepid, with only moderate economic growth, and the pessimists around the table worried the economy might be faltering. Moreover, despite the growth in production, the economy was in a "jobless recovery." The unemployment rate had actually risen since the end of the recession. And inflation had been exceptionally low—often a symptom of economic weakness, since firms are reluctant to raise prices when demand is soft. Stock prices remained depressed in the aftermath of corporate governance scandals at the telecommunications company WorldCom, the energy trader Enron, and the accounting firm Arthur Andersen.

As usual, Greenspan got the last word in the economic go-round.

He proposed that we refrain from further cuts in our target for the federal funds rate, but state in our closely watched postmeeting statement that "the risks are weighted mainly toward conditions that may generate economic weakness." In central bank speak, that would signal to the financial markets that we were worried about the slow pace of the recovery and thought that the next rate change was more likely to be down than up. Greenspan's remarks were the transition to a second opportunity for each person to speak, the "policy go-round," and effectively served as both the closing of the first round and the opening of the second round. Under Greenspan, this second round was usually brief and consisted of little more than participants stating their agreement with (or very occasionally their opposition to) his recommendation. This time, I concurred.

Unfortunately, the economy showed little sign of strengthening by the time of my second FOMC meeting, in September. Some participants noted that rising concern about a possible war with Iraq seemed to be making businesses and households extra cautious. We also discussed whether inflation was falling too low. People tend to think low inflation is a good thing, because it means that they can afford to buy more. But very low inflation—if sustained—also comes with slow growth in wages and incomes, negating any benefit of lower prices. In fact, inflation that is too low can be just as bad for the economy as inflation that is too high, as Japan's experience starkly illustrated. The drag on the economy from very low inflation or deflation might be so great that even lowering short-term interest rates to zero may not provide enough stimulus to achieve full employment. When my turn came to speak, I acknowledged that easing rates might further heat up already hot sectors such as housing but said I leaned toward a rate cut as a preemptive strike against the risk of falling into deflation.

We also debated whether the "zero lower bound"—the fact that interest rates cannot be reduced below zero—meant we were "running out of ammunition." Cutting the federal funds rate wasn't the only conceivable tool for spurring growth, as staff research papers had been exploring for several years and as I had argued at Princeton. But Greenspan downplayed the zero-bound concern. He suggested that, if the federal funds rate did hit zero, the Committee would be able to find other ways to further ease monetary policy, though he did not at that point say exactly how.

In any case, Greenspan once again argued against an immediate cut, though he suggested one might be necessary before the next regularly scheduled meeting. I went along even though I had been leaning toward a rate cut. The Committee seemed headed in the direction of further cuts and I did not think the precise timing that important. But two other members of the Committee voted against Greenspan. Surprisingly, one was Ned Gramlich. Board members typically have a higher threshold for voting against the chairman than do Reserve Bank presidents, perhaps because the Washington-based governors have more opportunity to argue their case between meetings. The other dissenter was Bob McTeer of the Federal Reserve Bank of Dallas, who had earlier earned the nickname "The Lonesome Dove."

WITH TWO FOMC MEETINGS under my belt, I felt ready to begin speaking in public. On October 15, 2002, in New York, I asked what monetary policy should do, if anything, about asset-price bubbles. The question was timely. A stock market boom and bust had helped trigger the 2001 recession, and we were seeing continuing increases in house prices.

Most people think they know what a bubble is, but economists have no exact definition. The term usually refers to a situation in which investors bid the price of a class of assets well above its "fundamental" value, expecting that they can resell at a still higher price later. I waded into the contentious debate over whether central banks should deliberately raise interest rates to try to deflate a bubble.

I raised two concerns about that strategy. First, identifying a bubble is difficult until it actually pops. Nobody ever knows for sure the fundamental value of an asset, which depends on many factors, including how the economy is likely to perform in the distant future. Indeed, if bubbles were easy to identify, investors wouldn't get caught up in them in the first place.

Second was the problem the FOMC confronted in 2002: what to do when one sector, such as housing, is hot but the rest of the economy is not. Monetary policy cannot be directed at a single class of assets while leaving other financial markets and the broader economy untouched. I cited the stock market boom of the late 1920s. New York Fed president Benjamin Strong, the Fed's de facto leader at the time, resisted increasing interest rates to squelch the stock market, on the grounds that the effects of higher rates could not be confined to stocks. He drew an analogy: Raising rates would be like spanking all his children just because one child—the stock market—had misbehaved. When Strong died in 1928, his successors abandoned his hands-off approach and raised rates. The ultimate results of this decision were not only the stock market crash of 1929 (in a tragic sense, the Fed succeeded in its effort to cool the market) but also a too-tight monetary policy that helped cause the Depression.

Do the problems with using monetary policy to pop bubbles mean that central banks should ignore bubbles as they are forming? No, I argued. First, sometimes bubbles will cause the overall economy to overheat—when higher stock prices encourage stockholders to increase their spending, for example—leading to unsustainable growth and higher inflation. In that case, monetary policy can lean against the bubble and help stabilize the broader economy at the same time. Mark Gertler and I had made a similar argument in a paper we presented at the Fed's Jackson Hole conference in 1999. Second, and critically, central banks and other agencies can fight bubbles by other means, such as regulation, bank supervision, and financial education. Or, as I put it in my speech, "Use the right tool for the job."

In November—in a speech entitled "Deflation: Can 'It' Happen Here?"—I addressed the question that the FOMC had debated in September: Would the Fed run out of ammunition if inflation fell very low and interest rates were cut to zero? I said that central banks should do whatever they could to avoid deflation. For example, they can set a goal for inflation above zero to provide a buffer, or safety zone, against deflation. Advanced-economy central banks generally aimed for inflation of about 2 percent rather than zero, though in the Fed's case the goal wasn't stated explicitly. I also argued that it was important to get ahead of deflation by cutting rates preemptively if necessary.

But if deflation did arrive, what then? Even when short-term interest rates were close to zero, I said, central banks could do more. I suggested several methods to bring down longer-term interest rates, such as mortgage rates, thereby providing additional economic stimulus, even when short-term interest rates could not be cut further.

The deflation speech saddled me with the nickname "Helicopter Ben." In a discussion of hypothetical possibilities for combating deflation, I mentioned an extreme tactic—a broad-based tax cut combined with money creation by the central bank to finance the cut. Milton Friedman had dubbed the approach a "helicopter drop" of money. Dave Skidmore, the media relations officer and former Associated Press journalist who edited my speeches when I was a Board member and later chairman, had advised me to delete the helicopter-drop metaphor. But I was unconvinced. I had, after all, referred to it in my writings as an academic. "It's just not the sort of thing a central banker says," he told me. I replied, "Everybody knows Milton Friedman said it." As it turned out, many Wall Street bond traders had apparently not delved deeply into Milton's oeuvre. They didn't see my remarks as a hypothetical discussion by a professor; they took it as a policymaker's signal that he was willing to push inflation too high, which would devalue their bonds.

DEFLATION AND FRIEDMAN'S IDEAS were at the center of a third speech early in my tenure, at the University of Chicago. The occasion was a ceremony honoring Milton on his ninetieth birthday. I knew Milton when I taught at Stanford and he was at Stanford's Hoover Institution. A tiny man, he always seemed to have a smile on his face.

He loved to talk economics with anybody, even a young assistant professor like me. It was from his work with Anna Schwartz that I had
learned that the Federal Reserve's failure to keep the economy from
sinking into deflation had been a major cause of the Depression. With
that in mind, I reminded the audience that I was now at the Fed and
ended by saying, "I would like to say to Milton and Anna: Regarding the Great Depression. You're right, we did it. We're very sorry. But
thanks to you, we won't do it again."

CHAPTER 4

In the Maestro's Orchestra

As a junior member of the Maestro's orchestra, I found life during the waning years of the Greenspan Fed to be as quiet or as busy as I cared to make it. It was also at times strangely isolating, even for someone used to the solitude of academic research. I traveled reasonably often to give a speech, to visit a Reserve Bank, or to represent the Board in a meeting abroad. But most days I worked alone in my office. I arrived early, parking in a garage in the basement of the Eccles Building. Some days Don Kohn's bicycle would occupy the parking space next to mine.

On a typical day, between meetings I read reports, followed economic and financial developments, and worked on speeches or on academic research left incomplete when I moved to Washington. The staff was more than happy to help with speeches or even to write them, but I preferred to draft my own and then revise based on staff comments. Several governors had CNBC on their TVs all day, but I found that distracting. Instead I periodically checked the Bloomberg screen in my office or read the staff market updates.

When I joined, the full Board met infrequently; much of the substantive work was done by committees. We did convene every other Monday morning for a staff briefing on economic, financial, and international developments. Governors asked questions after the staff presented. As a professor, I had been used to asking speculative or hypothetical questions at seminars, but at the Fed I quickly acquired more discipline. Once I asked an idle question at a briefing. By the end of the day, the staff had sent me a ten-page memo that answered the question under four different sets of assumptions and included a bibliography. After that I only asked questions when I really needed the answer.

At Princeton, I often dropped into a colleague's office to try out a new idea or to chat. At the Fed, outside of scheduled meetings, I did not see fellow Board members much—unless I made an appointment. Board members' offices are arrayed at intervals along a long carpeted hallway with vaulted ceilings and the hushed ambience of a library. Each office has an outer office occupied by an administrative assistant. Rita Proctor, a confident and efficient Fed veteran, was assigned to work with me. She quickly took me in hand, educating me about "how things are done" at the Board. At Princeton I had shared an assistant with other faculty members. I demanded so little of Rita's time that she volunteered to work for Mark Olson as well.

Another difference between academic life and life as a policy-maker was the dress code. As a professor, I often wore jeans to work. I wasn't used to wearing a suit every day, especially in the summer heat of Washington. Of course, I understood that formal dress was just a way of showing that you took the job seriously. But at a talk before the American Economic Association, I made the tongue-in-cheek proposal that Fed governors should be allowed to signal their commitment to public service by wearing Hawaiian shirts and Bermuda shorts.

Life outside the office was as quiet as life inside it. On weekends I was either at home in Princeton or on the road on Board business. Friends from academia dropped by. But on most weekday nights I returned to an empty apartment and phoned Anna to catch up on life in New Jersey. My apartment in Georgetown was close to a couple of Vietnamese restaurants that I frequented. When I didn't go out, I would microwave a Hot Pockets sandwich and eat it in front of a *Seinfeld* rerun. Sometimes I'd stroll over to Blues Alley, a jazz club across the street, or to a three-story Barnes & Noble bookstore a few blocks away. During off-hours, I read fiction and nonfiction, all subjects—history, biology, math, rarely any economics. I couldn't immediately indulge my primary extracurricular obsession—baseball—because it was not until 2005 that the Montreal Expos moved to Washington, changing their name to the Nationals.

I received invitations to receptions at embassies and the like but I turned down most. I did enjoy attending several dinner parties at the home of Greenspan and his wife, Andrea Mitchell. The chairman displayed a sly and sometimes self-deprecating sense of humor that was rarely visible in public. He told us, for example, about his marriage proposal to Andrea, which was so riddled with Greenspanian ambiguity that she couldn't figure out what he was asking. Andrea regaled us with stories of her adventures as an international correspondent for NBC News. Board alumni, including former senior staff as well as retired governors, formed an informal club that extended outside the institution's walls. Mike Kelley, a former Board member who lived with his wife, Janet, in the nearby Watergate complex, threw a reception around Christmas each year that drew everybody in town with current or past Fed connections.

At work, I had relatively few one-on-one conversations with Chairman Greenspan. I occasionally asked to see him in his office, and he sometimes invited me to lunch in his personal dining room. Although we got along fine, I suspect that he saw me as too academic, and consequently naïve about the practical complexities of central banking. That opinion was not without merit. And doubtless in FOMC meetings and speeches I harped on the need for policy transparency too much for his taste.

I was awed by Greenspan's reputation and record, but I also perceived shortcomings that a conventionally educated academic could be expected to see in someone who is largely self-taught. He had learned much of his economics on the job, as a consultant. After a master's degree at New York University, he had enrolled in a PhD program at Columbia University under the mentorship of former Fed chairman

Arthur Burns, a pioneer in the empirical analysis of recessions and recoveries. Greenspan dropped out of graduate school in the early 1950s after his consulting business took off. Much later, in 1977, he received a doctorate on the basis of a collection of past articles rather than a conventional dissertation. He was shrewd and knew a remarkable number of esoteric facts, but his thinking was idiosyncratic and less conceptual than I was used to. His famous libertarianism (he had been a disciple of novelist and philosopher Ayn Rand) would show in offhand remarks, but he tended toward the pragmatic in making monetary policy.

Despite differences in our worldviews, I liked and admired the chairman. He was invariably cordial, and he seemed eager to discuss any economic issue. Once I went to see him about twenty minutes before an FOMC meeting—I forget the precise reason. When I entered his office, Greenspan was sitting at his desk eating oatmeal, a napkin tied around his neck. We began to discuss my point, and in the midst of his animated response he realized that we were five minutes late for the meeting, a significant breach of protocol. He ripped off the napkin and hustled into the boardroom through the door from his office. I took the circuitous route through the hallway to the boardroom's main entrance.

Many outsiders at the time viewed the FOMC as a rubber stamp for Greenspan. I learned quickly that this was not the case. If the chairman had particularly strong views, his recommendation would almost certainly become policy. His personal prestige and the Fed tradition of deferring to the chairman would usually be enough. That had been the case in the late 1990s, when he had argued against interest rate increases because of his conviction that rapid productivity gains, which gave the economy more room to grow, made raising rates premature. (That call, featured in a book by Bob Woodward, helped earn Greenspan the title of the Maestro.) But he always knew where the center of the Committee was, and he generally accommodated members' views—if not completely, then through clever compromises or vague promises to act at some future meeting.

On substance, Greenspan and I agreed on many things. He was passionate, as was I, about maintaining the Fed's independence from short-term political pressures. The chairman made policy decisions in an apolitical, nonpartisan way. Like me, he also believed that monetary policy is a powerful tool, and he was prepared to act forcefully when warranted. We agreed on the benefits of low and stable inflation, and we largely agreed that monetary policy could remain effective even if short-term interest rates reached zero. Greenspan also shared my views that monetary policymakers could not reliably identify asset-price bubbles or safely "pop" them by raising interest rates.

Our thinking diverged in several areas. I championed, and he distrusted, formal policy frameworks like inflation targeting, which were intended to improve the Fed's transparency. He had even made jokes about his own strained relationship with transparency. He told a Senate committee in 1987, "Since becoming a central banker, I have learned to mumble with great incoherence. If I seem unduly clear to you, you must have misunderstood what I said." Also, he did not put much stock in the ability of bank regulation and supervision to keep banks out of trouble. He believed that, so long as banks had enough of their own money at stake, in the form of capital, market forces would deter them from unnecessarily risky lending. And, while I had argued that regulation and supervision should be the first line of defense against asset-price bubbles, he was more inclined to keep hands off and use after-the-fact interest rate cuts to cushion the economic consequences of a burst bubble.

THROUGHOUT MOST OF the 1990s the Fed presided over an economy with employment growing strongly and inflation slowly declining to low levels. The Fed was thus meeting both parts of its congressional dual mandate to pursue maximum employment and price stability. In contrast, when I arrived at the Fed, we saw risks to both sides of our mandate. On the employment side, we had the jobless recovery to contend with. On the price stability side, we faced a problem unseen in the United

States since the Depression—the possibility that inflation would fall too low or even tip into deflation, a broad decline in wages and prices.

In the past, the end of a recession had typically been followed by an improving jobs market. But during the two years after the recession that ended in November 2001, the U.S. economy actually lost 700,000 jobs, and unemployment edged up from 5.5 percent to 5.8 percent even as output grew. Many economists and pundits asked whether globalization and automation had somehow permanently damaged the U.S. economy's ability to create jobs. At the same time, inflation had been low and, with the economy sputtering, Fed economists warned that it could fall to 1/2 percent or below in 2003. Actual deflation could not be ruled out.

Worrying about possible deflation was a new experience for FOMC participants. Ever since the end of the Depression, the main risk to price stability had always been excessive inflation. Inflation spiraled up during the 1970s. Paul Volcker's Fed ended it, but at a steep cost. Within a few months of Volcker's becoming chairman in 1979, the Fed dramatically tightened monetary policy, and interest rates soared. By late 1981, the federal funds rate hit 20 percent and the interest rate on thirty-year fixed-rate mortgages topped 18 percent. As a consequence, housing, autos, and other credit-dependent industries screeched to a halt. A brief recession in 1980 was followed by a deep downturn in 1981–82. Unemployment crested above 10 percent, a rate last seen in the late 1930s.

After succeeding Volcker in 1987, Alan Greenspan continued the fight against inflation, although he was able to do so much more gradually and with fewer nasty side effects. By the late 1990s, the battle against high inflation appeared to be over. Inflation had fallen to about 2 percent per year, which seemed consistent with Greenspan's informal definition of price stability: an inflation rate low enough that households and businesses did not take it into account when making economic decisions.

The Great Inflation of the 1970s had left a powerful impression on

the minds of monetary policymakers. Michael Moskow, the president
of the Federal Reserve Bank of Chicago when I joined the FOMC,
had served as an economist on the body that administered the
infamous—and abjectly unsuccessful—Nixon wage-price controls,
which had attempted to outlaw price increases. (Predictably, many
suppliers managed to evade the controls, and, where they couldn't,
some goods simply became unavailable when suppliers couldn't earn
a profit selling at the mandated prices.) Don Kohn had been a Board
staff economist in the 1970s under Fed chairman Arthur Burns, on
whose watch inflation had surged. Greenspan himself had served as
the chairman of President Ford's Council of Economic Advisers and
no doubt shuddered to remember the Ford administration's inef-
fectual Whip Inflation Now campaign, which encouraged people to
wear buttons signifying their commitment to taming the rising cost
of living. With Fed policymakers conditioned to worry about too-
high inflation, it was disorienting to consider that inflation might
be too *low*. But it was a possibility that we would soon have to take
seriously.

The federal funds rate, after the rapid cuts in 2001, had been left
unchanged at 1-3/4 percent for most of 2002. But by the November 2002
FOMC meeting, my third since joining the Fed, the case for another
rate cut was gaining strength. After a brief upturn during the summer,
job creation was stalling again. I agreed that we needed to cut interest rates to support job growth. Additionally, I said, a rate cut would
help avoid further declines in the already low inflation rate. Greenspan
had come to the same conclusion. "We are dealing with what basically is a latent deflationary type of economy," he told us. "It's a pretty
scary prospect, and one that we certainly want to avoid." Greenspan
proposed, and the Committee supported, a significant half-percentage
point cut in the federal funds rate target, to 1-1/4 percent. Our postmeeting statement indicated that, with the rate cut, the "risks are balanced," meaning that future rate changes were about equally likely to
be up or down.

The economy seemed to pick up for a few months, but by the time of our March 2003 meeting the recovery again seemed stalled. Shockingly, the Labor Department reported private payrolls had contracted by 308,000 jobs in February. "With recoveries like this, who needs recessions!" said Dallas Fed president Bob McTeer.

U.S. forces had invaded Iraq a few days before the meeting. Businesses and households were reluctant to invest or borrow until they saw how the invasion would play out. My colleagues and I also were uncertain about the economic consequences of the war, especially its effect on energy prices. At Greenspan's urging, we decided to wait before considering further action. In our postmeeting statement, we said uncertainty was so high that we couldn't usefully characterize the near-term course of the economy or monetary policy. That unprecedented assertion probably added to the public's angst about the economy.

I HARBORED THE HOPE that aspects of my academic work would contribute to our debate. In particular, because accurate communication about policy becomes especially important as short-term interest rates approach zero, my work on inflation targeting and the need for policy transparency appeared even more relevant. In March 2003 I began a series of speeches on the topic.

Although inflation targeting was controversial within the FOMC, I wasn't worried about ruffling feathers by speaking about it outside the walls of the Fed. Board members and Reserve Bank presidents regularly give speeches on topics ranging from monetary policy to banking regulation. Speech texts are sometimes circulated in advance for comment or as a courtesy, but they do not have to be cleared by the chairman or anyone else. Except in rare circumstances, there is no coordination of topic or message. Speakers are expected to make clear that they are expressing their own views and not those of the Committee as a whole. FOMC participants also observe a "blackout period," just before and just after scheduled FOMC meetings, in which they refrain from discussing current monetary policy and the economic outlook. The practice helps keep markets calmer around meetings.

I began my March 2003 speech by observing that, despite a global trend toward inflation targeting that included advanced economies, emerging markets, and even economies transitioning from communism, few in the United States understood or appreciated its benefits. "Discussions of inflation targeting in the American media remind me of the way some Americans deal with the metric system—they don't really know what it is, but they think of it as foreign, impenetrable, and slightly subversive," I said.

One reason for skepticism was that inflation targeting seemed to neglect half of the Fed's dual mandate (maximum employment) in favor of the other half (price stability). Despite its name, however, inflation targeting was not only about inflation control. Inflation targets generally need be met only over periods of several years, leaving plenty of scope for monetary policy to react to an increase in unemployment. This version of inflation targeting—what economists and central bankers call "flexible inflation targeting"—couples longer-term inflation discipline with shorter-term flexibility to counter economic weakness. Virtually all central banks that target inflation are "flexible" inflation targeters.

Indeed, it seemed to me that an inflation target, if accepted as credible by markets and the public, would give the Fed more rather than less room to respond to an economic slowdown. If the markets and the public are confident that the Fed will act as needed to meet its inflation target over time—or, as economists put it, if the public's expectations of inflation are "well anchored" at the target—then the demands of wage- and price-setters will tend to be moderate. Moderate wage and price demands would in turn allow the Fed to fight rising unemployment aggressively with less concern that inflation might get out of control.

In the context of 2003, the communications benefits of inflation targeting seemed particularly salient. Facing the possibility of deflation, we needed to stimulate economic demand and nudge inflation a bit higher. But, with the federal funds rate approaching zero, we had little scope left to ease policy in the conventional way, by reducing the federal funds rate further. In any case, the funds rate, by itself, is relatively unimportant. The interest rates that really matter for the economy, such as mortgage rates or corporate bond rates, are much longer-term. These longer-term rates are not under the Fed's direct control. Instead, they are set by participants in financial markets.

With little room to cut the funds rate further, how could we put downward pressure on longer-term rates? One way was to convince market participants that we intended to keep the short-term rate that we controlled low for a relatively long time. In setting longer-term rates, market participants take into account their expectations for the evolution of short-term rates. So, if short-term rates were expected to be lower for longer, longer-term rates would tend to be low as well. Suppose, I argued, that the Fed had a numerical inflation target, and that actual inflation was projected to remain well below target. In that situation, investors would infer that we needed to keep short-term rates low for quite a while. As a result, longer-term rates would be lower than would otherwise be the case, stimulating demand and pushing inflation up toward our target.

Without inflation targeting or a coherent communications framework, the Fed had what I called a Marcel Marceau communications strategy. The idea was watch what I do, not what I say. That might have been adequate in normal times. Markets can infer how the Fed is likely to behave based on how it has behaved in the past. However, in 2002 and 2003, with interest rates and inflation quite low, markets didn't have enough examples of Fed behavior in similar circumstances. Inflation targeting, I argued, could help fill the information vacuum.

The inflation-targeting dispute at the Fed had been going on for a while. Greenspan had staged a debate on the topic at the January 1995 FOMC meeting to sound out the Committee's position before testifying at congressional hearings. During my time as a rank-and-file Board member, however, Greenspan remained firmly opposed. He also appeared concerned about achieving consensus among the seven Board members and twelve Reserve Bank presidents on what inflation target to set and how to characterize our plans for achieving the target. Finally, as a veteran of political battles, he hinted at his reluctance to change the framework for monetary policy without congressional authorization. Thus, although as a group we endlessly discussed the increasingly evident need for more effective communication, and sometimes mentioned inflation targets, we knew it wasn't going to happen unless Greenspan changed his views.

AS THE WAR in Iraq proceeded, uncertainties ebbed somewhat and we got a clearer look at the state of the economy. Leading into the May 2003 meeting, we didn't like what we saw. Payrolls continued to decline after the big drop in February, bringing the cumulative three-month loss through April to 525,000 jobs. Moreover, inflation continued to edge lower. Without a well-established communications framework, we struggled to convey our commitment to keep monetary policy easy until inflation increased and job growth resumed.

The FOMC's communications had indeed followed a long and tortuous journey. Until 1994, the Committee had made no postmeeting statement, not even when the decision was to change the federal funds rate. Instead, market participants had to guess at the FOMC's decision by watching developments in short-term money markets. Starting in February 1994, Greenspan issued a postmeeting "chairman's statement," usually drafted with the help of Don Kohn. However, Committee members soon recognized the effect that the statement could have on markets, and, over time, they became increasingly involved in its drafting. The statement also grew longer as the Committee tried to communicate its leanings without necessarily committing to a specific action.

The statement we issued after our May 2003 meeting included a key new sentence, one that reflected the Committee's growing concerns about deflation. We said that "the probability of an unwelcome substantial fall in inflation, though minor, exceeds that of a pickup of inflation from its already low level." The statement, though convoluted, focused attention on too-low inflation and, most importantly, conveyed that substantially lower inflation would be "unwelcome"—in stark contrast to the past forty years, when declining inflation was invariably viewed as good. Effectively, the Committee was saying that we had an inflation target—but without giving a number—and that we were concerned that inflation would fall below it.

The markets got the message. Expecting easier monetary policy, or at least a continuation of the current level of ease, traders bid down longer-term interest rates, adding more stimulus to the economy. The yield on ten-year Treasury securities, at 3.92 percent on the day before the meeting, fell as low as 3.13 percent by mid-June. Thirty-year fixed rate mortgages fell from 5.7 percent to 5.2 percent. Notably, we had attained this result through words only. At our June meeting, we followed up by cutting the federal funds rate, from 1-1/4 percent to 1 percent—the lowest level since the Fed had begun using the rate as a policy instrument in the 1960s.

Around this time, I used my speeches, including one in May in Japan, the poster child for deflation, to raise awareness that inflation could be too low as well as too high. In July, at the University of California, San Diego, I said the Fed must take even a small risk of deflation seriously and make clear that it was prepared to prevent it. Explaining our policy intentions was key. "The success of monetary policy depends more on how well the central bank communicates its plans and objectives than on any other single factor," I said. Of course, I saw the adoption of a numerical inflation target as the cleanest way to make our policy intentions clear.

The FOMC wasn't ready to take that step, but we spent many hours debating how to communicate our policy plans. In the statement after our August meeting, we offered guidance, albeit vague, on our own expectations for monetary policy. We said we expected we would maintain low interest rates for "a considerable period." The goal of that phrase was to keep longer-term interest rates low by influencing market expectations for short-term rates.

As the FOMC was pushing for a stronger recovery, we got some help from fiscal policy. In May 2003, the Bush administration won new tax cuts from Congress, on top of tax cuts approved in 2001. The bill put cash into people's pockets by cutting taxes on wages and on personal interest and dividends. To the extent they spent their tax cuts, demand for goods and services would increase, thus encouraging more production and hiring.

IN NOVEMBER, TIM GEITHNER replaced Bill McDonough as president of the New York Fed. The New York Fed president, as the vice chairman of the FOMC, has an important voice in monetary policy and—because many of the nation's largest banks are headquartered in New York—in banking supervision as well. I would ultimately become a big fan of Tim's, but when I first met him I was underwhelmed. Tim is slight, soft-spoken, and looked if anything younger than his forty-two years. He had neither professional credentials in economics nor experience as a bank supervisor. What he had was unqualified support from heavy hitters including former Treasury secretaries Larry Summers and Bob Rubin, as well as the chairman of the New York Fed's board—Pete Peterson, a former commerce secretary under Richard Nixon and the cofounder of the Blackstone private equity firm. I was skeptical about giving someone such an important job based on recommendations rather than on qualifications and a record of sustained accomplishment.

It turned out, however, to have been the right appointment. Tim did not have a doctorate but he had the equivalent of a PhD in financial crisis management. After working at Henry Kissinger's global consulting firm, he had joined the staff of the Treasury Department in 1988. He rose quickly, impressing Rubin and Summers with his intelligence and savvy and playing an important role in the Treasury's efforts to put out financial fires around the world, most notably the Asian financial crisis in 1997.

By the December 2003 meeting, Geithner's first, the economy looked stronger. Impressively, a preliminary estimate put economic growth in the third quarter at more than an 8 percent annual rate. FOMC participants during the go-round were upbeat. Several noted that the "considerable period" language appeared to be helping to keep longer-term interest rates down. "It's very evident that our effort to communicate that message has succeeded," Greenspan said. Despite the improved outlook, inflation remained too low for us to feel confident that deflation risks had been eliminated; and unemployment was still at 6 percent. The FOMC kept the funds rate at 1 percent and continued to project that policy accommodation would be maintained for a considerable period.

MY APPOINTMENT TO the Board in August 2002 had been to serve what was left of Mike Kelley's term, which would expire on January 31, 2004. White House officials had made no firm commitment but said I would receive strong consideration if I wanted a new term. It seemed too soon to return to Princeton, and so, during the summer of 2003, I asked to be reappointed. I soon received word that the reappointment had been approved. Princeton extended my two-year leave to three years but made clear it would not grant further extensions.

Attendance was sparse at my confirmation hearing before the Senate Banking Committee, on October 14, 2003, even though I appeared with Roger Ferguson, who was being nominated for another four-year term as Board vice chairman. As he usually did, Senator Jim Bunning of Kentucky, a Baseball Hall of Fame pitcher, criticized the Fed. He would continue to throw high and inside at me and other Fed officials for his remaining years in Congress. Bunning asked for assurances that Ferguson and I would not "rubber-stamp" Greenspan's decisions. I replied that I had been generally comfortable with the direction of policy, but noted that I had staked out independent positions on issues like inflation targeting. The nominations moved to the full Senate and Roger and I were reconfirmed without fanfare.

———

BY THE TIME of the first FOMC meeting of 2004, in late January, the economic outlook had brightened further still. The economy had grown at better than a 6 percent annual rate in the second half of 2003, and unemployment, at 5.7 percent in December, seemed to be on a mild downtrend. On the other hand, job growth remained flat and inflation was still very low. Ned Gramlich, who had dissented in favor of easier monetary policy in September 2002, proved to be a bellwether by swinging to the hawkish camp that worried about keeping interest rates too low for too long. He said a pattern of vigorous growth was spreading throughout the economy and it was time to start gradually reducing monetary stimulus. Greenspan too was optimistic that, even with less support from monetary policy, the economy could continue to improve.

Managing our communications had been critical in the easing process, and it would be equally important for a successful tightening of policy. As a first step in reducing stimulus, we dropped the assertion in our postmeeting statement that we would maintain low rates for a considerable period and said, instead, that we thought we could "be patient in removing" easy policy. Markets apparently missed the hint that we were moving, albeit slowly, toward tightening policy. Both short- and long-term interest rates changed little.

The economy continued to improve through 2004. Meanwhile, we continued to fiddle with the statement language. At the May meeting, we dropped "be patient" and said we thought easy policy could "be removed at a pace that is likely to be measured." We were signaling now not only the timing of the next rate increase (soon) but also the pace of subsequent increases (slow). In June, we abandoned our reliance on language alone and agreed, without dissent, to raise the target for the federal funds rate from 1 percent to 1-1/4 percent. It was the first increase since May 2000, before the recession had begun. Continued strength in job creation and receding deflation risk justified the action. Initial rate increases by the Fed can sometimes jar financial markets, but in this case market participants anticipated the move. They were seeing the same improvements in the economy that we observed and, with help from our statements, were guessing correctly how monetary policy would respond.

"The economy has come a long way in the past year, and . . . we should pause to take some satisfaction in the Federal Reserve's contribution to the turnaround," I said at the June meeting. "Our policy actions, reinforced by innovations in our communication strategy, helped provide crucial support to the economy during a dangerous period."

After sputtering for a year and a half, the recovery over the second half of 2003 and through 2004 went from jobless to job-creating. At the same time, inflation went from worryingly low levels to something closer to 2 percent—high enough to provide a buffer against deflation but not so high as to interfere with the healthy functioning of the economy. If we hadn't supported the economy by lowering interest rates and through our communication, the recovery would have been more halting, unemployment would have been higher for longer, and deflation risks would have been much higher.*

True to our word, the FOMC would increase rates at a "measured pace" over the next two years. By Greenspan's last FOMC meeting in January 2006, the Fed had raised the federal funds rate to 4-1/2 percent. Nevertheless, the economy continued to create jobs with modest inflation. The unemployment rate in Greenspan's last month in office was 4.7 percent, and inflation was trending just under 2 percent.

The Maestro looked to have done it again. At the Kansas City Fed's annual Jackson Hole symposium in August 2005, his last as chairman, he was hailed as the greatest central banker in history.

---

* Data revisions suggest the deflation risk may have been slightly less than we thought at the time, although inflation was certainly very subdued. Policymakers must of course make their decisions based on the data available at the time. Moreover, given the economy's weakness, inflation was at risk of dropping meaningfully further.

CHAPTER 5

The Subprime Spark

E ven as the United States enjoyed what appeared to be a Goldilocks economy (not too hot, not too cold) and Alan Greenspan was receiving accolades for a successful eighteen-year run, dangerous risks were building. These risks are clear now in hindsight but were less so at the time.

Toward the end of my tenure as chairman, I was asked what had surprised me the most about the financial crisis. "The crisis," I said. I did not mean we missed entirely what was going on. We saw, albeit often imperfectly, most of the pieces of the puzzle. But we failed to understand—"failed to imagine" might be a better phrase—how those pieces would fit together to produce a financial crisis that compared to, and arguably surpassed, the financial crisis that ushered in the Great Depression.

A few people had warned about various risks but few, if any, economists—or, for that matter, policymakers or financial executives—had assembled all the pieces into a coherent whole. Future Nobelist Robert Shiller of Yale warned of a possible bubble in house prices in his 2005 book *Irrational Exuberance*. Even earlier, in 2003, at the annual Federal Reserve Bank of Kansas City conference in Jackson Hole, Wyoming, Claudio Borio and William White of the Bank for International Settlements (BIS) wrote that long periods of financial calm could lead investors and financial institutions to become complacent and take excessive risks. Their arguments echoed ideas published decades earlier by the economist Hyman Minsky, who believed that, absent a crisis, risks in the financial system tend to build up. In 2005, also at Jackson Hole, University of Chicago economist (and later governor of India's central bank) Raghuram Rajan spoke about poorly designed compensation arrangements that might lead asset managers to take excessive risks. Of course, as always seems to be the case, many commentators also warned about imminent crises that did not occur, such as the return of high inflation or a collapse of the dollar in the face of the nation's large trade deficit.

If a hurricane knocks down a house, you can blame it on the strength of the hurricane or on structural deficiencies in the house. Ultimately, both factors matter. A destructive financial crisis is analogous. There are the immediate causal factors, or triggers—the hurricane. But the triggers cannot cause extensive damage without structural weaknesses, the vulnerabilities of the system itself—a house with a weak foundation.

The financial crisis of 2007–2009 had several triggers. The most important and best known is the rapid run-up and subsequent collapse in housing prices and construction. As is also widely appreciated, the housing boom and bust was in turn fueled by a widespread breakdown in discipline in mortgage lending, particularly in subprime lending (lending to borrowers with weak credit records).* Other, less-emphasized, triggers included excessively risky lending to commercial real estate developers and a huge global demand for financial assets perceived to be safe—a demand that incentivized Wall Street to construct and sell complicated new financial instruments that would ultimately blow up.

Many accounts of the financial crisis focus almost entirely on the triggers, particularly the housing bust and irresponsible subprime lending. These triggers, like a powerful hurricane, would have had

---

*   Typically, subprime borrowers had FICO (Fair Isaac and Company) scores of 620 or less, which made them ineligible for regular (prime) mortgages, unless they made significant down payments.

destructive effects in any scenario. But in the absence of key structural vulnerabilities in the financial system itself, the hurricane would not have come nearly so close to bringing down our entire economy. The American financial system had become increasingly complex and opaque, the financial regulatory system had become obsolete and dangerously fragmented, and an excessive reliance on debt—particularly short-term debt—had rendered the system unstable under pressure. The extraordinary complexity of the interaction of triggers and structural vulnerabilities helps explain why so few people anticipated the full nature and extent of the crisis.

But even if housing and subprime lending were only part of the story, they nevertheless were critical elements. It's accordingly important to understand how the Fed saw the developments in those areas before the crisis and why we and other regulators were not more effective in defusing the growing risks.

THE EVOLUTION OF housing finance offers as good an illustration as any of the sea changes in the financial system from the mid-twentieth century to the early twenty-first century. Decades ago, it was common for bankers to take deposits from people they nodded hello to at the grocery store and to make mortgage loans to people in neighborhoods within a thirty-minute drive of the bank. Community bankers, or the local representatives of larger banks, often knew personally the people to whom they were lending and had good information as well about the collateral (the home) that backed the loan. They usually kept those loans on their own books, giving them every incentive to try to make sound lending decisions.

By the time I arrived at the Fed in 2002, the traditional model of mortgage lending had been largely replaced by a sleeker, shinier version. In theory, the changes to the traditional model were improvements, designed to address weaknesses of the older system. New technologies, like computerized credit records and standardized credit scores, made mortgage lending more efficient and more competitive, reducing costs and expanding the range of borrowers that lenders could serve. More-over, firms that made mortgage loans were no longer mostly limited to lending funds raised by deposits, as had once been the case. Instead, they could sell their mortgages to third parties, who packaged them together and sold the newly created securities to investors—a process called *securitization*. Securitization allowed mortgage lenders access to an enormous pool of global savings to fund new loans. The suppliers of funds also saw benefits. The new mortgage-backed securities (MBS) could be structured in ways that increased diversification—by com-bining mortgages from different regions of the country, for example—and could be sliced into segments, or *tranches*, to accommodate the risk preferences of investors.

The advantages of the new model (sometimes called the originate-to-distribute model) were real. But by the early 2000s, the system was also facilitating, or even encouraging, risky and irresponsible behavior. Because mortgage originators no longer expected to retain the loans they made for very long, they cared less about the quality of those loans. Often, they delegated the responsibility of arranging loans to brokers with no more skin in the game than a month-to-month lease on an office in a strip mall. Brokers, often paid by commission, raced to connect as many borrowers as possible with mortgage originators. As in the traditional model, sometimes the originator was a commer-cial bank or savings and loan. But often, the originator of the loan was a nonbank company financed by Wall Street through various forms of short-term lending—a source of funding that could disappear literally overnight.

As the chain from borrower to broker to originator to securitizer to investor grew longer, accountability for the quality of the underlying mortgages became more and more diffused. Ultimately the complex securities, blessed by supposedly independent rating agencies (pri-vate firms paid by the issuers of securities to grade those very securi-ties), were purchased by investors ranging from U.S. pension funds to German banks to sovereign wealth funds owned by Asian or Middle

Eastern governments. Most investors did not independently analyze the securities they bought and had limited understanding of the risks involved. In some cases, unethical investment firms intentionally palmed off bad mortgage securities on investors. But many securitizers did not themselves appreciate the risks of the products they were selling. One study found that many Wall Street managers engaged in securitized finance had aggressively increased their personal investments in housing from 2004 through 2006, on the expectation that house prices would continue to rise.

For a time, these arrangements seemed to work well for both borrowers and investors. Investors liked that they could purchase highly rated assets with higher yields than government debt. Mortgage borrowers benefited from lower origination costs and increased credit availability. Indeed, thanks to the easy availability of subprime mortgages with low monthly payments, at least initially, many more Americans were participating in what the housing industry and politicians liked to call the American dream of homeownership. What happened if a homeowner couldn't pay the mortgage when the introductory interest rate reset higher? The assumption was, with house prices moving ever upward, a homeowner could refinance into a new mortgage or, as a last resort, sell the house and repay the loan. If a homeowner defaulted, investors in mortgage-backed securities would be protected because the house would be worth more than the mortgage. Diversification and the magic of financial engineering spread the risk thin and dispersed it around the world.

What if house prices fell precipitously and a lot of homeowners defaulted? No one really knew—but it seemed very, very unlikely. Until, of course, it happened.

IN THE YEARS FOLLOWING the 2001 recession, my colleagues at the Fed and I were paying close attention to developments in housing and mortgage markets, but we saw pluses as well as minuses. Robust home construction helped bolster otherwise sluggish economic growth, and rising home values supported consumer confidence. Chairman Greenspan often noted that homeowners' borrowing against the equity in their homes was an important source of consumer spending. We talked more about banks' profitability and improved capital positions than about their risks from mortgage lending. Indeed, the banking system seemed exceptionally strong. Not a single bank failed in 2005, the first year without a failure since the inception of federal deposit insurance during the Depression. Industry-wide, banks reported high profits and low credit losses.

We were not entirely unaware of or unconcerned about the risks to housing or the financial sector more generally. For example, at several FOMC meetings, Boston Fed president Cathy Minehan said she worried that low interest rates could be inducing investors to "reach for yield," that is, to make excessively risky investments in the hope of earning higher returns. Atlanta Fed president Jack Guynn regularly reported on overheated housing markets in Florida (part of his district) and fretted that his region's banks would be hurt by their lending to construction companies. Sue Bies, who became the head of the Board's bank supervision committee in August 2002, voiced serious concerns about troubled subprime mortgage loans and their potential effects on lenders and borrowers. At several meetings, Board members Ned Gramlich and Roger Ferguson quizzed the staff about the risk of bubbles.

Greenspan himself was clearly aware of potential financial risks. At the January 2004 meeting he worried openly about low interest rates on bonds issued by companies with weak credit, a signal that investors might be underestimating risks. "We are vulnerable at this stage to fairly dramatic changes in psychology," he said. "We are seeing it in the asset-price structure. The structure is not yet at a point where 'bubble' is the appropriate word to describe it, but asset pricing is getting to be very aggressive."

For my part, I argued for more systematic monitoring of threats to the financial system. At the March 2004 meeting, I said we ought to follow the lead of the Bank of England and other major central banks by publishing a quarterly or semiannual "financial stability report." Such a report would warn investors about possible dangers and pressure us, and other regulators, to take action as needed. I acknowledged we might be tempted to paint a benign picture to avoid stirring public concern. But, I said, "financial conditions do change, and it's our collective responsibility both to monitor those changes and to communicate truthfully to the public what we see."

As house prices continued to increase, the FOMC paid more attention. The FOMC heard a special staff presentation on the topic at its June 2005 meeting. I did not attend, having left the Fed by that time for a job in the White House, but I doubt that I would have been more foresighted than those who were there. Today the transcript of that meeting makes for painful reading. The staff presentation was set up as a debate. Staff economists on the pro side argued for the existence of a national housing bubble. They pointed out that house prices had risen far more quickly than rents. If you think of a house as an investment, in addition to being a place to live, then rents and house prices should rise at a similar pace. Housing was like a company whose earnings were flat but whose stock price kept rising—the hallmark of a bubble.

Taking the con side of the debate, other staff members downplayed the possibility of a bubble—or suggested that, if a bubble existed, the economic risks it posed were manageable. Rising house prices were justified, they said, by growing consumer income and confidence, relatively low mortgage rates, and local zoning restrictions that increased the value of housing in desirable locations. To the extent that any mispricing existed, historical experience suggested that it would correct slowly, perhaps through an extended period of stagnant prices. And, the staff economists argued, if housing prices did fall, interest rate cuts by the Fed could cushion the blow to the broader economy.

Most policymakers at the meeting, like most staff economists, downplayed the risks. Sue Bies again took a relatively more pessimistic view, worrying about poor lending practices such as increased reliance on adjustable-rate mortgages with low initial "teaser" rates, and "interest-only" mortgages in which borrowers did not pay down their loan principal. These practices could lead to losses at banks and other lenders, she said. But she did not see the threats to housing or banking as extraordinarily large.

Shortly before the special FOMC discussion, Greenspan had started to speak publicly about "froth"—a collection of small, local bubbles—in the housing market. The mantra of real estate agents— "location, location, location"—seemed to apply. It was easy to conceive of a housing bubble in one metro area, or even across several regions of the country. It was more difficult to imagine a nationwide boom and bust in house prices because local conditions varied. (Rating agencies assumed that combining mortgages from different parts of the country in securitized credit products would protect investors—a critical mistake.) Ultimately, the size of the housing boom and bust did vary considerably by region and by city, with the "sand states" (like Florida, Nevada, and Arizona) having much larger bubbles than, say, midwestern states. But the magnitude and geographical extent of the boom were large enough that the effects of the bust were felt nationally.

Greenspan's froth comments were among several veiled warnings in 2005 of imbalances in both financial and housing markets. In his February Humphrey-Hawkins testimony to Congress, he said, "history cautions that people experiencing long periods of relative stability are prone to excess." In August of the same year, at Jackson Hole, he suggested people could be paying too much for stocks, bonds, and houses, which meant they weren't taking adequate account of the riskiness of those assets. "History has not dealt kindly with the aftermath of protracted periods of low risk premiums," he said. A month later, he warned that exotic forms of adjustable-rate mortgages to subprime borrowers could, in the event of what he called "widespread cooling in house prices," expose both borrowers and lenders to significant losses. Markets, which had briefly quaked in 1996 when Greenspan mused publicly about "irrational exuberance," shrugged off these valedictory year ruminations. House prices rose 15 percent in 2005, on top of a 16 percent increase in 2004. Meanwhile the stock and bond markets ended 2005 about where they had begun.

CLEARLY, MANY OF US at the Fed, including me, underestimated the extent of the housing bubble and the risks it posed. That raises at least two important questions. First, what can be done to avoid a similar problem in the future? Improved monitoring of the financial system and stronger financial regulation are certainly part of the answer. A second question is even more difficult: Suppose we had done a better job of identifying the housing bubble in, say, 2003 or 2004? What, if anything, should we have done? In particular, should we have leaned against the housing boom with higher interest rates? I had argued in my first speech as a Fed governor that, in most circumstances, monetary policy is not the right tool for tackling asset bubbles. That still seems right to me.

The jobless recovery and the risk of deflation that followed the 2001 recession were real and serious problems. Greenspan believed, and I agreed, that the first priorities for monetary policy should be to help the job market and to avoid slipping further toward deflation. An example of what can go wrong when a central bank focuses too much on asset prices occurred some years later. Swedish central bankers raised interest rates in 2010 and 2011 in response to concerns about rising mortgage debt and house prices, even though inflation was forecast to remain below their target and unemployment was high. As a result, the Swedish economy fell into deflation, forcing the central bank to cut rates from 2 percent to zero over the next three years—an embarrassing reversal.*

Some have argued—most prominently, Stanford economist John

---

*   In February 2015 the Swedish central bank was forced to go even further to fight deflation, by beginning purchases of government bonds and setting a negative interest rate on bank reserves.

Taylor—that I've depicted the choice between achieving the Fed's inflation and employment goals, on the one hand, and letting the air out of the housing bubble, on the other, too starkly. Taylor argues that somewhat higher interest rates during the early 2000s could have cooled the bubble while still keeping inflation on track and bringing unemployment down. He has contended that the Fed could have avoided the worst of the housing bubble by setting monetary policy in accordance with a simple rule that he developed.

Could monetary policy during the early 2000s have been easy enough to achieve our employment and inflation goals while simultaneously tight enough to significantly moderate the housing boom? It seems highly implausible. Modestly higher interest rates, as implied by Taylor's rule, would have slowed the recovery while likely having only small effects on house prices. Research at the Fed in 2010 showed that following Taylor's rule over 2003–2005 would have raised the initial monthly payment of a typical borrower with an adjustable-rate mortgage by about $75. According to surveys conducted at the time, many people were expecting double-digit gains in house prices. An extra $75 doesn't seem like enough to have significantly affected those buyers' behavior. In any case, the Fed did begin tightening steadily in June 2004, but house prices continued to rise sharply for several more years.

Many who argue that interest rates should have been raised earlier to control house prices implicitly assume that monetary policy that was too loose caused the housing boom in the first place. But it's easy to identify factors other than monetary policy that contributed to the boom. Robert Shiller, who correctly predicted both the dot-com stock bubble and the housing bubble, attributed the housing bubble largely to psychological factors rather than low interest rates. He noted in 2007 that house prices began to accelerate rapidly in the United States around 1998, well before the Fed's 2001 rate cuts. Sharp increases in house prices occurred at about the same time in other countries, including in countries (like the United Kingdom) that ran more restrictive monetary policies than the United States.

Additionally, the remarkable economic stability of the latter part of the 1980s and the 1990s—a period that economists have dubbed "the Great Moderation"—likely bred complacency. The generally successful monetary policies of those decades probably contributed to the Great Moderation and thus may have contributed to the bubble psychology indirectly. But monetary policy cannot intentionally foster economic instability to guard against future complacency.

Yet another factor driving house prices was a tidal wave of foreign money that poured into the United States. These inflows—largely unrelated to our monetary policy—held down longer-term rates, including mortgage rates, while increasing the demand for mortgage-backed securities. Other countries with large inflows of foreign capital, like Spain, also experienced housing booms. When longer-term interest rates failed to rise after the Fed tightened monetary policy in 2004–2005, Greenspan called it a "conundrum." In speeches, I tied the conundrum to what I called the "global savings glut"—more savings were available globally than there were good investments for those savings, and much of the excess foreign savings were flowing to the United States. Additional capital inflows resulted from efforts by (mostly) emerging-market countries like China to promote exports and reduce imports by keeping their currencies undervalued. To keep the value of its currency artificially low relative to the dollar, a country must stand ready to buy dollar-denominated assets, and China had purchased hundreds of billions of dollars' worth of U.S. debt, including mortgage-backed securities.

IF MONETARY POLICY was not the right tool for addressing a possible house-price bubble, then what was? In my 2002 speech, I had said that financial regulation and supervision should be the first line of defense against asset-price bubbles and other risks to financial stability. If those more focused tools are used effectively, then monetary policy can be left free to pursue low inflation and unemployment. Unfortunately, in this instance, regulatory and supervisory tools were not used effectively, either by the Fed or by other financial regulators. Without doubt, that contributed importantly to the severity of the crisis.

Banking regulation and supervision, broadly speaking, have two purposes: first, to ensure that banks are financially sound and, second, to protect consumers. At the Board, the Division of Banking Supervision and Regulation managed safety-and-soundness regulation and supervision. The Division of Consumer and Community Affairs focused, among other duties, on writing rules to protect consumers and examining banks for compliance with those rules. Either or both of these sets of powers could have helped address the buildup of risks in housing and mortgage markets. They did not. The question is why.

Booming house prices in the early 2000s seemed to go hand in hand with risky mortgage lending, including subprime lending, but also lending involving bad underwriting practices (no verification of borrower income, for example) or with special features (like interest-only payments) that were risky for weaker borrowers. Risky mortgage lending increased the demand for housing, pushing prices higher. At the same time, the more house prices rose, the less careful lenders became. By far the worst loans were made in 2005, as house prices were nearing their peak, and in 2006, just as prices began to reverse. Indeed, by 2006 and 2007, some borrowers were defaulting on loans after making only a few, or even no, payments.

Subprime lending was not new in the early 2000s, but its share of total mortgage lending was rising steadily. In 1994, fewer than 5 percent of new mortgages were subprime, but by 2005 subprime's share of originations had risen to about 20 percent. Moreover, a substantial portion of subprime loans originated in the early 2000s were adjustable-rate mortgages. The interest rate on these loans initially was set low, typically for two or three years. After that, it adjusted to move in line with market rates. These teaser rates, together with very low down payments in many instances, made it possible for borrowers with poor credit to buy homes that, under ordinary circumstances, they could not afford. Both borrowers and lenders counted on bor-

rowers being able to refinance before the interest rate on their mortgage reset higher. But refinancing was only an option so long as house
prices (and thus homeowners' equity) kept rising.

Regulators, including the Fed, were aware of these trends, but, in
retrospect, we responded too slowly and cautiously. I don't think the
slow response can be attributed to ill-prepared examiners, the foot soldiers who interacted most closely with the banks. Like any large organization, the Fed had stronger and weaker employees, but the general
quality of the supervisory staff was high. I also don't think that key
Fed staff were captured by the firms they regulated, in the sense that
they perceived it to be in their own career or financial interest to go
easy. They were, however, open to arguments that regulatory burden
should not be excessive and that competitive market forces would to
some extent deter poor lending practices. Maintaining the appropriate balance between bank safety, on the one hand, and the availability
of credit, on the other, is never easy, and the Fed and other regulators
probably tipped too far in the direction of credit availability. Station-
ing on-site teams of examiners at the same large banks for protracted
periods could have made them too willing to accept the prevailing
assumptions and biases at the institutions they supervised.

A perennial problem at the Fed was the difficulty of maintaining consistent, tough supervisory practices across the twelve Federal
Reserve districts. Ultimately, the Board is responsible for bank supervision, but the Reserve Banks housed the examiners who oversaw
banks day in, day out. Reserve Banks often chafed at directions from
Washington, arguing that they were better informed than the Board
staff about conditions in their districts. Indeed, the Reserve Bank
presidents succeeded in resisting a 2005 attempt by Sue Bies to make
supervision more centralized.

Although regulatory philosophy and management issues at the
Fed played a role, some of the greatest barriers to effective supervision
lay outside the Fed, in the broader structure of financial regulation.
The U.S. financial regulatory system before the crisis was highly frag-

mented and full of gaps. Important parts of the financial system were inadequately overseen (if overseen at all) and, critically, no agency had responsibility for the system as a whole. The reasons for this fragmentation were both historical and political. Historically, regulatory agencies were created ad hoc in response to crises and other events—the Office of the Comptroller of the Currency during the Civil War, the Federal Reserve after the Panic of 1907, and the Federal Deposit Insurance Corporation and Securities and Exchange Commission (SEC) during the Depression. Politically, conflicts between competing power centers within government (congressional committees with overlapping jurisdictions, state versus federal regulators) and special interests, such as the banking and housing lobbies, have routinely blocked attempts to rationalize and improve the existing system.

The result was a muddle. For example, regulation of financial markets (such as the stock market and futures markets) is split between the SEC and the Commodity Futures Trading Commission, an agency created by Congress in 1974. The regulation of banks is dictated by the charter under which each bank operates. While banks chartered at the federal level, so-called national banks, are regulated by the OCC, banks chartered by state authorities are overseen by state regulators. State-chartered banks that choose to be members of the Federal Reserve System (called state member banks) are also supervised by the Federal Reserve, with the FDIC examining other state-chartered banks. And the Fed oversees bank holding companies—companies that own banks and possibly other types of financial firms—independent of whether the owned banks are state-chartered or nationally chartered. Before the crisis, still another agency, the Office of Thrift Supervision (OTS), regulated savings institutions and the companies that owned savings associations. And the National Credit Union Association oversees credit unions.

Institutions were able to change regulators by changing their charters, which created an incentive for regulators to be less strict so as not to lose their regulatory "clients"—and the exam fees they paid. For example, in March 2007, the subprime lender Countrywide Financial, by switching the charter of the depository institution it owned, replaced the Fed as its principal supervisor with the OTS, after the OTS promised to be "less antagonistic." The OCC at times actively sought to induce banks to switch to a national bank charter. Both the OCC and the OTS benefited the institutions they regulated by asserting that the institutions were exempt from most state and local laws and regulations.

This fragmentation of financial regulation often limited the ability of federal regulators to monitor system-wide developments. For example, in 2005, only about 20 percent of all subprime mortgages were made by banks and savings institutions under federal supervision. Another 30 percent of subprime loans were made by nonbank subsidiaries of federally regulated institutions. The remaining 50 percent of loans were originated by independent mortgage companies chartered and supervised only by the states. A few states—Massachusetts and North Carolina are often cited—did a good job in overseeing nonbank mortgage lending. Lacking resources and political support, most did not.

Even the regulatory oversight of mortgage securitization was split among agencies. The Office of Federal Housing Enterprise Oversight (OFHEO) regulated the government-sponsored companies that securitized mortgages (Fannie Mae and Freddie Mac), while the SEC oversaw the Wall Street investment banking firms that also created various securities backed by mortgages (known as private-label securitization). Like the Indian folktale of the blind men and the elephant, each regulator was aware of only part of the problem, and some parts were not examined at all.

It didn't help that many financial institutions, in their rush to embrace profitable new products and markets, did a poor job of measuring and managing the risks they were taking on. A spate of mergers among financial institutions, each with its own information system, exacerbated the difficulty. Large banks, it turned out, were exposed to the risk of mortgage defaults not only through the mortgages on their balance sheets but through many other channels, including through securitized assets they held or guaranteed. The systems that firms used to measure their exposures could not keep up with the rapid changes in the holdings of various subsidiaries, the many channels of risk exposure, or the extent to which the risks interacted.

The Fed and other regulators pushed banks to improve their systems for assessing and measuring their risks. And Sue Bies, at industry forums, regularly promoted the virtues of comprehensively assessing risks for the firm as a whole, rather than looking at risks only for each separate part of the business. But, in truth, in the years just before the crisis, neither banks nor their regulators adequately understood the full extent of banks' exposures to dicey mortgages and other risky credit. The experience of the Great Moderation had led both banks and regulators to underestimate the probability of a large economic or financial shock.

Meanwhile, constrained by bureaucratic, legal, and political barriers, regulatory agencies struggled to keep up with fast-moving changes in financial products and practices. The federal bank regulators (the Fed, the OCC, the FDIC, and the OTS) often responded to new issues by issuing official "guidance" to banks. Guidance has less legal force than regulations, but it still carries considerable weight with bank examiners. In the years before the crisis, regulators issued guidance on subprime lending (1999 and 2001), low-down-payment real estate lending (1999), real-estate appraisal practices (2003 and 2005), predatory (abusive) lending (2004 and 2005), and lending against home equity (2005). The federal agencies also proposed in 2005, and finalized in 2006, guidance on the "nontraditional" features (like the option to skip payments) that had become prevalent in subprime mortgages. Yet most of the guidance and rules weren't tough enough or timely enough.

Bureaucratic inertia, as well as legal and political impediments, slowed the issuance of guidance. When the regulatory agencies issued guidance jointly, the usual case, they had to reach agreement first within their own ranks and then across agencies. Promulgating rules, and sometimes also guidance, required an elaborate legal process that included periods for affected parties to comment and the agencies to respond. Whenever rules or guidance threatened the interests of favored groups, political pressure followed. In the summer of 2005, for example, regulatory agencies became concerned that some banks, especially smaller banks, were making and holding too many commercial real estate loans—which financed the construction of office buildings, shopping malls, apartment complexes, and housing developments. The agencies proposed guidance pushing banks to limit their risks in this area. Though an improvement over existing practices, the draft guidance wasn't particularly strict. Janet Yellen, then president of the San Francisco Fed, whose examiners were trying to rein in commercial real estate lending in red-hot markets in the West, later derided the final version. "You could take it out and rip it up and throw it in the garbage can. It wasn't of any use to us," she said in 2010.

Even so, the proposed guidance drew fierce resistance from community bankers, who relied heavily on profits from commercial real estate lending. Community banks, though a small part of the banking system, have disproportionate political clout. Thousands of letters of protest poured in, and a House Financial Services subcommittee held a hearing. The regulators pushed back against the lobbyists and politicians but spent months assuring critics (and themselves) that the guidance could achieve its objectives without overly crimping smaller banks. All of the back-and-forth meant the agencies did not issue the final guidance until the end of 2006, at least a year and a half after the problem had been identified.

WHILE IT WAS trying to protect banks from themselves, the Fed also was attempting to protect consumers from banks. Sue Bies's counterpart for consumer protection was Ned Gramlich. Ned had chaired the Board committee that oversaw the Division of Consumer and Community Affairs for four years when I arrived in 2002, and he would hold that position until he left the Board in 2005. I was a member from shortly after I arrived until the spring of 2005, with Sue Bies serving for much of that time as the third member. Humane and thoughtful, Ned felt strongly about consumer protection and was skeptical of simplistic free-market dogma. Nevertheless, despite his presence, here too regulation and supervision fell short.

Congress had tasked the Fed with writing regulations implementing many of the most important laws designed to protect financial services consumers, such as the Truth in Lending Act, which governs disclosures to borrowers. However, the responsibility for enforcing the Fed's rules was dispersed among many federal and state agencies, overseeing various types of institutions. The Fed directly enforced its own rules only in the state-chartered banks that had joined the Fed System (about 900 out of 7,500 commercial banks in total at the end of 2005) and at about 5,000 bank holding companies (many of which were shell companies created only to serve as an umbrella over a group of subsidiary companies).

Unfortunately, the consumer division had a relatively low status within the Board and lacked the resources of the supervisors focused on safety and soundness. Chairman Greenspan did not put a high priority on consumer protection. He distrusted what he saw as heavy-handed interventions in the financial services marketplace, although he readily supported improvements in consumer disclosures and in financial education, which he thought helped markets operate more efficiently.

My assignment to the consumer committee reflected my lack of seniority, but I didn't object. Although I had little experience with regulation, I thought the work would be interesting and saw it as a way to help average Americans. I joined my colleagues in regular meetings with the Board's advisory council on consumer issues and with other outside groups, and I tried to educate myself about the complex rules overseen by the Board.

Philosophically, I did not view myself as either strongly pro- or anti-regulation. As an economist, I instinctively trusted markets. Like

Greenspan, in most cases I supported clear disclosures about financial products and financial education for consumers rather than banning practices outright. On the other hand, as adherents of the relatively new field of behavioral economics emphasized, I knew that psychological as well as economic factors motivate human behavior. Realistically, behavioral economists would say, people don't have the time or energy to puzzle out all the contractual details of their mortgages. Consequently, sometimes it may be better simply to ban practices that are not in consumers' interest. The government doesn't allow sales of flammable children's pajamas, for example, no matter how clear the warning label. Over time I would become more sympathetic to the behavioral view. Later, during my chairmanship, the Fed would begin routinely testing the understandability of proposed disclosures (for credit card terms, for example) with actual consumers—an obvious step but an innovation for regulators. We found it was almost impossible to write sufficiently clear disclosures for some financial products. Like flammable pajamas, some products should just be kept out of the marketplace.

DURING MY FIRST two years as chairman, in 2006 and 2007, I would hear repeatedly at congressional hearings that the Fed had been "asleep at the switch" in protecting consumers earlier in the decade. The critics often focused on our failure to use our authority, under the Home Ownership and Equity Protection Act (HOEPA), to outlaw abusive mortgage lending practices. The story of the Fed and HOEPA isn't uplifting, but there's more to it than has been portrayed.

HOEPA, passed by the Congress with Federal Reserve support in 1994, targeted so-called predatory lending practices used by unscrupulous companies to cheat borrowers, particularly elderly, minority, and low-income borrowers. Examples of predatory practices include bait-and-switch (borrowers receive a different type of loan than they were told to expect); equity stripping (lending to borrowers without enough income to repay, with the intent of ultimately seizing their homes);

loan flipping (racking up loans and fees by encouraging repeated refi-nances); and packing (charging borrowers at mortgage origination for unnecessary services).

HOEPA was based on the premise that mortgage loans with very high interest rates were more likely to be predatory. The law required additional disclosures from lenders making high-cost loans and gave the borrowers additional protections not afforded to others. For exam-ple, it limited the use of pre-payment penalties that trapped borrowers in high-cost loans by making it costly for them to refinance. It also specified that investors who purchased high-cost loans could be liable for violations, which discouraged securitization. Importantly, the law applied to mortgages made by any originator—independent mortgage companies, for example—not only those regulated by the Fed or other federal agencies.

In December 2001, the year before I joined the Board, the Fed expanded the definition of a high-cost loan by the maximum extent permitted by law, thereby extending HOEPA protections to more loans. This change, prompted by a series of hearings held by the Fed on predatory lending, increased the share of subprime first mortgages covered by HOEPA from about 12 percent to about 26 percent.

Before the crisis, a controversy sprang up over a provision in HOEPA that authorized the Fed to prohibit practices it found to be "unfair or deceptive." Crucially, this provision applied to all mortgages, not just high-cost loans. In essence, this part of HOEPA gave the Fed a blank check to ban any mortgage practice it thought unfair—although, again, not the authority to enforce the ban, which fell to the federal or state supervisor of each lender. In 2001, in addition to extending high-cost protections to more loans, the Fed had banned three specific practices it deemed unfair or deceptive, the most important being loan flipping. It did not, however, ban other dubious practices, such as making loans without adequately verifying the borrower's income or ability to repay.

In part, the Fed's reluctance to impose blanket prohibitions grew out of the strong distinction that bank regulators, consumer advocates, and politicians made between subprime lending and predatory lending. In contrast to predatory lending, which was universally condemned, with good reason, the increase in lending to borrowers with blemished credit histories was widely extolled. Ned Gramlich, in praising the Fed's expansion of HOEPA protections in 2001, said: "We tried to make our amendments narrow and selective so as not to impede the general growth of the legitimate subprime mortgage market."

Why the support for subprime lending? Historically, lenders had often denied low-income and minority borrowers access to credit. Some lenders redlined whole neighborhoods, automatically turning down mortgage applications from anyone who lived in them. To fight redlining, Congress in 1977 passed the Community Reinvestment Act, which requires bank regulators to encourage banks and savings and loans to serve the entire community where they do business. The law provided some impetus to lend in lower-income or minority neighborhoods, but for various reasons subprime lending ultimately became economically attractive even to lenders, such as independent mortgage companies, not subject to the law. For example, the elimination of usury laws allowed lenders to charge risky borrowers higher interest rates. And, improvements in information technology, combined with the development of standardized credit scores (which summarized complicated credit histories into a single number), facilitated cheap automated lending decisions.

Subprime lending was widely seen as the antidote to redlining—and thus a key part of the democratization of credit. It helped push the U.S. homeownership rate to a record 69 percent by 2005, up from 64 percent a decade earlier. Many of the new homeowners were African Americans and Hispanics, and people with low incomes. As suggested by Ned Gramlich in 2001, federal bank supervisors, including the Fed, tried to avoid interfering with the "legitimate" subprime market—even after the shoddy practices employed in much subprime lending became evident.

Beyond the concerns about inhibiting subprime lending, as distinguished from predatory lending, Greenspan and senior Fed attorneys were reluctant as a matter of principle to aggressively use the HOEPA "unfair or deceptive" authority in a broad-brush way. In public remarks and letters to Congress before and immediately after I joined the Board, Greenspan worried that banning certain categories of practices, which by definition did not take into account the particular circumstances of each mortgage transaction, could have unintended consequences. Instead, the Fed would make case-by-case determinations of whether practices were "unfair or deceptive" as examiners looked at each bank. It could also be claimed, with some justification, that the HOEPA authority did not extend to poor underwriting practices (such as the failure to document income), which were undesirable but not necessarily predatory in intent.

I don't recall that the issue of how to use the unfair-or-deceptive authority was ever formally discussed during my time as a governor, but I was aware of the "case-by-case" approach and did not object. It seemed logical to me that categorical bans could have unintended results. For example, if we had used our unfair-and-deceptive authority to impose strict requirements for documenting borrowers' capacity to repay, then community bankers' ability to make "character loans" based on their personal knowledge of borrowers might be eliminated. That could squeeze out potentially creditworthy borrowers and further erode the competitiveness of community banks. The Fed also took the position that the case-by-case approach would in time provide the information necessary to decide whether categorical bans of certain unfair practices were warranted.

Whatever the validity of these arguments in the abstract, in practice we used our unfair-or-deceptive authority infrequently, and we failed to stop some questionable practices. The hole in our logic was that, as lending standards deteriorated, the exception became the rule. To preserve the ability of bankers to make character loans, for example, the Fed did not ban low-documentation loans. But then, many lenders failed to get adequate documentation even for borrowers they did not know. Similarly, we didn't categorically ban certain types of exotic mortgages, such as those requiring payment of interest only, because they were appropriate for some borrowers. But some lenders offered those types of mortgages to people without the financial wherewithal or sophistication to handle them. Given the bureaucratic barriers to the rapid development of effective interagency guidance, the Fed's unfair-or-deceptive authority, although far from the ideal tool, was probably the best method then available to address unsafe mortgage lending. Early in my term as chairman, the Fed would make extensive use of the authority. Of course, by that time much of the damage had been done.

Although the HOEPA controversy turned on the Fed's ability to write rules about mortgage lending practices, rules aren't useful unless they are enforced. Enforcement engaged Ned Gramlich early on. He observed frequently that, because of the fragmentation of the regulatory system, the enforcement of consumer protection laws was highly uneven. Banks and savings institutions with insured deposits were regularly examined by federal regulators, including the Fed. However, many bank holding companies owned subsidiaries that were not banks or savings institutions funded by deposits—companies that made personal loans to consumers, or mortgage companies financed through Wall Street, for example. These subsidiaries were mostly overseen by state regulators, who generally had few resources, or by the Federal Trade Commission (FTC). The FTC, too, had few resources; moreover, its responsibilities extended far beyond financial matters and included enforcement of antitrust laws and investigations of scams emanating from all manner of businesses. It operated by responding to complaints and did not conduct regular examinations. Finally, lenders that were neither banks nor owned by a bank holding company were beyond the reach of federal banking regulators and were overseen, if at all, only by state regulators and the FTC.

Ned recognized that, barring congressional action, not much could be done at the federal level about independent mortgage companies and other firms not affiliated with banks or bank holding companies. His focus instead was on nonbank lenders owned by bank holding companies. In principle, the Fed, as the overseer of the umbrella bank holding company, had the right to enforce its rules on their subsidiaries, even if those subsidiaries were not banks. And indeed, in one egregious case, the Fed had intervened. In 2004, the Fed hit CitiFinancial, a subsidiary of Citigroup that offered unsecured personal and home equity loans, with a $70 million penalty and a remediation order for a range of violations.

CitiFinancial was an exception, though. The overhaul of financial regulation by Congress, which resulted in the Gramm-Leach-Bliley Act of 1999, presumed that the Fed should defer to the primary regulator of a holding company subsidiary (say, a state regulator in the case of a nonbank mortgage company) and send examiners into the subsidiary only if evidence suggested that the primary supervisor was overlooking significant problems. The purpose of this approach, dubbed "Fed lite," was to avoid double oversight by the Fed of firms that had another regulator.

Ned believed that the Fed should routinely examine nonbank subsidiaries of holding companies for consumer protection violations, not just when obvious problems with state regulation surfaced. Three months before he died, in 2007, Ned told the *Wall Street Journal* that he proposed the idea privately to Chairman Greenspan around 2000. Ned said that Greenspan opposed it, "so I didn't really pursue it." Greenspan told the newspaper he didn't remember the conversation with Ned but acknowledged his opposition to the idea. He said he was worried about the cost of examining large numbers of small institutions, the risk of undermining legitimate subprime lending, and the possibility that borrowers might get a false sense of security from lenders that advertised themselves as Fed-inspected.

I would hear Ned mention the enforcement issue on subsequent occasions, but to my knowledge he didn't press it very hard, even internally. I think he, too, had mixed feelings about the rise of subprime lending. As Ned's *Subprime Mortgages: America's Latest Boom and Bust* (2007) suggests, although he saw the risks earlier than many others, he continued to see positive aspects of subprime lending as well, including the opportunity for increased homeownership. But, while not foreseeing all that would occur, Ned unquestionably did see more, and do more, than the rest of us on the Board.

Would routine exams of holding company subsidiaries by the Fed, as Ned had proposed, have made a difference? Probably yes, although the difference might not have been large, because of the Fed's sensitivity to the distinction between predatory lending and subprime lending. The Fed, in any case, could not examine the freestanding mortgage companies. In 2007, after I became chairman, the Fed, in coordination with state and federal regulators, would examine nonbank subsidiaries of bank holding companies for compliance with consumer protection laws.

By then, as with many of the steps we and other regulators took in 2006 and after, it was too late. With inadequate oversight, greedy and unethical lenders had made hundreds of thousands of bad mortgage loans. Those loans would ultimately expose the vulnerabilities of a fragile financial system. U.S. house prices would plunge more than 30 percent from the spring of 2006 to the spring of 2009 and would not begin a sustained recovery until early 2012. The percentage of subprime mortgages seriously delinquent or in foreclosure would soar from just under 6 percent in the fall of 2005 to more than 30 percent at the end of 2009. Those mortgages had been bundled and sliced and diced into complex instruments and distributed around the world. No one really knew where the losses would surface.

CHAPTER 6

Rookie Season

Early in 2005 Greg Mankiw announced he was leaving his post as chairman of President Bush's Council of Economic Advisers (CEA) to return to teaching at Harvard. Greg—whom I had known since graduate school—called and asked if I had any interest in succeeding him.

For an economist with a policy bent, being a member, let alone chairman, of the CEA is one of the most interesting jobs in Washington. Created in 1946, the council functions as the White House's internal economic consulting firm. It consists of a chairman and two members. About two dozen additional economists, most on temporary leave from a university or from the Fed or other government agencies, make up the staff. A few recent college graduates or graduate students serve as research assistants.

The council is not usually thought of as overtly political—it exists to provide the administration with objective economic advice—but it was certainly more political than the rigorously nonpartisan Fed. It would be easy for a CEA chairman with a political tin ear to get into trouble. Mankiw himself had ignited a short-lived media controversy by speaking favorably about outsourcing jobs to other countries— "a new way of doing international trade," he called it. I had to think about whether I would be comfortable in the job. Thus far in my short Washington career, no one at the White House seemed interested in applying any litmus tests when considering me. The screening of my political views had consisted of White House staff asking whether I was registered as a Republican voter and my exchange with Bush about the school board.

I thought of myself as a moderate Republican—liberal on social issues, more conservative on fiscal and defense, with the standard economist's preference for relying on market forces where possible. I had read Ayn Rand, Greenspan's guru, as a teenager, but I had never gone overboard on libertarianism. I believed (and still do) that respect for the rights of individuals must be balanced with support for families, communities, and other institutions that promote the values of society and provide for the common good. I thought that I would fit in reasonably well with the "compassionate conservatism" but pro-market agenda of President Bush. I knew that, as in any administration, I would have to hew to White House talking points, even when I did not fully agree with them. But at the CEA I would also see firsthand the sausage-making of economic policy, as idealized economic analyses met the rough-and-tumble of Washington politics. And, with the president having just been reelected, I could expect to be involved in new policy initiatives.

With both kids now away at college (Alyssa was attending St. John's College in Annapolis), Anna was ready for a change of scene. We had bought a town house a dozen blocks east of the Capitol. Anna had received an offer to teach Spanish at the National Cathedral School, a private girls' school in northwest Washington. Taking the new position in the third and final year of my leave from Princeton also meant that I would have to resign my tenured professorship. In terms of job security, I was moving in exactly the wrong direction: from a job with lifetime tenure, to a job as Federal Reserve governor that carried a fourteen-year term, to the Council of Economic Advisers, where I served at the pleasure of the president. But I was eager to work in the White House.

Once nominated, I stopped attending FOMC meetings to avoid any appearance of administration influence on monetary policy decisions. The March 2005 meeting, at which we raised the federal funds rate target to 2-3/4 percent, was my last as a governor. I appeared before the Senate Banking Committee on May 25 and was confirmed by the full Senate on June 21. Between Mankiw's departure and my confirmation, Harvey Rosen—a friend and Princeton colleague who had been a member of the council under Mankiw—served as chairman. Harvey, a quiet academic, seemed well liked in the White House. I took this as a good omen. Harvey introduced his wife and two adult children at his going-away party. "Pollsters say that only one out of four Jews vote Republican," he said. "My family is a perfect microcosm of that finding." Deputy Chief of Staff Karl Rove cracked up.

Both member positions on the council needed to be filled. Working with CEA's chief of staff, Gary Blank, I found two strong candidates: Katherine Baicker, a Harvard-trained rising star in health economics; and Matt Slaughter of Dartmouth College, a versatile economist who specialized in trade and globalization. We also recruited economists from academia and government to serve as visiting staff. Fortunately, permanent staff members provided continuity. This included Steve Braun, a former Fed staffer who single-handedly produced the council's macroeconomic forecasts.

For years the council had been housed at the Eisenhower Executive Office Building next to the White House. A grand nineteenth-century building in the French Empire style, it had once housed the State, War, and Navy departments. My high-ceilinged office directly overlooked the entrance to the West Wing. Unfortunately, extensive renovations to the building had forced most of my staff to relocate to a prosaic office building a block away. I wanted to be close to the West Wing and also in close touch with my staff, so I found myself frequently walking between the White House complex and our temporary headquarters.

The council is a remarkably flat organization, with everyone working collaboratively regardless of title or seniority. I sometimes coauthored policy memos with research assistants fresh out of college. The pace was much faster than at the Fed. Despite our limited resources we covered a wide range of issues, including topics that were only partly economic, like immigration or climate change. We prided ourselves on writing thoughtful and well-referenced memos in a few hours. We also monitored economic data and news and provided daily updates to the White House. I reviewed everything that we sent to the West Wing. I knew economic jargon would be ignored, so we worked hard to be clear. As chairman, I represented the Council at the daily 7:30 a.m. White House staff meetings, led by Chief of Staff Andy Card and Karl Rove in the Roosevelt Room. (Rove took to calling me "Doctor Data" at the meetings, but it didn't really catch on.) Rove usually called on me to summarize economic developments, so I arrived in my office by 7:00 a.m. to review the overnight news. My staff and I frequently worked late into the evening, dining on take-out meals from a nearby Subway.

White House economic policy discussions were organized by Al Hubbard, director of the National Economic Council (NEC). The NEC was created during the Clinton administration to play a role analogous to those of the National Security Council (which handles foreign policy and military issues for the White House) and the Domestic Policy Council (which covers noneconomic domestic issues, like education). The NEC was charged with collecting economic policy views from throughout the executive branch, resolving differences, and making recommendations to the president. A gangly, energetic man with a distinctive resonant laugh, Hubbard (no relation to Glenn Hubbard) was a great policy traffic cop. A businessman rather than an economist, he was always willing to acknowledge when he didn't know something and usually deferred to me on technical economic matters. He also made sure that the CEA had a chance to comment whenever economic issues were discussed.

I had a friendly, though not particularly close, relationship with President Bush. (I was invited once, but only once, to the Bush ranch in Crawford, Texas, where I declined an invitation to go running in hundred-degree heat.) I regularly briefed the president and vice president in the Oval Office (usually weekly), with eight or ten other senior staff in attendance. President Bush was a quick study and asked good questions, but he would not hide his impatience if the presentation was too basic or otherwise uninteresting. Sometimes he or the vice president would relay follow-up questions via Hubbard or Hubbard's deputy, Keith Hennessey.

Morale at the White House was good. Bush was loyal to his staff, including an inner circle that went back to his days as governor of Texas, but he was also supportive to others, like me, with less history with the Bush team. He told us frequently it was a privilege to be working in the White House and we should think about that every day. He paid several surprise visits to the CEA's offices to shake hands and talk to staff members.

Famously, Bush liked to tease. Once, when I was making a presentation in the Oval Office, the president walked over to me and lifted my pants leg. With a professor's finely honed sartorial sense, I was wearing tan socks with a dark suit. "You know," he said sternly, "this is the White House, we have standards." I replied that I had bought the socks at the Gap, four pairs for ten dollars, and wasn't he trying to promote conservative spending habits in the administration? He nodded, deadpan, and I went on with the presentation. The next day, I attended another Oval Office meeting. When the president entered, every member of the economic team in the room—plus Vice President Cheney—was wearing tan socks. The president tried to pretend that he didn't notice, but before long he burst out laughing. Keith Hennessey masterminded the prank.

Good morale or no, the period was difficult. Some of the president's initiatives advanced, including several trade deals, and he negotiated a major highway spending bill with Congress. Important groundwork was laid for the eventual reform of Fannie Mae and Freddie Mac. But Bush's proposal to add private accounts to Social Security went nowhere, as did his comprehensive immigration plans.

AFTER HURRICANE KATRINA ravaged New Orleans and the Gulf Coast in August 2005, killing more than 1,800 people, CEA economists put in long hours. Richard Newell, an energy economist now at Duke, provided us with a continuous stream of information on the conditions of refineries and pipelines and on gasoline shipments and shortages. The CEA also wrestled with the problem of developing economically sensible reconstruction plans for the city. On a C-SPAN call-in show about the administration's plans for rebuilding New Orleans, I got carried away discussing the economic costs of the hurricane and various strategies for rescuing the local economy. The first caller commented: "You know, I think you're so involved in all the numbers that you've forgotten the human beings involved." It was a good lesson: Never forget the people behind the numbers.

As CEA chair, I also occasionally testified before congressional committees, delivered speeches on economic policy issues, and met with print reporters. However, the White House asked me only infrequently to appear on TV and never involved me in a political event. I'm not sure whether that was because I was an inadequate spokesperson (as the C-SPAN experience suggested) or because they knew I might be considered to succeed Greenspan and didn't want me to appear too political.

When I did speak in public, the rapid increases in house prices proved one of the thorniest issues. I didn't know how house prices would actually evolve so I avoided making public forecasts. I noted that at least some of the house price appreciation was the result of fundamental factors such as growing incomes and low mortgage rates. I was certainly aware, and occasionally pointed out in both internal and external discussions, that housing, like any asset, could not produce unusually high returns indefinitely. But I thought a slowdown or modest reversal of house price appreciation was more likely than a sharp decline. Nevertheless, with Steve Braun's help, I analyzed the possible economic consequences of a substantial drop in house prices and a resulting decline in homeowners' equity. In an Oval Office presentation, Steve and I concluded that the effects on household spending would produce a moderate recession, similar to or perhaps somewhat deeper than the eight-month-long 2001 recession. We failed to take sufficient account of the effects of falling house prices (and the resulting mortgage delinquencies) on the stability of the financial system.

MY NOMINATION TO the CEA fueled speculation about whether I would be considered for the Fed chairmanship when Greenspan's term ended in January 2006. The CEA had been a stepping-stone to the Fed chairmanship for Greenspan, who had served President Ford, and Arthur Burns, who had served President Eisenhower. When I was eventually named Fed chairman, Princeton economist and *New York Times* columnist Paul Krugman called my time at the CEA "the longest job interview in history." But I didn't take the possibility seriously when I was considering the CEA job. When my Princeton colleague Alan Blinder asked about my prospects of becoming Fed chairman, I downplayed the idea, saying the probability of that happening was "maybe 5 percent." I never politicked for the job and never discussed it with President Bush.

In his last years in office, Greenspan was considered so indispensable that during a Republican presidential primary debate in 1999 John McCain said that if the chairman died, he would prop him up in a chair, put some dark glasses on him, and keep him in office. I suspect President Bush would have reappointed Greenspan—almost eighty years old but still sharp and active—if he could have. But the law says a Federal Reserve Board member can serve no more than one complete fourteen-year term. Greenspan had originally been appointed to a partial term on the Board, then was reappointed to a full term in 1992. That meant that he would be ineligible to serve on the Board after January 2006 and thus disqualified from continuing as chairman. Alan had served more than eighteen years, four months short of breaking the record established by William McChesney Martin, who served as chair through most of the 1950s and 1960s.

The president created a committee headed by Vice President Cheney to recommend a successor to Greenspan. It included Al Hubbard, Andy Card, and White House personnel director Liza Wright. I know little about the committee's deliberations. Journalists (and online betting sites) speculated that Marty Feldstein, Glenn Hubbard, and I were the leading contenders. Feldstein, the instructor of my introductory economics class at Harvard, had a distinguished academic career and had served as CEA chair under President Reagan. At that time he had clashed with Treasury secretary Don Regan and others in the administration when he voiced concern about the budget deficits generated by Reagan's tax cuts. Rumor had it that the controversy, though more than twenty years in the past, would hurt Feldstein's chances. I thought Glenn Hubbard, who after serving as CEA chairman had gone on to serve as the dean of Columbia University's Graduate School of Business, was the favorite. He had a close relationship with the president and had helped devise Bush's signature tax cuts. Glenn had also been active in Republican politics. My own case seemed to rest primarily on my relatively brief Fed experience and my writing and speeches on monetary and financial issues. Both Feldstein and Hubbard were known primarily for work on fiscal policy rather than monetary policy.

In September 2005, the search committee invited me to an interview in the vice president's office. Pretending to read the *Wall Street Journal*, I sat impatiently in the waiting room in the West Lobby of the White House. As visitors passed through, I remember thinking that this probably wasn't the best way to keep the interview under the radar. I was called in about twenty minutes past the appointed time. The meeting itself took maybe a half hour. Mostly we talked about my prior experience and my qualifications. I said that if I were not chosen to be Fed chairman I would be happy to stay at the CEA as long as the president wanted me there.

Weeks passed with no word, and I became convinced that I would be staying at the CEA. When Andy Card asked me to see him for five minutes before the morning staff meeting, I figured that my hunch would be confirmed. Instead, Card asked me whether I would like to serve as chairman of the Fed. I asked for a few hours to think about it but I think it was clear to both of us that I planned to accept.

I called Anna as soon as I left Card's office. "Oh no," she said, in tears. "I was afraid this would happen." Anna had a better idea than I did of the mental, emotional, and physical demands the job would make on both of us. But she would stand by me, for which I will always be grateful. Over the next eight years, a frequent conversation in our house would consist of Anna criticizing a journalist or politician who had gotten it all wrong, with me in the incongruous position of explaining why the person in question might not have been *entirely* wrong.

On October 24, President Bush, Greenspan, and I walked into the Oval Office to the clicking of cameras. Anna, Joel, and Alyssa were already seated, almost obscured by the reporters and their cameras and boom microphones. The president announced the nomination. When my turn came, I thanked the president and Chairman Greenspan, who I said had "set the standard for excellence in economic policymaking." In a hint of my hope to introduce inflation targeting and to increase Fed transparency, I said that best practices in monetary policy had evolved during the Greenspan years and would continue to evolve. But I also said that my first priority would be to maintain continuity with Greenspan's policies. Implicitly, I was promising to continue the gradual increase in interest rates that he had begun in June 2004.

The whole thing took less than eight minutes.

ONCE AGAIN I went through the vetting process, including even more extensive questioning by the FBI. On November 15, 2005, for the fourth time in three and a half years, I went before the Senate Banking Committee for a nomination hearing. My reception was warm and I was approved by the full Senate, with only Senator Bunning registering his opposition. The Senate not being known for haste, however, the confirmation vote came on the last day of Greenspan's term, January 31.

On the next day, February 1, 2006, in the boardroom, I became the fourteenth chairman of the Federal Reserve when I was quietly sworn in by Vice Chairman Roger Ferguson in the presence of a few governors and staff. There would be a formal swearing-in ceremony as well, on February 6 in the two-story atrium of the Eccles Building. In addition to family members, Alan Greenspan, Paul Volcker, and President Bush attended. It was only the second time that a president had visited the Federal Reserve since the dedication of the building by Franklin D. Roosevelt in 1937.

After Roger swore me in, I moved my books and papers into the chairman's high-ceilinged office, lighted by an elegant central chandelier. In an early organizational meeting, a staff group organized by senior adviser Lynn Fox showed up in my office, all wearing tan socks in a reprise of the joke Keith Hennessey and I had played on President Bush. My new desk was a nineteenth-century antique donated by the late John LaWare, a former Board member. Computer screens, a Bloomberg terminal, and a television screen would soon surround the scarred wooden desk, giving my work area the ambience of a cockpit. Built-in bookcases held my small library, including many books brought from my office at Princeton, such as Bagehot's *Lombard Street*. At one end of the room, an American flag and a flag bearing the Federal Reserve's symbolic eagle flanked a fireplace. Two tall windows looked out over a manicured lawn toward the National Mall. Next to the fireplace, a door led into the reception area, where Rita Proctor was already organizing the files.

Unlike my predecessor, I intended to use email. To avoid being deluged, I needed a pseudonym. Andy Jester, an IT specialist for the Board, suggested Edward Quince. He had noticed the word "Quince" on a software box and thought "Edward" had a nice ring. It seemed fine to me, so Edward Quince it was. The Board phone book listed him as a member of the security team. The pseudonym remained confidential while I was chairman. Whenever we released my emails—at congressional request or under the Freedom of Information Act, for example—we blacked out the name.

As I settled in, the first substantive issue I tackled was the Fed's capacity to respond to a financial emergency. Even before being sworn in, I had met with senior staff members to discuss our contingency plans. Led by Roger Ferguson and Don Kohn, the Board staff had since 9/11 considerably improved the Fed's readiness to deal with a crisis. I was determined to build on that work. I asked for daily reports on developments at major financial firms and, after the staff started providing them, I carried them on a flash drive on my key ring.

Following up on my earlier idea that the Fed should prepare a financial stability report, I also named a committee of senior staff members to make periodic presentations to the Board about potential concerns in the financial system. Similar work was going on under Tim Geithner at the New York Fed. However, the resources committed to these efforts were modest and the effect on policy choices was ultimately limited.

From the start I also focused on the political aspects of the job. Working with the Board's legislative affairs office, headed at the time by Win Hambley, I began inviting key members of Congress to the Fed for breakfast or lunch. We focused first on members of the Fed's oversight committees—the Senate Banking Committee and the House Financial Services Committee—but our outreach was wide and bipartisan. My first meeting, only two weeks after being sworn in, was with Representative Barney Frank of Massachusetts, the senior Democrat on House Financial Services. I also frequently met members in their offices or briefed an entire committee in private. I learned a lot about the ongoing debates in Congress, particularly on budgetary matters and financial regulation, and became more familiar with the legislative process.

Building ties to Congress would take work, but my relationships with people at the White House were already good. Over the next few years I would lunch periodically with the president, the vice president, and various advisers in the small dining room off the Oval Office. Following Greenspan's practice, I also shared a weekly breakfast or lunch with the Treasury secretary. When I began, that was the good-humored and expansive John Snow, a former railroad executive. In addition, the full Board met for an informal lunch once a month with the Council of Economic Advisers. Eddie Lazear, a labor economist I knew from my time at Stanford, would succeed me as CEA chair. I would also meet occasionally with Al Hubbard and Keith Hennessey—who would later succeed Hubbard as NEC director—and others in the administration. They included my "neighbor" Secretary of State Condoleezza Rice, whose building was next to the Fed's. We shared common experiences as Stanford faculty members and had both served in the Bush White House.

Another early priority was forging cordial working relationships with international policymakers. I already knew Mervyn King, the governor of the Bank of England. We had shared an office at MIT in 1983, when we were both visiting professors there. We had a pleasant reunion over lunch at the Fed in late March. Little had we known, as relatively junior faculty members, that we would each have responsibility for one of the world's most important currencies. In April, I had my first one-on-one encounters with Bank of Japan governor Toshihiko Fukui, European Central Bank president Jean-Claude Trichet, and Bank of Mexico governor Guillermo Ortiz when they were in Washington for the spring meeting of the International Monetary Fund, located a few blocks from the Board.

International meetings, especially with my fellow central bankers, would occupy a substantial part of my time as chairman. We gathered a half-dozen times a year at the Bank for International Settlements. (The Fed chairman and vice chairman generally attended alternate meetings.) Located in Basel, Switzerland, the BIS was created in 1930 to help manage Germany's World War I reparations payments. When the effort to force reparations collapsed, the BIS repurposed itself as a bank for central banks (investing reserves, for example) and as a place where central bankers could gather to discuss issues of common interest. After a day of formal meetings on the global economy, monetary policy, and financial regulation, we repaired to the BIS dining room for long, frank conversations over gourmet four-course dinners (each course with its own wine). For generations, the world's central bankers have formed a sort of club, of which I was now a member.

When I wasn't lunching with the secretary of the Treasury, a member of Congress, or an international official, I ate in the Board's cafeteria, waiting in line with my tray and sitting at a table wherever I could find an open seat, as I always had as a governor. I was now the chairman, but I thought it was important to continue to hear from staff members at all levels. For exercise, I worked out on a rowing machine and with weights or shot baskets in the Board's small gym a couple times a week, as I had as a governor. The basketball court was a converted squash court. A two-on-two game was the largest it could accommodate.

MY RETURN TO the Board reunited me with Michelle Smith, head of the Public Affairs office, with whom I had worked as a governor. A charming Texan, Michelle had advised three Treasury secretaries— Lloyd Bentsen (who had given her her first job in Washington), Robert Rubin, and Larry Summers; then Alan Greenspan—and now me. She had cut her teeth on media relations, at which she excelled, but during my tenure she also served as a chief of staff, helping to manage my schedule and public appearances. Sociable and outgoing, Michelle always knew if a governor was unhappy with an assignment or a staff member had a personal problem, and I would count on her to fill me in when I needed to know.

Michelle and I planned numerous public speeches during my first year, as well as visits to the twelve regional Reserve Banks. I would actually make it to eleven. I had to cancel my visit to the Atlanta bank to attend an economic summit in China in December. For my first speech as chairman, on February 24, I returned to Princeton and spoke to an audience of faculty and students. To strengthen my credibility as an inflation fighter and dispel the Helicopter Ben nonsense,

I focused on the economic benefits of low inflation—an easy topic for a central banker. As I had as a governor, I would continue to spend a lot of time on preparing speeches—in central banking, speeches aren't just about policy, they are policy tools—but, with more limited time, I relied much more on staff for first drafts and revisions.

I also prepared for the required semiannual testimony to Congress just two weeks after my swearing-in. The staff sent me thick notebooks of briefing materials on every area of Fed responsibility. I knew I would also get questions on issues outside the Fed's immediate purview. Responding to them could be tricky. I met with staff to discuss potential answers. Washington policymakers typically prepare for hearings through "murder boards," in which staff members pretend to be lawmakers and the policymaker practices his or her answers. I disliked such playacting and preferred a straightforward conversation. I already knew from my experience with Congress that lawmakers often asked leading questions intended to elicit support for some favorite policy proposal. Many of them were lawyers, so it was inevitable that they would ask questions for all sorts of purposes, but rarely because they were curious about the answer.

Greenspan had gotten himself in trouble in 2001 by seeming to endorse tax cuts proposed by the incoming Bush administration. In testimony, he had said that cutting taxes was preferable to accumulating large budget surpluses, which were forecast at the time. Greenspan did not go so far as to endorse the administration's specific proposals, but his many qualifications were soon forgotten. In early meetings with me, Harry Reid, the Democratic leader in the Senate, would refer with some bitterness to Greenspan's supposed endorsement of the tax cuts. Reid's message was clear enough: I should keep my nose out of fiscal affairs.

I couldn't sensibly discuss the economy while ignoring fiscal policy, so I decided to talk about fiscal issues in very broad terms—for example, emphasizing the need for a reasonable balance of taxes and spending, but saying it was up to Congress and the administration to determine how to achieve that balance. I would sometimes cite the "law of arithmetic," meaning that, by definition, the government's budget deficit equals spending minus revenue. Members of Congress sometimes spoke as if it were possible to increase spending, cut tax revenue, and reduce the deficit all at once—a mathematical impossibility.

In appointing me, the Bush White House had obviously focused on my background in macroeconomics and monetary policy and chosen to overlook my lack of practical experience as a bank supervisor. Experienced Board members were serving on the bank supervision committee, but I took the responsibility seriously and asked the Board's supervisory staff to brief me regularly. I had a lot to learn. Early on, I met with fellow regulators like Marty Gruenberg, then serving as acting chairman of the Federal Deposit Insurance Corporation, to discuss current developments.

No amount of advice can prepare you for a job like Fed chairman. You have to learn as you go, sometimes painfully. Early on, I had breakfast with Greenspan in the chairman's dining room. I asked him for any tips he might have. With a straight face, but eyes twinkling, he told me that when dining with an official guest, it was important to sit where you could see the clock. That way you'd know when the meeting was over. It was his only advice. New York City Mayor Michael Bloomberg was more to the point: "Don't screw up," he said, at a dinner we attended together.

I SLEPT FITFULLY the night before my first testimony as chairman on February 14. Although I would testify dozens of times over the next eight years, I always disliked it. Testimonies were sometimes endurance contests, requiring as much as four or five hours of uninterrupted concentration. I made it a point not to drink anything for at least a couple of hours before the testimony began, so I did not have to ask for a break. Even more stressful was the need to calibrate answers knowing that they would be parsed not only by the members of Congress in front of me but by the media, the markets, and the public. My days as a professor helped me stay unruffled most of the time. After a question or statement, I would consider how I might respond to an economics student. By assuming the role of teacher, I could usually ignore any antagonism or ulterior motives behind the questions.

In my first hearing, I delivered a generally upbeat message. The economy had grown by more than 3 percent in 2005, a vigorous pace, and the unemployment rate had fallen below 5 percent. We expected healthy economic growth to continue in 2006 and 2007. Inflation remained under control. With the economy apparently needing little help from monetary policy, we were continuing our campaign—begun in mid-2004—of hiking our target for the federal funds rate by a quarter percentage point at each meeting. It now stood at 4-1/2 percent.

I noted that housing was slowing. That was to be expected, I said, and wasn't inconsistent with solid overall economic growth, because other sectors seemed likely to take up the slack. But, I warned, given that house prices and construction had soared over the past several years, they could decelerate more rapidly than we expected. We didn't know how housing would evolve but I promised that the Fed would monitor it closely.

My first FOMC meeting as chairman was scheduled for March 27–28—two days instead of the usual one. Under Greenspan most FOMC meetings were a single day, which in practice meant about four hours of actual meeting time, allowing our statement to be released precisely at 2:15 p.m. The Committee met for two days twice a year, in January and June, with the extra day usually dedicated to staff presentations on a special topic. I wanted more two-day meetings to allow extra time for deliberation, a point I raised in one-on-one conversations that I had with every FOMC participant during my first few weeks as chairman. We agreed initially to double the number of two-day meetings, to four each year (out of eight).

I also made changes in the meeting format intended to further one of my goals—reducing the identification of the Fed with the chairman by making it clear that monetary policy decisions were vested in the

Committee, not a single person. I decided to summarize Committee members' thoughts on the economic outlook before giving my own— to show that I had heard and was considering their views. And during the policy deliberations that followed the economic outlook discussion, I would speak last rather than first, as Greenspan had always done. My intent was to avoid unnecessarily suppressing member opinions. The Fed is a strong and deep organization, and I wanted people to understand that extensive analysis and debate go into every decision.

As an academic, I had always valued frank discussion, which allowed new ideas to surface and be thoroughly vetted. For that reason I tried to encourage more spontaneous exchanges among Committee members, who had become accustomed to reading prepared statements. I introduced a convention, common at academic conferences, that participants could raise two hands to ask for immediate recognition to offer a short question or comment. We called the practice a "two-handed intervention." I would also sometimes ask colleagues to amplify a particular remark. These initiatives helped, but our discussions never became as free-flowing as I hoped. Nineteen people is perhaps too large a group for informal debate.

I did get one early indication that my depersonalization campaign was working. When Alyssa returned to college in fall 2006, a friend asked her what her father did for a living. "Well," Alyssa said, "actually, my dad is the chairman of the Federal Reserve." According to Alyssa the friend, dumbstruck, replied: "Your dad is Alan Greenspan?!"

WITH THE DEPARTURE of Greenspan and the resignation of Ned Gramlich in August 2005, five of the seven Board seats were occupied: by Roger Ferguson (vice chairman), Sue Bies, Mark Olson, Don Kohn, and me. By the end of June 2006, both Ferguson and Olson had left. Ferguson would ultimately go on to head TIAA-CREF, which manages retirement funds for teachers and other professionals. Olson resigned to head the Public Company Accounting Oversight Board, a nonprofit corporation created by Congress after the Enron accounting scandal to oversee auditors. The following year, Sue Bies would retire to her home in South Carolina, although she would remain active on corporate boards.

The White House nominated three new governors in 2006. I was pleased to have been closely consulted during the process, and I was happy with the president's choices. White House aide Kevin Warsh and University of Chicago economist Randy Kroszner joined the Board within a month after I was sworn in. Rick Mishkin, my former coauthor, arrived in September. I had served with Kevin at the White House, where he covered banking and financial issues for the National Economic Council. Before the White House, he had worked on mergers and acquisitions for the investment bank Morgan Stanley. At thirty-five, Kevin was the youngest person ever to serve on the Federal Reserve Board. His youth generated some criticism, including from former Board vice chairman Preston Martin, but Kevin's political and markets savvy and many contacts on Wall Street would prove invaluable.

Randy's scholarship focused on banking and finance, and, like me, he had a strong interest in economic history, including the Depression. We had gotten to know each other at academic conferences before I came to the Fed. He would take over the leadership of the bank supervision committee when Sue left.

Rick, with his high energy and sometimes off-color sense of humor, was the antithesis of the staid banker one might imagine serving on the Federal Reserve Board. Having worked with him, though, I knew that he had thought deeply about monetary and financial issues and had strong convictions. I expected Rick would be an ally on the FOMC and help me nudge the Fed toward inflation targeting.

In a final change, at my suggestion, the White House nominated Don Kohn as vice chairman, to succeed Roger. Don and I had joined the Board on the same day three and a half years earlier, and now we would work together to lead it.

Despite the addition of three new members in 2006, with Sue Bies's departure a year after I became chairman, once again only five of the seven Board seats were filled. For various reasons, most notably the routine blocking of Fed nominees in the Senate, we would function with only five members for most of the next three and a half years.

AT THAT FIRST FOMC meeting of my chairmanship, in March 2006, my colleagues and I were upbeat. We saw the cooldown in housing as mostly good news. A decline in construction and the flattening of house prices would let some air out of any potential bubble and help slow overall economic growth to a more sustainable level, reducing the risk that inflation might become a problem. We voted unanimously to increase the target for the federal funds rate by a quarter of a percentage point to 4-3/4 percent, the fifteenth consecutive quarter-point increase.

From this point on I knew policy might get a little more difficult. The federal funds rate was very close to what we assessed to be a normal level. But the economy still seemed to be running a little hot and energy prices had moved up, making us a bit concerned about inflation. A few more rate increases might make sense. But the end of tightening seemed in sight.

Then I made a rookie mistake—actually two mistakes. I wanted to create flexibility for us to deviate from the quarter-point-increase-per-meeting pattern that we had followed since June 2004. Soon it might make sense to leave rates where they were for a meeting or two while we assessed the economy's prospects. I signaled that possibility in my testimony to the Joint Economic Committee (a committee with members from both the Senate and House) on April 27. I said that "at some point in the future" the FOMC "may decide to take no action at one or more meetings in the interest of allowing more time to receive information relevant to the outlook." I added, "Of course, a decision to take no action at a particular meeting does not preclude actions at subsequent meetings."

My message seemed clear enough. I was saying that at some

point—not necessarily the next meeting—we might skip raising rates to allow more time to assess the situation, but that doing so wouldn't necessarily mean the tightening was over. Assuming that my words would be taken at face value was my first mistake. Markets dissected my every syllable for the coded message they knew must be there. They decided that I had announced an immediate end to the rate increases, and reacted sharply, with longer-term interest rates falling and stocks rising. I was upset by the miscommunication. Given the apparent momentum of the economy, I thought it reasonably likely that we'd need at least one more rate increase.

The following Saturday evening I attended the White House Correspondents' Dinner in a banquet hall of the Washington Hilton, along with several thousand other people. The Correspondents' Dinner is one of several large, glitzy media dinners on Washington's social calendar. I disliked all of them but I *really* disliked the Correspondents' Dinner. Originally intended as an opportunity for Washington correspondents and politicians to relax and mingle socially, the dinner was in practice an orgy of table-hopping and celebrity-watching, with the buzz of voices continuing even through the program. (Attending once as a governor, I had been disappointed when I could not hear what turned out to be one of Ray Charles's last live performances.) I went to the dinners for a while. Greenspan had always done so. I thought it was expected, and that it might help me to meet some of the other attendees.

At a reception before the Correspondents' Dinner that particular weekend, I met Maria Bartiromo, the well-known anchor of the CNBC business news cable channel. She remarked that the market had taken my comments to the Joint Economic Committee as a signal that Fed rate hikes were over. Thinking that we were off the record, I told her that I was frustrated by market participants' inability to grasp the plain English meaning of my statement. Second mistake.

The following Monday, as I was working in my office, my Bloomberg screen showed a sudden drop in the stock market. I was puzzled, but shortly thereafter learned the reason. Bartiromo had reported her conversation with me, in particular my concern that my testimony had been misinterpreted. Markets reacted instantly.

A wave of criticism followed, including from Senator Bunning at my next congressional testimony in May. Michelle Smith and Anna tried in their own ways to help me keep it all in proportion, but I felt terrible. The effects of my slip on the markets were transient, and I didn't expect any meaningful economic damage. But I had been working to establish my personal credibility, following in the footsteps of the legendary Greenspan, and it seemed possible to me at the time that the gaffe had irreparably damaged public confidence in me. In time the storm blew over, but I had learned an important lesson about the power that my words now carried.

Years later, before a speech I was giving to the Economic Club of New York, Bartiromo apologized to me. I told her truthfully that it had been more my fault than hers.

WE WOULD END UP raising rates twice more in 2006, in May and June, bringing the federal funds rate to 5-1/4 percent. Economic growth appeared to be moderating, in large part because of slowing housing construction. We noted in our statements that the decline in housing might quicken. But as before, we saw a gradual deceleration in housing as consistent with more balanced and stable growth.

Meanwhile, unemployment remained below 5 percent, and inflation had picked up. In part, the higher inflation reflected increases in oil prices, which staff economists expected would have only a temporary effect on overall inflation. However, many FOMC participants worried that inflation might develop some momentum. The Committee unanimously supported the rate increases. In June, we said "some inflation risks remain"—implying that we had not yet made up our minds whether to end our tightening campaign or to raise rates. The decision would depend on economic developments, especially on the persistence of inflation.

The next meeting, in August, was my first as chairman that required a tough policy call. Both the data and anecdotal reports from businesspeople suggested that inflation pressures continued to build, even excluding volatile energy prices. We had no official numerical target for inflation at that time, but the recent inflation data had shown price increases consistently exceeding what many FOMC participants had indicated was their comfort zone—2 percent or a little less. Also, wages were rising more rapidly than before, which, while good for workers, also meant that firms would be facing higher production costs and thus greater pressure to raise prices. Many participants supported another interest rate increase, or at least a postmeeting statement signaling strongly that another increase could occur in the future.

After seventeen consecutive quarter-point increases, and after consulting with Don Kohn, Tim Geithner, and other Committee members, I resolved to pause our rate-hiking campaign. I didn't think we should rule out future increases, but I didn't think we should strongly signal further increases, either. Economic growth was slowing and housing construction continued to fall. We did not know how fast housing would contract, or how much flatter house prices might affect homeowners' spending. I also knew that it took time for interest rate changes to have their full effect on the economy. We had already raised rates quite a bit, and it was possible that our prior rate hikes, over time, would be enough to calm inflation. I proposed that we leave the federal funds rate unchanged, while hedging our bets a little by continuing to acknowledge in our statement that "some inflation risks remained." The Committee agreed, except for Richmond Fed president Jeff Lacker, consistently one of the FOMC's most hawkish members.

THE END OF rate hikes was not the only consequential economic policy event of the summer of 2006. In July, Henry ("Hank") Paulson became President Bush's third Treasury secretary, after Paul O'Neill and John Snow. Rangy and athletic, with a broken pinky finger that sticks out at an odd angle, Hank looked like the Dartmouth all-Ivy football lineman he had been when he earned the nickname "the Hammer." Nearly bald, with blue eyes behind wire-rim glasses, Paulson projected a restless energy that took me some time to get used to.

Hank worked briefly in the White House during the Nixon administration but had spent almost all his career at the investment bank Goldman Sachs, the final years as CEO. One of Hank's strengths as CEO was his interest in and knowledge of China, the world's most important emerging market. As Treasury secretary, he would set up a semiannual Strategic Economic Dialogue with Chinese officials, which I regularly attended. Although Hank earned hundreds of millions of dollars at Goldman, I admired that he and his wife, Wendy, lived modestly, spending much of their free time bird-watching and pursuing conservationist activities. A Christian Scientist, Hank doesn't smoke or drink.

President Bush had chosen captains of industry as his first two Treasury secretaries, but—political considerations aside—having someone with financial services experience made more sense. The work of the Treasury is overwhelmingly on financial and fiscal policy, neither of which a nonfinancial CEO would be expected to know well.

Hank and I continued the weekly Fed-Treasury breakfasts, sharing among other things an affinity for oatmeal. We hit it off well, notwithstanding the sharp differences in our backgrounds and personalities. It was academic rigor meeting street smarts, which Hank possessed in abundance.

PART II
THE CRISIS

CHAPTER 7

First Tremors, First Response

On August 15, 2007, I took a few minutes between conference calls and market updates to email my brother, Seth. Anna and I would have to cancel our planned vacation with him and other family members the following week in Myrtle Beach, South Carolina.

"You can probably guess why," I wrote.

The beach trip was a family tradition. I hated to give it up. My parents, like many owners of small businesses, took almost no time off. Yet nearly every summer they found a free week to take me, Seth, and my sister, Sharon, to Myrtle Beach. As adults, my siblings and I had continued the practice with our parents and our own children. I had my planned beach reading picked out: *The New Bill James Historical Baseball Abstract*. But it wasn't to be this year.

"Sorry to hear that. Good luck with all that's going on," Seth replied.

"All that's going on" was something of an understatement. After months of uncertainty, the troubles in housing and subprime mortgage lending were now deepening into a much more serious financial threat—something with the potential to derail, or worse, what *Fortune* magazine had declared only a month earlier to be "the greatest economic boom ever." The previous week, on August 9, BNP Paribas, France's largest bank, had barred investors from withdrawing money from three of its investment funds that held securities backed by U.S. subprime mortgages. BNP Paribas said that it could not determine the value of its funds because of the "complete evaporation of liquidity" in the markets for those securities. In other words, investor distrust of subprime-backed securities was so great that potential buyers had withdrawn from the market entirely.

A wave of panicky selling in markets around the world followed. Investors were realizing that they did not know exactly who held subprime-related securities, had little reliable information about the loans that backed those securities, and could not anticipate which financial entity might be next to deny them access to their money. Since the French bank's announcement in Paris, key parts of the global credit markets looked as though they might seize up, with potentially grave economic consequences. A further blow occurred on August 15, the day of my email to Seth, when an analyst suggested that the largest mortgage lender in the United States, Countrywide Financial, might be facing bankruptcy. The Dow Jones industrial average fell steeply to a four-month low.

AT THAT POINT, the Fed had been working for some time to assess the causes and consequences of the subprime mortgage bust—and, more broadly, the housing slowdown. Our housing experts circulated frequent updates on the mortgage market and on home sales, prices, and construction. We viewed some cooling in what had been an over-heated sector as inevitable and even desirable. But in the early months of 2007, my second year as chairman, the cooldown was beginning to appear much less benign.

Housing, as I told the Joint Economic Committee in March 2007, had entered a "substantial correction." Mortgage delinquencies were on the rise, particularly for subprime loans with adjustable rates. And, particularly worrying, early defaults (defaults that occur shortly after a loan is made) had soared. As investors soured on mortgages, potential homeowners, especially those with weaker credit records, were finding loans increasingly difficult to get. Yet the economy as a whole contin-ued to expand and create new jobs. Indeed, economic growth would exceed our expectations in the second and third quarters of 2007, with output expanding at close to a 4 percent rate, according to contemporaneous reports, while unemployment remained low. What was the bottom line? I offered committee members my tentative conclusion: "At this juncture . . . the impact on the broader economy and financial markets of the problems in the subprime market seems likely to be contained."

By the time I emailed Seth in mid-August, I knew I had been quite wrong, of course. The phrase "likely to be contained" would dog me. But at the time my conclusion was widely shared within the Fed, as well as by most market participants and media commentators. We believed the housing slowdown and subprime mortgage problems would affect the economy primarily through two channels: first, by reducing jobs in construction and in industries related to housing, like home furnishings, and, second, by damping consumer spending. (Falling prices make homeowners feel less wealthy and reduce their ability to tap the equity in their homes—either by "cash-out" refinancing or through home equity loans.) The basic logic was the same as Steve Braun and I had applied in 2005 at the Council of Economic Advisers, when we estimated the effects of a housing price bust in our presentation to President Bush.

Steve's and my presentation proved wrong because we did not take into account the possibility that losses on subprime mortgages could ultimately destabilize both the U.S. and global financial systems. Even by early 2007, that outcome seemed remote. Only about 13 percent of outstanding mortgages were subprime. And fixed-rate subprime mortgages were performing reasonably well, as were prime loans and so-called Alt-A mortgages (mortgages with credit quality somewhere between subprime and prime). Adjustable-rate subprime mortgages, where delinquencies were climbing as introductory teaser interest rates expired, constituted only about 8 percent of all outstanding mortgages. Even if subprime mortgages defaulted at extraordinarily high rates, we calculated, the resulting financial losses would be smaller than those from a single bad day in global stock markets.

Moreover, the nation's banks seemed ready to withstand any spillover from housing. The Federal Deposit Insurance Corporation had reported in late 2006 that continued strength in most parts of the economy was offsetting the effect on banks of the "pronounced weakness" in housing. "FDIC-insured institutions continue to ride a string of six consecutive years of record earnings," the agency reported. "Bank capital levels remain at historic highs, while loan performance has slipped only slightly from record levels. Only one FDIC-insured financial institution has failed over the past two and a half years." Bank stocks were also performing well, a sign of investor confidence in the industry.

The FDIC's observation that bank capital levels remained historically high was comforting. Capital—which represents the stake of a bank's owners, or shareholders—acts as a buffer against losses. Imagine a hypothetical bank that made $100 in mortgage loans, with $90 of the funds lent coming from deposits. The remaining $10 of needed funding was raised from the bank's shareholders—that is, the bank's capital. If the bank lost $5 on the mortgages, its shareholders would be hurting—their $10 stake would now be worth only $5—but the bank would still be solvent, able to pay back its depositors if they withdrew their money. If instead the bank had funded its lending with less capital, say $5, and $95 in deposits, then a loss of $5 or more on the bank's mortgage lending would wipe out the shareholders and put the bank out of business. Ample capital accordingly implies that the banking system can withstand significant losses and continue to extend credit to households and businesses.

Seen from the vantage point of early 2007, the economy's good performance, combined with the relatively small size of the subprime mortgage market and what appeared to be a healthy banking system, led me and others at the Fed to conclude that subprime problems—though certainly a major concern for affected communities and the housing sector generally—were unlikely to cause major economic damage. But we failed to anticipate that problems in the subprime mortgage market could trigger an old-fashioned financial panic, albeit in a new, unfamiliar guise.

THE RECURRING FINANCIAL panics in the nineteenth and early twentieth centuries often began with bank runs triggered by events that, considered alone, didn't appear serious enough to cause a systemic crisis. The Panic of 1907, for instance, had modest origins. A group of speculators suffered a big loss after they tried, unsuccessfully, to corner the stock of the United Copper Company. The speculators were known to have close connections to New York City banks and trust companies (banklike financial institutions). Depositors had no idea whether their particular institution had financed the speculators, and in an era before federal deposit insurance, naturally they lined up to withdraw their cash. The runs spread, sparking a nationwide financial panic that contributed to a serious recession. The ultimate economic costs of the panic far outweighed the magnitude of the trigger—a failed scheme by a handful of speculators.

Today, depositors almost never line up at tellers' windows to take out their cash. Since 1934, the federal government has protected bank depositors against losses, up to a limit, even if their bank fails. But that didn't mean that runs were history. As we were learning in August 2007, they now occurred in different forms.

Over the past few decades, a network of diverse nonbank financial firms and markets, dubbed the shadow banking system by economist Paul McCulley, had developed alongside the formal banking system. The shadow banking system included nonbank lenders like mortgage companies and consumer finance companies, as well as companies operating in securities markets, such as investment banks. These firms relied on short-term funding other than government-insured deposits. Commercial banks, too, increasingly supplemented their insured deposits with uninsured funding, including short-term lending between banks in the so-called interbank market.

This short-term, uninsured financing—typically provided by institutional investors, like money market funds or pension funds—is called *wholesale funding*, to distinguish it from the bank deposits of individuals, known as *retail funding*. But, like retail funding in the days before deposit insurance, wholesale funding is potentially subject to runs. Many of the complex securities that proved troublesome during the crisis were financed, directly or indirectly, by wholesale funding, mostly in the form of *commercial paper* or *repurchase agreements*.

Commercial paper—short-term debt with a typical maturity of thirty days or less—has been used by both financial and nonfinancial companies since at least the mid-1800s. Traditionally, commercial paper has been unsecured—repayment is based only on the promise of the borrower and not on collateral. Thus, only well-established, creditworthy companies could issue it. However, the years before the crisis saw a rapid expansion in the use of a new form of commercial paper—so-called asset-backed commercial paper (ABCP).

ABCP was issued by a type of shadow bank known as a conduit, also called a special-purpose vehicle. A conduit is a legal entity set up (usually by a bank or other financial institution) to hold mortgages, credit card debt, auto loans, and many other forms of credit, as well as more complex securities that combined different types of loans (so-called structured credit products). ABCP was asset-backed in the sense that, if necessary, the conduit could presumably sell off its loans and securities to repay the ABCP it had issued.

A repurchase agreement—a *repo*, for short—is technically a sale and repurchase of a security, but it functions as a collateralized loan, usually with short maturity, often only overnight. A firm that wants to borrow cash in the repo market offers Treasury securities, mortgage-backed securities, corporate bonds, or other financial assets as collateral. When the repo agreement comes due, the borrower (a Wall Street investment bank, say, or a hedge fund) can renew, or "roll over," the loan with the same lender (a money market fund, for example) or another one. If for some reason the borrower can't pay back the loan on time, the lender is free to sell the securities.

Even though wholesale funding is not government-insured, most market participants and regulators saw it as relatively impervious to runs. Repos were considered particularly safe, because, even if the borrowing firm went bankrupt, the collateral protected the lender. But when subprime mortgages began to go bad, wholesale funding providers were forced to consider anew the riskiness of the borrowing firms and the complex and opaquely structured securities that they sometimes offered as collateral.

Many lenders had been relying on credit ratings to evaluate collateral. The ratings were issued by private firms—the best known were Standard & Poor's (S&P), Moody's, and Fitch—that were paid by the securities issuers. When losses started surfacing in even highly rated mortgage-related securities, lenders understandably lost faith in the ratings. Unable to evaluate the risks of complex securities on their own, they pulled back from lending against any type of security that included even a small amount of subprime or other risky mortgages. They behaved like grocery shoppers who, after hearing reports of mad cow disease, decide to avoid all beef even though only a minute fraction of cattle are affected.

When retail depositors run, they simply withdraw their money. Runs by wholesale funding providers are more complicated because, as an alternative to withdrawing their money completely, they can ask for greater protections or more favorable terms. As a first step many commercial paper lenders, for example, shortened the term for which they would lend, to as little as overnight. Repo lenders had the option of asking for more collateral per dollar lent or refusing to lend against riskier or more complex securities. As in a traditional run, however, the outcome was that shadow banking entities (including conduits) found it increasingly difficult to obtain funding. As a result, they came under growing pressure to shrink, for example, by selling assets or refusing to extend new credit.

Just as the bank runs of the Panic of 1907 amplified losses suffered by a handful of stock speculators into a national credit crisis and recession, the panic in the short-term funding markets that began in August 2007 would ultimately transform a "correction" in the subprime mortgage market into a much greater crisis in the global financial system and global economy.

ALTHOUGH THE EARTHQUAKE struck in August in the form of BNP Paribas' announcement that it had suspended withdrawals from its subprime mortgage funds, we had felt the first significant tremors of the coming crisis in June. Two mortgage-heavy hedge funds run by Bear Stearns—the fifth-largest Wall Street investment bank—began to suffer large losses. In response, the Bear funds' repo lenders demanded more collateral or simply refused to lend. On June 7, Bear froze redemptions by investors in the funds. Bear had no legal obligation to bail out its funds, which were in separately incorporated entities—"off-balance-sheet" vehicles. But the company was concerned about maintaining good relationships with the lenders to the funds, many of them other investment banks. So, it propped up one of the funds with a $1.6 billion loan. On July 31, both funds declared bankruptcy, and Bear lost most of what it had lent. In addition, Bank of America had, for a fee, guaranteed some of the assets in the Bear funds. It ended up losing more than $4 billion. The travails of Bear's hedge funds made short-term lenders wary of funding any mortgage-related investment, particularly the complex and difficult-to-evaluate structured credit products that mixed various types of mortgages and often other forms of credit.

In late July, subprime woes surfaced overseas. Rhineland, an off-balance-sheet vehicle funded by ABCP, had been created in 2002 by the German bank IKB, a midsized business lender. Rhineland's managers had made heavy bets on U.S. mortgages, including subprime mortgages, as well as on complex securities partially backed by mortgages. Concerned about those bets, lenders refused to renew Rhineland's commercial paper. IKB guaranteed a substantial part of Rhineland's funding, and, as outside funders withdrew, IKB in effect became the unwilling owner of Rhineland and its bad assets, which in turn brought IKB to the brink of failure. Ultimately, with the prodding of German regulators, the German banking group that controlled IKB bailed out the bank. But the Rhineland debacle made lenders more concerned about other conduits funded by ABCP. ABCP funding would soon begin to shrink rapidly, from about $1.2 trillion at the end of July 2007 to about $800 billion by the end of the year. When conduits lost funding, their sponsors had two options (other than allowing the conduit to go bankrupt). The sponsors could sell off some of the conduits' assets or they could themselves fund the conduits, which both exposed the sponsors to losses and increased their own funding needs.

Over the summer, we tracked the increasing strains in short-term funding markets. We were hampered because we had no authority to obtain confidential data from investment banks (like Bear Stearns), which were regulated by the Securities and Exchange Commission, or over foreign banks not operating in the United States (like IKB), or over hedge funds, which were largely unregulated. We worried that a retreat by wholesale funding providers would force more firms and investment vehicles to sell mortgage assets in "fire sales," pushing down prices and spreading the problem to other firms holding similar assets. Unfortunately, we could see little more to do at the time other than monitor market developments. Perhaps the stresses in funding markets would recede. Perhaps they wouldn't.

We discussed the market turbulence at the FOMC meeting on August 7. The day before, American Home Mortgage Investment Corporation, the nation's tenth-largest mortgage lender, had been brought down by its losses on some of the more exotic forms of adjustable-rate mortgages, in which it specialized. We also noted that markets had shifted slightly toward the view that the FOMC eventually would cut interest rates to offset the risks that recent financial turmoil posed to the economy.

But, at that point, the broader economy didn't seem to need help from lower interest rates. Job growth had been relatively steady, if unspectacular, and unemployment remained very low, at 4.4 percent. Moreover, oil prices, which had risen to a record $78 a barrel at the end of July, had pushed overall inflation to an uncomfortably high level of 5.2 percent at an annual rate over the April–June period. Even the doves on the Committee had to worry at least a bit that stimulating faster growth with rate cuts could generate higher inflation. Some FOMC members, I knew, continued to believe we had made a mistake a year earlier when, at my urging, we had halted a two-year series of inflation-damping interest rate increases.

We voted unanimously to hold the federal funds rate target at the past year's level of 5-1/4 percent, but our postmeeting statement reflected our competing worries. We acknowledged that recent market volatility had increased the risks to economic growth. But we repeated that inflation remained our "predominant" policy concern. The sharpest debate at the meeting turned on the seemingly narrow point of whether or not to keep the word "predominant" in the statement. Several around the boardroom table—including New York Fed president Tim Geithner and San Francisco Fed president Janet Yellen— argued for deleting the word, a step that would have caused markets to increase the odds of an interest rate cut later in the year. Most of the remaining members feared that removing "predominant" would signal insufficient concern about inflation. Some worried about appearing to overreact to what so far had been relatively modest market turmoil. I believed that the majority of the FOMC members still were more concerned about inflation than risks to economic growth, and so I supported retaining "predominant" as better reflecting the sense of the Committee. The reality that small changes in the phrasing of the FOMC's statement could have important effects on policy expectations sometimes led us to spend what seemed like an inordinate amount of time on the choice of a single word.

ON THURSDAY, AUGUST 9, the sun had been up for nearly two hours and the temperature was already in the mid-80s when I stepped outside my home shortly after 7:00 a.m. I climbed into the rear of a chauffeured black SUV for the fifteen-minute ride to the office. Hank Paulson and I were scheduled to share breakfast in my private dining room.

The BNP Paribas announcement had come earlier that morning. Almost as worrisome as the suspension of withdrawals from its sub- prime funds was the bank's judgment that the troubled assets in its funds could not be fairly valued. A Catch-22 was developing: Investors were unwilling to buy securities they knew little about. But without market trading, there was no means to determine what the securities were worth. I received sketchy information and an early indication of market conditions from staff emails as I prepared to meet Paulson. It was already late in the trading day in Europe, where markets had reacted very badly to the BNP Paribas announcement, with interest rates on short-term bank borrowings spiking and stock prices falling. American markets, for the most part, were not yet open, but the avail- able information implied that we were in for a bad day.

The European Central Bank had already taken steps to try to coun- ter the tumult. Ironically, the problems with U.S. subprime mortgages were being felt more strongly in Europe than in the United States, although we knew the market distress could easily cross the Atlantic. Markets had ultimately absorbed the July announcement of IKB's sub- prime woes. But, unlike the regional IKB, BNP Paribas was a global player. If it was infected by the subprime virus, who else was? And how fairly valued were other types of asset-backed securities? Securitiza- tion was supposed to disperse risk by packaging thousands of loans into securities, which could then be further sliced into segments and sold around the world. Increasingly, however, it was instead seen as an agent of global contagion.

As distrust grew, banks hoarded cash and lent to each other only reluctantly, causing the federal funds rate, the rate at which banks lend to each other overnight, to rise above the 5-1/4 percent target the FOMC had affirmed two days earlier. Increased demand for dollars from foreign banks added to the stress. At breakfast, Hank and I dis- cussed developments in Europe and agreed to keep in close touch. That morning, I emailed Brian Madigan, who had succeeded Vince Rein- hart as head of the Board's Division of Monetary Affairs, to instruct the New York Fed to buy large quantities of Treasury securities on the open market. The cash that the sellers of the securities received from us would end up in banks, meeting the banks' increased demand for cash. If banks had less need to borrow, the federal funds rate should move back to target and the pressures in short-term funding markets should ease. If all went well, we could withdraw the cash from the system in a day or two.

Walter Bagehot's lender-of-last-resort concept argues that central banks should stand ready during a panic to lend as needed, which in turn should help stabilize financial institutions and markets. Later that morning, consistent with Bagehot's advice and my instructions to Brian, the New York Fed injected $24 billion in cash into the financial system. Conditions in the European financial system—closer to the BNP Paribas spark—were even worse, and the ECB had injected even more cash, 95 billion euros ($130 billion). For both central banks, the goal was to ensure that financial and nonfinancial firms would have adequate access to short-term funding. Over the next week, the central banks of Canada, Japan, Australia, Norway, and Switzerland would conduct similar operations.

We issued a statement the next morning, Friday, August 10, on the heels of an emergency conference call of the FOMC. It had been the Committee's first unscheduled call during my chairmanship and the first since the start of the war in Iraq four years earlier. The Board convened at 8:45 a.m. in the Special Library, a dark, musty room with floor-to-ceiling book-lined shelves. We sat at a table that had served the first Federal Reserve Board in 1914. Metal nameplates showing the places of the original members were still screwed into its sides. The Reserve Bank presidents joined the meeting by video. A large screen displayed the presidents in a configuration that reminded me of the old TV game show *Hollywood Squares*.

The bureaucratic tone of our August 10 statement belied its potential power. "The Federal Reserve is providing liquidity to facilitate the orderly functioning of financial markets," we said. "As always, the discount window is available as a source of funding." The discount window (once literally a teller window manned by a lending officer, but no more) is the facility through which the Fed provides overnight loans to deposit-taking institutions, including commercial banks and savings and loans. The interest rate charged is called the discount rate. After issuing the statement, we added $38 billion more to the financial system through securities purchases. Again, reflecting greater stress in European markets, the ECB did more, injecting 61 billion euros ($84 billion).

Similar statements from the Fed had helped calm markets after the stock market crash in 1987 and again after the 9/11 attacks in 2001. This time the problems ran deeper and the statement did not have its hoped-for effect. Investors remained reluctant to provide short-term credit and shifted their money into safer and more liquid assets, like short-term Treasury securities. Commercial paper issuance (especially of asset-backed commercial paper) had fallen sharply and maturities had shortened dramatically, often to only a day or two, as lenders aimed to tie up their money for the shortest time possible. Ominously, the problems with subprime mortgages were prompting the reevaluation of other types of credit as well. Wholesale funders were becoming more wary of medium-quality Alt-A mortgages, second mortgages (used by some homeowners to cash out the equity in their homes), and some commercial real estate mortgages. If funding conditions continued to tighten, firms and investment vehicles that held these securities might be forced to dump them on the market for whatever they could get. Fire sales would drive the prices of these assets down further and make financing even more difficult to obtain, both for the selling firms and for firms holding similar assets.

BY THE TIME I emailed Seth to cancel our vacation it was clear that the Fed needed to do more—but what? In response to current events, people often reach for historical analogies, and this occasion was no exception. The trick is to choose the right analogy. In August 2007, the analogies that came to mind—both inside and outside the Fed—were October 1987, when the Dow Jones industrial average had plummeted nearly 23 percent in a single day, and August 1998, when the Dow had fallen 11.5 percent over three days after Russia defaulted on its foreign debts. With help from the Fed, markets had rebounded each time with little evident damage to the economy. Not everyone viewed these interventions as successful, though. In fact, some viewed the Fed's actions in the fall of 1998—three quarter-point reductions in the federal funds rate—as an overreaction that helped fuel the growing dot-com bubble. Others derided what they perceived to be a tendency of the Fed to respond too strongly to price declines in stocks and other financial assets, which they dubbed the "Greenspan put." (A put is an options contract that protects the buyer against loss if the price of a stock or other security declines.)

Newspaper opinion columns in August 2007 were rife with speculation that Helicopter Ben would provide a similar put soon. In arguing against Fed intervention, many commentators asserted that investors had grown complacent and needed to be taught a lesson. The cure to the current mess, this line of thinking went, was a repricing of risk, meaning a painful reduction in asset prices—from stocks to bonds to mortgage-linked securities. "Credit panics are never pretty, but their virtue is that they restore some fear and humility to the marketplace," the *Wall Street Journal* had editorialized, in arguing for no rate cut at the August 7 FOMC meeting.

Of course, investors were desperate to escape the "fear and humility" that the *Journal* editorial writers wanted to inflict on them. Perhaps the most colorful plea for looser monetary policy had been a screaming on-air rant by CNBC TV personality Jim Cramer on August 6. Michelle emailed me about the video. "I should warn you—he's not at all respectful of you," she wrote. I suspected that was an understatement. I never watched it. When the criticism devolves into name-calling or screaming, I pass.

Though I ignored Cramer, I was hearing from others whose views demanded greater attention. "Conditions in the mortgage market are the worst I've ever seen and are deteriorating day by day," former Board member Lyle Gramley wrote in an email forwarded by Don Kohn. "I am not one to cry wolf," Gramley added. After leaving the Board in 1985, Gramley had worked for more than a decade for the Mortgage Bankers Association of America and had served on Countrywide's board. He spoke with expertise, but perhaps also from a perspective influenced by his post-Fed positions.

It's a truism that market people "talk their book"—that is, argue for policies that benefit their own investments or interests. That's a fact of life that I always tried to keep in mind when hearing outside views. But I could not easily dismiss the concerns of Gramley and many other contacts with similar messages. I knew that financial disruptions—if allowed to snowball—could choke off credit to households and businesses and in worst-case scenarios send the economy into a tailspin. At the same time, I was mindful of the dangers of moral hazard—the risk that rescuing investors and financial institutions from the consequences of their bad decisions could encourage more bad decisions in the future.* I wanted to avoid the perception of a "Bernanke put" if at all possible.

We needed the right tool—a tool that would break the run mentality, calm market fears, and allow financial assets, from stocks to subprime mortgages, to reprice to their fundamental values without markets freezing or prices overshooting on the way down. We were close to settling on a plan that at first we had rejected, namely, making changes to our discount window policies to encourage banks and savings institutions to borrow from us.

Banks had largely ignored the come-and-get-it hint in our August 10 statement. As an alternative, the FOMC could have cut the federal

---

*   The idea of moral hazard came from writings about insurance, where it referred to the tendency of people whose property is insured to make less effort to avoid loss or accident.

funds rate, but that would have had broad economic effects, including possibly fueling inflation. Lending through the discount window was a more precise tool focused on the specific issue we faced: the growing scarcity of short-term funding. However, we faced two problems.

The first was the stigma associated with borrowing from the Fed. As Bagehot advised, we routinely charged a "penalty" rate on our discount window loans. At the time, that interest rate, the discount rate, was 6-1/4 percent—one percentage point above our target for the federal funds rate, the interest rate that a bank would pay another to borrow overnight. Under normal conditions, the penalty rate encourages banks to look first to private markets for funding, rather than relying on the Fed. But a side effect of this arrangement was that banks feared they would look weak if it became known that they had borrowed from the Fed—and that would make it even harder for them to attract private funding. Why would a strong bank pay the penalty rate if it didn't have to? We kept the identity of discount window borrowers strictly confidential, but banks worried that money market participants—by observing their behavior, or perhaps through careful analysis of the Fed's balance sheet figures—could guess when a bank had come to the window. Nearly all discount window loans were, and are, to sound institutions with good collateral. Since its founding a century ago, the Fed has never lost a penny on a discount window loan. Nevertheless, the perceived stigma of borrowing from the discount window was and remains a formidable barrier to its effectiveness. If banks won't borrow because they fear that doing so might send a bad signal about their financial health, then having a lender of last resort does little good.

The second problem, in addition to stigma, was that the financial system had outgrown the discount window. The Federal Reserve Act stipulates that, under normal circumstances, only depository institutions—banks and savings institutions—are eligible to borrow from the Fed. But in recent decades, the shadow banking system, with its reliance on wholesale funding rather than insured deposits, had come to play an increasingly prominent role in credit markets. Our discount window could not directly help nonbanks that had lost their funding, limiting our ability to stop panics.

So, even though we had been thinking about ways to encourage greater use of the discount window, we feared they wouldn't work. It could be like throwing a party that nobody attended. If we took highly visible steps to bring banks to the window, and they had no effect, it could shake confidence in the Fed's ability to fashion an effective response to the crisis and thus fuel the panic.

However, by August 16, financial conditions had deteriorated to the point where we were ready to be more aggressive. Tim Geithner, Don Kohn, and I conferred that morning with our central bank counterparts in Europe, Canada, and Japan. I scheduled another emergency conference call of the FOMC at six o'clock that evening. To try to overcome stigma, we decided we would make discount window loans more attractive by halving the interest rate penalty. Banks would be able to borrow at a half percentage point, rather than a full point, above the FOMC's target for the federal funds rate. We'd also try to persuade some leading banks to borrow at the window, thereby suggesting that borrowing did not equal weakness. To encourage credit to flow at terms longer than overnight, we would offer loans through the discount window for up to thirty days and indicate that we'd be liberal about renewing the loans as needed. And a new FOMC statement acknowledging increased risks to economic growth and saying we were "prepared to act as needed" would signal our willingness to push down interest rates more generally if necessary to prevent the financial upset from spilling over into the economy.

We considered cutting the discount rate more than a half percentage point, a step advocated by Rick Mishkin, but we were balancing two competing concerns. If we didn't cut the discount rate enough, banks, worried about stigma, wouldn't borrow. But, if we cut it too much, smaller banks—who can't borrow overnight funds in the open market as cheaply as larger banks—might overwhelm the Reserve Banks with requests for relatively small loans, which we were not pre-

pared to handle administratively. We might have to turn away would-
be borrowers.

We announced the discount rate cut and issued the FOMC's new
statement at 8:15 a.m. on Friday, August 17. Short-term funding markets, unfortunately, showed little immediate reaction, but the stock
market soared reflexively. Futures on the S&P 500 index jumped 3.6
percent within 46 seconds of the announcement. "The market thinks
Bernanke is a rock star!" Bob Pisani of CNBC declared (prematurely,
to say the least).

My FOMC colleagues and I worked the phones and shared our intelligence by email. As predicted, bankers remained nervous about the
potential stigma of borrowing from the Fed. Boston Fed president Eric
Rosengren reported that Ron Logue, chief executive of State Street, was
reluctant to borrow. State Street was the largest bank in the district, so
if the Boston Fed reported a large surge in discount window borrowing,
speculation would naturally fall on Logue's institution. He asked Rosengren if the weekly district-by-district reporting of loan totals could be
eliminated. But changing our accounting procedures without warning,
even if legally feasible, would hardly have inspired confidence. A Texas
banker advised Dallas Fed president Richard Fisher that if the Fed could
persuade some "big boys" to use the discount window, "it could be a life-
changing event in removing the stigma."

At 10:00 a.m., Tim and Don hosted a conference call with the
Clearing House Association, an organization of the nation's major
commercial and investment banks, and told them that we would consider borrowing at the discount window "a sign of strength." That evening, Tim relayed word from his on-site supervisors at Citibank that
its managers had authorized the bank to borrow from the window. On
Wednesday, August 22, Citi announced it was borrowing $500 mil-
lion for thirty days; JPMorgan Chase, Bank of America, and Charlotte,
North Carolina–based Wachovia also announced that they had each
borrowed $500 million. Our weekly report the next day showed dis-
count window borrowing of $2.3 billion on August 22, up from $264
million a week earlier.

The Fed's Board also sent letters to Citigroup, JPMorgan, and Bank of America granting temporary exemptions from Section 23A of the Federal Reserve Act, which normally prevented them from funneling discount window credit to nonbank components of their companies, such as subsidiaries engaged in consumer finance or securities trading. Our goal was to increase the supply of short-term funding to the shadow banking system. Because transactions between a bank and its holding company could put the bank's insured deposits at risk, the FDIC needed to sign off. I reached out to FDIC chairman Sheila Bair.

Sheila, a Kansas Republican and protégé of former senator Bob Dole, had been appointed to the FDIC by President Bush in June 2006. She had been teaching at the University of Massachusetts–Amherst, but she had government experience as well, including at the Treasury Department. A prairie populist, she inherently distrusted the big Wall Street banks and the government agencies charged with overseeing them—most especially the Fed and Treasury. She could be turf-conscious and hard to work with, but I also couldn't help but grudgingly admire her energy, her political acumen in pursuing her goals, and her skill in playing to the press. And I appreciated the crucial role her agency played in the regulatory system. When circumstances required cooperation among the Fed, Treasury, and FDIC, it often fell to me to make the call to her, as it did this time. I didn't want an unintentional slight on my part to impede good policies.

Sheila responded to our request for 23A exemptions by the end of the day that we announced the rate cut. I emailed, thanking her for the prompt response. "Amazing what a little credit crisis can do to motivate," she replied.

Unfortunately, our initial success in ramping up our discount window lending did not persist. The four big banks that trumpeted a collective $2 billion in borrowing from the Fed also—with stigma doubtless in mind—made very clear in their announcements that they didn't need the money. Five weeks later, discount window borrowing had fallen back to $207 million, a little less than it had been before we eased the terms of borrowing.

AS WE WERE working our way toward cutting the discount rate, the problems of Countrywide, the source of nearly one in five mortgages made in the United States, had remained on the front burner. Examiners from three agencies—the Federal Reserve, the FDIC, and the Office of Thrift Supervision—had been trying to determine whether the lender, with its large subprime portfolio, could remain afloat.

On August 16, nervous depositors queued at a branch of its savings and loan near its Calabasas, California, corporate headquarters. Many left reassured after they were told the deposits were FDIC-insured. But Countrywide faced a bigger threat: The company's commercial paper and repo lenders had refused to renew their loans on August 2. Raising funds by selling some of its assets would not solve its problems. The value of the suspect mortgages it held had fallen sharply—if buyers could be found at all. To avoid bankruptcy, Countrywide drew $11.5 billion from previously established emergency lines of credit with major banks—every penny that was available to it.

On August 10, I had asked Brian Madigan and Roger Cole, director of our Division of Banking Supervision and Regulation, to evaluate whether Countrywide was systemically important. In other words, would the firm's failure endanger the entire financial system? "What would its failure do to major banks or investment banks? To the mortgage market?" I had asked.

It was the first time that I had to pose such questions about a large financial institution. I emailed Madigan and Cole less than an hour after receiving an oddly upbeat note from OTS director John Reich. Reich, a former community banker as well as a former longtime aide to Senator Connie Mack of Florida, was an ardent advocate of deregulation. In 2003, then vice chairman of the FDIC, Reich had posed proudly at a press event, holding garden shears in front of a stack of paper wrapped in red tape—representing the regulations he was charged with enforcing.

Just before leaving his office for a planned two-week vacation, Reich sought to reassure me, Fed Board member Randy Kroszner, Sheila Bair, and a fourth bank regulator—John Dugan, director of the Office of the Comptroller of the Currency—that rumors of Countrywide's imminent bankruptcy were untrue. He acknowledged that the lender faced a liquidity challenge, but, putting a positive spin on the many recent failures of mortgage lenders, he wrote, "the longer-term looks positive, as their competition has greatly decreased."

Reich would soon back a request from Angelo Mozilo, Countrywide's white-haired, unnaturally tanned CEO. Mozilo wanted an exemption from the Section 23A rules that prevented Countrywide's holding company from tapping the discount window through a savings institution it owned. Sheila and the FDIC were justifiably skeptical, as was Janet Yellen at the Federal Reserve Bank of San Francisco, in whose district Countrywide's headquarters were located. Lending indirectly to Countrywide would be risky. It might well already be insolvent and unable to pay us back. The day after the discount rate cut, Don Kohn relayed word that Janet was recommending a swift rejection of Mozilo's request for a 23A exemption. She believed, Don said, that Mozilo "is in denial about the prospects for his company and it needs to be sold."

Countrywide found its reprieve in the form of a confidence-boosting $2 billion equity investment from Bank of America on August 22—not quite the sale that Janet thought was needed, but the first step toward an eventual acquisition by Bank of America. Countrywide formally withdrew its request for a 23A exemption on Thursday August 30 as I was flying to Jackson Hole, Wyoming, to speak at the Kansas City Fed's annual economic symposium. The theme of the conference, chosen long before, was "Housing, Housing Finance, and Monetary Policy."

I HADN'T SPOKEN publicly about the economy since delivering the Board's twice-a-year monetary policy report to the House and Senate in back-to-back hearings in July. With credit-market problems beginning to slow the economy, market participants would be looking for any sign that we were planning to broadly reduce short-term interest rates. We were definitely moving in that direction. Indeed, two days prior to my departure for Jackson Hole, I had been debating with Don and Tim whether to cut rates without waiting for the next scheduled FOMC meeting on September 18. Markets weren't expecting an inter-meeting move, though, and we were concerned that a surprise cut might lead traders to believe we were even more worried than they had thought.

"Going sooner risks, 'What do they know that we don't,'" Don wrote in an email to Tim and me. He recommended waiting until the FOMC meeting, but then cutting the federal funds rate by a half a percent, double the generally expected decrease.

In the cloistered world of central banking, the Kansas City Fed's two-day symposium at Jackson Lake Lodge was a major international event. For the past twenty-five years, just before Labor Day, top policymakers and staff from the Fed, international central bankers, well-known academic and private-sector economists, and leading U.S. economic journalists had been attending. The participants—about 110 in all—spent mornings debating monetary policy and the state of the global economy under elk-antler chandeliers. Evenings were given over to banquet dinners and entertainment. Afternoons were for enjoying the spectacular surroundings. From the rear of the lodge lay the glorious sight of the snow-capped Grand Tetons. On clear days, Jackson Lake's icy waters were visible. Every year, Don led a strenuous hike into the mountains that became known as the Kohn Death March. The less fit, or less ambitious, could fly-fish, take a boat ride on the lake, or simply sit on the veranda observing, through binoculars, moose and elk grazing on the highland meadows that stretched toward the mountains.

As a professor at Princeton, I had been pleased to occasionally receive one of the coveted invitations to Jackson Hole, but as chairman I was already looking at the meeting as something of a chore. I was always happy to talk economics, but it's difficult to have useful, free-flowing discussions in the glare of intense media coverage. I was acutely aware that any slip would be echoed and amplified, so I limited my participation to delivering my prepared remarks.

The turbulent markets of August 2007 made those risks even greater. Michelle Smith, after conferring with me, Don, and Tim, took the unusual step of emailing the Reserve Bank presidents asking them to refrain from media interviews. Also unusually, most complied. Randy Kroszner flew to Jackson Hole early to avoid having all of the Board members in the air and out of reach on the day before the conference. And we dispatched a team of computer specialists who would wire a conference room at the lodge to permit us to review market conditions as needed.

I arrived at the lodge late Thursday afternoon and, after a market-review meeting, headed to a dinner that always precedes the business sessions of Friday and Saturday. It was a somber event. Our friend and colleague Ned Gramlich was gravely ill with leukemia. He had been scheduled to address the symposium but his illness had prevented him from making the trip. Anna and I had only recently seen Ned and his wife, Ruth, at a brunch hosted by Lyle Gramley and his wife, Marlys. Ned knew then that he didn't have much time left, but he was upbeat and happy to spend time with friends. In my welcoming remarks at the conference dinner I noted that we would miss not only Ned's insights but also his warmth and generosity of spirit. At the luncheon on Saturday, David Wilcox, the Board's deputy research director and a close friend of Ned's, would read Ned's prepared speech. The topic was the boom and bust in subprime lending.

In my own speech the next morning, August 31, I had to walk a fine line. I wanted to put a rate cut squarely on the table. But I had to avoid damaging the comity of the FOMC by explicitly signaling a rate cut before members could debate and vote on it.

I described the toll that the housing downturn and associated financial stress had taken on the economy and reminded my listeners— pointedly, I thought—that "well-functioning financial markets are essential for a prosperous economy." To douse the idea that the FOMC might act solely to bail out Wall Street, I said, "It is not the responsibility of the Federal Reserve—nor would it be appropriate—to protect lenders and investors from the consequences of their financial decisions." But, I promised, the Federal Reserve "will act as needed to limit the adverse effects on the broader economy that may arise from the disruptions in financial markets." I was addressing multiple audiences simultaneously—trying to convince critics that we were motivated by a desire to help Main Street Americans while hoping to persuade investors not to overreact by retreating from all forms of private credit.

Market reaction was positive but subdued. Many traders apparently had hoped for an explicit signal that rate cuts were imminent. Dow Jones columnist Laurence Norman summed it up: "Like a hungry Oliver Twist accepting his gruel at the poor house . . . markets . . . made it clear they wanted more."

So it was that, even before the last of the attendees departed, Don and Tim and I were thinking about how to persuade our colleagues to do more to protect American jobs and livelihoods from turmoil on Wall Street. We wanted them to support a broad-based cut in short-term interest rates at the next FOMC meeting and, if necessary, to consider unorthodox measures. Tim and I left the conference early. Don stayed to hear the Saturday morning speakers. In an email, he recapped a particularly gloomy presentation by Martin Feldstein. Don, far from an optimist himself, thought that Feldstein's outlook was too dark. But, he confessed, "I wasn't that disturbed. . . . I saw it as a useful softening up of FOMC members."

Back in Washington we were ramping up what I was calling "blue-sky thinking." By focusing on discount window lending rather than on standard monetary policy as our response to the crisis, we had already departed somewhat from convention. But I was determined to go further if necessary. We could not let the fear of appearing unorthodox prevent us from attacking the problem with any tool available. That Sunday, in an email to Don, Tim, and Board member Kevin Warsh, I laid out the case for doing more and summarized ideas that had been percolating among policymakers and staff.

One intriguing proposal was to establish a currency swap line with the European Central Bank—effectively, a facility through which the Federal Reserve would provide dollars to the ECB, with the repayment collateralized by euros. Its purpose would be to help insulate U.S. markets from financial turbulence in Europe. Though the ECB was providing euros to the continent's money markets, much financial activity in Europe is transacted in dollars. Establishing a currency swap line with the ECB (or another foreign central bank) would provide it with dollars that it could subsequently lend to the commercial banks in its jurisdiction, reducing the scramble by foreign banks for dollar funding that had been disrupting U.S. markets. A swap line with a foreign central bank wouldn't be politically popular, but it could prove essential to protecting our own economy. Don initially had been skeptical, saying he needed to see a better case for why the ECB couldn't use its own dollar reserves for its lending. But Tim had been more open, arguing that establishing swap lines with the ECB and two or three other major central banks could reduce the need for foreign banks operating in the United States to borrow dollars directly from the Fed. Instead, they could borrow from their home-country central banks, which would be responsible for managing the loans and would be on the hook for any losses.

I also discussed a staff proposal to set up two facilities to auction Federal Reserve loans—one for depository institutions and the other for nondepositories, such as the Wall Street investment banks. It seemed possible that setting the interest rate on loans through an auction in which potential borrowers bid for funds, rather than fixing a rate as we currently did with the discount rate, might reduce the stigma of borrowing from the Fed. Borrowers could claim that they were paying a market rate, not a penalty rate. And, because it takes time to conduct an auction and determine the winning bids, borrowers would receive their funds with a delay, making clear that they were not desperate for cash.

Last on the blue-sky list was forcing banks to disclose more information about their condition and, importantly, about affiliated off-balance-sheet vehicles that had become linchpins of shadow banking. What they disclosed might be scary, but at least participants in the money markets could again realistically assess lending risks, and extend or not extend credit on that basis, instead of pulling back from all counterparties out of fear.

One of these items in particular—letting nondepository institutions like investment banks participate in auctions of Federal Reserve loans—would require a leap over a particularly high psychological hurdle. We would have to invoke the little-known Section 13(3) of the Federal Reserve Act, which authorized the Reserve Banks to lend to virtually any creditworthy person or entity. We hadn't used the authority since the Great Depression. I knew it was a hard sell, but I wanted the idea to remain under consideration.

"Staff arguments do not persuade me to drop this option from the playbook altogether," I wrote in the email to Don, Tim, and Kevin after Jackson Hole. Broadening Federal Reserve lending beyond depository institutions could be necessary in a financial system that had become less bank-centric. "But I agree that it should be filed under the 'Hail Mary' section," I wrote.

CHAPTER 8

One Step Forward

The turbulence that buffeted financial markets in August appeared to have eased just a bit when the Federal Open Market Committee met on September 18, 2007. The stock market had more than regained the ground it lost in August, and funding and credit markets were a little calmer.

Still, the situation was far from normal. Issuance of asset-backed commercial paper had declined further and interest rates on it had moved higher. In the repo market, lenders were demanding more collateral for their loans, even when the collateral was of relatively high quality. And banks remained skittish. The premium they charged each other to borrow for longer than overnight remained elevated, and they were growing reluctant to lend, even to household and corporate borrowers with sterling credit histories. Meanwhile, the economic news was downbeat, with the Labor Department having reported a loss of 4,000 jobs in August, the first monthly drop since 2003.

THE WEEK BEFORE the FOMC meeting, Anna and I had attended a small memorial gathering for Ned Gramlich at the Gramlichs' elegant apartment overlooking Rock Creek Park and downtown Washington. Ruth was gracious despite her grief. Ned had died on September 5, just days after his prepared remarks were read at Jackson Hole. Later in the month, in accordance with Ned's wishes, I would speak at his memorial service. As it ended, a New Orleans jazz band marched into the church, playing a raucous version of "When the Saints Go Marching In."

By the morning of the FOMC meeting, Washington's oppressive summer heat had eased. The weather was pleasant as my SUV turned into the Board garage. From there I rode a wood-paneled elevator to the second-floor Board members' offices.

I had been working to line up support on the FOMC for more action to cushion the economy from the effects of credit market turbulence. As it turned out, the hawks and doves flocked together this time—more or less. After the meeting we announced that the Committee had voted unanimously to cut the target for the federal funds rate by a half-percentage point, to 4-3/4 percent. It was the first cut in four years. Market expectations had been for only a quarter-point cut, so the announcement caused stocks to jump and bond yields to fall.

Some of the hawks—Jeffrey Lacker of the Federal Reserve Bank of Richmond and Richard Fisher of Dallas—had argued for a smaller rate reduction, but the rotation of votes among the Reserve Bank presidents left both of them without a vote in 2007. The often hawkish Thomas Hoenig of Kansas City and Bill Poole of St. Louis were voters that year, but neither dissented. They said they hoped that taking more action sooner would forestall the need for, and expectation of, greater interest rate reductions later. The hawks were at least slightly reassured by a modest recent improvement in inflation data, as well as by the staff's forecast of sub-2 percent inflation in both 2008 and 2009.

Of course, we knew how difficult it is for economists to peer into the future. The Board's research director, Dave Stockton, a fine forecaster of long experience, with an equally fine—and dark—sense of humor, reminded us what a messy business it was. "I thought I would invite you to don your hair nets and white butcher smocks and join me for a tour of the sausage factory," he quipped, before discussing the analysis underlying the staff projections.

The Fed's economic models, and economic forecasting models in general, do a poor job of incorporating the economic effects of financial instability, in part because financial crises are (fortunately) rare enough that relevant data are scarce. In 2007, Fed researchers were

actively trying to overcome that difficulty by looking at other indus-
trialized countries, like Sweden and Japan, that had relatively recently
suffered significant financial crises. In discussing the challenges he and
his team faced, Stockton reminded us of 1998, when staff forecasters
had lowered their projections for U.S. economic growth in response to
market turmoil triggered by the Russian debt default. But credit flows
in the United States were not much affected and the economy weath-
ered the storm. Six months after the onset of the Russian turbulence,
the staff reversed course and revised forecasts upward.

"I think it's fair to say that part of our mistake in 1998 was a failure
to appreciate just how strong the U.S. economy was when we entered
that period," Stockton said.

As in 1998, staff forecasters had marked down their economic projections in response to the financial tumult, though only modestly.
Were they on the verge of making the same mistake, projecting too
much economic weakness as the result of financial stresses—or perhaps the opposite one, of projecting too little? The latest unemployment
rate—4.6 percent in August—was still quite low despite the loss of
jobs reported for the month. On the other hand, the financial disruptions now were showing up in mortgage lending, while in 1998 they
had played out mostly in the stock and bond markets. The connection
of house prices and mortgage availability to the Main Street economy
was much more direct. Only about one in five households owned stocks
directly and even fewer owned bonds, while roughly two-thirds owned
rather than rented their home. The ongoing decline in home prices and
sales, by reducing construction and consumer spending, could slow the
wider economy, which would lead to further weakening in housing,
and so on. I warned that this vicious circle could unleash "the makings
of a potential recessionary dynamic that may be difficult to head off."

Rick Mishkin, from the same corner seat I had occupied when
Greenspan was chairman, put it more bluntly: "Though we may not be
allowed to mention it in public, we have to mention the r-word because
there is now a significant probability of recession."

Credit disruptions could spell trouble for the economy. But whether we were looking at something analogous to the Depression or something much milder was hard to determine. Thus far, the stress in credit markets seemed much more like the stress during the Russian debt crisis in 1998 than 1929. Indeed, for a while the New York Fed circulated a daily data comparison that suggested that the current crisis was effectively a replay of 1998. I was comforted that market volatility was still within the bounds of recent experience. But, with so much uncertainty about the outlook, I believed we needed insurance in the form of a larger than usual cut in the federal funds rate. Most of the hawks accepted that argument but wanted to make clear that the Committee wasn't committed to further cuts. I insisted on a more forward-leaning message. "I think what the market wants to hear is that we get it, and that we're here, that we are ready to move as needed," I said.

As in August, we again discussed the issue of moral hazard—the notion, in this context, that we should refrain from helping the economy with lower interest rates because that would simultaneously let investors who had misjudged risk off the hook. Richard Fisher warned that too large a rate cut would be giving in to a "siren call" to "indulge rather than discipline risky financial behavior." But, given the rising threat to the broader economy, most members, including myself, Don Kohn, Tim Geithner, Janet Yellen, and Mishkin, had lost patience with this argument. "As the central bank, we have a responsibility to help markets function normally and to promote economic stability broadly speaking," I said.

While we went through with the larger than expected interest rate cut, we delayed taking action on another front. The blue-sky thinking that had emerged in August—and which had been carried forward by the staffs of the Board and the New York Fed—had resulted in a two-pronged proposal. The first was a proposed new facility that would auction twenty-eight-day discount window loans to banks, both U.S. and foreign, operating in the United States. This was the Board's responsibility.

The second prong, which was under the authority of the FOMC as a whole, was currency swap lines with the European Central Bank and the Swiss National Bank. Through the swap lines, we could provide dollars to the two central banks, collateralized by euros and Swiss francs, respectively. The central banks could then lend the dollars to banks and other financial institutions in their jurisdictions. Having the ECB and the Swiss National Bank conduct auctions of dollar credit in parallel with ours should, we anticipated, reduce the pressures we were seeing in U.S. money markets—particularly in the morning (East Coast time), when European banks were still open and were trying to borrow dollars in New York.

Discussions with the Europeans on the details of coordinating credit auctions in the United States and Europe—and the timing of the announcement—continued until the day before the September FOMC meeting. The ECB, in particular, was sensitive to any aspects of a currency swap arrangement that might imply that the Fed was riding to the rescue of European markets. We, in turn, wanted to avoid an incorrect inference that we were lending to potentially risky foreign private banks rather than creditworthy central banks. In light of the ECB's diffidence and the modest improvements we were seeing in money market functioning, we chose to hold off. Both the auction program and the swap lines would remain on the shelf a bit longer.

Our September rate cut drew the usual mix of praise and criticism. The *Wall Street Journal*'s editorial writers sneered at it, without actually taking a stand for or against. The next morning, my old Harvard professor Martin Feldstein, whose gloomy presentation at Jackson Hole had caught Don Kohn's attention, offered his congratulations for our having engineered a unanimous vote for a "bold and I think correct" move.

Barney Frank, the chairman of the House Financial Services Committee, and Chris Dodd, chairman of the Senate Banking Committee, both issued statements. Barney said he was pleased at the rate cut but displeased that the FOMC statement, in his view, still put too much weight on inflation risks. Dodd referred to an August 21 meeting he'd had with me and Hank Paulson in a way that seemed to insinuate that he deserved some credit for bringing pressure to bear on me. At the time I had told him that I was prepared to use every tool at my disposal, if necessary, and now, less than a month later, he was depicting my comment as an ironclad promise to cut the federal funds rate—not at all what I had intended. The Federal Reserve strives to make its decisions independently from political considerations, so I wasn't particularly happy about the comments.

One potential critic of our interest rate cut was noticeably silent—Mervyn King, the governor of the Bank of England. In the summer of 2007, he had spoken in strong opposition to central bank interventions. In August, when the Fed and the ECB were trying to relieve financial strains by providing tens of billions of dollars and euros to the money markets, the Bank of England had remained on the sidelines. On September 12, in a report to the British parliament, Mervyn, without naming names, sharply criticized the ECB and the Fed. "The provision of such liquidity support . . . encourages excessive risk-taking, and sows the seeds of future financial crises," he wrote. In other words, there would be no Bank of England put. Mervyn's concern explained why the Bank of England had not joined the ECB and the Swiss National Bank in proposing currency swap agreements with the Fed.

By the time of our September 18 announcement, however, Mervyn appeared to have changed his mind. On the day after our meeting, the Bank of England for the first time announced it would inject longer-term funds (10 billion pounds, or roughly $20 billion, at a three-month term) into British money markets. Later in the crisis I observed, "There are no atheists in foxholes or ideologues in a financial crisis." Mervyn had joined his fellow central bankers in the foxhole.

The source of Mervyn's conversion was the arrival of the global financial crisis on Britain's High Streets. On September 14, the Bank of England had acted to stem a depositor run by lending to Northern Rock, a mortgage lender based in Newcastle upon Tyne, in northeast

England. It was the first bank run in Great Britain since the infamous collapse of Overend, Gurney, and Co. in 1866, an event that had inspired Bagehot to publish his classic treatise. Northern Rock had expanded rapidly by raising funds in money markets and on the Internet rather than from local depositors. When the firm lost access to money markets and was unable to sell mortgages into a disappearing securitization market, it began to founder. The Bank of England agreed to lend to Northern Rock, but, when that was reported by the BBC, frightened depositors ran—a good illustration of the consequences of the stigma of borrowing from a central bank. Britain lacked government deposit insurance, relying on an industry-funded program that only partially protected depositors. Soon after the Bank of England's intervention, the government announced it was guaranteeing all deposits at Northern Rock. In February 2008, it would take Northern Rock into public ownership.

TWO DAYS AFTER the FOMC meeting, on September 20, I testified before Barney Frank's House Financial Services Committee, along with Hank Paulson and Housing and Urban Development secretary Alphonso Jackson. The subject was finding ways to stem the rising tide of mortgage foreclosures—a vital, and politically contentious, discussion. Foreclosures—especially foreclosures on homes financed by subprime mortgages with adjustable rates—had been rising for two years. We expected that foreclosures would continue to increase as the teaser rates on many mortgages reset at substantially higher levels. And with home prices falling, borrowers who had put little money down to buy their homes could no longer easily refinance to avoid the higher payment.

A few members of Congress pushed for direct federal aid to help homeowners in trouble, but most had little appetite for spending substantial taxpayer funds on the problem. The administration was doing what it could to reduce foreclosures without new federal spending. President Bush had recently turned to the Depression-era Federal Housing Administration (FHA) in an effort to help people who had recently missed payments on adjustable-rate subprime mortgages. Under the plan, those borrowers would be able to refinance into an FHA-insured fixed-rate loan with a lower payment. Mortgage insurance premiums from the borrowers, not the taxpayers, would pay the cost of the program. The president also had asked Hank Paulson and Alphonso Jackson to work on a private-sector foreclosure avoidance initiative, which would be called Hope Now. The administration ultimately enlisted lenders covering 60 percent of mortgages, investors, trade organizations, and mortgage counselors in a voluntary effort to keep borrowers in their homes.

At the Fed we did what we could, offering advice to the administration and Congress when we thought we could be helpful. I spoke often both within the Fed and in public about the urgent need to avoid "unnecessary" foreclosures—those in which a reduction in the monthly payment or other modifications stood a good chance of keeping the borrower in the home. But, as a central bank without the authority to undertake fiscal spending programs, the Fed had only limited ability to help homeowners in trouble. At that point, our best available tool (other than pushing down short-term interest rates, which we were reserving for broader economic objectives) was our bank supervision powers. Earlier that month we had joined with other regulatory agencies in issuing supervisory guidance aimed at mortgage servicers. These companies, often owned by banks, collect monthly payments and forward them to the owners of the mortgages, including the owners of mortgage-backed securities. They also deal with delinquent borrowers, for example, by modifying payment terms or initiating foreclosures. We urged servicers to work with distressed borrowers. Because foreclosures cost time and money, and because foreclosed homes rarely resell for good prices, modifying troubled mortgages to keep borrowers in their homes could make sense for lenders as well as borrowers. Our message to the mortgage industry was that supervisors wouldn't criticize them if they gave struggling homeowners a break. The Reserve Banks also worked behind the scenes in their regions, offering technical assistance and other support to the many nonprofit groups around the nation that were trying to counsel and help homeowners.

Unfortunately, institutional barriers and operational complexities sometimes prevented loan modifications that would otherwise make sense. For example, the legal agreements that governed many mortgage-backed securities required that most or all of the investors agree to a modification, a high hurdle. Many borrowers had taken out second mortgages with lenders other than the issuer of their first mortgage, and each lender was typically reluctant to offer a modification without concessions from the other. Servicers were overwhelmed by the volume of troubled mortgages, which require far more time and expertise to manage than mortgages in good standing. Servicers also received limited compensation for handling loan modifications, so they lacked both the incentives to undertake modifications and the resources needed to manage them effectively. And, of course, not all mortgages could be successfully modified. Certain borrowers could not make even substantially reduced monthly payments for reasons other than rate resets, including job loss, illness, or divorce.

As I had before, I pointed out at the hearing that modifying delinquent mortgages could benefit both lenders and borrowers, but there didn't seem to be much consensus for action. Politically, averting foreclosures could be framed as protecting Main Street from Wall Street. But many voters evidently saw the issue as favoring irresponsible borrowers at the expense of the responsible.

A DAY LATER, Anna and I attended a party—in the courtyard of a stately mansion once the home of early nineteenth-century naval hero Stephen Decatur—for Alan Greenspan's newly released memoir, *The Age of Turbulence: Adventures in a New World*. Greenspan, who largely avoided public encounters with the press while in office, had promoted the book with an appearance on CBS's *60 Minutes* on the eve of the FOMC meeting. When asked by the interviewer about the Fed's response to the financial crisis, he was graciously evasive and said he wasn't certain he would have done anything different and that I was "doing an excellent job." I hoped he was right. I didn't say it then, but as the financial crisis gathered steam, I couldn't help but reflect on the irony of the title Greenspan chose for his book.

Financial conditions continued to improve modestly in the weeks after the September FOMC meeting. The rate cut and our earlier efforts to add liquidity seemed to have helped wholesale funding markets. And interest rates on interbank loans showed that lending banks felt a little more comfortable about the ability of borrowing banks to repay. The stock market continued to rebound—with the Dow closing at a record 14,165 on October 9.

Not all the news was positive. Wall Street analysts were abuzz with pessimistic speculation about upcoming earnings reports at large financial companies. And, on September 28, the Office of Thrift Supervision shut down NetBank Inc., founded in suburban Atlanta in 1996 as one of the nation's first Internet-only banks. It was the largest savings and loan failure since the S&L crisis of the 1980s.

By the middle of October, the bad news Wall Street analysts had anticipated started to materialize. The credit rating agencies Moody's and Standard & Poor's continued to downgrade subprime mortgage–backed securities, and the prices of the securities continued their downward trek. During the week of October 15, three big banks—Citigroup, Bank of America, and Wachovia—reported steep declines in profits after write-downs of bad loans and mortgage-backed securities. The week ended with a stock market sell-off on Friday, October 19, the twentieth anniversary of the 1987 crash. The Dow fell 367 points to its lowest close since the day before the September 18 rate cut. It recovered somewhat in subsequent days, but the high-water mark reached earlier in the month would not be regained until years later.

A few hours after the market closed on October 19, Board member Kevin Warsh sent along a disturbing rumor that Merrill Lynch, a Wall

Street securities firm overseen by the Securities and Exchange Commission, was about to report much greater losses than it had earlier previewed—an unusual event. Kevin saw the sharp revision as a bigger problem than the losses themselves. It suggested that credit markets were deteriorating so rapidly that even large financial firms were having difficulty valuing their holdings. On October 24, Merrill Lynch reported the biggest quarterly loss in its ninety-three-year history, $2.3 billion, and disclosed for the first time that it had $15 billion in complex collateralized debt obligations (CDOs)—backed by subprime mortgage securities—on its books.

As the name suggests, CDOs consisted of various forms of debt, which were bundled and sold to investors. CDOs were initially embraced as a means of providing enhanced diversification and tailoring the degree of risk to each investor's preferences, but now they were suffering the same loss of confidence as other complex financial instruments. Merrill had created the CDOs to sell to investors, but it had kept some highly rated tranches of the securities for its own portfolio. Ratings no longer reassured potential buyers, and the values of the CDO tranches had fallen sharply. On October 30, Merrill CEO Stan O'Neal resigned.

AS THE OCTOBER 30–31 FOMC meeting approached, the key question—as in September—was how much would Wall Street turbulence hurt the "real" economy—where Americans worked, shopped, and saved for the future. Consumer spending was holding up surprisingly well. Except for housing, other economic bellwethers, such as new claims for unemployment benefits, had come in on the strong side, too. As at the previous meeting, the staff was projecting only a modest slowdown in economic growth.

The hawks on the Committee pointed to two developments that increased their anxiety. First, the foreign exchange value of the dollar had weakened (a trend that, if sustained, could make imports more expensive and raise inflation). Second, the day before the meeting, the price of crude oil had shot above $93 a barrel, which, after adjusting for inflation, broke a record set in 1981 during the oil crisis. Nevertheless, the staff's inflation forecast hadn't changed much. Dave Stockton explained that the dollar's decline was not expected to have a lasting effect on import prices and that the staff expected energy prices to reverse course.

Considering the risks to both economic growth and inflation, we had two basic options for monetary policy. We could buy more "insurance" against the dangers posed by rocky credit markets with a further cut to the overnight interest rates. Or, we could lean against still worrisome inflation risks by standing pat and awaiting further developments. In a speech at the Economic Club of New York on October 15, I had been careful to avoid signaling either way. Nevertheless, the New York Fed's latest survey of Wall Street firms suggested that markets expected a quarter-point cut.

I told the Committee that the decision was a "very, very close" call for me. I acknowledged that inflation was a concern and said the markets could probably withstand the surprise if we held our target rate steady. But I came down on the side of cutting the rate. "The downside risks are quite significant, if the housing situation, including prices, really deteriorates," I said. However, in a concession to the hawks that I would later regret, I agreed to a shift in language that signaled we weren't eager to cut rates again absent a change in the data. We cut the federal funds rate to 4-1/2 percent and said that, with that action, "the upside risks to inflation roughly balance the downside risks to growth." Tom Hoenig of Kansas City dissented anyway. He said it was easy to cut rates, often a popular move, but difficult to raise them later if you have made a mistake. The balanced-risks language was enough to satisfy the other hawkishly inclined voter, Bill Poole of St. Louis. The vote in favor of the action and statement was 9–1.

AFTER THE FOMC announcement, Chris Dodd—who was then seeking the Democratic Party nomination for president—again issued a statement implying a link between our action and his August meeting with Paulson and me. That irritation aside, in late 2007 and into 2008, my greater concern was that Dodd was sitting on three Federal Reserve Board nominations. The president in May 2007 had nominated Betsy Duke, a community banker from Virginia Beach, and Larry Klane, a senior executive of Capital One Financial Corp., to fill two vacancies on our seven-member Board. With the departure of Mark Olson in June 2006 and Sue Bies in March 2007, the Board not only was short-staffed, we also had no one with practical banking experience. Incumbent Randy Kroszner, meanwhile, had been nominated for a new fourteen-year term. He had been serving out Ned Gramlich's term, which would end on January 31. The three nominees had had a joint confirmation hearing before the Senate Banking Committee on August 2, but Dodd had shown no inclination to allow the nominations to proceed.

By September 26, I knew that we were going to have to deal with uncertain financial and economic prospects without a full Board. Brian Gross in the Fed's legislative affairs office had talked to Betsy, who had heard about a comment by Dodd that there was "no way all three nominees are going to be confirmed." Brian, who had long experience in Washington, looked at the glass as at least one-third full. "By ruling out 'all three nominees,' I think it does rule in at least one," he said in an email. In the meantime, though, Dodd let the nominees dangle.

As the months passed, living in nomination limbo wore on Randy. By law, even after his term expired, he could continue to serve until someone else was confirmed in his place. But it was hard to feel like a full member of the Board under those circumstances. Randy was filling an important role in overseeing the Fed's efforts to improve its banking supervision and consumer protection. And with the nominations apparently on hold, we couldn't afford to lose another Board member. I would invite him to a symphony at the Kennedy Center in January and try to buck up his morale. Since the Fed opened its doors in 1914 the Board had never had fewer than five members in office. Around the same time, I was also worried that we would lose Rick Mishkin. Rick had asked whether he could, while serving at the Fed, work on a new edition of his very well-regarded (and lucrative) textbook on money and banking. The answer from the Office of Government Ethics was no. I asked if he would consider staying on nevertheless.

Both Randy and Rick were important contributors to the Board's work—but I faced a procedural challenge in ensuring that their views were heard. Federal open-meeting laws regard any gathering of four or more Fed Board members as an official meeting. Any such interaction must be both publicly announced and, unless certain requirements are met, open to the public. Don Kohn, my vice chairman, with his long experience at the Fed, and Kevin Warsh, with his many Wall Street and political contacts and his knowledge of practical finance, were my most frequent companions on the endless conference calls through which we shaped our crisis-fighting strategy. Tim Geithner, as president of the New York Fed, was also involved in most of our discussions, but not being a Board member he didn't trigger the open-meeting law. Inviting Randy or Rick to join these conversations would have made the calls official meetings subject to the sunshine law—not a great venue for blue-sky thinking and strategizing. I tried to keep Rick and Randy apprised of developments through one-on-one lunches and frequent email exchanges.

IN THE OCTOBER FOMC meeting we also discussed the first substantial step toward my most cherished pre-crisis priority—making the Fed's monetary policy process more transparent and systematic. I had long advocated that the Fed adopt flexible inflation targeting—a strategy that set a specific target for inflation but also respected the maximum employment part of our mandate. Finally, I was in a position to do more than talk.

Early in my chairmanship, I had asked Don Kohn to lead a subcommittee of the FOMC to evaluate ways the Fed could improve its monetary policy communications, including, perhaps, by adopting an inflation target. In 2003, Don and I had taken opposite sides on inflation targeting at a symposium at the Federal Reserve Bank of St. Louis. But Don had described himself as a skeptic rather than an opponent. If Don, who commanded enormous respect from his colleagues, could find ways to alleviate his own concerns, he would move toward my position and others would follow.

Don's group included Janet Yellen, whose experience as a monetary policymaker extended back to a term on the Board in 1994–96, and Gary Stern, who was then the longest-serving Reserve Bank president, having been at the helm in Minneapolis since 1985. The subcommittee stopped short of recommending that we formally adopt inflation targeting. But, based on its work, reviewed by the FOMC in June 2007, I proposed moving in that direction by publicly releasing numerical information about what Committee members meant by "price stability" and by publishing more extensive and more frequent economic projections. The two steps, in combination, would help markets form more accurate expectations about future monetary policy and the path of interest rates.

The FOMC had been releasing economic projections since 1979 as part of its twice-a-year report to Congress. Don's subcommittee had looked at doubling the number of forecasts to four a year and releasing them more quickly. The subcommittee also had examined a subtle but significant step toward a formal inflation objective—extending the forecast period for economic growth, inflation, and unemployment to three years, from two. At least under normal circumstances, three years is enough time for monetary policy to achieve (or come close to) the Committee's desired level of inflation. By announcing a forecast for inflation three years out, the Committee would effectively be telling the world its numerical target for inflation. It was indirect, but I was confident that market participants would understand the point.

Don's subcommittee hadn't forgotten about the employment half of the Fed's mandate. That issue, however, was more complicated. Ultimately, inflation is determined almost entirely by the tightness or ease of monetary policy, so the FOMC could target the inflation rate at whatever level we thought made most sense. The maximum sustainable level of employment, however, is determined by a host of factors—ranging from the demographics of the labor force, to the mix of workers' skills, to technological developments—and cannot be arbitrarily set by monetary policymakers. As an additional complication, economists cannot know the maximum sustainable level of employment with any certainty but must estimate it based on historical experience. Having a fixed employment target in parallel to the fixed inflation target was consequently not feasible. Nevertheless, monetary policymakers' predictions of the unemployment rate three years out would at least give a general sense of what level of employment policymakers thought they could achieve without generating inflationary price and wage increases.

Ideally, the whole Committee would have agreed on the projections. Policy committees in several countries, the United Kingdom being one leading example, publish collective forecasts. But we could not count on the diverse (and geographically dispersed) Federal Open Market Committee, with its nineteen participants when all positions are filled, being able to agree on a single forecast. Instead, following existing practice, we asked each individual participant to submit his or her own projections for economic growth, inflation, and unemployment, assuming that their preferred monetary policy was followed. We publicly reported both the full range of projections for each variable and the "central tendency" of the projections (the range of projections with the three highest and three lowest projections excluded).

The first set of projections under the new system would show most FOMC members forecasting inflation in three years (in 2010) to be between 1.6 percent and 1.9 percent. Most expected an unemployment rate at the end of 2010 of 4.7 percent to 4.9 percent. It wasn't unreasonable to draw the conclusion that the Committee was aiming for inflation a little less than 2 percent and that it thought unemployment couldn't dip too much below 5 percent without running the risk of overheating the economy. For this purpose it didn't much matter whether the forecasts were accurate—the purpose of the longer-term forecasts was to disclose the direction in which, ideally, the Committee would like to steer the economy.

Now all that remained was to announce the new system. In mid-September Tim Geithner—ever the pragmatist—had urged me to consider postponing the launch of the new framework until my semi-annual testimony before Congress in February. He argued that a period of financial fragility wasn't the best time to introduce a new monetary policy regime, and that the staff shouldn't be distracted from crisis fighting. And, he said, there was "a real risk this will get lost in the noise of other stuff." After some thought, I decided that the fall of 2007 was as good a time as any.

Our announcement options narrowed when Greg Ip published a story containing the gist of our plan in the *Wall Street Journal* on October 25. I decided that we would announce on November 14, and that I would follow our press release with a speech the same morning to the Cato Institute, a libertarian think tank.

Before we announced, we needed to touch base with Barney Frank and Chris Dodd, the chairs of our oversight committees. I believe strongly in central bank independence when it comes to the implementation of monetary policy, but the proposed changes had implications for the goals Congress had established by law. Consultation was entirely appropriate. I called Barney myself. Laricke Blanchard, then head of our legislative affairs office, reached out to an economist on the staff of Dodd's committee. Barney was concerned that any step toward an inflation target would downgrade the Fed's employment objective. But he at least provisionally accepted my argument that the changes were aimed primarily at achieving greater clarity. With those boxes checked, I proceeded to lay out my case for greater openness in monetary policy at the Cato Institute.

The new communications practices for monetary policy played to generally favorable reviews in the newspapers and among economists, but, as Tim Geithner had predicted, it soon was "lost in the noise of other stuff."

CHAPTER 9

The End of the Beginning

The markets continued their roller-coaster ride through November as investors tried to assess the worsening crisis. Much of their concern focused on major financial companies. Sharp declines in the prices of mortgage-related securities and other credit products continued, forcing many firms to report large write-downs. Meanwhile, funding costs continued to rise in both the United States and Europe.

The losses were large. Citigroup revealed on November 4 that it was preparing to write down its subprime-related holdings by $8 billion to $11 billion. It also said that its chief executive, Chuck Prince, had "elected to retire." Prince had in 2003 succeeded Sanford Weill, who in 1998 had reinvented Citi as a financial services supermarket by merging the insurance conglomerate Travelers Group Inc. with the bank holding company Citicorp. Prince was the second CEO of a financial behemoth, after Merrill's O'Neal, to fall to the crisis. In light of the size of the losses, he said that "the only honorable course" was to step down. Just four months before his ouster, in an interview with a *Financial Times* reporter in Japan, Prince had uttered words that would become emblematic of his industry's complacency on the eve of the crisis: "When the music stops . . . things will be complicated. But as long as the music is playing, you've got to get up and dance. We're still dancing."

As would become clear over the next few months, Citi had compounded its problems by conducting a substantial portion of its operations through separately incorporated off-balance-sheet entitles called structured investment vehicles (SIVs), which collectively accounted for more than a third of its holdings. SIVs, which Citi invented in 1988, were similar to other types of off-balance-sheet vehicles, though somewhat more conservatively structured. SIVs didn't have much capital to absorb losses, but their funding was typically more stable than other vehicles, with less reliance on asset-backed commercial paper and relatively greater use of longer-term debt, with maturities of up to five years. They also held a wider range of assets. Many SIVs had little or no exposure to subprime loans, and, typically, they held considerable amounts of easily sold (liquid) assets, such as Treasury securities. It's perhaps not surprising, then, that, up until this point, SIVs had performed reasonably well. Between 2004 and 2007, the SIV sector tripled in size, and, just prior to the crisis, thirty-six SIVs held almost $400 billion in assets.

However, in the second half of 2007, SIVs started coming under pressure. Unsurprisingly, the first to run into trouble had substantial subprime holdings. But investors soon began withdrawing funds from SIVs with minimal or no subprime assets as well, an indication of just how deep investor mistrust was becoming. As their funding dried up, the SIVs had to sell assets rapidly to repay investors. By the end of November 2007 SIVs had liquidated 23 percent of their portfolios, on average. Over the following year, virtually every SIV would default, be restructured, or be taken back on its sponsor's balance sheet.

But that wasn't the end of the story. The faltering SIVs also had direct effects on banks, like Citi, that had served as their sponsors. Sponsors advised SIVs and sometimes extended backup credit lines. On paper, the sponsors recognized no potential loss exposure other than through the credit line. Indeed, SIVs and other off-balance-sheet vehicles appealed to banks because the supposed reduction in loss exposure meant the banks could hold less capital against SIV assets. However, the sponsoring banks (and their regulators) hadn't counted on "reputational risk." As outside funding became unavailable and

SIVs threatened to collapse, sponsoring banks found that it wasn't so easy to separate their reputations from those of their progeny. In many cases, the sponsors scrambled to prop up their SIVs, for fear that the collapse of those vehicles would hurt the parent bank's public image and reputation with investors. But propping up off-balance-sheet vehicles meant taking responsibility for their losses.

On November 5, the day after Citi announced its write-downs, Fitch Ratings said it was reviewing the financial strength of the so-called monoline insurers. These nine U.S. firms, including MBIA Inc., Ambac Financial Group, and Financial Guarantee Insurance Company (FGIC), were little known outside the industry but played an important role. They insured bonds and other securities, paying off policyholders in the event of a default; they were called "monolines" because this was essentially their only business. Their traditional business had been insuring corporate and municipal bonds, but over time they had expanded to offering insurance on securities backed by mortgages and other types of credit. Just as a property insurer suffers losses when a major earthquake or hurricane destroys thousands of properties, the monolines experienced large losses due to losses on subprime and other securities. That is what had prompted Fitch's review.

If the ratings companies took away the monolines' triple-A ratings, as seemed likely, it would affect not only the insurers. Firms that had purchased insurance from the companies would have to recognize the reduced value of that insurance by writing down the values of insured securities on their own books. Here was another familiar feature of classic financial panics: contagion. Weak firms infect other firms that have lent to them or that rely on them for guarantees or other forms of support. Trouble in the monolines consequently led to sharp drops in the stock prices of many financial firms.

A few days after the Fitch announcement, Boston Fed president Eric Rosengren reported several conversations with hedge fund managers. They were particularly concerned about the potential effect of monoline downgrades on the municipal bond market, which had so far been relatively untouched by the crisis. Of the $2.5 trillion in secu-rities insured by the monolines, about $1.5 trillion were municipal bonds, used to finance the construction of schools, roads, and bridges. Even with no change in the financial conditions of the issuing states and cities, municipal bond ratings could slip if the ratings of the mon-olines were downgraded.

Morgan Stanley, the white-shoe investment banking firm and an inheritor of the legacy of financier J.P. Morgan, added to the prevail-ing gloom with an announcement on November 7 that it, too, would write down its subprime holdings—by $3.7 billion. It would more than double that figure, to $9.4 billion, in a subsequent announcement on December 19. Wachovia and other large firms followed with more losses and write-downs.

On a positive note, many firms raised capital, much of it from abroad, which at least partially filled the holes in their balance sheets. In October, Bear Stearns had initiated a partnership with the state-owned CITIC Securities Co. of China. Citigroup in November raised capital from the Abu Dhabi Investment Authority. In December, Mor-gan Stanley would tap the Chinese sovereign wealth fund, and Merrill Lynch a Singapore government investment company. These and other foreign government investments in U.S. financial firms drew scrutiny from Congress. Lawmakers should have been pleased that capital had arrived to strengthen the wobbly American financial system. Instead, they worried about foreign influence on U.S. institutions. Yet for the most part these investments were passive and left control of business decisions to the existing shareholders and management.

Despite the occasional pieces of good news, including a strong jobs report for October, the economic outlook deteriorated in the weeks following the October 30–31 FOMC meeting. Funding pres-sures rose sharply midmonth and the stock market slid about 8 percent in the three weeks following the meeting. More important, the Main Street economy was increasingly feeling the effects of the financial disruptions. Home construction continued its steep descent as mortgage credit tightened, foreclosures spread, and house prices fell. Household spending weakened in the face of falling income and confidence, as well as high oil prices. The reasonably good pace of economic growth that we had seen for most of the year was clearly not going to continue.

By mid-November, markets began to assume that the FOMC would soon cut interest rates again. But a press interview by Bill Poole, the president of the St. Louis Fed, and a speech by Board member Randy Kroszner, both voting members of the Committee, caused them to reassess, at least temporarily. Poole, who had joined the majority in voting for rate cuts in September and October, told Dow Jones Newswires on November 15 that he saw the economic risks as roughly balanced between higher inflation and weaker growth (as the Committee's October 31 statement had suggested), and that it would take new information to change his mind. Randy, in a speech the next day in New York, agreed.

It seemed to me that Bill had intended to send the signal he sent, while Randy's message was probably inadvertent. Randy had followed a long-standing practice of FOMC members who want to avoid sending market signals by paraphrasing the October 31 statement, the most recent Committee pronouncement on the outlook for the economy and monetary policy. But financial and economic conditions were changing rapidly, and it now seemed likely that the FOMC had not yet done enough to offset the housing decline and the credit crunch. Moreover, Randy, unlike Bill, was seen as a centrist rather than as a committed hawk or dove. Fed watchers read his remarks as offering more information about the views of the FOMC as a whole.

I had consciously taken a democratic approach in leading the FOMC. I wanted people to understand that a wide range of views and perspectives were being taken into account as we made important policy choices. I saw the public airing of differences among FOMC participants as generally helpful, despite complaints that free speech sometimes created cacophony. But I also knew that a decisive and clear message would be needed at times. With uncertainty about the economic outlook and our strategy for monetary policy high, this was one of those times. I was in Cape Town, South Africa, the weekend of November 16–18, attending a meeting of the Group of 20 (G-20), a forum for the central bank governors and finance ministers of nineteen countries and the European Union. On Monday, the nineteenth, at 2:43 a.m. Washington time, the BlackBerrys of the directors of the Board's three economic divisions buzzed with an incoming email from me: "I think it would be good to give the market more guidance about our thinking leading up to the Dec FOMC." My plan was to use a speech scheduled for November 29 in Charlotte. Don Kohn had a scheduled speech in New York the day before and could reinforce the message.

Our guidance was this: Financial stresses had materially weakened the outlook for the economy and we were prepared to respond. Don answered Fed critics who saw our interest rate cuts as rescuing the Wall Street firms and big banks from their poor judgment. "We should not hold the economy hostage to teach a small segment of the population a lesson," he said. In my remarks, I acknowledged that the economic outlook had been "importantly affected over the past month by renewed turbulence in financial markets" and that we would "take full account" of both incoming economic data and ongoing financial developments.

Markets received our message loud and clear, with the Dow surging more than 400 points from the day before Don spoke to the day after I spoke. We looked at the stock market not because we wanted to move it by a particular amount, but because its reaction was a good measure of whether or not our policy message had been understood.

The clarity of our message collided, however, with the opaque economic outlook. Markets scaled back rate-cut hopes generated by Don's and my speeches after the release of a relatively positive employment report on December 7, the Friday before the meeting. Employers had added 94,000 jobs in November and the unemployment rate was steady at 4.7 percent. Whatever the ill effects of financial turmoil, it was still not fully evident in the job market, whose health had a much more direct effect on most Americans than volatility on Wall Street.

Notwithstanding the seemingly benign jobs situation, the Board's economists told the FOMC at the December 11 meeting that they had marked down their growth forecast for 2008 to a sluggish 1.3 percent. And Dave Stockton acknowledged that even this gloomier forecast could prove too optimistic because it showed the economy avoiding a recession. He joked that he was trying not to take personally a recent HR office decision to increase the frequency of staff drug tests: "I can assure you . . . we came up with this projection unimpaired and on nothing stronger than many late nights of diet Pepsi and vending-machine Twinkies." Whether or not the staff was operating under the influence, it turned out to be the wrong call. A year later, with the substantial benefit of hindsight, the National Bureau of Economic Research would declare that what we now call the Great Recession had begun in December 2007.

Given what we knew, we moved cautiously. The FOMC voted 9–1 in December to cut the target for the federal funds rate by only a quarter point, to 4-1/4 percent. We deleted the balanced risks language from our statement, which had created the impression that we were done with rate cutting, but we avoided any new language that might seem to promise additional cuts. This time the dissenter was a dove— Eric Rosengren. He had argued for a half-point cut, along with Board member Rick Mishkin. Rick also had been inclined to dissent, but, at my request, he did not. I thought that a strong vote for the Committee's action would avoid sending mixed messages to fragile markets. However, with my support, Rick would soon speak publicly about the dangers posed to the economy by continued financial stress.

I had been torn about the rate decision. In the end I asked the Committee to approve a quarter-point reduction because I was concerned that a half point would be viewed as a lurch and a signal of greater worry about the economy. "I am quite conflicted about it, and I think there is a good chance that we may have to move further at subsequent meetings," I said.

On a second front, we dusted off and implemented the plans we had shelved in September to auction discount window credit to banks and for central bank swap lines. In the process, we created the first of many crisis-related acronyms—TAF, for Term Auction Facility (the word "term" referring to the fact that loans would be for terms longer than overnight). We started relatively small, by central banking standards. We planned two $20 billion auctions of discount window loans of approximately one-month maturities. We said we'd conduct two more auctions, of unspecified size, in January—and then see if we wanted to continue. To relieve pressure in dollar funding markets in Europe, we established temporary currency swap lines, for six months, with draws limited to $20 billion by the European Central Bank and $4 billion by the Swiss National Bank.

With both the TAF and the currency swaps in place, we were entering what Don Kohn, an avid sailor, called uncharted waters. We were acutely aware of the risks of failure. TAF auctions were, by design, intended to overcome the stigma of borrowing from the Fed. But what if stigma, which had kept banks away from the discount window, attached to the auctions, too? We also recognized that providing short-term loans to banks, while reducing funding pressures, would not erase subprime mortgage losses. (We hoped, though, that by reducing the need for stressed institutions to sell their assets, we might slow the price declines in mortgage-backed and other securities.) Similarly, we worried that our first tentative step on the swap lines might not be big enough to significantly reduce the strains in Europe. "This may not work. I don't want to oversell it," I told the FOMC. "If we do it, we are just going to have to give it a try and see what happens."

WE THOUGHT THAT our actions at the December 11 meeting would be roughly in sync with investor expectations. The market reaction

quickly told us otherwise; by the end of the day the Dow Jones industrial average had fallen 294 points. Apparently, some in the markets
had hoped for a larger rate cut, and many expected a stronger hint in
our statement that more rate cuts were in train. "There is a growing
sense the Fed doesn't get it," said David Greenlaw, an economist at
Morgan Stanley, which had already begun forecasting a recession.

Much of the negative reaction resulted from a communications
misstep. After the FOMC meeting, we didn't immediately announce
our new currency swap lines or the creation of the TAF, even though
reporters had been speculating since early December about the possibility of some action aimed at money market functioning. Inferring
that no announcement meant no new actions, market participants
grew even more concerned that the Fed wasn't being proactive enough.

We had agreed to delay announcing the new programs until the
following morning because we wanted to coordinate with six other
central banks that would be issuing statements. The ECB and the
Swiss National Bank, our partners in the swap lines, were planning
to announce they would provide banks in their jurisdictions with
dollar funding, while the Bank of England and the Bank of Canada
would announce new steps to provide liquidity in their own currencies. The central banks of Sweden and Japan took no action but
planned to express their support. I thought coordinating our statements would provide greater clarity to markets and potentially boost
global confidence.

The logistical decision had a subtext, however. ECB president Jean-
Claude Trichet wanted the TAF and swaps announcements out at the
same time to foster the impression that the swap lines were part of a
solution to a U.S. problem, rather than an instance of the Fed helping out Europe. His goal was to avoid highlighting the dollar-funding
difficulties faced by European banks. A career French civil servant,
educated in elite schools and a former governor of the French central bank, Trichet was gentlemanly, diplomatic, and always attentive
to public messaging. Beneath his sometimes grandfatherly demeanor,

however, he also had considerable skills as a political infighter and was an excellent judge of market psychology.

I had some sympathy for Jean-Claude's concerns. The subprime mortgage securities at the heart of the financial crisis had originated in the United States. But, in truth, the turmoil in dollar funding markets was his problem, too. As it turned out, not only did the $24 billion initially distributed through the swaps go to Europe, all but about $3 billion of the $40 billion distributed in the first two TAF auctions went to European and other foreign institutions operating in the United States, with German banks leading the way. Foreign bank branches in the United States aren't eligible for U.S. deposit insurance and thus couldn't rely—as did U.S. banks—on a stable funding base of deposits. By law, however, our discount window is open to all banks operating in the United States. That makes sense because U.S. businesses and households rely on loans from both foreign and domestic banks. A liquidity crunch at the U.S. operations of a foreign bank would hurt their U.S. customers.

SHORTLY AFTER THE December FOMC meeting, I began brainstorming with Don Kohn, Tim Geithner, Kevin Warsh, and Michelle Smith about how we could avoid seesawing market expectations in the run-up to meetings. At one point we discussed whether I should hold regular news conferences. News conferences are routine in Washington—and routine for many other central banks. But they would be a big step for the Fed. Paul Volcker had called one, on October 6, 1979, a Saturday, to announce his anti-inflation campaign. But that was considered extraordinary.

I already was painfully aware that the Fed chairman's remarks can easily be misunderstood or overinterpreted. And I knew that if we began holding regular news conferences, there would be no going back. Nevertheless, I was eager to explore the idea. Don suggested a slow start, with twice-a-year news conferences in April and October that would complement my monetary policy testimonies in February and July. I also raised the heretical idea, at least for the Fed, of doing on-the-record newspaper interviews every other month. I knew that the ECB president granted regular media interviews, rotating by country around the currency zone. Caution prevailed that weekend. We agreed on nothing more than that Don, Tim, and I should continue to try to shape markets' policy expectations through more strategic timing of our speeches.

THE WEEK AFTER the FOMC meeting, we turned our attention to a promise I had made early in my tenure as chairman—strengthening regulations protecting mortgage borrowers. Though most mortgages were made by institutions supervised by other federal agencies or the states, the Fed's rules applied to all lenders. With a few exceptions, the Fed had resisted spelling out the acts and practices it deemed "unfair and deceptive" under HOEPA, the Home Ownership and Equity Protection Act, preferring a "case-by-case" approach. Many at the Fed had believed that blanket prohibitions of certain practices could have unintended consequences, inadvertently making legitimate loans illegal or at least difficult to obtain.

By late 2007, however, it was clear that some practices had to be banned, unintended consequences or not. On December 18, the Board proposed a rule prohibiting lenders from making loans without considering borrowers' ability to repay and requiring lenders to verify borrowers' incomes and assets. These bits of common sense had been discarded in the frenzy of the housing boom, and in a system in which loan originators could effectively pass any problems on to the unwitting purchasers of mortgage-backed securities. We also proposed limits on penalties imposed on borrowers who prepaid their mortgages.

The rule-writing process, with its rounds of public comment, could be maddeningly slow. We had launched our effort to rewrite our HOEPA rules with hearings conducted by Randy Kroszner over the summer of 2006. We would not propose new rules until December 2007, however, and final rules were not adopted until July 2008. The final rules in turn would not be fully implemented by the industry and the supervisors until October 2009. By that point, of course, subprime lending had already virtually ended.

The Board meeting to propose the new HOEPA rules also represented a modest step forward in openness. For the first time, television cameras recorded the entire meeting. Before then, public Board meetings had essentially been print media–only affairs, with broadcasters permitted to film, without sound, for only the first few minutes.

ANNA AND I spent the holidays in Washington, taking time off when we could. On the Friday before Christmas, we lunched with the security agents who protected us, an annual tradition. With twenty-four-hour-a-day security, we spent a great deal of time with Bob Agnew, his deputy, Ed Macomber, and the other agents, and we considered them friends. Anna would often surprise me with facts that she had learned about agents' families or their backgrounds that they would never share with me. From the time that I cut my thumb in the kitchen to the time I was accosted by a self-described independent journalist wielding a video camera at an awards dinner of the United States–Mexico Chamber of Commerce in May 2011, the team was always there to help. In April 2008, six hundred demonstrators from National People's Action, a network of grassroots organizations advocating racial and economic justice, arrived in a caravan of buses and protested in front of our home. The agent on duty, Charles Briscoe, stood alone, blocking our front door. After twenty minutes or so he persuaded the protesters to leave. The police were never called.

From various holiday destinations (Tim and his family were in Bali, Don was visiting family in Seattle), the crisis management team kept in touch through conference calls and by email. On the afternoon of December 31, I poured out my worry and frustration to Don and Tim in a long email. "I have become increasingly concerned that our policy rate is too high . . . with very little insurance for what are, to my mind, some large and growing downside risks," I wrote. Market players had been criticizing us for "being too indecisive and too slow to respond to the gathering storm." Politicians, I predicted, would soon join them. "Part of this game is confidence, and looking clueless and uncertain doesn't help."

I had found it difficult to choose, at the December meeting, between a quarter-point and a half-point rate cut. Now I knew we needed to do more. A December 28 report had shown an unexpectedly sharp 9 percent drop in sales of new houses in November, to a twelve-year low. The housing collapse and credit problems could feed on each other and fuel a more general downturn. I told Don and Tim that house price decreases were "starting to sink in" with consumers, and surveys showed that consumer confidence had declined to levels seen in previous recessions. I proposed a special videoconference meeting of the FOMC. If the economic data remained soft, particularly the employment data, we should cut rates twice in January—by a quarter point at the videoconference and another quarter point at the meeting scheduled for January 29–30. Tim and Don, in separate replies, cautioned once again against a rate move between regularly scheduled FOMC meetings, an action that would usually be taken in response to an emergency. Tim wrote that it was difficult to judge whether a surprise rate cut earlier in the month would reassure or roil markets. "They want agility and force, but they also want predictability and steadiness," he said.

We continued our long-distance debate into New Year's Day. I pointed out that, at the late January meeting, the FOMC vote would rotate to two hawkish Reserve Bank presidents—Richard Fisher of Dallas and Charles Plosser of Philadelphia. We'd have a better chance of minimizing dissenting votes against a half-percentage point reduction in January—or even a three-quarters percentage point cut, if necessary—by acting in two steps. Don agreed that I had made a convincing case for at least scheduling an early January conference call, but he was keeping an open mind about whether we needed to act at it. "I'd be more comfortable if there was a demonstrable loss of [market] confidence," he wrote.

When the FOMC videoconference began at 5:00 p.m. on January 9, I had decided not to ask for an intermeeting rate cut. I thought we could get about the same effect, with less damage to the FOMC's deliberative process, if I used the call to build a consensus for a large rate cut at the next scheduled meeting. I could then send a strong signal in my speech the next day. I told the Committee that it looked like we were headed into a recession. I noted that the staff had again cut its economic growth forecast for 2008, to a scant 1 percent, and that the unemployment rate had risen from 4.4 percent in March to 5 percent in December. The economy had never been able to crawl along at a 1 percent growth rate without lapsing into recession, and unemployment had never increased by that much without presaging a much greater rise. "The concern I have is not just a slowdown but the possibility it might become a much nastier episode," I said.

Don and Tim, I knew, would have supported an intermeeting move, as would doves such as Janet Yellen and Eric Rosengren. But other FOMC members, such as Jeff Lacker of Richmond, did not want to appear to be responding to a single economic report. The Labor Department had reported on January 4 that employers had added a disappointingly low 18,000 jobs in December. The afternoon of the employment report, amid press stories that the Bush administration was considering a fiscal stimulus package, I had attended a meeting at the White House with President Bush, Hank Paulson, and other top economic officials. On our FOMC conference call, senior Board staff and even some Committee members, including Gary Stern of the Minneapolis Fed, worried about the "optics" for central bank independence if a Fed rate cut followed less than a week after the well-publicized White House meeting.

The videoconference ended at about 7:00 p.m. and I turned to finalizing the luncheon speech I would deliver the next day. That evening and the next morning, I conferred with Don, Tim, Kevin, and senior staff. We sweated every word. Should I say that additional rate cuts "may be necessary" or "may *well* be necessary"? Should I say that we stood ready to take "*substantive* additional action" to support growth or "*meaningful* additional action"? The absurdity of our discussion did not escape us, but we had learned through bitter experience that a single word often mattered. Our goal was to send the markets as clear and strong a signal as possible, while still allowing us enough wiggle room to change course if necessary.

The day of the speech, I visited the Board's barber shop for a haircut and beard trim from Lenny Gilleo (the "Hairman of the Board," according to his business cards). Lenny leased a small shop in the basement of the Martin Building and had been cutting what was left of my hair since I had joined the Board in 2002. He had trimmed the hair of Alan Greenspan, Paul Volcker, and Arthur Burns before me and dispensed wisdom on politics, monetary policy, and baseball. A sign on his wall read: "My money supply depends on your growth rate."

Back in my office, I opted to use the language options we judged to be a shade stronger—"may *well* be necessary" and "*substantive* additional action." The message was received. The speech, at the Mayflower Hotel (scene of my ignominious National Spelling Bee performance in 1965), solidified Wall Street analysts' expectations for a half-point interest rate cut at the end of the month, instead of a quarter point.

Stocks rallied, supported not only by my speech but also by reports that Bank of America would take over the troubled mortgage lender Countrywide. Optimists saw the $4 billion takeover as a sign of a possible bottom in the subprime crisis and good news for Bank of America, which was acquiring Countrywide's sprawling mortgage origination and servicing business at what was considered a cheap price. Pessimists wondered if Bank of America, the nation's largest bank as measured by deposits, wasn't buying a parcel of ticking time bombs in the form of future losses.

AS WE AT THE FED came to grips with the need to counter the cumulating economic weakness with more aggressive monetary policy, the administration was contemplating fiscal remedies. Since November,

Hank Paulson and I had been discussing whether some form of fiscal stimulus—such as a temporary cut in Social Security and Medicare payroll taxes—might boost the economy. I told Hank a broad-based tax cut could prove particularly helpful at this point, with homeowners struggling to meet monthly mortgage payments. I also pushed the idea of using federal loan guarantees or other incentives to induce state and local governments to speed up job-creating infrastructure projects. Word came back, though, that the Council of Economic Advisers thought the infrastructure idea impractical. The objection, essentially, was that there were not enough "shovel-ready" projects that could be undertaken in a short time.

As politically independent central bankers, we had to walk a fine line. We believed that the country was best served if we made monetary policy free of political interference, so long as we were accountable for reaching the goals Congress set for us. And we couldn't expect elected leaders to honor the long tradition of Fed autonomy if we tried to exert influence on fiscal matters not within our purview. At the same time, we had a lot of expertise at the Fed. I thought we should be willing to offer advice, at least in private, if it would be helpful and we could avoid becoming embroiled in a partisan fight. In that spirit, just as I had met with Paulson and President Bush on January 4, I met privately on January 14 with the top Democrat in the House, Speaker Nancy Pelosi, who on January 8 had called for stimulus legislation. Shortly afterward, a Bloomberg News story appeared reporting that I supported fiscal stimulus. It was attributed to an anonymous Democratic aide. I did think that some kind of stimulus plan would be a good idea, as I would testify to the House Budget Committee on January 17, but with caveats that the anonymous aide apparently had omitted. The leak annoyed but didn't surprise me; I had learned that's how Washington works.

Board staff at first advised me to avoid taking any kind of position on fiscal stimulus. Then, after I resisted their advice, they asked me to consider advocating that any stimulus be conditioned on an objective trigger, such as the size of job losses. They were still predicting an economic slowdown in 2008, rather than an outright recession, and they weren't convinced fiscal stimulus was justified. "A positive word from you would give this locomotive a big shove out of the station," warned David Wilcox, who had served at Treasury during the Clinton administration and had sharper political instincts than most Fed career economists. In this case, though, I wasn't so sure. I doubted that my words would have the weight of Greenspan's, and in any case it seemed to me that Congress is ruled first and foremost by interests and ideology, not by the advice of experts or supposed experts, including the chairman of the Fed.

In the end, I testified that "fiscal action could be helpful in principle" if it could be implemented quickly, focused on affecting the economy over the short term, and be explicitly temporary to avoid increasing the long-term deficit. I expressed no preference for whether the stimulus should take the form of tax cuts, spending increases, or both. I—a Republican appointee, albeit at a nonpartisan institution—was delivering the same message that Larry Summers, a former Treasury secretary under President Clinton, had delivered more concisely the day before to the Joint Economic Committee. "A stimulus program," he said, "should be timely, targeted, and temporary." On January 18, the day after my testimony, the president proposed a $150 billion stimulus package, consisting mostly of temporary tax cuts for individuals, families, and businesses.

AS I PREPARED for the budget testimony, I was regretting my decision of a week earlier to refrain from insisting on an intermeeting rate cut. The drumbeat of bad financial news continued: more big write-downs at Merrill Lynch and Citigroup, deepening troubles at the monoline insurers, and repeated sharp drops in stock prices. The wider economy looked shakier, too: Retail sales had declined in December. On January 15, the day of the retail sales release, I emailed Don and Tim: "If I could pull the trigger [on a rate cut] myself, I would do it this week." They talked me off the ledge that morning. I would wait until the scheduled meeting, but I soon began lining up support for a very large rate cut—at least three-quarters of a percentage point. The following week, an unanticipated event—in the form of what Don had earlier called "a demonstrable loss of confidence"—would give us a reason to act.

The Board was closed on Monday, January 21, for Martin Luther King Jr. Day. I was in the office that morning. Like my father, I grew distracted and unhappy when I could not usefully occupy my time. This character trait ("flaw" is probably a better word) had caused some tension with Anna early in our marriage. But we had struck a deal: I would work in the morning on weekends and holidays and in the afternoon and evening devote my full attention to family and recreation. On this particular holiday, I would not return home until long after dark.

On arrival I checked the Bloomberg screen in my office and saw that a wave of selling, originating in the Far East, was sweeping across European stock markets. Futures markets were predicting a steep 3.5 percent drop when U.S. stock markets reopened the next day. I called Tim Geithner. He was already checking in with his market contacts. Kevin Warsh emailed: "Should we do a markets call?" I agreed that we should. I called Don. He was on the road but thought he could make an 11:00 a.m. call. I emailed dial-in numbers to Don, Tim, Kevin, Michelle Smith, Bill Dudley (the markets chief in New York), and Brian Madigan. Brian headed to the office. (I don't know when Brian slept. I can't remember ever sending him an email, day or night, without getting a response in ten minutes.)

We decided to convene the full FOMC by videoconference that afternoon and propose an immediate rate cut of three-quarters of a percentage point, with a statement suggesting more to come at the end of the month. I sat down at my computer terminal, banged out the first draft of the statement, and circulated it for comment. Brian then set about arranging the videoconference, including trying to track down the two Board members and eleven Reserve Bank presidents not on the morning call. By 3:15 p.m., everyone had been reached except Rick

Mishkin. Charles Plosser of the Philadelphia Fed was traveling in Florida but could participate using a secure line at the Jacksonville branch of the Atlanta Fed. Gary Stern of the Minneapolis Fed would participate from Chicago. We set the conference time at 6:00 p.m. The staff reached Rick shortly before 4:00 p.m. He was on the top of a mountain, cross-country skiing at Lake Tahoe, and wouldn't be able to get to a secure phone line in time.

The videoconference began with a report on markets from Bill Dudley. Bill, affable and with a quick laugh, had a PhD in economics from Berkeley. He had been the chief economist for Goldman Sachs for ten years before Geithner hired him to succeed Dino Kos as head of the Open Market Trading Desk at the New York Fed. He understood macroeconomics and monetary policy, but he also knew how Wall Street worked.

U.S. stock values had declined nearly 10 percent during the first three weeks of the new year, Bill said, and futures prices suggested stocks could open an additional 5 percent lower on Tuesday. We didn't know what was driving the latest selling wave. Bill mentioned the Merrill Lynch and Citigroup write-downs of the previous week and the possible spillover of the monoline insurers' troubles into the municipal bond market. His European contacts were citing the growing odds of a U.S. recession and its likely effect on their economies.

I told the Committee our job wasn't to protect stock investors. But, I said, the sharp stock declines "reflect a growing belief that the United States is in for a deep and protracted recession." That belief was creating a worrisome dynamic: Investors were withdrawing from risk and lenders were withdrawing from lending. A large and immediate cut in our target for the federal funds rates might help arrest the dynamic.

"We are facing, potentially, a broad crisis," I said. "We can no longer temporize. We have to address this crisis. We have to try to get it under control. If we can't do that, then we are just going to lose control of the whole situation."

Bill Poole objected: "Whenever we act between meetings, we set a precedent." Markets would anticipate a Fed rate cut whenever stocks declined significantly. Tom Hoenig, the other hawk with a vote, was torn. He understood the need to break markets' bad psychology and to get ahead of the deteriorating economy but continued to worry about inflation. Don, Tim, Eric Rosengren, Kevin Warsh, Randy Kroszner, and Charlie Evans of Chicago supported my proposal. Don, the conciliator, said, "We could look panicky. . . . But I think the greater risk would be in not acting."

The Committee voted 8–1 to cut the federal funds rate to 3-1/2 percent (from 4-1/4 percent) and issue a statement promising to "act in a timely manner as needed." Poole dissented; Hoenig didn't. It was the FOMC's biggest rate cut since 1982 and its first move between meetings since September 11, 2001. We announced our decision before markets opened on Tuesday. The Dow Jones nevertheless plunged 464 points. But then it rebounded, closing down 128 points, or 1 percent.

Some of the commentary on our action focused on a perceived shift in my leadership style. Depending on the perspective of the commentator, the surprise rate cut was either evidence of a new decisiveness or a vacillation in the face of pressure from the markets. I believed I hadn't changed—circumstances had. In earlier months, I had emphasized the importance of considering all points of view and developing consensus. But, in a crisis, collaboration must give way to stronger direction. I was determined to offer that direction as needed.

On January 24, news emerged that cast doubt on our decision. Société Générale (SocGen), France's second-largest bank, announced that unauthorized futures trading by a single employee, later identified as Jérôme Kerviel, had caused a $7.2 billion pre-tax loss. The bank had uncovered the loss after questioning Kerviel on January 19 but kept mum in public to give itself time to unwind its trading positions. Now it looked as if at least part of the Martin Luther King Jr. Day sell-off in Europe might have resulted from a one-off event. We had no idea the rogue-trading bombshell was coming. In fact, on a conference call the morning of January 19 Paris time, senior SocGen managers in Paris and New York had told New York Fed supervisors that the bank would report positive earnings for the fourth quarter, even after taking write-downs on its subprime mortgage exposure.

Some commentators said we had been stampeded into unnecessary action, but I had become convinced even before the market turbulence that we needed to get ahead of the curve with larger rate cuts. Some of the criticism took a personal turn. I had been in office only two years and still had two years left in my term, yet journalists began to speculate on whether I would be reappointed by a new president (who wouldn't take office for another year). The *New York Times* asked Senator John McCain of Arizona, a presidential hopeful and fellow Republican, how I was doing. "It's not clear yet," he replied. Meanwhile, Reuters suggested that if a Democrat won the White House, he or she would choose my replacement from among Janet Yellen, Larry Summers, and my former Princeton colleague Alan Blinder.

Reuters quoted House Financial Services Committee chairman Barney Frank as saying a Democratic president "might find someone who's more in tune with Democratic views." Upon seeing the quote, Barney directed a senior aide to call the Board's general counsel, Scott Alvarez, to say he had not meant to indicate dissatisfaction or call for my replacement. He had thought he was stating the obvious—that a new president would have the option to appoint a new Fed chairman when my term expired. If it had been anyone but Barney, I might have doubted the explanation. Barney has a sharp tongue, but he is direct and honest. When he means to criticize you, he leaves no doubt. The next day he issued a six-paragraph clarification. He said he was embarrassed by his "rookie mistake." His prompt apology was an extraordinary and rare act in Washington. I admired him for it.

In the week leading up to the January 29–30 FOMC meeting, I laid the groundwork for another interest rate cut. Staff economists continued to call for slow growth rather than an outright recession, even nudging up their growth forecast slightly. But the risks to growth seemed significant to me, and we cut our target for the federal funds rate another half-percentage point, to 3 percent. We also tweaked the language of our statement. While it still leaned toward additional rate cuts in the future, it also acknowledged the sharpness of the recent cuts and the possibility that those cuts might be sufficient for the time being.

The vote was 9–1. Richard Fisher told us he had prayed over his decision but couldn't join the majority. He was worried about inflation, which had ticked up in the second half of 2007, even when volatile food and energy costs were excluded. And he didn't want to react to financial turmoil. "When the market is in the depressive phase of . . . a bipolar disorder, crafting policy to satisfy it is like feeding Jabba the Hutt—doing so is fruitless, if not dangerous, because it will simply insist upon more," he said.

Within the majority, views differed over whether we had cut our federal funds rate target enough. Most believed it probably would provide sufficient support if the economy followed staff projections and skirted a recession. But Rick Mishkin scoffed at the glimmers of optimism around the table. "It reminds me a little of one of my favorite scenes in a movie, which is Monty Python's *Life with* [sic] *Brian*," he said. "I remember the scene with them there all on the cross, and they start singing, 'Look on the Bright Side of Life.'"

Rick's instincts proved correct. But at the time we were balancing competing concerns. We were worried about inflation. We knew it was difficult to assess the effect of financial turbulence on the broader economy. And we didn't want to overreact to financial stress and thereby exacerbate moral hazard in markets. Still, over the six months from August 2007 to January 2008, we had slashed our target interest rate to 3 percent from 5-1/4 percent, an earlier and more rapid response than any other major central bank. We also established innovative lending programs to ease pressures in funding markets. At the end of January 2008 it seemed that our response might now be correctly calibrated. We couldn't be sure, but we hoped we might just have reached the beginning of the end of the crisis. As it turned out, we were only at the end of the beginning.

CHAPTER 10

Bear Stearns: Before Asia Opens

The Senate Banking Committee had moved its hearing from the usual room to a more spacious venue, Room G50, on the ground floor of the Dirksen Senate Office Building. Once an auditorium, G50 was packed nonetheless that morning, April 3, 2008. Bright television lights shone on the green felt of the witness table. I sat behind it with Chris Cox, chairman of the Securities and Exchange Commission; Treasury undersecretary Bob Steel (subbing for Hank Paulson, who was on a trip to China); and Tim Geithner. The senators looked down from a raised platform. On the floor between the witness table and the dais, a dozen or more photographers jostled for better shots.

I waited, my hands folded atop my prepared statement—a glass of ice water to my left, a gooseneck microphone and a timer to my right, a small sign with my name in front of me. I reminded myself to remain calm and deliberate. In the hubbub, committee chairman Chris Dodd, whose shock of thick silver hair gave him the look of a senator straight out of central casting, banged his gavel for order. Ten minutes after the scheduled 10:00 a.m. start time, the room quieted and the hearing began.

"We are not in our traditional hearing room, and the size of the crowd in the room is evidence of the reason why," Dodd began.

The senators and audience were there to hear our firsthand account of the Federal Reserve's decision in mid-March—during what Dodd called "this momentous four-day period"—to lend $30 billion in taxpayer funds to prevent the failure of the eighty-five-year-old Bear

Stearns Companies, the nation's fifth-largest Wall Street investment bank. Additionally, to stem the panic that gripped financial markets, we had opened our lending, normally reserved for commercial banks and savings institutions, to Bear Stearns's Wall Street competitors. In both actions, we had declared the existence of "unusual and exigent circumstances."

Dodd continued, evidently savoring the drama. "There can be no doubt that these actions taken in order to calm financial markets that appeared to be teetering on the brink of panic have set off a firestorm of debate." I was glad he seemed to be assuming our good intentions. Then he asked, "Was this a justified rescue to prevent a systemic collapse of financial markets or a $30 billion taxpayer bailout, as some have called it, for a Wall Street firm while people on Main Street struggle to pay their mortgages?"

Dodd's question hung in the air as the members of the committee made their opening statements. Richard Shelby of Alabama, the senior Republican, focused on legal issues. How is it, he asked, that the Federal Reserve had "unilateral regulatory authority" to extend the government's safety net to previously unprotected investment banks? "The committee here today," he intoned in his soft drawl, "needs to address whether the Fed or any set of policymakers should have such broad emergency authority going forward."

When all the members had spoken, Dodd addressed me, attempting to lighten the mood: "Chairman Bernanke, you have spent quite a bit of time in Congress these last few days. I suggested in private before the hearing that we might find an office up here for the chairman, he has been here so often over the last number of days."

I thanked him, and I began to explain what had happened leading up to and during the weekend of March 15–16.

Only six weeks before that crucial weekend, after an unprecedented, rapid series of interest rate cuts and some creative use of our lending authority, we had been feeling a bit better about the prospects for the economy and financial system. Our rate cuts in January seemed well justified, given the subsequent report that the United States had unexpectedly lost 17,000 jobs that month. Fiscal help was on the way as well. The president signed a bipartisan tax cut on February 13, in time for the coming tax-filing season. Between April and July, individuals would receive tax rebates of up to $300 and families with children, up to $1,200.

The day after the president had signed the tax cut, I tried to strike a balance in Senate testimony. I predicted "a period of sluggish growth, followed by a somewhat stronger pace of growth starting later this year as the effects of monetary and fiscal stimulus begin to be felt." But I cautioned that "downside risks remain" and promised that the Fed would "act in a timely manner as needed to support growth." Alan Greenspan generated financial wire headlines the same day when he told a Houston conference that the economy was "clearly on the edge" of a recession.

I wasn't willing to use the r-word in public at that point, even though the risk of a downturn was clearly significant. I didn't have the freedom of expression that Alan enjoyed as a private citizen again. John Maynard Keynes had observed that emotions often drive economic decisions—"animal spirits," he called them. I wanted to paint a realistic picture, but, with Keynes's insight in mind and with consumer sentiment approaching a sixteen-year low, I did not want to add unnecessarily to the prevailing gloom by talking down the economy.

Animal spirits, sentiment, psychology, whatever you want to call it, was central to the economic and financial story in February and March. Consumer sentiment was in decline, and financial market sentiment was plummeting. Nervous buyers and lenders were shunning more and more classes of securities, including securities with no relation to subprime mortgages, such as municipal bonds, securities backed by student loans, and low-rated bonds used to fund corporate buyouts. This lack of discernment meant one thing: A panic was building. And the economy and credit markets were increasingly mired in their own destructive feedback loop—bad economic news fueled financial turmoil, and the turmoil in turn disrupted the flow of credit that powered economic activity.

The troubles of the monoline insurers deepened. One of the most prominent, Ambac Financial Group, had lost its AAA credit rating on January 18. Prodded by New York State insurance regulators, eight big banks and Wall Street firms were negotiating a rescue. Another monoline insurer, FGIC, was downgraded on January 30, and a third, MBIA Inc., looked like it might be next. Our ad hoc crisis management team—Don Kohn, Tim Geithner, Kevin Warsh, and I, along with general counsel Scott Alvarez, monetary adviser Brian Madigan, and other staff—was following the situation closely.

The monolines' guarantees of subprime securities were behind their ratings downgrades. Because the monolines also insured municipal bonds, however, investors grew wary of those bonds as well. We brainstormed about ways to help the muni market, which was largely an innocent bystander of the ongoing financial mayhem. We had authority to purchase some types of shorter-term municipal bonds (six months or less in maturity) in the New York Fed's market transactions, but any substantial lending to states or cities would require us to use our 13(3) authority. After a meeting with other regulators and Treasury officials, Don summarized the cautious consensus against bailing out the muni market: "Monitoring and helping affected parties get together is the federal government's proper role—they don't require any explicit support or bailout." Kevin seconded him: "I think we want to avoid suggesting any sort of intervention."

Financial turmoil had spread to another obscure, but significant, credit market—the market for so-called auction-rate securities, many of which the monolines also insured. Introduced in the mid-1980s, auction-rate securities were long-term bonds that, for the buyer, functioned like safe, easy-to-sell short-term securities. They were issued mostly by state and local governments, student-loan authorities, and nonprofit organizations such as hospitals. Buyers included corporations, retirement funds, and wealthy individuals. Issuers got to borrow long-term but pay a (generally lower) short-term interest rate; investors received a rate slightly higher than those paid on other low-risk short-term, but simpler, securities. The rates on the securities were not fixed but were reset in regular auctions, held every one to seven weeks. Investors could sell their securities at one of these auctions and take the cash. New investors could buy in. If an auction failed for a lack of new buyers, the issuer had to pay a penalty rate to investors stuck with the unwanted securities.

Auctions almost never failed. If there weren't enough buyers, as happened on occasion, the big investment and commercial banks who sponsored the auctions usually stepped in as back-up bidders. Except in mid-February 2008, when they refused to buy. Many of the sponsoring institutions were wary of adding auction-rate securities to balance sheets already stuffed with other hard-to-sell complex debt instruments. On February 14, an astonishing 80 percent of the auctions failed for lack of investor interest. Issuers with good credit records suddenly faced steep interest penalties through no fault of their own. The Port Authority of New York and New Jersey, for instance, saw its interest rate nearly quintuple from 4.2 percent to 20 percent.

Elsewhere in the market, financial dominoes had continued to fall. On February 11, the venerable insurance giant AIG disclosed in an SEC filing that its auditors had forced it to take a $5 billion write-down on its holdings of derivatives tied to subprime mortgages. (Derivatives are financial instruments whose value depends on the value of some underlying asset, such as a stock or a bond.) Three days later, the massive Swiss banking firm UBS reported an $11.3 billion loss for the fourth quarter of 2007. It attributed $2 billion of the loss to a write-down of its exposure to Alt-A mortgages. UBS's write-down of its Alt-A mortgage securities forced lenders with similar securities to do the same. Given the level of investor distrust and the vagaries of generally accepted accounting principles, the valuations of the most pessimistic firms and investors seemed to be determining asset prices industrywide.

Two hedge funds with assets totaling more than $3 billion, managed by the London-based Peloton Partners and run by former Goldman Sachs traders, failed on February 28. On March 3, Santa Fe, New Mexico–based Thornburg Mortgage, with $36 billion in assets, was missing margin calls—demands from nervous creditors for additional collateral in the form of cash or securities. Thornburg specialized in making adjustable-rate jumbo mortgages (mortgages above the $417,000 limit on loans purchased by Fannie and Freddie) to borrowers with strong credit. But it also had purchased securities backed by now-plummeting Alt-A mortgages. On March 6, an investment fund sponsored by the Carlyle Group, a private equity firm whose partners moved in Washington's inner circles, also failed to meet margin calls. The fund's $22 billion portfolio consisted almost entirely of mortgage-backed securities issued and guaranteed by Fannie and Freddie. The holdings were considered very safe because investors assumed Fannie and Freddie had the implicit backing of the federal government. But the Carlyle fund had paid for its securities by borrowing more than $30 for every $1 in capital invested in the fund. It could absorb only very small losses. By Monday, March 10, it had unloaded nearly $6 billion in assets—yet another fire sale.

Peloton, the Carlyle fund, and Thornburg had something in common: Lenders in the repo market were reluctant to accept their assets as collateral—assets they had routinely accepted in the past. Until the previous summer, repos had always been considered a safe and reliable form of funding—so reliable that a company like Thornburg felt comfortable using them to finance holdings of long-term assets, like mortgages. Because longer-term interest rates are usually higher than short-term rates, this strategy was usually profitable. It's effectively what a traditional bank does when it accepts deposits that can be withdrawn at any time and makes loans that won't be paid off for months or years.

But Thornburg wasn't a bank, and, of course, its borrowings were not government-insured. When concerns about Thornburg's assets surfaced, nervous repo lenders began to pull back. In what was becoming an increasingly common scenario, some repo lenders shortened the term of their loans and demanded more collateral per dollar lent. Others wouldn't lend at all. With no means to finance its holdings of mortgages, even its high-quality jumbo mortgages, Thornburg found itself in serious trouble—much like a bank suffering a run in the era before deposit insurance.

Senator Jeff Bingaman of New Mexico called and left a message for me on behalf of Thornburg cofounder Garrett Thornburg on the afternoon of March 3. (Special pleading from members of Congress on behalf of specific constituents was not unusual and would become more common as the crisis wore on.) When Bingaman called, I was en route to Orlando, Florida, to deliver a speech on foreclosure mitigation at a community bankers' convention the next day. Bingaman wanted to know if the Fed would declare a Section 13(3) emergency so it could lend to Thornburg and other institutions that could no longer use their AAA-rated collateral in the repo market. I knew the staff would be skeptical, but I was starting to think the time to break out the Hail Mary section of our playbook was drawing near.

"Don't say no immediately," I instructed Brian Madigan, who was preparing to call Garrett Thornburg on the Fed's behalf. "I would like to at least discuss it." When I got back to Washington the next day, I called Thornburg. I was sympathetic. He and his company were caught up in a panic not of their own making. But in my heart I knew that use of our emergency authority could only be justified when it served the broad public interest. Whether the firm was in some sense deserving or not was irrelevant. Lending to Thornburg would overturn a six-decade practice of avoiding 13(3) loans—a practice rooted in the recognition of the moral hazard of protecting nonbank firms from the consequences of the risks they took, as well as the understanding that Congress had intended the authority to be used only in the most dire circumstances. The failure of this firm was unlikely to have a broad economic impact, and so we believed a 13(3) loan was not justified. We would not lend to Thornburg, and it would fail.

CONGRESS HAD ADDED Section 13(3) to the Federal Reserve Act in 1932, motivated by the evaporation of credit that followed the collapse of thousands of banks in the early 1930s. Section 13(3) gave the Federal Reserve the ability to lend to essentially any private borrower. At least five members of the Board needed to certify that unusual and exigent circumstances prevailed in credit markets. The lending Reserve Bank also had to obtain evidence that other sources of credit were not available to the borrower. And importantly, 13(3) loans, as with standard discount window loans, must be "secured to the satisfaction" of the lending Reserve Bank. In other words, the borrower's collateral had to be sound enough that the Federal Reserve could reasonably expect full repayment. This last requirement protected taxpayers, as any losses on 13(3) loans would reduce the profits the Fed paid each year to the Treasury and thus add to the budget deficit. But the requirement also limited the interventions available to the Fed. Invoking 13(3) would not allow us to put capital into a financial institution (by purchasing its stock, for example) or to guarantee its assets against loss.

The Fed used its 13(3) authority during the Depression, but only sparingly. From 1932 to 1936, it made 123 such loans, mostly very small. The largest, $300,000, was made to a typewriter manufacturer; another, for $250,000, was extended to a vegetable grower. As the economy and credit markets improved in the latter part of the 1930s, the Fed stopped making 13(3) loans.

BY THE END of February, I was convinced that we needed to address the mounting funding problems faced by shadow banking entities that relied on repos and commercial paper. Around this time, Lehman Brothers CEO Dick Fuld had urged the Board to include Wall Street investment banks like his own in our regular TAF auctions of discount window loans to commercial banks—a step that would require us to invoke Section 13(3). In a phone call on February 28, Lloyd Blankfein,

Paulson's successor at Goldman Sachs, told me he thought that broader access to the discount window would help both the investment banks themselves and the markets. I was most concerned about the markets. Firms squeezed for funding were reacting by dumping securities and other assets indiscriminately. Everyone seemed to be trying to sell and almost no one seemed to want to buy, sending prices into a tailspin. "Our situation seems to be getting trickier by the day," I wrote in an email to Tim Geithner.

At 8:30 a.m. Friday morning, March 7, the financial markets, already fragile, would learn what we had learned confidentially the evening before—that the nation's payrolls had fallen by 63,000 jobs in February, the second consecutive decline. Dave Stockton's staff was now projecting a recession in the first half of the year and little or no growth in the second half.

The jobs news was a tangible indication that financial instability, contracting credit, and falling confidence were seriously damaging the economy. Instead of waiting until the following week, as originally planned, we decided to announce, before the markets opened Friday morning, two new measures aimed at increasing the availability of short-term funding. First, we'd increase our March auction of twenty-eight-day discount window loans to $100 billion, from the $60 billion we had announced a week earlier. Second, to make investors more comfortable holding mortgage-backed securities guaranteed by Fannie and Freddie, we said that we would accept those securities in monetary policy operations with the twenty securities dealers that regularly conducted transactions with the New York Fed. These so-called primary dealers, which included the five large stand-alone investment banks (Goldman, Morgan Stanley, Merrill, Lehman, and Bear Stearns), would be able to swap Fannie and Freddie securities for cash from the Fed for twenty-eight days. The emphasis on mortgage securities was a new twist on the New York Fed's usual operations, which generally involved only Treasury securities, and its staff had planned to start at $10 billion a week. I spotted the figure in a memo hastily circulated to the FOMC Thursday evening. Relative to the enormous size of the mortgage market, the number seemed small to me. I emailed Geithner and he agreed. A half-hour later, we were at $25 billion a week, or $100 billion for the month of March.

The bad employment report and our new liquidity measures competed for markets' attention on Friday. The Dow fell 147 points, but, in a positive sign for our newest initiatives, the difference (or spread) between interest rates on Fannie and Freddie's mortgage-backed securities and the rates on Treasury securities had narrowed—a sign that investors weren't shunning the mortgage securities to the extent that they had been.

WE PLANNED TO announce additional measures on Tuesday, March 11. First, we'd increase our two swap lines with foreign central banks by half—to $30 billion for the European Central Bank and to $6 billion for the Swiss National Bank. More importantly, starting in two weeks, we'd vastly expand our lending of Treasury securities from the Fed's balance sheet to the primary dealers—up to $200 billion. Since 1969, the Fed had been lending a modest amount of Treasury securities, in exchange for other Treasury securities of different maturities and issuance dates, in an effort to ensure that traders could acquire the specific Treasury securities that best met their needs. In a significant new step, we would now also lend Treasury securities against collateral that included not only Fannie and Freddie mortgage-backed securities but also the so-called private-label mortgage securities packaged by investment banks and other private firms.

We'd been talking about such a move for months. The program would put plenty of Treasuries, the most readily accepted collateral in the repo market, in the hands of the dealers and other market participants. The recipients could then take the Treasury securities to the repo market and obtain funding. By helping the dealers maintain access to funding, we would also be increasing their ability to lend to other market participants, thereby supporting the flow of credit to households and businesses. And we hoped that, by accepting AAA-rated private-label mortgage securities as collateral, even at depressed market prices, we'd encourage wholesale funding providers to begin trusting them again as well. This last feature—lending to primary dealers against private-label mortgage securities—meant that we'd have to at last invoke Section 13(3).

Over the weekend, Don Kohn—who was attending a central bankers' meeting in Basel—paved the way for the expansion of the swap lines and encouraged central banks without U.S. swap lines to announce their own liquidity measures as we announced ours. Meanwhile, in Washington, I made the case to FOMC members for lending Treasury securities to the primary dealers against a range of mortgage collateral. We proposed calling the new program the Term Securities Lending Facility, or TSLF—the latest Federal Reserve acronym. "This is unusual but so are market conditions," I wrote in an email. "I strongly recommend that we proceed with this plan." I needed a yes vote from all five Board members. Also, because it concerned the New York Fed's transactions on behalf of itself and the other Reserve Banks, I needed a majority vote of the FOMC.

I had a sense that we were making history when I opened yet another unscheduled FOMC call at 7:15 p.m. on Monday, March 10. I explained that some of the new market turmoil was a natural reaction to bad economic reports, but that some of it could be attributed to what I called "self-feeding liquidity dynamics." In other words, fear begat fear. The steps we had taken the previous Friday and the measures we would announce on Tuesday aimed to mitigate or break that dynamic. Bill Dudley reviewed the deteriorating financial situation, mentioning Peloton, Thornburg, and the Carlyle fund, and added, "There were rumors today that Bear Stearns was having funding difficulties." With nearly $400 billion in assets, Bear was roughly six times the size of Peloton, Thornburg, and the Carlyle fund—combined. Jeff Lacker spoke against the TSLF. He opposed targeting Fed policy at a particular class of assets—mortgage securities in this case—and warned that this precedent would make it difficult to resist pressure from Congress to bail out other sectors.

In reply, Don Kohn quoted one of the central bankers from the weekend meeting in Basel: "Sometimes it is time to think the unthinkable," the central banker had said. Don added, "I think that time is here for us right now."

"We're crossing certain lines," I acknowledged. "We're doing things we haven't done before. On the other hand, this financial crisis is now in its eighth month, and the economic outlook has worsened quite significantly. . . . I think we have to be flexible and creative in the face of what really are extraordinary challenges."

The FOMC approved the TSLF, 9–0. Lacker didn't have a vote that year. His fellow hawks who did—Richard Fisher of Dallas and Charlie Plosser of Philadelphia—went along, despite misgivings. Board member Rick Mishkin, who had missed the FOMC's emergency call on Martin Luther King Jr. Day while cross-country skiing, was skiing in Finland and had missed this vote, too. Before the Tuesday morning announcement, he registered his approval as a Board member for invoking Section 13(3). "This is bad karma," he emailed. "Maybe I should never leave the Board and then financial conditions will improve."

OUR MARCH 11 announcement described the TSLF in technical financial language and lacked any mention of emergency powers or 13(3) authority. (We worried that trumpeting the invocation of emergency powers last used in the Depression would deepen the panic.) But market participants applauded the new facility. They recognized that its creation showed our willingness to lend to financial institutions that weren't banks but which had become critical to the flow of credit and to the smooth operation of financial markets. The Dow rose 417 points that day, its biggest jump in more than five years. Despite the short burst of euphoria, Bear Stearns stock, already hammered, eked out only a 67-cent gain, closing at $62.97—a far cry from the all-time intraday high, fourteen months earlier, of $172.69. The stock had plunged in the morning but recovered after SEC chairman Chris Cox told reporters that his agency "had a good deal of comfort" with the capital cushions of the big five investment banks, including Bear.

But Bear's situation wasn't improving. Moody's had just announced it was downgrading fifteen bond deals sponsored by a Bear fund that specialized in Alt-A mortgages. Moody's wasn't downgrading the firm itself. Nevertheless, fears that Bear might run out of cash to pay its creditors were spreading. Its eighty-year-old former chief executive, the balding, burly, cigar-chomping Alan Greenberg, told the cable station CNBC that rumors of a cash squeeze at Bear were "totally ridiculous."

BEAR STEARNS HAD been a Wall Street fixture since 1923, when it was founded by Joseph Bear, Robert Stearns, and Harold Meyer. It survived the stock market crash of 1929 without having to lay off a single employee. Over the years, it built a reputation as a scrappy firm that took risks in markets where others feared to venture. During World War II, when Franklin Roosevelt commandeered the railroads to move war matériel, the firm bought up the deeply discounted debt of railroad companies. It subsequently sold the debt at an immense profit, after the war, when it became clear that the companies wouldn't be nationalized. Bear made a practice of hiring talented outsiders overlooked by its competitors. Greenberg called them "PSDs"—Poor but Smart employees with a deep Desire to get rich. Greenberg, the son of an Oklahoma City clothier, started at Bear as a clerk in 1949, working his way up to CEO in 1978. His nickname was Ace; he was an avid bridge player and an amateur magician (card tricks were a particular favorite). In 1993, he handed over the reins to James "Jimmy" Cayne, a former professional bridge player hired by Greenberg in 1969 as a stockbroker.

Cayne, a college dropout, cemented Bear's outsider reputation in 1998 when he refused to join fourteen other large banks and investment firms in the $3.6 billion rescue of the hedge fund Long-Term Capital Management, even though Bear was the firm that held LTCM's

In the Roosevelt Room of the White House, October 14, 2008. On the far side of the table, left to right, comptroller of the currency John Dugan, SEC chairman Christopher Cox, Treasury secretary Hank Paulson, me, FDIC chairman Sheila Bair, and New York Federal Reserve president Tim Geithner. (Official White House photograph by Eric Draper)

Marriner S. Eccles Building, the headquarters of the Board of Governors of the Federal Reserve System in Washington, D.C. Construction was completed in 1937. (Federal Reserve Photograph, Britt Leckman)

The two-story atrium of the Eccles Building. Marriner Eccles served as Federal Reserve chairman from 1934 to 1948. (Federal Reserve Photograph, Britt Leckman)

President Bush and Anna look on as Board vice chairman Roger Ferguson swears me in as Alan Greenspan's successor as chairman, February 6, 2006, in the Eccles Building atrium. (Official White House photograph by Kimberlee Hewitt)

A week after the White House announced my nomination to be Federal Reserve chairman, former chairman Paul Volcker, six foot seven, embraces me and the then-current chairman, Alan Greenspan, October 31, 2005, in a dining room at the Federal Reserve. (Federal Reserve Photograph, Britt Leckman)

The Federal Open Market Committee (FOMC) confers around the Board's twenty-seven-by-eleven-foot mahogany and black granite table, March 2009. At far side of table, left to right: Bill Dudley, deputy FOMC secretary Debbie Danker, me, Don Kohn, Kevin Warsh, Betsy Duke, Dan Tarullo, Richard Fisher, Jim Bullard. With back to camera, left to right, staff economists Brian Madigan, Nathan Sheets, Michael Leahy, Dave Stockton, Dave Reifschneider, Joe Gagnon, and Bill Nelson. (Federal Reserve Photograph, Britt Leckman)

In my office, with the Board's communications director, Michelle Smith, in May 2010. (Mary F. Calvert / ZUMA Press / Newscom)

Working at my desk, February 2013. (Federal Reserve Photograph, Britt Leckman)

On the steps outside the U.S. Treasury, April, 11, 2008, with, left to right, Masaaki Shirakawa of the Bank of Japan, Jean-Claude Trichet of the European Central Bank, Mario Draghi of the Bank of Italy, and Mervyn King of the Bank of England. (Brendan Smialowski / Getty Images)

Chatting with Representative Barney Frank of Massachusetts, chairman of the House Financial Services Committee, July 21, 2009. (Andrew Harrer / Bloomberg via Getty Images)

Meeting with Senator Chris Dodd of Connecticut, chairman of the Senate Banking Committee, in his office, February 6, 2008. (Alex Wong / Getty Images)

With Treasury secretary Tim Geithner, lunching in his dining room, November 2009. (Photograph by Dan Winters)

Walking to a press conference in the Rose Garden, September 19, 2008, with, left to right, President Bush, Christopher Cox, and Hank Paulson to announce the administration's request for taxpayer funds to fight the financial crisis. (Win McNamee / Getty Images)

With Board member Kevin Warsh (center) and Board vice chairman Don Kohn, on the balcony overlooking the veranda of Jackson Lake Lodge, Wyoming, August 2008, at the Federal Reserve Bank of Kansas City's Economic Symposium. (Andrew Harrer / Bloomberg via Getty Images)

With Stan Fischer, governor of the Bank of Israel, at Jackson Lake Lodge, August 2012. Stan was my thesis adviser at MIT. (AP Photo / Ted S. Warren)

With Hank Paulson before the House Financial Services Committee at the height of the crisis, September 24, 2008. (AP Photo / Charles Dharapak)

Explaining the Federal Reserve's strategy for eventually shrinking its balance sheet, before the House Financial Services Committee, March 25, 2010. Communications director Michelle Smith in background, right, and media relations officer Dave Skidmore, left. (AP Photo / Manuel Balce Ceneta)

The FOMC, March 2009. Reserve Bank presidents standing, left to right: Bill Dudley, Eric Rosengren, Jim Bullard, Charlie Evans, Tom Hoenig, Richard Fisher, Gary Stern, Sandy Pianalto, Jim Lockhart, Charlie Plosser, Jeff Lacker, and Janet Yellen. Board of Governors members seated, left to right: Elizabeth Duke, Kevin Warsh, me, Don Kohn, and Dan Tarullo. (Federal Reserve Photograph, Britt Leckman)

Chatting with President Obama before his announcement of my nomination to a second term as Fed chairman at Oak Bluffs Elementary School, Martha's Vineyard, Massachusetts, August, 25, 2009. (Official White House photograph by Pete Souza)

When interest rates are rising, cartoonists often depict the Fed chairman as the Grinch. This one, from *the* Indianapolis Star, *in 2008, takes the opposite approach. We struggled to explain the logic behind our extraordinary efforts to support the economy.* (Gary Varvel Editorial Cartoon used with the permission of Gary Varvel and Creators Syndicate. All rights reserved)

Cartoon lampooning Texas governor Rick Perry's remarks at a Republican presidential primary event in Iow *August 2011. Perry said he would "treat me pretty ugly down in Texas" if the Fed continued to support the economy with forceful monetary policy.* (Nate Beeler, courtesy of Cagle Cartoons)

AT HOME WITH
BEN BERNANKE

SIPNESS

A cartoon from The New Yorker *magazine, October 7, 2013. In reality, Anna strove to make our home an oasis from the pressures of the Fed, where a slip of the tongue could send financial markets gyrating.* (David Sipress, *The New Yorker* Collection / The Cartoon Bank)

"And if you think that every time you open your mouth around here everyone is going to dance to your tune, you've got another thing coming, Mr. Federal Reserve!"

MORE STIMULUS!

ECONOMY

BERNANKE

DAVE GRANLUND © www.davegranlund.com

A cartoon from October 2008 underscores the deep public and political skepticism about the ultimate effects of the Federal Reserve's unorthodox efforts to calm the financial crisis and revive the economy. (Dave Granlund © www.davegranlund.com)

Cartoon accompanying Paul Krugman's New York Times Magazine *column headlined, "Earth to Ben Bernanke," April 24, 2012.* (Kelsey Dake)

accounts and cleared its trades. The New York Fed had arranged the private-sector bailout when the highly interconnected fund's trading strategies blew up in the aftermath of the Russian debt default. Greenberg remained at the firm after Cayne became CEO and was still there, as chairman of its executive committee, in March 2008. Together, the two men had presided over Bear's plunge into mortgages.

Bear's stock peak coincided with the start of a steep two-year slide in U.S. house prices. In addition to packaging mortgages into securities and marketing those securities, the firm was both an originator of mortgages (through subsidiaries) and a holder of mortgage-backed securities. Its managers were bullish on both subprime lending and structured credit products and invested accordingly. The business had helped propel Bear to a fifth straight year of record earnings in 2006. But the unraveling of its two subprime mortgage hedge funds in June 2007 had hurt investor confidence. As a consequence, Bear decided to rely less on (uncollateralized) commercial paper for short-term funding and more on (collateralized) repo borrowing. Repo lenders would be less likely to run if the firm's troubles worsened, they assumed. At the end of 2007, Bear was borrowing $102 billion in repo and less than $4 billion via commercial paper.

Bear reported its first-ever loss in the fourth quarter of 2007. In January, Cayne, 73, resigned as CEO. He had often been absent from the office, at bridge tournaments and golf outings, when Bear was dealing with its imploding subprime mortgage funds. Alan Schwartz, a polished investment banker who had run Bear's mergers and acquisitions business, took over. He would occupy the CEO suite for two months.

SCHWARTZ'S TRYING WEEK turned nightmarish after Monday, March 10, when the firm held roughly $18 billion in cash reserves. By close of business Wednesday its cash was down to $12 billion. On Thursday the firm's liquidity began to drain away in earnest. Hedge funds and other brokerage customers started withdrawing funds, the firms with whom Bear normally traded derivatives were refusing to transact, and lenders were getting ready to stop renewing Bear's repo the next morning. Uncertain about Bear's near-term survival, some repo lenders refused to lend to it even against Treasury securities, the safest possible collateral. The company ended the day with about $2 billion in cash, but by the next day that too would surely be gone. If Bear had been an old-fashioned bank, its depositors would have been at its door. In this new world, the clamoring was electronic, but it was just as dangerous as a traditional run.

That evening, an attorney working with Schwartz telephoned Jamie Dimon, the CEO of JPMorgan Chase, to request a loan that would allow Bear to open on Friday. JPMorgan, the nation's third-largest bank holding company at the end of 2007, was Bear's clearing bank, serving as in intermediary between Bear and its repo lenders, and thus was familiar with its holdings. JPMorgan countered that it might be interested in buying some of Bear's financial assets or business lines but made no commitment. Schwartz called Tim Geithner and told him Bear was in danger of not having the cash to meet its obligations and might have to file for bankruptcy in the morning. Tim sent a team to examine Bear's books, as did Dimon.

What if Bear did file for bankruptcy the next morning? As midnight approached, Don, Tim, senior staff, and I tried to come up with something we could do to cushion the blow at least a little. Brian Madigan submitted some options, the strongest of which was to publicly declare the existence of "unusual and exigent circumstances" and to stand ready to lend directly to Wall Street investment banks, a new application of 13(3) powers. It might stop the run from spreading beyond Bear. If the emergency aspects of TSLF had been deemphasized before, here they would be explicitly acknowledged. Tim proposed that we also cut the discount rate by a further half percentage point, bringing it even with the federal funds rate, to encourage bank borrowers to come to the Fed.

The news from the New York Fed and JPMorgan teams in the early morning hours was grim. Bear's balance sheet appeared full of toxic surprises and JPMorgan concluded it would need more time to evaluate the holdings. In the meantime, it told us it could not lend to Bear without Fed assistance. Even with its vaunted "fortress balance sheet," which at $1.6 trillion was four times larger than Bear's, JPMorgan was unwilling on its own to stand behind it.

JPMORGAN CHASE'S ROOTS extended to the earliest years of the United States. In its modern incarnation it was largely the product of the merger, in 2000, of J.P. Morgan & Co. and Chase Manhattan Corp. Chase traced its history to 1799, when Aaron Burr founded Manhattan Co. to compete with Alexander Hamilton's Bank of New York. J.P. Morgan & Co. had been established in 1871 by J. Pierpont Morgan, the financial savior of Wall Street during the Panic of 1907.

James "Jamie" Dimon—silver-haired despite his relative youth—had been the CEO of JPMorgan since the end of 2005. The grandson of a Greek banker, he had enjoyed early success. (He was celebrating his fifty-second birthday with family at a Greek restaurant the night he received the call from Bear's attorney.) After earning an MBA at Harvard in 1982, he got his start in finance as an assistant to Sandy Weill at American Express Co. He later helped Weill build Citigroup into a financial supermarket. After the two men had a falling-out in 1998, Dimon rebuilt his career in Chicago, rising in 2000 to CEO of Bank One, the fifth-largest bank in the country at the time. He returned to New York when JPMorgan merged with BankOne in 2004. At the end of 2005 he was named CEO of the combined company, and a year later he became chairman of the board as well. I found him to be smart and very tough. (His heavy New York accent contributed to that impression.) He understood the severity of the crisis early on and was determined to steer his bank through the maelstrom.

I WENT TO BED Thursday as work continued in New York, slept fitfully for a few hours, and woke on Friday for a 5:00 a.m. call with Don, Kevin, Tim, Hank Paulson, and Bob Steel. I dialed in from the kitchen table in our Capitol Hill town house. Bear seemed unlikely to make it through the day without help. The TSLF, through which Bear could have borrowed Treasury securities, wouldn't be operating until March 27. We ran through the options.

Tim proposed a plan to keep Bear open that the New York Fed's general counsel, Tom Baxter, believed wouldn't require the use of 13(3). JPMorgan, as the clearing bank between Bear and its repo lenders, would be holding a large amount of Bear's securities during the day. Tom suggested that we lend to JPMorgan, a deposit-taking commercial bank eligible to borrow from the discount window. With Bear's securities as collateral, JPMorgan would then lend the Fed's cash to Bear. Our loan would be nonrecourse, meaning that if Bear didn't repay, JPMorgan was off the hook, and we'd be stuck with Bear's securities. Basically, the plan was for the Fed to take the place of Bear's fleeing repo lenders. However, the Board's general counsel, Scott Alvarez, had a different legal interpretation. Because the loan was effectively for the benefit of Bear, he said, we would have to invoke 13(3).

I thought Scott's reading made the most sense, at least in terms of the spirit of the statute. I put great trust in Scott's advice. I had always thought of lawyers as tied up in formalisms, but Scott impressed me as deeply knowledgeable and concerned about both the underlying logic of the law and the policies the law was intended to implement.

An hour or so into the call, SEC staffers joined but not Chris Cox, who apparently didn't have the dial-in information. The call continued for about two hours as the sky changed from dark to light. At one point my security detail rang the doorbell. They had expected me to be out an hour earlier and wanted to be sure I was all right. I told them to stand by. Back on the call, Don, Tim, Hank, and I discussed what to do. Was Bear so large and entwined in the financial system that its collapse would substantially worsen the panic and, perhaps, lead to failures of other major firms? In other words, was Bear systemically important? We hadn't put Thornburg Mortgage in that category. This was a much more difficult judgment.

As always when difficult decisions loomed, I tried to think of prec-
edents. Two came to mind. In 1990, the government had declined to
intervene when Drexel Burnham Lambert had gone down in flames
amid a junk-bond trading scandal. It was the nation's fifth-largest
investment bank when it got into trouble, just as Bear was in 2008. But
Drexel's troubles were idiosyncratic, unrelated to a broader systemic
crisis. Moreover, Drexel was far less interconnected than Bear to major
firms through derivatives contracts and other financial relationships.
Fed officials under Alan Greenspan had reviewed the Drexel situation carefully and decided—correctly, it turned out—that its demise
would not pose risks to the broader financial system. They let it go.
In contrast, in 1998 the Fed had judged that markets in the wake of
the Asian crisis and Russian default were too fragile to withstand the
disorderly unwinding of the large, complex, and highly interconnected
Long-Term Capital Management. The New York Fed, led at the time by
Bill McDonough, had accordingly engineered a private-sector rescue,
without government funds. The hedge fund would be liquidated in an
orderly way less than two years later.

We didn't have time to arrange a nongovernment rescue of Bear
that morning, but we were reasonably sure that its unexpected bankruptcy filing would ignite even greater panic. Bear had nearly 400 subsidiaries, and its activities touched almost every other major financial
firm. It had 5,000 trading counterparties and 750,000 open derivatives
contracts. The problem of how to handle troubled financial institutions like Bear has been labeled TBTF—too big to fail. But size alone
wasn't the problem. Bear was big, but not that big compared to the
largest commercial banks. Actually, it was TITF—too interconnected
to fail.

Among Bear's creditors were prominent money market funds that
catered to mom-and-pop investors. We worried about the broader
effects on confidence if those funds, supposedly very safe, began to
take losses. A bankruptcy proceeding would also lock up the cash of
many other creditors, potentially for years. Additionally, the unwind-

ing of Bear's derivatives positions could prove chaotic—both because of the sheer number and complex features of the derivatives contracts and because Bear's derivatives counterparties would have to scramble to find new hedges for the risks opening up in their portfolios.

But the biggest risks lay in the $2.8 trillion tri-party repo market. (In the tri-party repo market, a clearing bank intermediates between repo lenders and borrowers. In the very large and quite opaque bilateral repo market, investment banks and other financial firms arrange repo transactions among themselves. Bear borrowed mostly in the tri-party market.) When Bear's repo lenders refused to renew their loans, JPMorgan, as the company's clearing bank, would face a stark choice: either lend to Bear itself and risk tens of billions in JPMorgan shareholders' dollars, or start selling the collateral on behalf of Bear's creditors. A decision to dispose of the collateral in a fire sale (the likely outcome) would, in turn, drive securities prices further down, leading to a new wave of losses and write-downs. Worse yet, others in the tri-party repo market, fearful of losses or of having their funds tied up, might resolve not to lend to any borrower. The remaining four major investment banks would be particularly vulnerable, and the failure of Bear could lead to runs on those firms as well. My own greatest fear, if Bear collapsed, was that the repo market might break down entirely, with disastrous consequences for financial markets and, as credit froze and asset prices plunged, for the entire economy.

Baxter's lending plan offered a means of getting Bear to the weekend, when we'd have breathing room to work on a longer-term solution. As Scott Alvarez advised, though, we would take the extra step of invoking our 13(3) authority to make the loan. I insisted, also, that the Fed could not go further without the administration's agreement. We felt reasonably confident we'd be repaid if we made a collateralized loan to Bear, but it was a risk nonetheless. If we weren't repaid, taxpayers would suffer. Thus, the plan under discussion was at least partly a fiscal matter. Hank excused himself to check with President Bush, rejoining the conference call a short while later. We had the president's support.

At around 7:00 a.m. it became clear that time was running out. As

Tim reminded us, the repo markets would open at 7:30 a.m. The Federal Reserve was the only institution with the authority to intervene and I was its head. I had listened carefully on the call. I saw many risks, but the risks to the repo market—a market few Americans had even heard of—loomed largest. "Let's do it," I said. After covering a few operational issues, I hung up the phone, finished getting ready for work, and walked out the door to the waiting security detail. I emailed Rita Proctor, "Pls order a couple of muffins and oj for me. I'll be in in 10 mins."

At 9:15 a.m., the Board met and voted, 4–0, to authorize the New York Fed to lend to JPMorgan so it could provide financing to Bear Stearns. Since we had invoked 13(3), we could have lent directly to Bear, but the paperwork prepared in New York overnight, in line with Baxter's idea, was for the back-to-back loan. There wasn't time to draw up new documents. The Board also delegated to me its authority to permit the New York Fed to lend to other securities dealers if necessary. It wasn't—at least that Friday. Though we had invoked 13(3) in creating the TSLF, the extension of credit to Bear was the first actual use of the authority to extend funds since 1936. Rick missed that vote as well. He was in transit from Finland. The Federal Reserve Act required five votes—but we had an out. An amendment added to the act as a precaution after the 9/11 terrorist attacks, when Roger Ferguson was the only Board member in Washington, permitted 13(3) actions on "the unanimous vote of all available members."

Stocks plunged initially on the news, with the Dow falling as much as 300 points before recovering somewhat. Investors were wondering who was next. Bear's share price fell to $30, from $57, and the run of its creditors and customers continued. We ended up lending the company $13 billion. But we got to the weekend. From there, it was a race to find a longer-term solution "before Asia opens," specifically before Asia's largest stock market opened Monday morning in Tokyo (Sunday evening in New York).

I SPENT A hectic weekend in my office, talking to staff and monitoring developments. Tim, the Fed's eyes and ears on Wall Street, stayed in touch with Dimon. We were looking to JPMorgan either to buy Bear or make an investment that would stabilize it. The private investment firm J. C. Flowers & Co. was also considering whether to make an offer. But it soon became apparent that only JPMorgan had the financial wherewithal to get the deal done before Monday. By Saturday evening, Dimon told Tim he was prepared to pay $8 to $12 a share for Bear's stock. Meanwhile, Deborah Bailey, the deputy director of the Board's banking supervision division, reported that the New York Fed would be sending teams to work with the SEC in reviewing the cash positions of the other big investment banks. "Monday looks like it will be a very difficult day for some of the IBs," she wrote, "but particularly for Lehman." Lehman was the fourth-largest investment bank and it was widely expected to be the next target of speculative attack if Bear went down.

On Sunday, Tim called. He had spoken to Dimon. The deal was off. Dimon wasn't willing to take on Bear's substantial subprime mortgage holdings. Tim started exploring with Paulson and Dimon what it might take to reverse the decision. As I was digesting the news, Michelle Smith forwarded an email from former Treasury secretary Larry Summers—her former boss in the Clinton administration (and Tim's). Now a Harvard economics professor and a managing director at the hedge fund D. E. Shaw, Larry had emailed Tim but hadn't heard back and was asking Michelle to pass on his message.

Larry is known for being blunt, to put it mildly, and he seemed to be warning against rescuing Bear. He said he had spoken at length to someone who had been inside the firm for most of Saturday. "The Fed may well be on a path that: 1) will fail to contain systemic risk, 2) will invite legitimately all kinds of charges of 'helping friends,' 3) be negative for moral hazard," he wrote to Michelle. "Happy to explain to you, ben, tim or anyone else." He continued, "At minimum please pass on to Ben the following: having embarked on unprecedented bear bail out, fed must succeed or its cred will be in tatters." He concluded, "Good luck to you all. L."

With Larry's email, the "firestorm of debate" that Chris Dodd would reference at the April 3 hearing had already begun. Larry's point about moral hazard was a good one. But he didn't need to explain it to us. (Nor did he need to explain that, if we failed, our credibility would be in tatters. We knew that.) We wanted creditors that funded financial institutions, large as well as small, to be careful about where they put their money. That they might not, because they expected any failing firm to be bailed out, was the moral hazard problem. In the short run, though, we couldn't risk a general panic in the repo market and other funding markets. The result, we knew full well, could be frozen credit flows, with all the consequences that would have for the economy and for ordinary Americans.

Senator Dodd offered to help over the weekend by calling Bill Daley, a friend of Jamie Dimon's, with the goal of persuading Dimon to return to the negotiating table. Dimon apparently knew Daley, a Commerce secretary in the Clinton administration and a brother of Chicago Mayor Richard M. Daley, from his days at BankOne. As it turned out, we didn't need Dodd to make the call. By early afternoon, Tim and Hank had worked out a deal with Jamie. JPMorgan would buy Bear Stearns, paying $2 each for shares that had been worth nearly $173 in January 2007. With the need to contain moral hazard in mind, Hank had pressed for a very low share price. He did not want us to be perceived as bailing out Bear's owners, its shareholders. Importantly, in the weeks ahead, during the wait for approval by the shareholders of both firms, JPMorgan would stand behind all of Bear's obligations. Without a credible guarantee, the run on Bear Stearns would continue and the company might collapse before the acquisition could be consummated.

What changed Dimon's mind about acquiring Bear? The answer would prove to be the deal's most controversial aspect. To make the deal work, we agreed to lend up to $30 billion, without recourse, taking as our security $30 billion of Bear's assets, mostly mortgage-related securities judged by the rating agencies to be investment-grade. Dimon had made clear that otherwise the deal would be too big and too risky for

JPMorgan. BlackRock, an asset management firm headed by the veteran Wall Street analyst Larry Fink, was hired by the New York Fed to look at the assets. It advised that the Fed could reasonably expect to get its money back if it held the assets for several years. BlackRock's assessment allowed Tim, the president of the Reserve Bank that would do the actual lending, to affirm that the loan was "secured to the satisfaction" of the Reserve Bank. Our judgment about the asset values was founded on our confidence that we would ultimately be able to stabilize the financial system. If we succeeded, then the value of the assets we were lending against should ultimately be sufficient to repay the Fed's loan with interest. If we did not succeed, the outcome was uncertain. Because any losses to the Fed would reduce our payments to the Treasury, we would have liked the Treasury to guarantee our loan, but, without congressional authorization, it did not have the authority to do so. We settled for a promise of a letter from Paulson expressing the administration's support.

That afternoon and evening, Don and I worked the phones, alerting counterparts around the world to our plans. I called Jean-Claude Trichet at the European Central Bank, Mervyn King at the Bank of England, and Toshihiko Fukui of the Bank of Japan. They were supportive, and relieved that Bear's collapse would be averted. We also wanted my two predecessors as chair—often quoted by the press—to understand what we had done and why. Don called Greenspan and I called Volcker. "Spoke to him, he's fine," I reported back. Notwithstanding my assessment, Volcker would soon publicly express concerns.

The Board met at 3:45 p.m. on Sunday. In addition to declaring unusual and exigent circumstances and approving the loan against Bear's $30 billion in assets, the Board also approved an important new lending facility—the Primary Dealer Credit Facility, or PDCF. It would allow the primary dealers to borrow from the Fed, just as commercial banks had always been able to do. And the collateral that we accepted for such loans would be much broader than the collateral accepted at the TSLF for a loan of Treasury securities.

We created the PDCF to reduce the risk of a disruptive failure of a primary dealer. And, having access to the PDCF should allow the primary dealers to "make markets"—that is, stand ready to buy and sell financial assets. More liquid markets would function better and would reduce destabilizing price swings. We also hoped that, by effectively providing a backstop funding source for repo borrowers (primary dealers are both repo borrowers and repo lenders), we could promote confidence and keep that market functioning.

In addition to creating the PDCF, we opened the liquidity spigot another turn for commercial banks, increasing the maximum maturity of discount window loans from thirty days to ninety days. And we cut the discount rate (the interest rate on discount window loans) by 1/4 percent, to 3-1/4 percent—just 1/4 percent higher than the target for the federal funds rate.

In the months that followed our before-Asia-opens announcement, the New York Fed negotiated fiercely over the set of assets that would collateralize our loan, ensuring we would be protected as much as possible. In the meantime, Bear's shareholders were so furious at the $2 share price that Dimon was worried that they would reject the deal when the time came to vote on it. He renegotiated and agreed to pay $10 a share, an offer that Bear's shareholders accepted on March 24.* Tim and I had persuaded a reluctant Hank not to stand in the way of Dimon's higher offer. It's true that the lower price would have sent a stronger message: that we were interceding to protect the system, not the owners of the firm. But if Bear shareholders rejected the deal, it would be the night of March 13 all over again—with us wondering whether the American financial system would implode over the next few days.

We negotiated a better deal for the Fed as well. The $30 billion in Bear Stearns assets would be placed in a limited liability corporation created by the New York Fed, which would allow us to structure

---

* Dimon had a further incentive to raise his offer: A lawyer's drafting error committed JPMorgan to guarantee Bear Stearns's liabilities for up to a year, even if the shareholders voted down the merger. The mistake increased Bear's shareholders' bargaining power.

our assistance as a loan against collateral, as required by 13(3). It was named Maiden Lane LLC, after a street outside the New York Fed's fortresslike building in lower Manhattan. We would lend $29 billion to Maiden Lane and JPMorgan would lend $1 billion. JPMorgan would take the first $1 billion in losses, if any. Of course, Maiden Lane looked uncomfortably like the off-balance-sheet SIVs that Citigroup and others had used to bet on subprime mortgages. One big difference was that we included it on the Fed's balance sheet and reported publicly on its market value every quarter. The deal would work out for the Fed and taxpayers in the end. Our loan was repaid, with $765 million in interest; in addition, as of early 2015, Maiden Lane held assets worth an additional $1.7 billion in profit for the Fed and, consequently, for the taxpayer. The important thing was not the return on the loan—it was that the financial system and the economy, at least for a time, were spared enormous disruption.

The Bear rescue nevertheless was heavily criticized, especially after Dimon increased the offer to Bear's shareholders. The commentary focused on the unfairness of bailing out Wall Street (a sentiment with which I agreed) rather than on what would have happened had we not acted. In an April speech, Paul Volcker declared that the Fed in the Bear Stearns deal had taken actions "that extend to the very edge of its lawful and implied powers, transcending in the process certain long-embedded central banking principles and practices." I took slight comfort from the fact that he hadn't said we had gone *over* the edge of our lawful power. Really, he was warning that the private-sector excesses and regulatory deficiencies that had led to what he called "the mother of all crises" must end. I agreed with him about that, and also that we had gone to the edge of our lawful and implied powers. My concern was that those powers, even if pushed to the limit, might not be enough to handle the next blowup.

THE FOMC MET on March 18, two days after JPMorgan agreed to buy Bear Stearns. Dave Stockton and his staff explained why they now believed that the economy was entering a recession. In light of the worsening economic outlook and the ongoing financial stresses, I recommended a substantial rate cut of three-quarters of a percentage point, bringing the target for the federal funds rate down to 2-1/4 percent. The FOMC approved it, with two hawks—Richard Fisher and Charlie Plosser—voting no. On April 30, the FOMC would cut the rate another quarter point, to 2 percent.

The Bear Stearns action brought a period of relative calm to financial markets. In late March, the investment banks reported earnings that beat market expectations. In a vote of confidence in the U.S. financial system, big commercial banks and the investment banks were able to raise an impressive $140 billion in new capital by the end of June. Funding conditions improved, and borrowing through the PDCF by the primary dealers, after spiking above $37 billion in late March, shrank to zero by the start of July. The stock market reflected the better tone of credit markets. The Dow closed at 12,263 on March 31, virtually unchanged from its level before the Bear Stearns crisis. By May, the Dow had climbed to 13,058, within 8 percent of its October 2007 peak. Most importantly, the economy showed signs of modest growth. The Commerce Department on July 31 would report that the economy grew by almost 1 percent in the first quarter and a hair below 2 percent in the second quarter. With lower interest rates and the temporary tax cuts, we had at least some hope that the economy would avoid a recession after all.

ALL OF THIS was unknown on April 3 as I tried to explain, under the camera lights at the Senate hearing on Bear Stearns, why we had intervened. I knew that the more thoughtful senators on the panel understood—some of them would later tell me so—but the temptation to make political hay was too great for many. Why were we bailing out Wall Street when so many ordinary Americans needed help?

Wall Street and Main Street are interconnected and interdependent, I explained. "Given the exceptional pressures on the global economy and financial system, the damage caused by a default by Bear Stearns could have been severe and extremely difficult to contain," I said. And the damage would have surely extended beyond financial markets to the broader economy. Without access to credit, people would not be able to buy cars or houses, and businesses would not be able to expand or, in some cases, even cover current operating costs. The negative effects on jobs and incomes would be fast and powerful.

Why were we creating moral hazard by rewarding failure? ("That is socialism!" Senator Bunning had roared.) I pointed out that, even with our action, Bear Stearns lost its independence, its shareholders took severe losses, and many of its 14,000 employees likely would soon lose their jobs.

"I do not think it is a situation that any firm would willingly choose to endure," I told Senator Tim Johnson of South Dakota. "What we had in mind here was the protection of the financial system and the protection of the American economy. And I believe that if the American people understand that we were trying to protect the economy and not to protect anybody on Wall Street, they would better appreciate why we took the actions we did."

One thing was clear. From now on we would be facing two challenges in dealing with the crisis. The first would be to do the right thing. The second would be to explain to the public and politicians why what we did was the right thing.

IN RETROSPECT, was it the right thing? Some economists have argued that it was a mistake. Our actions restored a degree of calm in financial markets, but for less than six months. Ultimately, much of what we feared would happen if Bear collapsed came to pass when Lehman Brothers filed for bankruptcy in September 2008. Some would say in hindsight that the moral hazard created by rescuing Bear reduced the urgency of firms like Lehman to raise capital or find buyers.

In making the decisions we made in March 2008, we could not know all that would transpire. But even in hindsight, I remain comfortable with our intervention. The enormously disruptive effect of Lehman's failure in September, I believe, confirmed our judgment in March that the collapse of a major investment bank—far from being the nonevent that some thought it might be—would severely damage both the financial system and the broader economy. Our intervention with Bear gave the financial system and the economy a nearly six-month respite, at a relatively modest cost. Unfortunately, the respite wasn't enough to repair the damage already done to the economy or to prevent panic from breaking out again in the fall.

I also believe that critics overstate the contribution of moral hazard from the Bear intervention to the resurgence of the crisis in the fall. As I told Senator Johnson, no firm would willingly seek Bear's fate. And financial firms, including Lehman, did indeed raise substantial capital over the summer. Moreover, as nearly happened to Bear, Lehman was done in by an overwhelming run on the firm. The occurrence of the run shows that Lehman's creditors and counterparties worried it would not be rescued. In other words, Lehman was subject to market discipline.

It cannot be denied, though, that these are difficult questions, and we would debate them among ourselves as spring turned to summer in 2008.

Fannie and Freddie:
A Long, Hot Summer

The Bear Stearns rescue was followed by a period of relative calm, but we remained wary. Powerful destructive forces had been set in motion. Home prices continued to fall. More delinquencies and foreclosures were sure to follow—with the losses flowing through to mortgage-related securities. We did not know how large the losses would be or where they would show up. But we knew more shoes could drop.

Our bank supervisors would relay a steady flow of bad news all summer long. IndyMac, based in Pasadena, California, and the nation's seventh-largest savings and loan, was teetering. It had been deeply involved in the Alt-A niche of the mortgage market, one level above subprime. IndyMac was overseen by the Office of Thrift Supervision. Since it had government-insured deposits, the FDIC monitored it as well. Normally we wouldn't have been involved, but the possibility that IndyMac might come to the Fed's discount window led the San Francisco Reserve Bank to dispatch two examiners. Based on their reports, Deborah Bailey of the Board's banking supervision division told me on July 1 that she didn't see how the company could survive much longer. "Retail deposits have been running since Friday, the company is tracking it hourly," she wrote. "The company is shrinking and selling off assets as fast as it can." Now, nearly a year into the financial crisis, even insured depositors could be spooked. Like a cadre of grim reapers, the FDIC's specialists in bank resolution were preparing to seize the lender.

Even more than private-sector lenders like IndyMac, we were concerned about the world's two largest holders of residential mortgages, the government-sponsored enterprises (GSEs) Fannie Mae and Freddie Mac. Congress had created Fannie and Freddie to support homeownership. Both started out as federal agencies, Fannie during the Great Depression, in 1938, and Freddie in 1970. However, both were later converted by Congress to shareholder-owned corporations— Fannie in 1968 and Freddie in 1989. Although legally private, Fannie and Freddie were regulated by and maintained close ties to the federal government, were exempt from all state and local taxes, and had a line of credit from the Treasury.

Their platypus status, as both private corporations and de facto government agencies, was flawed from inception. Effectively, the arrangement created a "heads I win, tails you lose" situation, with shareholders enjoying the profits earned by the companies but with taxpayers ultimately responsible for losses.

Fannie and Freddie had achieved some success in their mission to promote homeownership. They purchased mortgage loans from banks, savings institutions, and other mortgage originators and packaged the loans into mortgage-backed securities. They sold MBS to a wide range of investors, from insurance companies to pension funds to foreign central banks. For a fee, Fannie and Freddie guaranteed their MBS against borrower defaults, so purchasers faced no credit risk. Through bundling mortgages and selling the resulting securities, Fannie and Freddie allowed the world's savings to pour into the U.S. housing market. This huge inflow likely made mortgages cheaper and easier to get, thereby promoting homeownership, although precisely by how much was contentiously debated.

The benefits of Fannie and Freddie, such as they were, came with significant risks to the housing market, the financial system, and the taxpayer. The greatest risks originated in what was probably a deliberate ambiguity on the part of Congress when it created the GSEs. Officially, if Fannie or Freddie went broke, the U.S. government had no obligation to protect those who had lent directly to the companies or purchased their MBS. Consequently, the federal budget did not recognize the risk of having to bail out one or both GSEs. In Washington, where the official figures shape reality, omitting this possible cost from the budget allowed successive Congresses and administrations to ignore it.

And yet, investors assumed that the government would never let Fannie or Freddie fail, for fear of the damage to the U.S. housing market, financial markets in general, and the economy. This belief in an implicit government guarantee in turn enabled the GSEs to borrow at interest rates not much above those at which the government itself could borrow. The regulator of Fannie and Freddie, the Office of Federal Housing Enterprise Oversight, following congressional instructions, had long required the companies to hold only small capital cushions against possible losses. Still, investors' confidence in the GSEs and the implicit guarantee had remained largely unshaken through the ups and downs of the economy and the housing market.

Their ability to borrow cheaply made Fannie and Freddie hugely profitable in normal times. In one particularly lucrative strategy, they used the proceeds of their cheap borrowing to buy and hold hundreds of billions of dollars' worth of MBS, including many of the very MBS they had issued and guaranteed. The rate the GSEs earned on the MBS they held was higher than the implicitly subsidized rate they paid to borrow. It seemed like the ultimate free lunch—an ongoing flow of profits with no apparent risk. Congress too shared in the free lunch, in that it could require the GSEs to use some of their profits to support housing programs in members' districts. Fannie and Freddie also spent some of their profits on lobbying and political contributions, cementing the cozy relationship. Their clout had largely protected them during a series of accounting scandals between 2003 and 2006, when earnings overstatements resulted in enormous bonuses for some of the companies' top executives.

The companies also worked hard to maintain a good relationship with the Fed, notwithstanding (or perhaps because of) the concerns we often expressed about the risks they posed. We received regular research reports, some commissioned from prominent economists, that invariably concluded the GSEs were safe as houses, so to speak. Early in my chairmanship, I met with their executives and economists several times to discuss the housing market and the GSEs themselves. Both companies' CEOs were relatively new at that point. Richard Syron, a former president of the Federal Reserve Bank of Boston, had taken over at Freddie Mac in late 2003. Bespectacled, with a heavy Boston accent, Syron seemed well aware of (and a little apologetic about) the inherent conflicts arising from the GSEs' status. Daniel Mudd, a decorated former marine and the son of former CBS television news anchorman Roger Mudd, had taken the helm at Fannie a year later as interim CEO, following the resignation of Franklin Raines (a victim of Fannie's accounting scandal). Mudd, more hard-charging than Syron, struck me as someone who would aggressively defend his company's interests.

Critics, including the Government Accountability Office and the Congressional Budget Office, had often warned about the possibility that the government might one day have to bail out one or both GSEs. Alan Greenspan, with the assistance and urging of the Board staff, had spoken out frequently. When I became chairman, I continued the criticism, arguing that the GSEs' low levels of capital posed risks both to the taxpayer and to the financial system as a whole.

When the mortgage crisis began in 2007, it appeared at first that the GSEs might help stabilize housing, as they and their supporters expected and promised. Investment banks and other private firms had been creating their own, unguaranteed mortgage-backed securities. In many cases, these so-called private-label securities were constructed out of mortgages—known as nonconforming mortgages—that the GSEs would not securitize, either because they were bigger than the maximum size legally allowed by Congress or because they did not meet the GSEs' quality standards. Investor demand for new private-label MBS evaporated when the poor quality of many of the underlying mortgages was revealed. At that point, banks and other lenders originating nonconforming mortgages had no choice but to keep them on their own books. Most originators had limited capacity or desire to do so. That meant only conforming mortgages eligible for sale to Fannie and Freddie were available to sustain the housing market. In the summer of 2008, Fannie and Freddie owned or had guaranteed about $5.3 trillion in U.S. mortgages—about half of all those outstanding. With the demise of their private-sector competition, the GSEs had become even more indispensable.

But how strong were the companies, really? The GSEs' vaunted underwriting standards, it would turn out, did not ensure that the companies would acquire only high-quality mortgages. Fannie and Freddie were not allowed to buy subprime and other exotic mortgages directly from originators. However, anxious about the competition posed by private-label MBS, and eager for the high returns that lower-quality mortgages seemed to promise, they bought and held private-label MBS that included subprime and other lower-quality mortgages. By some estimates, the GSEs had bought about one-third of the $1.6 trillion in lower-quality, private-label mortgage-backed securities issued from 2004 through 2006. The CEOs of both companies strongly supported this strategy and remained resolute even as losses in lower-quality mortgages began to mount.

As house prices continued to decline, delinquencies and defaults increased to levels not seen since the Depression, and not only among subprime borrowers. In early June, our economists told me that they expected 2.2 million homes to enter foreclosure in 2008, up from 1.5 million in 2007. Mortgage delinquencies were a double whammy for Fannie and Freddie: They lost money both on the mortgages they held on their balance sheet as well as on the mortgages held by others that the companies had guaranteed.

With their profits turning to losses, Fannie and Freddie slashed the dividends they paid to their shareholders, and their stock prices plummeted. Stock investors had never expected to be protected by the government's implicit guarantee, and they were not. The implicit guarantee did keep most investors from abandoning the companies' MBS and debt, but even there confidence was waning, notably overseas. Foreign central banks and sovereign wealth funds (such as those that invest the earnings of oil-producing countries) had loaded up on Fannie and Freddie MBS because they were considered close substitutes for U.S. government debt and were highly liquid—easily bought and sold. In 2008, China alone held more than $700 billion in GSE mortgage-backed securities, slightly more than it held in long-term U.S. Treasuries.

As doubts grew about the GSEs, both Hank Paulson and I received calls from central bank governors, sovereign wealth fund managers, and government officials in East Asia and the Middle East. Were the companies safe? Would the U.S. government stand behind them? Several of my callers had not realized that the government did not already guarantee the GSEs. News coverage had alerted them to the risk. I was as reassuring as I could be, but I was not in a position to offer guarantees, implicit or otherwise.

With so much risk still in the system, Hank and I were eager to focus Congress on the gaps in financial regulation. On July 10, Paulson and I testified before Barney Frank's House Financial Services Committee about the need for comprehensive reforms. Highlighting the problems inherent in piecemeal supervision of the financial sector, Paulson suggested that Congress make the Fed responsible for the overall stability of the financial system, an important feature of regulatory reforms the Treasury had proposed in March. The proposal seemed to meet with a generally favorable response. (Barney said that the Fed was not ideal for the role but that it was the best alternative. He cited as his authority the comedian Henny Youngman: "How's your wife?" Youngman was asked, to which he replied, "Compared to what?") Both Hank and I called for a more orderly system that could wind down large financial firms on the verge of failure. Barney hoped legislation could be completed early in 2009, but that did not seem realistic to me.

Events moved much more quickly than the congressional debate. On the Monday before the testimony, Fannie's and Freddie's stock prices had dropped sharply when an industry analyst speculated that, as the result of an accounting change, the companies might have to raise tens of billions in new capital. Few doubted that lax accounting rules and regulatory standards had allowed the companies to hold very little capital relative to the potential losses on the mortgages they held or guaranteed.

Meanwhile, the FDIC seized IndyMac at the end of the week. The failure would cost the FDIC about $13 billion. In its wake, OTS Director John Reich and Senator Chuck Schumer of New York engaged in mutual finger-pointing. The run had begun in earnest after June 26, when Schumer said in a letter to Reich and the FDIC that IndyMac posed "significant risks to both taxpayers and borrowers." Reich issued a press release complaining that Schumer's letter had provoked the run. Schumer responded that the run was caused by regulators' failure to prevent IndyMac's "poor and loose lending practices." Both had valid points. IndyMac was in deep trouble and would have certainly failed in any case. But in a financial crisis, the words of government officials carry extraordinary weight.

Fannie and Freddie would need shoring up, and soon, although—as IndyMac's collapse had illustrated—Treasury and the Fed had to be cautious not to acknowledge that fact in so many words. The implicit guarantee notwithstanding, investors were wary of new debt issued by the GSEs, and rumors were spreading among market participants that the Fed would soon open its discount window to them. I certainly did not want to do that. How ironic would it be for the Fed to help rescue the GSEs after all the years spent criticizing them? Moreover, I saw the GSEs as the responsibility of Congress and the administration. After Reuters reported a rumor July 11 that I had spoken to Dick Syron about opening the discount window to the GSEs, I emailed the Reserve Bank presidents. "There was absolutely no truth to the rumor," I wrote. "I wanted to be clear on this point." My plan instead was for our examiners to independently evaluate the GSEs' condition. Whatever course we chose would need to be based on the best possible information.

The Fed and the Office of the Comptroller of the Currency had struck an agreement with OFHEO, the GSE regulator, to "deepen our mutual understanding" of the risks the GSEs were facing. In other words, bank regulators would look closely at the GSEs' books. Don Kohn hoped the effort could be kept quiet, to avoid stirring market fears. With that objective in mind, the Fed and OCC examiners reviewed the GSEs' data at OFHEO's offices rather than going physically into the companies.

My resolve against backstopping Fannie and Freddie didn't last long. On the day of IndyMac's failure, the GSEs' stock prices, especially Fannie's, fell sharply despite supportive words from President Bush and Secretary Paulson. They had lost close to half their value in a single week. Meanwhile, scenes of depositors lining up to withdraw their money from IndyMac played over and over on cable television, and oil prices hit a record $145 per barrel. In the midst of all this bad news, Paulson called to tell me that he had obtained the president's permission to ask Congress for help with Fannie and Freddie.

Hank kept us up to date on his progress with Congress and on his conversations with management at Fannie and Freddie. With mortgage losses rising and investor confidence in the GSEs dropping, he saw no alternative to asking Congress to authorize whatever financial support might be necessary to stabilize the companies. He was worried, however, that the very act of proposing the legislation, by revealing the government's deep concerns, could set off a run on the companies. He asked me whether the Fed would provide a temporary credit line to Fannie and Freddie until legislation was in place.

I agreed, with reluctance. To lend to Fannie and Freddie, which were not banks and thus not eligible to borrow at our regular discount window, we'd invoke yet another rarely used lending authority, this one under section 13(13) of the Federal Reserve Act. Our authority under section 13(13) was more limited than the 13(3) authority we had used to rescue Bear Stearns. Under 13(13), our loans must be collateralized by Treasury securities or securities guaranteed by an "agency" such as Fannie and Freddie. But both authorities could be used only in unusual and exigent circumstances—13(3) by law and 13(13) by Board regulation. Hank emphasized that our credit line would be temporary and precautionary. And, as was the case with all Fed loans, any extension of credit would be fully secured by collateral. I consulted with Board members, who all agreed that maintaining the stability of Fannie and Freddie was paramount. The Board met on Sunday, July 13, and invoked 13(13), giving the New York Fed the go-ahead to lend to Fannie and Freddie if necessary. We acted, we said in a press release, "to help ensure the ability of Fannie Mae and Freddie Mac to promote the availability of home mortgage credit during a period of stress in financial markets."

Hank made his pitch to the Senate Banking Committee on July 15. SEC chairman Chris Cox and I sat at his side. Paulson asked Congress for "unspecified"—meaning unlimited—authority for the administration to purchase the GSEs' securities and stock. Hank explained that unlimited authority would so reassure markets that he might be able to avoid using it. "If you've got a squirt gun in your pocket, you may have to take it out. If you've got a bazooka, and people know you've got it, you may not have to take it out," he said. Sometimes market fears can be self-fulfilling, and a strong demonstration can avoid the worst outcomes. I was reminded of the military doctrine of "overwhelming force" as the way to prompt quick surrender and minimize casualties.

A bipartisan measure to backstop the GSEs passed the House on July 23 and the Senate on July 26, and President Bush signed it into law on July 30. The legislation also included reform measures that GSE critics had long advocated—stronger capital requirements and a new, more powerful regulator, the Federal Housing Finance Agency (FHFA, or "fuff-a," in Beltwayese) to replace OFHEO. If it had been five years earlier, GSE critics would have celebrated the reforms as real progress. But in the summer of 2008, given the condition of Fannie and Freddie and of financial markets, the reforms would prove largely irrelevant. All that mattered was the backstop.

THE NEXT FOMC MEETING, on August 5, 2008, would be Rick Mishkin's last. It would also be the first for Board member Betsy Duke, who had been nominated by President Bush in May 2007, along with Larry Klane of Capital One Financial Corp. I was sorry to see Rick return to Columbia University. He had been an early and ardent supporter of strong measures to counter financial turbulence. To keep the mood light at his going-away luncheon, all I had to do was read from Rick's previous remarks to the FOMC. For example, he had once described his ambivalence about a close FOMC vote: "As you know, sitting on a fence and having a fence right in that anatomically uncomfortable position is not a good place to be."

Betsy had spent most of her career in community banking in Virginia (although, after a series of acquisitions, she found herself working for Wachovia). She was a welcome addition to the Board— friendly and good-hearted, but blunt when she needed to be. I often relied on her terrific good sense. She also brought a practical banker's perspective, a valuable complement to the economists on the Board and the FOMC. I swore her in just before the meeting began. She had waited fifteen months for Senate confirmation, while Larry Klane's nomination was blocked by Democrats after community activists complained of his employer's subprime lending practices. Klane had called me several times to express his deep frustration and disappointment.

Randy Kroszner's Board term had expired at the end of January and Democrats refused to confirm him to a new term. With Betsy's nomination the exception, the Senate seemed to be creating a regrettable convention, that no one could be confirmed to the Fed's Board in the last year to eighteen months of the president's term. (In 1999, ahead of the 2000 presidential election, one of Chris Dodd's Republican predecessors as Senate Banking Committee chairman, Phil Gramm, had blocked President Clinton's nomination of Roger Ferguson to a second Board term. After the election, President Bush renominated him.) I was grateful that Randy agreed to continue serving until a replacement was sworn in. But it was unfortunate that, largely for political reasons, two Board seats remained unfilled, leaving us shorthanded during a difficult period.

At the FOMC meeting, Bill Dudley focused his briefing on Fannie and Freddie. The bill signed into law the week before had helped avert a meltdown in the markets for GSE-guaranteed mortgage-backed securities as well as the debt the GSEs issued to finance their portfolios. But, for the housing market, the measure was at best a palliative. Even though the new law allowed the GSEs to support the mortgage markets by increasing their MBS portfolios, they were shrinking their holdings to reduce risk. And, despite the "bazooka" written into the legislation, foreign investors had also retreated from buying GSE securities. The reduced demand for MBS helped push mortgage rates higher. Notwithstanding our sharp cuts to the federal funds rate, thirty-year fixed-rate mortgages hovered around 6-1/2 percent, up from 5-1/2 percent at the start of the year.

I had asked Bill to discuss the state of the Federal Reserve's balance sheet in his briefing. We were facing what might prove to be a critical question: Could we continue our emergency lending to financial institutions and markets, while at the same time setting short-term interest rates at levels that kept a lid on inflation? Two key elements of our policy framework—lending to ease financial conditions, and setting short-term interest rates—could come into conflict.

When the Fed makes a loan, taking securities or bank loans as collateral, the recipient of the loan deposits the funds in a commercial bank. The bank in turn adds the funds to its reserve account at the Fed. When banks hold substantial reserves, they have little need to borrow from other banks, and so the interest rate that banks charge each other for short-term loans—the federal funds rate—tends to fall.

But the FOMC targets that same short-term interest rate when making monetary policy. Without offsetting action, our emergency lending—by increasing the reserves that banks held at the Fed—would tend to push down the federal funds rate and other short-term interest rates. Since April, we had set our target for the federal funds rate at 2 percent—the right level, we thought, to balance our goals of supporting employment and keeping inflation under control. We needed to continue our emergency lending and at the same time prevent the federal funds rate from falling below 2 percent.

Thus far, we had successfully resolved the potential inconsistency by selling a dollar's worth of Treasury securities from our portfolio for each dollar of our emergency lending. The sales of Treasuries drained reserves from the banking system, offsetting the increase in reserves created by our lending. This procedure, known as sterilization, allowed us to make loans as needed while keeping short-term interest rates where we wanted them.

But this solution would not work indefinitely. We had already sold many of our Treasury securities. If our lending continued to expand—and the potential appetite for our loans at times seemed infinite—we could run out of Treasuries to sell, making sterilization infeasible. At that point, the funds injected by any additional loans would increase the level of bank reserves, and we could lose control of interest rates. This concern was very much on our minds, and it provided additional ammunition to FOMC participants who were uncomfortable with our growing array of lending programs.*

David Wilcox followed Dudley's briefing. Wilcox told the FOMC that the Bush administration's temporary tax cuts had helped the

---

* The Treasury helped us solve this dilemma to some extent, by raising money in debt markets and depositing the proceeds with the Fed. Its Supplementary Financing Program (SFP) pulled cash out of the private sector and allowed us to finance our emergency lending without increasing bank reserves. However, the SFP varied in size, and had to be drawn down when the government approached its statutory debt limit. Thus, it was not a reliable solution to our problem. And, as officials of an independent central bank, we didn't like to be dependent on Treasury's help in setting monetary policy.

economy grow at a moderate clip earlier in the year, but that weak job data and renewed financial turmoil led the staff to expect growth in the second half of 2008 of a half percent or less. In a particularly worrisome development, our quarterly survey of bank loan officers had revealed that banks were tightening the terms of their loans, especially loans to households, very sharply. The staff maintained its view, first laid out in April, that the economy was either in or would soon enter recession.

At the same time, we could not completely dismiss inflation concerns. Oil prices had fallen to $120 per barrel from their record high of $145 in July. However, staff economists still saw inflation running at an uncomfortable 3-1/2 percent in the second half of the year. Even excluding volatile food and energy prices, the staff expected inflation to pick up to around 2-1/2 percent, more than most FOMC members thought was acceptable. Like all central bankers, we were always alert to the possibility that households and firms might lose confidence in our commitment to price stability. Indeed, responding to perceived inflation risks, the European Central Bank had just a month earlier raised interest rates despite slowing economic growth and continuing financial pressures. Still, I sided with the members concerned about the debilitating effects of financial stress on economic growth and employment. We agreed to keep our target interest rate unchanged and wait for more information. Only Dallas Fed president Richard Fisher, who wanted to raise the federal funds rate immediately, voted no.

It was a good result, but the 10–1 vote understated rising hawkishness on the Committee. I vented in an email the next day to Don Kohn: "I find myself conciliating holders of the unreasonable opinion that we should be tightening even as the economy and financial system are in a precarious position and inflation/commodity pressures appear to be easing." The subject line of the email had been "WWGD?"—meaning "What Would Greenspan Do?" Don, who had been Greenspan's closest adviser before becoming a Board member, reassured me that my management of the FOMC was going about as well as could be expected, given the circumstances. "It's not clear that the squeaky wheels represent the majority on the Committee," he wrote. And he reminded me that things hadn't always gone smoothly for Greenspan. After a honeymoon period of three meetings without dissent in 1987, the Maestro had faced dissents in nineteen of his next twenty-one meetings.

To someone accustomed to watching a legislative body, or the Supreme Court, where close votes are hardly unusual, my concern about having a few dissents on the Committee—which at full strength has twelve voting members—might seem strange. But FOMC tradition called for consensus decision making, and in that context a "no" vote represents a strong statement of disagreement. Most central banks strive to present a united front, although there are exceptions—like the Bank of England, where the governor (the equivalent of the Fed chairman) is sometimes outvoted. Part of a central bank's ability to influence financial conditions—and by extension the economy—depends on whether markets believe it will follow a consistent policy path. Too many dissents, I worried, could undermine our credibility.

AUGUST IS USUALLY slow in Washington, with Congress in recess and many federal workers on vacation. Like the previous August, however, August 2008 was hectic at the Fed. I did not even bother to plan a vacation, although I did try to take in the occasional Nationals game. Baseball would remain one of my few respites—at least for a handful of hours at a time—as the financial crisis intensified. I had been a Nats fan since the team had arrived in Washington in 2005. Unfortunately, there was no turning off my BlackBerry, and I was often forced to look for a quiet corner of the stadium to take a call. One Sunday afternoon, I found refuge in the stadium's first-aid area; two nurses watched me curiously as I spoke in low tones.

On August 6, Kevin Warsh reported on a breakfast meeting with Fannie CEO Daniel Mudd. Third-quarter results would be "miserable"— with losses triple what the market expected. Mudd was concerned the company might not have enough capital, a change from his earlier, more confident tone. I heard from our supervisors that Freddie, too, would be announcing significant losses, although Dick Syron continued to insist that the company would raise $5.5 billion of capital. (It never did, although Fannie did follow through on a promise to raise $7.4 billion.) On August 11, Hank and Treasury staff members came to the Eccles Building for a meeting about the GSEs, with Bill Dudley and others from the New York Fed joining by phone. Despite the July reforms, the GSEs' capital was not going to cover the likely losses.

The July legislation had included a provision that the Fed consult with FHFA, the new GSE regulator, about Fannie's and Freddie's financial condition. On August 14, Don, Kevin, and I, along with several of our supervisors, met with FHFA director Jim Lockhart and his staff to discuss how we could build on the informal arrangements set up earlier in the summer. I liked Lockhart, a numbers guy who had previously served as the chief operating officer for the Social Security Administration, and who had consistently pointed out that Fannie and Freddie were undercapitalized. But he was clearly torn between his concerns about the GSEs and the normal inclination of an agency head to protect his staff's prerogatives. As a general matter, I tried to be sensitive to other agencies' turf concerns, on the grounds that doing so was more likely to foster cooperation and good policy in the end. But the situation at the GSEs was getting more dire by the day. "The GSEs have been running with such low capital levels and dysfunctional and confused internal dynamics for so long that I have felt that they could blow up at any time," Kevin Warsh wrote in an email.

The GSEs' troubles were further undermining fragile financial markets and quashing any hope of a recovery in housing. Without invoking any extraordinary authorities, we had the power to purchase MBS guaranteed by the GSEs, and I asked Bill Dudley whether we should start doing that as a way to help housing. Dudley was initially skeptical. It might be technically difficult to efficiently buy and manage the GSE securities, and (as he had explained at the FOMC meeting) we had limited room on our balance sheet to buy more securities while still maintaining control of monetary policy. He agreed, though, to look into the idea.

INDYMAC AND FANNIE and Freddie weren't the only big financial institutions on our radar that summer. We were also watching Washington Mutual, WaMu for short, a mortgage lender based in Seattle. The OTS was WaMu's lead regulator. The FDIC, as deposit insurer, also monitored it, as did the San Francisco Fed, in case it asked for a discount window loan.

WaMu was founded in 1889 with the goal of helping the city recover from the great Seattle Fire, which had destroyed its entire business district. Over the next century, WaMu survived numerous traumas, including the bank runs of the Great Depression, only to flirt with failure during the savings and loan crisis of the 1980s. The lesson the company took from the 1980s was that long-term viability required growth and diversification, which it achieved largely by purchasing other companies. Nobody bought into that philosophy more than WaMu CEO Kerry Killinger, a former stock analyst. Distinguished by dyed sandy-brown hair that he arranged in a careful comb-over, Killinger, nicknamed "the Energizer Banker," took over in 1990 at the age of forty. Through a remarkable series of acquisitions, he set out to make WaMu the nation's number-one home lender, eventually making it the country's second-largest mortgage lender, behind Countrywide. I had encountered Killinger at meetings of the Federal Advisory Council, a group (including one banker from each Federal Reserve district) created by the Federal Reserve Act to advise the Board. Even in these staid meetings, Killinger's energy and strong opinions came through.

Expansion, if it is too rapid, can also be dangerous. As early as 2004, the OTS expressed concern about whether WaMu was doing enough to integrate its many acquisitions. Worse, as part of its growth strategy WaMu plunged into subprime lending; in time, it began to suffer significant losses. In March 2008 our supervisors reported that WaMu was calling an emergency board meeting to consider possible responses, including the sale of the company. Its board had hired Lehman Brothers to help identify potential acquirers.

By the summer of 2008, it seemed questionable whether the company would survive. Nonetheless, the OTS believed that its problems, though serious, were manageable. The more conservative FDIC—always sensitive to any risk to the deposit insurance fund—wanted to intervene. Our people sided with the FDIC. I worried that the OTS was focused too much on preserving a regulatory client and not enough on the broader risks to the system. I had been glad to hear from John Reich on August 2 that Killinger was being replaced. It sounded like the OTS was taking the matter seriously after all.

Don Kohn watched WaMu and reported regularly. Tension between the OTS (under Reich) and the FDIC (under Sheila Bair) continued. Bair wanted WaMu to look actively for potential acquirers—ideally more than one or two. This would ensure that the company could sell itself for a reasonable price and thereby avoid an FDIC payout. Sheila informed OTS that she was going to approach Wells Fargo and JPMorgan, to gauge their interest—just in case. But, as Don reported, OTS officials "went ballistic" and accused the Fed and the FDIC of "being fronts for JPM." Sheila backed off—for the moment.

IN THE SECOND HALF of August, the Jackson Hole conference loomed. My speech this year would be especially closely watched, and I badgered the staff and various Board members to read draft after draft. I wanted it to provide a road map for monetary policy while at the same time acknowledging the especially high level of uncertainty.

On Thursday, August 21, the select group of conference participants converged on Jackson Lodge. The sight of the snow-capped Grand Teton range was awe-inspiring, as always. Also unchanged from previous years: media trucks with their satellite dishes pointing skyward, tents set up on the lodge terrace for interviews, and TV reporters standing in front of the mountains as they spoke to the cameras.

Fed technicians had again set up an information center in a meeting room. Warsh, Geithner, Kohn, and I frequently left the formal proceedings to discuss the latest market data and developments regarding Fannie and Freddie. We tried to remain inconspicuous by leaving the conference at different times. I also found time to meet with foreign central bankers to update them and hear their views and concerns.

The news on the GSEs was not good. The Fed and OCC supervisors agreed that a realistic assessment of the two companies would leave them insolvent. A team from the investment bank Morgan Stanley was reviewing the GSEs' books for Treasury and was coming to a similar conclusion. If intervention became necessary, the most likely alternatives seemed to be receivership (bankruptcy) or conservatorship, an alternative to bankruptcy in which the companies would continue to operate under the direction of their regulator.

On Friday morning, I began my speech by observing that continued financial stress, a weakening economy, and a jump in inflation had created "one of the most challenging economic and policy environments in memory." I tried to set market expectations for steady monetary policy: We would keep policy easy to support the economy, but we would also do what was necessary to ensure price stability. I also explained why we had intervened with Bear Stearns and laid out an approach to avert future crises. As before, I argued that financial regulation should take a more system-wide approach, to detect risks and vulnerabilities that might be missed by the current, fragmented regulatory oversight.

After my remarks, the rest of the conference focused on the causes and effects of the financial crisis. Gary Gorton of Yale University argued that we were seeing a financial panic similar in structure to, though differing in many details from, the panics of the nineteenth and early twentieth centuries. I agreed. Indeed, we saw our responses to the panic as fulfilling the classic central banking role of lender of last resort. Other speakers and conference participants took a less generous view. Our Bear Stearns intervention came in for a good bit of criticism. A few participants argued that letting a big financial firm fail would be good for the financial system. Willem Buiter of the London School of Economics unrelentingly attacked both our monetary policy and our lending programs. Too-easy monetary policy would lead to serious inflation, he said. In an email to Michelle Smith and Dave Skidmore I half-jokingly suggested that I ought to make a public bet with Buiter on the inflation rate over the next year. They quickly quashed that idea. (But I would have won the bet if it had been made.) There was certainly no consensus at the meeting about the economy or about our response thus far, and little appreciation of what lay ahead.

On Friday evening I attended, with other conference participants, a small dinner at the Jackson Hole home of Jim Wolfensohn, a former president of the World Bank and business partner of Paul Volcker's. We talked about the events of the past year. Wolfensohn asked the gathering whether what we were experiencing would be a chapter or a footnote in the economics textbooks of the future. Most of the attendees thought it would be a footnote. I declined to answer, but I was still hoping against hope for the footnote.

SEPTEMBER 1 WAS Labor Day, but, given the urgency of the situation at the GSEs, our work went on. Representatives of the Treasury, Fed, and FHFA met all three days of the long weekend, in a large conference room across from the Treasury secretary's third-floor office. Dress was casual and staff came and went. Besides me, the Fed's representatives included Don Kohn, Kevin Warsh, Scott Alvarez, and Tim Clark, the bank supervisor who was leading the Fed's review of Fannie's and Freddie's books.

A war room at Treasury was appropriate—after all, Congress had given Paulson the bazooka. As Hank moved from one issue to another, pressing for solutions or more analysis, I could see why he had been an effective CEO. Like a general planning a surprise attack in hostile territory—not a bad metaphor for what we were discussing—Hank wanted to be sure that we had thought through every possibility. We believed that taking control of Fannie and Freddie was the only way to stabilize them. Doing so in a weekend, without advance warning or leaks, was going to be difficult enough. But Hank also asked the Treasury and Fed staff to think through how to keep the two companies operating effectively after the takeover. Lawyers briefed us about the alternatives for taking control, and we debated the structure of the guarantees that the Treasury would offer for GSE debt and GSE-sponsored MBS. Another concern: What if the GSEs decided to fight the takeover? If they resisted, what damage could a period of legal uncertainty do? What could we do to make sure the companies retained key employees?

The spillover effects of a takeover were also hard to anticipate. For example, many small banks held significant amounts of GSE stock, and I worried that a takeover that further reduced the value of that stock might cause community bank failures. I asked our staff to try to estimate community banks' exposure to the GSEs, but with limited data their answers involved a lot of guesswork.

Planning continued through the week, with the Treasury, Fed, and FHFA teams reconvening at Treasury at 8:00 a.m. Thursday, September 4. Tim Clark's team of examiners once more confirmed that Fannie and Freddie were effectively insolvent. The OCC and the outside consultants from Morgan Stanley concurred. The time had come to fire the bazooka. Hank, Jim Lockhart, and I agreed to set up a meeting with the CEOs and senior executives of Fannie and Freddie, rehearsing what each of us would say.

The showdown came the next day in an unprepossessing conference room at the FHFA headquarters, less than a block from the White House and the Treasury. We had avoided leaks about the meeting until *Wall Street Journal* reporter Damian Paletta spotted me entering FHFA by the front door. He flashed the news on the *Journal*'s financial wire. Daniel Mudd and Dick Syron were visibly shocked when Paulson told them that the U.S. government was going to put the two companies into conservatorship. Conservatorship, rather than receivership, would ensure that the companies would continue to perform their vital role in supporting housing. Conservatorship also protected the holders of Fannie's and Freddie's debt and MBS, which would be necessary to avoid creating a panic in global financial markets. The Treasury would inject capital into the companies as needed to keep them solvent.

I spoke next. I emphasized the gravity of the economic situation and the national interest in stabilizing housing and financial markets. Markets were questioning the companies' fundamental solvency, and for good reason, I said. We needed to remove the uncertainty about Fannie and Freddie to avoid even greater financial volatility. At the same time, for the sake of the U.S. housing market, the companies had to remain going concerns. Lockhart followed, discussing the details of his findings and the steps his agency would be taking. Paulson told the CEOs to explain to their boards that one way or the other the companies would be taken over. Hank must have been convincing, because Mudd and Syron didn't resist.

We had decided to replace them. Hank's lifetime of contacts in the financial services industry came in handy here. By Sunday we were ready to announce that Mudd would be succeeded at Fannie by Herb Allison, a veteran of Merrill Lynch who at that time was heading the TIAA-CREF pension fund. Syron's replacement, David Moffett, came from the management ranks of the Minneapolis-based U.S. Bancorp. Hank characterized the jobs to Allison and Moffett as opportunities for public service.

After the initial shock, the takeover was well received in most circles, including by many in Congress. Investors, including foreign central banks, were relieved that the U.S. government's implicit guarantee of agency debt and agency-guaranteed MBS had been made explicit. The Treasury also announced that it would be purchasing modest amounts of MBS and that it would provide a liquidity backstop for the GSEs, eliminating the need for the line of credit extended by the Fed. (We would keep the line in place anyway, as a precaution, although it would never be used.) Investors became more comfortable holding

GSE-backed MBS and mortgage rates fell by a half percentage point over the next two weeks. Fannie and Freddie stock prices, however, fell close to zero. As we expected, many smaller banks were among these stockholders, and we had to provide assurances that their supervisors would work with them to ensure that they had adequate capital.

Former Fed chairman Paul Volcker aptly summarized the state of play in an interview around that time. "It is the most complicated financial crisis I have ever experienced, and I have experienced a few," he said. Volcker had dealt with financial dustups on his watch, including the debt crisis in developing countries in 1982 and, in 1984, the largest-ever U.S. bank failure, of Continental Illinois, a record that would stand only a little while longer.

CHAPTER 12

Lehman: The Dam Breaks

O f all the firms that came to grief in 2007 and 2008, none was more controversial or emblematic of the crisis than Lehman Brothers—a storied investment bank with roots extending to the pre–Civil War South.

Lehman was founded in 1850 as a cotton brokerage by three Jewish brothers (Henry, Emanuel, and Mayer) who had emigrated from Bavaria to Montgomery, Alabama. The brothers relocated their headquarters in 1868 to New York City, where they helped found the New York Cotton Exchange. In the early 1900s, Lehman shifted to investment banking, arranging the financing needed by growing companies in the nation's rising industries, from aviation to motion pictures. The Lehman family became important in New York politics, with Herbert Lehman, Mayer's son, serving as lieutenant governor of New York during Franklin D. Roosevelt's governorship, then succeeding to the governorship when FDR became president in 1933.

The Lehman franchise appeared to have come to an end in 1984 when American Express acquired it and merged the firm with its retail brokerage, Shearson, to create Shearson Lehman. But after years of backbiting between Lehman executives and the parent company, Amex restored the original Lehman Brothers name to the division in 1990 and spun it off as an independent company in 1994.

The responsibility for recapturing Lehman's past luster fell to its new CEO, Dick Fuld, who had joined Lehman Brothers as a commercial paper trader in 1969. An intensely competitive, wiry man with deep-set eyes and a volatile temperament, Richard Fuld Jr. (nickname:

the Gorilla) projected the opposite of the traditional gentility of invest-ment bankers. But he accomplished what he set out to do, multiplying the firm's profits many times over. After the 9/11 attacks severely dam-aged the firm's headquarters at 3 World Financial Center, he purchased a midtown Manhattan building from archrival Morgan Stanley, and within a month Lehman was up and running again. In 2006, a *Fortune* magazine article lauded Lehman's "greatest run ever" over the previ-ous decade. "So complete has Fuld's makeover of Lehman been that he is more like a founder than a CEO," the magazine said. By 2008, Fuld was the longest-serving CEO of a major Wall Street firm.

Fuld's commitment to his firm was evident in every discussion or encounter I had with him. He saw the firm's success as a personal vali-dation. In the same vein, every short sale of Lehman stock or investor question about the quality of Lehman's assets stung him like a per-sonal affront. (Effectively, a short sale is a bet that the value of a stock will go down—the opposite of purchasing a stock, which is a bet that the value will go up.) But, as of the summer of 2008, Fuld's "greatest run ever" was coming to an end.

Lehman Brothers had two problems. First, like Bear Stearns, the firm depended heavily on short-term, uninsured repo funding, though it did have an important advantage over Bear: access to Fed-eral Reserve loans through the Primary Dealer Credit Facility, which had been created the weekend JPMorgan agreed to acquire Bear. The PDCF reduced Lehman's vulnerability to unexpected cash outflows. However, like the discount window for commercial banks, the PDCF carried some stigma (no firm wanted to admit that it needed to borrow from it). Lehman borrowed seven times from the PDCF in March and April, in amounts as high as $2.7 billion, but then stayed away.

Lehman's second, more fundamental problem was the quality of its $639 billion in assets as of the end of May. Fuld and his lieutenants had been aggressive even by pre-crisis Wall Street standards, propelling the company into commercial real estate, leveraged lending (lending to already indebted firms to finance takeovers and other speculative activ-ity), and private-label mortgage-backed securities. In the process, they

had blown through the company's established guidelines for controlling risk. Substantial profits and executive bonuses followed. But, as real
estate crashed, the values of many of these assets plunged. Other companies suffered losses, of course, but Lehman's losses were particularly
severe, and its reservoirs of capital and cash were smaller than most.
Moreover, Fuld and his team seemed in denial about how badly their
bets had gone wrong. Compared to many of its peers, Lehman was slow
to mark down the values it assigned to questionable real estate assets.
Egged on by critics like David Einhorn, the contrarian manager of the
hedge fund Greenlight Capital, investors and rival firms were growing
increasingly skeptical of Lehman's judgment of the value of its holdings.

The SEC supervised Lehman's principal subsidiaries, which were
broker-dealers—firms that buy and sell securities. U.S. law permitted Lehman's parent company, Lehman Brothers Holdings, to operate unsupervised—by the SEC or any other agency. However, to meet
requirements imposed by European authorities, the Lehman parent
voluntarily agreed to supervision under the SEC's Consolidated Supervised Entities program. Not surprisingly, this voluntary arrangement
was less strict than one required by law might have been.

Despite a sincere effort, the SEC was not well suited to supervising
the investment banks. It was, and remains, primarily an enforcement
agency. SEC lawyers enforce laws, like those prohibiting broker-dealers
from misappropriating funds from customer accounts or requiring
truthful disclosures about securities products, and punish violations.
They are not there to ensure that firms are well run. The SEC was not,
in other words, a supervisory agency like the Fed or the Office of the
Comptroller of the Currency, whose examiners focus on the overall
safety of the banks they oversee in addition to their compliance with
consumer protection rules.*

---

* In congressional testimony in March 2010, Mary Schapiro—who would become the
SEC chair in January 2009, succeeding Chris Cox—would acknowledge that the SEC's
voluntary supervision of Lehman and other investment banks fell short. The program,

Although the Fed was not responsible for supervising investment banks and in fact lacked the authority to do so, we did gain some access to Lehman after the Bear Stearns rescue. With the establishment of the PDCF, we had leverage to request information from Lehman because it might want to borrow from us. Moreover, the SEC was looking to the Fed for help. After JPMorgan Chase bought Bear, the New York Fed staff conferred frequently with the SEC and Lehman—up to three times per day. We would eventually send a small number of bank supervisors to Lehman and the other remaining investment banks. At first, the relationship between the agencies was bumpy. Fed supervisors were reluctant to share what they learned with the SEC division in charge of enforcing securities laws out of concern that doing so would make the investment banks unwilling to cooperate. Chris Cox and I negotiated a memorandum of understanding, signed on July 7, that laid out ground rules, and the coordination between the agencies improved.

Without doubt, Lehman needed capital. How much was difficult to determine. The company and its critics profoundly disagreed on the value of its complex investments. Investors and accounting standard setters had embraced more widespread application of the mark-to-market approach, under which valuations are determined by prices on the open market. But for some assets, such as individual loans to particular companies, an active market might not exist; or if it did, it might have very small numbers of buyers and sellers. Prices in such small markets are less reliable, especially in a panic. Often, valuations came down to whose assumptions you preferred to believe.

Valuation controversies notwithstanding, that investors lacked confidence in Lehman was not in dispute, and in the end that was what mattered most. Tim Geithner and, especially, Hank Paulson had been

---

she said, "was inadequately staffed almost from the very beginning" and "really required more of a banking regulators' sort of approach" rather than the SEC's "disclosure and enforcement mentality."

concerned about Lehman's viability since well before Bear Stearns, and Hank had been pressing Fuld to raise more capital for at least a year. After Bear, and in light of a sequence of downgrades of Lehman's credit rating, the Fed and the Treasury ratcheted up pressure on Fuld, telling him that he needed either to raise new capital or find a partner willing to buy a large stake in his company. Tim was the Fed's principal contact with Fuld. Geithner and Fuld spoke on the phone some fifty times between March and September, and Fuld kept Tim informed about the leads he was pursuing. Hank—who often made dozens of calls in a day—also spoke often with Fuld. Based on their conversations, both Hank and Tim believed Fuld didn't have a realistic view of what his firm was worth even as he actively considered many options.

If Lehman had been a midsize commercial bank, forcing Fuld to raise more capital would have been straightforward: Either the company met the supervisors' expectations or the FDIC would have taken it over and paid off depositors as necessary. But neither the Fed nor the FDIC had the authority to take over Lehman, nor could the FDIC deposit insurance fund be used to cover any losses. Legally, the government's only alternative, if Lehman couldn't find new capital, would have been trying to force the firm into bankruptcy. But that was a nuclear option. Because of Lehman's size, its extensive interconnections with so many financial firms and markets, and the already shaky state of investor confidence, we knew that forcing it into bankruptcy could unleash financial chaos.

On Monday, June 9, Lehman had announced a $2.8 billion second-quarter loss (its first since splitting from American Express in 1994) but also said that it planned to raise $6 billion in capital by selling new stock. Don Kohn told me that he thought the new capital "should stabilize the situation, at least for a time." "But," he warned, "there are deeper problems." The large surprise loss had undermined Lehman's credibility and raised questions about what else it might be hiding. Don said a "hedge fund type" had told him a Wall Street consensus had formed that Lehman's days were numbered. "The question is when and how they go out of business, not whether," Don wrote. Once again I worried about self-fulfilling prophecies: If concerns about Lehman's viability became sufficiently widespread, other firms would stop doing business with it and make recovery impossible.

We wanted Lehman to have enough cash and easily sellable liquid assets to fund itself for a while if it lost access to the repo market. In May, the New York Fed and the SEC had worked together to evaluate the ability of the remaining four independent investment banks (Goldman Sachs, Morgan Stanley, Merrill Lynch, and Lehman) to withstand a run. We subjected them to "stress tests" under two hypothetical scenarios to see if they had enough liquidity to survive in circumstances like those Bear Stearns had faced in March. One of the two scenarios was dubbed "Bear" internally—it tried to capture the actual stresses faced by Bear Stearns. The second, milder scenario was dubbed "Bear Light." With the Bear Stearns experience in mind, we assumed that repo lenders could run, even though repo borrowing is collateralized.

Although two of the investment banks (Morgan Stanley and Goldman) had enough liquid assets to get through Bear Light, none passed the Bear test. We pushed the companies to fix the problem, telling Lehman in particular that it needed at least $15 billion more in liquid assets. Lehman reported an increase in its liquidity by some $20 billion by the end of July, and it sold some of its real estate. As it turned out, however, not all the extra liquidity was really available for an emergency; much of it had already been committed as collateral. And, as credit losses mounted, Lehman's solvency and longer-term viability remained in doubt.

In late August, Fuld floated the idea of dividing Lehman into two pieces: a "good bank," which would retain the company's best assets and its operating businesses, and a "bad bank," which would hold the company's troubled commercial mortgages and other real estate assets. Within Lehman, the two units were referred to as "Cleanco" and "Spinco." Lehman would put capital into the bad bank and try to raise additional financing for both parts of the company. Paulson immediately made clear that the government had no authority to put money into the bad bank, as Fuld proposed. The good bank–bad bank strategy can be successful under the right conditions. The good bank—shorn of its questionable assets—may be able to raise new capital, while the bad bank can be financed by speculative investors at high interest rates and wound down, with assets being sold off over time. Fuld said that he hoped to divest Lehman's bad assets and make up the losses by selling one of the company's most valuable subsidiaries, its asset management unit, Neuberger Berman. Some thought it could fetch $7 billion to $8 billion. However, the plan, even if it ultimately proved workable, would take months to complete. It was time Fuld didn't have.

Concurrent with Fuld's newly offered plan, the state-owned Korea Development Bank had proposed acquiring a significant stake in Lehman. Fuld had been talking to the Koreans for several months. Other possible suitors included China's CITIC Securities, two Middle Eastern sovereign wealth funds, the MetLife insurance company, and the British bank HSBC. On September 8, criticism of the deal by the main Korean financial regulator spurred the Korea Development Bank to retract its proposal, and none of the other possible deals came to fruition. Fuld also approached investor Warren Buffett, with no success. Lehman's stock price continued to drop (the news from Korea alone caused it to fall from $14.15 per share to $7.79 per share in one day), making raising new capital even more difficult.

With would-be investors shunning Lehman, the Fed and the Treasury in early September focused on finding another company to take it over. Paulson had been in touch with Bank of America CEO Ken Lewis, who was known to want an investment bank. Lewis played it close to the vest. He might be interested in Lehman, but it would depend on the company's condition and, possibly, on the government's willingness to help. Lewis raised another concern. Although he had not been pressured by the government to acquire Countrywide, he believed that in doing so he had contributed to the stability of the broader financial system. As I would hear from our supervisors, Lewis was accordingly upset that—contrary to what he believed were commitments from the Fed—the Richmond Fed, his immediate supervisor, was pressing his bank to raise more capital. He wanted to know whether, given the criticism, the Fed would let him buy Lehman.

Board general counsel Scott Alvarez and I investigated Lewis's complaint. The concerns expressed by the Richmond Fed seemed reasonable. Bank of America had recently raised $20 billion in capital, but its acquisition of Countrywide exposed it to potentially large mortgage losses. The Richmond Fed had a good case for pushing Bank of America to add more capital, for example, by retaining more of its earnings and paying out less to shareholders. Importantly, though, based on the information available, Richmond supervisors did not rule out another acquisition, if it made sense for Bank of America. That was good news. It meant that one of our best options for avoiding the collapse of Lehman remained viable.

Fuld's frenetic attempts to strengthen his firm were not bearing fruit and the endgame looked to be approaching. On September 9, Board economist Patrick Parkinson told me that on September 18 Lehman would disclose another substantial loss—$3.9 billion for the third quarter. He added that Geithner and Cox planned to tell Fuld that, if he didn't raise capital, he would have to consider bankruptcy. Their goal was to shock Fuld into action. We were also concerned about the company's funding, including its reliance on about $200 billion from the tri-party repo market. Eric Rosengren, who had good contacts in the mutual fund industry, reported that key lenders were already pulling back from Lehman. "They would move more quickly," Eric wrote, "but they do not want to be blamed for triggering an event." Meanwhile, JPMorgan, Lehman's clearing bank for repo funding, demanded an additional $5 billion in collateral.

Wednesday, September 10, began with more dour conference calls and meetings. Lehman had no promising leads for raising capital. Rosengren reported that if the credit agencies downgraded Lehman, some lenders were saying that they would have to pull away completely.

It seemed increasingly obvious that finding a purchaser—or at least a major investor willing to buy a large part of the company—might be the only way to avoid Lehman's collapse. No new buyers had surfaced. Ken Lewis and Bank of America still seemed the best bet.

Unfortunately, given all that was going on, I had a longstanding commitment to visit the St. Louis Fed. Normally, I found Reserve Bank visits—and the chance to meet local board members, employees, and business leaders—valuable. But with Lehman unresolved and a regular FOMC meeting coming up the next week, I regretted that I had agreed to this one. That evening I attended a dinner for past and present members of the St. Louis Fed board. Early the next morning, in my hotel room and not yet dressed, I received a call from Hank Paulson. He was worried that Lewis was getting cold feet. Would I call him?

I reached Lewis and we talked for about twenty minutes. I urged him to continue with his evaluation of Lehman's books and its fit with Bank of America. I reiterated a message already sent by the supervisory staff—his bank needed to strengthen its capital over time, but we did not think that Bank of America's current capital position would preclude its acquisition of Lehman, provided the deal made business sense. Lewis agreed to continue to look at Lehman and bring a team to New York. I felt encouraged. His reaction to the financial storm was to look for bargains rather than to hunker down.

Bespectacled, quiet, and reserved, Lewis had nevertheless maintained the hard-charging style of his predecessor, Hugh McColl. Through a series of aggressive acquisitions, in Florida, Texas, and elsewhere in the South, McColl—a former marine from South Carolina—had transformed NCNB (North Carolina National Bank) into a regional powerhouse called NationsBank. In 1998, four years after Congress substantially reduced restrictions on banks branching across state lines, McColl's bank became the first with coast-to-coast operations when it acquired Bank of America, which had been founded in 1904 in San Francisco by the legendary A. P. Giannini. Though NationsBank was the acquirer, it took the better-known name of the acquired company. After McColl retired in 2001, the Mississippi-born Lewis took over. He had joined NCNB in 1969 as a credit analyst, after putting himself through Georgia State University. As CEO, he focused mostly on consolidating the acquisitions made under McColl's leadership, although his acquisition of FleetBoston in 2004 gave Bank of America a foothold in New England.

I FLEW BACK to Washington on Thursday, September 11. The FOMC meeting was scheduled for Tuesday, September 16, and, with my focus on Lehman, I had not prepared as much as usual. Don offered to help me. Between the two of us, on Friday we called most of the Reserve Bank presidents to discuss policy choices, and I also visited with the other Board members.

The economic outlook appeared little changed from August. The combination of rising inflation and a slowing economy continued to pose the classic central banker's dilemma. We could not simultaneously damp inflation with higher interest rates and stimulate growth with lower interest rates. Consumer prices were up a troubling 5.4 percent from a year earlier, reflecting both high commodity prices and more broad-based pressures. But at the same time, after a surprisingly strong spring, the economy was clearly weakening. The unemployment rate had jumped sharply in August—to 6.1 percent from 5.7 percent the month before.

The rise in inflation had stirred up the FOMC hawks. Before the August 5 meeting, the private-sector boards of three Reserve Banks—Kansas City, Dallas, and Chicago—had recommended raising interest rates. Generally, the private-sector boards are heavily influenced by the views of the local Reserve Bank president, so these "recommendations" signaled, none too subtly, the positions of at least three FOMC participants. The hawks were backed by the usual suspects, including the *Wall Street Journal* editorial page, which thundered against our "reckless easing." The doves had been pushing back. They argued in public remarks that financial turmoil was diluting the effect of monetary medicine and that a stronger dose was needed. Banks were tightening credit standards, they pointed out, and important interest rates like the rate on car loans had not fallen by as much as the Federal Reserve's target rate.

From my consultations, I concluded that the center of the Committee favored holding policy steady, at least for now. I shared that view and was working to prevent a victory for the hawks. The wait-and-see approach appeared to have been winning the day abroad as well. The European Central Bank, after its rate increase in July, had held steady in August. The Bank of Canada and the Bank of England had also made no changes to their key interest rates.

BY FRIDAY, SEPTEMBER 12, the media were widely reporting the government's efforts to find a solution for Lehman. Fuld continued to talk about his good bank–bad bank plan and the possibility of selling Neuberger Berman, but the markets weren't listening. Lehman's stock had sold for $4.22 at the end of trading on Thursday, 7 percent of its value in February. Worse, a broad-based run appeared to be under way. So many customers and counterparties were demanding cash or additional collateral that the firm was unable to process the requests.

On Friday morning I had breakfast with Hank at the Treasury. We agreed we had to do what we could to avoid a messy failure of Lehman. I did not press him on statements the Treasury had leaked to the effect that Hank had ruled out putting government money into Lehman.* I knew that those statements were partly the product of Hank's frustration—understandably, he didn't like being the public face of Wall Street bailouts—and partly tactical, an effort to incentivize the private sector to come up with its own solution. I also

---

*   Paulson, in his memoir, said Geithner did press him on the issue: "Tim expressed concern about my public stand on government aid: he said that if we ended up having to help a Lehman buyer, I would lose credibility. But I was willing to say 'no government assistance' to help us get a deal. If we had to reverse ourselves over the weekend, so be it."

knew that any government money would come from the Fed, not the Treasury.

Most importantly, I knew from my experience of working with Hank that he would do whatever he could to avoid the horrific consequences we knew Lehman's failure would bring. We had worked together to rescue Bear Stearns in March, and we continued to believe that had been the right decision. Lehman was 50 percent bigger than Bear had been on the eve of its acquisition and at least as interconnected (its derivatives "book" was twice the size that Bear's had been). Moreover, financial markets and the economy were, if anything, more fragile now. We still worried about the stability of the repo market—the most important motivation for my support of the Bear rescue. Lehman's repo borrowings were twice what Bear's had been.

It appeared that Lehman's fate would be determined over the weekend. Tim Geithner invited the CEOs of major financial institutions to a meeting Friday evening at the New York Fed. Lehman and Bank of America, as a potential acquirer, were excluded. Attendees included the heads of the other major investment firms—Lloyd Blankfein of Goldman Sachs, John Thain of Merrill Lynch, and John Mack of Morgan Stanley—as well as the heads of major U.S. banks, including Jamie Dimon of JPMorgan Chase, Vikram Pandit of Citigroup, and Bob Kelly from Bank of New York Mellon. Foreign banks at the table included Credit Suisse (Brady Dougan), the French bank BNP Paribas (Everett Schenk), the Royal Bank of Scotland (Ellen Alemany), and the Swiss bank UBS (Robert Wolf).

Tim's goal was a deal that would save Lehman. The process would move on two tracks. On the first track, teams of specialists would evaluate Lehman's assets and try to determine its true value. A team from Bank of America had already made a start. We were encouraged that some interest in Lehman was now arriving from a new quarter, the British bank Barclays. One of the world's largest and oldest banks (it traced its roots back to 1690), Barclays, like Bank of America, wanted to increase its presence in investment banking.

On the second track, the Wall Street CEOs would, in cooperation with the Fed, the Treasury, and the SEC, try to develop alternative plans for Lehman. Most likely, we thought as the weekend began,
the CEOs would provide financial support or guarantees to assist the
acquisition of Lehman by either Bank of America or Barclays. Alternatively, in the absence of a single purchaser, we would look for some
cooperative arrangement through which the industry as a whole might
prevent the disorderly collapse of the firm. The analogy to the rescue of
Long-Term Capital Management again came to mind. Almost exactly
ten years earlier, the New York Fed had provided a group of financial
CEOs a meeting venue (and sandwiches and coffee), but no financial
assistance. With the Fed acting as a facilitator, the CEOs chipped in
enough money to allow LTCM to wind down gradually.

As in the LTCM episode, in September 2008 we hoped the private
sector could find a solution for Lehman, if it came to that. But this
time the CEOs had far more concern about the stability of their own
companies. Moreover, stresses at Merrill Lynch and the massive insurance company AIG were becoming increasingly evident, and some
participants worried that Lehman would be only the first of a series of
market shocks. Getting them to contribute funds, particularly to help
competitors, might prove difficult.

MEANWHILE, AS WHAT became known as Lehman weekend
approached, popular, political, and media views were hardening against
the idea of the Fed and the Treasury taking extraordinary measures
to prevent the firm's failure. It seemed that the most that would be
tolerated was our perhaps looking for a private-sector buyer. At their
nominating convention in early September, rank-and-file Republicans
had been unequivocal: no bailouts. The powerful senior Republican
on the Senate Banking Committee, Richard Shelby, echoed that view.
(President Bush and Senator John McCain, the Republican presidential nominee, held more nuanced positions.)

The media piled on. London's respected *Financial Times* noted the government takeover two weeks earlier of Fannie Mae and Freddie Mac, adding, "Further such rescues should be avoided like the plague." The *Wall Street Journal* opined: "If the feds step in to save Lehman after Bear and Fannie Mae, we will no longer have exceptions forged in a crisis. We will have a new de facto federal policy of underwriting Wall Street that will encourage even more reckless risk-taking." Our challenge that weekend went beyond finding a solution for Lehman. We would have to do so in the face of bitter criticism.

Some of the critics were ideologues (the free market is always right) or uninformed (the economy will be just fine if a few Wall Street firms get their just deserts). Some simply railed against the unfairness of bailing out Wall Street giants but not the little guy on Main Street. Personally, I felt considerable sympathy for this last argument. (I would wince every time I saw a bumper sticker reading "Where's my bailout?") But it was in everyone's interest, whether or not they realized it, to protect the economy from the consequences of a catastrophic failure of the financial system.

The opponents' most substantive argument was that, whatever the short-run benefits of bailouts, protecting firms from the consequences of their own risky behavior would lead to riskier behavior in the longer run. I certainly agreed that, in a capitalist system, the market must be allowed to discipline individuals or firms that make bad decisions. Frank Borman, the former astronaut who became CEO of Eastern Airlines (which went bankrupt), put it nicely a quarter-century earlier: "Capitalism without bankruptcy is like Christianity without hell." But in September 2008 I was absolutely convinced that invoking moral hazard in the middle of a major financial crisis was misguided and dangerous. I am sure that Paulson and Geithner agreed.

"You have a neighbor, who smokes in bed. . . . Suppose he sets fire to his house," I would say later in an interview. "You might say to yourself . . . 'I'm not gonna call the fire department. Let his house burn down. It's fine with me.' But then, of course, what if your house is made of wood? And it's right next door to his house? What if the whole town is made of wood?" The editorial writers of the *Financial Times* and the *Wall Street Journal* in September 2008 would, presumably, have argued for letting the fire burn. Saving the sleepy smoker would only encourage others to smoke in bed. But a much better course is to put out the fire, then punish the smoker, and, if necessary, make and enforce new rules to promote fire safety.

The firefighting argument applied equally well to Lehman Brothers. We had little doubt a Lehman failure would massively disrupt financial markets and impose heavy costs on many parties other than Lehman's shareholders, managers, and creditors, including millions of people around the world who would be hurt by its economic shockwaves. In the many discussions in which I was involved, I never heard anyone from the Fed or the Treasury suggest that letting Lehman fail would be anything other than a disaster, or that we should contemplate allowing the firm to fail. We needed to put the fire out.

Tough talk in the negotiation was still required, of course. If the private-sector participants were certain that the government would swoop in with a solution, they would have little incentive to commit their own funds. Tim Geithner, in talking points prepared for the Friday evening meeting and sent to me for my approval, proposed to give the CEOs plenty of incentive to come up with their own plan to prevent Lehman's collapse.

"A sudden and disorderly unwind could have broad adverse effects on the capital markets, with a significant risk of a precipitous drop in asset prices," he proposed to tell them. "The financial community needs to come together to fashion an orderly resolution. . . . I cannot offer the prospect of containing the damage if that doesn't occur." Tim was clear about the risks of letting Lehman fail, and I believe that most or all of the CEOs appreciated the risks as well.

What Tim wanted, what we all wanted, was for the CEOs to act in their own and the broader interest and work with the government. As his talking points indicated, he would ask them to lend their analytical talents and provide capital if necessary. The Fed would facilitate necessary regulatory approvals and provide regular collateralized lending (which was within our powers) but not "extraordinary credit support." The term "extraordinary credit support" was vague, which I assume was Tim's intention. The gathered CEOs might presume that, even if Lehman was deeply insolvent, the government would find some way to fill the hole. By offering lending but no extraordinary credit support, we would be pushing back against that presumption. As a central bank, we had the ability to lend against a broad range of collateral, but we had no legal authority to overpay for bad assets or otherwise absorb Lehman's losses.

The weekend was a blur. Paulson, Geithner, Cox, and Kevin Warsh were in New York for the negotiations. With the possibility that the Board would have to meet over the weekend to approve the acquisition of Lehman, I remained in Washington, spending most of my time in my office. Michelle Smith brought sandwiches. We used frequent conference calls to keep the Treasury, the Fed, and the SEC on the same page. (The speakerphone on the coffee table in my office on which I took the calls began to figure in my dreams.) I catnapped on the burgundy leather sofa in my office, going home, briefly, late on Friday and Saturday.

The reports I received on Friday evening and Saturday morning were discouraging. Both Bank of America and Barclays had found losses in Lehman's balance sheet to be much bigger than expected. They were looking for the government to put up $40–$50 billion in new capital. I asked Tim whether they were overstating the numbers as a ploy to obtain a better deal or as an excuse to end negotiations. Tim acknowledged the possibility but reminded me that other firms, including Goldman Sachs and Credit Suisse, were independently reviewing parts of Lehman's portfolio, in preparation for the possibility that, as part of a larger solution, certain assets might be sold or used as collateral for loans. The third-party firms had independently estimated the values of Lehman's assets—especially the commercial real estate—at well less than Lehman's values.

As much as I wanted to avoid Lehman's failure, the reports gave me pause about our two strategies—finding a buyer or building a consortium. None of the firms represented in the New York Fed's conference room was in terrific financial shape. Would combining shaky balance sheets through an acquisition (by a single firm or a consortium) lead to a stronger financial system, or would it simply result in an even bigger blowup later? My mind went back to my own studies of the Great Depression of the 1930s. The most catastrophic financial failure of that period was the collapse of the Kreditanstalt, the largest bank in Austria, in May 1931. Its failure toppled other banks and, perhaps, helped derail nascent economic recoveries in the United States and Europe. One reason for its failure had been an earlier forced merger with another, weaker Austrian bank, whose own losses had helped pushed the larger bank over the edge.

At this point in the crisis, the U.S. institution with the strongest balance sheet, with the greatest capacity to borrow and invest without raising concerns about its creditworthiness, was the federal government. To me, it seemed increasingly likely that the only way to end the crisis would be to persuade Congress to invest taxpayer funds in U.S. financial institutions. I began to make this point on our conference calls over the weekend.

As Saturday wore on, it became evident that Lehman was deeply insolvent, even allowing for the likelihood that fire sales and illiquid markets had pushed the values of its assets to artificially low levels. Fuld would later claim Lehman wasn't broke, but the capital figures he cited were based on the firm's inflated asset valuations and greatly overstated the true capital. Lehman's insolvency made it impossible to save with Fed lending alone. Even when invoking our 13(3) emergency authority, we were required to lend against adequate collateral. The Fed has no authority to inject capital or (what is more or less the same thing) make a loan that we were not reasonably sure could be fully repaid.

We could have used our lending powers to facilitate an acquisition, but Lehman's financial weakness was also a big problem for any firm considering buying it. Whatever the long-run benefits of gaining Lehman's business, its losses would be tough for the acquirer to absorb in the near term. I hoped that we would get some help from the CEOs who had assembled in Tim's conference room. But they were unenthusiastic, being acutely aware that their own resources were limited and might well be essential to their survival if the crisis worsened.

Bad news arrived on other fronts. The private equity firm J.C. Flowers & Co., run by billionaire former Goldman Sachs partner J. Christopher Flowers, reported that AIG was also in dire trouble. Losses in its massive derivatives positions were resulting in calls for more collateral by its counterparties. And of course, the three investment banks other than Lehman—Merrill Lynch, Morgan Stanley, Goldman Sachs—had considerable reason for anxiety if Lehman failed. The market seemed poised to attack the weakest remaining member of the herd.

After Lehman, that was clearly Merrill Lynch, which had made many of the same investment mistakes. Established in 1914, Merrill had done more than any other firm to, in founder Charles Merrill's phrase, "bring Wall Street to Main Street." It prospered in the years after World War I, betting on the success of motion pictures and chain stores. Before the 1929 stock market crash, Merrill famously warned clients to get out of debt. His firm survived the Depression and by 1941 was the world's largest securities house. However, Merrill had bet heavily on residential and commercial mortgage lending just as the real estate boom was turning into a bust. After Stan O'Neal resigned as CEO in October 2007, he was replaced by John Thain, the former CEO of the New York Stock Exchange.

I tried to prepare for the FOMC meeting on Tuesday but found it difficult to concentrate on the meeting materials. In between calls with New York, I did what I could to keep others in the loop on the Lehman negotiations. I spoke with the Fed Board members and Reserve Bank presidents and several members of Congress. I avoided false optimism, but I did not want to appear defeatist, either. At 10:00 a.m. on Saturday, I held a conference call with foreign central bankers, including Mervyn King of the Bank of England, Jean-Claude Trichet of the ECB, and Masaaki Shirakawa of the Bank of Japan. Trichet was particularly exercised about the possibility that no solution for Lehman might be found; he said the company's failure would lead to a "total meltdown." I told him I agreed and that we would do everything we could. King gave me an important piece of information: He had heard that the Financial Services Authority, which supervised Britain's banking system, was very concerned about bringing Lehman's bad assets into Barclays, particularly given uncertainties about the flagship British bank's own condition. I asked if he could weigh in on the issue and he said he would try.

Sunday morning's news was worse than Saturday's. Bank of America was now definitely out of the running for Lehman. (Ken Lewis would later report that he had told Paulson that Lehman's assets were worth $60–$70 billion less than their official valuation.) The small silver lining was that Lewis was negotiating with Thain to acquire Merrill Lynch, which he viewed as both in better shape than Lehman and a better fit for Bank of America. Bank of America had a huge retail banking footprint, and Merrill, whose army of brokers was nicknamed the "thundering herd," had the largest retail operation of any of the investment banks. Paulson had strongly encouraged Thain to consider Lewis's offer, and Thain—an experienced Wall Street operator—knew which way the wind was blowing. Taking Merrill off the market would mean one less large investment bank in danger of failing, although if Merrill was secured the pressure would likely shift to the remaining two firms, Morgan Stanley and Goldman.

Moreover, the Barclays option for Lehman was looking less and less likely. As Mervyn King had warned, the Financial Services Authority was reluctant to approve the acquisition. The authority, led by Callum McCarthy, worried that, if Barclays acquired Lehman, the responsibility for its bad assets would ultimately wind up on the British government's doorstep. This could be the case if the acquisition forced a bailout of Barclays. Given the seriousness of the threat posed to global financial stability by a Lehman bankruptcy, I had expected that the British could be brought around. That did not seem to be happening.

A difference between U.S. and UK securities law—first brought to my attention by King, then confirmed by Geithner—also posed a problem. Under British law, Barclays would not be allowed to guarantee Lehman's liabilities until after the acquisition was approved by Barclays' shareholders, a process that could take weeks or months. The JPMorgan acquisition of Bear Stearns had calmed markets because JPMorgan was able to guarantee Bear's liabilities while shareholder approval was pending. With no unconditional guarantee in place for Lehman, a run could destroy the firm, even if Barclays agreed to a deal in principle. Hank reported that he had appealed to his British counterpart, Alistair Darling, chancellor of the exchequer, for a waiver of the shareholder approval requirement. Darling refused to cooperate, on the grounds that suspending the rule would be "overriding the rights of millions of shareholders." Moreover, he shared McCarthy's concern that, if Barclays acquired Lehman, the British taxpayer might end up footing the bill for bad investments made by an American company, a hard thing to explain to Parliament.

A call from Tim dashed my remaining hopes. He said that there was no buyer for Lehman. He confirmed that Bank of America was negotiating with Merrill Lynch. Barclays would not be able to resolve its regulatory issues in time to guarantee Lehman's liabilities. I asked Tim whether it would work for us to lend to Lehman on the broadest possible collateral to try to keep the firm afloat.

"No," Tim said. "We would only be lending into an unstoppable run." He elaborated that, without a buyer to guarantee Lehman's liabilities and to establish the firm's viability, no Fed loan could save it. Even if we lent against Lehman's most marginal assets, its private-sector creditors and counterparties would simply take the opportunity to pull their funds as quickly as possible. Moreover, much of the company's value—certainly the part that had initially interested Lewis and Bank of America—was as a going concern, based on its expertise, relationships, and reputation. In a full-blown run, already well under way, the firm's going-concern value would be lost almost immediately, as customers and specialized employees abandoned ship. We would be left holding Lehman's bad assets, having selectively bailed out the creditors who could exit the most quickly, and the firm would fail anyway. "Our whole strategy was based on finding a buyer," Tim said. It was a question of practicality as much as legality. Without a buyer, and with no authority to inject fresh capital or guarantee Lehman's assets, we had no means of saving the firm.

It was a terrible, almost surreal moment. We were staring into the abyss. I pressed Tim for an alternative solution, but he had none. It seemed the next step would be to prepare for a bankruptcy, which would be filed shortly after midnight on Sunday night. "All we can do," Tim said, in a classic Geithner-ism, "is put foam on the runway." The phrase itself conveyed what we all knew: Lehman's collapse, like the crash landing of a jumbo jet, would be an epic disaster, and, while we should do whatever we could, there wasn't much we could do.

Knowing that Lehman's collapse would likely cause short-term lending markets to freeze and increase the panicky hoarding of cash, we increased the availability of funding from the Fed. At an emergency meeting at noon on Sunday, the Board substantially broadened the range of assets acceptable as collateral for Fed loans. To backstop the repo market, we said we would accept any asset that was normally used as collateral on the private repo market. We also expanded the size of some of our lending programs and temporarily relaxed Section 23A restrictions on the ability of banks to provide financing to affiliated securities dealers. Bagehot's advice still guided us: We were fighting a financial panic by providing essentially unlimited short-term credit to fundamentally solvent financial institutions and markets. We would also continue to lend to Lehman on a day-to-day basis, to the extent that it had acceptable collateral, to facilitate Barclays' purchase of Lehman's broker-dealer subsidiary (a relatively healthy, but relatively small, part of the firm). Barclays would repay us when the acquisition was completed. All these steps, I thought, might help reduce the effect of Lehman's failure.

In the short run, unfortunately, our efforts would be like throwing a few buckets of water on a five-alarm fire. Lehman's failure fanned the flames of the financial panic, and the bankruptcy proceedings would drag on for years—more proof, if it were needed, that traditional bankruptcy procedures are entirely inadequate for a major financial firm that fails in the midst of a financial crisis.

For Wall Street old-timers, the events of the weekend would evoke some nostalgia. Two iconic Wall Street firms that had survived world wars and depressions, Lehman and Merrill, had disappeared in a weekend. I felt no nostalgia at all. I knew that the risks the two firms had taken had endangered not only the companies but the global economy, with unknowable consequences.

A few Board members and senior staff were still in the building on Sunday evening. Some of the staff were assisting efforts to unwind some of Lehman's derivatives positions, in the hope of reducing the chaos that we knew would follow the company's filing. I updated my colleagues and made a few more calls to foreign central banks and to Capitol Hill. I joined yet another conference call with the New York Fed and the Treasury. Then I went home.

CHAPTER 13

AIG: "It Makes Me Angry"

L ehman's bankruptcy filing, at 1:45 a.m. Monday, September 15, reverberated through financial markets—at first abroad, then in the United States. Don Kohn, Kevin Warsh, Tim Geithner, and I convened a 9:00 a.m. call to assess the market developments. By day's end, the Dow Jones industrial average would plummet 504 points, its worst one-day decline in seven years. AIG's stock price would drop by more than half. And shares for Morgan Stanley and Goldman Sachs, the two remaining independent investment banks, would lose an eighth of their value.

Even though the stock market would be the focus of that evening's financial news, as it was on most days, we were far more concerned with funding markets, including the repo and commercial paper markets, where the cost of borrowing would as much as double on Monday. Swings in stock prices can have modest economic consequences, at least in the short term. But the economy would remain at great risk until funding markets, which supplied crucial credit to financial and nonfinancial companies alike, began to operate normally again.

Rather than lend to a company or financial institution that could default, investors fled to the safety of U.S. Treasury securities on Monday, demanding as little as a 0.21 percent rate to lend to the government for one month. Banks hoarded cash and the federal funds rate spiked to 6 percent—far above the FOMC's 2 percent target—until the New York Fed could flood money markets with a temporary infusion of $70 billion that morning.

At 10:00 a.m., staff economists, as usual on the day before an FOMC meeting, briefed the Board on the economic outlook. We could speculate, but it was too soon to know the extent of the wider damage from the weekend's events. At 6:00 p.m., Senator Obama, by this time the Democratic nominee for president, called for an update. I told him that the economic consequences of the Lehman failure, while uncertain, could be very serious. He listened carefully and asked a few questions. His tone was subdued, and if he had any opinions he kept them to himself. We also discussed Fannie and Freddie. I talked up their recent takeover by the government as an essential, positive first step toward stabilizing the housing market. I said that the clearest message of recent events was that Congress would need to overhaul the financial regulatory system. We agreed on that, but we also agreed that nothing was likely to happen until after a new president was inaugurated in January.

AS THE LEHMAN drama played out over the weekend, we had also been keeping an eye on AIG, whose trillion-dollar insurance operations spanned 130 countries. CEO Robert Willumstad, who had joined AIG three months earlier, after long experience at Citigroup, had told Tim the previous Friday that the company could soon run out of cash. On Friday evening, AIG executives had asked Board staff members about the possibility of a loan from the Federal Reserve. They warned about the prospect of an imminent downgrade of the company's credit rating, which would lead to even more demands for cash and collateral as counterparties sought to protect themselves from a possible default.

We had no responsibility for regulating or supervising AIG; nevertheless, we had it on our radar over the summer. AIG's biggest business was selling ordinary life insurance and property insurance, and its U.S. operations were overseen primarily by state regulators. These regulators were supposed to ensure that AIG's subsidiary companies were properly run and prepared to meet the claims of policyholders. However, the holding company that tied together AIG's many businesses (including its foreign operations and businesses not involved in insurance) was not subject to oversight by insurance regulators. Because it happened to own a small savings and loan, the gargantuan holding company came under the regulatory purview of the small and understaffed Office of Thrift Supervision—an incredible mismatch of expertise and resources. Until the days leading up to Lehman weekend, the OTS hadn't hinted that AIG might be in serious trouble, although Willumstad's appointment in June had come after the company reported significant losses on securities tied to subprime mortgages.

AIG GOT ITS START in China in 1919, when an adventurous twenty-seven-year-old college dropout from California, Cornelius Vander Starr, quit his job as a clerk at a steamship company in Yokohama, Japan, and moved to Shanghai. There he founded a general insurance company, the American Asiatic Underwriters, in a two-room office. In 1967, after decades of impressive expansion, Starr created the holding company AIG to serve as an umbrella for businesses in North America, Europe, Latin America, and the Middle East as well as Asia. Maurice "Hank" Greenberg succeeded Starr as CEO in 1968 and took the company public a year later. The son of a taxi driver from the Bronx, Greenberg ran away from home at seventeen to fight in World War II and helped to liberate the Dachau concentration camp. Described as "dominant, brilliant, irascible, short tempered, controlling, obsessive," he transformed AIG into the largest insurance company in the world.

AIG's principal threat to U.S. financial stability came not from its regular insurance operations but from its large-scale entry into the derivatives business. In 1987, Greenberg had created a subsidiary of the holding company called AIG Financial Products, or AIG FP. Although AIG FP traded many types of financial instruments, by the late 1990s a centerpiece of its business amounted to selling insurance by a different name. The customers were U.S. and European banks and other financial institutions that wanted protection against the possibility of large losses in their collateralized debt obligations, which packaged together many types of private debt (in this case, mostly mortgages and other real estate–related debt). In exchange for regular payments—insurance premiums, essentially—AIG agreed to make good any losses to those securities exceeding specified amounts. This insurance was offered through derivatives called credit default swaps.

It looked like a win-win proposition. Because of AIG's high credit rating, its CDO insurance customers did not insist that AIG put aside significant reserves against loss. Meanwhile, the banks and other institutions buying this insurance were able to show their regulators that they had secured protection against the possibility of large losses on their CDOs, which in turn allowed them to reduce the capital they held to meet regulatory requirements. AIG did not increase its capital when it sold protection, so the total amount of capital in the financial system standing behind the CDOs was effectively reduced.

A well-run insurance company, under the watchful eye of its regulator, will protect itself from the risk of catastrophic loss by holding substantial capital and reserves, limiting its exposure to any single risk, and selling off part of the risks it assumes to other insurers (a practice known as reinsurance). From an economic point of view, AIG FP was selling insurance, but it was effectively unregulated and its transactions were not subject to rules that governed conventional insurance. Nor did it take precautions on its own, which left it unprepared for the shock of the crisis.

Hank Greenberg had long been aware of the riskiness of AIG FP's derivatives positions. In 1993, after the unit stumbled badly and lost $100 million on a single bet, he decided to replace the subsidiary's founding president, Howard Sosin. Greenberg reportedly told the new president, Tom Savage: "You guys up at FP ever do anything to my triple-A rating, and I'm coming after you with a pitchfork." But Greenberg was evidently unwilling or unable to curtail AIG FP's risky activities. Most of the credit default swaps that brought AIG FP to grief were originated between 2003 and 2005. Greenberg lost his own job in March 2005. The AIG board forced him to resign after the Securi-

274 THE COURAGE TO ACT

ties and Exchange Commission and the Department of Justice discovered fraudulent accounting practices that ultimately cost the company a ratings downgrade and a $1.6 billion fine. Greenberg was replaced by longtime AIG executive Martin J. Sullivan. Sullivan in turn was replaced by Willumstad, who had joined AIG's board after Greenberg's resignation.

AIG FP's risk was compounded by the difficulty in valuing its highly complex positions, in part because the securities that the company was insuring were themselves so complex and hard to value. As early as 1998, *Fortune* magazine reported, "Fact is, many Wall Streeters have given up really analyzing this company: it is so complex that they think it inscrutable. They just fall back on faith, telling themselves that Greenberg will keep turning out earnings." When Robert Willumstad became CEO, he announced his intention to focus on core insurance businesses. If those plans had been completed (Willumstad had suggested an announcement could be made in September), it seemed possible that AIG FP, along with other odd components like the company's airplane leasing business, could be sold off or gradually dismantled.

The OTS, AIG's nominal regulator, showed little concern about the riskiness or opacity of AIG FP. In a July 2007 review, the OTS judged AIG FP's risk-management program adequate and called the level of credit risk it faced moderate. The OTS noted that the securities that AIG FP was insuring were highly rated by the credit agencies, and added that the subsidiary had stopped offering protection on transactions with subprime exposure in December 2005. Based on this review, the OTS saw little reason to take action. However, although AIG had not added to its bets after 2005, neither had it taken steps to reduce or hedge its existing subprime exposures.

WILLUMSTAD WAS BUSY over Lehman weekend. His company needed a great deal of cash, fast. He worked with Eric Dinallo, the New York State supervisor of insurance companies, on a plan to obtain $20 billion for AIG's holding company from its subsidiaries. He and his team were also trying to raise funds from private equity firms, including J.C. Flowers & Co. and Kohlberg Kravis Roberts (KKR).

Like Lehman, AIG seemed slow to comprehend the gravity of its position. On Saturday morning, Don Kohn reported that the company viewed its predicament as a temporary cash crunch and, notwithstanding its talks with J.C. Flowers and KKR, it wasn't considering selling core assets (such as one of its insurance subsidiaries) or finding a partner to make a major investment. I was concerned that the company was not taking its own situation seriously enough and told Don to try to get them to develop a specific and credible plan to address their problems. Reluctantly, I was already considering the possibility that we would have to step in. "I would be willing to consider lending to them against good collateral," I wrote Don, "if we have explicit and public commitments regarding the actions they will take to wean themselves and restore stability."

Don recommended that we wait and see what private-sector solutions might emerge, in the spirit of the strategy that Hank and Tim were taking with Lehman. He acknowledged that short-term Fed lending to help AIG meet its cash crunch might ultimately prove necessary but said we should do everything possible to avoid that outcome. I agreed.

On Sunday, even as Lehman was unraveling, AIG again commanded our attention. Every time we heard from the company and its potential private-sector rescuers, the amount of cash it needed seemed to grow. The value of the securities that AIG had insured was dropping, and its counterparties were demanding more collateral to protect themselves should the company prove unable to meet its commitments. Moreover, AIG—through another subsidiary—had unwisely doubled down on its bet on the mortgage market by investing in large quantities of private-label mortgage-backed securities, whose value was now also sharply declining. AIG had financed its holdings of private-label MBS through a form of financing called securities lending—for practical purposes, an activity equivalent to borrowing in the repo market—using securities owned by its subsidiary insurance companies as collateral. The providers of the funding to AIG had the right to demand the return of their cash on one day's notice, and, as the concerns grew about AIG's stability, many of them exercised that right. By Sunday evening, it looked like AIG needed $60 billion in cash to meet its contractual obligations. By Monday morning, some projections of the company's cash needs exceeded $80 billion.

Meanwhile, AIG's negotiations with potential investors had not gone well. On Sunday morning, J.C. Flowers and KKR made offers for parts of the company, but AIG's board rejected them as inadequate. And as estimates of the company's cash needs grew, the interest of potential buyers waned. With the company apparently days away from being unable to pay its creditors, its representatives—including its vice chairman, Jacob Frenkel, a onetime University of Chicago economist and former governor of the central bank of Israel—began passing the word to Don Kohn and others that it likely would need Fed assistance to survive.

By Monday we had little doubt about the magnitude of the danger that AIG posed. The company was so large and interconnected with the rest of the financial system that the ramifications of its failure would be massive, if hard to predict. With financial markets already in turmoil, what would the collapse of the world's largest insurance company do to investor confidence? What, indeed, would it do to public and investor confidence in the insurance industry, which itself constituted a large part of the financial system? I, for one, did not want to find out.

Early Monday afternoon, Paulson denied at a White House news conference that the government was working on a loan for AIG. "What is going on right now in New York has got nothing to do with any bridge loan from the government. What's going on in New York is a private-sector effort," he said. At that point Hank, frustrated by our inability to save Lehman and trapped between growing anti-bailout rage and the prospect of a collapsing financial system, was still hoping against hope for a private-sector AIG deal. But that outcome looked more and more unlikely.

At 5:00 p.m. Monday, Mike Gibson, a Board economist who would later head our banking supervision division, filled me in on a call he and other Board staff had had with AIG, the New York state insurance regulator, and the New York Fed. AIG's plan was evolving. Its executives had stopped talking about a private equity deal, Mike said. They were hoping now for a Federal Reserve loan collateralized by a grab bag of assets ranging from its airplane-leasing division to ski resorts.

As the panic worsened, problems metastasized. I received a message from the San Francisco Fed, reporting that Washington Mutual would be downgraded by S&P and likely also by Fitch. "Deposits are 'slipping,'" the report added. "No lines or signs of chaos, but a definite reduction in deposits." Don reported that he and Randy Kroszner had spoken again with both John Reich at the OTS and Sheila Bair at the FDIC. Sheila, concerned about the risks that WaMu posed to the deposit insurance fund, continued to push for a sale of the company as soon as possible. Nonfinancial companies were also feeling the pressure. I was told that Ford Motor Company, which relied on the commercial paper market to finance much of its daily operations, was concerned about its funding and wanted to talk to us. I felt like I was juggling hand grenades. Financial panics are a collective loss of the confidence essential for keeping the system functioning. If we couldn't find a way to stabilize the situation soon, I thought, it would get radically worse.

Tim Geithner and staff at the New York Fed worked late into the night on Monday, trying to find a solution for AIG. (Tim's energy and ability to concentrate for long stretches always astonished me. His metabolism seemed supercharged. At FOMC meeting breaks he would inhale doughnuts, but nevertheless remained slim.) Michelle Smith reported that Tim thought "there's some real possibility" the AIG rescue would fail. I called Tim and we agreed it made sense for him to skip the FOMC meeting the next morning and stay in New York to keep working on AIG. His first vice president, Christine Cumming, would represent the New York Fed at the meeting.

ON TUESDAY MORNING, an hour before the scheduled start of the FOMC meeting, I was on a conference call about AIG that included Paulson, Geithner, and Board members Kevin Warsh and Betsy Duke. With the private equity firms out of the picture and no nibbles from investment banks that had reviewed AIG's assets, the solution—if there was one—would have to involve Fed lending. Tim outlined a plan to save the company that had been developed overnight. Paulson and I urged him to push ahead and to get back to us as soon as possible.

The call ran long, making me nearly half an hour late to the FOMC meeting. Normally, I entered the boardroom precisely at the stroke of nine. This morning, curious looks greeted me as I hurried to my seat at the table. With so much still unresolved and with time from the meeting already lost, I did not share much, only noting that the markets were "continuing to experience very significant stresses" and that AIG was an increasing concern. That, I said, explained Geithner's absence.

Monetary policy and the Lehman fallout were not the only topics of the meeting. As planned, I also asked the Committee for authority to provide additional currency swap lines to other central banks. A shortage of dollars abroad was among the factors driving up short-term interest rates for both U.S. and foreign banks. Expanding the swaps program would allow us to supply more dollars to foreign central banks, who could then lend to their own domestic banks, with the hope of calming those funding markets. The Committee expanded the limits on the existing swap lines with the European Central Bank and the Swiss National Bank and authorized new swap lines with the Bank of England, the Bank of Canada, and the Bank of Japan.

Bill Dudley's briefing on the markets was grim. The Dow, after falling nearly 4-1/2 percent on Monday, had resumed its decline. Short-term borrowing costs continued to increase rapidly. Pressure was also mounting on Goldman Sachs and Morgan Stanley. Their funding was drying up, other firms were reluctant to enter into derivatives contracts with them, and hedge funds and other important customers, worried that one or both companies might follow the path of Lehman, were moving their accounts elsewhere. Perhaps even worse, panicked investors were reportedly pulling out of a money market fund called the Reserve Primary Fund. If withdrawals spread to other money market funds, it would open a new front in the crisis.

Money market funds, which are regulated by the SEC, are mutual funds that generally invest in very safe and liquid assets, like short-term Treasury securities and highly rated commercial paper. They mimic bank accounts by allowing check-writing and by fixing the price of a share at $1—meaning investors could reasonably expect to suffer no losses. Many individual investors kept some cash in money funds, usually in connection with a broader brokerage account. Institutions, including corporations, municipal governments, and pension funds, also found money funds to be a convenient place to park their cash.

The Reserve Primary Fund—which was managed by Reserve Management, the company that opened the first money market fund in 1971—took more risks than many, which allowed it to pay higher returns on average. The higher returns attracted investors, and the fund grew rapidly. However, as we would learn, the Reserve Primary Fund had invested about $785 million in Lehman's commercial paper. With that commercial paper now essentially worthless, the Reserve Primary Fund's assets were now worth less than $1 per share. In the jargon of Wall Street, it had "broken the buck," the first mutual fund to do so in fourteen years. Hoping to escape before the Reserve Primary Fund's managers decided to halt withdrawals at the fixed price of $1 per share, investors had started pulling out their cash, and a run on the fund had begun. About $40 billion would be withdrawn by the end of the day on Tuesday, almost two-thirds of the fund's value. In subsequent days the run would spread to other money market funds, threatening the stability of the entire industry and endangering the cash holdings of households, corporations, and nonprofit organizations. And, with money flowing out of the funds, financial institutions and nonfinancial companies alike would have difficulty selling the commercial paper they depended upon to meet payrolls and finance inventories.

But these concerns, as serious as they were, were not the greatest that we faced that day. "Of course, we have the issue of AIG," Bill continued. AIG, although not a bank, was also experiencing something like a run. Lenders and other counterparties were increasingly reluctant to deal with it, and the firms that had purchased AIG insurance on their collateralized debt obligations were demanding more cash as a guarantee that AIG would make good on its commitments. The race was on to find a solution, but neither Bill nor I had anything concrete yet to report.

With time very short, the rest of the meeting was compressed. Many participants saw signs of further slowing in the economy and saw inflation concerns as a bit reduced. I reiterated my view that we were probably already in a recession. At the end of the discussion we modified our planned statement to note market developments but also agreed, unanimously, to leave the federal funds rate unchanged at 2 percent.

In retrospect, that decision was certainly a mistake. Part of the reason for our choice was lack of time—lack of time in the meeting itself, and insufficient time to judge the effects of Lehman's collapse. Don and I had worked hard the previous week to achieve a consensus for the relatively neutral course of no change in our target interest rate, which seemed the right decision given what we knew then. In a shortened meeting, trying to change that outcome could have provoked a contentious split. There was also substantial sentiment at the meeting in favor of holding our fire until we had a better sense of how the Lehman situation would play out. Consequently, I did not push to cut rates, even though some financial market players expected that we might.

AS WE DISCUSSED monetary policy in Washington, Geithner and his team in New York rushed to draft terms for lending AIG the cash—now up to $85 billion—necessary to avoid its imminent failure. Unlike Lehman, AIG appeared to have sufficiently valuable assets—namely, its domestic and foreign insurance subsidiaries, plus other financial services companies—to serve as collateral and to meet the legal requirement that the loan be "secured to the satisfaction" of the lending Reserve Bank. Still, in lending to AIG we would be crossing a new line, and not only because AIG was an insurance company. Unlike every other loan the Fed made during the crisis, the collateral would not be loans or securities but the going-concern value of specific businesses. AIG's collateral was thus harder to value or sell than the collateral we normally accepted, and the protection it afforded was reduced by the fact that, if the AIG holding company failed, its subsidiaries serving as collateral would also lose substantial value. But we didn't see an alternative. The marketable securities available to AIG were not nearly sufficient to collateralize the size of the loan it needed.

Geithner's proposed terms for the loan—which drew heavily on the work of bankers he had asked to explore options for private financing for AIG—included a floating interest rate starting at about 11.5 percent. AIG would also be required to give the government an ownership share of almost 80 percent of the company.

Tough terms were appropriate. Given our relative unfamiliarity with the company, the difficulty of valuing AIG FP's complex derivatives positions, and the extreme conditions we were seeing in financial markets, lending such a large amount inevitably entailed significant risk. Evidently, it was risk that no private-sector firm had been willing to undertake. Taxpayers deserved adequate compensation for bearing that risk. In particular, the requirement that AIG cede a substantial part of its ownership was intended to ensure that taxpayers shared in the gains if the company recovered.

Equally important, tough terms helped address the unfairness

inherent in aiding AIG and not other firms, while also serving to mitigate the moral hazard arising from the bailout. If executives at similarly situated firms believed they would get easy terms in a government
bailout, they would have little incentive to raise capital, reduce risk, or
accept market offers for their assets or their company. The Fed and Treasury had pushed for tough terms for the shareholders of Bear Stearns
and Fannie and Freddie for precisely these reasons. The political backlash would be intense no matter what we did, but we needed to show
that we got taxpayers the best possible deal and had minimized the
windfall that the bailout gave to AIG and its shareholders.

My job was to help sell the deal to official Washington, insofar as
that was possible. The first and most important sale would be to my
own Board. I had briefed the Board members on AIG and the work
at the New York Fed during a break in the FOMC meeting, and when
the FOMC meeting ended, a Board meeting commenced—first in my
office, then, as the Reserve Bank presidents headed for their planes, in
the boardroom. By the time the meeting had moved to the boardroom,
we had received copies of Geithner's proposed set of terms, and Tim
had joined the meeting by phone.

A critical question was whether the proposed $85 billion line of
credit would in fact save the company. For us, the ultimate disaster
would be to lend such an enormous amount and then see the company collapse. We didn't know for sure, but, based on both outside and
internal reviews, we believed AIG as a whole was likely viable even
though it lacked the cash to meet immediate demands. AIG FP was
like a hedge fund sitting on top of a giant insurance company, and it,
along with the securities lending operation, was the principal source
of AIG's cash drain. If AIG FP had been a stand-alone company there
would have been no hope. But the insurance subsidiaries and other
businesses owned by AIG were for the most part healthy, as far as we
could tell, and their value potentially offered the necessary collateral
to secure our loan.

There was some circularity here: If the loan to AIG helped stabilize financial markets, then AIG's companies and assets would likely retain enough value to help repay the loan over time. But if financial conditions went from bad to worse, driving the economy deeper into recession, then the value of AIG's assets would suffer as well. And, in that case, all bets on being repaid would be off. We had to count on achieving the better outcome.

We also considered whether we could let AIG go and hope financial markets would stabilize anyway. With the markets reeling from Lehman's failure, the answer was obvious, at least to me. AIG was about the size of Lehman and Bear Stearns combined and, like those firms, deeply interconnected with the global financial system. Its failure would create chaos in so many ways: by raising doubts about the solvency of its creditors and derivative counterparties, which in many cases were critical financial institutions; by imposing losses on holders of its commercial paper (losses on Lehman's commercial paper had already triggered the run on money market funds); and by draining available cash from state funds set up to protect customers of failing insurance companies. (In some cases, state guarantee funds relied on after-the-fact assessments of the industry, so the cash would have to come directly from other insurance companies.) The drain on state insurance funds, together with the likely seizure of AIG's insurance subsidiaries by state regulators if AIG declared bankruptcy, would in turn reduce confidence in the rest of the insurance industry. We might see a wave of policy redemptions and a funding crunch for other insurance companies. AIG's many other financial activities included insuring popular investment products in retirement plans. A rapid sell-off of AIG's assets would also cause stock and bond prices to fall further, pushing more companies toward insolvency. And doubtless there were consequences we hadn't even considered yet.

I saw no alternative to the loan, conditional on the AIG board's accepting our terms. All five Fed Board members voted to approve it, fulfilling the requirement to invoke 13(3). The minutes of the meeting summarized our rationale, albeit blandly, given the circumstances:

"Board members agreed that the disorderly failure of AIG was likely to have a systemic effect on financial markets that were already experiencing a significant level of fragility and that the best alternative available was to lend to AIG to assist in meeting its obligations in an orderly manner as they came due. Board members also agreed that the terms of the loan should protect the interests of the U.S. government and the taxpayers."

The next stop on that seemingly endless Tuesday, September 16, was a 3:30 p.m. meeting at the White House, where Paulson and I had previously arranged to update the president on the general state of the markets. We had even more to talk about than we had expected. Also attending were Vice President Cheney; Chris Cox of the SEC; Walt Lukken of the Commodity Futures Trading Commission; Erik Sirri, a senior SEC staff member; and various Treasury and White House officials, including the president's chief of staff, Josh Bolten, formerly the director of the Office of Management and Budget; my successor as chair of the Council of Economic Advisers, Eddie Lazear; and the current budget director, Jim Nussle. We made our presentation to a hushed room. After asking a few questions, the president said that we should do what was necessary, and that he would try to provide political support. He suggested that we talk to Congress as well.

We agreed, and at 6:30 p.m. Paulson and I met with the congressional leaders, including Senate majority leader Harry Reid, House minority leader John Boehner, and Senate Banking Committee chairman Chris Dodd. Judd Gregg, the senior Republican on the Senate Budget Committee, arrived in a tuxedo without a tie. House Financial Services Committee chairman Barney Frank wore a rumpled shirt with the tail hanging out. Everyone stood. The room was so small it lacked a table and chairs.

Paulson and I briefly explained the situation and again took questions. I don't recall any of the legislators disputing the need to intervene. Barney Frank wanted to know where the Fed was going to get the $85 billion to lend to AIG. I didn't think this was the time to explain the mechanics of creating bank reserves. I said, "We have $800 billion," referring to the pre-crisis size of the Fed's balance sheet. Barney looked stunned. He didn't see why the Fed should have that kind of money at its disposal. I explained that the Fed, under 13(3), had the authority to make loans as necessary to stem financial crises; and that was precisely what we were trying to do.

We would be doing it on our own responsibility, as Harry Reid would make clear. I believe that most of the attendees understood why we had little choice. But we could expect little if any public support from Congress.

BETWEEN MEETINGS I was briefed several times on developments in New York. Willumstad had presented Geithner's terms, now approved by the Fed Board, to his own board. In the course of the discussions, Hank had also told Willumstad that he would be replaced by Ed Liddy, who had served as president of Allstate from 1999 to 2005. I doubt Willumstad could have done a great deal more to avoid AIG's problems, given his short tenure. But we believed that the magnitude of AIG's debacle demanded new leadership. Willumstad accepted the decision without protest.

AIG board members reacted to Geithner's terms with dismay. They shouldn't have been surprised, given the terrible situation that the company had created for itself, for the Fed, and, most importantly, for the U.S. financial system and economy. "We are faced with two bad choices," Willumstad reportedly told his board. "File for bankruptcy tomorrow morning or take the Fed's deal tonight." The board asked Geithner if the terms could be negotiated. Tim said no—that he was prepared to let AIG go if it rejected the terms. I strongly supported Tim's position and told him so; we had gone as far as we could go, and the terms being offered were completely reasonable, given the circumstances. Still, I admired Tim's poker player cool. We all knew how important it was to prevent AIG's collapse.

Just before 8:00 p.m., Tim's deadline, Willumstad phoned to tell him the deal would be accepted. Tim called to let me know. All that was needed now was to put out the press release. Before reviewing it with Michelle Smith, I thought once more about what we were doing. Things had been moving so fast, with little time for careful reflection. But I concluded that there was no choice. By 9:00 p.m., the news of our rescue was moving on financial news services.

NO ONE (INCLUDING ME) felt much sympathy for AIG. It got itself into trouble. Congress, which had shown little ability to agree on any subject, soon united in virulent opposition to this bailout. In the months that followed I would testify many times before angry legislators trying to explain why we had to do what we did. Congress, of course, was only reflecting American public opinion.

Moreover, because of the enormous losses that AIG would incur in the following quarters, the deal would have to be restructured several times. Ultimately the U.S. government (the Fed and the Treasury combined) would make investments and loan commitments totaling $182 billion to prevent AIG from failing. At the time of our initial rescue of AIG, I kept my emotions in check and tried to view the situation analytically, as a problem to be solved. But, once I fully understood how irresponsible (or clueless) AIG's executives had been, I seethed. "It makes me angry. I slammed the phone more than a few times on discussing AIG," I would later say in a television interview. "I understand why the American people are angry. It's absolutely unfair that taxpayer dollars are going to prop up a company that made these terrible bets . . . but which we have no choice but [to] stabilize, or else risk enormous impact, not just in the financial system, but on the whole U.S. economy."

Looking back now, I am only partly consoled by the fact that the government ultimately recouped all that it invested in AIG, and more. The Fed and the Treasury realized a combined gain of nearly $23 billion. That's a testament to good work by the company's new leaders— including CEO Robert Benmosche, who followed Liddy—and the Fed and Treasury teams that monitored AIG after our loan was made. But, importantly, it was also because our interventions would ultimately stabilize the financial system, allowing AIG and other financial institutions to find their footing.

In a remarkable demonstration of chutzpah, former AIG CEO Hank Greenberg, as head of the investment vehicle Starr International Co., which owned a substantial stake in AIG, would file a $25 billion lawsuit three years later accusing the U.S. government of imposing unfairly punitive terms in the bailout. He made this argument despite the fact that AIG's own irresponsible actions were the source of its predicament, and despite the fact that the AIG board voluntarily accepted the Fed's terms, recognizing that bankruptcy would leave the shareholders with nothing. As it turned out, because of the bailout, the AIG shareholders eventually regained control of a profitable company. Thousands of other companies, like Thornburg Mortgage, did not receive similar help during the crisis and failed as a result.

LEHMAN WEEKEND, WHICH ultimately became Lehman-AIG week, transformed a year-old crisis, already exceptionally severe, into the worst financial panic in our nation's history. Because Lehman failed but AIG was saved, questions persist. Did the government make a conscious decision to let Lehman fail, and, if so, why did it go on to save AIG? Additionally, if Lehman had somehow been saved, would a substantial part of the ensuing crisis have been averted?

Many have argued that Lehman could have been saved, as Bear Stearns had been and as AIG would be, and that letting Lehman go represented a major policy error. Yet the Fed and the Treasury did not choose to let Lehman fail. Lehman was not saved because the methods we used in other rescues weren't available. We had no buyer for Lehman, as we'd had for Bear Stearns—no stable firm that could guarantee Lehman's liabilities and assure markets of its ultimate viability. The Treasury had no congressionally approved funds to inject, as they'd had in the case of Fannie and Freddie. Unlike AIG, which had sufficient collateral to back a large loan from the Fed, Lehman had neither a plausible plan to stabilize itself nor sufficient collateral to back a loan of the size needed to prevent its collapse. And Lehman's condition was probably worse than reported at the time, according to the bankruptcy examiner's report in 2010. As we would learn, the company used dubious accounting transactions to inflate its reported ratio of capital to assets. It also significantly overstated the cash it had available to pay creditors. Ultimately, in bankruptcy, Lehman's bond-holders would receive only about 27 percent, and its other unsecured creditors only about 25 percent, of what they were owed. Total losses to creditors have been estimated at close to $200 billion.

Some have contended that converting Lehman into a bank hold-ing company overnight, as was done later for other investment banks, could have saved it. But that wouldn't have solved its problems. Lehman already could borrow short-term from the Fed through the Primary Dealer Credit Facility. A short-term infusion of cash wouldn't have been enough. Given the size of its losses, it needed to find a buyer or a major long-term investor, or a consortium of investors. Fuld had been unable to attract major investors in months of trying, and none were to be found on that final, fateful weekend.

If a means of saving Lehman did exist, given the tools then avail-able, we were not clever enough to think of it during those frenetic days. Dozens of people were involved in both New York and Washing-ton, and no one has ever reported a meeting or a call in which Hank, Tim, or I discussed whether or not to save Lehman—as we did, for example, with both Bear Stearns and AIG. We already knew Lehman needed to be saved. We lacked the means to do so.

I understand why some have concluded that Lehman's failure was a choice. In a way, it is a sort of backhanded compliment: We had shown such resourcefulness to that point, it is hard to imagine that we could not have come up with *some* solution to Lehman. Even a few participants in the September 2008 FOMC meeting, such as Jim Bul-lard of the St. Louis Fed, Jeff Lacker of Richmond, and Tom Hoenig of

Kansas City—none of them involved in the discussions over Lehman weekend—inferred, approvingly, that letting Lehman go was a choice rather than an unavoidable outcome.

Paulson's declarations that no government money would be used to save Lehman, both before and during the weekend, also understandably fuel the belief that we chose to let Lehman fail. Hank had various reasons for saying what he said, including his personal and political discomfort with becoming the face of unpopular bailouts of too-big-to-fail institutions. However, I am sure that tactical considerations were an important motivation for his statements. We very much wanted the private sector to take the lead in rescuing Lehman, either through an acquisition or through a consortium of private-sector firms. But the private sector would have little incentive to incur the costs of a solution if they were sure that the government would ultimately step in. Hence the need to talk tough. Finally, Hank's statements were to some extent beside the point, in that Fed loans were the only government funds available. It would have been the Federal Reserve's decision—not Hank's or the Treasury Department's—whether to make a loan, had a loan of sufficient size to save the firm been judged feasible.

In congressional testimony immediately after Lehman's collapse, Paulson and I were deliberately quite vague when discussing whether we could have saved Lehman. We spoke about the true, but ultimately irrelevant, fact that financial firms had more time to prepare for Lehman's collapse than for a Bear Stearns failure. But we had agreed in advance to be vague because we were intensely concerned that acknowledging our inability to save Lehman would hurt market confidence and increase pressure on other vulnerable firms. Today I wonder whether we should have been more forthcoming, and not only because our vagueness has promoted the mistaken view that we could have saved Lehman. We had good reason at the time to be concerned about runs on Goldman Sachs and Morgan Stanley and possibly other firms. Nevertheless, our caginess about the reasons for Lehman's failure created confusion about the criteria for any future rescues. Would it have been better for market confidence to have admitted that we were unable to save Lehman? Or was it better to maintain ambiguity, as we did, which suggested we still had the capacity to carry out future interventions? I don't know.

While we did all we could to save Lehman, I feared at the time that avoiding the firm's failure might only delay the inevitable. Today I'm confident that my instinct was right. By Lehman weekend, the ability of the Fed to keep rescuing major financial firms, alone and without support from Congress, was fast coming to an end. As Bill Dudley had emphasized to the FOMC, the Fed's balance sheet could not expand indefinitely without compromising our ability to implement monetary policy. More importantly, though, political tolerance for what Milton Friedman's former coauthor Anna Schwartz called the Fed's "rogue" operations had reached its limits. In short, even if it had somehow been possible for the Fed on its own to save Lehman, and then perhaps even AIG, we would not have had either the capacity or the political support to undertake any future financial rescues.

Even as we came to the end of our resources, the increasingly evident weakness of the system—losses still to come, lack of capital, evaporating confidence—went well beyond Lehman. The United States had had several very bad hurricane seasons in the previous years, and on Lehman weekend I imagined a series of hurricanes coming up the coast, one after the other. But these hurricanes, rather than being named Katrina or Rita or Gustav, were named AIG and Merrill Lynch and Morgan Stanley and Goldman Sachs and Washington Mutual and Wachovia and Bank of America and Citigroup and . . . How could the Fed hope to deal with this colossal crisis on its own, with no remaining tools and no political support? As I said on conference calls over Lehman weekend, we should stop fooling ourselves: The time had come to go to Congress. There was simply no historical precedent for solving a financial crisis of this magnitude without significant taxpayer dollars and the political will to undertake the effort.

As it turned out, even the risk of a once-in-a-century economic and financial catastrophe wasn't enough for many members of Congress to rise above ideology and short-run political concerns. Despite the chaos that followed Lehman's failure and the obvious implications for the economy, Congress would need more than two weeks and two tries to pass legislation that ultimately provided the money necessary to stop the crisis. It seems clear that Congress would never have acted absent the failure of *some* large firm and the associated damage to the system. In that sense, a Lehman-type episode was probably inevitable.

If historians eventually agree that saving Lehman would not have avoided subsequent failures, the intensification of the crisis, the resulting recession, or the need for hundreds of billions of taxpayer dollars from Congress, then perhaps the question of whether the company's collapse that weekend was avoidable will become moot. Nevertheless, I do not want the notion that Lehman's failure could have been avoided, and that its failure was consequently a policy choice, to become the received wisdom, for the simple reason that it is not true. We believed that Lehman's failure would be extraordinarily disruptive. We did everything we could think of to avoid it. The same logic led us to rescue AIG, where (unlike for Lehman) our makeshift tools proved adequate.

CHAPTER 14

We Turn to Congress

Newspapers on Wednesday, September 17, splashed the rescue of AIG across their front pages in type usually reserved for declarations of war. The political and media worlds were trying to arrive at a conventional wisdom on the events of the past few days, and the early returns did not favor us. Most editorialists and economists on Monday and Tuesday had supported what they saw as a principled decision to let Lehman fail. Consequently, many viewed the subsequent decision on AIG as an inconsistent reversal, rather than what it was: a different response to different circumstances.

Even economists generally well disposed to the Fed were critical. "The government drew a line with Lehman and then erased a portion of the line," said Vincent Reinhart, formerly the director of the Board's Division of Monetary Affairs, where he had coauthored several papers with me. Adam Posen, another former coauthor who would go on to be a leading policy dove at the Bank of England, wrote, "This is very bad news and it is a very confused precedent. AIG has been bleeding capital and liquidity for months. Anybody in their right mind could have gotten out." And Carnegie Mellon professor Marvin Goodfriend, a former Richmond Fed economist whom I knew well, said of the Fed, "You don't have any rules and you are trying to set the rules in the middle of the game." I was sure we had made the right call, but the hostile reaction from informed observers put me on notice. We were going to have a tough time convincing Congress, the media, and the public. I was also dismayed that some people who had known or worked with me—like Reinhart, Posen, and Goodfriend—seemed disinclined to give us the benefit of the doubt.

Politicians, as usual, tried to have it both ways. On the one hand, they knew that bailouts were intensely unpopular, and many did their best to take advantage of (and reinforce) the perception that the Treasury and the Fed were putting Wall Street ahead of Main Street. Jim Bunning compared the Fed, unfavorably, to Hugo Chávez, the socialist Venezuelan dictator. A Dow Jones wire story captured the mood: "For one day at least in this politically charged election season, Democrats and Republicans on Capitol Hill appear to have buried the hatchet. Right into Ben Bernanke." On the other hand, more thoughtful legislators like Barney Frank realized that they themselves might soon be called upon to make unpopular decisions, and so their comments were more cautious. (However, as usual, Barney could not resist a joke. At a hearing later that week, he proposed that Monday, September 15—the day between Lehman's failure and AIG's rescue—be designated "Free Market Day." "The national commitment to the free market lasted one day," Barney said. "It was Monday.")

In the financial world, short-term funding markets were barely functioning. Banks were hoarding cash rather than making loans, and withdrawals from money market funds were accelerating—especially from so-called prime money market funds, which invest in a range of mostly short-term assets, including commercial paper issued by financial and nonfinancial firms. Much of the cash flowing out of prime funds was moving into "government-only" money funds that invested solely in Treasury bills and other government liabilities viewed as ultrasafe. In the three weeks between September 10 and October 1, $439 billion would run from the prime funds, while $362 billion would flow into the government-only funds—an unprecedented shift.

I arrived at work on September 17 around 7:00 a.m. After a long-scheduled breakfast with Florida congressman Connie Mack, great-grandson and namesake of the famous manager of the Philadelphia Athletics, I updated colleagues inside and outside the Fed on the AIG rescue. At 9:45 a.m., joined by Don Kohn, Kevin Warsh, and Tim Geithner, I spoke via conference call to the governors of the Bank of Canada (Mark Carney), the Bank of England (Mervyn King), the European Central Bank (Jean-Claude Trichet), and the Bank of Japan (Masaaki Shirakawa). All of them were pleased that, after the Lehman debacle, we had been able to avoid AIG's failure. All agreed that the disorderly collapse of another large, interconnected financial firm should be avoided at all cost. I expressed confidence—perhaps more than I felt—that the AIG deal would work.

The aftershocks from Lehman's failure and AIG's near miss were pounding financial markets around the world, and each of the governors had increased his bank's lending in an effort to quell the panic. We also collectively confirmed that the expanded currency swap lines approved by the FOMC on Tuesday would be jointly announced at the opening of business in Europe on Thursday. I told the other central bankers I appreciated their support. It was more than lip service. Each of us was acutely aware of the responsibilities we faced as well as the political and media minefields ahead. We all knew that we would meet those challenges more effectively if we worked together rather than operating in isolation.

After the international call, at Michelle Smith's suggestion, I briefed the FOMC by videoconference. Michelle had been hearing all morning from frustrated Reserve Bank presidents asking for more information. They were besieged by press inquiries and calls from their board members and needed to know how to respond. I explained the terms of the loan to AIG and the reasons for it. Tim and Bill Dudley also commented and took questions. I had trouble gauging the presidents' reaction. Most seemed to appreciate that extraordinary times justified extraordinary measures. But some expressed concerns about the action itself, which looked like an inconsistent lurch, as well as about the political backlash against the Fed that was already building.

Since the Board decides whether to invoke the Section 13(3) emergency lending authority, it was entirely appropriate—and necessary, as a practical matter—to inform the presidents about the details after the fact. Nevertheless, during the videoconference I felt a tension that we dealt with throughout the crisis: I wanted to involve as many of my colleagues as possible, to get both useful advice and greater buy-in. But during this most intense phase of the crisis, at least, the need to move quickly often trumped the benefits of broad consultation.

After lunch, at Michelle's request, I took calls from reporters. If we were going to hold our own in the court of public opinion, we needed to get our side of the story out. Generally, I spent the most time with the beat reporters who wrote regularly about the Fed, including Jon Hilsenrath of the *Wall Street Journal*, Greg Ip of the *Economist*, Krishna Guha of the *Financial Times*, Neil Irwin of the *Washington Post*, John Berry of Bloomberg, Steve Liesman of CNBC, and Ed Andrews of the *New York Times*. I knew that these more specialized reporters were best equipped to understand and then explain what we were doing and why. Other media would pick up on their reporting.

Not that these folks necessarily took what we told them at face value. *Wall Street Journal* editor and columnist David Wessel once told me that if a reporter was doing a good job, the officials the reporter was covering felt relieved when he or she was reassigned. Some of the reporters I dealt with over the years would have handily met Wessel's criterion. But overall, I thought we usually received a fair hearing from the beat reporters. We were more likely to see an unfair or inaccurate story from journalists who did not usually cover the Fed and were, consequently, less well informed.

Throughout Wednesday we paid particularly close attention to Goldman Sachs and Morgan Stanley. As the two remaining independent investment banks, they were the subject of intense market scrutiny and speculation. Both companies had stronger franchises and healthier balance sheets than Bear Stearns, Lehman, and Merrill Lynch. But, like the other firms, they needed to find funding every day to finance their securities holdings and to meet demands for collateral.

As we now fully appreciated, lenders, customers, and counterparties were reluctant to deal with a company whose stability they doubted. If confidence in the firms continued to decline, we could see the equivalent of a run on one or both of them.

Goldman and Morgan Stanley had long histories. Goldman was founded in 1869 in lower Manhattan by Marcus Goldman, the son of a Jewish cattle dealer in Bavaria. Goldman brought his son-in-law Samuel Sachs into the firm in 1882, and the company prospered into the new century. Goldman Sachs nearly failed after the 1929 stock market crash but recovered under the leadership of Sidney Weinberg, who, after dropping out of school, had started at Goldman as a janitor's assistant at age sixteen.

Goldman had long been associated with the political establishment. Critics dubbed it "Government Sachs." Sidney Weinberg was a confidante of FDR, and Presidents Eisenhower and Johnson reportedly followed his recommendations for appointments of Treasury secretaries. Bob Rubin, secretary of the Treasury under President Clinton, had been a top executive at Goldman, as Hank Paulson had been. In the world of central banking, Mario Draghi (governor of the Bank of Italy, later president of the ECB), Mark Carney (governor of the Bank of Canada and, later, the Bank of England), and Bill Dudley (the New York Fed's markets chief and later president) were also Goldman alumni. Gary Gensler, the head of the Commodity Futures Trading Commission at the time, had also worked at Goldman. Not surprisingly, the close connections have led to concerns about undue influence. I understand the concern. On the other hand, it seems unrealistic to expect government agencies to effectively regulate markets or industries if no one in the agency has relevant experience in that market or industry. I can only say that the Goldman alumni with whom I worked brought not only substantial financial expertise to their government duties, as one would expect, but also a strong dedication to the public interest.

The current Goldman CEO, Lloyd Blankfein, and I had been

undergraduates at Harvard together, though I did not know him well there. He then earned a law degree from Harvard and, after a few years of lawyering, went to work for Goldman as a precious metals salesman in London. He had grown up in a housing project in Brooklyn; his father sorted mail at the post office and his mother was a receptionist for a burglar alarm company. During my time as chairman I met with Blankfein occasionally to discuss issues related to Goldman and to hear his views on the markets and the economy. Lloyd was obviously very bright, and I found his insights into market developments particularly useful. That said, I intentionally avoided developing close personal relationships with anyone on Wall Street, not only because of the Fed's regulatory responsibilities, but to avoid being influenced by the groupthink that seemed too often to develop in the financial halls of power.

Morgan Stanley was born of the breakup of J.P. Morgan & Company in 1935, after passage of the Glass-Steagall Act forced the separation of commercial banking (making loans) and investment banking (underwriting stocks and bonds). J.P. Morgan's grandson, Henry Morgan, and Harold Stanley, a J.P. Morgan partner, lent their names to the new firm, which instantly joined the ranks of Wall Street's elite. In 1997, in a departure from its traditional business, the firm merged with the retail brokerage Dean Witter Reynolds, acquiring the Discover credit card franchise in the process. But Morgan remained engaged in underwriting and trading securities. It became the biggest U.S. securities firm by market value in 1998, although its earnings recovered less quickly from the dot-com crash than those of other firms. After a series of power struggles, John Mack, a long-time Morgan Stanley executive, became CEO in 2005.

Mack, the sixth son of Lebanese immigrants (the family name was originally Makhoul), grew up in Mooresville, North Carolina, where his father ran a general merchandise store. He attended Duke University on a football scholarship. Mack was seen in the industry as aggressive and charismatic; in the period before the crisis he boosted Morgan

Stanley's profits by increasing risk and taking on more debt. Kevin
Warsh, whose first job had been at Morgan Stanley, followed the firm
closely and kept us apprised of developments.

MEANWHILE, WASHINGTON MUTUAL'S troubles finally were coming
to a head. It had been on death watch for months, but disagreements
between the Office of Thrift Supervision and the Federal Deposit
Insurance Corporation had delayed the resolution. FDIC chairman
Sheila Bair pressed WaMu to sell itself, notwithstanding continued
resistance from the OTS, which believed the company could survive
on its own. JPMorgan Chase seemed the most likely acquirer, but several other firms had also expressed interest. It looked like negotiations
would wrap up over the weekend.

We were also getting worrisome reports about Wachovia. The bank
had been underperforming for several years. In June, its board had
ousted its CEO, Ken Thompson. Ken, a smart, gregarious native of
Rocky Mount, North Carolina, where he was a star athlete in high
school, had spent his entire career at the bank, starting thirty-four
years earlier at a predecessor institution, First Union Corp. I got to
know Thompson during the time he sat on our Federal Advisory
Council, and he struck me as knowledgeable and thoughtful. But he
had made the same mistake that many of his peers had made, aggressively pushing his bank into risky real estate lending. In 2006 Wachovia acquired Golden West Financial Corporation for $25 billion and
inherited a portfolio of mostly lower-quality residential mortgages.
Golden West had popularized the option adjustable-rate mortgage,
which initially allows the borrower to make payments so small that
the loan balance can grow rather than shrink. Wachovia's merger with
Golden West and Bank of America's acquisition of Countrywide were
strikingly similar. Wachovia had also expanded strongly in commercial real estate and construction lending. But now the losses and mark-
downs were accumulating, and Wachovia watched as its uninsured
funding melted away.

I WAS GROWING weary of putting out fires one by one. We needed a more comprehensive solution to the crisis, and that meant asking Congress for taxpayer dollars. I had made that point on calls over the weekend, during discussions of Lehman and AIG. Wednesday evening, on a call with Hank, Tim, Chris Cox of the SEC, and others, I pressed the point again. The Fed couldn't do it alone. As we looked ahead, many major financial institutions, and indeed the entire economic and financial system, were at serious risk. To secure the necessary authority, the fiscal firepower, and the democratic legitimacy needed to stop the crisis and avoid unthinkable outcomes, we had to go to Congress.

Hank was initially noncommittal. He knew that he and his team would have to lead the effort to develop a legislative proposal and sell it to Congress. It would not be easy. The bailouts had angered the voters and thus the politicians. Main Street had not yet even felt the full effect of Wall Street's woes. But the alternatives all seemed worse. By Thursday morning Hank would come around to the view that we could not hope to contain the crisis without help, and he agreed to seek legislation.

Chris Cox, meanwhile, wanted to ban short-selling of financial company stocks. John Mack, like Dick Fuld of Lehman before him, had complained that short-selling was threatening to destabilize his company. Stop short-selling, Cox suggested, and we would remove one threat to firms under pressure.

Paulson seemed prepared to support Cox. I had doubts. Short-selling is part of how a healthy market determines prices. A trader who is optimistic about a company buys its stock. Short-selling the company's stock is a way for a pessimist to express a contrary opinion. Short-sellers, at times, are the sharks in the financial ocean: They thrive by preying on the weakest companies. That's normally healthy for the ecosystem—it allows stock prices to reflect a full range of views. On the other hand, these were hardly normal times. I wanted to think about it. I was pleased to learn on the call that Mack was in serious talks with the Chinese sovereign wealth fund, for a second investment on top of its investment in December 2007, and a Chinese bank. Raising capital would be the best way for Morgan Stanley to restore market confidence.

Thursday, September 18, was another tough day, but it proved to be a turning point. Inauspiciously, it began at a gastroenterologist's office. He wondered if my stomach upset might be caused by stress. More encouraging was an email from the baseball statistics genius Bill James, relayed by Chuck Blahous, an economic adviser in the White House. "Tell Ben to hang in there," James wrote. "At some point the people who are saying it can't get any worse HAVE to be right."

The expansion of currency swap lines with other major central banks had been announced. All told, adding together the limits of the swap lines, we stood ready to provide nearly $250 billion to calm dollar funding markets around the world.

Calls with Treasury and the SEC filled the morning and early afternoon. Cox again pushed to ban short sales of financial stocks. Pressure on the stock prices of Morgan, Goldman, and other firms seemed to be growing, some of it likely coming from short-sellers. Although I still had lingering doubts, I agreed not to oppose a temporary ban. Cox would take the idea back to his commission for consideration.

We discussed the money market funds at length. Even some of the largest, best-known money funds were reporting significant outflows. The runs had the potential to inflict serious economic damage, not only by adding to the market panic but also because many large corporations depend on money funds to buy their commercial paper. A pullback by the money funds would hurt the ability of companies like General Electric or Ford to finance their daily operations. We were already hearing that only the highest-rated firms could sell commercial paper, and even these for terms of only a day or two. Meanwhile, firms shut out (or worried about being shut out) of the commercial paper market drew down their bank lines of credit, putting additional pressure on cash-short banks and making them even less willing to lend to other customers. Financial turmoil was now having clear and demonstrable effects on the nonfinancial part of the economy, threatening production and employment.

We needed to stop the bleeding. The Board, the New York Fed, and the Boston Fed had been working on a new facility to provide the money market funds with the cash they needed to pay off their investors. But it was technically and legally complicated. Rather than lending directly to the money funds, we would lend to banks on favorable terms, on the condition that they purchase less liquid asset-backed commercial paper from money funds—a significant share of the assets held by the funds. That would funnel cash to them, without violating legal restrictions on the Fed's purchasing securities directly from the money funds.

On the call that morning, Paulson proposed also using Treasury's Exchange Stabilization Fund to guarantee the money market funds, much as the FDIC guarantees ordinary bank deposits. If investors in the funds believed their money was safe, they would have no reason to run. I thought this idea was excellent. The Exchange Stabilization Fund was created during the Depression to allow the Treasury to manage the dollar's value in foreign exchange markets. (If the Treasury wanted to curb a rapid increase in the dollar's value, for instance, it would sell dollars and buy euros or yen, thus increasing the supply of dollars. If it needed to slow a fall in the dollar's value, it would sell euros or yen to buy dollars.) While what Paulson was proposing was not an intervention in the foreign exchange market, in the past the fund had been used for purposes only indirectly connected to managing the dollar's value. Most notably, it was used in 1995, when Bob Rubin and Larry Summers were leading President Clinton's Treasury Department, to lend $20 billion to Mexico to help stabilize the plummeting peso.

Because money market funds hold many foreign assets—they are a principal source of dollar funding for European banks—it would not be difficult to argue that stopping the runs on the money funds would help to stabilize the dollar. Moreover, Paulson's plan likely would not involve actual spending or lending. If the backstop restored investor confidence, then the run should stop without any money leaving the stabilization fund. Indeed, because money market funds were charged a premium for the insurance, the Treasury would earn a profit from the program.

We continued to discuss what we should request from Congress. By now, everyone agreed that the crisis had become too big for the Fed and Treasury to handle without money appropriated by Congress. But, assuming Congress agreed, what was the best way to deploy the funds? Historically, governments have often ended banking crises by injecting capital into (that is, buying stock in) viable firms, so-called good banks. In some cases, troubled firms were made into good banks by separating their bad assets into newly incorporated vehicles—bad banks. The bad banks would be separately financed and, over time, would sell off their low-quality loans. I was inclined toward that approach, including having the government invest directly in banks in exchange for newly created stock. It seemed the simplest and most direct way to restore the banking system to solvency, to provide reassurance to investors and the public, and to support the flow of credit to households and businesses.

The economic logic of putting public capital into financial institutions aside, Hank had serious reservations. He feared that partial government ownership of banks would look socialistic, or like more bailouts, and thus would prove a political nonstarter. He believed, in particular, that House Republicans would never accept a plan that looked like a government takeover of banks. Going to Congress with a proposal only to have it turned down would devastate market confidence. He also worried that proposing government capital injections would panic existing bank shareholders. They would fear having their ownership stake diluted, or even expropriated if public capital injections became the first step toward nationalization—the complete takeover of banks by the government. Our tough treatment of the shareholders of Fannie, Freddie, and AIG would offer little comfort to bank shareholders facing what they might see as the prelude to a government takeover. If existing shareholders took fright and sold their stock, bank share prices would slide, closing off any possibility of raising new capital from the private sector. Finally, Hank was concerned (as we all were) that banks that were partially or fully nationalized might find it difficult to reestablish profitability and return to private status.

Paulson proposed instead to use appropriated funds to buy bad assets from banks—effectively, a good bank–bad bank strategy for the whole system. He believed that government purchases of bad assets would not only take those assets out of the system but also put a floor under the prices of similar assets remaining on banks' books. That floor would strengthen banks and help them raise capital more easily from private investors. His idea had its origins in a Treasury staff memo entitled "'Break the Glass' Bank Recapitalization Plan." Quietly circulated in April, the memo discussed several strategies for bank stabilization but focused on buying $500 billion of mortgage-backed securities from financial institutions via auctions. Professional asset managers would be hired to manage the purchased securities and eventually resell them to private investors, with the goal of getting the best possible return for the taxpayers.

The break-the-glass memo was a useful exercise but it lacked detail, particularly on how the government would decide which assets to buy and how much to pay. After the memo's circulation, Federal Reserve economists considered various types of asset-buying programs in more depth. They were concerned that asset buying would be complicated and might take a long time to develop and implement. They also were unable to find an exact precedent in earlier financial crises that could serve as a model. During the Swedish banking crisis of the 1990s, often cited as an example of a successful policy response, the government had purchased bad assets but only in conjunction with government injections of new capital into banks.

Nevertheless, I understood why Hank preferred this approach; and I believed that, since Hank would be the one persuading Congress to act, his views deserved some deference. If I had learned one thing in Washington, it was that no economic program can succeed, no matter how impeccable the arguments supporting it, if it is not politically feasible. Moreover, if the asset purchases raised the prices of troubled assets, as I believed they could, the system would be recapitalized indirectly. Most importantly, Hank assured me that the authority to purchase assets would be written broadly enough to allow the government to purchase equity shares in banks—that is, to inject government capital, my preferred approach—if that turned out to be best.

WE HAD A PLAN; the next step was to sell it. At 3:30 p.m., Paulson, Cox, and I met again with the president in the Roosevelt Room at the White House, together with staff from the White House and other agencies. Kevin Warsh joined me. Once everyone was gathered, the president entered from the Oval Office and sat at his usual spot in the middle of one side of the long table. The participants had already found their places as indicated by printed name cards. I am pretty sure the president knew everyone and could have dispensed with the name cards, but protocol is powerful. As had become usual, Paulson, Cox, and I sat directly across from the president.

Hank and I updated him on market developments, including the runs on the money market funds. We emphasized the urgent need to control the crisis before the economy suffered more damage. At Hank's request, I repeated my judgment that the Fed was nearing the end of its resources to stop the run on the financial system and that a comprehensive attack on the crisis using funds authorized by Congress was probably the only workable approach. We then reviewed the Treasury and Fed proposals to restore confidence in the money funds and Chris Cox's proposed ban of short-selling. Finally, and most importantly, we turned to Hank's proposal to ask Congress for money to buy bad assets.

For the second time in three days, we had come to President Bush to request his support for radical and unprecedented intervention in the American financial system. As a Republican with a strong predilection for letting the markets sort things out, the president couldn't have been happy with the options we offered. He knew that it would be difficult to get his own party's support. But, in the spirit of the approach that Franklin Roosevelt had taken three-quarters of a century earlier, he agreed that preserving the free market in the long run might require drastic government intervention in the short run. Once again, the president expressed his full support for us. We were grateful. Once again, Congress would be our next stop.

After I returned to my office, I called Speaker Pelosi and asked if Hank, Chris Cox, and I could meet with congressional leaders that evening. She said she would try to arrange it. At 6:00 p.m. Senator Obama called. I explained our strategy. He promised to be as supportive as possible. With the election little more than six weeks away, what happened in the financial markets and in the Congress could be important wild cards in what appeared to be a close contest. For the Fed, the situation was tricky: We needed to work closely with the administration and push for a legislative solution without appearing to be partisan.

Every Thursday afternoon the Fed reports on its balance sheet. Once a boring, under-the-radar release, it had become newsworthy for the information it provided on our lending. This Thursday, the report reflected deepening stress in the financial system. Lending to securities brokers through the Primary Dealer Credit Facility had reached a record $60 billion, up from zero the previous week. (A week later, PDCF borrowing would total $106 billion.) Meanwhile, borrowing by banks through the discount window rose by $10 billion from the previous week, to $33.5 billion. Over the next week, discount window loans would rise to nearly $40 billion, not far below the $45.5 billion borrowed the day after 9/11.

A FEW MINUTES BEFORE 7:00 p.m., Paulson, Cox, and I arrived at Room H-230 in the Capitol, a small conference room near Speaker Pelosi's office. The sun was beginning to set on the Mall as we took our places at a wooden conference table. Pelosi, Senate majority leader Harry Reid, and House minority leader John Boehner sat across from us. Other members, including the top-ranking members of the Senate Banking Committee and the House Financial Services Committee (roughly a dozen overall), were seated around the table. Paulson said a few words, then asked me to elaborate on the risks we faced.

I had no prepared remarks. With no notes, I don't remember everything I said, although attendees later repeated much of it to the press. I wanted to convey the absolute necessity of quick action. I said that we risked a global financial meltdown, and that it might occur in days rather than weeks. I fully believed every word I said and I think the members could see that. The room was very quiet.

I then turned to the economic implications of a financial meltdown—for the country and their own constituents. Here, I tried for a balanced, even cautious, view. I didn't want to be accused of hyperbole or of sparking panic. Although I drew an analogy to the Great Depression, when the unemployment rate had peaked at 25 percent, I also talked about the less severe but still very deep economic declines that had followed financial crises in Japan and Sweden. Based on those experiences, I said, if action was not taken immediately, we could expect a sharp recession and significant further declines in the stock market and other asset prices. Unemployment could rise from the current 6 percent to 8 or 9 percent, I said, with large nonfinancial companies like General Motors joining financial companies in bankruptcy.

I think it is fair to say that I made an impression. It's probably also fair to say that, as dire as my warnings were, I underestimated the potential damage. No global financial crisis this large had been seen at least since the Depression, if ever. We had little basis for assessing the magnitude of its fallout. But my academic research and reading of history convinced me that the effects could be large, even catastrophic. As I spoke, I remember feeling quite calm. The only way forward, I believed, was to be as focused, deliberate, and methodical as possible.

We needed to gain and keep legislators' confidence that we had a plan that would work.

The legislators asked many questions. How much money would be needed? How would it be used? Would aid to financial companies come with requirements to lend and restrictions on executive pay? How would we help homeowners and other innocent bystanders hurt by the crisis? When would the administration propose legislation? We answered as best we could. Paulson mentioned the idea of using the appropriated funds to buy bad assets from banks but did not provide detail. When the meeting ended at close to 9:00 p.m., I snuck out without being snagged by reporters. My escape was made easier by the fact that the congressional leaders were perfectly happy to talk.

Despite all the bad news, I left the meeting feeling encouraged. I told Michelle Smith that I saw a developing consensus for action. The markets also were encouraged: The Dow Jones industrial average ended the day up 410 points as rumors about a possible comprehensive response to the crisis circulated.

ON FRIDAY, SEPTEMBER 19, the Board met at 7:30 a.m. I had already explained that the Treasury intended to use the Exchange Stabilization Fund to guarantee the money market funds. But we believed our program to encourage banks to buy asset-backed commercial paper from money funds could also help stop the run, and we approved it. The money funds could use the cash received to meet withdrawals without having to sell their commercial paper or other assets into a falling market. Once again, we were fulfilling our fundamental role as a central bank by lending in the face of financial panic, albeit indirectly in this case. Because some of the largest funds were headquartered in Boston, we asked the Federal Reserve Bank of Boston, headed by Eric Rosengren, to run the program.

In the meantime, the central banks of Sweden, Norway, Denmark, and Australia were asking for currency swap lines. The FOMC had delegated the authority to initiate swaps to a committee consisting of

Don, Tim, and me. We approved the requests and informed FOMC members. We left negotiation of the details to Bill Dudley and his team. Bill was also busy monitoring markets, helping to oversee various lending programs, and conducting the Fed's market operations to maintain the federal funds rate near the FOMC's 2 percent target. I commented to Don that Bill "must be a one-armed paperhanger up there." In truth, we all felt like that paperhanger. As science fiction writer Ray Cummings once said, "Time is what keeps everything from happening at once." During the past month, it had felt like time was not doing its job.

Later that morning, Paulson, Cox, and I stood next to President Bush in the Rose Garden as he defended the rescues of Fannie, Freddie, and AIG. He also cited the Fed's injections of "much-needed liquidity into our financial system" through our lending and in coordination with other central banks.

"These were targeted measures designed primarily to stop the problems of individual firms from spreading even more broadly," he said. "But these measures have not been enough, because they have not addressed the root cause behind much of the instability in our markets—the mortgage assets that have lost value during the housing decline and are now restricting the flow of credit." He then described the initiatives we had discussed in the Roosevelt Room the previous day.

Markets liked what they heard. Short-term Treasury yields, which had plunged to a post–World War II low, rose very sharply. The three-month yield went from 0.07 percent to 0.92 percent between late Thursday and late Friday. This was good news. Traders were willing to sell ultrasafe Treasury bills in favor of other assets. At the same time, corporate funding costs dropped significantly, and outflows from money market funds slowed. The stock market rose more than 3 percent, bringing the Dow back to less than 1 percent below its closing level a week earlier, just before Lehman weekend. Stocks of financial companies, which were expected to benefit from the ban on short-selling, rose about 11 percent. We had also announced that the New York

Fed would support the housing market by purchasing the short-term debt of Fannie and Freddie, which they issued to finance their purchases of mortgages. We bought $8 billion on Friday, helping to push down interest rates on those securities by a significant 0.6 percent. The broadly positive reaction reflected relief that at last we had a comprehensive plan to fight the crisis, whatever its specific elements might be.

I spent the rest of the day explaining the proposals the president had outlined to reporters, fellow central bankers, and Congress. It was difficult to read legislators' reactions, but already I could tell that it was not going to be easy to enlist them in what they would undoubtedly perceive as a massive taxpayer bailout of Wall Street rather than as a critical step for stabilizing the economy.

I also met with a few staff and Board members to further think through design issues for Paulson's proposal to purchase bad assets. Treasury had offered few specifics, and we wanted to understand the trade-offs of different approaches. The best historical analogy we could find was the Resolution Trust Corporation (RTC), which had successfully liquidated the assets of failed savings and loans following the S&L crisis of the 1980s. But the RTC differed from Paulson's plan in a crucial way. Assets came to the RTC automatically when a savings and loan failed. It did not have to figure out how much to pay for those assets. In contrast, Paulson planned to buy troubled assets from solvent financial institutions—but at what price?

That question would prove to be the biggest roadblock to asset purchases. Should the government pay the current market price, or something else? If the government paid the current, depressed market prices (assuming that market prices could even be determined in such a dysfunctional environment), the program might do very little to restore bank solvency. Perversely, all financial institutions might be forced to mark down their assets to the government prices, which would worsen their financial condition, at least in terms of the official accounting measures. Alternatively, the government could pay a higher-than-market price—say, the estimated price that might prevail under more normal market conditions. As a patient investor, the government could wait for values to better reflect the assets' longer-term returns. That would certainly help the banks, but would it be fair to the taxpayer if the government had to pay prices above those of the current market with the possibility of taking a loss when it came time to sell the assets? In the coming weeks, the Fed and Treasury would exhaustively analyze how to conduct auctions and value assets, but how best to set purchase prices remained a key question.

The urgency to act on so many fronts, together with the complexity of the problems we faced, exhausted all of us. That week, many senior staff worked through the night. We knew the choices we were making were vitally important. As Brad DeLong, an economics professor at the University of California, Berkeley, put it in his blog: "Bernanke and Paulson are both focused like laser beams on not making the same mistakes as were made in 1929. . . . They want to make their own, original, mistakes."

ON FRIDAY EVENING, I heard through Fed supervisors that Goldman Sachs wanted to change its legal status, from a securities holding company to a bank holding company. As the name suggests, a bank holding company is a company that owns one or more banks. Goldman owned a small deposit-taking institution based in Utah, a so-called industrial loan company. The industrial loan company could quickly be converted to a bank, thus meeting the minimum requirement for Goldman to be a bank holding company. This change in legal status would have only one effect of consequence: Goldman would now be supervised by the Fed instead of the SEC. Goldman's executives believed that they could reduce the risk of a run on their short-term funding simply by announcing that the Fed would oversee their activities. Their motivation was incorrectly reported at the time as a move to secure access to Fed lending, but Goldman's broker-dealer subsidiary already had access to Fed lending through the PDCF.

On Sunday, the Board approved Goldman's application, and a similar application by Morgan Stanley, which had become very concerned about the stability of its funding. We allowed the changes in status to take effect immediately. At the same meeting, the Board permitted the London-based broker-dealer subsidiaries of Goldman, Morgan Stanley, and Merrill Lynch to borrow at the PDCF. Their New York offices already could borrow from the PDCF. Our action allowed the companies to use collateral held in London without transferring it to New York. These steps eased funding strains for both Goldman and Morgan. I saw that as evidence that, at least for these two companies, the crisis had aspects of a self-fulfilling panic—investors refusing to lend and counterparties refusing to transact only because they feared others would do the same. The conversions of Goldman and Morgan Stanley to bank holding companies—together with the failure of Lehman and the acquisitions of Bear Stearns and Merrill Lynch—brought the era of freestanding investment banks to a sudden conclusion.

Goldman and Morgan Stanley did not count on their new status as bank holding companies to secure their stability. Both companies also pursued new strategic investors. A week later, Goldman announced a $5 billion investment by Warren Buffett.

A man of wit and—despite his immense wealth—personal modesty, the Sage of Omaha had a connection to Washington that I hadn't realized. His father served in Congress, so young Warren started some of his first businesses in Washington. According to Buffett, as a boy he organized several paper routes into a single business, making the other delivery boys his first employees. He told me that the Christmas cards he sent his customers each December read: "Merry Christmas. Third notice!" Buffett supported the Fed throughout the crisis and thereafter, boosting both the Fed's political standing and my morale. I like to think that Warren's consistent backing reflected his personal regard, but it could not have been lost on him that his support for beleaguered policymakers, by improving market sentiment, was good for the economy and, consequently, for his own investments. Certainly, by investing in Goldman at that particular moment, Buffett cast a critical vote of confidence in the U.S. economy, considerably reducing the stress on Goldman (and, indirectly, Morgan Stanley). His investment, on highly favorable terms, also paid off quite well for his shareholders.

As for Morgan Stanley, the deal they had been discussing with the Chinese did not work out. But in mid-October, Mitsubishi UFJ, Japan's largest financial group, announced it would invest $9 billion. Before signing the papers, the financial group asked for and received assurances from Secretary Paulson that the U.S. government would not subsequently expropriate the Japanese stake in Morgan Stanley. With that investment in Morgan, and Buffett's in Goldman, the two newly minted bank holding companies would be much less of a concern for us (and for the markets).

As the Sunday Board meeting suggests, weekends no longer had much meaning at the Fed (or the Treasury). I had tickets for a Nationals game on Sunday afternoon but instead found myself at a meeting, along with Hank, in Senator Bob Corker's office with six Republican senators. We explained the Treasury's proposal and possible alternatives. The discussion had useful moments, but Senator Bunning, who seemed constantly angry and was always angriest with the Fed, delivered a diatribe and walked out. The thrust of it was that the Fed could not be trusted to fix a crisis that, in his view, it had created through excessively easy monetary policy and poor regulation.

ON FRIDAY EVENING, the Treasury had sent congressional leaders a three-page synopsis of its proposed legislation. Paulson asked for $700 billion to purchase troubled assets. The figure was fairly arbitrary. It was an enormous sum, but (as Paulson pointed out) it was small in comparison to the roughly $11 trillion in outstanding residential mortgages, not to mention other real-estate-related assets such as commercial real estate and construction loans. The problem was gigantic, and the response would have to be proportionate. On the other hand, the $700 billion would not be government spending in the usual sense but rather the acquisition of financial assets. If all went well, the government would eventually sell the assets and recoup most or all of the money.

Lawmakers reacted with consternation to the Treasury's proposal. In his own account, Paulson says he intended the three pages as an outline for discussion and assumed that Congress would fill in the details. However, many in Congress took the short proposal, written in the form of draft legislation, as a demand for essentially unlimited powers without oversight. This would not fly, although it was not Hank's expectation in the first place. The proposal, dubbed TARP (for Troubled Asset Relief Program), was off to a bad start.

CHAPTER 15

"Fifty Percent Hell No"

On Tuesday, September 23, four days after Hank Paulson and I stood with the president in the Rose Garden, Hank and I were once again side by side. Across from us sat the visibly angry members of the Senate Banking Committee. They greeted the proposal for TARP with deep skepticism. How was the $700 billion program supposed to work? Would ordinary Americans see any benefit?

Under the camera lights and the stern glare of committee members, I did something that I had never done before and would never do again at a congressional hearing: I spoke extemporaneously from rough notes that I had jotted down just that morning rather than from a prepared text. I had agreed to support asset purchases, and I believed I was the right person to explain how they could strengthen financial institutions and stabilize the financial system while also treating taxpayers fairly. The economics professor in me took over.

"Let me start with a question," I said. "Why are financial markets not working? Financial institutions and others hold billions in complex securities, including many that are mortgage-related. I would like to ask you for a moment to think of these securities as having two different prices. The first of these is the fire-sale price. That is the price a security would fetch today if sold quickly into an illiquid market. The second price is the hold-to-maturity price. That is what the security would be worth eventually when the income from the security was received over time. Because of the complexity of these securities and the serious uncertainties about the economy and the housing market, there is no active market for many of these securities. And, thus, today the fire-sale price may be much less than the hold-to-maturity price."

Asset purchases could help, I continued, if the government paid prices somewhere between the fire-sale and hold-to-maturity prices— that is, prices that were low but nevertheless closer to what sellers could obtain in a properly functioning market. Financial institutions could sell assets at the intermediate prices, and value the assets still on their books at those prices, without taking losses that threatened to exhaust their remaining capital. At the same time, prices lower than long-run, hold-to-maturity values would ensure that the taxpayers got their money back if, as we anticipated, the program helped restart the economy and the housing market.

The government would not have to calculate the fire-sale and hold-to-maturity prices of the assets, I argued. Prices between those two extremes would emerge automatically in auctions in which the government participated as a substantial buyer, perhaps along with buyers from the private sector. As evidence that this could work, I observed that the very announcement of the asset-purchase proposal had caused the prices of subprime mortgage assets to jump.

I believed then, and still do, that this way of thinking about asset purchases made the most sense. Sheila Bair also supported the idea. Of course, setting up fair and effective auctions for highly complex, difficult-to-value securities posed significant conceptual and operational problems.

For nearly five hours, the senators pressed us, raising questions and making suggestions of their own. Jack Reed, a financially savvy Democrat from Rhode Island, said taxpayers should share the profits if purchasing assets pushed up financial institution stock prices. In the middle of the hearing, Chris Dodd, the chairman of the committee, briefly noted a point that Hank hadn't—that nothing in the bill prohibited the government from acquiring equity stakes in institutions. Reed's and Dodd's comments suggested they weren't necessarily averse to partial public ownership of banks, although they seemed to think of it as a way to improve the returns to taxpayers rather than as a means of forcing restructuring or giving the government control over banks. In response, I encouraged the senators to give the administration broad flexibility in how it could use the $700 billion, depending on changing conditions and the outcomes of different approaches.

Senators repeatedly sounded the theme of fairness to Main Street. Mike Enzi, Republican from Wyoming, asked about small banks that did not have bad assets to sell to the government. Wouldn't we be rewarding failure by buying assets from the mostly larger financial institutions who made many of the worst loans? Actually, many small banks did hold bad assets, but in pointing out that deeply troubled banks would benefit most from the program, Enzi was highlighting yet another instance of the conflict between doing what was necessary to save the system and avoiding moral hazard. Several senators said executive pay at any financial institution benefiting from the program should be restricted. Others, including Dodd, pushed for doling out the money in tranches rather than all at once, thereby allowing Congress to stop the program if it was not satisfied with the results. It was a long and difficult hearing, but I thought we had made progress.

The next day, Wednesday September 24, felt like cruel and unusual punishment. I faced two more grueling hearings—one before the Joint Economic Committee and another before Barney Frank's House Financial Services Committee—as well as contentious meetings with the House Republican Conference—essentially, all the Republican members of the House—and the Senate Democratic Caucus. The morning before, House Republicans had angrily rebuffed an appeal from a delegation that included Vice President Cheney, White House Chief of Staff Josh Bolten, Keith Hennessey of the National Economic Council, and Kevin Warsh from the Fed.

Hank and I did our best with the House Republicans, but we had no better luck than the vice president's delegation. Lawmakers lined up behind microphones on each side of the large caucus room to vent. Their message: Bailing out Wall Street fat cats would be a gross injustice, a gift from Main Street to Wall Street. One member told us that he had spoken to small-town bankers, auto dealers, and others in his district with knowledge of the "real" U.S. economy. So far, he said, they had not seen any meaningful effects of the Wall Street troubles. "They will," I said to him. "They will." Developments on Wall Street, remote as they might seem, had the potential to choke off credit to small businesses and entrepreneurs and cripple the economy, I said. But most of the legislators were skeptical. I worried that Congress would act decisively only when the economic damage was apparent, large, and in all likelihood irreversible.

Throughout the day I hammered home the argument that deteriorating credit conditions posed a grave threat. "Credit is the lifeblood of the economy," I told the House Financial Services Committee. If the financial conditions didn't improve, "we're going to see higher unemployment, fewer jobs, slower growth, more foreclosures. . . . This is going to have real effects on people at the lunch-bucket level."

The perception that the financial crisis was not Main Street's concern was not our only problem: The asset-purchase plan remained difficult to explain and controversial for several other reasons. Some outside economists said that it would either not help (if assets were purchased at low prices) or would be unfair to taxpayers (if the prices were high). That criticism ignored my argument that auctions would produce prices between low fire-sale prices and higher hold-to-maturity prices. Others saw problems in designing auctions, because of the complexity and diversity of the securities to be purchased. I thought that objection, though legitimate, could be answered as well. But, despite our best efforts to make the case for asset purchases, I saw little evidence of an emerging consensus in favor of them and widespread confusion about how they would work.

Even as I explained asset purchases, I tried to preserve the administration's flexibility. I thought an oversight board could be empowered to make changes as needed. I didn't know how the crisis would evolve, so to a certain extent I was trying to have it both ways: supporting

Hank's strategy, while trying to retain an option for direct government capital injection or other approaches.

When Hank and I met with Democratic senators in the Capitol, they seemed no more inclined toward the Treasury plan than Republicans. The main difference, not surprisingly, was that Republicans wanted the government to do less (stand aside and let the system adjust on its own) and Democrats wanted the government to do more (act directly to help Main Street and to reduce executive compensation).

After the last meeting, exhausted and dispirited, I went home. Anna and I watched President Bush on TV, addressing the country. His plea for decisive action to end the crisis was effective, I thought. But by this point, on this issue, I was not an objective observer.

THURSDAY MORNING, September 25, market conditions were improving a bit. The Treasury and Fed programs to stabilize the money market funds appeared to be working. Outflows from prime funds had largely ceased. The commercial paper market also seemed to be functioning better. Still, both financial and nonfinancial companies continued to face challenges obtaining funding.

Meanwhile, the president had given Paulson a free hand to negotiate with Congress, and Hank began hectic rounds of shuttle diplomacy. The independent and nonpartisan Fed had no standing to be actively involved in political deal making. So we watched developments carefully and stood ready to respond to questions and make suggestions. I took calls from legislators. Most were looking for a politically acceptable way to do what had to be done.

The key questions at this point, it seemed to me, were how best to structure asset purchases, if any, and whether we should instead shift our focus to capital injections or something else. But as the debate grew ever more contentious, most legislators seemed unwilling or unable to grapple with the core issues. Instead, Hank found himself negotiating a range of auxiliary issues: restrictions on executive compensation, disbursing TARP money in tranches, helping troubled mortgage borrowers (very important but unlikely to end the crisis in time to avoid a meltdown), details of program oversight, and the treatment of small banks.

The fight over compensation illustrated the tensions between political and economic imperatives. Many in Congress wanted to cap pay at financial institutions that benefited from taxpayer dollars. The political appeal was clear, and, once again, I certainly understood why people were angry. Even before the crisis, many people saw financial executives' big paychecks as unfair. Now, with financiers' excessive risk taking having helped drive the economy into a ditch, the unfairness was stark. But, as a practical matter, if the conditions for participation in TARP were too onerous, firms would do what they could to stay away. We could not force a bank to take capital. If strong banks avoided the program, then weaker banks would not want to participate, either, since doing so would mark them as weak in the eyes of customers and creditors. That dynamic would doom our efforts to failure. Moreover, the proposed restrictions on executive compensation made no distinction between the executives running financial companies when they foundered and their successors trying to clean up the mess. We needed skilled and experienced professionals to come in and quickly restructure troubled firms. There weren't many like Ed Liddy, who had agreed to run AIG for a dollar a year.

In worrying about the practical aspects of the plan more than political considerations, I may have been tone-deaf. But most of my colleagues on the front lines, including Hank and Tim, seemed to share my perspective. Tim, in particular, complained about the "Old Testament" attitude of politicians who seemed more interested in inflicting punishment than in avoiding impending disaster. We were fine with bad actors getting their just deserts, but we believed it was better to postpone the verdict on blame and guilt until the fire was out. I had also over the years seen a great deal of feigned outrage in Washington, and I didn't feel like playing that game. I focused on solving the problems we faced and avoided sweeping populist indictments of bankers, in part because I knew that there was plenty of blame to go around, including at the Fed and other regulatory agencies and in Congress. Perhaps my low-key approach hurt us politically, but I was not comfortable proceeding in any other way.

The presidential election created further complications. In an ill-advised move, Republican Senator John McCain had suspended his campaign to come to Washington, supposedly to address the crisis. But the crisis was too large and complex for one senator to solve, even a nominee for president. We worried that one or both candidates would try to use the crisis for political advantage, complicating any potential deal in the Congress.

At McCain's request, President Bush convened a meeting at the White House on Thursday evening. I decided not to go. I didn't want to compromise the Fed's political independence by getting involved in the details of legislative disputes. All the other key players did attend, including the president, Hank, both presidential candidates, and congressional leaders of both parties. They had a chance to strike a deal. Both candidates had broadly endorsed Hank's plan, and the Senate Banking Committee had issued a set of bipartisan principles that included limits on executive compensation and giving the government equity stakes in companies receiving aid. President Bush tried to push the meeting toward an agreement, but it devolved into acrimony and disarray. Election politics and Republican resistance, especially in the House, prevented a deal. The Democrats, besides their substantive concerns, were miffed at having to provide most of the votes to pass an unpopular measure proposed by a Republican administration. McCain, despite having asked for the meeting, seemed unwilling to work actively for a solution.

One impediment was a proposal by Eric Cantor and several other House Republicans to replace asset purchases with an insurance program. For a fee, the government would insure assets against losses. I never understood the appeal. Cantor argued that his proposal would save taxpayers money, but he eventually conceded that it would not work for the most complex securities, which were the heart of the problem. Insuring those assets required setting a value for them as well as a fair premium. It was no simpler than asset purchases. Moreover, unlike purchases, insurance gave the taxpayer little upside if the assets appreciated. To gain a few additional Republican votes, the final bill included an optional version of Cantor's plan that would never be deployed.

On the left, legislators and economists pushed for helping homeowners in trouble rather than purchasing assets. I had no doubt that avoiding unnecessary foreclosures would benefit both borrowers and the broader economy, and I had often said so. But developing a cost-effective program, without being unfair to borrowers who had faithfully paid their mortgages, would take considerable time. With the financial system perhaps only days or weeks from collapse, we needed rapid action.

While both campaigns were in contact with the Fed, Obama seemed more interested in my views than McCain was. Obama called me for updates and had visited my office in late July. He was already leading in the polls at that point. I greeted him on his arrival at the Board garage and we rode up together in the small elevator, jammed in with security agents and staff. At our meeting we discussed recent developments but also steps he might take as president to reform financial regulation and strengthen the economy. I was pleased that he made a point of emphasizing his support for the Federal Reserve's independence. (He also charmed Rita Proctor and other administrative staff who gathered near my door, speaking briefly to each.)

McCain, on the other hand, seemed to be grasping for the right political stance. I had a favorable impression of McCain, a straight talker and an effective senator. (And Anna and I enjoyed meeting his mother, Roberta, at the time nearly a hundred years old, at a performance of the impressive Marine Corps Silent Drill Platoon at the Marine Barracks on Capitol Hill.) Given his military background,

McCain seemed more comfortable with foreign policy and military matters than with economics, but he was experienced and smart enough to know that, with the financial system near collapse, a laissez-faire approach wouldn't work. But he was vulnerable, both because his Republican base detested any government action that looked like a bailout and because the crisis and the proposed response occurred during a Republican administration.

He certainly did not think through his decision to suspend his campaign to come to Washington. He arrived without clear buy-in on a plan from Republican congressional leaders. On the Saturday after the White House meeting he called me at home and asked a few questions, indicated his support for the administration's proposal, and confessed his chagrin about any problems his intervention might have caused. He promised to "keep my head down." At one point, he compared the recurring explosions in the financial sector to IEDs, the military's acronym for improvised explosive devices.

The Board staff worked hard with senior staff from the Treasury and the New York Fed to design an effective asset-purchase program. I followed the work closely. At my urging, the staff also engaged outside experts on auction design. Despite these efforts, experienced members of my staff remained concerned about whether the government, as Hank hoped, could buy enough assets quickly enough to calm the crisis. "The problem . . . is a mismatch between rhetoric and reality," David Wilcox wrote to me. "I am becoming more convinced by the week that the need for large-scale capital infusion is drawing nearer. I don't think we're there yet, but we're getting closer."

ON THURSDAY, THE day of the ill-fated White House meeting, Don Kohn relayed news from Sheila Bair: JPMorgan had made a bid for Washington Mutual. Sheila was pleased because JPMorgan's acquisition involved no cost to the FDIC and no losses to uninsured depositors, such as corporations and municipalities. However, as a condition of the deal, not only WaMu's shareholders but also the holders of the company's senior debt—debt that was supposed to be paid first, before any other type of unsecured debt—would suffer significant losses.

I and others at the Fed, including Tim Geithner and Randy Kroszner, worried that forcing senior debt–holders to take losses, while the right and usual thing to do in normal times, would be a mistake in our current circumstances. It would create even more uncertainty about how the government would treat failing firms and make it harder for other banks to issue new debt. Senior debt had been protected at Fannie and Freddie and AIG, for example. Tim, whose relationship with Sheila was strained at best, was particularly exercised about the decision, but the Fed had limited leverage on this issue. The deal was negotiated largely between the FDIC and JPMorgan. JPMorgan indicated the deal was off if it had to make good on WaMu's senior debt, and Sheila adamantly opposed allowing the deposit insurance fund to incur any costs to protect senior debt–holders. (Sheila was tenacious about protecting the deposit insurance fund, which was admirable; but sometimes it seemed that she put the fund ahead of the interests of the broader financial system.) As justification for her position, Sheila could point out that the Federal Deposit Insurance Corporation Improvement Act of 1991, FDICIA for short, required the FDIC to resolve failing firms at the lowest possible cost to the deposit insurance fund. The requirement could be suspended only if the FDIC, the Fed, and the Treasury all agreed that doing so endangered the stability of the entire financial system. This "systemic risk exception" had never before been invoked.

The Office of Thrift Supervision bowed to the inevitable and shut down WaMu, allowing it to default on its senior debt and other liabilities. The FDIC seized the company's assets and assured depositors they would be protected. JPMorgan completed the transaction overnight, paying the FDIC $1.9 billion for WaMu's banking operations and loan portfolio. It was the largest bank failure in U.S. history. To strengthen its own position, JPMorgan raised $11.5 billion in additional capital by issuing new common stock. That Jamie Dimon's bank could raise capital in this environment was itself a show of strength.

Whether the FDIC's decision to impose losses on WaMu's senior debt–holders worsened the crisis is controversial. Sheila has strongly defended the action. She told the Senate in April 2010 that the resolution went smoothly. And in another forum that year she said, "It was below the fold if it was even on the front page . . . barely a blip given everything else that was going on."

My view, shared by others at the Board like Randy Kroszner, was that the WaMu decision, while perhaps not catastrophic, probably did hasten the fall of the next financial domino—Wachovia. By this time, Wachovia was headed by Bob Steel, a Goldman alum who, having served for twenty-one months as Paulson's undersecretary for domestic finance at the Treasury, had replaced ousted Wachovia CEO Ken Thompson in July 2008. Wachovia's fundamental problem was a large portfolio of low-quality mortgages. After WaMu's senior debt–holders suffered losses, unsecured creditors started to run from Wachovia and other struggling banks. By noon on the day after the WaMu failure, creditors were refusing to roll over Wachovia's short-term funding, including commercial paper and repo.

On Friday morning, September 26, I saw Paulson for breakfast at the Treasury. Hank told me he was becoming optimistic about getting a deal on TARP. Importantly, he also seemed more open to the idea of the government's injecting capital into financial institutions, either by "co-investing" with the private sector or through some type of auction. When I got back to my office I immediately emailed Geithner, Kohn, Kroszner, and senior staff including Wilcox. "He has been very resistant" to capital injection, I wrote. "Today he switched gears and said he thought those were fine ideas." However, Hank said he would not change his legislative strategy. He would continue to emphasize asset purchases in public discussion while simultaneously pressing for maximum flexibility in the use of TARP funds. I nevertheless encouraged

Fed staff members to redouble their efforts to determine how best to structure public capital injections. "Very good chance they will actually be relevant," I wrote.

Scott Alvarez, Brian Madigan, and our legislative team were tracking another provision in the TARP bill that would give us the ability to control short-term interest rates even as our interventions, such as our swaps with foreign central banks, caused our balance sheet to grow. In 2006, Congress had granted the Fed the authority to pay banks interest on the reserves that they hold at the Fed. However, for budgetary reasons, the authority had been set to become effective five years later, in 2011. But we asked, as part of the TARP legislation, that we be allowed to pay interest on reserves immediately.

We had initially asked to pay interest on reserves for technical reasons. But in 2008, we needed the authority to solve an increasingly serious problem: the risk that our emergency lending, which had the side effect of increasing bank reserves, would lead short-term interest rates to fall below our federal funds target and thereby cause us to lose control of monetary policy. When banks have lots of reserves, they have less need to borrow from each other, which pushes down the interest rate on that borrowing—the federal funds rate.

Until this point we had been selling Treasury securities we owned to offset the effect of our lending on reserves (the process called sterilization). But as our lending increased, that stopgap response would at some point no longer be possible because we would run out of Treasuries to sell. At that point, without legislative action, we would be forced to either limit the size of our interventions, which could lead to further loss of confidence in the financial system, or lose the ability to control the federal funds rate, the main instrument of monetary policy. The ability to pay interest on reserves (an authority that other major central banks already had), would help solve this problem. Banks would have no incentive to lend to each other at an interest rate much below the rate they could earn, risk-free, on their reserves at the Fed. So, by setting the interest rate we paid on reserves high enough, we could prevent the federal funds rate from falling too low, no matter how much lending we did.

AFTER BREAKFAST WITH Hank, I called Mervyn King and Jean-Claude Trichet to broach the idea of a joint interest rate cut. To my knowledge, major central banks had never coordinated interest rate cuts, and I thought that joint action would send a powerful signal of international unity. Mervyn, who after his early reticence to intervene had become a supporter of aggressive action, was somewhat more open to my idea than Jean-Claude. Both promised to think about it. I told Don and Tim that a joint rate cut looked possible but some further persuasion might be needed, especially for the ECB. Don replied that he would discuss the issue with the second-in-commands at the two central banks and suggested bringing the Canadians and the Japanese into the negotiation.

The United States was not alone in suffering from fragile financial institutions and markets. Since the run on Northern Rock the previous September, both the British and the continental Europeans had been putting out large financial fires. We learned on Friday that the giant Belgian-Dutch financial firm Fortis, a 775-billion-euro company that combined banking and insurance, was in dire straits, the result of investments in collateralized debt obligations and a mismanaged takeover of parts of the Dutch bank ABN AMRO. On Saturday, Don Kohn reported on a call from ECB vice president Lucas Papademos. "Fortis is a mess," was Don's summary. Papademos told Don that ING, a multinational firm headquartered in Amsterdam, and BNP Paribas, the French bank whose August 2007 announcement blocking withdrawals from its subprime mortgage funds had helped set off the financial crisis, were bidding for Fortis. But, he told Don, the deal probably wouldn't get done over the weekend, and the ECB was worried about how the markets would react.

The Europeans acted more promptly than Papademos had expected. On Sunday, the governments of Belgium, the Netherlands, and Luxembourg collectively injected more than 11.2 billion euros ($16 billion) of capital into Fortis. The ECB also lent dollars to Fortis, drawing on the swap line with the Fed. In an even bigger intervention, Germany's second-largest commercial property lender, Hypo Real Estate, received government and private guarantees totaling about 35 billion euros ($50 billion). Other problem institutions included the British lender Bradford & Bingley (partially nationalized at the end of September, using procedures developed for Northern Rock) and the German-Irish bank Depfa (a Hypo Real Estate subsidiary that was nationalized by the German government). The Belgian bank Dexia, which had made a large loan to Depfa, would be bailed out on September 29.

BACK IN THE United States, Wachovia was deteriorating even more quickly than we had anticipated. At the time the fourth-largest bank holding company in the United States, Wachovia was an even bigger financial bomb, potentially, than either Washington Mutual or Lehman. Its subsidiary banks had substantial uninsured liabilities, including unsecured debt, wholesale funding, and foreign deposits. Moreover, unlike WaMu, Wachovia conducted significant business activities outside its bank subsidiaries, in affiliated companies like its securities dealer or in the holding company itself (which had issued more than $50 billion in long-term debt).

Sheila Bair, who well understood the risks that Wachovia's collapse would pose, wanted to find a buyer for the whole company: the parent company, the nonbank affiliates, and the bank subsidiaries. Kevin Warsh had been leading an effort to evaluate the possibility of a merger between Goldman Sachs and Wachovia. However, that option disappeared as Goldman grew nervous about the losses embedded in Wachovia's balance sheet.

Citicorp and Wells Fargo also had expressed substantial interest. Merging Wachovia into another big bank wasn't ideal. It would increase the overall concentration in the banking industry, already dominated by the largest firms, and might also weaken the acquiring company. Still, given the circumstances and our rapidly shrinking options, it seemed the best solution. One consolation was that Citicorp and Wells Fargo had relatively little presence in the Southeast, where Wachovia was strongest. Consequently, a merger with either of the two wouldn't weaken regional competition for deposits and lending.

Managing Wachovia consumed the weekend, culminating in another all-night negotiation from Sunday to Monday, September 28–29, involving the holding company, its potential acquirers, and three regulators—the FDIC, the Fed, and the Office of the Comptroller of the Currency (which regulated Wachovia's largest bank). On Sunday morning, the prospects for a clean acquisition by either Citi (then the nation's largest bank holding company, about two and a half times larger than Wachovia) or Wells (the sixth largest—about three-quarters of Wachovia's size) looked good.

Citi's new CEO, the mild-mannered, urbane Vikram Pandit, then fifty-one, was aggressively pursuing Wachovia. Pandit struck me as sharp and sensible, although a number of supervisors (especially those at the FDIC) had reservations about his qualifications to lead Citi. He had spent most of his career in securities trading, at Morgan Stanley, rather than in traditional commercial banking. He had taken the helm at Citi in December 2007 after Chuck Prince (of "we're still dancing" fame) was pushed out. Pandit grew up in central India, came to the United States at sixteen, and earned degrees in electrical engineering before switching to business and completing a doctorate in finance at Columbia University. His mission at Citi was to refocus the ailing behemoth on its core strengths as a global commercial bank while ditching Citi's bad assets and improving its risk management.

Pandit's rival for Wachovia was the irascible and opinionated Dick Kovacevich, veteran chairman of Wells Fargo. Kovacevich had started his banking career at Citi and was CEO of the Minneapolis-based Norwest Corp. when it bought and assumed the name of San Francisco's Wells Fargo in 1998. Kovacevich had skillfully managed the integration of the two companies' operations and had avoided the riskiest subprime mortgages that had gotten many of its competitors into trouble. He had given up the CEO title the year before to his long-time number two, John Stumpf, and had been set to fully retire at the end of the year. But, a month short of his sixty-fifth birthday during the negotiations over Wachovia, he was looking for one more big deal.

After showing initial enthusiasm, though, Kovacevich decided on Sunday to back away, apparently out of concern over potential losses from Wachovia's commercial loans. Whether Wells would return to the negotiations, and if so on what terms, was unclear. That left Citi as potentially the sole bidder.

Because Wachovia included a large bank subsidiary, the government possessed a tool that had not been available with Lehman. The FDIC could purchase or guarantee some of the bank's assets, which could make the company as a whole more attractive. However, as in the case of WaMu, the law required the FDIC to resolve the bank at least cost to the deposit insurance fund, unless suspending the rule was necessary to avoid a substantial risk to the broader financial system. Doing so required the approval of two-thirds of the FDIC's board, two-thirds of the Federal Reserve Board, and the Treasury secretary, after consultation with the president.

Sheila had told me she thought a Wachovia deal could be done without government assistance, but, just in case, the Fed Board on Sunday afternoon approved a systemic risk exception, for the first time since enactment of the FDICIA law seventeen years earlier. We notified the FDIC. Meanwhile, Paulson got the president's approval. Don and I persuaded Sheila that the system could not withstand the failure of another major firm, and that invoking the exception would provide important flexibility in the negotiations. Josh Bolten, the president's chief of staff, called her Sunday evening to express White House support for invoking the exception. This time, Sheila accepted our arguments. The FDIC board acted early the next morning, completing the necessary approvals.

Sunday's all-night vigil involved many calls and meetings with exhausted staff. Kovacevich had gone to ground at the Carlyle Hotel in New York City, where he was monitoring developments. Citi executives seemed more eager. They coveted Wachovia's more than 3,300 bank branches and its nearly $420 billion in deposits, a reliable and low-cost source of funding. But Citi had problems of its own and wanted the FDIC to limit the losses it might inherit from Wachovia. Sheila asked the Fed and the Treasury to shoulder some of the risk. I was sympathetic and eager to get a deal done, but at the time I didn't see a way for the Fed to help. With the TARP legislation not completed, the Treasury had no money, either. In the end, the FDIC agreed to guarantee any losses in Wachovia's $312 billion loan portfolio beyond $42 billion. In return, the FDIC would receive preferred stock in Citi, as well as the option to buy additional stock and thereby benefit from any increase in Citi's stock price.

With that, Citi agreed to acquire all of Wachovia's liabilities— deposits and debt—as well as all of its loans. When Sheila's staff assured her that the FDIC was unlikely to lose money on the acquisition, and that the official accounting for the transaction would reflect that conclusion, she signed off. As Hank Paulson would note in his memoir, while he was struggling to obtain $700 billion from Congress to help the entire financial system, the FDIC had agreed to guarantee $270 billion in loans for a single bank and nobody seemed to notice. In this case, I thought Sheila had done well balancing her responsibility to protect the deposit insurance fund with the need to avoid a systemic financial crisis. I congratulated her and her staff.

But the story wasn't over. After the sale to Citi was announced on Monday but before it was final, Kovacevich and Wells Fargo came back with an offer for Wachovia that did not require loss protection by the FDIC. Wells Fargo's reentry was motivated in part by an IRS notice issued on September 30, which increased the tax advantages that Wells expected if it completed the acquisition. Sheila much preferred the Wells offer, both because of the reduced risk to the FDIC and because she saw Wells as the stronger pair of hands. She encouraged new negotiations between Wachovia and Wells.

Once again the Fed and the FDIC were at odds. We thought Sheila's desire to get a better deal for the FDIC fund had trumped other important considerations. Future negotiations could be jeopardized if the government refused to honor the agreement with Citi that it had helped to arrange. And we worried that the demise of the existing deal would fan market fears about Citi, which already had trumpeted the acquisition as strengthening its franchise.

On Thursday evening, October 2, Don let me know that Sheila was pressing forward on the Wachovia-Wells merger. She was "completely unconcerned about integrity of auction process" or the market uncertainty about Citi that could result from revoking the earlier deal, Don said. That message was the prelude to yet another night of negotiation. Lawyers for Wachovia and Wells worked feverishly. Meanwhile, Citi was in the dark. Kevin Warsh emailed me just before midnight that Bob Steel (possibly with Sheila) would call Citi after Wachovia's board had approved the deal with Wells. "Expect C to be outraged and to threaten legal action in the am . . . Our message: Wells took offer to Wachovia (no blessing from us) and FDIC gave them license," Kevin wrote.

At 3:00 a.m. on Friday, October 3, Don Kohn emailed: "Sheila and Bob called Vikram. . . . Vikram went 'nuts.' Sheila defended the decision saying better deal for 'the fund.' Not pretty. . . . will make for tricky markets in the am." Later, Vikram called me and vented bitterly. He urged us to block Wachovia's deal with Wells. Like all bank holding company mergers, it required the approval of the Fed's Board. He warned that Citi could be in danger if its own deal didn't go through, because markets had come to believe Citi needed Wachovia's deposits to survive. I also heard from Robert Rubin, the former Treasury secretary, now a senior counselor and board member at Citi. He thought that Citi might be able to improve its offer and get back in the game.

Tim weighed in strongly on Citi's side. He acknowledged that Wells Fargo's offer was superior but argued that allowing the deal to be scuttled at this point would destroy the government's credibility as an honest broker. He warned that the United States would look like a banana republic if the government arbitrarily reneged. In contrast with the WaMu deal, the Fed's authority over holding company mergers gave us some leverage. (Because WaMu was a savings institution, and JPMorgan's bank, which acquired WaMu, was a nationally chartered bank regulated by the Office of the Comptroller of the Currency, Fed approval had not been required in that case.) However, the law requires specific findings for rejecting a merger of holding companies. We had to find, for instance, that a merger would hurt competition in local banking markets or that the banks involved had not met their responsibilities to invest in local communities. None of these criteria provided much basis for favoring Citi over Wells. The real issue, whether Wachovia's acceptance of Wells's offer had violated its provisional agreement with Citi, was a matter for the courts, not the Federal Reserve.

We worked for compromise. To help mollify Citi, we supported allowing it to increase its deposit base by acquiring Wachovia's branches in several northeastern states. In exchange, Citi agreed not to try to block the merger of Wells and Wachovia, although it would continue to seek damages of $60 billion from Wells. The Fed Board approved the merger of Wachovia and Wells Fargo on October 9. I spent several hours assuring senators and representatives from North Carolina that the merger did not mean the end of the bank's role as a major employer in Charlotte. To the contrary, I told them, avoiding the collapse of Wachovia should help preserve local banking jobs as well as avoid much more serious economic consequences for the country.

AS REGULATORS TENDED to the Wachovia negotiations, Paulson had continued his discussions with congressional leaders about TARP. Early Monday morning, September 29, he called to report that they shook hands at 1:00 a.m. Hank's experience as a Wall Street dealmaker had paid off. He had successfully resisted significant changes to the legislation. The money would be disbursed in two $350 billion tranches. Congress could prevent the second tranche from being used only by passing a bill and sustaining it over the president's veto. If the program lost money after five years, the president would have to propose a plan for recovering the losses through fees on the financial services industry. There would be multiple oversight bodies, including a special inspector general and a congressional oversight panel, and also a board of cabinet-level officials (I would end up being the chair) that would advise on how best to use the funds.

The deal included Senator Jack Reed's idea of using stock warrants (the right to purchase common stock at a fixed price) to give taxpayers a share of the gains if participating companies rebounded. It also required Treasury to develop a plan to help mortgage borrowers in trouble. The three-page plan that Treasury had sent to the Congress was now more than a hundred pages of legislation. The critical elements of the Treasury proposal—the authorization of funding and the flexibility to use the money as needed—were intact. The final bill also retained the provision moving up the effective date of the Fed's authority to pay interest on bank reserves. After Paulson announced the deal, both presidential candidates guardedly lent their support.

Meanwhile, on an FOMC conference call Monday morning, I updated the Reserve Bank presidents on Wachovia developments, as well as the implications of our newfound interest-on-reserves authority. I also asked the Committee to more than double our currency swap lines with major foreign central banks to $620 billion, which it did. The crisis was hitting European banks even harder than those in the United States. On Monday alone, the stock price of Anglo Irish Bank plunged 46 percent, Dexia fell by 30 percent, Germany's Commerzbank and Deutsche Postbank by 23 and 24 percent, respectively, and Sweden's Swedbank by 19 percent. I could hardly imagine a clearer vote of no confidence.

But the most important event of September 29 would be the congressional vote on TARP. Americans wanted us to end the financial crisis, but we had failed to persuade them that pouring hundreds of billions of taxpayer dollars into the financial system was the solution. Senator Jon Kyl of Arizona told me that his constituent calls on TARP were running fifty-fifty: "fifty percent no, fifty percent hell no." Editorialists and op-ed writers generally supported the legislation, though often with thumb and forefinger firmly pinching their nostrils. "The alternative to this admittedly imperfect and highly uncertain program could be much, much worse," the *Washington Post* wrote.

I thought that the bill would pass, given that the leaders of both parties had signed off. But late Monday morning, Kevin Warsh, who was monitoring Hill developments, sent a troubling email: "FYI. Last thing we need but there is a real House GOP problem in coming up with enough votes such that Speaker delivers on her side." The syntax of the sentence, composed I'm sure in haste, was a little garbled, but the message was clear: Republican support was thin and Speaker Pelosi's troops, who did not want Democrats to be seen as the party of TARP, were not willing to make up the difference.

Two hours after Kevin's email, it was clear that the House would defeat the bill. House leaders kept the vote, originally scheduled for fifteen minutes, open for forty minutes, hoping to persuade "no" voters to switch. When the gavel banged at 2:10 p.m., the yeas were 205 and the nays, 228. I had watched the progress on the television in my office, together with the market reactions on my Bloomberg screen. I felt like I had been hit by a truck. So did the stock market. The Dow Jones industrial average plunged nearly 778 points—its worst-ever one-day decline in point terms, a record that still stands. In percentage terms, it was down 7 percent, the worst since the first trading day following the 9/11 attacks. Meanwhile, the S&P 500 fell by almost 9 percent. In all, $1.2 trillion in value vanished from the U.S. stock market in a single day.

The House vote seemed a crippling setback to our efforts to end the crisis. But constituent support for TARP increased significantly as people saw their 401(k) retirement accounts shrinking—or their "201(k) accounts," as they were being called. Sobered congressional leaders regrouped and tried again. They sweetened the bill by including a temporary increase (later made permanent) in deposit insurance, from $100,000 to $250,000 per account. The Senate passed the bill, 74–25, on Wednesday, October 1, and the House, 263–171, on Friday, October 3. The president signed it that afternoon.

The administration had a powerful new weapon, and, finally, primary responsibility for restoring financial stability would no longer rest solely with the Fed.

CHAPTER 16

A Cold Wind

The bloodletting in financial markets continued during the week after the president signed the TARP legislation (known formally as the Emergency Economic Stabilization Act). Stock prices sometimes swung up and down by hundreds of points in an hour, driving indicators of market volatility to record levels, but always the prevailing trend was down. From Friday, October 3, to Friday, October 10, the Dow Jones industrial average lost 1,874 points, a shocking 18 percent. I tilted the Bloomberg screen in my office away from my desk so that I wouldn't be distracted by the flashing red numbers.

Notwithstanding the enactment of TARP, confidence in financial institutions had nearly evaporated, and even strong nonfinancial companies found credit extremely difficult to obtain. The week before, General Electric, a top-rated conglomerate with both financial and nonfinancial arms, had been forced to raise $3 billion in capital from Warren Buffett before lenders would roll over its commercial paper. Interest rates on corporate bonds and the cost of insuring against corporate default shot skyward—a sign that traders were expecting the slumping economy to bring down more companies.

In public I described what was happening as the "worst financial crisis since the Great Depression," but privately I thought that—given the number of major financial institutions that had failed or come close to failure, its broad-based effect on financial and credit markets, and its global scope—it was almost certainly the worst in human history. Whether the financial crisis would touch off the deepest economic downturn since the Depression, or something even worse, remained an open question. The data depicted an economy sinking ever further. The Fed's regular survey of bank loan officers during the first half of October would show that banks were sharply tightening their lending terms and credit flows to families and businesses were drying up. Employers had shed 159,000 jobs in September—the ninth straight monthly decline. Unemployment, still only mildly elevated at 6.1 percent, was clearly headed for a sharp rise.

The deepening slump was evident not only in government statistics but also in what we were hearing from business and community leaders around the country. In mid-October, Governor Betsy Duke went to San Francisco to meet with the Reserve Bank's private-sector board and an advisory panel of businesspeople from around the region. "The comments are stunning and terrifying," Betsy wrote me in an email. "Across the board every business reporting a complete 'hunkering down.' They are canceling every capital project and discretionary program possible. Credit is increasingly unavailable. . . . Small businesses and non-profits . . . are missing payrolls and shutting down. I would plead to do anything possible to restore confidence in the entire financial system."

The economic effects of the crisis spread rapidly, without regard for national borders. In November, while in São Paulo for an international meeting, I made time to meet with the CEOs of the largest Brazilian banks and other local business leaders. "In early September everything was fine," one of the CEOs told me. "Then all of a sudden everything stopped. No borrowing, no investment. It was like a cold wind blew through the economy."

FOR SEVERAL WEEKS, Hank Paulson and I had been debating the relative merits of purchasing troubled assets versus injecting capital into distressed banks. In our private conversations, Hank had moved toward my preferred strategy—capital injections, in which the government would acquire stock and thus partial ownership of banks. Capital injections would strengthen banks directly, by increasing the buffer available to absorb losses. In contrast, purchases of troubled assets would strengthen banks indirectly and only to the extent that they raised the prices of the assets that banks held.

On October 1, when we had lunch with President Bush, Hank himself had raised the possibility of using some TARP funds to provide new capital to banks as well as for purchasing assets. The TARP legislation was written broadly enough to permit either strategy or both, and Hank was keeping his options open. But, within a week after the president signed the TARP, Hank had clearly shifted away from asset purchases. Whatever the merits of the strategy in the abstract, it was becoming clear that financial markets and the economy were deteriorating too quickly. There just wasn't enough time to design and implement an effective asset-purchase program.

It probably helped that the British, led by Prime Minister (and former finance minister) Gordon Brown, also appeared to be converging on a plan that included government capital injections via purchases of stock in large banks. They announced their plan on Wednesday, October 8. On the same day, Paulson met with journalists and released a statement noting that, among other authorities, TARP gave the Treasury the power to put capital into banks. "We will use all of the tools we've been given to maximum effectiveness, including strengthening the capitalization of financial institutions of every size," he said.

Economists and editorial writers generally approved of recapitalizing banks, but the political blowback was fierce. As we met with legislators, Hank and I had emphasized the need for flexibility to adapt to changing circumstances. News reports had noted that the TARP legislation encompassed a variety of approaches, including capital injections. Senator Dodd had pointed that out at his committee's September 23 hearing. Nevertheless, many members of Congress regarded the new emphasis on capital injection as a bait and switch. Fair or not, that perception further increased politicians' animosity toward the TARP.

In retrospect I wonder whether I should have insisted earlier and more vigorously on persuading Congress to accept capital injections. Perhaps so, although Hank's arguments about political feasibility and possible market reactions rang true to me at the time. In any case, the initial emphasis on asset purchases was not a ploy: We and the Treasury had made a serious effort to implement an asset-purchase program. Fed staff had worked diligently to find an approach that would both stabilize the financial system and treat taxpayers fairly. But they ultimately concluded that, given the difficulty of establishing fair prices for complex, diverse assets, an effective program might take the Treasury many weeks to set up. Another staff concern was that, with more and more assets coming under suspicion, spending every penny of the $700 billion in TARP money on toxic assets might not be enough to stabilize the system. Providing $700 billion of new capital, on the other hand, would increase the capital of the banking system by half or more, reassuring creditors and customers and bolstering banks' confidence to lend. If strengthening financial institutions stimulated private investors to put capital into banks as well, then so much the better.

As Hank showed increasing openness to capital injections, a Board staff team—led by David Wilcox—developed alternative implementation strategies. One approach, co-investment, aimed at involving private investors. Bank regulators and the Treasury would determine which banks needed capital, then capital-short banks would have a chance to find private investors. Those that could not would be required to take TARP capital. Hank liked the co-investment idea but ultimately opted for a simpler, government-capital-only plan on the grounds that, in the fall of 2008, capital markets were effectively closed to the great majority of banks. However, the basic approach that Wilcox and his team developed would resurface later.

I was glad that Hank was now prepared to use TARP to put capital into banks. I expected that fatter capital cushions, by reducing the risk of bank failures, would reduce fear and panic in the markets. But I also knew that in chaotic conditions, when asset values swing wildly, increased capital alone may not restore confidence. Government guarantees might also be needed. We had seen how a Treasury guarantee had ended a run on money market funds a month earlier, and FDIC-insured depositors had stayed with their banks throughout the crisis. But, in the twenty-first-century banking system, deposits were only one avenue for bank financing. Recognizing that, Britain, Ireland, and Greece had begun guaranteeing all bank liabilities (including longer-term debt) as well as deposits.

The Fed, though it could lend to banks against good collateral, had no authority to guarantee their debts directly. I discussed, with Fed staff, an idea for indirectly guaranteeing short-term interbank loans, a narrow subset of transactions. Instead of lending directly to each other, banks could use the Fed as an intermediary. The lending bank would make a deposit at the Fed, which would in turn lend to the borrowing bank. The use of the Fed as an intermediary would eliminate the consequences (for the borrowing bank) of a default by the lending bank and thus possibly revive the market for short-term interbank loans. This strategy, though it appeared to be legally permissible, looked to be operationally unwieldy and difficult to implement reasonably quickly. Fortunately, a better and more natural alternative surfaced. The FDIC had potentially broad guarantee powers, if it chose to use them.

Hank and I met with Sheila Bair on Wednesday, October 8, at the Treasury (with Tim Geithner on speakerphone). We hoped to persuade Sheila to guarantee the liabilities of the entire banking system through the deposit insurance fund. To do that, her board would have to join the Fed and the Treasury in declaring a systemic risk exception for all banks—not just one bank, as we had done to facilitate Citigroup's ultimately scuttled acquisition of Wachovia. Sheila, who became pricklier as events pushed her into taking steps further out of her comfort zone, has described the meeting as an "ambush." I wouldn't call it that. Our goal was only to broach the subject to the policymaker who, in this case, had the authority to act. We certainly did not expect an immediate commitment.

And Sheila was indeed noncommittal. She said she doubted that, even after declaring a systemic risk exception, she had the legal authority to guarantee all bank liabilities. She also doubted that her $35 billion deposit insurance fund would prove a credible backstop for trillions of dollars of bank debts and deposits. We pointed out that if broad guarantees helped prevent future bank failures, the deposit insurance fund would be far more secure.

The next morning, Sheila emailed Hank, Tim, and me. Upon reflection, she had concluded that blanket guarantees of the system were not necessary. Her staff believed that banks had enough capital and earnings to cover anticipated losses, which should be sufficient to restore confidence over time. She worried that bank guarantees could have unintended consequences, including sucking money away from money market funds. (I believed that the Treasury's guarantee of money funds had alleviated that concern.) She was also concerned that weak banks might use guaranteed funds to finance go-for-broke risk taking, keeping the profits if they were lucky and dumping the losses on the deposit insurance fund if they were not. She concluded that it was better to use TARP funds to both invest in bank stock and provide any guarantees of bank liabilities that the Treasury deemed necessary. The FDIC could then fulfill its normal function of dealing with individual bank failures, which she saw as likely to remain manageable.

Tellingly, nowhere in the email did she argue that the FDIC lacked the necessary authority; and, despite her reservations, Sheila and her staff were working seriously on a guarantee plan. On Friday she sent a counterproposal. The FDIC would invoke the systemic risk exception and guarantee newly issued bank debt only—not existing debt, and not debt issued by bank holding companies. The guarantee would require a 10 percent co-pay by investors. That is, if a bank defaulted on debt covered by the guarantee, the investor would be on the hook for 10 percent of the loss. Also, the FDIC would cover senior debt only, not lower-priority debt, such as subordinated debt. (Subordinated, or junior, debt cannot be repaid until the claims of senior debt–holders are fully satisfied.) Banks would pay fees for the FDIC guarantees. In addition, the FDIC would insure accounts, such as business checking accounts, that were not already covered by regular deposit insurance.

The Fed had traditionally opposed expanding deposit insurance, on the grounds that it would increase moral hazard. But during the crisis, insuring checking accounts used by businesses, municipalities, and nonprofit organizations, at least temporarily, made a lot of sense. Without it, these entities might rapidly shift their deposits from smaller banks perceived to be at risk to banks perceived as too big to fail. However, imposing a 10 percent co-pay on the debt guarantee and excluding the liabilities of bank holding companies didn't seem workable. Potential bank debt buyers wouldn't want to risk even 10 percent of their money, particularly since they had the alternative of buying the debt of banks in Europe, where some countries had already fully insured all bank liabilities.

Negotiations continued for several days. With a lot of hard staff work, we reached an agreement. On October 13, the FDIC board unanimously invoked the systemic risk exception and approved broad guarantees. The Fed's Board invoked the exception the same day. The FDIC would fully insure new senior debt issued by both banks and their holding companies (no 10 percent haircut) for maturities of more than thirty days and less than three years. Coverage under the Temporary Loan Guarantee Program (TLGP), as it would officially be called, was free for the first month. To leave the program, banks had to actively opt out (few did). Participating banks paid moderate fees for the protection, with higher fees for guarantees of longer-term debt. As Sheila had originally suggested, the plan also extended deposit insurance to accounts used by businesses, governments, and nonprofits. I sent Sheila a letter promising that Fed supervisors would watch vigilantly for risky behavior by banks whose debts had been guaranteed.

In time, 122 banks and bank holding companies would issue $346 billion in guaranteed debt under this program, giving banks the security of longer-term funding and shoring up confidence in the banking system. The FDIC lost $150 million on its debt guarantees and $2.1 billion on the extended deposit insurance, but it collected more than $11 billion in fees, for a net gain to its insurance fund of $9 billion.

EVERYTHING STILL SEEMED to be happening at once. While the discussions about capital injections and bank guarantees were progressing, the Fed was also busy working on a new program to support the commercial paper market. Since the eruption of the crisis in 2007, lenders had become very cautious about buying commercial paper, funding only the most creditworthy issuers. Money market funds had become particularly skittish buyers after Lehman defaulted on its commercial paper. From just before Lehman weekend to the middle of October, commercial paper outstanding had fallen by about one-sixth, or $300 billion. Maturities on more and more of the paper had shrunk to a day or two, increasing the risk that borrowers would be unable to roll over their financing.

September 2008 was not the first time that dysfunction in the commercial paper market had prompted Fed action. In June 1970, the railroad company Penn Central unexpectedly declared bankruptcy and defaulted on its commercial paper. Worried lenders soon refused to roll over the paper of many other firms; corporate borrowing in the commercial paper market dropped by more than 9 percent over the next three weeks. The Fed stemmed the slide by lending to banks through its discount window and encouraging the banks, in turn, to lend to customers that had lost access to the commercial paper market.

In 2008, though, discount window lending to banks wasn't likely to help. Banks were lending as little as possible. We needed a more direct way to backstop the commercial paper market. We could invoke our emergency 13(3) authority and lend directly to firms unable to roll over their commercial paper, but that seemed a step too far. We wanted to restore the proper functioning of the commercial paper market, not replace it with our own lending.

In the Bear Stearns rescue, we created a legal entity to hold some of

Bear's risky assets, and the Fed lent to that entity. Several staff meetings with lots of blue-sky thinking, at both the Board and the New York Fed, led to the proposal of a similar solution. The Board could create a new legal entity called the Commercial Paper Funding Facility, or CPFF, which could buy commercial paper with funds provided by the Fed under its 13(3) authority. Hank and I had discussed the basic idea at our October 1 lunch with the president.

We needed to break the mentality that was prompting commercial paper buyers to lend for only a few days at a time (if they were willing to lend at all). Buyers lending at very short maturities hoped to be the first to the door if anything went wrong, leaving the buyers who had lent at longer maturities holding the bag. It was yet another example of run psychology. With the Fed acting as a backstop for commercial paper, including commercial paper with longer maturities, we might be able to restore confidence to both lenders and borrowers.

We soon faced an unexpected hitch. Loans made by the Federal Reserve, we knew, must be "secured to the satisfaction" of the Reserve Bank making the loan—in the case of the CPFF, the New York Reserve Bank. Firms that issue commercial paper are legally obligated to repay, but by longstanding practice the paper is rarely backed by explicit collateral, such as marketable securities. Could a loan to the CPFF, whose only assets were commercial paper, be considered adequately secured?

When we announced our plan to create the CPFF, we thought we had the solution to that problem. I had asked Hank to contribute TARP money to the new facility. If the TARP funds were first in line to absorb losses, then Fed loans to the CPFF would be adequately secured, meeting the legal requirement. Hank appeared to react positively, and we had counted on TARP money to make the CPFF work. But, to my chagrin, either I misunderstood Hank or he and his staff changed course. Over the next few days Fed staff and Treasury staff talked but didn't reach agreement. Paulson later wrote that he declined to put TARP funds in the CPFF because he hadn't wanted the revamped commercial paper facility to be the TARP's first program, although why that was such an important consideration I don't know. Hank did like the general approach we proposed, though, and it became a model for later Fed-Treasury collaborations.

We had already announced the CPFF, and now, unexpectedly, TARP money was unavailable. We scrambled to find a way to ensure that our loans to the facility would be adequately secured. It took some lengthy meetings and calls, but eventually we found a workable formula. First, we stipulated that the CPFF would be allowed to buy only the most highly rated commercial paper (which, unfortunately, left out some important companies). We also required firms that wanted to sell their commercial paper to the facility to pay an up-front fee and an interest rate high enough to hasten their return to the regular market as conditions normalized. The fees were put in a reserve against possible losses. Finally, we limited our risk by capping the amount of commercial paper any one firm could sell to the CPFF. With these conditions in place, the Board and the New York Fed were willing to stipulate that loans to the CPFF were adequately secured. During its existence, the facility would suffer no losses and turn a profit for taxpayers, collecting $849 million in fees.

DURING THE CONGRESSIONAL debate around TARP, many lawmakers, especially Democrats, had argued passionately for helping homeowners facing foreclosure. As passed, the TARP bill required the government to modify mortgages it acquired through asset purchases. More importantly, the bill also authorized the use of TARP money for foreclosure prevention programs.

These provisions were just the latest effort to do something about the foreclosure epidemic. In July, Congress had also passed a program, called Hope for Homeowners—not to be confused with Hope Now, the voluntary private-sector initiative from the year before. H4H, as the new program was known inside the Beltway, authorized the Federal Housing Administration to refinance up to $300 billion of troubled mortgages, after imposing losses on the private-sector holders of the mortgages. At the Fed, we thought that the approach, advocated by Barney Frank and others, was promising. Refinancing would take the troubled mortgages off lenders' books (after appropriate recognition of losses) while reducing monthly payments for borrowers. The Fed, along with other agencies, was assigned to oversee the program. Betsy Duke, who was now spending much of her time on housing issues, represented the Board.

The program failed. Only a few hundred borrowers even applied. Crucially, Congress had been unwilling to spend much on loan modifications. It made the terms for FHA refinancing unattractive for lenders, who mostly refused to participate. Congress's tightfistedness was a nod to fiscal rectitude, but it also reflected the fact that many people apparently regarded helping troubled homeowners as "one more bailout" of irresponsible actors. I found that attitude remarkable. By this time the foreclosure epidemic had spread well beyond those who had knowingly purchased homes they could not afford. With the economy tanking and credit drying up, millions of people were either having trouble making their mortgage payments or knew someone who was. Moreover, helping troubled borrowers could benefit not only the borrowers themselves but also neighborhoods blighted by foreclosed homes, the broader housing market (where foreclosures and forced sales were depressing prices and construction), and the overall economy.

AS WE WORKED to implement new programs at home, I kept a close watch on the economies and financial systems of our trading partners. The cold wind was blowing very strongly abroad, particularly in Europe.

I continued urging other major central banks to join us in a coordinated interest rate cut. I believed that the rate cuts themselves would support global economic growth and that the demonstration of unity would cheer the markets. When I had talked to Mervyn King and Jean-Claude Trichet on September 26, they had been interested but had also had reservations. The European Central Bank in particular had still been nervous about inflation. However, as financial conditions and the economic data worsened, resistance melted. Other central banks wanted to join in.

A coordinated rate cut presented tricky logistical problems. Each central bank involved had to arrange a special meeting or conference call with its policy committee. Then we had to coordinate the timing and wording of our announcements, all without giving any hint in advance of the market-moving news that was coming.

The Federal Open Market Committee met by videoconference late in the afternoon of Tuesday, October 7. Two FOMC hawks—Richard Fisher and Charles Plosser—happened to be in New York, so they joined Tim Geithner at the New York Fed for the call. "I just wanted to point out that I have assembled a historic coalition in New York of hawks on both sides of me today," Geithner joked. Fisher, ever the Texas chauvinist, deadpanned, "Mr. Chairman, we enjoy visiting Third World countries." And Plosser responded, "We just thought we would outflank him, but we haven't succeeded."

Small levities aside, the meeting had a dark tone. Bill Dudley described an "extremely dangerous and fragile" financial environment. In addition to more than doubling the cap on our swap lines with other central banks, to $620 billion, we had responded with a sixfold increase in scheduled auctions of discount window credit to banks in the United States—to $900 billion. The goal, as always, was to ensure banks access to funding despite the turmoil in credit markets. The huge amounts showed the size of the problem. But, despite all our efforts, panic persisted and credit remained frozen.

I told the FOMC that the financial situation posed enormous and growing economic risks. A coordinated response, showing the resolve and cooperation of major central banks, could have a stronger effect on the U.S. and global economies than if we acted alone. I also believed that concerted action could provide cover for other central banks to cut rates, notably the ECB, which was heir to the hawkish tradition of Germany's Bundesbank. The FOMC voted unanimously to cut the federal funds rate by a half percentage point, to 1-1/2 percent.

The back-and-forth on the choreography with other central banks culminated in a call that included me, Trichet, King, Mark Carney of the Bank of Canada, and Masaaki Shirakawa of the Bank of Japan. Finally, on October 8, at 7:00 a.m. New York time, the Fed, the European Central Bank, the Bank of England, the Bank of Canada, the Swiss National Bank, and Sweden's Riksbank each announced interest rate cuts of half of a percentage point.* The Bank of Japan, with its policy rate already near zero, expressed strong support. We did not coordinate with the People's Bank of China, but it, too, cut rates that morning. It felt good to pull off such a complicated piece of theater. The psychological effect of the world's major central banks acting in concert would, I hoped, prove as important as the stimulus provided by the rate cuts themselves.

Yet as dramatic as the coordinated rate cut was, it did not solve the global financial system's fundamental problems: unremitting panic and growing unease about the health of major financial institutions. The Dow Jones industrial average rose 180 points after we announced the coordinated cuts but ended down 189 points, or 2 percent, for the day. Markets were sending an unmistakable signal: More force was needed, and soon.

SO FAR, the global response—outside of central banks—had largely been ad hoc and country by country. The Europeans had bailed out even more financial firms than we had but had not developed a comprehensive response. German rhetoric about the moral hazard of bailouts—despite the rescues of Hypo Real Estate and IKB—hamstrung cooperation on the continent. Meanwhile, some countries were com-

---

*   After the cuts, the policy rates at the other central banks were: ECB, 3-3/4 percent; Bank of England, 4-1/2 percent; Bank of Canada, 2-1/2 percent; Sweden's Riksbank, 4-1/4 percent.

plaining about spillover effects. When Ireland announced on September 29 that it was guaranteeing the deposits and debt of its banks, the British worried that Irish banks would drain funds from British banks. That led the British to follow nine days later with their own guarantee of bank liabilities.

Some small countries with large banks simply lacked the resources to go it alone. For example, tiny Iceland, with its 300,000 people, was also home to three large banks with operations extending to other Nordic countries, Britain, and the Netherlands. By early October, all three banks had collapsed, wiping out their shareholders (mostly domestic) and bondholders (mostly foreign). We had declined Iceland's request for a currency swap line, as did the European Central Bank and Bank of England. Iceland's financial institutions had few ties to U.S. financial institutions, and their problems were in any case too severe to be solved by currency swaps.

An opportunity to strengthen global cooperation arrived on Friday, October 10, as the world's finance ministers and central bank governors converged on Washington for the regular fall meeting of the member countries of the International Monetary Fund (IMF) and the World Bank. The two institutions, which trace their origins to an international conference in Bretton Woods, New Hampshire, in 1944, were intended to promote international economic cooperation, with the IMF focused on maintaining economic and financial stability and the World Bank on fostering growth in developing countries. With 188 nations as members, these institutions had also become important venues for international consultation and policy coordination.

A series of smaller meetings led up to the broader gathering. First, on Friday, was the Group of Seven (G-7): the United States, Canada, Japan, France, Germany, Italy, and the United Kingdom. On Saturday, the larger G-20 would meet. In addition to the major industrial countries, it included the most important emerging-market economies, among them China, India, Brazil, Mexico, and Russia. The G-20's policy role had been growing with the global economic weight of the

emerging-market economies. However, because the G-7 countries were
home to most of the world's largest financial institutions and financial
markets, I expected that on this occasion the G-7 meeting would be
the more important. It turned out to be the most consequential international meeting that I would attend during my time as Fed chairman.

We met in the Treasury Department's Cash Room, a two-story
marble hall with enormous brass chandeliers directly across from the
Treasury's main entrance. Opened for business in 1869, it was used
for financial transactions with bankers and the public through 1976.
Now it was the scene of formal events and social gatherings. For the
G-7 meeting, long tables had been arranged in a square, with country
placards at the seats. Interpreters were available but not necessary for
the U.S. delegation; all discussions would be in English. Deputies and
assistants moved in and out of the room, and aides, security agents, and
other support personnel milled about in the hallway outside. As was
customary, Paulson, the finance minister of the host country, presided.

International meetings are often sleepy affairs, occasions useful
primarily for policymakers and senior staff members to maintain communications with their international counterparts. The same agenda
topics recur meeting after meeting. The same platitudes are repeated.
Deputies write and agree in advance to the postmeeting communiqué,
drafted in fuzzy bureaucratic language aimed at winning unanimous
support.

The tone of this meeting was anything but sleepy. Unlike no previous moment since the 1930s, the global economic system itself seemed
at risk. Most of the finance ministers and central bank governors
assembled blamed the United States for the crisis. Whose financial
deregulation had subjected the world to the depredations of "cowboy capitalism"? Whose subprime mortgages had infected the assets
of financial institutions around the world? Who had let Lehman fail?
On this last point, Jean-Claude Trichet, in his ringing Gallicized English, was particularly eloquent, passing around a chart that showed
the sharp deterioration in funding markets that had occurred after

Lehman weekend. Others echoed Jean-Claude, and for a moment it seemed the meeting might degenerate into finger-pointing.

In a global crisis, the United States was the natural leader. But our country's prestige and credibility were at a low ebb. The early schadenfreude of other advanced countries at the U.S. crisis had morphed into anger when the effects of the crisis spread globally and gathered force. Who were we to give advice? We heard this message both from the G-7 and, perhaps even more consistently, from emerging-market officials at the G-20 meeting on Saturday.

Despite those tensions, the G-7 representatives were determined to work together. Too much was at stake for the group to leave Washington without at least the outlines of a coordinated response. And, despite some testy rhetoric, the people at the table respected each other. We knew we were among the few who could stop the bleeding. Breaking protocol established over many years, we ignored the meeting agenda and launched into a freewheeling and substantive discussion.

I had been thinking about what should be done for some time. On the Wednesday before the meeting I had finished drafting a set of principles that I hoped the G-7 would adopt. They were basic, but I believed they encompassed the responses that had calmed panics many times in the past. In brief, I wanted the assembled officials to pledge to cooperate to stabilize financial markets, restore the flow of credit, and support global economic growth. Toward those objectives, I wrote, the countries represented at the meeting should provide necessary short-term loans and capital for their banks, collaborate on supervising banks operating internationally, and permit no more failures of systemically important institutions. And I wanted us to pledge to restart critical markets for mortgage-backed securities, commercial paper, and interbank lending. With Treasury's support I submitted my list of proposed policy commitments to the deputies working on the communiqué.

The principles resonated with the ideas that others brought to the table. In the final statement issued by the G-7, my initial list was shortened to five points. First, the member nations promised to prevent more Lehmans—that is, to prevent more failures of systemically important institutions. (The United States could credibly make this promise after the enactment of TARP.) Second, we pledged to work to unfreeze funding markets (the Fed's commercial paper facility being an example of such an attempt). Third, we committed to recapitalizing banks to promote the flow of credit. Fourth, we said we would put deposit insurance in place to protect ordinary depositors and maintain confidence in banks. (This point was not on my original list because the United States had long had federal deposit insurance. But it was an issue for Europe, where most countries lacked comprehensive deposit insurance.) And, fifth, we promised to work to restart securitization, so that mortgages and other types of credit could be funded by investors.

The participants left the G-7 meeting with their resolve restored. In the United States, we were moving beyond the ad hoc responses of the pre-Lehman period. Mobilization had been slow, but I believed we now had the chance to mount a systematic attack on the crisis at the global level.

GLOBAL POLICYMAKERS LIVED up to their promises. Most importantly, on Sunday evening the eurozone countries agreed to implement capital injections and guarantees for their banks. Austria, France, Germany, Italy, the Netherlands, Portugal, Spain, and Sweden announced bank debt guarantees similar to the one proposed by the FDIC in the United States. An even larger group expanded their deposit insurance systems. A few countries, including Norway and Spain, announced that they would buy assets as well. On Monday, the United Kingdom essentially nationalized two of its largest banks, the Royal Bank of Scotland and HBOS. For the most part, the plans adopted followed the G-7 principles.

In the United States, work on Treasury's plan to recapitalize banks, dubbed the Capital Purchase Program (CPP), continued into

Columbus Day—Monday, October 13. With Paulson's change of heart, the Fed and Treasury were now on the same page with regard to the need to inject capital into banks, and the FDIC and the Office of the Comptroller of the Currency agreed to support that approach. To avoid stigma, which could be fatal to our plans, we wanted a program that would appeal to all banks, not only weak ones. If accepting CPP capital was perceived as a sign of weakness, then banks would do all they could to avoid taking it, and we would not be able to put enough capital into the system to end the panic and restart the flow of credit. We needed to set conditions that were fair to taxpayers but not so punitive that they dissuaded stronger banks from accepting capital.

We also needed to avoid the appearance of a government takeover of the banking system, one of Paulson's original concerns. We agreed that capital injections would take the form of the government purchasing newly created, nonvoting preferred stock. Because the stock was nonvoting, the government wouldn't control the operations of the banks receiving help, except for the executive pay restrictions required by the TARP bill. Because the government's stock was preferred, it would be first in line to receive dividends, ahead of common shareholders. In addition, as required by the legislation, the government would receive warrants that would allow taxpayers to share the gains if bank stock prices rose. The government would receive a dividend on its shares of 5 percent per year for three years. The dividend would then jump to 9 percent to encourage banks to replace government capital with private capital, which we hoped would be plentiful by that point.

To ensure widespread participation, including by stronger banks, we needed the nation's leading banks to take part. (I was reminded of our efforts to bring banks to the discount window in August 2007.) Hank summoned nine CEOs to his large conference room on Columbus Day afternoon. On one side of the room's long oval table sat Jamie Dimon of JPMorgan, Dick Kovacevich of Wells Fargo, Vikram Pandit of Citigroup, Ken Lewis of Bank of America, Lloyd Blankfein of Goldman Sachs, John Mack of Morgan Stanley, John Thain of Merrill Lynch, Ronald Logue of State Street, and Bob Kelly of Bank of New York Mellon. Paulson, Sheila Bair, Tim Geithner, Comptroller of the Currency John Dugan, and I sat across from the CEOs. Hank and I said it was important that strong as well as weak banks participate. Sheila told the CEOs about the bank debt guarantees. Tim reviewed the amount of capital proposed—up to 3 percent of each bank's risk-weighted assets. Hank asked the CEOs to commit to taking the capital, consulting with their boards as necessary.

John Mack of Morgan Stanley scrawled his acceptance immediately on a sheet of paper and pushed it across the table. Dick Kovacevich of Wells Fargo, feisty as always, insisted his bank didn't need any capital but finally agreed to consult his board. Vikram Pandit said that this was cheap capital and the banks should be glad it was available. Ken Lewis of Bank of America urged the group not to haggle over details but to go along in the interest of the system. Ultimately, all the banks took the recommended amounts of capital, totaling $125 billion, or half the $250 billion initial commitment to the Capital Purchase Program. Merrill Lynch, which would declare large losses later that year, took its own tranche of capital even though it was scheduled to be acquired by Bank of America.

The news from Europe and leaks about the new capital program in the United States created euphoria on the stock market. On Monday, the Dow Jones industrial average jumped 936 points (11 percent) to 9,387—partially recovering from the previous week's 1,874-point loss. It was the index's largest one-day gain in percentage terms in seventy-six years.

ON TUESDAY MORNING, Hank, Sheila, and I stood in the Treasury's Cash Room at a press conference. Paulson described the new Capital Purchase Program. Asset purchases were still on the table but would be delayed. Sheila described the FDIC's expansion of deposit insurance and its program to guarantee bank debt. Finally, I elaborated on the Fed's Commercial Paper Funding Facility, which would begin purchasing commercial paper in two weeks, on October 27.

We were still months away from stability, but, together with the steps taken abroad, a coherent and powerful strategy was finally taking shape.

CHAPTER 17

Transition

When Barack Obama defeated John McCain on November 4, 2008, I marveled that the election of the first African American president came less than forty years after I had attended segregated schools in Dillon. I also was reminded of the economic uncertainty caused by the four-month transition between the Hoover and Roosevelt administrations in 1932–33, which prompted a constitutional amendment that shortened by two months the wait between the election and inauguration of a new president. Even with this shorter transition, the handoff from George W. Bush to Barack Obama would complicate the management of a crisis not yet under control. At the Federal Reserve, exempt from the wholesale personnel changes facing the Treasury and other cabinet departments, we resolved to provide as much policy continuity as possible.

Important decisions loomed. Should the Bush administration ask Congress for the second half of the TARP funds? Should TARP money be used to help struggling auto companies? What could be done to assist homeowners behind on their mortgage payments? On these and other matters, the incoming and outgoing administrations had to figure out how to cooperate without violating the maxim that there can only be one president at a time.

IN THE MEANTIME, Paulson focused on getting Treasury's Capital Purchase Program up and running. The nine large banks represented at the Treasury Department's October 13 meeting had taken $125 bil-

lion in new government capital, leaving half of the $250 billion allo-
cated for other banks. It took some time to work out the details about
how to provide capital to smaller institutions. It was not a given that
banks would willingly participate, but demand for TARP capital was
strong from banks of all sizes, and by the end of 2008, the Treasury's
investments in banks were approaching $200 billion.

The capital program was a major step forward in stabilizing the
banking system. And it didn't seem particularly unpopular with the
broader public, by the standards of crisis-era programs. Executive
compensation limits at firms receiving government capital helped
politically, without being so tight that they discouraged broad participation. It also helped politically that banks of all sizes, including community banks, could avail themselves of government capital, so long
as their regulators judged them to be viable. Still, politicians, worried
about defending their vote for the TARP, pressed the Treasury and the
Fed for evidence that the capital program was working. The question
was most often phrased, "Are banks lending the money they're getting
from TARP?"

It seems like a simple question, but it's not. Money is fungible: One
dollar is like any other. Consequently, asking whether a particular loan
is made with a TARP dollar or some other dollar the lender obtained
elsewhere does not mean much. Moreover, capital's purpose is mainly
to absorb possible losses, which in turn makes banks more willing to
risk making loans. A better way to ask the question would have been,
"Is the availability of TARP capital allowing banks to make more loans
than they otherwise would have made?"

Even that question was difficult to answer. How could we prove a
counterfactual—what would have happened if there were no TARP?
I had no doubt that the TARP, together with all the other measures,
had prevented a financial meltdown that would have plunged the economy into an extraordinarily severe and protracted recession, or even
a depression. True, bank lending after the introduction of the capital
program was much lower than before the crisis, but that was hardly

a fair comparison. The recession greatly reduced the number of businesses and households seeking credit and the number of those who could qualify for credit in the first place.

A Board staff team, led by senior economist Nellie Liang, gathered data and developed metrics for assessing the TARP's effect on bank lending. But we never found a measure that was both comprehensive and easy to explain. Moreover, while we wanted banks to lend, we didn't want them to make bad loans. Bad loans had gotten us into the mess in the first place. For that reason, setting lending targets for banks who took TARP capital, as some politicians advocated, didn't seem wise. Our strategy, admittedly difficult to explain in a sound bite, was to lean against the excessive conservatism of lenders and examiners that typically followed a lending boom and bust. With the other federal bank regulators, we encouraged banks to lend to creditworthy borrowers. We also pressed our examiners to strike an appropriate balance between encouraging reasonable prudence and ensuring that creditworthy borrowers could get loans.

Meanwhile, the Fed's new Commercial Paper Funding Facility had quickly proved its value. By the end of the day on October 29, two days after it opened for business, it had purchased $145 billion in three-month commercial paper. A week later, it held $242 billion and, at its peak in January 2009, $350 billion. The program halted the rapid shrinkage of this crucial funding market and helped return interest rates on commercial paper to more normal levels.

Even with these important new tools and policy initiatives, the financial system was still reeling from the Lehman shock. Investors, whose fears a year earlier had centered on subprime mortgages, were shying away from funding virtually any type of private credit, such as credit card loans and auto loans. They had little reason to think that these other types of credit would suffer similar losses, and they never did. But, like subprime mortgages, these forms of credit also were routinely bundled into securities and sold to investors, leading to guilt by association. The sharp drop in investor demand for these asset-backed securities posed still another risk to the whole economy.

In response, we collaborated with the Treasury to develop yet another program. We invoked Section 13(3) again and announced the TALF (for Term Asset-Backed Securities Loan Facility) on November 25. But, given the complexities involved in setting up the facility, it would not extend its first loan until four months later. Under the TALF, we would lend for terms of up to five years to investors who would buy AAA-rated securities backed by credit card loans, student loans, auto loans, commercial mortgages, and loans guaranteed by the Small Business Administration. Our loans would be without recourse, meaning that the borrower could give us the asset-backed securities they had purchased in lieu of fully repaying the loan. That provided "downside protection" for the borrowers. But turning over the securities to us before maturity would make sense only if the return on the securities dropped below the cost of the loan.

We took measures to protect ourselves. Investors could borrow only a portion of what they paid for securities. Thus, they would incur the first losses, if any, and had "skin in the game." Further, taking the step it had declined to take with the Fed's commercial paper facility, the Treasury provided $20 billion out of the TARP as capital to support Fed lending of up to $200 billion. The TARP money would be next in line, after the private sector, to cover any losses. As it turned out, none of the securities financed by the TALF would ever be "put" back to the Fed. The program took no losses and returned profits to the taxpayer.

THE OUTGOING BUSH and incoming Obama administrations—with advice from the Fed and FDIC—also wrestled with home foreclosures. The problem was escalating as millions of homeowners lost their jobs and millions more found themselves "underwater," with their homes worth less than the amount they owed on their mortgages. Once largely confined to subprime mortgages with teaser rates, foreclosures now were rising even for plain vanilla prime mortgages. The economic

and social costs extended well beyond lenders' losses and the pain suffered by displaced families. Empty, foreclosed homes blighted entire
neighborhoods, pushing down the value of nearby homes and reducing local tax bases.

Hank Paulson's voluntary Hope Now program, launched in October 2007, had made a creditable start at reducing foreclosures. However,
without government funding, its scope was necessarily limited. The
subsequent Hope for Homeowners plan, enacted in July 2008, provided
for refinancing through the Federal Housing Administration, but Congress effectively sabotaged it by imposing onerous requirements and
fees that discouraged both homeowners and lenders from participating.

Meanwhile, the Fed had sponsored or cosponsored more than 100
foreclosure-prevention events across the country. The Federal Reserve
Bank of Boston, for instance, helped organize a massive workshop in
August 2008 in Gillette Stadium (home of the New England Patriots
football team) that brought together more than 2,200 distressed borrowers with lenders, servicers, and counselors. We worked with the
nonprofit NeighborWorks America to help communities minimize the
blight created by foreclosures.

After the election, with a new administration coming in and with
the TARP money available for foreclosure relief, it seemed a good time
for new ideas. Sheila Bair had been pushing hard for more action to
prevent foreclosures. After the FDIC took over IndyMac in July 2008,
it began modifying mortgages that the lender had owned or serviced.
It capped the mortgage payments of borrowers in trouble at 31 percent
of their income. That was accomplished through a variety of strategies,
including reducing the interest rate on their loans, forgiving part of
the principal owed, and extending the maturity of the mortgage (say,
from thirty to forty years).

It seemed a worthwhile effort, but, as we debated options during
the transition, it was also too early to judge its success. As of late 2008,
only a few thousand modifications of IndyMac mortgages had been
completed. We didn't know whether the modifications would stick or

ultimately result in another default. (A later FDIC assessment would find that two-thirds of seriously delinquent IndyMac loans would re-default within eighteen months of having been restructured.) Nevertheless, in mid-November, what became known as the FDIC's IndyMac protocol was adopted in modified form by Fannie and Freddie. Sheila also pressed the administration to use TARP funds to offer lenders guarantees as an incentive to adopt the IndyMac guidelines. If a borrower with a modified mortgage subsequently defaulted, then the government would make up half the loss.

I didn't always agree with Sheila's views, but I had to admire her political talent. Ignoring the administration's normal policy process, and by using the media and lobbying on Capitol Hill, she persuaded (mostly Democratic) legislators to endorse her plan—including House Speaker Nancy Pelosi and Senator Dodd. But Sheila came very close to characterizing anyone not fully in support of her plan as an opponent of foreclosure relief in general. I recall Hank being very exercised by a *New York Times* story criticizing the Treasury for failing to immediately act as Sheila advised and comparing it to the Federal Emergency Management Agency after Hurricane Katrina.

At the Fed, we agreed wholeheartedly with the goals of Sheila's plan but questioned some of the specifics. Deputy research director David Wilcox and his team compared alternative strategies. Among several flaws, the FDIC's guarantee plan seemed unnecessarily generous to lenders. In its original form, it provided a perverse incentive for lenders to modify the mortgages of the borrowers with the least capacity to remain current, since if the borrower re-defaulted the lender would pocket the government guarantee payment and could still foreclose on the home.

Fed economists proposed alternative plans, including variants of the FDIC's IndyMac protocol, that they believed would achieve more sustainable modifications at lower cost to the government. We also suggested that the Fed and Treasury could create a new special-purpose vehicle to buy at-risk mortgages in bulk from lenders and investors.

Under our plan, this new government entity would be capitalized by $50 billion from the TARP and could borrow from the Fed. The mortgages it purchased would then be modified by independent specialists, not by private-sector lenders and investors, and refinanced by the Federal Housing Administration.

Hank had his doubts about Sheila's plan to use TARP funds to partially guarantee modified mortgages, for reasons similar to ours. But his time as Treasury secretary was short, so he focused his team on analyzing competing proposals without making recommendations. Larry Summers, who had been chosen to head Obama's National Economic Council, weighed in with a memo to the president-elect on December 15, in consultation with other Obama advisers. Like the Fed, Larry favored fixing the Help for Homeowners program to make it more attractive to both lenders and borrowers. He also shared the Fed's concerns about the FDIC's plan to compensate lenders for re-defaults of modified mortgages. He instead supported incentives for lenders to reduce interest rates on troubled mortgages. Larry's memo did not address the Fed's idea of having a special-purpose vehicle buy troubled mortgages in bulk, but he let us know that he didn't like the political optics of the government foreclosing on people, which would sometimes occur if the new government entity took responsibility for modifying mortgages. Final decisions would have to await the swearing-in of the new president and his new Treasury secretary.

MONETARY POLICYMAKING CONTINUED without regard to presidential transitions. Ongoing market turmoil had given us plenty to discuss at the FOMC meeting of October 28–29, just before the election. Buyers remained in full retreat. From the September FOMC meeting until the day before the October meeting, the Dow Jones index fell nearly 2,900 points, losing about a quarter of its value. The market's volatility was mind-boggling; after its sharp declines, the Dow soared almost 900 points on the first day of our meeting, without any obvious good news to explain the jump.

Falling prices for houses and stocks, and tightening credit, in turn accelerated the decline in the economy. Household and business confidence—the "animal spirits" so important to economic growth—seemed to be in free fall. The University of Michigan's well-known survey of households showed consumer sentiment at its lowest point in almost thirty years. Board economists forecast a recession that would last through the middle of 2009. Their guess about the timing would prove accurate, but, as with most outside forecasters, neither the staff nor most FOMC participants yet appreciated how extraordinarily deep the downturn would be. We know now that the U.S. economy shrank at a 2 percent annual rate in the third quarter of 2008, an astonishing 8.2 percent rate in the fourth quarter (the worst performance in fifty years), and a 5.4 percent rate in the first quarter of 2009. It was easily the deepest recession since the Depression. Inflation, meanwhile, was falling rapidly, reflecting a $30-per-barrel drop in oil prices and overall weakness in the economy.

Dismal markets and shrinking economies were now a global phenomenon, in emerging-market and advanced economies alike. Russia had suspended trading to try to stop the slide in its stock market, and Mexico had spent 15 percent of its foreign exchange reserves in an effort to arrest the fall of the peso. Japan's Nikkei stock index hit a twenty-six-year low on the first day of our late-October meeting. Given the American origins of the crisis, it was ironic that global investors, desperate for assets perceived to be safe, were snapping up dollar-denominated assets, particularly Treasury securities. The activity had pushed up the dollar's value by a remarkable 9 percent since the last time we had met. With the U.S. economy declining rapidly, the rise in the dollar was hardly good news. It made U.S. exports more expensive and thus less competitive on world markets.

We expanded our currency swap lines yet again at the meeting by adding four carefully chosen emerging economies: Mexico, Brazil, South Korea, and Singapore. We chose these countries based on their importance to U.S. and global financial and economic stability, declining requests for swaps from several others. The additions brought the total number of our central bank swap lines to fourteen. Two weeks earlier, we had removed the limits on draws by the European Central Bank, the Bank of England, the Swiss National Bank, and the Bank of Japan, reflecting both the demand for dollars in Europe and Japan and our close relationships with those central banks.

The case for cutting interest rates further looked strong. I told the Committee that the steps taken so far to end the crisis had probably not yet reached their full effect. Nevertheless, I argued, we were facing what looked likely to be a deep and protracted recession, and it demanded bold action. The Committee approved, without dissent, a 1/2 percent cut in the federal funds rate, lowering it to 1 percent—the same level we had reached at the height of our concerns about deflation in 2003.

The prior evening, I had met with the Reserve Bank presidents at their usual pre-FOMC dinner. They were deeply worried about the political risks created by our interventions, particularly the bailout of AIG. And although the 13(3) lending programs were the responsibility of the Board, not the FOMC, some of the presidents felt that I hadn't consulted them enough. Every president wanted assurances that they would be kept in the loop, if for no other reason than to have answers to the inevitable questions posed at their public appearances. Given the pace of recent events, I had had good reasons to depart from the careful consensus-building style that I preferred. But the presidents' concerns were reasonable, and I offered to hold biweekly videoconferences to update them on any Board initiatives, as well as financial, economic, and legislative developments.

WE HAD HOPED that capital infusions under the TARP would end the dreaded weekend rescues of faltering financial giants. Unfortunately, worsening economic conditions and mounting losses continued to press on weaker institutions. AIG, the recipient of the Fed's $85 billion bailout in September, was one of them. We had already tacked on a loan of an additional $37.8 billion in early October, to help AIG finance its holdings of private-label (not guaranteed by the government) mortgage-backed securities. But even that was not enough. The company's losses had ballooned in the third quarter to more than $24 billion. To survive, the firm needed capital as well as some relief from the tough loan terms its board had accepted in the initial bailout in September.

Letting AIG fail was not an option, for the same reasons that we had intervened two months earlier, so we restructured the terms of the rescue and, in the process, increased its size (including Treasury funds) to more than $150 billion. Paulson at first wanted the Fed to provide all the funding for the new deal, but Geithner and I convinced him that the Fed couldn't do it alone. AIG needed a major infusion of capital, which, with private markets effectively closed, could only come from the Treasury. On November 10 the Fed and the Treasury announced a restructured AIG bailout, which included the purchase of $40 billion of preferred stock by the Treasury. AIG did not qualify for the Capital Purchase Program, which was broad-based and aimed at strengthening relatively healthy, not troubled, firms. We required it to accept stricter conditions, including a higher dividend payment on the Treasury's stock. As part of the restructuring, AIG repaid the supplementary loan the Fed had made in October, and we were able to reduce our original credit line to AIG from $85 billion to $60 billion. In exchange, we agreed to substantially lower the interest rate we charged and extend the time for repayment from three years to five.

To cap future risks to AIG's stability the Board, by invoking Section 13(3) once again, allowed the New York Fed to create and finance two new legal entities, to be called Maiden Lane II and Maiden Lane III. The New York Fed would lend $22.5 billion to Maiden Lane II, which in turn would acquire the private-label residential mortgage securities that had inflicted so many losses on AIG. Maiden Lane III, with a New York Fed loan of $30 billion, would buy from AIG's counterparties the collateralized debt obligations insured by AIG's Financial Products division. By acquiring the CDOs, we effectively closed out the insurance policies that had brought AIG to the brink in September. Tim Geithner likened the removal of troubled assets from AIG to a tourniquet, intended to stop the hemorrhaging. By that analogy, our loans and Treasury's capital were transfusions. I hoped they would be enough to save the patient—again, not out of any care about AIG, but for the sake of the broader system. In particular, we wanted to avoid further credit rating downgrades of AIG, which would automatically lead to massive new demands for collateral and cash.

To protect the Fed, we hired outside asset managers to value the securities we were acquiring. AIG provided $1 billion to absorb the first of any losses in Maiden Lane II, as well as an additional $5 billion to absorb the first losses in Maiden Lane III. The two new vehicles would appear on the Fed's balance sheet with the market values of the securities they held, updated quarterly. On Sunday, the day before the November 10 announcement, Paulson and I had sat in his office and called congressional leaders, explaining the new package and why we had little choice but to implement it. As was often the case with Congress, pushback was minimal at the time. It would come later.

Stuffed with new capital and relieved of many of its troubled assets, AIG seemed stable, at least for the moment. But the restructuring also reignited anti-bailout outrage (some real, some intended for the TV cameras) that we had faced after the original rescue. I understood the anger, especially since the bailouts had not averted what now looked to be a serious recession. But I had no doubt that keeping AIG afloat was essential to prevent the crisis from metastasizing yet further. Moreover, helping AIG to remain viable was the best—really, only—way that we could get back the money the taxpayers had put into the company.

Our Maiden Lane III purchases of the CDOs that AIG had insured raised a new issue, which perhaps I should have anticipated but didn't. In buying the insured securities, we had essentially allowed AIG's counterparties—most of them large financial institutions, some of them foreign—to receive the full benefit of the insurance. As these facts sunk in, we were pilloried by Congress and the media for conducting "backdoor bailouts." Why had we not insisted that those counterparties, which included companies like Goldman Sachs, bear some losses?

I was so intensely focused on controlling the panic that initially this criticism befuddled me. The New York Fed had broached the idea of voluntary payment reductions to some of the counterparties, without success (not surprisingly). As we would point out repeatedly, we had no legal means to force reductions. AIG's counterparties had contracts to receive the insurance payments, which were no less valid than the claims of AIG's other creditors or the customers who held more traditional kinds of insurance policies with the company. Applying supervisory pressure to the counterparties to accept reduced payments, as many critics said we should have done, would have been a clear abuse of our authority. And many of the counterparties were foreign institutions outside our jurisdiction, whose national regulators in some cases backed their refusals to take reductions.

We also faced criticism for not immediately disclosing the identities of the CDO counterparties. Although we had legitimate reasons, our decision in that case was tone-deaf. We had initially focused only on the legalities, including provisions of the Uniform Trade Secrets Act, which did not permit us to make such unilateral disclosures. And we worried about the subsequent willingness of counterparties to do business with AIG. After being pounded by Congress and the media for weeks, however, we asked AIG to disclose the names of the counterparties, which it promptly did.

I did my best to explain our actions and defend our response. Michelle Smith had by this time abandoned the Fed's traditionally conservative communications strategy and was bringing me proposals for engaging more intensively with the media and the public, including an invitation to speak and take questions from reporters at the National Press Club (I would appear there in February). I cooperated with John Cassidy of *The New Yorker* magazine on a lengthy piece that offered one of the first inside looks at how the Fed had battled the crisis. And I increased the pace of my public speaking, picking high-profile venues around the country to describe the many steps that we were taking to fight the crisis and how they fit together. I also testified regularly to congressional committees and stayed in frequent contact with legislators in off-the-record meetings or on the phone. I focused on party leaders and members of our oversight committees, but, except in cases of unresolvable schedule conflicts, I always accepted requests to meet or call from any member of Congress.

AIG WAS NOT the only corporate patient in intensive care. Within a few weeks, Citigroup also looked to be on the brink. Since its founding in 1812 as the City Bank of New York, Citi has remained a powerful but controversial institution, involved in nearly every financial panic the country has experienced. It almost collapsed after facing crippling losses on loans to Latin American countries in the 1970s and 1980s, and, again in the 1990s, when its U.S. commercial real estate loans soured. It survived thanks to a $590 million capital infusion from Saudi Arabian prince Al-Waleed bin Talal in 1991. After its historic 1998 merger with Travelers Group, Citi became the nation's largest bank holding company, but, by the end of September 2008, it had slipped to second behind JPMorgan Chase. The company had retreated somewhat from the "financial supermarket" vision of Sandy Weill, but it remained enormous, with total global assets hovering above $2 trillion.

Citi was sprawling and complex, with many lines of business and operations in dozens of countries. Its managers struggled to forge a coherent strategy. Our supervisors had been particularly concerned about the bank's ability to identify and measure its risks on a company-wide basis. Its management weaknesses and risky investments left it exceptionally vulnerable. Its problems had been made worse after some of its structured investment vehicles lost their outside funding and were brought onto its balance sheet. Sheila Bair had sharply criticized Citi's management, including CEO Vikram Pandit, and its board of directors, headed by Richard Parsons. How much of Citi's troubles could be blamed on Pandit is debatable; he had become CEO only the previous December. But Sheila was right that Citi was a weak organization and that the Fed and the Office of the Comptroller of the Currency had not done enough to fix it.

Citi had gotten a lift from $25 billion in capital that Pandit had accepted at the Columbus Day meeting at Treasury, but its condition remained precarious. Market concerns about the company were again escalating as the overall economy deteriorated. Its bank subsidiary, Citibank, relied heavily on $500 billion in foreign deposits, which were not insured by the FDIC, and on wholesale funding—both potentially subject to runs. Indeed, increased access to U.S.-based, FDIC-insured deposits had been a principal reason behind Citi's pursuit of Wachovia. In a pattern that we had seen many times, Citi's less stable funding sources began to pull away.

On Thursday, November 20, I entertained Board members in my dining room at the Fed for our annual Thanksgiving lunch. It was a pleasant occasion, but calls about Citi had already begun that morning and would continue through the weekend. Rumors were spreading that Citi was looking to sell itself, although it was not clear what institution could make such a huge acquisition.

A further complication arose on Friday, when President-elect Obama announced his intention to nominate Tim Geithner to be his Treasury secretary. Although Tim had not previously been part of Obama's inner circle, he had been asked during the campaign to brief the candidate about the crisis. Obama had obviously been impressed. Following the announcement, Tim immediately recused himself from his crisis-fighting duties at the New York Fed, as well as from monetary policy decisions. But he would remain in close touch with us in his new capacity as adviser to the president-elect.

This time without Tim, we again debated how to stabilize a giant financial company in danger of collapse. At the G-7 meeting in Washington in mid-October, we had committed publicly to avoiding the failure of any more systemically critical institutions. Citi easily met that criterion, but Sheila initially said she thought that Citi could be allowed to fail. I suspect she was being provocative, and in any case she ultimately joined our effort to prevent the company's collapse. I did agree with Sheila that Citi was being saved from the consequences of its own poor decisions. But, as we couldn't say often enough, we weren't doing this for Citi, its executives, its creditors, or anyone on Wall Street, but in the interest of overall economic and financial stability.

As before, we found ourselves in "before-Asia-opens" mode, with the inevitable conference calls, spreadsheets, and collective mood swings as possible solutions were proposed and shot down. The availability of the TARP reduced the pressure somewhat. On the other hand, not only were we negotiating with Citi, but the Treasury, Fed, and FDIC also were negotiating about each agency's share in the rescue. The leaders and staff of each of the agencies felt tapped out—politically, financially, and often physically—and under pressure. It didn't help that Citi was maddeningly slow in responding to our requests for information, further reducing our confidence in the company's management. At one point Sheila emailed: "Can't get the info we need. The place is in disarray. How can we guarantee anything if citi can't even identify the assets?" Despite these tensions, the stakes involved kept us on track. I'm sure that everybody involved in the negotiations, even Sheila, knew that, in the end, letting Citi go was not an option. We would all have to make concessions to find a workable solution.

We announced the package to stabilize Citigroup late Sunday evening, November 23. It included an additional $20 billion of TARP capital, in the form of preferred stock that paid the government an 8 percent dividend rather than the 5 percent required by the Treasury's Capital Purchase Program. In addition, we agreed to provide a "ring fence" (a backstop guarantee) for a $306 billion portfolio of Citi's troubled assets, which included residential and commercial mortgage-backed securities. Citi would bear the first $37 billion of losses from this portfolio, including $8 billion of existing reserves set aside against those losses. The government would bear 90 percent of any additional losses, with Treasury (through the TARP) shouldering the

first $5 billion of government's share, and the FDIC the next $10 billion. In exchange for this guarantee, the Treasury and the FDIC would
receive preferred stock in Citi. In the unlikely scenario that the losses
became so severe as to exhaust the Citi, Treasury, and FDIC commitments, the Fed would make a backup loan equal to 90 percent of the
remaining assets, taking all of the assets as collateral. As part of the
deal, Citi agreed to virtually eliminate its stock dividend and to adopt
mortgage modification procedures advocated by Sheila and the FDIC
to reduce unnecessary foreclosures. The FDIC's participation in this
arrangement required the agencies to invoke, again, the systemic risk
exception to the requirement that FDIC interventions be conducted at
least cost. The market liked the deal, at least initially. Citi's stock price
soared nearly 60 percent.

Why did we ring-fence Citi assets, rather than just add more capital? The ring fence, modeled on the deal that the FDIC had struck
when Citi was trying to acquire Wachovia, was intended to protect Citi
from a worst-case scenario. Eliminating the relatively small risk that
Citi could suffer extreme losses reassured investors while requiring a
relatively smaller commitment of dwindling TARP funds.

Of the $350 billion that made up the first tranche of the TARP,
Paulson had already committed $250 billion to the Capital Purchase
Program, $40 billion to AIG, and now $20 billion in new capital for
Citi. He was facing demands to help homeowners and auto companies, and it was surely important to keep some money available for
emergencies. The obvious solution was to ask Congress to release the
second $350 billion of the TARP, but, concerned about the politics and
whether Congress would go along, the Bush administration had not
yet made the request.

IN THE WAKE of the Citi episode, on Tuesday, November 25, the Fed
made an announcement that foreshadowed the next phase of our
response to the crisis. We said that we planned to buy up to $500 billion
in mortgage-backed securities guaranteed by Fannie, Freddie, and the

Government National Mortgage Association, or Ginnie Mae. (Ginnie Mae is wholly owned by the government, unlike Fannie and Freddie, which had been owned by private shareholders before their takeover by the Treasury.) We also announced plans to buy up to $100 billion of the debt issued by Fannie, Freddie, and other government-sponsored enterprises to finance their own portfolios. We were motivated by our concerns about housing. Uncertainty had driven buyers from the MBS market. Investors didn't know how long the government would support Fannie and Freddie or how much worse housing would get. Moreover, some financial institutions, short of liquid assets and capital, were actively dumping MBS on the market—pushing up mortgage rates. Our purchase program would provide increased demand for MBS while signaling the government's commitment to the companies. Even though we would not actually purchase any MBS until January, the announcement itself had a powerful effect on investor confidence. The spread between yields on MBS issued by Fannie and Freddie and yields on longer-term Treasury securities fell by 0.65 percentage points within a few minutes of the press release, a large move. Rates on thirty-year mortgages dropped from around 6 percent at the end of November to around 5 percent at the end of December.

With the mortgage market deteriorating, I had wanted to announce the MBS purchases as soon as possible. We discussed what we needed to do to authorize the program. An existing FOMC directive allowed the New York Fed to purchase MBS guaranteed by Fannie, Freddie, or Ginnie, so long as the purchases were consistent with the Committee's monetary policy decisions. No further FOMC approval was needed, argued Brian Madigan, the Board's Monetary Affairs Division director, so long as we took other steps to keep the federal funds rate at the target level. But the Board's general counsel, Scott Alvarez, argued, and Brian and I were persuaded, that a program of this size and importance should be undertaken with FOMC approval, if only to maintain good relations. I had not forgotten the Reserve Bank presidents' concerns about insufficient consultation.

We briefed the FOMC in a video conference about the proposal and its rationale. Afterward, Don and I worked the phones to see if FOMC participants would support it and, if so, whether they would be okay with an announcement before the next meeting. Confident that we had the Committee's support, we announced the plan to purchase MBS. The Committee formally ratified the program at its December meeting, with actual MBS purchases to begin about a month later.

Despite Don's and my calls before the announcement, several presidents remained unhappy. They believed that, given the significance of the decision, I should not have announced the program before the FOMC formally voted. I had been motivated by the need to act quickly, but, on reflection, I decided that they had a point. At the January 2009 FOMC meeting I acknowledged that I had made a mistake in making the announcement with only informal approval and promised I would follow a more deliberative process in the future. We agreed that asset purchases would be subject to the same degree of FOMC oversight as changes in short-term interest rates had been.

WHEN BANK OF AMERICA CEO Ken Lewis had declined to buy Lehman in September, the silver lining was that he agreed to acquire Merrill Lynch, which well might have been the next domino to fall. Lewis sealed the deal, without government assistance, with Merrill CEO John Thain. The Fed Board approved the merger on November 26 and the shareholders of both companies approved on December 5.

Paulson and I had been relieved at Merrill's apparent stabilization, so we were shaken to learn in mid-December that the deal was threatening to come undone. Lewis asked for a meeting, and, on December 17, we heard for the first time that Bank of America was thinking about walking away. Lewis told us that Bank of America had only recently determined that Merrill was likely to suffer much greater than anticipated losses in the fourth quarter (it would eventually announce a $15.3 billion loss). Lewis said he was considering invoking a clause in the contract with Merrill—known as the material adverse change clause, or MAC clause. It permitted Bank of America to rescind the agreement if Merrill's condition proved materially worse than had been represented at the time the contract was signed.

Lewis's news meant that we were potentially facing yet another massive blow in our battle to control the crisis. If the merger did not go through, Merrill would certainly face an immediate run by funders, customers, and other counterparties, a run that could easily spread to Bank of America as well. As we had just seen, the funding pressure on Citi could be attributed in part to its failure to merge with Wachovia. I also felt certain that, if Lewis walked away from the deal, the wider panic would escalate, which could not be good for Bank of America. I wondered what he could be thinking.

After consulting with Scott Alvarez and our bank supervisors, I became even more convinced that Lewis's plan to invoke the MAC clause made no sense. From both a business and a legal perspective, the case for using the clause seemed exceptionally weak. Bank of America had been afforded ample opportunity to analyze Merrill's assets before the shareholder vote—no one had claimed that Merrill had misrepresented its holdings—and changes in market conditions were explicitly excluded as a basis for invoking the MAC clause. If Lewis tried to use the clause, he likely would provoke extended litigation that Bank of America would ultimately lose. During the litigation, both companies would no doubt be under intense market pressure, and in the end Bank of America would likely be forced to acquire a much weakened or even insolvent Merrill Lynch.

The Fed supervised Bank of America's holding company, but we had no authority to compel the company to go through with the merger. When Lewis asked me to send a letter to his board instructing them to consummate it, I declined. Legally, the decision had to be Bank of America's. We were also careful not to advise Lewis on the disclosures to his shareholders about Merrill's losses, the merger plans, or his negotiations with the government. Hank and I did make clear that we thought that invoking the MAC clause was a terrible idea for both Bank of America and the financial system. We also told him what we had already said publicly: We would do what was necessary to prevent any more failures of systemically important financial institutions. With that general assurance, Lewis persuaded his board to go through with the merger, which was completed on New Year's Day.

During the month that followed Lewis's visit to Washington, we worked to determine what the merged company would need to remain viable. I suspected that securing government help was probably one of Lewis's objectives when he threatened to invoke the MAC clause. That aside, Merrill's losses were large and Lewis had reason to be concerned about the stability of the combined companies, particularly because Bank of America had substantial losses of its own. We had shored up AIG and Citi. Investors likely would next probe Bank of America for weakness. We wanted to act before we were forced to do so by a run.

With advice from Kevin Warsh and numerous supervisory and legal staff—including staff from the Richmond Fed, Bank of America's immediate supervisor—we and the Treasury put together a package modeled on the Citi transaction. Hank put in $20 billion more TARP capital into the merged company, charging the same 8 percent dividend rate that Citi and AIG were paying. As in the Citi deal, the Treasury, Fed, and FDIC invoked the systemic risk exception. We ring-fenced a $118 billion portfolio, made up mostly of assets from the former Merrill Lynch. Similar to Citi, Bank of America was responsible for the first $10 billion of losses and 10 percent of any beyond that. Treasury would cover subsequent losses, up to a maximum of $7.5 billion. The FDIC took the next $2.5 billion. The Fed promised to make a loan equal to 90 percent of any assets remaining after all other funds had been exhausted. For this protection, Bank of America would give the government $4 billion in preferred stock upon implementation of the ring fence. We announced the package on January 16, 2009. Kevin Warsh ended an email to me, "Happy inauguration day, Mr. President!" The incoming administration faced plenty of problems, but it looked like Bank of America would not be one of them.

Both the Citi and Bank of America ring fences reassured the market but would never cost the Treasury, the FDIC, or the Fed any money. Indeed, in May, Bank of America would ask the government not to implement the ring fence agreement, saying it did not expect losses to exceed the $10 billion it was obliged to cover. We would allow Bank of America to cancel the deal, but only after it agreed to pay the government a $425 million termination fee as compensation for bearing some of the bank's risk over the period since the announcement.

Controversy would dog the Bank of America episode, however. Bank of America shareholders criticized Lewis for not disclosing Merrill's losses earlier. Hank and I were accused of abusing our authority by allegedly forcing Bank of America to go through with the deal. The House Committee on Oversight and Government Reform, chaired by Democrat Edolphus Towns of New York, with Darrell Issa of California the senior Republican, would air the issues in a fraught hearing on June 25. In a meeting just before the hearing, Ohio Democrat Dennis Kucinich told me that they "hadn't been able to pin any securities law violations" on me but that I should expect a tough hearing anyway. Hank and I were sworn in, as if we were witnesses in a criminal trial. I explained that we had sought to persuade Lewis to go through with the merger but that the decision remained in his hands, and his board's, as did the responsibility for disclosing Merrill Lynch's losses to shareholders. The hearing ended after three and a half hours of bombast and insinuation. The committee's accusations gained no traction, and it did not pursue the matter further. However, in September 2012, Bank of America would agree to pay nearly $2.5 billion to settle claims that it had misled shareholders about the acquisition.

DURING DECEMBER 2008, executives of the Big Three automakers in Detroit, and others on their behalf, had asked Congress for help. The Fed also received calls from auto executives, who clearly were very worried about whether their firms could survive the next few months. The companies were suffering the combined effects of the recession and their poor strategic choices, including the failure to adapt their cars and trucks to the high gas prices of the previous few years. But they were also experiencing something like a slow run. Suppliers and other creditors were demanding cash in advance for fear that one or more companies would fail. Congress had considered various ways to help, but no solution had emerged.

After initial congressional attempts to provide help failed, Senate majority leader Harry Reid, House Speaker Nancy Pelosi, Senator Chris Dodd, and other members of Congress called on the Fed to lend to the auto companies. We were extremely reluctant. We believed that, consistent with the Fed's original purpose, we should focus our efforts on the financial panic. We were hardly the right agency to oversee the restructuring of a sprawling manufacturing industry, an area in which we had little or no expertise. And, unlike the financial emergencies that required quick responses, the threats to the auto industry were unfolding more slowly, giving Congress time to debate options. If Congress decided not to act, it didn't seem legitimate for the Fed to effectively overrule its decision.

Fortunately, the issue became moot when Paulson and President Bush agreed to use TARP funds for GM and Chrysler (Ford decided not to participate), as well as for their financing arms. President Bush announced the investments from the Roosevelt Room on December 19, and the Obama administration would follow through. The commitment of funds to the auto companies left little doubt that the second $350 billion tranche of the TARP would be needed. Four days before we announced the Bank of America package, on January 12, President Bush had requested the second tranche, relieving the incoming president of that politically distasteful responsibility, and Congress did not block it.

THE DECEMBER 16 FOMC meeting was pivotal, so I extended it to two days, beginning on Monday, December 15. Unemployment had risen to 6.7 percent in November and payrolls had declined by more than half a million that month, an enormous drop. And it looked like we were hurtling into an abyss. On December 1, the National Bureau of Economic Research had officially confirmed that the U.S. economy had entered a recession a year earlier, helping to trigger a 680-point drop in the Dow. Board economists forecast the economy would shrink rapidly in the fourth quarter and the first quarter of 2009—pushing the unemployment rate to 7-3/4 percent by March and above 8 percent by the end of 2009. Even that dire forecast would turn out to be considerably optimistic.

We were ready to cut the federal funds rate target further, from 1 percent. In 2003, we had been reluctant to cut much below that level, in part because of concerns that money market funds and other institutions would not be able to function normally at such low rates. Nevertheless, at this meeting we ended up specifying a target range for the funds rate between zero and 1/4 percent. It was a tough call for some of the hawks, who had resisted rate cuts since the beginning of the crisis, and the discussion ran long. Charles Plosser noted that he was voting yes "with some reluctance." Richard Fisher voted no initially, but during a break for lunch, with only minutes left before the vote was publicly announced, he told me that he wanted to change his vote. I announced the vote change when the Committee reassembled, explaining that Richard had switched "in order to maintain a united front."

The decision was historic. It meant that the FOMC had accepted that economic conditions required a funds rate near zero. In that respect, the United States had become Japan, where short-term rates had been pinned near zero for years.

Now that the funds rate was essentially zero, we could no longer ease monetary policy by simply cutting the funds rate target. We'd have to find another way. We discussed possible options at length at the December meeting, echoing our debates in the last years of Greenspan's chairmanship, when the funds rate had reached 1 percent and we were worried about deflation. The discussion also reflected the themes I had raised in my 2002 Helicopter Ben speech about deflation and unconventional monetary tools. Even though the overnight interest rate was essentially at zero, longer-term rates were higher. If we could push down longer-term interest rates, we could stimulate the demand for housing, autos, and capital investment. Increased spending in turn should put more people to work and help stave off deflation.

We focused on two tools. The first—large-scale asset purchases, or LSAPs, as the staff dubbed them—could involve buying hundreds of billions of dollars' worth of securities to hold on our balance sheet. We were already entering that business with the Committee's formal approval of the $600 billion in GSE mortgage-backed securities and debt announced three weeks earlier. Besides buying these securities, we could also step up our purchases of Treasury securities, which we already routinely bought and sold in smaller amounts as part of normal monetary policy operations. I had broached the possibility of systematically buying large quantities of Treasuries in a speech a few weeks earlier in Austin, Texas, and we said in our December FOMC statement that we would evaluate the possibility—a fairly strong hint to the market. Our goal in buying longer-term securities, like Treasury bonds, would be to lower the interest rates on them and put downward pressure on other longer-term rates, providing additional stimulus to the economy.

The second tool we discussed was communications strategy, or "open-mouth operations." With short-term interest rates essentially at zero, we could hope to convince the public and the markets that we would keep short-term rates low for a long time. That, in turn, should help push down longer-term rates, because expectations about future short-term rates influence investors' decisions on what yields to accept on longer-term securities. We also talked once again about an explicit numerical inflation target, something that I had been advocating since I arrived at the Fed in 2002. In the current circumstances—with inflation likely to drop very low during the recession—setting an explicit objective could help convince markets that policy would remain easy for as long as needed to return inflation to our target. We knew, though, that setting a numerical target would be a big step, both economically and politically, and we agreed only to further discussions. For this meeting's statement, we embraced qualitative language. In an echo of the Greenspan-era phrases "considerable period" and "likely to be measured," we said we anticipated that weak economic conditions likely would warrant exceptionally low levels of the federal funds rate "for some time."

TIM GEITHNER, having recused himself after the incoming administration announced its intention to nominate him as Treasury secretary, did not attend the FOMC meeting. As was customary for any departing member of the FOMC, however, we roasted and honored him at a postmeeting dinner. I teased Tim about his inclusion in a *New York Daily News* article headlined "Hotties of the Obama Cabinet" but concluded by thanking him for his work over the past year and a half. "You have been just the sort of person anyone would want alongside them in the financial crisis foxhole," I said. Jeff Lacker, a frequent intellectual sparring partner of Tim's, speaking on behalf of the Reserve Bank presidents, ribbed him about his apparent willingness to bail out anybody at any time. Tim replied in kind, characterizing Jeff's frequently expressed view that the various bailouts were themselves a cause of market disruptions as the theory that "firefighters cause fires." It was mostly good-humored, but tinged by the underlying tensions in the Committee during a very difficult period.

Tim's departure would be a significant loss to the Fed. I would miss the profanity-laced intensity that he brought to our deliberations and his distinctive aphorisms: "plan beats no plan," "foam on the runway," "Old Testament thinking," and more. I was nevertheless pleased that I would be gaining an able partner in the new administration. In choosing Tim, the president-elect showed that he was willing to take some political heat to get the adviser he wanted. Tim had patiently explained to Obama why he would be a bad choice for the Treasury, most importantly because of the baggage he would bring as an architect of unpopular bailouts. He had recommended Larry Summers, one of his mentors, instead. But Obama had made up his mind and pressed Tim to accept, which he eventually did.

Anna and I had gotten to know Tim's gentle and down-to-earth wife, Carole, a social worker and the author of a young-adult novel. Carole's reaction to Tim's nomination was about the same as Anna's to my Fed chair nomination—deep unhappiness born of knowing what the job was likely to entail for both her husband and the family. Like Anna, Carole had no interest whatsoever in the putative glamor of being the spouse of a national policymaker. By this time I understood Carole and Anna's concerns well. When Tim's nomination was announced and the stock market jumped, I jokingly congratulated him on the "Geithner rally." He and I both knew how fickle market (and media) judgments can be.

Tim's troubles would start early, when some errors he had made in calculating his taxes during a stint at the International Monetary Fund became a centerpiece of his confirmation hearing. Despite the bumps, and there would be more, Tim would remain cool in the face of adversity. His great strength, cultivated over his years in government, was his focus on getting the policy right, whatever the obstacles. He attracted smart and dedicated people, and he emphasized a team approach—his standard for hiring staff was "no jerks, no peacocks, no whiners." I also appreciated Tim's limited patience for Washington bloviating and spin doctoring, although I knew that it would sometimes hamper his effectiveness in his new, more political role as Treasury secretary.

I was pleased with Obama's other choices for economic policy appointees as well. I had known Larry Summers for decades. While I had stumbled into economics in college, it seemed that Larry had been groomed from childhood to be a star in the field. Both his parents were economists, and two uncles—Kenneth Arrow and Paul Samuelson— had won Nobel Prizes. As National Economic Council director, Larry seemed likely to stake out and defend his own views rather than play the role of policy traffic cop that Al Hubbard had performed so well in the Bush White House. But his analytical skills, particularly his ability to detect weaknesses in an argument, would make everyone around him better and lead to better policy.

For my old position as chair of the Council of Economic Advisers, Obama would nominate Christina Romer, my former colleague at Princeton and neighbor in Rocky Hill, New Jersey. A talented economic historian, now at Berkeley, she had, like me, published papers on the Great Depression. She knew that passive, orthodox policymaking greatly worsened the Great Depression, and, like me, she tended to favor aggressive, unconventional policies in the face of dire threats to financial and economic stability.

The president-elect also would nominate a new member of our Board, Dan Tarullo. He would fill the seat occupied by Randy Kroszner, which would force Randy—who never won Senate confirmation to a second term—to leave in January 2009. Dan, a Georgetown University law professor who specialized in financial regulation, had served in various roles in the Clinton administration and had led the transition team's economic issues working group. I had not worked with Dan before, so I invited him to meet with me. I was impressed by his knowledge of the Fed and his interest in our work. I thought he would be a natural to take over the bank supervision committee after Randy's departure. I was less sure of how well Dan, a lawyer among economists, would fit into the FOMC, but he would more than hold his own in monetary policy debates, digging particularly deeply into labor market issues. After his confirmation on January 27—by a vote of 96 to 1, with only Senator Bunning voting no—the Board would consist of Betsy Duke, Kevin Warsh, Dan, Don Kohn, and me, with two seats still empty. (During the week between Randy's departure and Dan's swearing-in, the Board would be left with only four members for the first time in its history.)

The transition from one administration to another involved departures as well as new faces, of course. On Monday, January 5, I hosted a small dinner at the Fed in honor of Hank Paulson. Two past Treasury secretaries (Bob Rubin and Larry Summers), the incoming secretary (Tim Geithner), the two living past Fed chairmen (Paul Volcker and Alan Greenspan), and Board vice chairman Don Kohn attended. Hank was reflective. A lot had happened during his watch, and he seemed relieved it was ending. He had worked closely with the incoming administration and believed he had given Tim and his colleagues the means to continue the fight against the crisis—especially the money provided by the release of the second tranche of the TARP.

When he returned to his home near Chicago, Hank would be free to pursue his passions—China and environmental preservation. He would found an institute at the University of Chicago dedicated to building business and cultural ties between the United States and China. He would continue his frequent visits to that country and would publish a book about the economic opportunities there. On the ecological side, Hank and his wife, Wendy, continued both their hobbies (they are avid birdwatchers) and their philanthropy. They funded a foundation to preserve Little St. Simons Island off the coast of Georgia.

On January 20, 2009, Anna and I attended the inauguration of the new president on the steps of the Capitol. It was the first inauguration for both of us. My security detail escorted us through ranks of police officers into a small, ornate room in the Capitol where we waited with FBI director Robert Mueller and his wife, Ann, until it was time to take our seats behind the speaker's podium. In front of us, as far as we could see, an enormous crowd covered the Mall. We waited, shivering in the gusty wind and 28-degree cold. Finally the ceremony began. Aretha Franklin sang "My Country, 'Tis of Thee," Chief Justice John Roberts administered the oath of office, and the new president began his first inaugural address.

The president had campaigned on hope, even as the nation faced economic calamity, and he sounded that theme again. "We remain the most prosperous, powerful nation on earth," he said. "Our workers are no less productive than when this crisis began. Our minds are no less inventive, our goods and services no less needed than they were last week, or last month, or last year. Our capacity remains undiminished. . . . Starting today, we must pick ourselves up, dust ourselves off, and begin again the work of remaking America."

Sitting with Anna on the dais, listening to those words, I hoped that the inauguration would mark an opportunity to regather our collective strength and determination to help restore the prosperity of the United States and the world.

CHAPTER 18

From Financial Crisis
to Economic Crisis

The frenetic autumn of 2008 had tested the mettle and skills of the staff and leadership throughout the Federal Reserve System. As the pressure rose and it seemed the bad news would never end, I saw exhaustion in everyone's face. Senior staff stayed on call pretty much 24/7, and employees at all levels were prepared to work as many hours as needed. Brian Madigan, at the office all hours of the day and night, grew so pale that colleagues worried about his health. Family and personal lives took a backseat. One weekend, Michelle Smith's six-year-old son, Henry, hid her continually buzzing BlackBerry and was crestfallen when she found it. Yet morale remained high—people knew that they were doing essential work, and they took pride in their professionalism and expertise. As often as possible, we engaged in free-flowing, problem-solving meetings—blue-sky thinking. These sessions produced some of our best ideas, and even when they led nowhere they kept us focused. A group of economists took to calling themselves, proudly, I think, "the nine schmucks" when, after one lengthy blue-sky session, as memo writing and research assignments were doled out, I joked, "How come the same nine schmucks get stuck with all the work each time?" I worried, though, about how long we could sustain our efforts.

I tried to appear, and in fact be, calm and deliberate, though my insides often churned. (Geithner once called me "the Buddha of central banking," which I took to be a compliment, although with Tim you were never quite sure.) As I told Michelle, a frequent sounding board, financial panics have a substantial psychological component. Projecting calm, rationality, and reassurance is half the battle. It was overwhelming, even paralyzing, to think too much about the high stakes involved, so I focused as much as I could on the specific task at hand—preparing for a speech or planning a meeting.

Anna made our home life an oasis, and she pushed me to take care of myself and to take time off. At her suggestion and after consulting a doctor, I eliminated gluten from my diet, and digestive issues that bothered me early in the crisis eased. She was far from an avid baseball fan but was always willing to go to Nationals games with me. In exchange, I went with her to dance performances at the Kennedy Center. She did small things like buying an aromatherapy diffuser to scent our house with rosemary, lavender, and other fragrances. (Typically, I might not have noticed if she hadn't pointed it out.) And she always kept me grounded: At dinner, I would tell her about some multi-billion-dollar action that the Fed had taken, and she would say, "That's nice," and remind me to take out the garbage and the recyclables. We also shopped for groceries together on weekends, trying unsuccessfully to be inconspicuous as our security agents trailed behind.

Our two dogs, Scamper (an ancient beagle-basset) and Tinker (a small, friendly dog of indeterminate breed), provided some diversion. They would see me to the door in the morning, then return to their perches by the living room window, overlooking a courtyard. During the crisis I wished more than once that I could skip the office and sit with them for the day.

In 2008, Anna fulfilled a longtime dream, starting an educational program for urban kids in Washington, which she named Chance Academy. As the number of children in the program grew over the next few years, she would add part-time teachers, and parents would volunteer their time in lieu of paying the small tuition. We covered most of the costs ourselves, with occasional help from friends and foundations. Anna spent sixty hours a week or more on the project at no pay and loved what she was doing. It was a relief to hear about her daily experiences when I came home. I believed the Federal Reserve was helping people, but Anna could see the benefits of her efforts much more concretely and immediately in the progress and joy of her students.

THE SWEARING-IN OF the president indeed marked a new phase in the battle against the crisis. His team brought different ideas, but the bigger transition was that the crisis itself was becoming less purely financial and more economic in nature. Fittingly, President Obama aimed his first major policy initiative at arresting the devastating economic contraction—now more than a year old. As new (and old) Keynesians would predict, collapsing private demand—consumer spending, home purchases, capital investment—had sent production and employment reeling. As Keynes had first suggested in the 1930s, in an economic slump public spending could replace private spending for a time. With the economy still in free fall and with short-term interest rates already near zero, the economy certainly needed fiscal help—increased government spending, tax cuts to promote private spending, or both. I had said so (albeit in my usual cautious central bank speak) during the fall, to the point that the *Wall Street Journal* editorialized that I had effectively endorsed Obama for president. I wasn't endorsing a candidate, I was endorsing a program, just as I had supported President Bush's fiscal stimulus (in the form of tax cuts) that had passed in early 2008.

On February 17, less than a month after his inauguration, Obama signed a major fiscal package, the American Recovery and Reinvestment Act of 2009. The $787 billion bill included $288 billion in tax reductions to help spur consumption and investment—most notably, a temporary reduction in Social Security payroll taxes—as well as $144 billion in aid to state and local governments, mostly to support spending on education and Medicaid (the principal government program to provide health services to the poor). The remaining $355 billion was spread among diverse federal spending programs, including $40 billion for extended unemployment benefits and $105 billion for infrastructure investment.

I am sure that the Recovery Act helped create jobs and slow the economic contraction—a conclusion shared by our own staff and the nonpartisan Congressional Budget Office. Nevertheless, the recovery would be slow and protracted. In retrospect, some economists (including Obama's CEA chair, Christy Romer) have said that the stimulus package was too small. Within the Fed, some of our fiscal specialists expressed that concern at the time. Over the next few years, I came to agree that, from a purely economic perspective, the program probably was too small.

I know it's hard to think of a $787 billion package as small, but its size must be compared with its objective of helping to arrest the deepest recession in seventy years in a $15 trillion U.S. economy. Also, several considerations reduced the impact of the program. First, the headline figure overstated the program's effective size to some degree. For example, some of the Medicaid spending and certain tax fixes included in the bill likely would have occurred anyway. Second, and importantly, much of the effect was offset by spending cuts and tax increases undertaken by state and local governments. With economic activity contracting, the income, sales, and property tax revenues of state and local governments fell sharply. Many of these governments operate under laws requiring balanced budgets, so they responded to the lost revenue by laying off workers (including thousands of teachers, police, and firefighters), raising tax rates, and canceling capital projects. The federal stimulus package aided state and local governments but not nearly enough to make up for the budget crunch they faced.

Defenders of the package maintain that it was the largest politically feasible option. They may well be right. (Three Republicans supported it in the Senate and none in the House.) Voters usually cheer tax cuts and increased spending on social programs and infrastructure, at least when they benefit directly. But the huge budget deficit generated by the package—and by recession-induced declines in tax revenues and automatic increases in social spending (on unemployment benefits and food stamps, for instance)—worried many Americans. It didn't help that some voters likely perceived the stimulus as a "Christmas tree" that funded legislators' pet projects, regardless of their merit. Perhaps if the package had been more clearly focused and sold as a way of strengthening America's infrastructure and improving the economy's long-run productive potential, it would have been more broadly supported. But it's hard to know.

THE OBAMA ADMINISTRATION in its early weeks also focused on rolling out plans for reducing mortgage foreclosures. After extensive conversations and debates during the transition between administrations, Tim and his team had settled on a strategy. On February 18, President Obama unveiled the Making Homes Affordable program. It had two main components. The first, called the Home Affordable Refinance Program (HARP), would help underwater homeowners who were current on their payments to refinance into mortgages with better terms and lower monthly payments. It echoed some aspects of a proposal by Columbia University professors Christopher Mayer and Glenn Hubbard. (It was Hubbard who, as an adviser to President Bush, had invited me to interview for a seat on the Board of Governors.) With lower payments, an underwater homeowner would have a better chance of staying current. However, only mortgages owned or guaranteed by Fannie and Freddie, which were indirectly controlled by the government, were eligible.

The second component, the Home Affordable Modification Program (HAMP), would target homeowners who had already missed payments. Unlike HARP, HAMP was financed by TARP funds and included homeowners whose mortgages were not owned by Fannie and Freddie. Borrowers with a monthly debt burden exceeding 31 percent of their gross monthly income would be eligible for a trial loan modification, which could be converted into a permanent modification if they were able to keep up with their payments during the trial period.

HAMP would pay private mortgage servicers a fixed sum for each permanent modification they completed. To encourage sustainable modifications, servicers also would receive ongoing payments when borrowers proved able to remain current on their modified mortgages.

I remained perplexed that helping homeowners was not more politically popular. But Americans apparently were no more disposed to bail out their neighbors than they were to bail out Wall Street. Indeed, television personality Rick Santelli's famous rant about homeowner bailouts on the cable station CNBC is thought by some to have been a trigger of the Tea Party movement. In February 2009, Santelli, commenting from the floor of the Chicago Mercantile Exchange, turned to traders and shouted (ungrammatically), "How many of you people want to pay for your neighbor's mortgage that has an extra bathroom and can't pay their bills, raise their hand." A chorus of "No!" rose from the trading floor. "President Obama, are you listening?" he asked.

IN THE FIRST months of the new administration, completing the stabilization of the banking system remained a top priority. Short-term funding markets had improved noticeably, in large part because of the Fed's lending programs. But, despite the new TARP capital and the arrangements to prop up Citi and Bank of America, market confidence in banks remained shaky. The share prices of the largest banks nosedived in January and February—by about 80 percent, in the case of Citi and Bank of America, by half or more for other large banks. The cost of insuring large banks' debt against default also remained worryingly high, suggesting that market participants saw the failure of another major institution as quite possible. The weakening economy and continuing worries about bank losses were probably the main factors behind market concerns, but uncertainty about what the new administration's plans would mean for bank investors and creditors didn't help.

During the transition and in the days after he took office, Tim called frequent meetings with the Treasury, the Board, the FDIC, and the Office of the Comptroller of the Currency to discuss our options.

The New York Fed, which supervised many of the largest bank holding companies, usually joined by phone. Sheila Bair of the FDIC and John Dugan of the OCC were being retained by the new administration. Bill Dudley left his position as manager of the Open Market Trading Desk to replace Tim as the president of the New York Fed.

At first, we and incoming Treasury officials focused on strategies for shoring up the banking system, including further injections of capital, asset purchases, and new forms of guarantees. In late December, Don Kohn had reported on work at the New York Fed in all these areas, and on the day after the inauguration, Board staff walked me through a long list of potential strategies.

Sheila and the FDIC also developed proposals, including the creation of an "aggregator bank"—essentially, a government-owned bank that would buy or guarantee troubled bank assets. Sheila also proposed that banks be allowed to issue so-called covered bonds, with an FDIC guarantee. Covered bonds, common in Europe but rarely seen in the United States, are bank-issued bonds backed by specific, high-quality assets, usually mortgages. If a loan backing a covered bond goes bad, the bank must replace it with another, sound loan. Consequently, covered bonds are safer for investors than standard asset-backed securities, in which defaults of the underlying assets can result in losses to investors.

At the Fed, we supported putting more capital into the banks and were also receptive to covered bonds. We had a concern about Sheila's plan for an aggregator bank: She wanted the Fed to finance it with 13(3) lending. We certainly didn't rule out the possibility, but we knew that lending to an aggregator bank would further expand our balance sheet (then at about $2.1 trillion, more than double its pre-crisis level), adding still more reserves to the banking system and possibly further complicating our conduct of monetary policy. To address this issue, we asked Treasury officials whether they would support legislation to allow us to sell our own short-term debt (which we provisionally called Fed bills) directly to the public. Issuing our own short-term debt, as many central banks do, would allow us to finance our lending without creating bank reserves and so give us better control over the federal funds rate. Treasury officials were skeptical. They doubted Congress would approve (I had to agree), and they were reluctant to have a new type of government obligation competing with Treasury securities in the marketplace, which could complicate Treasury's financing of the national debt. Their concern about competition also made them skeptical of Sheila's covered bonds, which, under her proposal, would be sold with the "full faith and credit" of the U.S. government and thus would be effectively equivalent to U.S. government debt.

Always overhanging these discussions was a concern that bank losses might yet outstrip the capacity of the TARP, even though Congress had released the second $350 billion installment. Getting the most bang for the buck out of TARP funds was therefore critical. As with the original debate about asset purchases versus capital injections, that consideration seemed to weigh in favor of putting more capital into banks, perhaps on an as-needed basis rather than in the broad-based manner of the Capital Purchase Program.

Once confirmed as Treasury secretary, Tim became the final decision maker when it came to disbursing TARP funds. He encouraged robust interagency discussion and creative thinking, but ultimately he discarded many of the options we had evaluated in favor of a relatively simple package. He proposed putting the largest, most systemically important banks through what he originally called a "valuation exercise"—later called the "stress test." It would estimate how much capital those banks would need to withstand a deep recession, one even deeper than what we were experiencing, together with significant further deterioration in financial markets. If market analysts found the estimates credible, the stress test would increase confidence in the banks that passed. Banks that came up short would get a chance to raise capital privately; if they couldn't, Treasury would fill the hole with TARP funds. Either way, we hoped, customers, counterparties, and potential investors would know the banks were viable.

In addition to the stress tests, Tim proposed vastly expanding the capacity of the Fed's TALF program—created to unfreeze the market for asset-backed securities—to up to $1 trillion (from $200 billion), and broadening it to accommodate more types of assets, such as loans to finance business equipment. The new ceiling, which seemed unlikely to be reached, was intended to convey the strength of the government's commitment to unfreezing the important market for asset-backed securities. We agreed to the expansion of TALF so long as Treasury provided additional capital from the TARP to protect the Fed in the event of losses.

Tim also wanted the TALF to include older, "legacy" assets, such as existing private-label mortgage securities, as a way of increasing prices and improving liquidity for those assets. We resisted that step, worried about the effects on the size of our balance sheet and because we wanted the program to focus primarily on new credit extension. Eventually, we did make a limited exception for highly rated legacy securities backed by commercial real estate mortgages. To ensure that the valuations of those mortgages were up to date, we required them to be re-rated and repackaged into new securities. We made the exception because we believed that supporting the market for existing commercial MBS would help revive that market, which at the time was moribund, and thus help restart the flow of credit for new commercial projects.

Additionally, Tim proposed a new Treasury program, without Fed involvement, targeting other legacy assets. Under the PPIP—for Public-Private Investment Program—private investors would receive loans from TARP to finance their purchase of existing assets, such as private-label residential MBS and structured credit products created before the crisis. The investors would also put their own money at risk, and they and the government would share any profits made from later reselling the assets. The program gave private investors, rather than the government, the responsibility for deciding which assets to buy and how much to pay, thereby avoiding having the government determine prices for toxic assets. The investors had strong incentives to make smart choices, since their own returns depended on the assets they chose and their ability to keep down the costs of acquiring them. It had been a long time coming, but the Treasury had finally found a way to fulfill Paulson's original vision of using TARP funds to buy troubled assets, without overpaying for them.

Tim publicly introduced the stress-test idea, along with the expansion of the TALF and the creation of the Public-Private Investment Program, in a speech delivered February 10 in front of a phalanx of American flags in his department's marble-walled Cash Room. The strategy was more work-in-progress than a full-fledged plan, and financial markets reacted badly to the lack of detail. The Dow plunged 382 points that day. In a call with the FOMC to brief members in advance, I had predicted that the markets wouldn't like the lack of specificity. But, with confidence in banks diminishing by the day, I understood the urgency of announcing something. It didn't take long for the details to emerge: Two weeks after Tim's speech, the Fed and other bank supervisory agencies released plans for conducting the stress tests. On March 3, we provided more information about the expansion of the TALF, and, in late March, Treasury outlined the specifics of PPIP.

Conducting the stress tests, however, would take some time, and while we waited for the results, doubts about the banking system persisted. An ongoing question, actively debated by Tim and Larry Summers in the White House, was what to do if the test revealed a capital hole deeper than could be filled by the remaining TARP funds. Summers was pessimistic and presumed that, if the stress tests were to be credible, they would have to show catastrophic losses that would overwhelm the TARP. He accordingly favored nationalizing some troubled banks—that is, having the government take them over, lock, stock, and barrel. The idea was less outlandish than it would have seemed six or eight months earlier. A week after Tim announced the stress tests, no less a free-market champion than Alan Greenspan raised the possibility of temporarily nationalizing some banks—an event that might need to occur once in a hundred years, he said. Other prominent commentators, like Paul Krugman of the *New York Times*, agreed that it might be necessary. But Tim wanted to avoid nationalization, if at all possible, and I sided with him. "We don't plan anything like that," I told the House Financial Services Committee on February 25. I repeated my view in meetings at the Treasury and the White House.

I knew that nationalization might have some political appeal. It would look less like a bailout, and we could implement reforms at nationalized institutions without having to deal with private boards and shareholders. But, based on our recent experiences with the semi-nationalizations of Fannie, Freddie, and AIG, I believed in practice it would be a nightmare. Once nationalized, banks could be wards of the state for many years. Governments do not have the expertise to run banks effectively, and private investors are hardly likely to want to put money in banks that are government-controlled. And politics would almost certainly intrude—for example, nationalized banks might be pressured to extend credit to government-favored groups, irrespective of creditworthiness, which could lead to more losses and bailouts.

Whether there were feasible alternatives to nationalization, though, depended on the results of the stress tests. As the regulator of the large bank holding companies, the Fed took the lead. Coryann Stefansson, an associate director of the Board's supervision division, organized a comprehensive review. From February through May of 2009, our staff and the staff of other agencies bore an extraordinary burden. More than 150 Fed examiners, analysts, and economists worked evenings and weekends for ten weeks. We focused on the nineteen largest U.S.-owned bank holding companies, those with assets of $100 billion or more. Collectively, they held about two-thirds of the assets and half the loans in the U.S. banking system.

Stress testing itself was not a new idea. For years, both banks and their examiners had used the technique to analyze how, say, a given portfolio of assets might perform under adverse conditions. But, far more ambitiously, we aimed to conduct a single, rigorous test that covered all the big banks and all their assets simultaneously and using the same criteria. That way, we and the markets could both assess the overall health of each institution and compare each institution to its peers. (David Wilcox and his team had proposed a stress test of the banking system as part of the co-investment plan they presented to the Paulson Treasury in October 2008.) We asked each bank to provide detailed estimates of its likely losses and earnings over the next two years under two hypothetical economic scenarios: a baseline scenario corresponding to the consensus of private-sector forecasters, and an adverse scenario that assumed significantly worse economic and financial conditions. Our supervisors and economists intensively reviewed the reported results for consistency and plausibility, using statistical and economic models to analyze the data. When we were comfortable with the estimated revenues and losses, we then calculated how much capital a given bank would need under each of the two scenarios.

Then, as previously arranged with the Treasury, we told the banks that they had six months to raise enough capital to allow them to remain viable and continue to lend normally, even in the adverse scenario. If they were unable to raise the required capital from private markets within sixth months, they would have to take capital from the TARP under conditions imposed by the Treasury.

We also decided to make public, in considerable detail, the stress test results for each bank, including each bank's projected losses for each type of asset. The banks objected strongly, and some of our veteran supervisors were uneasy. The release of this information would contravene the practices of generations of bank examiners at the Fed and every other bank regulatory agency, where "supervisory confidentiality" was sacrosanct. In normal times, assurances of confidentiality increase banks' willingness to cooperate with examiners by allaying any concern that their proprietary information would be obtained by competitors. In the atmosphere of fear and uncertainty that prevailed in early 2009, we could not dismiss the possibility that disclosing banks' weaknesses could further erode confidence, possibly leading to new runs and further sharp declines in bank stock prices. Fed Board members agreed, however, that releasing as much information as possible was the best way to reduce the paralyzing uncertainty about banks' financial health.

Our test was tough as well as transparent, and markets judged the results to be highly credible—in part because we reported loss estimates more severe than those of many outside analysts. For example, we projected, in the hypothetical adverse scenario, that banks would suffer loan losses of 9 percent over the next two years, higher than the actual losses in any two-year period since 1920, including the years of the Great Depression. But equally important, I think, was that government capital from the TARP could be tapped to help any bank in serious trouble. The availability of backstop capital gave the regulators the right incentives: Without it, we might have been suspected of going easy on weaker banks, for fear of inducing runs. With the backstop, investors could see that we had every reason to be tough, to ensure that troubled banks would be forced to take all the capital they needed to remain stable.

Because most banks tested were found to be either adequately capitalized or reasonably near to being adequately capitalized, the test substantially increased confidence in the banking system. After the release of the results in May, the private sector became willing once again to invest in U.S. banks. By November, the tested banks would increase their collective capital by $77 billion. Ten of the nineteen institutions needed more capital, but only GMAC, General Motors' financial arm, couldn't raise it on its own. Treasury injected $3.8 billion in TARP capital into GMAC (later renamed Ally Financial); this was in addition to $12.5 billion in previous injections. The cost of insuring against defaults by large financial institutions fell sharply as confidence returned.

The stress test was a decisive turning point. From then on, the U.S. banking system would strengthen steadily—and, eventually, the economy would follow.

———

AS I WRITE, six years after the end of the most intense period of the financial crisis, politicians, journalists, and scholars continue to debate its causes and consequences. Why did the crisis happen? What made it so bad? Were the policy responses the right ones? What would have happened if governments around the globe hadn't ultimately contained the crisis?

New insights will certainly emerge in coming years, just as Milton Friedman and Anna Schwartz, writing in the 1960s, fundamentally changed our understanding of the Great Depression. However, as we battled an extraordinarily complicated crisis, we didn't have the luxury of waiting for the academic debates to play out. We needed a coherent framework to guide our responses.

For me, as a student of monetary and financial history, the crisis of 2007–2009 was best understood as a descendant of the classic financial panics of the nineteenth and early twentieth centuries. Of course, the recent crisis emerged in a global financial system that had become much more complex and integrated, and our regulatory system, for the most part, had not kept up with the changes. That made the analogies to history harder to discern and effective responses more difficult to devise. But understanding what was happening in the context of history proved invaluable.

Based on the historical parallels, I believed then and believe now that the severity of the panic itself—as much as or more so than its immediate triggers (most prominently, subprime mortgage lending abuses and the house price bubble)—was responsible for the enormous financial and economic costs of the crisis. Despite the feeling at times that we were working with chewing gum and baling wire, our policies (and the Treasury's and the FDIC's) drew heavily on classic prescriptions for fighting financial panics, and they ultimately eased the crisis. If they hadn't, historical experience suggests that the nation would have experienced an economic collapse far worse than the very severe slump we endured.

THE DETAILS OF earlier banking panics in the United States differed substantially, but major panics tended to follow a consistent story line. Many were preceded by a credit boom that made both lenders and borrowers more vulnerable to financial shocks. And most began with one or more triggering events that led depositors to worry about their banks, such as the failure of the stock market speculation scheme that touched off the Panic of 1907.

In a panic, runs on a few institutions soon become contagious. Contagion can occur through several channels. When bad news about one institution emerges, for example, depositors naturally wonder whether other institutions with similar asset holdings or business models might be in trouble as well. Also, financial institutions are interconnected, regularly lending to each other and transacting through a variety of business relationships. Consequently, like a row of dominoes toppling, one institution's failure may cause others.

Perhaps the most dangerous channel of contagion, however, is a fire sale of assets. Financial institutions facing runs must quickly obtain cash to satisfy their depositors or other creditors. If they cannot borrow the necessary cash, they must sell assets. First they jettison the easy-to-sell assets, such as government bonds. Then they try to liquidate the difficult-to-sell assets—like loans to individual businesses. If many institutions are trying to unload difficult-to-sell assets at the same time, then the market prices of those assets will plunge. As asset values fall, institutions' financial conditions deteriorate further, increasing their creditors' fears and possibly leading to even more widespread runs.

A firm that does not have the cash to meet its current obligations is said to be illiquid. An illiquid firm need not be insolvent; that is, the value of its assets may still exceed the value of its liabilities, even if it lacks ready cash. However, in a panic, the distinction between illiquidity and insolvency quickly blurs. On the one hand, depositors and other short-term lenders likely would not run if they did not suspect their bank might be insolvent and thus likely to default. On the other hand, in a panic, even initially sound firms may be forced into insolvency, as fire sales and any economic slump resulting from the panic depress the value of their assets. Major panics involve both illiquidity and insolvency, and so both short-term lending and injections of capital may be required to end them.

When a serious panic occurs, significant damage to the broader economy is almost inevitable. Amid fear and uncertainty, investors want to hold only the safest and most liquid assets. Lenders become ultraconservative, so credit disappears or remains available only to the best borrowers at high cost and under stringent conditions. The prices of riskier assets, like stocks and corporate bonds, may also fall sharply, reducing household wealth and companies' access to new capital. As credit tightens and asset prices fall, firms and households hit the pause button. Hiring, investing, and spending fall precipitously, pushing the economy into recession.

This basic scenario was repeated many times in the United States until the reforms of the Great Depression—especially the institution of deposit insurance. The U.S. financial system then entered a lengthy period of relative calm, but significant financial crises did occur in Japan, the Nordic countries, and emerging markets in Latin America and East Asia. Economists intensively studied the Asian and Latin American crises of the 1980s and 1990s but did not think that those countries' experiences were particularly relevant to the United States. The emerging-market countries had underdeveloped financial systems and, as small economies dependent on international trade and investment, were much more vulnerable to so-called external shocks, such as sharp changes in international capital flows. Economists, including me, also studied the experiences of the Nordic countries and Japan, but we concluded that institutional, economic, and political differences made those countries special cases. We should have listened to Mark Twain, who is reputed to have said that history does not repeat itself, but it rhymes. Although the recent crisis took place in a radically different financial and economic context, it rhymed with past panics.

LIKE MOST EARLIER CRISES, the panic of 2007–2009 followed a credit boom, in this case concentrated in mortgages made to borrowers with lower credit scores but showing up in other areas, such as commercial real estate, as well. Also like earlier crises, the panic began with identifiable triggers, such as the BNP Paribas announcement in August 2007 that investors would not be allowed to withdraw their money from three of its funds. This announcement and others contributed to investors' growing realization that subprime mortgages, and the structured credit products that bundled them, could suffer significant losses in spite of high credit ratings.

The defining characteristic of a panic is a widespread run on financial firms. The introduction of federal deposit insurance in 1934 had supposedly eliminated the possibility of bank runs. But that did not take into account the evolution of the market for short-term funding in the years before the crisis, particularly the growth in wholesale funding such as repo agreements and commercial paper.

The search by firms and institutional investors for better ways to manage their cash holdings fueled the growth of wholesale funding. Someone with extra cash to lend can always deposit it in a bank, but deposit insurance (limited, before the crisis, to $100,000 per account) afforded little protection to holders of much larger amounts of cash. Corporations, pension funds, money market funds, insurance companies, and securities dealers looked for alternatives to bank deposits. Both commercial paper and repo agreements were widely viewed as safer and more convenient than uninsured bank deposits.

Meanwhile, interest in wholesale funding on the other side of the market—firms looking to borrow cash—was also growing. Banks found wholesale funding a cheap and flexible (and less tightly regulated) supplement to ordinary deposits. The nonbank financial institutions at the core of the shadow banking system (such as investment banks, securities dealers, and structured investment vehicles) could not accept insured deposits. They depended heavily on wholesale funding. They used it to finance holdings that included longer-term, illiquid securities. By the eve of the crisis, the financial system's reliance on wholesale funding exceeded its use of insured deposits. At the end of 2006, insured deposits totaled $4.1 trillion, while financial institutions' wholesale funding amounted to $5.6 trillion, including repos of $3.8 trillion and commercial paper of $1.8 trillion. In addition, banks held uninsured deposits (including foreign deposits and large certificates of deposit) of $3.7 trillion.

Because much wholesale funding—including asset-backed commercial paper and repos—was directly or indirectly collateralized, firms and regulators saw little risk of runs. But collateral reassures lenders only if it is known to be of good quality and can be easily sold. Treasury securities, which carry no credit risk and are traded in a deep and liquid market, are ideal collateral. But wholesale funding grew more rapidly than the available supply of Treasuries and other high-quality collateral. At the same time, high-quality securities were greatly prized by global investors seeking security and liquidity, including foreign central banks and sovereign wealth funds. The result was a shortage of safe, liquid assets.

In response, Wall Street firms, seeing a profit opportunity, employed financial engineers to convert riskier and less liquid assets into seemingly safe assets in large quantities. To do so, they packaged loans and securities of varying credit quality, then sliced the packages into lower- and higher-quality components. The higher-quality tranches carried AAA credit ratings, bestowed by rating agencies that were paid by the securities issuers and that often consulted with the issuers on the securities' design. These structured credit products provided both new collateral and seemingly attractive assets for investors around the world, including many financial institutions, looking for higher-yielding but also highly rated securities.

But, while structured credit products seemed for a time to meet the heavy demand for safe assets, they had a critical defect: The cash flows they gave investors depended in complicated ways on the performance of hundreds or thousands of varied loans or securities. This complexity reduced the ability of investors to independently judge the structured products' quality. Some potential purchasers insisted on more information and greater transparency, but most took the easy way and relied instead on the credit ratings. When AAA-rated securities that contained subprime mortgages began to go bad, those investors did not have their own analysis to fall back on. Contagion reared its ugly head. Just as depositors in 1907 ran on any bank with a whiff of a connection to the bankrupt stock speculators, investors a century later pulled back en masse from any structured credit product that might carry the subprime virus.

The most intense runs took place in the market for asset-backed commercial paper, which had shrunk rapidly after the BNP Paribas announcement in August 2007. In the repo market, runs did not always take the form of a complete refusal to lend. For example, repo lenders might demand more collateral for each dollar lent, refuse to accept certain types of securities as collateral, or be willing to lend only overnight instead of for longer periods. And, because repo lending is based on the current market value of the collateral, declines in asset values led immediately to declines in available repo funding. Overall, wholesale funding for all financial institutions fell from $5.6 trillion at the end of 2006 to $4.5 trillion by the end of 2008, with most of the decline coming at nonbank institutions.

The investment vehicles set up to hold complex structured securities, like Citigroup's structured investment vehicles, were particularly hard hit by the run. Most were forced to seek assistance from the financial institutions that created them. Ultimately, the losses in off-balance-sheet vehicles would be almost entirely absorbed by their sponsors.

In addition to the run on wholesale funding, financial firms confronted other demands for cash. Banks that had offered credit lines to their institutional and corporate customers now saw those lines drawn to their limits. Counterparties to derivatives contracts demanded more collateral. Hedge funds and other institutional customers of investment firms closed their accounts, withdrawing cash and securities. Banks refused to lend to each other in the interbank market. In a panic, cash is king. Investors and firms try to maximize their holdings of short-term, safe, and liquid assets.

The funding crunch forced fire sales—particularly of the structured credit products that no one now wanted. The prices of those assets plummeted, forcing financial institutions to mark down the value of similar assets still on their books. As the panic progressed, illiquidity morphed into insolvency. The firms that were most thinly capitalized or had taken the greatest risks either failed or teetered on the brink of insolvency, increasing the fear in the markets.

The interconnectedness of the financial system also promoted contagion: The failure of Lehman directly touched off a run on money market funds because one of them, the Reserve Fund, had suffered significant losses on its holdings of Lehman's commercial paper. Investors eventually refused to finance securities backed with assets completely unrelated to mortgages, like credit card debt, student loan debt, and government-insured small business credit—assets that they should have had no reason to fear, except for the contagion sweeping the markets.

The skyrocketing cost of unsecured bank-to-bank loans mirrored the course of the crisis (Figure 1). Usually, a bank borrowing from another bank will pay only a little more (between a fifth and a half of a percentage point) than the U.S. government, the safest of all borrowers, has to pay on short-term Treasury securities. The spread between the interest rate on short-term bank-to-bank lending and the interest rate on comparable Treasury securities (known as the TED spread) remained in the normal range until the summer of 2007, showing that general confidence in banks remained strong despite the bad news about subprime mortgages. However, the spread

FIGURE 1: The Cost of Interbank Borrowing Soared
During the Crisis

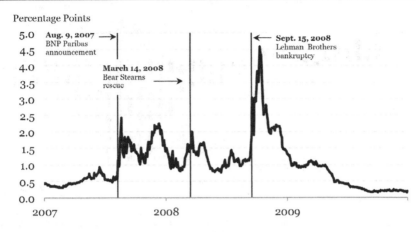

The line tracks the TED spread, a measure of distress in credit markets. It is the difference between the rate paid on three-month interbank loans as represented by the London Interbank Offered Rate (LIBOR) and the interest rate paid on three-month Treasury bills. The TED spread showed that credit risk increased sharply at key points in the crisis. Source: Federal Reserve Bank of St. Louis

jumped to nearly 2-1/2 percentage points in mid-August 2007 as the first signs of panic roiled financial markets. It soared again in March 2008 (corresponding to the Bear Stearns rescue), declined modestly over the summer, then shot up when Lehman failed, topping out at more than 4-1/2 percentage points in mid-October 2008. As the government's policy response took effect, the spread declined toward normal levels by mid-2009.

All this financial turmoil had direct consequences for Main Street America. The recession began in December 2007, a few months after the onset of the crisis. Even so, job losses (Figure 2) were relatively moderate until the panic accelerated in early fall 2008. Then the job market collapsed. During the last four months of 2008, 2.4 million jobs disappeared, and, during the first half of 2009, an additional 3.8 million were lost. Payrolls continued to decline through the rest of the year, but less precipitously.

FIGURE 2: The Job Market Collapsed After the Crisis Intensified

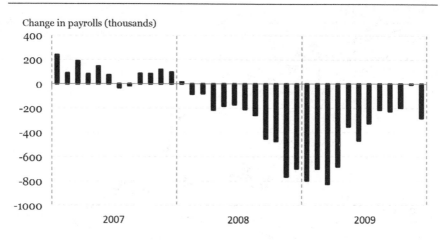

The bars show modest gains in U.S. payrolls through 2007, moderate declines as the Great Recession began, and then a very steep drop when the crisis intensified in September 2008. Job losses slowed as financial stability returned. Source: Bureau of Labor Statistics

Household consumption also tracked the course of the financial crisis. Adjusted for inflation, it was about flat in the first half of 2008. However, consumption fell by 2.9 percent (at an annual rate) in the third quarter of 2008, with the biggest decline in September, the month Lehman failed. As the crisis intensified, consumption dropped at a whopping 4.7 percent rate in the fourth quarter—the biggest quarterly drop since Jimmy Carter's credit controls (intended as an inflation-fighting measure) caused a collapse in consumer spending in 1980. Consumption continued its decline, at about a 1.6 percent rate, in the first half of 2009. Capital investment by businesses fell even more sharply, with the largest declines coming in the fourth quarter of 2008 and the first quarter of 2009. In short, the close correspondence between the intensification of the financial crisis and the worsening of economic conditions offers strong evidence that the magnitude of the panic at the height of the crisis was the most important reason for the severity of the Great Recession. The experiences of many countries, as documented by academic studies (including my own work on the international experience during the Depression), demonstrates that serious financial crises are typically followed by deep and protracted downturns.

The conclusion that the financial panic deeply hurt the economy does not rule out other contributing causes to the recession. The unwinding housing bubble that preceded the panic certainly reduced residential construction and, by lowering the value of homeowners' equity, depressed household wealth and spending. Indeed, the same historical and international evidence that links financial crises and ensuing economic slumps typically finds that those slumps are worse if the crisis is combined with a crash in real estate prices.

Some economists, though, believe the collapse of the housing bubble alone can explain the depth and persistence of the recession, and that the subsequent financial crisis was mostly a sideshow. It's more than an academic debate. Its resolution has strong implications for the choices we made in fighting the panic of 2007–2009 and for the decisions policymakers might make in the future. If the crisis truly was mostly a sideshow, then policymakers devoted too much of their effort and resources to stabilizing the financial system. Instead, according to this view, they should have focused almost exclusively on helping homeowners whose houses were worth less than their mortgages.

I agree that more should have been done to help homeowners, although devising effective policies to do that was more difficult than many appreciate. However, it seems implausible that the financial crisis had little to do with the recession. The timing alone argues against that hypothesis. The recession, which began in December 2007, followed the onset of the crisis in August 2007, and it became a truly deep recession only after the panic reached its peak, in September and October 2008. The plunge in fourth-quarter economic activity, at the peak of the panic, was the worst in a half century. The economic contraction ended in June 2009, shortly after the financial crisis calmed.

Moreover, the housing-only view takes as given the sharp decline in house prices over this period. Absent the financial crisis, it's not clear that house prices would have fallen so far or fast. They flattened out in 2006 but did not decline much initially (Figure 3). When the crisis emerged, in August 2007, they were only about 4 percent lower than they had been at the beginning of 2006. Conceivably, if not for the panic, the housing bubble might have deflated more gradually, as Fed forecasters had anticipated.

But by the time Bear Stearns was sold to JPMorgan, in March 2008, house prices had fallen nearly 10 percent from their pre-crisis level, and by the collapse of Lehman they had fallen an additional 9 percent. From Lehman, in September 2008, to May 2009, house prices fell 11 percent further. They remained basically flat through 2011 before starting to recover. This pattern suggests that at least some of the speed and depth of the house price decline can be attributed to the crisis and its economic effects, including falling employment and income,

FIGURE 3: Home Prices Plummeted Only After the Crisis Began

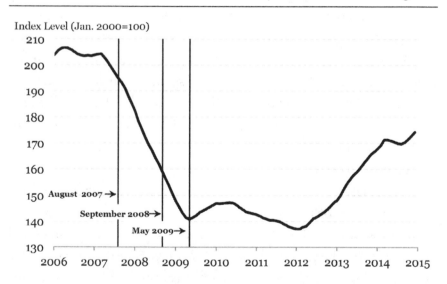

The figure shows that home prices in 20 major U.S. cities fell only modestly from the start of 2006 until August 2007 when the crisis began. The decline accelerated through the crisis but prices stabilized in May 2009, as the crisis abated. Home prices rebounded beginning in early 2012. Source: S&P/Case-Shiller 20-City Composite Home Price Index, Seasonally Adjusted tighter credit, and shattered confidence. Indeed, likely because of the crisis and the force of the recession, house prices seem to have overshot on the way down. (They rose more than 25 percent from May 2009 to early 2015.) In short, the financial crisis appears to have significantly accelerated and worsened the decline in house prices.

It took time for the Fed to recognize the crisis and gauge its severity. In responding, we had to avoid other potential risks, from higher inflation to increased moral hazard in financial markets. As we gained greater clarity, our knowledge of past financial panics guided our diagnosis of the new crisis and influenced the treatments we applied. The Federal Reserve's response had four main elements: lower interest rates to support the economy; emergency liquidity lending aimed at stabilizing the financial system; rescues (coordinated when possible with the Treasury and the FDIC) to prevent the disorderly failure of major financial institutions; and the stress-test disclosures of banks' condition (undertaken in conjunction with the Treasury and other bank regulators).

In September 2007, once it seemed clear that Wall Street's financial turmoil could threaten Main Street, we started cutting the target for the federal funds rate. We continued until we reduced the target to near zero and could go no further. From there, we would venture into uncharted waters by finding ways to push down longer-term interest rates, beginning with the announcement of large-scale purchases of mortgage-backed securities. The journey was nerve-racking, but most of my colleagues and I were determined not to repeat the blunder the Federal Reserve had committed in the 1930s when it refused to deploy its monetary tools to avoid the sharp deflation that substantially worsened the Great Depression.

Our emergency liquidity lending took many novel forms. When Congress created the Fed in 1913, it envisioned us lending to banks in a panic, thereby serving as lender of last resort. Changes in the financial system over the subsequent hundred years required us to counter a run by wholesale lenders and other short-term creditors, not depositors, and so to lend to a broad array of financial institutions, not just banks. Our efforts, often drawn from our blue-sky thinking, were widely seen as creative, even daring. But, in essence, we did what Congress had intended when it created the Federal Reserve, what Walter Bagehot had advised a century and a half earlier, and what central banks had always done in the midst of panics. When financial institutions lose their funding, central banks replace it by lending against collateral, thereby reducing the pressure to dump assets at fire sale prices. Bagehot never heard of an asset-backed security or a repurchase agreement, but I think he would have understood the principles we applied to damp contagion.

Bagehot probably had not considered the possibility that a central bank would serve as lender of last resort beyond the borders of its own country. But the global role of the dollar meant that turmoil abroad could spill over into U.S. markets. So, through swap lines with fourteen other central banks, we supported dollar-denominated funding markets in Europe, Asia, and Latin America. The swap lines were our largest single program, with nearly $600 billion outstanding at their peak. They would prove crucial in containing global contagion.

In a few instances, we went beyond Bagehot by using our lending authority to rescue large institutions on the brink of collapse, including Bear Stearns and AIG. As we emphasized at the time, we took those actions not out of any consideration for their shareholders, executives, or employees but because their failure would surely have led to greater financial contagion and fanned the fear and uncertainty already raging through the markets.

Finally, working with the Treasury and other banking agencies, we helped restore confidence in the banking system through the stress tests in spring of 2009. By providing credible information about banks' prospective revenues and losses, we helped pave the way for private investment in the banking system.

For much of the panic, the Fed alone, with its chewing gum and baling wire, bore the burden of battling the crisis. This included preventing the failure of systemically important institutions. Starting in July 2008, action by Congress facilitated a more comprehensive response. The Treasury was empowered to bail out Fannie and Freddie and later, through the TARP, to begin the recapitalization of the U.S. banking system. Measures such as the Treasury's guarantee of the money market funds and the FDIC's guarantee of bank liabilities also helped to calm markets.

Even as the financial panic subsided in 2009, the damage done by the crisis became increasingly apparent. The recession would deepen into the worst economic downturn since the Great Depression. Unemployment would peak at 10 percent in October 2009. A quarter of homeowners would owe more on their mortgages than their homes were worth. Lenders had begun 1.7 million foreclosures in 2008 and would initiate 2.1 million more in 2009 and 1.8 million in 2010. Worst of all, the crisis and its economic consequences dealt such a body blow to Americans' confidence that it threatened to become a self-fulfilling prophecy. The markets were calmer, but we still had our work cut out for us.

PART III
AFTERMATH

CHAPTER 19

Quantitative Easing: The End of Orthodoxy

It was March 7, 2009, and I was again back in my hometown of Dillon, South Carolina. Two and a half years had passed since Dillon had welcomed me, early in my chairmanship, for Ben Bernanke Day. This time, as I walked by rundown brick storefronts on Main Street, Scott Pelley of CBS's *60 Minutes* walked alongside. During the day, trailed by TV cameras, I met with students at Dillon's high school, visited my childhood home on Jefferson Street—it had been through several owners and a foreclosure since my family lived there—and attended the dedication of a highway interchange named in my honor. Appropriately, the exit at the Ben Bernanke interchange took the driver off Interstate 95 toward South of the Border, where I had once waited tables, then on to Dillon. I hope someday to hear a radio report that "traffic is light near the Ben Bernanke interchange."

As Pelley and I strolled along the sidewalk to a wooden bench near what was once my family's pharmacy, I tried to explain what the Federal Reserve does, how we were responding to the financial crisis, and what I expected for the economy. But, as I learned from many people after the program aired, the images of Main Street—as I had hoped—left the more lasting impression. "You know I come from Main Street. That's my background," I told Pelley. "And I've never been on Wall Street. I care about Wall Street for one reason and one reason only—because what happens on Wall Street matters to Main Street." I explained that if we failed to stabilize financial markets and restart the flow of credit, someone like my father, who once borrowed to build a new and larger store a block away from the original one, would be out of luck. When Pelley asked why I was doing a TV interview, a rare occurrence for a sitting Fed chairman, I replied: "It's an extraordinary time. This is a chance for me to talk to America directly."

I talked about how the Fed was helping to bring down mortgage rates, strengthen banks so that they could make loans again, and stabilize money market funds. "And I think as those green shoots begin to appear in different markets—and as some confidence begins to come back—that will begin the positive dynamic that brings our economy back," I said. Some have suggested that the phrase "green shoots" meant that in March 2009 I saw a strong economic recovery right around the corner. Of course neither I nor my colleagues at the Federal Reserve expected anything of the sort. I was referring to recent improvements in mortgage and other financial markets, which I believed would ultimately help the economy begin to recover. That forecast wasn't so bad. On March 9, just two days after the interview, the Dow Jones industrial average hit bottom, closing at 6,547, a near twelve-year low, and then began its long climb back. Financial conditions continued to improve over the spring, reflecting, among other factors, our monetary policy actions and the bank stress tests. The economic contraction would end in June of that year, although unemployment would continue to rise through October.

60 Minutes brought the Fed's story to a broad audience, something we desperately needed. I had come to the Fed as an advocate of transparency, mostly because I thought it would make monetary policy more effective if the markets and the public understood our thinking. But transparency about the Fed and our policies also was proving essential for the greater battle of winning the public's trust. Michelle Smith, our communications director, believed that the Fed's sphinx-like image had ceased to serve. "The public and the media deserve the opportunity to learn more about the individual, the policy choices, and the institution," she wrote during our discussions over the *60 Minutes* invitation. "Let's do it."

It was only the beginning. That year I would take students' questions at universities, write op-eds explaining the Fed's actions, and appear on a nationally televised town hall hosted by Jim Lehrer of PBS. Television appearances, in particular, were not my métier. I have crossed hosting *The Tonight Show* off the list of my post-Fed job possibilities. But I am glad that we reached out, and not only to explain the Fed's side of the story amid the barrage of negative coverage. Economic conditions in early 2009 were scary, and if I could explain what was happening and reassure people about the future, it could only help.

WITH MORTGAGE-BACKED SECURITIES purchases just getting under way, the FOMC did not take additional action at its first meeting of 2009. Only four governors attended. Randy Kroszner had recently left the Board and Dan Tarullo was not yet sworn in. As Tim's successor as president of the Federal Reserve Bank of New York, Bill Dudley also became vice chairman of the FOMC.

We were now treating every meeting as a joint meeting of the Board and the FOMC to stress cooperation between the overlapping bodies. A few Committee members remained uncomfortable about our alphabet soup of lending facilities. Jeff Lacker of the Richmond Fed frequently expressed the concern that our programs, including our plan to purchase mortgage-backed securities, were unnecessarily distorting markets. Since Adam Smith, economists have generally believed in the capacity of free markets to allocate resources efficiently. But most of my colleagues and I recognized that, in a financial panic, fear and risk aversion prevent financial markets from serving their critical functions. For now our interventions remained essential, I argued. With the support of most of the Reserve Bank presidents, the Board extended the emergency lending facilities for six months, to October.

At the FOMC meeting, our discussion of the economy was dour and most around the table expected we would need to take new steps soon. The deepening U.S. recession was spreading globally. Inflation, an important concern when the Committee had met six months earlier, was rapidly declining as spending plummeted and commodity prices fell. The prospect of improvement in the economy was nowhere in sight. "I think we ought to recognize that we could be at zero [interest rates] for quite a long time," I said.

BEFORE BECOMING CHAIRMAN, I had spoken about monetary policy after short-term interest rates reached zero. I was responding to a fairly widely held view that, once rates hit zero, it marked the exhaustion of monetary policy options. I had argued then to the contrary. Now the time had come to put my ideas into practice. We had reached the end of orthodoxy.

Our purchases of hundreds of billions of dollars of securities were probably the most important and definitely the most controversial tool we would employ. We usually referred to them as large-scale asset purchases, or LSAPs, but the financial world persisted in calling the tool quantitative easing, or QE.* The purchases of Fannie and Freddie debt in December 2008 and of mortgage-backed securities in January 2009 marked our first use of it. Purchases of Treasury securities would come next.

Our goal was to bring down longer-term interest rates, such as the rates on thirty-year mortgages and corporate bonds. If we could do that, we might stimulate spending—on housing and business capital investment, for example. In particular, our planned purchases of $600 billion of mortgage-related securities were intended to increase demand for the securities at a time when many investors were shy-

---

*   I tried, without success, to get the media and markets to use the term "credit easing," a phrase suggested by Dave Skidmore, rather than "quantitative easing." Quantitative easing was the term applied to (unsuccessful) Japanese programs earlier in the decade, which differed from our securities purchases in many respects. In particular, the Japanese QE programs were aimed at increasing the money supply, while the Fed focused on purchasing longer-term Treasury and mortgage-backed securities as a means of reducing longer-term interest rates.

ing away from them. By adding to the demand for MBS in particular we hoped to push down their yields, which would in turn cause the interest rates paid by individual mortgage borrowers to decline. Indeed, since financial markets are forward-looking, mortgage rates had started to fall in late November 2008—after our announcement but before any actual purchases were made.

Similarly, when we bought longer-term Treasury securities, such as a note maturing in ten years, the yields on those securities tended to decline. Of course, nobody in the private sector borrows at the same interest rate as the U.S. Treasury, the safest of all borrowers. But lower yields on Treasury securities generally spill over to other longer-term interest rates. For example, when considering a corporate bond, investors typically evaluate the yield on that bond relative to what they could earn on a Treasury of similar maturity. If the yield offered by the Treasury security falls, investors will usually accept a lower yield on the corporate bond as well. Moreover, when the Fed's purchases reduce the available supply of Treasuries, investors are forced to shift to other assets, such as stocks, leading the prices of those assets to rise. In buying Treasury securities, our ultimate goal was to precipitate a broad reduction in the cost of credit.*

At the next FOMC meeting, on March 18, 2009, the hawks and doves alike exuded pessimism. "I'm not sure what's going on. It looks pretty bleak," said Charlie Plosser. "The economic and financial news has been grim," agreed Janet Yellen. Fear about the stability of the banking system pervaded markets; the stock prices of even the stronger banks had declined sharply since the beginning of the year. Indeed, the Dow had fallen by almost half in less than eighteen months. The market losses not only destroyed enormous amounts of purchasing power, they stood as a constant reminder of the economy's terrifying

---

*   Ideally, we would have purchased private-sector debt, like corporate bonds and private-label MBS, affecting the rates on those securities directly. But, unlike most central banks, the Fed does not have that authority, except by invoking 13(3).

descent into the unknown. Payrolls had plummeted by 650,000 jobs in February as fearful employers laid off workers at an ever-faster pace. International trade was collapsing as more countries around the world fell into recession. We had to do more.

The most powerful step we could take would be to expand our securities purchases. I did not have a clear preference between buying more mortgage-backed securities and beginning purchases of Treasury securities. (Presumably, buying MBS would have relatively more effect on housing, while the effect of Treasury purchases would be more broad-based.) The policy alternatives I put on the table included both options. The discussion at the meeting—including the Reserve Bank presidents' reports from their deeply pessimistic business contacts—revealed even more alarm about the economy than I had expected. "One actually called me and said, 'Do you want some good news?'" Richard Fisher of Dallas reported. "And I said, 'Please.' He said, 'Call somebody else.'" The Committee's appetite for action was strong. "I think it's important that we do something big," said Charlie Evans. In the end, we agreed *both* to buy more MBS and to begin Treasury purchases. We were now fully committed to aggressive securities purchases—a program that would later become known as QE1.

The overall package was designed to get markets' attention, and it did. We announced that we planned to increase our 2009 purchases of mortgage-backed securities guaranteed by Fannie, Freddie, and Ginnie Mae to $1.25 trillion, an increase of $750 billion. We also doubled, from $100 billion to $200 billion, our planned purchases of the debt issued by Fannie and Freddie to finance their own holdings. We would also buy $300 billion of Treasuries over the next six months, our first foray into Treasury purchases. Finally, we strengthened our guidance about our plans for our benchmark interest rate, the federal funds rate. In January, we had said that we expected the funds rate to be at exceptionally low levels "for some time." In March, "for some time" became "for an extended period." We hoped that this new signal on short-term rates would help bring down long-term rates. The Committee approved the package unanimously. Even Jeff Lacker supported it, despite his concerns that purchasing mortgage-backed securities might channel credit away from worthy borrowers outside of housing.

A new era of monetary policy activism had arrived, and our announcement had powerful effects. Between the day before the meeting and the end of the year, the Dow would rise more than 3,000 points—more than 40 percent—to 10,428. Longer-term interest rates fell on our announcement, with the yield on ten-year Treasury securities dropping from about 3 percent to about 2.5 percent in one day, a very large move. Over the summer, longer-term yields would reverse and rise to above 4 percent. We would see that increase as a sign of success. Higher yields suggested that investors were expecting both more growth and higher inflation, consistent with our goal of economic revival. Indeed, after four quarters of contraction, revised data would show that the economy would grow at a 1.3 percent rate in the third quarter and a 3.9 percent rate in the fourth.

Other central banks would also adopt quantitative easing. The Bank of England started purchasing government bonds at about the same time that we announced the expansion of our QE program in March 2009. Ultimately, its program looked similar to ours, both in its emphasis on government bond purchases and in its size relative to the economy. The Bank of Japan, which had pioneered quantitative easing earlier in the decade, would both increase its purchases of government bonds and undertake a range of other programs to promote the flow of credit. However, during this period the European Central Bank would undertake only limited asset purchases, focusing instead on increasing its longer-term lending to banks.

MEANWHILE, SIX MONTHS after the original $85 billion bailout of AIG, the far-flung insurance behemoth staggered yet again. We had supplemented the first rescue with an additional $38 billion loan in early October 2008. In November of that year, working with the Treasury, we had restructured the bailout to include a $40 billion capital investment from TARP. But instead of stabilizing, the company lost an astonishing $62 billion in the fourth quarter, bringing its losses for 2008 to $99 billion, roughly equal to the annual economic output of Mississippi. To avoid a downgrade in AIG's credit rating, which would have triggered a new—likely bankruptcy-inducing—outflow of cash, the Fed and Treasury restructured the bailout once again in March 2009. We completed the new arrangements on a Sunday, one day before the company's announcement on March 2 of its huge fourth-quarter loss. The new deal included an additional $30 billion in TARP capital, bringing the total TARP investment to $70 billion, or 10 percent of the total congressional appropriation. And that figure didn't include the Fed's lending support.

The more than $180 billion that the U.S. government had committed through various programs to stabilizing AIG stirred public discontent, but a figure about one-thousandth as large ignited a much bigger firestorm. Newspapers on Sunday, March 15, quoting an unnamed senior administration official, reported that AIG would pay $165 *million* in bonuses to executives and specialists in the infamous Financial Products division, which had brought AIG to the brink of collapse. Outrage ensued. Republican senator Chuck Grassley of Iowa suggested that the AIG employees follow the "Japanese example" by apologizing, then resigning or committing suicide. Democratic representative Paul Hodes of New Hampshire said, "I think AIG now stands for arrogance, incompetence, and greed." Syndicated columnist Charles Krauthammer called for "an exemplary hanging or two." Violence indeed seemed possible. Death threats led the company to increase security around the suburban Connecticut offices of its Financial Products division and in neighborhoods where AIG executives lived. The House, in a measure of dubious constitutionality, voted to levy a confiscatory 90 percent tax on bonuses paid by companies receiving more than $5 billion in TARP funds. (The bill died in the Senate.)

The news of the planned bonuses accelerated the decline in our political standing. Barney Frank's House Financial Services Committee had not held a hearing on AIG in the six months since the bailout, but the bonuses prompted him to summon Tim Geithner, Bill Dudley, and me to a hearing on March 24. Members of Code Pink (a women's group formed originally to protest the Iraq War) sat behind us, dressed in pink shirts and life jackets. When TV cameras turned toward us, the protesters held up signs reading, "WHERE'S MY JOB?" and "BAIL ME OUT." Barney banged his gavel to begin and declared, "This is a very important public hearing. It will not be disrupted. There will be no distractions." A short while later, as Tim read his statement, Barney interrupted to admonish a protester: "Will you please act your age back there and stop playing with that sign?"

As I would explain at the hearing, I had only learned of the bonuses on March 10, when Board general counsel Scott Alvarez brought me the news. I knew immediately that AIG had presented us with yet another political and public relations disaster. I had tried to stop the payments, only to be told by the Fed's lawyers that the payments had been legally contracted and could not arbitrarily be rescinded. Our lawyers also cautioned against suing to block the payments, since AIG (and thus the taxpayers) would be subject under Connecticut law to punitive damages if we lost, as we probably would. In the end I had to settle for urging AIG CEO Ed Liddy to find a way to reduce the bonuses, and I encouraged Bill Dudley to send a letter making the same request.

As was so often the case during the financial crisis, the facts behind the AIG bonuses would turn out to be less clear-cut than they first appeared. The bonuses had been promised, before the bailout, to retain key employees, most of whom had nothing to do with the controversial actions that brought the company to the brink. Many had specialized expertise that was needed to safely unwind AIG's complex positions and, thus, to protect the taxpayers' investment in the company. That said, I certainly understood why an unemployed worker or a homeowner facing foreclosure would be outraged. Paying bonuses to employees of a company that had been bailed out by the taxpayers was an injustice that anybody could understand. No wonder people were angry. Practically, the episode provided one more reason that we needed better legal authority for winding down failing financial firms, including the ability to abrogate existing contracts.

Ultimately, some recipients voluntarily returned all or part of the bonuses, and Treasury appointed a lawyer, Ken Feinberg, to oversee compensation policies at firms that took TARP funds. Public anger eventually ebbed. But the political damage to the Fed from this and similar controversies lasted. In July 2009, a Gallup poll found that only 30 percent of those polled thought the Fed was doing an excellent or good job. We ranked last among nine federal agencies, behind even the IRS, which drew a 40 percent approval rating.

I often reminded myself that we weren't appointed to be popular. We were appointed, to the best of our abilities, to develop and implement policies that were in the long-run interest of the American people. Through the spring and summer, we continued working to support the economy and stabilize the financial system. I continued to come into the office seven days a week, using weekends to write and edit speeches or testimony or simply to reflect on recent developments.

However, I did take the first weekend of August off for the wedding of our son, Joel. (In setting the date, Joel and his fiancée, Elise Kent, had made sure that it wouldn't conflict with the Fed's Jackson Hole conference later in August.) Joel and Elise chose a hotel in sunny San Juan, Puerto Rico, for the wedding. It was a wonderful event and a welcome diversion. Among the many who attended were friends Joel had known since elementary school in New Jersey. A week later the newlyweds threw a party in Great Barrington, Massachusetts, the location of Simon's Rock College, where Joel and Elise had met. Among the guests was Ken Manning, now an MIT professor, who had persuaded me to leave Dillon for Harvard thirty-eight years before. Our daughter, Alyssa, then pursuing a postbaccalaureate program in Southern California that would lead her to medical school, attended both events. Anna and I were pleased that our kids were thriving, building their own lives far removed from the events that consumed the attention of politicians and policymakers in Washington.

EARLIER IN 2009, as I looked forward, I had considered how much longer I would serve as chairman. My term would end in January 2010, and I presumed that the president would decide over the summer whether to nominate me for another four years. I weighed whether I even wanted a second term. I had gotten more than I had bargained for when I signed up for the job—a global financial crisis and a deep recession. I was a lightning rod for critics, and their barbs were sometimes quite personal. I understood that criticism was part of the job, but it bothered me nonetheless. And maybe the critics were right. Despite all our efforts, we had avoided neither the crisis nor the recession. On darker days I wondered whether I was the right person for the job, and if remaining in the post was the right thing for the country and for the Federal Reserve.

On those days, I would sometimes find solace reading a quote attributed to Abraham Lincoln. Steve Bezman, the manager of the Board's parking garage, had given it to me on a 3 x 5 card. I kept it next to my computer. "If I were to try to read, much less answer, all the attacks made on me, this shop might as well be closed for any other business," Lincoln was quoted as saying, amid congressional criticism for military blunders in the Civil War. "I do the very best I know how—the very best I can; and I mean to keep doing so until the end. If the end brings me out all right, what is said against me won't amount to anything. If the end brings me out wrong, ten angels swearing I was right would make no difference."

Whether or not I wanted to continue, it wasn't clear that I would be offered reappointment. Media stories speculated that Larry Summers, denied the nomination to be Treasury secretary but named a top adviser to Obama, had been promised, or virtually promised, the Fed chairmanship. Board member Dan Tarullo, who had extensive connections within the administration, told Don Kohn that no promises had been made to his knowledge, but rumors persisted. I also heard secondhand that Larry had not been shy about criticizing our handling of the crisis, an indication to me that he was campaigning for the job.

As I deliberated, friends and colleagues offered support. Michelle Smith, Don Kohn, and others dismissed the notion that my leaving could be good for the Fed. Kevin Warsh, who had superb political judgment and particularly good connections among Republican lawmakers, told me that despite my battles with Congress, I was well regarded on the Hill. He was confident I could be confirmed, and in later months he would work to secure Republican support in the Senate. I appeared to have outside supporters as well. In November 2008, not long after the height of the crisis, the *Wall Street Journal* had reported that three-quarters of fifty-four private-sector economists polled supported my renomination. Subsequent surveys by the *Journal* gave even more encouraging results, although I knew full well that many considerations other than the views of economists would enter into the president's deliberations. Reappointment was certainly not assured, but neither did it seem impossible.

As I turned the question over in my mind during the spring of 2009, I concluded that I would be leaving critical tasks unfinished if I left. Although the worst of the financial crisis appeared to be over, much more remained to be done to restore normal conditions. The economy was still descending into the deepest recession since the Depression, and monetary policy would be critical to the recovery. The essential task of reforming the financial regulatory system was only beginning. And, importantly to me, the Federal Reserve—an institution for which I had the greatest respect—was at the nadir of its popularity, ripe for attack from the extremes of both the left and the right.

I certainly was not the only person equipped to tackle these problems, but it felt like desertion to leave. The searing experience of the past few years also had given me both the knowledge and the personal relationships to maintain the continuity required in a crisis. And, frankly, I wanted my efforts to be affirmed in the strongest conceivable way: through reappointment by a new president, one whose political allegiances were different from those of the president who had originally appointed me. Anna and I discussed the various considerations and my concerns at length. Despite her reluctance that I accept the chairmanship in the first place, she agreed that I needed to see through what I had started. I decided that I should try for another term.

As a close adviser to President Obama, Tim would certainly play a critical role in the decision. I didn't envy him. Tim and I had worked together in some of the darkest moments of the crisis, and I believed that he appreciated what we had accomplished and would support me. But Larry was Tim's mentor and now his colleague in the administration. And, although I got along well with the president, Larry certainly had a much closer relationship with him than I did—not unlike the relationship I had built with President Bush during my brief time in the White House in 2005.

In June, Tim asked about my plans and I told him I wanted to be reappointed. I also made clear that my second term, if I got one, would be my last. Two terms was about right for a Fed chairman, I thought, and in any case I doubted that I could tolerate the stress of the job for more than eight years. It is possible this declaration influenced Tim, because if I were to leave in January 2014, the president would still have the opportunity to appoint Larry if he chose—assuming, of course, that the president was reelected.

In the end, I don't know how the decision was made. In his own memoir, Stress Test, Tim writes that continuity in the middle of a crisis was an important consideration. President Obama certainly knew of my resolve to do whatever was necessary to help the economy recover. I had developed a good relationship with Rahm Emanuel, then the president's chief of staff; he undoubtedly would have counted Senate votes and reported that I was confirmable. My relative lack of political experience—other than my time on the school board and a brief stint at the Council of Economic Advisers—probably helped me. I was seen as having little partisan baggage. Keeping me at the Fed would also let Larry remain as Obama's close adviser. In any case, the decision soon came down: Tim told me the job was mine if I still wanted to stay on.

On Wednesday, August 19, in the early evening, Tim and I met with President Obama in the Oval Office. The chosen hour was after the press corps had left for the day and at a time when few staff were in the building. The meeting was brief. As always, the president was friendly and respectful. He praised the work that I had done and confirmed that he intended to renominate me. I told him what I had told Tim—that I wanted more time to complete unfinished business but that four more years would absolutely be my limit. He said he understood, then told me the decision would be announced soon. Half an hour later I emailed Michelle: "Saw BO. Thumbs up." Anna didn't cry this time when I relayed the news. She had known what was coming.

The next day, I flew to Jackson Hole for the annual Fed conference. As usual, I would give the keynote speech Friday morning. In it, I reflected on the year of crisis, an *annus horribilis* if there ever had been one. It was hard to believe that, less than twelve months earlier, we had not yet seen the takeover of Fannie and Freddie, the collapse of Lehman, the multiple bailouts of AIG, runs on the money market funds, the stabilization of Citi and Bank of America, the passage of the TARP, the introduction of quantitative easing, and so much more. We had come so close to the abyss. "Although we have avoided the worst, difficult challenges still lie ahead," I said. "We must work together to build on the gains already made to secure a sustained economic recovery."

Although the presentations at the conference focused on the crisis and economic outlook, much of the discussion during the meals and receptions was about who would lead the Fed for the next four years. I deflected questions. Many colleagues publicly expressed support for me, among them Marty Feldstein, my old professor at Harvard who had been a contender for the job when I was originally appointed. Intrade, the online gambling site, put my odds of reappointment at 79 percent.

Stan Fischer, my thesis adviser at MIT and, at the time, governor of the Bank of Israel, delivered the luncheon remarks on Friday. As he spoke, my security team called me out of the room. Curious looks followed my exit. Cell phone reception in the Wyoming mountains was spotty and the call that arrived had failed. Eventually I was able to return it. A White House aide let me know that the official announcement of my renomination would take place on Tuesday, at Martha's Vineyard, where the president and his family would be vacationing.

I broke the news to the senior Board staff attending the conference—including Dave Stockton, Brian Madigan, and Nathan Sheets, the director of the Board's international division—in the break room for employees of the Jackson Hole Airport. It had been set aside for us while we waited for the flight out. When I returned to Washington, I also called each member of the FOMC. At least for a few days, I felt that I had made the right decision.

Early Tuesday morning, August 25, accompanied by Michelle Smith and security agents Bob Agnew and Ed Macomber, I was driven to Andrews Air Force Base. A small, sleek jet owned by the air force brought us to Martha's Vineyard Airport. From there we proceeded to the Oak Bluffs School, where the announcement would take place. As instructed, I was wearing a blue blazer, slacks, and no tie. At 9:00 a.m. the president's convoy arrived, bristling with security and communications technology. Obama emerged from a black SUV, quickly threw on a blue blazer of his own, and offered me private congratulations. We stepped in front of the cameras. The president thanked me for helping bring the country and the world through one of the worst financial crises in history. He credited my background as a scholar of the Depression, my temperament, my courage, and my creativity. I thanked the president for his support, both for me personally and for a "strong and independent Federal Reserve." Then back to the airport. I was in my office in Washington in time for lunch.

I got another morale boost a few months later, on December 16, when I was named *Time* magazine's 2009 Person of the Year. Michelle had told me about the possibility several months earlier, and we had cooperated with *Time* reporter Michael Grunwald. I hoped that, like the *60 Minutes* episode, the story would humanize me and help people better understand the Federal Reserve and our actions. I think it did. Grunwald called me "the most important player guiding the world's most important economy" and credited the Fed with averting a second Depression. The magazine cover depicted my face on a stylized dollar bill.

BUT, ALONG WITH the praise, *Time* also observed that the Fed's actions had triggered a powerful political backlash. I had felt that backlash on December 3, when I went before the Senate Banking Committee for a grueling hearing on my nomination that ran from 10:00 a.m. until past 3:00 p.m. I had slept poorly and hoped that I would be able to maintain both my concentration and my cool. Chris Dodd, the chairman, supported my renomination. He praised the Fed's extraordinary actions under my leadership, although he also questioned whether the Fed should continue to have a central role in financial regulation. I was always puzzled by the combination of Dodd's apparently high personal regard for me and his willingness to blast the Federal Reserve, as if I had had nothing to do with the Fed's decisions and policies.

Richard Shelby, the senior Republican, was wholly critical. He complained about the bailouts, which he believed had done little more than increase moral hazard, and the size and riskiness of the Fed's balance sheet. "For many years I held the Federal Reserve in very high regard," he said in his soft Alabama drawl. "I had a great deal of respect for not only its critical role in the U.S. monetary policy, but also its role as a prudential regulator. . . . I fear now, however, that our trust and confidence were misplaced in a lot of instances." He then outlined the considerable challenges the economy still faced. "The question before us," he said, "is whether Chairman Bernanke is the person best suited to lead us out and keep us out of trouble." Despite his sometimes harsh words in public, Shelby, like Dodd, seemed to value his personal relationship with me. He often invited me to his office to chat with him alone or sometimes with a small group of Republican senators. His good-old-boy mannerisms belied a shrewd intelligence and cosmopolitan tastes. I once invited him to dinner and he chose one of the finest Italian restaurants in Washington. During our conversation, I was surprised to learn of his affinity for Wagnerian opera.

The Fed's (and my) nemesis, Senator Bunning, pounded on what he saw as our failures not only under me but also under Alan Greenspan, whose policies I had never sufficiently repudiated, in his view. Two weeks after the hearing, at a public discussion of my renomination among the Senate Banking Committee members, Bunning would deride the *Time* announcement: "Chairman Bernanke may wonder if he really wants to be honored by an organization that has previously named people like Joseph Stalin twice, Yasser Arafat, Adolf Hitler, the Ayatollah Khomeini, Vladimir Putin, Richard Nixon twice, as their person of the year," he said. "But I congratulate him and hope he at least turns out better than most of those people."

At my hearing I defended my record. I credited the Fed, in partnership with the Treasury, the FDIC, and the Congress, with averting financial and economic collapse. I pushed back against hyperbolic claims that the Fed and the Fed alone was responsible for the crisis, and that we should have both seen it coming and averted it completely. I pointed out the many steps we had taken to increase our transparency and explained why our monetary actions (slashing interest rates and buying securities) were both necessary and responsible. I conceded regulatory and supervisory failures by the Fed (we were hardly alone) but argued that we needed to retain our supervisory powers if we were to play our essential part in preserving financial stability. It was a tough day but I believed I had made my case.

Two months later, the committee voted, 16–7, to send my nomination to the full Senate. My support on the committee, as in the Senate as a whole, came mostly from Democrats, with the exception of Oregon's Jeff Merkley. Merkley told me in a phone call that he believed that

I was too implicated in the origins of the crisis to deserve his vote. I wondered whether anyone involved in federal economic policy before 2007 could entirely escape that charge. Four Republicans supported me: Bob Bennett of Utah, Bob Corker of Tennessee, Judd Gregg of New Hampshire, and Mike Johanns of Nebraska.

I admired each of these four and worked with them constructively throughout my tenure. Bennett, a senator with a patrician air, thoughtful and moderate, had voted for TARP and later lost in the Republican primary in part because of that vote. Gregg, a highly capable legislator, often stood up for the Fed in debates among Republicans, with important additional support coming from fellow Republican Lamar Alexander of Tennessee. Johanns, with whom I had worked during my time in the White House when he was secretary of agriculture, was reasonable and low-key and always gave me a fair hearing. My relationship with Corker was complicated by frequent policy disagreements. He was particularly unhappy with our quantitative easing, and he would later advocate the elimination of the employment side of the Fed's mandate. But he was one of the most economically literate members of the Senate, as well as one of those most willing to work across the aisle. He sought my views on a range of topics and would organize private meetings with other Senate Republicans so I could explain our actions.

These and a few other exceptions notwithstanding, the increasing hostility of Republicans to the Fed and to me personally troubled me, particularly since I had been appointed by a Republican president who had supported our actions during the crisis. I tried to listen carefully and accept thoughtful criticisms. But it seemed to me that the crisis had helped to radicalize large parts of the Republican Party. The late Senator Daniel Patrick Moynihan of New York once said that everyone is entitled to his own opinion but not his own facts. Some Republicans, particularly on the far right, increasingly did not draw the distinction. They blamed the crisis on the Fed and on Fannie and Freddie, with little regard for the manifest failings of the private sector, other regulators, or, most especially, of Congress itself. They condemned bailouts as giveaways of taxpayer money without considering the broader economic consequences of the collapse of systemically important firms. They saw inflation where it did not exist and, when the official data did not bear out their predictions, invoked conspiracy theories. They denied that monetary or fiscal policy could support job growth, while still working to direct federal spending to their own districts. They advocated discredited monetary systems, like the gold standard.

For me, these positions pushed the party further away from the mainstream and from traditional Republican views. I still considered myself a conservative. I believed in the importance of personal autonomy and responsibility and agreed that market economies were best for generating economic growth and improving economic welfare. But I had lost patience with Republicans' susceptibility to the know-nothing-ism of the far right. I didn't leave the Republican Party. I felt that the party left me.

Of course, the Democrats suffered their own delusions, especially on the far left (though if both the far right and the far left opposed me, I figured I must have been doing something right). Senator Bernie Sanders of Vermont, a self-described socialist who caucused with the Democrats, seemed to see the world as a vast conspiracy of big corporations and the wealthy. (Corporations and the wealthy have lots of power, certainly, but in the real world most bad things happen because of ignorance, incompetence, or bad luck, not as the result of grand conspiracies.) When I became chairman I resolved to be nonpartisan, which was appropriate for my role. My experiences in Washington turned me off from political parties pretty much completely. I view myself now as a moderate independent, and I think that's where I'll stay.

On January 28, 2010, after some active administration lobbying on my behalf as well as some arm-twisting by Chris Dodd, the full Senate voted, 70–30, to confirm me—not an especially close margin for many matters but nevertheless the closest vote by which any Fed chairman had ever been confirmed. I wasn't surprised. People were understandably dissatisfied with the economy and financial conditions, and Congress reflected that.

I was more disturbed by several phone calls I received from senators after the vote. Each had a common theme: The senator believed I was doing a good job but, for political reasons, had to vote against me. The callers seemed to believe that voting in opposition to their personal views for political reasons was perfectly natural. One call was striking. After the senator expressed his confidence in me and apologized for his no vote, I asked him why he voted as he did. "Well," he replied blithely, "sometimes you just have to throw some red meat to the knuckle-draggers."

Comments like that brought to mind an observation attributed to the comedian Lily Tomlin: No matter how cynical you become, you just can't keep up. If I could have, I would have stayed as far away from politics as possible. But, as head of the Federal Reserve, about to be sworn in for a new four-year term, I knew that politics would continue to occupy much of my time and energy.

Walking with students after a speech at Princeton University, September 24, 2010. Security agent Lou Harris, with lapel pin, far left, and agent-in-charge Bob Agnew, with lapel pin, to the immediate right of me. (AP Photo / *The Times of Trenton*, Martin Griff)

Delivering the first of four lectures on the Federal Reserve and the financial crisis at George Washington University, March 20, 2012. (AP Photo / Manuel Balce Ceneta)

Fielding a question from a reporter at my first quarterly press conference, April 27, 2011. (Federal Reserve Photograph, Britt Leckman)

With Maria Bartiromo of CNBC and Roger Ferguson, after a speech to the Economic Club of New York, November 20, 2012. Roger was the club's chairman. (The Economic Club of New York: photograph by Brian Stanton)

Mr Chairman

Thanks for Breakfast + the Visit

Ron Paul

With Representative Ron Paul of Texas, after breakfast at the Federal Reserve Board, May 9, 2012.

Protesters from Code Pink stand behind the witness table as I prepare to testify on the rescue of AIG, before the House Financial Services Committee, March 24, 2009. (Reuters / Kevin Lamarque)

CBS News correspondent Scott Pelley interviews me on bench outside the building that once housed my family's pharmacy on Main Street in Dillon, South Carolina, March 7, 2009. (CBS News / 60 Minutes)

My grandfather Jonas Bernanke, right, at the entrance to Jay Bee Drugs with a neighboring shopkeeper, Main Street, Dillon, South Carolina, early 1940s.

Jonas Bernanke, seated, second from right, with other Austro-Hungarian soldiers captured by the Russian Army, at the Rasdolnoe prisoner-of-war camp near Vladyvostok, Siberia, 1916.

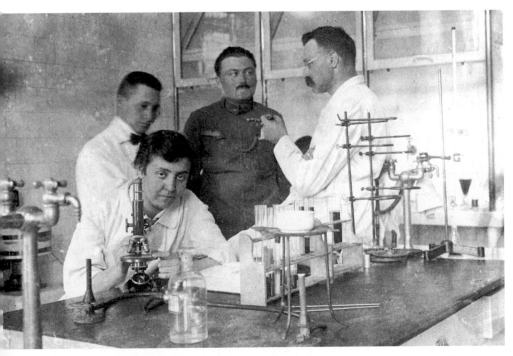

My grandmother Pauline (née Heiden) Bernanke at the microscope at the Franz Josef Hospital in Vienna, Austria, 1918. She was a medical student at the University of Vienna.

Home of my grandmother Friedman's family, the Rozas, in Lithuania.

My mother's parents, Herschel and Masia (née Roz) Friedman (Harold and Marcia), likely in the early 1920s.

My parents, Philip and Edna (née Friedman) Bernanke on their wedding day, June 15, 1952, in Charlotte, North Carolina.

As Fed chair, for security reasons, I was not allowed to drive. I missed it.

From the 1975 Harvard-Radcliffe yearbook. (Reproduced from the collections of the Harvard University Archives. Copyright 1975 Harvard Yearbook Publications)

Anna and I, shortly after our wedding. We were married on May 29, 1978, at Temple Israel in Boston.

Visiting my parents' home in Dillon, South Carolina, as a young professor.

In front of Princeton University's Woodrow Wilson School of Public and International Affairs. I chaired the economics department from 1996 to 2002. (Denise J. Applewhite, Courtesy of Princeton University)

Shaking hands with Washington Nationals third baseman Ryan Zimmerman, before the game, September 7, 2012. First baseman Adam LaRoche looks on. (AP Photo / Alex Brandon)

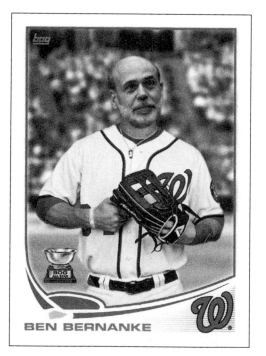
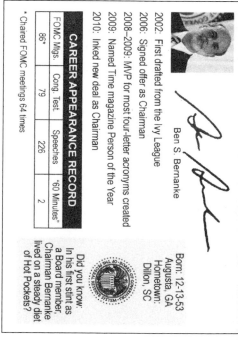

Mock baseball card prepared by the Board staff for my baseball-themed farewell reception, January 30, 2014. (Federal Reserve Photograph, Britt Leckman)

Posing with my guests before a farewell dinner for Treasury secretary Tim Geithner, January 17, 2014, at the Federal Reserve Board. Left to right, Alan Greenspan, Bob Rubin, Tim, Paul Volcker, me, Hank Paulson, Don Kohn, and Larry Summers. (Federal Reserve Photograph, Britt Leckman)

Janet Yellen, Paul Volcker, Alan Greenspan, and me at a ceremony commemorating the centennial of the Federal Reserve Act, December 16, 2013, in the boardroom. (Mark Wilson / Getty Images)

Ben — Thanks for your continued leadership and steady hand.

With President Obama, February 5, 2013, in the Oval Office. I affirmed that I did not want to be nominated to a third term as chairman. (Official White House photograph by Pete Souza)

My last Board meeting, January 27, 2014. Standing at the table, left to right, Board secretary Bob Frierson, Janet Yellen, and Dan Tarullo. (Federal Reserve Photograph, Britt Leckman)

President Obama applauds after announcing his nomination of Janet Yellen as the next chair of the Federal Reserve Board, in the State Dining Room of the White House, October 9, 2013. (AP Photo / Pablo Martinez Monsivais)

Anna and I at a farewell ceremony in the Eccles Building atrium, January 30, 2014. (Federal Reserve Photograph, Britt Leckman)

Board employees throng the ground floor of the atrium for the reception that followed the ceremony. (Federal Reserve Photograph, Britt Leckman)

Leaving the chairman's office for the last time, January 31, 2014. (Saul Loeb / AFP / Getty Images)

CHAPTER 20

Building a New Financial System

E ven as the fires of the financial crisis continued to rage, we were thinking ahead to what would need to be done after the flames burned low. The questions were both difficult and consequential: What should the new financial system, built on the ashes of the old, look like? Could we prevent future financial crises? Or, more realistically, what could we do to ensure that future crises would be arrested before they burned out of control?

As we considered these questions in late 2008 and early 2009, we drew from a global conversation on financial reform already under way. In August 2007, President Bush had asked the President's Working Group on Financial Markets (which consisted of the heads of the Treasury, the Fed, the Securities and Exchange Commission, and the Commodity Futures Trading Commission) to review the causes of the financial turmoil that, as it turned out, was just getting going. Internationally, in October 2007 the G-7 industrial countries had asked the Financial Stability Forum (which included central bankers, finance ministers, and regulators from major financial centers) to do the same. Even before the crisis began, in June 2007, Hank Paulson's team at Treasury had started work on a "blueprint" to reform the outmoded and balkanized financial regulatory structure in the United States.

The three reports generated by these separate efforts all would make useful recommendations, but of the three, Hank's "blueprint" was both the most ambitious and the most helpful to me for thinking about wholesale regulatory reform. It focused squarely on the daunting task of rationalizing the hodgepodge of federal financial regulatory agencies while eliminating overlap and closing gaps.

Hank's report, issued in March 2008, made both shorter- and longer-term recommendations, but its ultimate goal was to create a "three peaks" regulatory structure. The first peak would be a single, "prudential" regulator focused on ensuring the safety and soundness of individual financial institutions, such as banks, savings and loans, credit unions, and insurance companies. The report envisioned the Office of the Comptroller of the Currency as the agency primarily responsible for prudential supervision.

The second peak would be a new "conduct of business" agency charged with protecting consumers and investors served by banks and also nonbank entities ranging from securities dealers to mutual funds. The new agency would combine many of the existing powers of the SEC and the CFTC, and it would also take over most of the consumer protection authorities vested in the Fed and other banking agencies.

The first two elements of the Treasury plan essentially reorganized and expanded existing regulatory functions. The third peak was new. It called for an agency responsible for the stability of the financial system as a whole. The agency would also oversee critical infrastructure, such as the systems used by financial institutions for making payments or transferring securities. In Hank's proposal, this broad role would fall to the Fed, which would monitor the financial system and address any vulnerabilities it found. It would also have the authority to examine individual institutions, in cooperation with the prudential regulator, when doing so was necessary to meet the financial stability objective.

The Treasury plan stood out for its conceptual clarity about the main objectives of financial regulation and the institutional structure needed to attain them. But Hank (and we) understood that the blueprint's longer-term recommendations had to be viewed as aspirational. Congress would not take up reforms of this magnitude in a presidential election year. In any case, we knew that changes of this sort shouldn't be implemented in the middle of the crisis.

On March 27, 2008, four days before Hank unveiled his blueprint, candidate Obama in a speech at Cooper Union, a college in Manhattan, had laid out his own core principles for a twenty-first-century regulatory framework. He argued that the Fed should have supervisory authority over any institution that could borrow from it. Obama also urged streamlining overlapping regulatory agencies (without getting into specifics), strengthening capital requirements for banks, and creating a new oversight commission (analogous to Hank's financial stability regulator) to identify unanticipated threats to the financial system. I was glad to see Obama bringing these issues, normally below the radar for most voters, into the campaign debate. The principles in his speech seemed sensible and pragmatic to me.

Their many other constructive suggestions aside, the reports and studies of financial regulation completed before and soon after the onset of the crisis all failed to tackle what became one of the most pressing issues in the wake of Bear Stearns and Lehman: how to shut down a big, complex, financial firm without taking down the entire system with it. Hank and I had raised this critical concern at a hearing before Barney Frank's House Financial Services Committee in July 2008. But before Congress had an opportunity to give serious consideration to these issues, Lehman had failed, the financial world had changed yet again, and the TARP proposal soon would dominate legislative debate.

IN LATE 2008, amid the crisis firefighting, we at the Fed began working on our own proposals for financial reform. I wanted to have a well-formulated position before the legislative debates went into high gear. Kevin Warsh led a committee of Board members and Reserve Bank presidents that laid out some key principles.

Kevin's committee considered a more explicitly "macroprudential," or system-wide, approach to supervision and regulation. Historically, financial oversight had been almost entirely "microprudential"— focused on the safety and soundness of individual firms, on the theory that if you take care of the trees, the forest will take care of itself. In contrast, the macroprudential approach strives for a forest-AND-trees perspective. It looks not only at the health of individual institutions but also at factors that may affect the stability of the financial system as a whole, including linkages among institutions and risks that may span multiple institutions and markets. For instance, a few lenders overexposed to subprime mortgages aren't necessarily a systemic problem, but many institutions with significant subprime exposures may well be. The goal of macroprudential regulation is to identify and defuse more broad-based risks that may not be evident when looking at individual institutions in isolation.

Warsh's group also explored the concept of a financial stability supervisor to implement the macroprudential approach—an idea close in spirit to the third peak in Hank's blueprint for reform. By the fall of 2008, after witnessing firsthand the complex interactions among markets and firms that had so gravely worsened the crisis, I had been thoroughly persuaded that a system-wide approach to supervision was essential for financial stability in a modern economy. I raised the need for more holistic oversight of the financial system in a speech in March 2009 to the Council on Foreign Relations. I also pushed again for a new system for the orderly wind-down of systemically important non-bank financial firms like Lehman and AIG.

HANK WAS FOCUSED on addressing the immediate threats posed by the crisis until he left office in January 2009, which left the task of developing a legislative proposal for financial regulatory reform to now-Secretary Geithner and his team at Treasury. White House chief of staff Rahm Emanuel had initially pressed Tim, unrealistically, to produce draft legislation before a G-20 meeting scheduled for April 2009. "You never want a serious crisis to go to waste," was Rahm's motto. But the administration had higher priorities during the first hundred days, including its economic stimulus package and the bank stress tests. Also, hampered by the slow confirmation process for senior

Treasury officials, Tim was operating with a very lean staff. "Tim has nothing like a full team in place and they are simply overwhelmed," David Wilcox emailed early in February 2009. To help fill the gaps, we lent Treasury several senior staffers, including economist Patrick Parkinson, who had helped design some of our emergency lending facilities, and attorney Mark Van Der Weide, a specialist in banking regulation. Tim and I agreed that Pat would help the administration put together the legislative proposal. "Poor Pat has not been informed of this yet," I wrote to Kohn and others after a lunch with Geithner in late February. Pat accepted the assignment stoically.

Tim rolled out the administration's proposal on June 17, 2009, in an eighty-eight-page white paper. If passed, the plan would trigger the most comprehensive overhaul of federal financial law since the Depression. Yet the plan was also pragmatic. It did not try to remake the financial system or financial regulation from scratch but built instead on existing institutions and arrangements.

The administration, for instance, chose *not* to take a radical approach to the problem of too-big-to-fail financial institutions. Understandably, given public anger at bailouts, support had been gathering from both the right and the left for breaking up the largest institutions. There were also calls to reinstate the Depression-era Glass-Steagall law, which Congress had repealed in 1999. Glass-Steagall had prohibited the combination within a single firm of commercial banking (mortgage and business lending, for example) and investment banking (such as bond underwriting). The repeal of Glass-Steagall had opened the door to the creation of "financial supermarkets," large and complex firms that offered both commercial and investment banking services.

The lack of a new Glass-Steagall provision in the administration's plan seemed to me particularly easy to defend. A Glass-Steagall–type statute would have offered little benefit during the crisis—and in fact would have prevented the acquisition of Bear Stearns by JPMorgan and of Merrill Lynch by Bank of America, steps that helped stabilize the two endangered investment banks. More importantly, most of the institutions that became emblematic of the crisis would have faced similar problems even if Glass-Steagall had remained in effect. Wachovia and Washington Mutual, by and large, got into trouble the same way banks had gotten into trouble for generations—by making bad loans. On the other hand, Bear Stearns and Lehman Brothers were traditional Wall Street investment firms with minimal involvement in commercial banking. Glass-Steagall would not have meaningfully changed the permissible activities of any of these firms. An exception, perhaps, was Citigroup—the banking, securities, and insurance conglomerate whose formation in 1998 had lent impetus to the repeal of Glass-Steagall. With that law still in place, Citi likely could not have become as large and complex as it did.

I agreed with the administration's decision not to revive Glass-Steagall. The decision not to propose breaking up some of the largest institutions seemed to me a closer call. The truth is that we don't have a very good understanding of the economic benefits of size in banking. No doubt, the largest firms' profitability is enhanced to some degree by their political influence and markets' perception that the government will protect them from collapse, which gives them an advantage over smaller firms. And a firm's size contributes to the risk that it poses to the financial system.

But surely size also has a positive economic value—for example, in the ability of a large firm to offer a wide range of services or to operate at sufficient scale to efficiently serve global nonfinancial companies. Arbitrary limits on size would risk destroying that economic value while sending jobs and profits to foreign competitors. Moreover, the size of a financial firm is far from the only factor that determines whether it poses a systemic risk. For example, Bear Stearns, which was only a quarter the size of the firm that acquired it, JPMorgan Chase, wasn't too big to fail; it was too interconnected to fail. And severe financial crises can occur even when most financial institutions are small. During the Great Depression, the United States, with its thousands of small banks, suffered a much more severe financial crisis than did Canada, which had ten large banks and only a few small banks. (For that matter, Canada, whose banking system continues to be dominated by large institutions, also came through the recent crisis relatively well.)

With these considerations in mind, I agreed with the administration view that breaking up large firms was likely not the best way to solve the too-big-to-fail problem, at least not until other, more incremental options had been tried and found wanting. In particular, more important than limiting the size of financial institutions per se is ensuring that size confers no unfair advantages on large institutions, including no presumption of a bailout if they get into trouble. That's a difficult challenge. The administration's plan sought to address it in three ways.

First, it proposed tougher capital, liquidity, and risk-management standards for systemically important institutions—both banks and nonbanks (such as AIG and the Wall Street investment firms). If large, complex institutions posed more risk to the financial system, then they should be required to operate with a wider margin of safety. The stricter requirements, in turn, might spur large firms to assess whether the true economic benefits of their size exceeded the extra costs associated with tougher rules and capital requirements. If not, then market forces should, over time, lead those firms to get smaller and less complex, or at least not grow further.

Second, the administration proposed that the Fed supervise all systemically important financial companies—not only the big bank holding companies that it already supervised but also the big Wall Street investment banks and, potentially, large insurance companies and other major financial firms. Large and complex financial companies that happened not to be banks would no longer evade meaningful oversight.

Third, and critically, the administration's plan would give the government the legal tools to take over and dismantle, in an orderly way, systemically important financial institutions on the brink of failure.

The government would no longer have to choose between bailing them out or facing the dangers of a chaotic, Lehmanesque bankruptcy. These provisions seemed to me essential for ending the too-big-to-fail problem. Besides reducing the risk of another Lehman, the very existence of a credible mechanism for safely dismantling a systemic firm should reduce the potential benefits of being perceived as too big to fail. We had done what we had to do to stabilize systemically critical firms during the crisis, but nothing would please me more than being able to get the Fed out of the bailout business.

The proposal took another essential step by emphasizing the need for macroprudential regulation and supervision to complement the oversight of individual firms and markets. Tim had originally envisioned that the Fed would be responsible for monitoring the system as a whole, much as Hank's earlier plan had proposed. But Sheila Bair, who had the ears of key members of Congress, including Chris Dodd, had been lobbying aggressively against enhancing the Fed's authority. Sheila seemed prepared to concede to the Fed a role as the supervisor of very large institutions, as the administration had proposed. But she wanted a council of regulatory agencies—chaired by its own independent head, appointed by the president—to handle oversight of the system as a whole and, in particular, to decide which institutions the Fed should oversee. Under her proposal, the council also would be able to write rules for those institutions if it considered the Fed's regulations inadequate.

Neither Tim nor I was thrilled with Sheila's plan. The Fed already possessed the bulk of the government's expertise and experience needed to serve as the financial stability regulator, and another layer of decision making in the form of a council could inhibit rapid and effective responses to systemic risks. Ultimately, however, the administration's plan included a watered-down version of Sheila's idea. It proposed a Financial Services Oversight Council headed by the Treasury secretary, instead of a separate presidential appointee. This council wouldn't write rules or designate specific financial institutions as systemically critical, as Sheila had proposed, but would advise the Fed on which institutions should be designated and consult on the formulation of standards for those institutions. The council would also help member agencies keep informed about developments in parts of the financial system lying outside their immediate jurisdiction, provide a forum for the resolution of interagency disputes, and pool regulators' insights to help identify emerging financial risks.

By including a version of Sheila's proposal in the white paper, Tim and his administration colleagues had bowed to political reality. For one, Chris Dodd and Richard Shelby—far from giving the Fed more authority—were determined to strip us of our supervisory duties, leaving us responsibility for monetary policy alone. Dodd envisioned combining all of the bank supervisory agencies into one mega-agency. Reacting to Tim's plan, even with the inclusion of the regulators' council, Dodd said, "Giving the Fed more responsibility . . . is like a parent giving his son a bigger, faster car right after he crashed the family station wagon." I thought that Dodd's comments were less about principle and more a reflection of his assessment that bashing the Fed was politically popular. Shelby was also eager to leverage anti-Fed sentiments. However, even Barney Frank, who had leaned toward designating the Fed as the financial stability regulator, switched to the council-of-regulators concept after the controversy over the AIG bonuses erupted in mid-March. He judged that making the Fed the financial stability regulator had become politically impossible. I trusted Barney's political instincts and concluded that fighting the council proposal would be fruitless. In any case, I was getting more comfortable with the idea as I better understood how the council would work.

The administration's reform plan included a host of other measures. It sought to drag the shadow banking system, where so many of the bad securities had originated, into the sunlight. For example, it would require that mortgage lenders or securitizers retain some "skin in the game" (some of the credit risk should the loan default)—a particular goal of Barney Frank.

The plan would also strengthen the regulation of derivatives, such as those that had contributed to AIG's deep losses. Importantly, it would require that more derivatives transactions be standardized and cleared centrally on exchanges, rather than settled privately between the parties to the contract. Open and transparent derivatives trading would help regulators and others better understand the interconnections among firms and markets. Also, because most exchanges, backed by their members, guarantee that transactions will be honored even if one party to the transaction defaults, trading most derivatives on exchanges would help limit contagion if a large firm unexpectedly failed. To help ensure that the exchanges themselves operated safely, the Fed—in its capacity as systemic stability regulator—would gain new supervisory authority over exchanges and other organizations playing similar roles in the financial system.

IN CONTRAST TO Hank's blueprint, which had envisioned a radical simplification of the regulatory bureaucracy, the administration's more evolutionary proposal left the existing set of regulators largely intact. Political practicalities were an important consideration. For example, Tim and his colleagues opted not to propose merging the SEC and the CFTC, though many of the financial markets and instruments they regulated served similar purposes. (The SEC regulates corporate bond trading, while the CFTC oversees trading in bond futures contracts, for example.) Merging the SEC and CFTC was a political nonstarter because they were overseen by separate committees in Congress. The congressional oversight committees jealously guarded their turf because the market players regulated by the two agencies could be counted on to provide lucrative campaign contributions.

The plan did include two changes in the regulatory bureaucracy— one relatively minor, the other more significant. The minor change was the abolishment of the hapless Office of Thrift Supervision, the regulator of savings institutions. Two big S&Ls (Washington Mutual and IndyMac) had failed on its watch, and another (Countrywide) nearly failed. Also, nominally, the tiny thrift office had been responsible for overseeing AIG's far-flung operations. Under the administration plan, the thrift office's duties would be assumed by the other banking regulators.

The more significant change was the proposed creation of a Consumer Financial Protection Agency. A 2007 article by Harvard law professor Elizabeth Warren, who was later elected to the U.S. Senate from Massachusetts, provided the impetus. In the article, Warren had called for a Financial Product Safety Commission, which would protect consumers from faulty credit cards and defective mortgages, just as the Consumer Product Safety Commission protects consumers from toasters that burst into flames. Hank's 2008 blueprint had a somewhat similar idea, the "business conduct" agency, except that it would have protected stock and bond investors—as well as borrowers and users of financial services—from shady practices. (The administration proposed to leave investor protection with the SEC.) We had gotten an early hint that the new administration was leaning toward moving consumer protection duties outside the Fed when, about four weeks before the inauguration, Don Kohn reported on a conversation with Dan Tarullo, then a leader of Obama's transition team. Tarullo raised "the possibility of consumer migrating elsewhere," Don said.

I was ambivalent about the proposal for a new consumer protection regulator. The Fed, like the other bank regulatory agencies, enforced federal consumer protection laws in the institutions it supervised—roughly five thousand bank holding companies and more than eight hundred state-chartered banks that had joined the Federal Reserve System. We also wrote many of the detailed rules needed to implement consumer protection laws. I had acknowledged on numerous occasions that, for a variety of reasons, the Fed had not done enough to prevent abuses in mortgage lending before the crisis. But, under the leadership of division director Sandy Braunstein and with my strong encouragement, the Fed's consumer protection staff had made great strides. They were particularly proud of the regulations banning unfair mortgage lending practices adopted by the Board in July 2008 under the Home Ownership and Equity Protection Act, and of our sweeping reform of credit card regulations, approved in December 2008.

Our new credit card rules overhauled the disclosures required at account opening and on monthly statements, based on our extensive testing with consumers. They also protected card users from unexpected interest charges and required that they get a reasonable amount of time to make their payments, among other measures. Our reform would serve as the basis for the Credit Cardholders' Bill of Rights, which became the Credit CARD Act of 2009, passed by Congress in May at the urging of the Obama administration. A few news articles noted that the bill largely reflected regulations that the Fed had already adopted, but for the most part our contributions were ignored.

Still, I understood the Obama administration's argument for having a single agency devoted to protecting consumers of financial services. It was the one provision in their plan that they could unambiguously depict as a win for Main Street. Most central banks don't have a role in consumer protection, so I could hardly argue that it was at the heart of our mission. In terms of legislative priorities, I thought it more important for us to maintain our significant role as a safety-and-soundness bank regulator and to increase our role in macroprudential, systemic regulation. The tipping point for me may have been a meeting of the Board's Consumer Advisory Council, a panel that included both lenders and consumer advocates. I asked the council members whether they thought the Fed should keep its consumer protection authorities. Even though the members had worked closely with Fed staff for some years and had seen our increased activism, a sizable majority said they preferred a new agency. In the end, as in the case of Sheila's financial stability council, I didn't actively resist the administration's plan to take away the Fed's consumer protection authority.

Unsurprisingly, my decision caused dismay among affected staff members. Sandy Braunstein organized a town hall meeting so I could hear their concerns. I pointed out that, even if we fought, we were unlikely to win. I also explained that the law would likely give each of them the right to transfer to the new agency, retaining pay and seniority, if they chose. But it was a tough meeting. They all cared deeply about protecting consumers and had worked long hours to develop the new rules, only to receive what they perceived as a vote of no confidence. I understood and shared their frustration.

IN THE WEEKS after the release of the Treasury plan, Tim's staff put the administration's broad proposals into legislative form, and Barney Frank introduced a series of bills based on them. From mid-October through early December 2009, his committee met to consider amendments to the bills. Barney ultimately combined the results into one gargantuan bill—1,279 pages. It cleared the full House on December 11 by a vote of 223 to 202, with no Republicans in favor.

There were compromises along the way. In September, even before his committee considered the legislation, Barney had cut a deal with Camden Fine, president of the Independent Community Bankers of America, an organization representing more than five thousand community banks. Fine's bankers were wary of the new consumer agency. They did not want an additional bureaucracy to deal with. But Fine agreed not to lobby against it—so long as Barney exempted banks with less than $10 billion in assets (virtually all of Fine's members) from regular examination by the new agency. The consumer agency would still write the rules for all lenders, large and small, but would enforce the rules only in big banks. The Fed, the OCC, and the FDIC would continue to examine smaller institutions for compliance with the regulations.

Barney agreed to Fine's demand because he needed to split the banking industry on the question. United, it might have had the political strength to torpedo the consumer protection agency. The large banks continued to oppose it, but with popular anger at Wall Street still intense, few politicians were willing to stand with them, at least publicly. Moreover, virtually every member of Congress had at least one community bank in his or her district. Fine, a square-jawed former small-town banker from Missouri, as well as the former director of the state's tax division, was a shrewd and vigorous advocate for small banks. He believed, with justification, that they had little to do with causing the crisis and were in danger of being punished for big banks' sins. I met with him regularly and addressed his group's annual convention nearly every year that I was in office. In the fall of 2009, community bankers seemed to be one of the few outside groups backing the Fed.

In the meantime, we faced assaults on the Fed's independence from the far right and far left. Two such campaigns, though, were gathering momentum under the banner of transparency: one to "audit" the Fed, and the second to disclose which firms had borrowed from our discount window and our emergency lending facilities during the crisis. Both measures seemed reasonable on their face—and thus difficult to counter—but both posed serious threats to the Fed's effectiveness and ability to make policy free of political pressure.

I found the audit-the-Fed campaign the most frustrating—mostly because our books and operations are, and long have been, intensively audited. By constant disingenuous repetition of their "audit the Fed" slogan, however, and by intentionally inducing confusion about the meaning of the word "audit," proponents managed to convince people that we were somehow exempt from scrutiny. Who could be against auditing an organization with a balance sheet the size of the Federal Reserve's? In fact, the financial statements of the Reserve Banks are audited by a private outside accounting firm, and the Board's financial statement is audited by an outside firm retained by our independent inspector general's office. All this information, together with the auditors' opinions, is made public on the Board's website. And, as with most federal agencies, our inspector general's office conducts wide-ranging investigations and reviews of the Board's operations.

On top of this full range of financial audits, the Government

Accountability Office (GAO), which reports to Congress, evaluates the efficiency and integrity of all the Board's operations, with one crucial exception—monetary policy decision making. The GAO's reviews are not audits, in the common meaning of the term (a review of financial statements). Instead they review policy and performance. While often valuable, these reviews are quite different from an audit in the usual sense. Congress had decided in 1978 to exclude monetary policy—but not other Federal Reserve functions such as banking supervision—from GAO review. The exclusion reaffirmed the understanding that the Fed, to make monetary policy in the longer-term interests of the economy, must be free of short-term political pressure. In lieu of GAO reviews, Congress required regular reports and testimony on our actions in pursuit of the goals it had given us: maximum employment and price stability.

The careful congressional compromise between holding the Fed accountable, on the one hand, and protecting it from undue political pressure, on the other, would have been shattered by audit-the-Fed provisions, which would have allowed the GAO to review any aspect of monetary policy decision making, including second-guessing decisions made at particular meetings. Since GAO reviews are generally initiated by members of Congress and often reflect a political objective, the reviews could easily become vehicles of harassment. I exaggerate only slightly when I tell audiences that, if they are impressed with Congress's management of the federal budget, they should support audit-the-Fed legislation to give Congress the responsibility for making monetary policy as well.

The audit-the-Fed movement, in the House, was led by Ron Paul of Texas, an obstetrician-turned-congressman who retired from Congress after 2012. His son Rand Paul was elected to the Senate in 2010. The elder Paul, who ran for president on both the Libertarian and Republican tickets, spoke fondly of the gold standard. The audit-the-Fed leader in the Senate was Bernie Sanders from Vermont, the self-described democratic socialist. Paul and Sanders shared a strong populist streak. They distrusted technocratic institutions like the Fed, as well as what they saw as the excessive concentration of financial power in few hands. A dose of populism is healthy for any democracy. It reminds us that the government is supposed to serve the people and warns us to be wary of undue influence exerted by powerful elites in government and industry. Policymakers, including me, needed to hear those messages. But in extreme forms, on either the left or the right, populism can also lead to cynical manipulation of legitimate public anger and to contempt for facts and logical argument. When these aspects of populism dominate political discourse, good governance is nearly impossible.

I never worried particularly about my personal encounters with either Paul or Sanders. There was a refreshing purity to their views, which seemed often unaffected by real-world complexities. The principal difference between the two, other than their ideologies, was that Sanders had a tendency to shout until he was red-faced while Paul usually rambled amiably. Paul's thinking, though, veered toward conspiracy theories. To justify his push for intrusive GAO reviews of monetary policy, he alleged in a hearing in February 2010 that the Fed had supplied the cash used in the Watergate burglary and that the Fed in the 1980s had facilitated a $5.5 billion loan to Saddam Hussein, which the Iraqi dictator spent on weapons and a nuclear reactor. In surprise, I dismissed the allegations as "absolutely bizarre," a judgment later confirmed by an extensive investigation by the Board's inspector general.

Each man, compared with most politicians, could on occasion demonstrate disarming honesty. I told Paul, in a May 2009 hearing of the Joint Economic Committee, that auditing the Fed, as he and his allies construed it, seemed like an attempt to dictate to the Fed how to make monetary policy. In response, he readily acknowledged, "Of course, it's the policy that's the only thing that really counts." After the release of his 2009 book *End the Fed*, Paul stated plainly that he saw auditing the Fed as a "stepping stone" to eliminating it. I had cordial private discussions with the congressman, including over breakfast at the Fed. He was certainly sincere, but his thinking was dogmatic. He lacked a clear understanding of how the historical gold standard actually had worked (as opposed to the idealized version).

Paul, working on the House Financial Services Committee with Florida Democrat Alan Grayson, succeeded on November 19 in inserting an amendment removing the monetary policy exemption for GAO reviews—despite opposition from Barney and North Carolina Democrat Mel Watt, who would later head the agency overseeing Fannie Mae and Freddie Mac. (Grayson was a fitting partner for Paul. He was an extreme anti-Fed populist despite having earned multiple Harvard degrees, and he delighted in badgering me and other Fed representatives at hearings.) The next day, Warren Buffett, in a CNBC interview, warned Congress not to fool around with the Fed's independence. Senator Judd Gregg of New Hampshire threatened to filibuster any legislation with the Paul amendment when it reached the Senate.

Compared to the audit-the-Fed crowd, I had a bit more sympathy for lawmakers pushing us to disclose the identities of our borrowers. Transparency, in central banking and in government generally, is vitally important, especially when great power is being wielded. At the same time, I knew that immediate transparency in this instance would pose a serious problem during any future financial panic. If we were forced to immediately disclose the identities of borrowers, all but the most desperate banks would shun the discount window. That would cripple our ability to lend freely and thereby calm panics, as central banks had done for centuries.* Unfortunately, many of our critics conflated our more than fully collateralized, short-term liquidity loans to solvent institutions with the much longer-term loans associated with

---

*   An interesting earlier historical example of "stigma" occurred after the names of banks receiving loans from the Reconstruction Finance Corporation were published in newspapers in late August 1932. Economic historians judge that the RFC had some success in reducing bank failures during its first seven months in operation (February–August 1932) but that its effectiveness greatly diminished after loan recipients were identified.

the rescues of teetering institutions such as Bear Stearns and AIG. Our liquidity loans weren't gifts to individual institutions; they were an effort to replace funding that had evaporated in the panic. We lent to financial institutions because we wanted to keep credit flowing to their customers, including families and Main Street businesses.

Still, I understood when Bernie Sanders said it was difficult to go home and tell his constituents, "Your money was lent out and we don't know where it went." I decided to push the Fed's transparency envelope. For many years, as required by law, we had published a weekly summary of our balance sheet in a little-noticed release known internally as the H.4.1. Board staff had developed a new website, unveiled in February 2009, to make that information more accessible. It included detailed information about each of our crisis-era lending programs and an interactive chart showing balance sheet trends. I also asked Don Kohn to head an internal task force to review our transparency practices with the goal of releasing as much useful information as possible. In June 2009, we started issuing monthly reports on our lending that included new information on the number of borrowers, borrowing amounts by type of institution, and collateral accepted by type and credit rating. With the financial system and the economy far from out of the woods, however, we continued to resist naming names, even in the face of Freedom of Information Act (FOIA) lawsuits from Bloomberg News and Fox News.

WHILE THE LEGISLATION wound its way through Congress, we reflected on the shortcomings of our own banking supervision and began working to improve it. Turning once more to Don Kohn, I asked him to lead other policymakers and staff at the Board and Reserve Banks in developing a list of "lessons learned"—both for bankers and for our own examiners. Throughout 2009, implementing recommendations flowing from Don's project, we insisted that U.S. banks add loss-absorbing capital, increase their liquid assets that could be sold in a run, and improve risk management. We pushed our examiners, when they uncovered shortcomings, to press harder for corrective action and not to hesitate to bring concerns to top managers at banks.

Dan Tarullo led our supervision reform efforts. Deeply knowledgeable, stubborn, and sometimes impatient, Dan was in many ways the ideal person to take on the change-resistant Federal Reserve System. With my support, Dan reduced the supervisory autonomy of the Reserve Banks—the goal that Sue Bies had been unable to attain in 2005. His efforts resulted in greater consistency in supervision across districts and more coordinated oversight of the largest institutions. He was hard-charging and sometimes ruffled feathers, but the Fed's supervisory culture gradually began to change. Breaking down organizational silos within the Fed, we built on the multidisciplinary approach used in the big-bank stress tests in the spring of 2009, and, increasingly, our supervisors, economists, attorneys, accountants, and financial experts worked in teams. When Roger Cole retired in August 2009 as director of the Board's Division of Banking Supervision and Regulation, we replaced him with Pat Parkinson, the senior economist we had lent to Treasury to work on financial reform. Pat personified the wider perspective we were trying to bring to bank supervision. He had never worked as a rank-and-file examiner, but he possessed deep knowledge of the financial system and its role in the economy, and he brought "outsider's eyes" to directing the work of the division.

Besides changing our own culture, we also aimed to change the culture at the banks we oversaw, requiring senior managers and boards to pay more attention to factors that had led to excessive risk taking before the crisis. For example, we and the other bank regulators told the banks that compensation should be tied to long-term performance, not to short-term profits gained through risky bets. We applied that principle not only to senior executives but also to lower-level employees, such as traders and loan officers, whose decisions could put banks at risk.

CONGRESS'S WORK WAS naturally focused on domestic regulation, but new rules and tougher supervision for U.S. banks alone wouldn't ensure stability in a globalized financial system. Without international coordination, tougher domestic regulation might result only in banking activity moving out of the United States to foreign financial centers. Moreover, even if foreign jurisdictions adopted comparably tough rules, in the absence of international coordination those rules might be inconsistent with U.S. standards, which could fragment global capital markets and otherwise diminish the effectiveness of new rules. The potential solution to these problems lay in Basel, with the Bank for International Settlements. The BIS, besides being a gathering place for central bank governors, was also the host of an international forum called the Basel Committee on Banking Supervision. More than two dozen countries, including major emerging-market economies, were represented.

Early in September 2009, the Basel Committee began negotiations over new international requirements for both bank capital and liquidity. Dan Tarullo, Bill Dudley, and I represented the Fed in these discussions. The FDIC's Sheila Bair and Comptroller of the Currency John Dugan completed the U.S. delegation. The negotiations led to an agreement that would be known as the Basel III accord. The first Basel accord, completed in 1988 and now referred to as Basel I, had established the principle of risk-based capital—that is, that banks should hold more capital to absorb potential losses from risky assets, such as business loans, than they do to absorb potential losses from relatively safer assets, such as government bonds. However, over time, banks had found ways to circumvent Basel I's rudimentary risk weightings, either by loading up on assets that met the definition of low-risk under the rules but actually carried higher risk or by pushing riskier assets into off-balance-sheet vehicles (as Citi did with its SIVs). A second agreement, unveiled in 2004 and known as Basel II, established a more sophisticated (but also very complex) approach to calculating capital needs at the largest banks, overseen by the supervisors but relying in part on the banks' own risk models. These new rules for determining the amount of capital to be held against each type of asset (never fully implemented in the United States) were intended to discourage banks from gaming the system but did not aim to raise or lower the total amount of capital held by banks.

However, as we now were painfully aware, many banks around the world had come into the crisis without enough capital. Consequently, a primary goal of Basel III was to increase the capital held by banks, particularly the systemically important institutions whose operations crossed international borders. The new accord, released in December 2010, called for increased capital requirements in general and also an extra "countercyclical" capital buffer. The buffer would ensure that banks built up their capital in good times, so that they could absorb losses and keep lending in bad times. The following year, the Basel Committee would add a requirement that financial institutions deemed systemically important would have to hold more capital than other banks.

Basel III also established a new international capital requirement—a minimum leverage ratio—in addition to the risk-based requirements. A leverage ratio is simply the ratio of a bank's total capital to its total assets, without any adjustments for the riskiness of the assets. Unlike most other countries, the United States had required its banks to meet a minimum leverage ratio before the crisis, albeit at a relatively low level. Basel III extended the requirement to all internationally active banks; and U.S. regulators, including the Fed, would subsequently raise the leverage ratio for U.S. banks above the Basel minimum.

The leverage ratio, and where it should be set, stirred considerable controversy both in the international negotiations and domestically. Advocates of a high leverage ratio argued that the complex risk-based standards in Basel II and III are too easy for banks to manipulate—only the leverage ratio gives a real picture of bank capital, in their view. Opponents pointed out that a leverage ratio, unaccompanied by a risk-based requirement, allows banks to hold the same amount of capital against their riskiest assets as against their safest, which provides them an incentive to take on more risk. The reasonable compromise, I think, is to use both types of capital requirements, as we do in the United States, with the leverage ratio serving as a backstop—the suspenders to the belt of risk-based standards.

Basel III would ultimately tackle another important concern. During the crisis, some institutions met minimum capital standards but still came under significant pressure because they did not have enough cash and easily sellable liquid assets on hand to meet payment demands. For example, Wachovia Bank met regulatory capital standards but nearly failed (and had to be acquired by Wells Fargo) because its funding sources dried up. To address this issue, Basel III supplemented its tougher capital standards with new liquidity standards. By international agreement, banks would be required to hold enough cash and other liquid assets to survive all but the severest runs without having to turn to their central bank.

AS WE WORKED on Basel III, regulatory reform efforts continued in Congress. A month before the House passed Barney's bill, Chris Dodd had unveiled his own 1,136-page opus. Unlike Barney, he had not started with the administration's proposal, believing that only bipartisan legislation could clear the Senate, where the minority party has far more ability to block action in the House. Unable to entice Richard Shelby into real negotiations, Dodd released a discussion draft of his proposed legislation on November 10, 2009. Shelby denounced it at a Senate Banking Committee session on November 19. In particular, Shelby could not accept the creation of a new agency to protect consumers of financial services, which he saw as unduly burdensome to banks and insufficiently accountable to Congress.

As I went through Dodd's bill with the Board's lawyers, I was pleased to see that it included a mechanism for the FDIC to safely unwind failing systemically significant financial companies, a key provision of the administration plan and a high priority of mine. But I was dismayed to see that he had stuck with his plan to strip the Fed of virtually all of its duties other than monetary policy. In addition to losing both our consumer protection and bank supervision authorities, under Dodd's bill we would also have little role in ensuring systemic stability. Instead, Dodd had proposed a new financial stability agency, to be led by an independent chairman appointed by the president.

I defended the need for Fed involvement in both bank supervision and fostering financial stability in an op-ed column published November 29, 2009, in the *Washington Post*—a common tactic for Washington policymakers but quite rare for a Fed chairman. "The Fed played a major part in arresting the crisis, and we should be seeking to preserve, not degrade, the institution's ability to foster financial stability and to promote economic recovery without inflation," I wrote. I argued that the Fed offered a unique mix of expertise and experience that couldn't be replicated soon, if ever, at a new financial stability agency. Moreover, to serve as an emergency liquidity lender during a financial panic, we needed to understand both the sources of the panic and the conditions of firms that might borrow from us; for that, we needed some role in supervising financial institutions. Globally, post-crisis, the trend was toward central banks getting more, not less, responsibility for bank supervision and financial stability. For example, the Bank of England had lost the power to supervise banks in 1997 and, partly as a result, had been caught by surprise by the 2007 run on the mortgage lender Northern Rock. In 2012, Parliament would return bank supervision to the Bank of England and create a new Financial Policy Committee at the Bank, with responsibility for the stability of the British financial system as a whole. Similarly, the European Central Bank would be given an important new financial stability role and, in 2014, would begin supervising banks in the eurozone.

On January 6, 2010, Dodd announced that he would not seek reelection. His personal popularity and his influence in the Senate had eroded, in part because of a string of controversies, including allegations that Angelo Mozilo's Countrywide had refinanced mortgages on Dodd's homes in Connecticut and Washington at favorable rates. With no need to campaign, he could turn his full attention to one of the last important pieces of legislation in his thirty-six-year career in Congress. But Shelby's vocal opposition meant that there was a lot more work to do to develop a bill that the Senate would approve. That would take time. It gave us some months to make our case to senators, on and off Dodd's committee.

THE RESERVE BANK presidents were particularly alarmed at the prospect of losing bank supervision duties—one of the Reserve Banks' primary functions. The banks had already endured rounds of staff layoffs over the previous decade as many of the Federal Reserve's financial services, such as check clearing, were consolidated into fewer locations. In particular, with the advent of electronic check clearing, many employees who had once processed paper checks were no longer needed. Reserve Banks still participated in making monetary policy, distributed currency and coins, kept an eye on their region's economies, and engaged in community development efforts—but a large proportion of their remaining employees examined and supervised banks and bank holding companies.

From the start, some presidents were skeptical about the Board's commitment to keeping the full range of our supervisory authorities. Tim Geithner and the administration were insisting only that Congress retain Fed supervision of the thirty-five bank holding companies with $50 billion or more in assets. Tim was willing to move Fed oversight of state-chartered member banks elsewhere—as was Dan Tarullo, if that was the price of keeping oversight of the largest institutions. I agreed that supervisory authority over the largest banks was crucial to the Fed's ability to manage financial crises. However, I also wanted to retain supervision of the smaller bank holding companies, as well as the state-chartered member banks.

In part I was responding to the concerns of the Reserve Bank presidents, who saw the loss of supervision as an existential threat. But I also agreed with their substantive arguments. Losing the authority to supervise smaller banks could create a dangerous blind spot. Examining banks of all sizes, from all over the country, allowed us to better understand the industry as a whole and to detect potential problems earlier. Examining smaller banks also strengthened our connections with local communities and improved our ability to monitor economic developments at the grass-roots level, leading to better monetary policy. After all, who knows more about the local economy than a community banker? Whenever I could, I made the case for leaving the Fed's supervision of both big and small banks unchanged. I raised the issue during the dozens of congressional meetings arranged as part of my reconfirmation process, and I made phone calls to many more legislators over the winter and spring. I also pressed the issue at congressional hearings.

I knew I could count on strong support from the Treasury and the White House for keeping the largest banks. Indeed, Dodd's determination to freeze us out of bank supervision softened in large part because of a plea from President Obama during a meeting in the Oval Office. The bill Dodd would take to his committee in March 2010, in contrast with his November 2009 proposal, left us the supervision of bank holding companies with more than $50 billion in assets. Authority over smaller holding companies, in Dodd's bill, was to be split between the OCC and the FDIC. Supervisory responsibility over the state-chartered banks that were members of the Federal Reserve System would go to the FDIC.

We were making progress, but the Reserve Bank presidents remained deeply concerned about Dodd's latest proposals. The New York Fed supervised six of the top seven bank holding companies and ten of the top thirty-five. No other Reserve Bank supervised more than four of the top thirty-five, and two—St. Louis and Kansas City— supervised none. Kansas City, on the other hand, supervised 172 state-chartered banks, more than any other Reserve Bank. Not surprisingly, Kansas City Fed president Tom Hoenig, along with Richard Fisher of Dallas, led the Reserve Banks' campaign to preserve their role in banking supervision. Hoenig met with senators on his own and organized meetings and calls with his fellow presidents. On May 5, 2010, he and three other Reserve Bank presidents met privately with a group of legislators. His activities threatened to undermine our efforts to speak to Congress with something approaching a unified voice. Hoenig sent Board members and Reserve Bank presidents a summary of his meetings with senators and wrote, "The leadership of the Fed (especially the Chairman) must get aggressive." In fact, despite my understated style, I was as aggressive on this issue as on any during my time in Washington. In one phone call with Senator Bob Corker, I pushed for retaining Fed supervision of state-chartered member banks so forcefully that he upbraided me for acting like a lobbyist.

The Fed's tradition of collegiality ultimately prevailed, and Board members and Reserve Bank presidents were able to work together. In July 2009 the Board had hired a new congressional liaison director, Linda Robertson, who had served in a similar capacity in the Clinton administration's Treasury Department. A Capitol Hill veteran who seemed to know every single staffer and member we dealt with in Congress, Linda understood viscerally how the institution worked and how its members responded to incentives and pressures. She worked hard to make our case and to keep the presidents informed and singing, if not in perfect harmony with the Board, at least from the same hymnal.

In the end, despite some frictions, I credit the Reserve Bank presidents with helping the Fed navigate a period of great political peril. Many of them made good use of relationships with local legislators that they had cultivated over the years. Hawks like Hoenig reminded like-minded legislators that the Fed was not a monolith, and that their views on monetary policy were being represented within the institution. The Reserve Banks had also developed broad and deep ties in their districts through their private-sector boards, the boards of their twenty-four branch offices, members of advisory councils, and former directors. Thus, dozens of prominent citizens in each district belonged to what we liked to call "the Fed family." Many of them offered to go to bat for us in one capacity or another. Their efforts helped, although Linda strove to coordinate communications with Congress and to limit freelancing, which she feared would do more harm than good.

IN THE SENATE, Dodd never achieved his grand bipartisan bargain. He tried various tactics after Shelby's sharply critical statement in mid-November. He formed bipartisan teams of committee members to work out compromises on particular issues, with modest progress. When he and Shelby reached an impasse, he worked with Corker, a middle-ranking Republican on his committee. Still, Dodd couldn't strike a comprehensive deal, and when it finally came time, on March 22, to send the bill to the Senate floor, every Republican on his committee voted no. But his persistent efforts to reach across the aisle would pay off later in the spring. The full Senate approved regulatory reform legislation, 59–39, on May 20, with four Republican senators joining in support. The Senate bill, like the House bill, retained our supervisory authority over all bank holding companies and state-chartered member banks, thanks to an amendment on the Senate floor from Amy Klobuchar of Minnesota and Kay Bailey Hutchison of Texas (a friend and onetime political opponent of Richard Fisher's), as well as lobbying from Camden Fine's community banking trade group. Dodd also forged an agreement with Bernie Sanders, as a substitute for "audit the Fed," that increased disclosures and provided for a onetime review of the Fed's governance and crisis-era programs.

The next step, in June, was a conference between selected House members and senators to work out differences between the House and Senate bills. Each chamber adopted the resulting compromise, and President Obama signed the bill into law on July 21, 2010. I attended the signing ceremony in the Ronald Reagan building, a massive office complex a few blocks from the White House. I felt satisfied. The bill, which in the end hewed fairly closely to the administration proposal, was hardly perfect, but it was nevertheless a substantial accomplishment. By coincidence, that afternoon, I testified before Dodd's committee, delivering the chairman's usual twice-a-year report to Congress. The final legislation, I said, went a long way toward achieving its overarching goal: "reducing the likelihood of future financial crises and strengthening the capacity of financial regulators to respond to risks that may emerge."

Dodd soberly noted that it would take months and years for the Fed and other agencies to write the regulations to implement the law, known formally as the Dodd-Frank Wall Street Reform and Consumer Protection Act. "Much work remains to be done," I agreed. Indeed, by one estimate, the law required the agencies to write 243 new regulations, conduct 67 onetime studies, and write 22 new periodic reports—all of which had to be done by staff while they carried out their normal duties. Many of the rules were "multi-agency," meaning that as many as five or six agencies were required to reach agreement on them.

It seemed to me that the final legislation had struck sensible compromises on most of the contentious issues. Closing an important gap in oversight, the Fed would become the regulator of systemically important financial institutions—bank holding companies but also nonbanks such as the Wall Street investment firms and huge insurance companies like AIG. We would be required to devise tougher capital and other standards for firms in that category, but we would not choose which firms would be designated as systemically important. That job fell to a new body, the Financial Stability Oversight Council, made up of the heads of the many federal financial regulatory agencies (including the Fed) and chaired by the Treasury secretary, as the administration had proposed.*

An amendment from Senator Susan Collins of Maine ensured, among other things, that tougher capital standards would be applied not just to U.S. institutions but also to foreign-owned banks operating in the United States. This measure angered some foreign bankers and

---

*   The name was changed from the administration's June 2009 proposal, which would have named the body the Financial Services Oversight Council.

their regulators. Before Dodd-Frank, the Fed had relied on the parent companies abroad to provide financial support if a U.S. subsidiary ran into problems. But, as demonstrated by the heavy borrowing from the Fed by foreign-owned institutions during the crisis, U.S. subsidiaries of foreign banks needed to be able to stand on their own. The Board would go on to pass tough rules that force U.S. subsidiaries of foreign banks to meet requirements similar to those imposed on domestic banks.

The final bill, like the administration's original proposal, left the regulatory bureaucracy relatively intact. However, it did eliminate the Office of Thrift Supervision and create a Consumer Financial Protection Bureau. The deal that Barney Frank and Camden Fine had struck, shielding smaller banks from regular exams by the bureau, survived. The new regulator was called a "bureau," not an "agency," because, at the suggestion of Bob Corker, it became technically part of the Federal Reserve. That was in name only. The bureau was to be headed by a director who would be appointed by the president and confirmed by the Senate, and who consequently would act independently of the Fed. The Fed would have no power to hire, fire, or direct any of its employees; no power to delay or disapprove its rules; and no power to intervene in any of its examinations or proceedings. We were required, however, to pay its operating expenses indefinitely ($563 million in 2014). The unusual arrangement relieved the agency of having to go to Congress every year for approval of its budget. The bottom line for taxpayers was the same, though. Every dollar spent on the bureau's operations meant that the Federal Reserve returned one dollar less in net revenue to the Treasury.

The administration recruited Elizabeth Warren, who had proposed the new agency in 2007, to set it up and get it running. But implacable opposition from Republicans meant she would never be nominated to head it. She came to see me to discuss the transfer of staff and other resources from the Fed. We had a good conversation, and she seemed pleased with the cooperation that the Fed was providing. Her instincts were too populist for us to see eye to eye on policy, however, and when she became a senator from Massachusetts she would sharply and frequently criticize the Fed.

One of the most important reforms of the Dodd-Frank Act was the new authority to unwind failing, systemically important financial firms. Under the "orderly liquidation authority," the Treasury secretary, after consulting with the president and obtaining the approval of the Federal Reserve and FDIC boards, could turn over a collapsing firm to the FDIC. The FDIC could operate the firm and make good on its obligations to secured creditors (such as repo counterparties). The FDIC also could repudiate contracts, such as the AIG bonus contracts, and impose losses on unsecured creditors. The failing firm's senior executives would be fired, and shareholders would stand last in line to recover their investment. The FDIC could borrow any funds needed for winding down a big firm from the Treasury, but if it incurred losses, they would be recovered by levying an assessment on large financial firms. To help make the FDIC's job easier, big financial firms would file plans, dubbed "living wills," showing how they could be dismantled without destabilizing the financial system.

With the new orderly liquidation authority in place, the Fed would lose its ability to use the "unusual and exigent" clause, Section 13(3), to rescue individual institutions such as AIG and Bear Stearns. It was one authority I was happy to lose. We would still be able to use 13(3) to create emergency lending programs with broad eligibility, such as our lending program for securities dealers or the facility to support money market funds, although we'd have to obtain the Treasury secretary's permission first. I didn't consider that much of a concession, since I couldn't imagine a major financial crisis in which the Fed and the Treasury would not work closely.

Some aspects of the final legislation may have diminished our ability to respond to future financial panics, though. Under the compromise that Bernie Sanders worked out with Chris Dodd, we would have to publish the identities of future discount window borrowers—but with a two-year lag. We would begin doing that in September 2012. Lagged disclosure is a lot better than immediate disclosure, but the new disclosure requirements may still increase the stigma of borrowing from the Fed in a panic. The legislation also restricted the FDIC's authority to guarantee bank debt, as the agency had announced on the day after Columbus Day 2008. Now the FDIC would need congressional approval in addition to the concurrence of the Fed and the Treasury secretary—not an easy hurdle to clear, as we saw with the TARP vote. And the FDIC no longer could invoke the systemic risk exception for specific firms that had allowed it during the crisis to help stabilize Citigroup.

Other provisions affecting the Federal Reserve turned out, from our perspective, far better than the original proposals. Per the agreement between Dodd and Sanders, we would continue to be shielded from ongoing and potentially politically motivated GAO reviews of monetary policy decisions (no "audit the Fed"). But the legislation required two onetime GAO reviews—one of our lending during the crisis and the other of the Fed's unique governance system created a century ago by the original Federal Reserve Act. The review of our crisis lending, released in July 2011, would find that our programs were effectively designed and operated, and that all our loans had been repaid. The governance review focused on the nine-member Reserve Bank private-sector boards, which by law included bankers and others with financial industry experience. To avoid conflicts of interest, we had long had policies that prevented the Reserve Bank directors from involving themselves in bank supervisory and emergency lending decisions. The GAO would find that our policies were followed but would suggest we make them publicly available on Fed websites. Three of the directors on each Reserve Bank board are still, by law, chosen by bankers to represent the banks in the district. To prevent the appearance that bankers were choosing their own regulator, Dodd-Frank barred those three directors from taking part in the selection of Reserve Bank presidents, confining that duty to the remaining six directors.

As the administration had proposed originally, the final legislation tightened derivatives regulation and pushed more derivatives trading into the sunlight by requiring greater use of exchanges. The final law reached beyond the administration's original proposal with the addition of what became known as the Volcker rule, after its originator, former Fed chairman Paul Volcker. Paul, who once claimed that ATMs were the only worthwhile financial innovation in his time, believed that banks' trading in securities markets on their own account distracted them from their primary business of making loans. Moreover, he believed, it led them to take excessive risks, with losses ultimately ending up at the door of the taxpayer. His rule, endorsed by President Obama in January 2010, banned banking companies from short-term trading of many securities, derivatives, and commodity futures and options. It provided exceptions for trading government securities, for using derivatives to hedge (or reduce) a banking company's risks, and for trading on behalf of customers. In a sense, the Volcker rule was an effort to partially reinstate the Depression-era Glass-Steagall provision that had separated commercial and investment banking.

The Dodd-Frank Act left some unfinished business: The status of Fannie Mae and Freddie Mac remained unresolved, for instance, and the act did not address the vulnerability of money market funds and the repo market to runs. Nevertheless, the law does much good and stands as a remarkable accomplishment.

I believe that the many administration officials, lawmakers, and regulatory policymakers—and their staffs—who poured a year and a half of prodigious work into the legislation had been guided, knowingly or not, by a simultaneously high-minded and pragmatic sentiment that Woodrow Wilson voiced before he launched the effort that would establish the Federal Reserve System. "We shall deal with our economic system as it is and as it may be modified, not as it might be if we had a clean sheet of paper to write upon; and step by step we shall make it what it should be," Wilson said in his first inaugural address. Wilson's words continued to make good sense a century later.

CHAPTER 21

QE2: False Dawn

On February 3, 2010, six days after the Senate voted to confirm me to a second four-year term, I stood, with my right hand raised and Anna at my side, on a landing overlooking the Eccles Building's spacious atrium. Vice Chairman Don Kohn, my good friend and close colleague throughout the crisis, administered the oath of office. Board members, visitors, and hundreds of Board employees gathered on the ground floor, along the second-floor railing ringing the atrium, and on the broad marble steps of the staircases on either side.

"America and the world owe you a debt of gratitude," I told the staff. "We moved rapidly, forcefully, and creatively to confront the deepest financial crisis since the Great Depression and help prevent a looming economic collapse."

My gratitude was heartfelt. Our response to the crisis had been a team effort. But I was not declaring victory that day, not with more than fifteen million Americans unable to find work and millions more in danger of losing their homes. "We must continue to do all that we can to ensure that our policies are helping to guide the country's return to prosperity," I said.

The economy had begun to grow again during the summer of 2009, ending a year-and-a-half-long recession—the longest since the 1929–1933 downturn that marked the first leg of the Great Depression. The initial estimate for the last three months of 2009 showed output expanding rapidly. The growth, however, had not yet translated into a significant improvement in the job market. The unemployment rate, which had peaked at a twenty-six-year high of 10.2 percent in October, stood at 10 percent by the end of the year.* The situation called to mind the jobless recovery that had followed the 2001 recession. I wondered if we were seeing a replay.

Still, our lending programs and securities purchases—along with the Obama administration's fiscal stimulus and the bank stress tests— appeared to be having their intended effect. Financial conditions were improving, a bellwether for the broader economy. Stocks had substantially rebounded, funding markets functioned more normally, and the banking system—though by no means completely healthy—appeared to have stabilized. At least as far as the financial system was concerned, it was time to start unwinding our emergency measures.

We had taken the first step in June 2009, when the Board reduced the bank loans offered in the biweekly discount window auctions from $300 billion to $250 billion. By March 2010, we would phase out the auctions completely. We were also in the midst of normalizing the terms of our regular discount window lending to banks. By March, the typical maturity on the loans, which had been extended for up to ninety days during the crisis, would be back to overnight. And, with less reason to encourage banks to borrow from us, we would soon increase the interest rate on discount window loans by a quarter of a percentage point.

Lending under all but one of our various 13(3) facilities, including those aimed at stabilizing money market funds, the commercial paper market, and securities firms, had ended on February 1, as had the currency swap agreements with other central banks. Our only remaining special lending facility was the TALF. After June 30, 2010, it, too, would cease new lending. All told, the TALF lent $71 billion—below the program's original $200 billion limit and far below the expansion to $1 trillion in February 2009. Even so, it supported the origination of

---

*   The initially reported rates were revised in 2012 by the Labor Department to 10 percent in October 2009 and 9.9 percent in December 2009.

nearly 3 million auto loans, more than 1 million student loans, nearly 900,000 loans to small businesses, 150,000 other business loans, and millions of credit card loans.

I felt good about what we had accomplished with these programs. Less well known and certainly less controversial than the Bear Stearns and AIG rescues, our lending facilities had been essential in controlling the panic. And, although we made thousands of loans to a wide range of borrowers, every penny was repaid, with interest—and the Fed, and thus the taxpayers, profited by billions of dollars. Much more importantly, these programs prevented the financial system from seizing up and helped to keep credit flowing. Walter Bagehot would have been pleased.

Although FOMC members, hawks and doves alike, agreed it was time to wind down our emergency lending programs, they differed on when to begin rolling back our accommodative monetary policy. At the end of March, we would complete the securities purchases that we had promised a year earlier. We now held $2 trillion in Treasury securities, Fannie, Freddie, and Ginnie mortgage-backed securities, and Fannie and Freddie debt, up from $760 billion before we expanded QE1 in March 2009. In the meantime, we had kept the funds rate near zero and continued to predict, in our statement, that it would remain exceptionally low "for an extended period." The hawks, led by Kansas City Fed president Tom Hoenig (who had a vote in 2010), worried that this easy policy would eventually have bad side effects—if not higher inflation, then perhaps the return of excessive risk taking in financial markets. They pressed the Committee to think about how we might exit from our unusual policies.

With unemployment still near its peak and inflation quite low, I thought we were a long way from tightening policy. Two historical episodes—one seventy years old and one relatively recent—influenced my thinking. The first was the recession of 1937–1938, the so-called recession within the Depression. Expansionary monetary and fiscal policies had put the economy on the path of recovery after Franklin Roosevelt took office in 1933. But excessive fear of future inflation led, in 1937, to the tightening of both monetary and fiscal policy, despite the fact that unemployment was still high. Tax increases and a contraction in the money supply (caused in part by Fed policy) hurled the economy, which was still fragile, back into a steep decline. More recently, the Bank of Japan, eager to move away from zero interest rates, had tightened policy in 2000 and again in 2007. Each time, the move had proved premature and the bank was forced to reverse itself. Still, in the interest of good planning, I thought it made sense for the FOMC to discuss and agree on the mechanics of normalizing policy. And making clear that we had a workable strategy for tightening policy when the time came might ease the concerns of both the hawks inside the Fed and our external critics.

Barney Frank also thought that a public airing of exit issues would help. He invited me to testify on February 10 before his House Financial Services Committee. I wasn't enthusiastic, especially since I had the regular semiannual Monetary Policy Report testimony just two weeks later. I also was scheduled, the prior weekend, to attend a meeting of the G-7 finance ministers and central bank governors in Iqaluit, Canada, which would cut into my prep time. But testifying was easier than saying no to Barney.

Iqaluit, a city of about seven thousand, is the capital of the territory of Nunavut, in northern Canada, about two hundred miles below the Arctic Circle. Surrounded by snow and ice, it is accessible only by air in the winter. The austere setting seemed apt, given the policy goals of Canadian finance minister Jim Flaherty, the host, and some of his European counterparts. Now that the most chaotic phase of the crisis was over, they—like the FOMC hawks and some U.S. lawmakers—argued for less expansionary fiscal and monetary policies. Tim Geithner and I pushed back. We were skeptical that the progress so far was sufficient to warrant a change in course.

Our discussions in Iqaluit were punctuated by dogsled rides (I declined, but Mervyn King tried it) and a chance to see the inside of a real igloo and eat raw seal meat. (I went into the igloo but passed on the seal meat.) The weather held up nicely for our near-Arctic travel but then disrupted our return to Washington. While we were away, a major blizzard, later dubbed Snowmageddon, dumped two feet of snow on Washington and buried much of the mid-Atlantic region. Washington's airports closed and we spent an unplanned night in Boston before returning home.

Government offices were shut, but I wanted to prep for Barney's hearing on Wednesday. On Tuesday morning, staff members dressed in jeans, sweaters, and flannel shirts met with me in the Anteroom, a small but elegant conference room ringed with portraits of past chairmen. We reviewed questions I might be asked. Other staff members joined by conference call. As it turned out, federal offices did not reopen until Friday and the hearing was postponed until March. We posted my statement on the Board's website anyway. It explained how we would go about raising interest rates at the appropriate time if our balance sheet was still much larger than normal at that point, which seemed likely.

Prior to the crisis, the Fed affected the federal funds rate by changing the supply of bank reserves. In particular, to raise the funds rate, we would sell some of our securities. The payments we received would reduce bank reserves and leave banks with greater need to borrow on the interbank market. More borrowing by banks would in turn push up the federal funds rate, the interest rate on interbank loans. But our securities purchases under QE1 had flooded the banking system with reserves, to the point that most banks now had little reason to borrow from each other. With virtually no demand for short-term loans between banks, the funds rate had fallen close to zero. In this situation, moderate reductions in the supply of reserves would be unlikely to affect banks' borrowing needs and thus influence the federal funds rate. In short, the Fed's traditional method for affecting short-term interest rates in its pursuit of maximum employment and price stability would no longer work.

We needed new methods to raise interest rates when the time came, even if our balance sheet remained large. An important new tool had come as part of the TARP legislation, when Congress had given us the power to pay interest on banks' reserve accounts at the Fed. We had set that rate at 1/4 percent. If we wanted to tighten policy, we could increase it. Since banks would be unwilling to lend to each other or anyone else at a rate below what they could earn by holding reserves at the Fed, raising the interest rate paid on reserve accounts should raise the funds rate as well as other short-term rates.

To supplement that tool, we had also tested methods for draining reserves from the banking system without necessarily selling our securities. One of several methods was offering banks higher-yielding term deposits with longer maturities. A bank's reserve account at the Fed is similar to a consumer's checking account at a commercial bank. Like a consumer with a checking account, a bank can withdraw funds in its reserve account on demand. The term deposits we would offer could be thought of as analogous to certificates of deposit, or CDs. Like money held in a CD, reserves held as term deposits couldn't be used day to day, and this would effectively reduce the supply of available reserves in the banking system. Fewer available reserves should mean a higher funds rate. Another tool involved financing our securities holdings by borrowing from securities dealers and other nonbank lenders rather than through the creation of bank reserves. Again, fewer available reserves in the banking system should cause the funds rate to rise.

Of course, we could always tighten monetary policy simply by selling some of our securities, thereby unwinding the effects of quantitative easing. I was willing to consider selling our securities eventually, if the sales were very gradual and announced well in advance. But I saw this as a way of normalizing our balance sheet in the longer term, not as the primary tool for tightening policy. I worried that Fed securities sales would lead to volatile and hard-to-predict movements in interest rates, making them a less precise tool for managing financial conditions.

Our new methods were works in progress, but I had already seen enough to feel confident that tightening policy would pose no technical obstacles, even if our securities holdings remained much larger than before the crisis. I wanted both legislators and market participants to understand that. I also wanted them to understand that developing these exit tools did not mean we were contemplating an actual tightening of monetary policy anytime soon.

Besides their usual concerns about inflation, the FOMC hawks also worried that low rates might encourage investors, frustrated by low returns, to take excessive risks, possibly fueling new asset bubbles. I took that issue very seriously. After all that we had been through, I wanted to be sure that we were doing everything we could to maintain financial stability. And, as I had long argued, I believed that the first line of defense against speculative excesses should be regulatory and supervisory policies.

We had already heightened our scrutiny of the largest, most complex banks and our attention to risks in the financial system as a whole. Over 2010, we further increased our surveillance of the financial system—including parts we didn't regulate. Multidisciplinary teams produced analyses and reports, ranging from statistical studies to compilations of market chatter, and regularly briefed the Board and the FOMC. After the passage of the Dodd-Frank Act in July 2010, we created an umbrella organization within the Board—the Office of Financial Stability Policy and Research—to oversee and coordinate the staff's work. I chose Nellie Liang, an experienced and savvy financial economist who had helped lead the stress tests of large banks in 2009, as its first director. To a much greater extent than before the crisis, the FOMC had begun to pay attention to potential financial stability risks as it discussed monetary policy.

These new efforts to promote financial stability were far more ambitious than the work of the small staff group I had created in my early days as chairman. But I didn't want to oversell what we were doing. Systemic threats are notoriously hard to anticipate. If bubbles were easy to identify, for example, far fewer investors would get swept into them in the first place. But I was convinced that changing our approach would give us a better chance for success.

In particular, I urged Nellie and her staff not only to think through what they saw as the most likely outcomes but also to consider worst-case scenarios. I had come to believe that, during the housing boom, the FOMC had spent too much time debating whether rising house prices reflected a bubble and too little time thinking about the consequences, if a bubble did exist, of its bursting spectacularly. More attention to the worst-case scenario might have left us better prepared to respond to what actually happened.

Recognizing that financial shocks are often unpredictable, I also encouraged the staff to look for structural weaknesses in the financial system and to find ways to make it more broadly resilient. That idea was already motivating many of our reforms, such as requiring more bank capital, which strengthened the banking system's ability to absorb losses, no matter what the cause.

AFTER THE SNOW from the February blizzard melted, spring came a bit early to Washington; the cherry trees around the Tidal Basin hit peak bloom at the end of March. The economy remained quite weak, but I hoped that the green shoots I had observed in financial markets in my 2009 appearance on *60 Minutes* might soon spur a palpable improvement on Main Street. Unfortunately, it was not to be. Financial turmoil erupted again, this time in Europe, and with a virulence that threatened the U.S. economy and other economies around the globe.

The panic of 2007–2009 had hit Western Europe hard. Following the Lehman shock, many European countries experienced output declines and job losses similar to those in the United States. Many Europeans, especially politicians, had blamed Anglo-American "cowboy capitalism" for their predicament. (At international meetings, Tim and I never denied the United States' responsibility for the original crisis, although the European banks that eagerly bought securitized subprime loans were hardly blameless.) This new European crisis, however, was almost entirely homegrown. Fundamentally, it arose because of a mismatch in European monetary and fiscal arrangements. Sixteen countries, in 2010, shared a common currency, the euro, but each—within ill-enforced limits—pursued separate tax and spending policies.

The adoption of the euro was a grand experiment, part of a broader move, started in the 1950s, toward greater economic integration. By drawing member states closer economically, Europe's leaders hoped not only to promote growth but also to increase political unity, which they saw as a necessary antidote to a long history of intra-European warfare, including two catastrophic world wars. Perhaps, they hoped, Germans, Italians, and Portuguese would someday think of themselves as citizens of Europe first and citizens of their home country second.

Starting in 1999, eleven of the twenty-eight European Union countries, including Germany, France, Spain, and Italy, agreed to replace their marks, francs, pesetas, and lire with the euro, which would be managed by a single central bank, the European Central Bank. Existing national central banks would become part of a eurozone system, assuming roles roughly analogous to those played by Reserve Banks within the Federal Reserve System. With a single currency, doing business across national borders would become easier. For countries like Italy or Greece, with histories of inflation and currency devaluation, the new common currency had the additional benefit of conferring instant anti-inflation credibility—so long as the ECB was perceived by market participants to be sufficiently tough on inflation.

Every effort was made to ensure that it would be. Europe's newly created central bank was given a single mandate, to maintain price stability—in contrast to the Fed's dual mandate to foster job creation as well as low inflation. The ECB's headquarters were located in Frankfurt, the financial capital of Germany and the home of its national central bank, the Bundesbank. The symbolism was not subtle. The ECB was expected to adopt the "hard money" anti-inflation stance of the Bundesbank, not the more dovish approach that had characterized central banks in southern Europe. Before they could join the common currency, countries were required to achieve sufficiently low levels of government deficits and debt (as specified in an agreement known as the Stability and Growth Pact) as well as achieve modest inflation.

On the whole, the introduction of the euro was remarkably smooth. It quickly gained global acceptance second only to the dollar. More countries joined the original eleven. Europeans hoped that their new currency—in combination with the harmonization of regulations and the removal of restrictions on the movement of people, goods, and financial capital across European borders—would convey some of the same economic advantages enjoyed by the United States, with its single currency and open borders between states.

The eurozone, however, differs from the United States in one crucial respect. In the United States, the federal government tries to manage fiscal policy in the interests of the country as a whole, and the U.S. national debt is guaranteed by the country as a whole. In the eurozone, fiscal policy is set by the parliaments of each country. There is no supranational authority, analogous to the ECB, for tax and spending policies. This lack of fiscal integration and coordination, together with marked differences across Europe in labor market and other economic policies, ultimately spawned enormous problems.

The trigger of the European crisis had occurred in October 2009 but at the time drew little notice in the United States. Shortly after taking office, the new prime minister of Greece, George Papandreou, the son of a former prime minister and economics professor at Harvard and other universities, announced that the Greek budget deficit was far higher than the government had previously reported. The corrected figure showed the deficit to be close to 13 percent of a year's output, compared with the ceiling of 3 percent specified by the Stability and Growth Pact. Papandreou's shocking announcement struck at a core assumption of the pact—that member countries were able to monitor each other's budgets effectively. It also raised the question of why investors were willing to lend so much to the Greek government, at very low interest rates, in the first place.

Greece's easy access to international capital markets reflected the euro's success. By adopting the common currency in 2001, Greece had effectively turned its monetary policy over to the ECB. It borrowed in euros rather than in drachmas. No longer could it reduce the value of its debt through inflation or currency devaluation. Investors presumed Greece would abide by, or at least hew close to, the limits on government deficits and debt specified in the Stability and Growth Pact. Finally, even though the treaty that led to the creation of the euro forbade bailouts of governments, lenders came to believe that the eurozone countries would collectively aid a member rather than permit a default that could disrupt financial markets and jeopardize investor confidence in other borrowing countries. That was moral hazard at the country level, reminiscent of the implicit guarantee of Fannie Mae and Freddie Mac by the U.S. government. For these reasons, Greece had been able to borrow at interest rates very close to what Germany, the most creditworthy country, had to pay. But, as the world learned in October 2009, Greece had borrowed far beyond its means, all the while doctoring the statistics to obscure that fact. It soon became clear that, without outside help, Greece would default.

The eurozone grappled with how to respond, if at all. Superficially, allowing Greece to default made some sense. A small country on the periphery of Europe, it accounted for only a tiny share of eurozone trade and investment. Default would encourage investors to be more careful in the future, reducing moral hazard. And declining to intervene would avoid a voter backlash in countries that would be expected to finance any rescue, like Germany.

On the other hand, much as Lehman's failure had shaken the entire financial system, a Greek default could have far-reaching implications for Europe and the world. Although Greece was Europe's most profligate borrower, it was not the only country that had amassed substantial public and private debts. Private capital had poured into Spain before the crisis, financing a construction boom that had since busted. Ireland's promise in 2008 to protect its banks' creditors had resulted in massive government deficits when it had to bail out its large banks. Portugal's relatively weak economy had in turn weakened its fiscal position. And Italy's government debts were the highest in Europe. If Greece defaulted, investors might conclude that other overindebted eurozone countries were next. The interest rates those countries would have to pay might jump, triggering a cascade of debt crises.

The potential effects of a Greek default on the European banking system were also a concern. Many European banks had been severely weakened by the earlier crisis and remained short of capital. That posed a particularly serious threat to the eurozone economy because bank lending makes up a much larger share of overall credit in Europe than in the United States. Most European banks outside of Greece did not hold large quantities of Greek government debt (French banks were probably the most exposed), but they held substantial amounts of the debt, both public and private, of other vulnerable eurozone countries. If defaults spread beyond Greece, the stability of Europe's entire banking system could be at risk.

Finally, policymakers had to weigh what might happen if Greece, after a default, also abandoned the euro and returned to its own currency. One reason to do so would be to regain monetary policy independence, which might help the Greek government respond to the economic crash that was likely to follow a default. But if Greece left the euro, fears that other countries might follow would no doubt increase. Even the possibility that the eurozone might break apart would inflict damage. For example, bank depositors in a country thought to be at risk of leaving the euro would worry that their euro-denominated deposits might be forcibly converted to the new, and presumably less valuable, national currency. To avoid that risk, depositors might withdraw their euros from their own country's banks in favor of, say, German banks (which, in an era of cross-border branching, might simply mean walking a block down the street or clicking on a bank's website). These withdrawals could quickly degenerate into a full-fledged run on the suspect country's banks.

For these reasons, finance ministers and especially central bank governors in Europe generally, if grudgingly, concluded that they would have to assist Greece. ECB president Jean-Claude Trichet, who had decried the Lehman failure, was particularly adamant on this point and sought to persuade other European policymakers. Recognizing that financial instability would not be confined to Europe, Tim and I—in meetings, conference calls, and one-to-one conversations— pushed our European counterparts to address their problems as fast and as definitively as possible. The International Monetary Fund and countries outside Europe, also worried about possible spillover effects, likewise pushed for rapid resolution of the crisis.

As European leaders debated what to do, the consequences of not having a single fiscal authority for the eurozone became apparent. Discussions about sharing the burden of providing aid moved ponderously and revealed substantial disagreements. It took almost four months from Papandreou's disclosure of Greece's debts for the eurozone governments to promise help for Greece, and even then with few details. After more back-and-forth, Prime Minister Papandreou asked the eurozone countries for a bailout on April 23, 2010. By this time, reflecting rising default fears, yields on Greek ten-year bonds were about 6 percentage points higher than yields on comparable German bonds, up from 1 percentage point the previous October. On Sunday, May 2, European leaders announced a rescue package of 110 billion euros, about $145 billion. Two-thirds of the package would come from loans from individual European countries and one-third from the International Monetary Fund, fulfilling its role as lender to countries in danger of default.

However, markets saw the European effort as vague and insufficiently ambitious. The May 2 announcement did little to improve borrowing terms for Portugal and Ireland, whose bond yields were also rising, although not so far as Greek yields. In the United States, the Dow Jones industrial average rose on Monday, the day after the announcement, but then fell 7 percent over the rest of the week. And the people of Greece—the supposed beneficiaries of the agreement— saw the proposed rescue terms, including steep cuts in public spending, as unfair. Rioters spilled into Athens' streets, and, on May 5, three people died when a Greek bank was firebombed.

As the Dow's response to the announcement of the Greek package suggested, the United States was hardly isolated from Europe's financial woes. Volatility in U.S. stock markets in May 2010 was the highest since the period after Lehman, reflecting a global surge in fear and risk aversion. To assess the risk of financial contagion reaching the United States, Nellie Liang's group, together with the Fed's bank supervisors, worked long hours trying to assess U.S. exposures. The good news was that U.S. banks held relatively little European government debt, including Greek debt. On the other hand, many of them had extensive exposure to the major European banks and to the European economy more broadly—through loans to European businesses, for example. And U.S. money market funds had provided considerable funding to European banks, mainly for the banks' lending in the United States.

After the negative response to the May 2 announcement, European policymakers tried again. On May 7, they announced tougher enforcement of the curbs on government deficits and debt for all eurozone countries, together with a commitment to tighten their fiscal belts. On Sunday, May 9, they announced the creation of the European Financial Stability Facility and a related agency, with authority to borrow up to 500 billion euros on international capital markets. The funds, which were in addition to the 110 billion euros committed to Greece, could be used to help any eurozone country. In addition, the ECB made clear its readiness to buy government bonds of troubled countries, through its newly created Securities Market Program. The objective was to reduce interest rates on the bonds. The ECB would make modest purchases of bonds over the next several months before putting the program on hold. The program was not a form of quantitative easing, however, as the ECB would match its purchases of sovereign bonds with sales of other assets, leaving the overall size of its balance sheet unchanged.

On May 9, at the request of Jean-Claude Trichet, I called a videoconference of the FOMC to discuss renewing some of the currency swap lines we had closed three months earlier. I had also received concerned calls from Mervyn King and Masaaki Shirakawa. It was a delicate moment for the Fed. The Senate was preparing to vote on the Dodd-Frank Act. I worried that senators would see the renewal of the swaps as a bailout of foreign banks, despite the fact that the swaps involved no credit risk and would help prevent European financial turmoil from crossing the Atlantic. The potential legislative consequences aside, it seemed to me that the health of the U.S. economy was linked to what happened in Europe. Moreover, with its Securities Market Program, the ECB was taking some politically daring steps of its own. I also continued to believe that central bank cooperation could have benefits for confidence over and above the direct effects of our collective actions. Consequently, I pushed for, and the FOMC approved, the resumption of the swaps with the ECB, the Bank of England, the Swiss National Bank, and the Bank of Canada. To avert possible political fallout as best I could, I met with legislators, including at a private briefing of the Senate Banking Committee on May 11. To my relief, most of the attending senators seemed to appreciate that promoting global financial stability was in the interest of the United States.

Markets responded more positively than they had the previous week to the latest European actions, as well as to the news of the swap lines. Yields on Greek, Portuguese, and Irish government debt dropped sharply on Monday, and the Dow jumped nearly 400 points, about 4 percent, a sign that investors saw the threat to the U.S. economy as diminished. Still, over time, optimism about resolving Europe's problems faded. Investors worried that Greece would not be able to service its debt even with the aid package. Portugal's and Ireland's fiscal positions looked less and less healthy. Eventually, concerns about Italy and Spain, both much larger economies, arose as well. No one was sure whether Europe's resources and political will were sufficient to solve all these problems, or whether banks and other lenders would be forced to share in losses. Thus, after a brief respite, yields on the bonds of countries seen as at risk resumed their upward trek. The Dow again declined; U.S. stocks would fall 13 percent from the day that the Greek prime minister asked for aid in April until early July. European bank regulators conducted a stress test of the continent's banks in July. But, unlike the U.S. stress tests of the previous year, investors did not see the results as credible, and Europe's banks remained wary of lending, including to each other.

The crisis would still be rolling when, at an ECB conference in Frankfurt on November 19, I met with Jean-Claude Trichet. The center of financial turmoil had shifted from the United States to Europe. "Now, Jean-Claude, it is your turn," I told him. He laughed wryly. Nine days later, the IMF and the European Union, drawing on the facility it had established, agreed to an 85-billion-euro rescue of Ireland.

WHEN THE FEDERAL Open Market Committee had gathered for its April 27–28, 2010, meeting, just four days after Prime Minister Papandreou asked the rest of Europe for aid, I and most of my colleagues expressed guarded optimism about prospects for the U.S. economy. We discussed risks that European developments might pose to the United States, but to date those risks had not materialized. Unemployment remained very high—at 9.7 percent from January through March. But we hoped and expected that economic growth would continue to strengthen. We thought that nascent improvements in household spending and business capital investment should offset the ebbing effects of the Obama administration's 2009 fiscal stimulus—enough to bring unemployment down modestly by the end of the year. Inflation remained low—perhaps a bit too low—but we expected it to rise gradually.

Unfortunately, our projections increasingly looked too rosy as spring turned to summer. By the time of the next FOMC meeting, on June 22–23, the outlook was somewhat weaker than in April. Nevertheless, as planned, we continued to discuss ways to gradually shrink our swollen balance sheet at the appropriate time. A few of the inflation hawks argued for beginning to sell securities fairly soon, but most Committee members wanted to wait until the economic recovery was well and obviously under way. That was my position, too. Given the deterioration in the outlook, however, I thought we might be thinking too narrowly. It was fine to talk about our eventual exit from easy money, but we needed also to consider what we would do if the economy required more support.

A week after the meeting, Bill Dudley warned about an issue that, until then, had not given us much pause. When we ended QE1 at the end of March, we decided we would not replace our Fannie- and Freddie-guaranteed mortgage-backed securities as they matured. Our MBS holdings shrank when the mortgages underlying the securities were paid off—because of home sales or refinancings. Over time, the slow runoff would result in passive monetary tightening as our balance sheet declined. It seemed a minor concern. But Bill warned that a recent drop in mortgage rates, which had fallen from about 5 percent to 4.5 percent over the past two months, might well spark a mortgage refinancing wave that could lead to a more rapid runoff in our MBS and a significant, if unintended, tightening of monetary policy.

By the time of our August 10 meeting, the economy was clearly losing momentum. Unemployment had remained flat at 9.5 percent into the summer, and inflation was running around 1 percent, not in immediate danger of lapsing into deflation, but too low for comfort. As I had early in 2008, I warned that the economy likely could not sustain very low growth for long. If growth did not pick up enough to boost consumer and business confidence, the economy might tumble into a new recession. To me, with more fiscal help unlikely, it seemed clear that the economy needed more support from monetary policy.

Bill English, the new director of the Monetary Affairs Division, outlined the policy options for the Committee. Bill, like me, was a graduate of MIT and a student of Stan Fischer. A month earlier he had succeeded Brian Madigan, who retired after a thirty-year career at the Fed. I recommended, and the Committee accepted, the relatively modest step of halting the passive tightening that resulted from not replacing maturing MBS in our portfolio. To keep the size of the balance sheet constant, we agreed to begin purchasing additional longer-term Treasury securities as the MBS ran off. We were already replacing our Treasury securities when they matured. We decided to replace the MBS with Treasuries as well to accommodate Jeff Lacker and several other Committee members who advocated moving toward a portfolio consisting only of Treasuries, as had been the norm before the crisis. Though it would not generate many headlines, our decision to replace maturing MBS let markets know we were concerned about the economic outlook and hinted at our willingness to do more if it continued to slide. Tom Hoenig, who had been dissenting throughout the year, dissented again. He didn't think the economy needed more help from monetary policy, and he continued to worry that easy policy would increase risks to financial stability.

Our August 10 move was only a holding action. I knew that we needed to be ready to ease policy further and, importantly, that we needed to prepare the markets, the public, and the politicians for that possibility. I could do that on August 27 at the upcoming Jackson Hole conference. I decided to scrap my planned topic—the implementation of the Dodd-Frank Act—and instead talk about the economic outlook and our monetary policy options. I spent the weekend of August 14–15 working on the speech. In the absence of a decision by the FOMC, I could not make definitive promises. But just by discussing the possibilities at length I would send a signal that we were prepared to act.

Two weeks later, I stood at the podium in Jackson Lake Lodge. I made it clear that we still had tools available to support the economy. I said that we were determined to keep the recovery going and resist any descent toward deflation. I discussed further use of two policy options we had already employed—securities purchases and communication aimed at convincing markets that we would keep short-term interest rates low for a long time. Both options were meant to help spur economic growth and job creation by putting downward pressure on long-term interest rates. I added, though, that the benefits of further unorthodox policy steps should be weighed against their potential costs and risks.

We bided our time at the next meeting, on September 21, but with concerns about the sustainability of the recovery mounting, we made clear that action was close. We said that we were "prepared to provide additional accommodation if needed" to support the recovery and nudge inflation up to a more acceptable level.

THE SEPTEMBER MEETING was the first in many years without Don Kohn. Don, who was approaching his sixty-eighth birthday, had wanted to retire in the spring, at the end of his four-year term as vice chairman and after forty years in the Federal Reserve System. With at least two of the five Board seats vacant (except for one month) since Sue Bies's departure in March 2007, I had persuaded Don to stay on for one meeting more and then another, until I could persuade him no longer. For me personally and for the entire Fed, Don's retirement was a great loss. He is an outstanding economist and a wise policymaker, admired and trusted by colleagues throughout the Federal Reserve System and at central banks around the world. He knew the Fed and its history better than anyone. And throughout the crisis he provided steadfast moral support, leavened with dry, self-deprecating humor.

Without Don, the Board had only four governors. As had become routine, the Senate was again holding up nominees to fill the empty seats. President Obama had nominated Maryland's chief financial regulator, Sarah Bloom Raskin; MIT professor Peter Diamond; and Janet Yellen to the Board on April 29, but the summer had passed without action.

I had known Peter and Janet for decades (Peter had been on the

MIT faculty when I was a graduate student), and I strongly supported their nominations when Tim Geithner ran the names by me. I didn't know Sarah, but she came well recommended. A lawyer, she had previously served as counsel to the Senate Banking Committee. We were always looking for people who could bring knowledge of community banking to the Board, and Sarah ably filled the bill.

Janet Yellen had been nominated to fill the vice chair position being vacated by Don. Like me, she was an academic economist. She received her doctorate from Yale, where her thesis supervisor had been James Tobin, a leading Keynesian and Nobel Prize winner. Janet's Keynesian proclivities were clear in her research, which often focused on problems related to unemployment and wages. After graduate school and some time as an assistant professor at Harvard, she had taken a job at the Fed in Washington. There, in the cafeteria, she met George Akerlof, a shy and soft-spoken economist known for his creative research. Janet and George would become not only husband and wife but also coauthors and, for many years, colleagues on the faculty of the University of California at Berkeley. George would win the Nobel Prize for his work on how incomplete information on the part of buyers or sellers affects the functioning of markets.

Janet also had substantial policy experience. As I had, she served for two and a half years on the Fed's Board of Governors under Chairman Greenspan and as chair of the Council of Economic Advisers, in her case for President Clinton. In addition, she had served as the president of the San Francisco Reserve Bank since 2004. At the time, she was a leader of the FOMC doves, a role that reflected her longstanding concerns about high unemployment and the hardships it imposed on individuals, families, and communities. More than many on the Committee, she had recognized that the recession touched off by the crisis had the potential to be very deep and required a strong response. That said, based on knowing her and on her record on the Board in the 1990s when inflation was a concern, I also had little doubt that she would tenaciously defend price stability when necessary. She prepared for meetings meticulously and backed her positions with careful analyses and with frequent references to the research literature or to work done by her staff under her direction. Her contributions were always among the most substantive at the meeting. The room hushed when she spoke.

The Senate ultimately confirmed Sarah and Janet, with little opposition. I swore them in on October 4. Peter Diamond's nomination did not go well, despite his distinguished academic record. Peter had done important research in economic theory and in fiscal policy, Social Security, and labor markets. MIT had named him an Institute Professor—the highest rank on the faculty—and he was a past president of the American Economic Association. But Republicans on the Senate Banking Committee, led by Richard Shelby, viewed him as too liberal. They blocked his nomination and the Senate returned it to the White House in August 2010.

At this point most people would have given up, but Peter asked the president to renominate him. Shortly thereafter, we learned that Peter would share in a Nobel Prize for his work on labor markets. Shelby, who based his opposition in part on Peter's supposed lack of qualifications for the job, was implacable. "Unquestionably, the Nobel is a major honor. Yet being a Nobel recipient does not mean one is qualified for every conceivable position," he said. Meanwhile, prominent anti-tax-increase activist Grover Norquist's conservative Club for Growth announced that opposition to Diamond would be a key vote for their 2011 legislative scorecard, implying that yes voters risked being branded as insufficiently conservative. Peter would never be confirmed. In June 2011, he would withdraw his name, denouncing in a *New York Times* op-ed the "partisan polarization" in Washington. It was a real loss for the Fed and the country. The episode also showed that conservative animosity toward the Fed had not ended with the passage of the Dodd-Frank Act.

In March 2011, Janet would be succeeded as president in San Francisco by her research director, John Williams, a distinguished monetary economist whose research with Board economist David Reifschneider (one of the "nine schmucks") and others had helped us think about the monetary policy implications of the zero lower bound on interest rates. John would prove to be a centrist on the FOMC, and I would often use him as a barometer of Committee sentiment.

As the November 2–3 FOMC meeting approached, Bill Dudley and I used our public remarks to prepare markets for a second round of large-scale securities purchases. Bill, in an October 1 speech, said that the current situation—continued very high unemployment and declining inflation—was "wholly unsatisfactory." And he helped shape market expectations by putting a hypothetical $500 billion figure on the purchases. He estimated that purchases of that amount would have about the same stimulative effect as a cut in the federal funds rate of a half to three-quarters of a percentage point. I wasn't so specific in my own speech in Boston on October 15 but said, "There would appear—all else equal—to be a case for further action."

In the meantime, Janet and I worked to shore up support on the Committee, splitting the responsibility of calling each of the Reserve Bank presidents. I knew Tom Hoenig would dissent again. He was waging an increasingly public campaign, using what was, especially in the staid Federal Reserve culture, provocative rhetoric. In a speech the week before the meeting, he called our prospective securities purchases "a bargain with the devil." He was worried that the purchases would create financial instability and sow the seeds of too-high inflation. The previous month, *Businessweek* magazine had profiled Tom in a lengthy article—"Thomas Hoenig Is Fed Up"—and he appeared to be enjoying the attention. Over the years, Tom had impressed me as mild-mannered and civil. I respected his right to dissent, to ask tough questions, and to publicly explain his stance. But now I thought he risked undermining public confidence in the Fed and disrupting the Committee's deliberative process by staking out inflexible positions before hearing other Committee members' views.

Other presidents—including Richard Fisher of Dallas and Charles

Plosser of Philadelphia—shared Hoenig's skepticism about aggressive policy actions. But neither of them had a vote in 2010. Fisher didn't think more monetary support would help because he believed uncertainty created by political squabbling over the federal budget was discouraging businesses from investing and hiring. Plosser continued to worry about inflation and had little confidence in our ability to generate jobs by easing policy further.

I knew I could count on the support of Eric Rosengren of Boston, who did have a vote. And I thought that the other presidents voting that year, Jim Bullard of St. Louis and Sandra Pianalto of Cleveland, would support further action as well. It was Sarah Raskin's first regular FOMC meeting and Janet's first as Board vice chair. Janet favored strong action and I suspected that Sarah would, too, along with Dan Tarullo. Betsy Duke was much less optimistic about the likely benefits of future easing and worried about the risks associated with our growing balance sheet. Janet had dinner with Betsy, and Betsy agreed to support additional purchases, though without enthusiasm.

Kevin Warsh had substantial reservations. He was one of my closest advisers and confidants, and his help, especially during the height of the crisis in the fall of 2008, had been invaluable. He had supported the first round of securities purchases, begun in the midst of the crisis. Now that financial markets were functioning more normally, he believed that monetary policy was reaching its limits, that additional purchases could pose risks to inflation and financial stability, and that it was time for others in Washington to take on some of the policy burden. I met with him on October 8 and assured him we could cut the purchases short if we were dissatisfied with the results or if we saw signs of building inflation pressures. I told him that, in my public remarks, I would continue to emphasize that large-scale purchases had costs and risks as well as benefits. It was a good talk, but I wasn't sure I had convinced him. We met again on October 26 and he told me he would not dissent. But I knew it would be a difficult vote for him.

I thought that the case for action at the November meeting was very strong. Payroll employment had fallen during each month from June through September (the latest report available). True, much of the decline could be attributed to a onetime drop in federal employment as the 2010 census wound down. But nongovernment payrolls had averaged monthly gains of only 84,000 over the period, enough to accommodate recent graduates and other new job seekers but not enough to reduce the overall unemployment rate. At 9.6 percent, the rate was virtually unchanged from the start of the year. And, with the incoming data disappointing, it seemed likely that growth in 2011 would be too weak to reduce unemployment meaningfully. I was especially concerned about the corrosive effects of long-term unemployment. In September, more than 40 percent of the unemployed had been without a job for longer than six months. Their skills were getting rusty and they were losing their contacts in the working world. At the same time, on the other side of our mandate, inflation—already too low—looked to be flat or declining. Over the last six months, it had averaged only about 1/2 percent. Very low inflation or deflation would make full recovery even harder to achieve.

I believed the Committee could not stand by and risk letting the recovery stall out. Moreover, I did not think securities purchases had lost their effectiveness. Since I had begun publicly hinting in August that we might do more, financial conditions had improved, apparently in anticipation of additional policy action. The Dow had risen 12 percent and inflation expectations, as measured by the prices of inflation-protected bonds, had increased toward more normal levels. By itself, a new program of asset purchases was unlikely to be a game changer; it certainly would not create the millions of jobs we needed. But it would help, and it might even be the key to preventing the economy from sliding back into recession.

The FOMC voted to buy $600 billion of Treasury securities through June 2011, at a pace of about $75 billion per month. This second round of purchases, which the media quickly dubbed QE2, would raise our balance sheet to approximately $2.9 trillion, compared to less than $900 billion in mid-2007, on the eve of the crisis. As St. Louis Fed president Jim Bullard had urged since the previous summer, we had thought about an open-ended program, where we would vary the amount of securities purchases depending on the progress of the recovery and inflation pressures. But I worried that, with no anticipated end date, it would be hard for us to stop buying without shocking the market. We did say that we would regularly review the pace of purchases and adjust if changes in the economic outlook warranted, but in practice the bar would be high.

Surprising no one, Hoenig dissented—and, to boot, gave an interview the day after the meeting to Sudeep Reddy of the *Wall Street Journal* in which he criticized the Committee's action. He would also dissent, for the eighth and final time, at the December FOMC, marking the longest string of dissents by a Fed policymaker since 1980.

As he had promised, Kevin voted in favor, but the following week he delivered a speech in New York and published an op-ed in the *Wall Street Journal* that reflected his reservations. He argued that monetary policy alone could not solve the economy's problems, and he called for tax and regulatory reforms aimed at increasing productivity and longer-term growth. I agreed that other Washington policymakers should take more responsibility for promoting economic growth. Federal spending on infrastructure projects such as road building, for example, could have helped make our economy more productive in the longer term while putting people back to work right away. Yet nobody expected anything to happen on the fiscal front or in the other areas that Kevin highlighted, either. The reality was that the Fed was the only game in town. It was up to us to do what we could, imperfect as our tools might be.

Hoenig's comments had irked me, but, despite hearing from a few FOMC colleagues who were piqued at Warsh's op-ed, I was comfortable with it. I never questioned Kevin's loyalty or sincerity. He had always participated candidly and constructively, as a team player, in our deliberations. And I was grateful that he had voted for the second round of asset purchases despite his unease. I saw his public comments more as an indictment of policymakers outside the Fed than as an attack on Fed policies. Kevin would leave the Board three months later, but not because of any policy disagreement. We had agreed when he was appointed in 2006 that he would stay for about five years. We remain close to this day.

MARKETS SEEMED TO anticipate QE2 and take it in stride. I thought that we had successfully telegraphed our action. Nevertheless, I wanted to ensure that our aims were well understood. I had seriously considered conducting an unscheduled press conference after the November meeting, but decided that it risked disrupting markets. Instead, I spent several hours telephoning key reporters individually, answering questions on background. I also wrote an op-ed that was published November 4 in the *Washington Post*. Despite these efforts, I was unprepared for the blowback from policymakers abroad and politicians at home.

November 2, the first day of our meeting, was Election Day, and voters had dealt Democrats what President Obama called a "shellacking." After four years in the minority, Republicans took control of the House. As a result, Barney Frank would lose the chairmanship of the House Financial Services Committee to Alabama congressman Spencer Bachus. Republicans picked up seats in the Senate but remained in the minority there. Perhaps emboldened by the election results, Republican politicians and conservative commentators, including radio host Glenn Beck, hit our decision hard. Sarah Palin, who had never before demonstrated an interest in monetary policy, called on us to "cease and desist."

More troubling, to me, was a November 17 letter from the four top Republicans in Congress—John Boehner and Eric Cantor in the House and Mitch McConnell and Jon Kyl in the Senate. They expressed deep concerns about our action. Our asset purchases, they wrote, could "result in . . . hard-to-control, long-term inflation and potentially generate artificial asset bubbles." They offered no evidence to support their assertions. The letter came a day after Senator Bob Corker and Republican Representative Mike Pence of Indiana proposed legislation to remove the full employment part of the Fed's dual mandate, leaving price stability as the only objective of monetary policy. (The change in mandate, if it had been approved, would not have changed policy much, if at all; very low inflation alone justified highly stimulative policy.)

A few economists weighed in against our decision as well. The *Wall Street Journal* published an open letter on November 15 from twenty-three (mostly conservative) economists, commentators, and asset managers who argued that our securities purchases "should be reconsidered and discontinued." According to the letter, the policy was not necessary, would not work, and risked "currency debasement and inflation." Among the signatories were Michael Boskin of Stanford, who had chaired the Council of Economic Advisers under the first President Bush; historian Niall Ferguson of Harvard; Douglas Holtz-Eakin, a former director of the Congressional Budget Office; and John Taylor of Stanford. The media and politicians rarely pay attention to statements by economists, but unfortunately they do if the statements are sufficiently controversial (in the case of the media) or support preconceived views (in the case of politicians).

Foreign officials joined in the criticism. German finance minister Wolfgang Schäuble was translated as calling our decision "clueless." Others, particularly from emerging markets like Brazil and China, complained that our actions, if they succeeded in lowering longer-term interest rates in the United States, would create damaging spillover effects for their economies. Lower rates in the United States could spark volatile investment flows into emerging markets as investors looked for better returns. A week after our announcement, President Obama heard a torrent of criticism of QE2 while attending a G-20 summit in Seoul, South Korea. When I next met with him, two months later, I jokingly apologized for causing him so much trouble. He laughed and said that he wished we could have waited a week.

I had had an opportunity to explain our possible November action in advance at a meeting of G-20 finance ministers and central bankers in Gyeongju, South Korea, on October 23. I argued that, because we are an important trading partner for many countries, the rest of the world would benefit from a stronger U.S. recovery. I said that countries with sound monetary, budget, and trade policies could better withstand any short-term disruptions from our easing. Foreign central bankers, who well understood our aims, generally were more sympathetic to our actions than their more political peers in the finance ministries.

I was more worried by the domestic criticism than the foreign. The letter from the Republican leaders signaled a willingness to politicize monetary policy. I understood that this grew out of voters' understandable dissatisfaction with the economy, but it was also the product of confused or deliberately misleading statements about our policies, their objectives, and how they worked. Our difficulties were evident in an animated YouTube video featuring two creatures of indeterminate species hilariously but wholly inaccurately explaining "the quantitative easing." The video went viral, and by mid-December it had logged 3.5 million views.

The economic logic underlying all three—the cartoon, the letter from the congressional Republicans, and the economists' missive— was misguided and inaccurate. In particular, there was virtually zero risk that our policies would lead to significant inflation or "currency debasement" (a loaded term for a sharp decline in the value of the dollar). That idea was linked to a perception that the Fed paid for securities by printing wheelbarrows of money. But contrary to what is sometimes said (and I said it once or twice myself, unfortunately, in oversimplified explanations), our policies did not involve printing money—neither literally, when referring to cash, nor even metaphorically, when referring to other forms of money such as checking accounts. The amount of currency in circulation is determined by how much cash people want to hold (the demand goes up around Christmas shopping time, for example) and is not affected by the Fed's securities purchases.

Instead, the Fed pays for securities by creating reserves in the banking system. In a weak economy, like the one we were experiencing, those reserves simply lie fallow and they don't serve as "money" in the common sense of the word.

As the economy strengthened, banks would begin to loan out their reserves, which would ultimately lead to the expansion of money and credit. Up to a point, that was exactly what we wanted to see. If growth in money and credit became excessive, it would eventually result in inflation, but we could avoid that by unwinding our easy-money policies at the appropriate time. And, as I had explained on many occasions, we had the tools we needed to raise rates and tighten monetary policy when needed. The fears of hyperinflation or a collapse of the dollar were consequently quite exaggerated. Market indicators of inflation expectations—including the fact that the U.S. government was able to borrow long-term at very low interest rates—showed that investors had great confidence in the Fed's ability to keep inflation low. Our concern, if anything, was to get inflation a little higher, which was proving difficult to accomplish.

A second common misconception was that our hundreds of billions of dollars of securities purchases were a form of government spending, comparable to the Bush and Obama administrations' fiscal stimulus packages. This confusion led to some scary, though entirely misleading, claims about the cost of our policies to taxpayers. Our purchases were analogous to a financial investment made by a family—such as buying a stock or bond—rather than to a family's paying rent or buying gas. Indeed, since the interest paid by the securities we acquired exceeded the interest we paid on the additional reserves that banks deposited with us, our purchases would prove highly profitable for taxpayers.

The only useful response to the post-QE2 confusion, I believed, was more communication and explanation. I met with and called legislators, including critics such as Senators Shelby and Corker, Paul Ryan (the senior Republican on the House Budget Committee), and Dave

Camp (the senior Republican on the House Ways and Means Committee). In September I had held a town hall meeting for high school teachers. I made public appearances, including a second *60 Minutes* interview on December 5. But I knew that we would need to do more to get our message across.

CHAPTER 22

Headwinds

T he clock in my dining room in the Martin Building was ticking down to 2:15 p.m. It was April 27, 2011. Michelle Smith and her Public Affairs colleague Rose Pianalto—the sister of Cleveland Fed president Sandy Pianalto—waited with me. I sipped from a bottle of water and kept my eye on the clock. In a few minutes I would take the unprecedented step, for a Fed chairman, of beginning a series of regularly scheduled press conferences.

With no auditorium or television studio at the Board large enough for a press conference, we had decided to use our largest dining room, on the same floor as the cafeteria. (My small dining room had been pressed into service as a green room.) The logistical challenges of holding such a high-profile and market-sensitive event on live television were daunting, and Michelle and Rose, along with many other staff members, had been working for weeks trying to anticipate every contingency.

We had also carefully considered the staging of the event, aware that every detail could send a subliminal message. We wanted the feel of an economic seminar rather than a news conference in a more political venue. Consequently, I would not stand behind a podium but would sit at a desk (placed atop a platform to give the TV cameras at the back of the room a clear shot), with the assembled reporters seated at long tables. In a nod to Washington convention, though, I would be flanked by an American flag on my right and the Federal Reserve flag to my left.

I had rehearsed answers to possible questions with the staff, more than I normally would before congressional testimony. We expected reporters' questions to be more pointed and more technical than those usually asked by members of Congress. I was certainly not a novice in dealing with the press. I had taken questions from reporters after speeches at the National Press Club as well as in many off-the-record meetings with editorial boards and other groups of journalists. Nonetheless, I was nervous. It seemed as though the cable TV business stations had talked about nothing else for a week—and we had been swamped by requests to attend. Michelle invited about sixty reporters—one per news organization, including newspapers, magazines, wire services, network and cable TV, and radio. Foreign outlets also attended, including *Der Spiegel*, Agence France-Presse, TV Asahi of Japan, and *Korea Economic Daily*.

At 2:15 precisely I walked into the improvised studio to the clicking of cameras and took my seat. I looked over the rows of reporters and began a short statement.

We had been discussing the possibility of regular press conferences for some time, and the FOMC had endorsed the idea at the March 15 meeting. Many other central banks hold press conferences, some as frequently as monthly, and adopting the practice seemed the natural next step for increasing transparency at the Fed. As I had often remarked, monetary policy is 98 percent talk and 2 percent action. That's especially true when short-term interest rates hover close to zero and influencing expectations about future interest rates becomes critically important. Still, the backfire potential during a live, unscripted televised exchange with reporters was significant. Any wrong or unintended policy signal could roil markets. And we knew that once we began holding press conferences it would be difficult, if not impossible, to stop.

After the blowback that greeted our introduction of QE2 in November 2010, however, we needed more than ever to explain our policies clearly and effectively. We had announced on March 24 that I would hold four postmeeting press conferences a year, coinciding with FOMC participants' quarterly submissions of projections for economic growth, unemployment, and inflation.

In my opening statement, I said that we would complete, as promised, $600 billion of Treasury securities purchases under QE2 by the end of June, and that we continued to expect the funds rate to remain low "for an extended period."

It was premature to make a definitive judgment about the effects of QE2, but the early signs seemed promising. Financial conditions had eased considerably since I had first hinted at a second round of securities purchases at Jackson Hole eight months before. Stock prices had risen 27 percent, and spreads between the yields on corporate bonds and Treasury securities had narrowed (suggesting more willingness by investors to take on risk). Longer-term interest rates had fallen with the announcement of the program, as expected, but subsequently rose as investors became more confident about future growth and less worried about deflation. The pattern was similar to what we had seen after the expansion of QE1 in March 2009.

Improved financial conditions in turn seemed to be helping the economy. Payroll increases averaged close to 200,000 per month in February and March, and the unemployment rate, which had been a discouraging 9.8 percent in November, had dipped below 9 percent. I said that the FOMC expected the recovery to proceed at a moderate pace, with unemployment continuing to fall slowly, though some unforeseen developments—most importantly, the disastrous earthquake and tsunami that hit Japan on March 11—could temporarily weigh on growth. Besides inflicting tragic loss of life—some twenty thousand people died—the earthquake and tsunami disrupted global supply chains. The sudden shortages of critical parts limited the production of automobiles and other manufactured goods around the world. In a gesture of solidarity, the Fed and the Treasury had coordinated with the Japanese in a rare intervention in the foreign exchange market. The week after the quake, along with other G-7 countries, we bought dollars and sold yen to bring down the value of the yen and help make Japanese exports more competitive. It was our only foreign exchange intervention during my time at the Fed.

Inflation prospects posed some tricky issues. QE2 had been undertaken in large part because of our concerns about deflation risks, and now, less than six months later, those risks seemed to have dissipated—another apparent success for the program. But had we overshot? Gasoline prices had risen by almost a dollar per gallon, to $4, since the QE2 announcement. Food prices were also rising, propelled by global increases in the prices of major crops (wheat, rice, corn, and soybeans) and some weakening of the dollar.

After Neil Irwin of the *Washington Post* asked the first question at the press conference, about an apparent slowing of growth in the first quarter, Jon Hilsenrath of the *Wall Street Journal* asked if the Fed could or should do anything about the increasing costs of gas and food. Everyone was aware of our critics' repeated warnings that our securities purchases might cause out-of-control inflation. Should the Fed consider reversing its easy-money policies?

The appropriate monetary policy response to swings in energy and other commodity prices has long challenged central banks. Over the years, the FOMC has generally chosen to look through them and focus on more stable measures of inflation trends—such as so-called core inflation, which excludes energy and food prices. This approach has often been derided. As the question is usually put, "Don't you people at the Fed eat or drive?" Yes, we do, and the Fed has always equated price stability with low *overall* inflation, including inflation in energy and food prices.

We paid attention to core inflation because there is a lag between changes in monetary policy and their effect on the economy. We must take into account not only the current inflation rate but also the prospects for inflation a few quarters ahead, when the effects of policy decisions will actually be felt—much as a quarterback throws the football to where he expects his receiver to be, not where the receiver is at the moment the pass is released. Research shows that setting aside the most volatile prices leads to better predictions of overall inflation. We had faced a similar dilemma in the summer of 2008. Energy prices were rising sharply, though the economy was weak. We—correctly, in hindsight—had resisted raising interest rates.

I told Hilsenrath that we saw the recent increases in gasoline prices in particular as likely to be temporary, the result of factors mostly outside of monetary policy, including political unrest such as the Arab Spring (which had raised concerns about reduced oil supply). As best we could tell, neither the rise in oil prices nor the increases in crop prices seemed likely to translate into persistently higher overall inflation. Consequently, I said, no monetary policy response was warranted.

After about an hour, the press conference ended. It looked to have been a critical, and logistical, success.

SPEAKING OF CRITICAL SUCCESSES, in May 2011 the HBO movie *Too Big to Fail*, based on Andrew Ross Sorkin's book of the same title, told the story of the crisis. Paul Giamatti's version of me earned him an award from the Screen Actors Guild. To gather material for his characterization, Giamatti had visited me at the Fed. His father, Bart Giamatti, had been the commissioner of Major League Baseball. Our lunch conversation turned quickly to the game and we never talked about the Fed or the financial crisis. I guess he got what he needed, judging by the critical reception of his performance. While I have read Sorkin's book, I have never seen the movie. I avoided it, perhaps unfairly expecting an oversimplified treatment of complicated issues—not to mention the fact that it would feel strange to see myself portrayed on screen. When asked my opinion of the film, I would respond that I didn't need to see it; I had seen the original.

Around the time the movie came out, Bill Clinton invited me to meet with him. I had met Hillary Clinton during her time as senator and then secretary of state. Once, to lunch with her, I walked the block from the Fed to the State Department, accompanied by my security detail. She welcomed me warmly and we ate at a table for two that had been wheeled into a small private dining room. She conveyed her support for the Fed's actions during the crisis but listened more than she spoke, pumping me for my insights into the world's economies.

At my meeting with Bill, we spent more than an hour in the living room of the Clintons' home in Washington, near the Naval Observatory. He looked thin—after several heart surgeries, the most recent in 2010, he had reportedly become a vegan—but he conversed with great energy about politics, foreign affairs, and the economy. He too greeted me warmly and praised the Fed's response to the crisis. He urged me to continue my efforts to speak to the country, such as the *60 Minutes* interview and the news conferences. He said people were uncertain and afraid and needed to hear from someone who could explain what was happening. Americans would become more confident, he told me, if they understood better what was going on.

AS IT TURNED OUT, the FOMC correctly diagnosed the inflation situation in the spring of 2011. Gas prices would peak in early May and then fall the rest of the year. Overall inflation, including food and energy prices, would rise until September and then move steadily downward. However, once again we (along with private-sector forecasters) were too optimistic about economic growth. As in 2010, promising growth in the spring would give way to a summer swoon. Job gains would slow sharply—on average, only about 50,000 jobs were created each month in May, June, and July. The initial August report showed a complete stall in job growth. The unemployment rate, after its encouraging drop early in the year, would stagnate near 9 percent into the fall—a net improvement of only about 1 percentage point since the recession's official end two years earlier. Moreover, extensive revisions of previous years' data would show that the recession had been deeper and the recovery slower than we had thought. As of mid-2011, the country's output of goods and services had only just reached its pre-recession peak, and employment was more than six and a half million jobs below its peak. Economists are criticized for not being able to predict the future, but, because the data are incomplete and subject to revision, we cannot even be sure what happened in the recent past. Noisy data make effective policymaking all the more difficult.

We endlessly debated the economy's apparent inability to reach escape velocity—to reach the point where growth was self-sustaining. Unforeseen shocks like the Japanese earthquake and tsunami were insufficient explanation. I came to think of the other, more significant, barriers to growth as headwinds—factors that we had expected to slow the recovery but which were proving more substantial and more persistent than we had thought.

One headwind was the lingering effects of the financial crisis. Although U.S. financial markets and institutions had largely stabilized, credit was still tight. Only applicants with the best credit scores were getting loans. Tight credit meant the creation of fewer new businesses and fewer expansions of existing businesses—and thus fewer new jobs. Even households and firms that could borrow were declining to do so. Instead, they spent cautiously and focused on paying down debt. The situation, unfortunately, was confirming the financial accelerator theory that Mark Gertler and I had developed during my academic days. Our research suggested that recessions worsen the financial conditions of both borrowers and lenders, which restricts the flow of credit, which makes the downturn deeper and more protracted. As I told Mark, I would have preferred to see our theory disproven.

Tight credit contributed to another persistent headwind: the slow housing recovery. Normally, a rapid rebound in home construction and related industries such as realty and home improvement helps fuel growth after a recession. Not this time. Builders would start construction on only about 600,000 private homes in 2011, compared with more than 2 million in 2005. To some extent, that drop represented the flip side of the pre-crisis boom. Too many houses had been built, and now the excess supply was being worked off. Additionally, mortgage lending terms, too easy before the crisis, had swung to the opposite extreme. Potential borrowers, including many would-be first-time buyers, were being turned away. Other drags on home lending and construction included high numbers of foreclosures and distress sales, which held down home prices, and regulatory uncertainty—about the future of Fannie and Freddie, for instance.

Fiscal policy—at state, local, and federal levels—was also blowing the wrong way. After enacting President Obama's stimulus package in February 2009, Congress had shifted into austerity mode, echoing the trend in Europe. Meanwhile, balanced-budget requirements had forced state and local governments to cut jobs and construction as their tax revenues fell. This headwind was no soft breeze. Government employment usually rises during economic recovery, but this time public-sector jobs (excluding census workers) would fall by more than 750,000 from their peak before turning up. (More than 300,000 of those who lost jobs were teachers.) Fed staff had estimated that QE2 might create an additional 700,000 jobs. Tight fiscal policies were arguably offsetting much of the effect of our monetary efforts.

Speaking publicly about the fiscal headwind was a particular challenge. Government spending and taxation are outside the Fed's jurisdiction. On the other hand, fiscal policies were holding back the recovery and job creation and thus challenging our ability to meet our employment mandate. After long discussions with the Board staff, I decided on a two-pronged public approach. First, I would emphasize that the Fed, especially with short-term interest rates close to zero, couldn't do it alone. The economy needed help from Congress—if not from additional spending (on roads and bridges, for example), then at least in areas such as retraining unemployed workers. Second, I would point out that the federal deficit, while a serious matter, was primarily a longer-run concern, reflecting in large part the challenges of dealing with an aging population and rising health-care costs. Congress needed to focus its deficit fighting on these longer-term issues. Raising current taxes or reducing current spending would only slow the recovery without solving the longer-run problem.

IF THE CREDIT, housing, and fiscal headwinds were not a sufficient challenge for the economy, financial conditions deteriorated again during the summer of 2011, in part because of a resurgence of the European crisis. The bailouts of Greece in May 2010 and Ireland in November 2010 were followed by a package for Portugal (of 78 billion euros) in May 2011. Each country receiving aid was required to aggressively reduce its budget deficit and implement reforms to improve its economic competitiveness and efficiency. Ideally, imposing tough conditions on bailout recipients reduces moral hazard and leads them to correct the poor policies that got them into trouble in the first place. If the terms were not tough, other countries in similar straits wouldn't make the hard choices required to avoid having to ask for a bailout.

On the other hand, tough bailout conditions only work if the requirements make sense and if they can be implemented without causing the political collapse of the recipient government. Was Europe getting it right? The question was important for Europe, of course, but also for the rest of the world, which was linked to Europe financially and through trade. With Tim Geithner (at meetings and conference calls of international groups like the G-7 and the G-20) and on my own (at central bank meetings in Basel and elsewhere), I listened to hours of debate.

Tim and I largely agreed that Europe was getting it wrong. We did not hesitate to say so. Doubtless some countries needed to tighten their fiscal belts; and many countries in Europe, not only those receiving bailouts, could benefit from eliminating heavy-handed regulations that made their economies inefficient. For example, some countries make firing workers very difficult, which makes employers reluctant to hire in the first place. But Europe was on the wrong track, we thought, in several crucial respects.

Although austerity in the more troubled countries was probably unavoidable, given how indebted they were, it predictably pushed them deeper into recession. Unfortunately, the Europeans showed no inclination to offset necessary austerity in weaker countries by spending more and taxing less in countries, like Germany, that could afford to do so. Instead, Germany and other better-off countries also cut their budgets, purportedly to serve as examples to more benighted nations. As a result, fiscal policy for the eurozone as a whole was highly contractionary. The eurozone's macroeconomic approach seemed to boil down to "no pain, no gain," irrespective of whether the pain was actually achieving anything. At the same time, the ECB exacerbated the effect of this fiscal austerity by tightening monetary policy. When inflation rose above the ECB's target of "below but close to 2 percent," it twice raised interest rates, in April and July of 2011, despite high unemployment and continued financial stress. Unlike the Fed, it decided against looking through temporary increases in oil and crop prices. I found the decision hard to understand, although it was consistent with the ECB's response to higher oil prices in the summer of 2008, when it had also raised rates. Fiscal austerity throughout the eurozone, along with higher interest rates from the ECB, virtually guaranteed very slow growth in Europe as a whole and outright economic contraction and soaring joblessness in countries like Greece, Ireland, and Portugal.

Beyond concerns about near-term growth in Europe, Tim and I also believed too little was being done to address the basic structural problem of the eurozone: the mismatch of a single monetary policy and central bank with the uncoordinated fiscal policies of seventeen independent countries. (The membership had reached seventeen when Estonia joined the ECB at the start of 2011.) Some steps had been taken, including tougher enforcement of the rules limiting deficits. And no one expected European countries in the foreseeable future to become fiscally integrated like the states of the United States. Still, Europe's leaders would reject or put off plausible and constructive acts of fiscal cooperation— like undertaking joint infrastructure projects, creating a common fund to safely shut down failing banks, and sharing the risk of bank failures by establishing a eurozone-wide system of deposit insurance.

Another contentious issue concerned how to treat countries that, even after rigorous austerity, were unable to pay their debts. Should they be bailed out by other eurozone members and the International Monetary Fund? Or should private lenders, many of them European banks, bear some of the losses as well? The situation was analogous to the question of whether to impose losses on the senior creditors of Washington Mutual during the crisis. We (Tim, especially) had opposed that, because we feared that it would fan the panic and increase contagion. For similar reasons, we opposed forcing private creditors to bear losses if a eurozone country defaulted. Jean-Claude Trichet strongly agreed with us, though he opposed other U.S. positions. (In particular, he did not see much scope for monetary or fiscal policy to help the eurozone economy, preferring to focus on budget balancing and structural reforms.) On the issue of country default, though, Jean-Claude's worry, like ours, was that, once the genie was out of the bottle, lenders' confidence in other vulnerable European borrowers would evaporate.

The issue gained relevance over the summer as it became clear that Greece's imploding economy would prevent it from servicing its debts, despite its bailout. European politicians began to discuss forcing private lenders to take losses, along with official lenders (European governments and the IMF). They saw loss sharing as an antidote to moral hazard as well as a way to protect their taxpayers. In contrast, Trichet and the ECB argued strenuously against any default or restructuring of Greek debt that might prompt contagion. (Economics aside, Trichet also seemed to view default as inherently dishonorable.) Ireland and Portugal were safe from contagion for the moment, since, as recipients of official loans, they did not have to borrow on private markets. However, two much larger countries, Spain and Italy, could be at risk.

On July 21, European leaders assembled a new package for Greece, roughly doubling the 110 billion euros in loans approved in May 2010. But, for the first time, private holders of Greek debt were also forced to make concessions, in the form of lower rates and a longer repayment period. It was, in effect, a partial default. Predictably, private lenders soon began to pull back from the bonds of Italy and Spain. At the beginning of 2011, ten-year Italian bonds yielded 4.7 percent, and ten-year Spanish bonds 5.4 percent (both up from about 4 percent a year earlier). As discussions of Greek restructuring proceeded, those yields began to rise; by August 1, Italian bonds paid 6 percent and Spanish bonds 6.2 percent. Spanish yields then stabilized and declined, but by the end of the year the yield on Italian bonds was 7.1 percent, even though the ECB restarted its program of bond purchases in August.

A rise of a few percentage points in interest rates might not seem important. But higher interest costs directly increase government deficits. A vicious circle can set in: Lenders, fearful of default, demand higher interest rates, but the higher interest rates themselves make ultimate default more likely. Over the summer of 2011, more and more people were thinking the unthinkable—that the euro would collapse as countries defaulted and either withdrew or were expelled from the common currency. With already weakened European banks holding large quantities of government debt, country defaults could bring down the European banking system as well. It looked like a financial disaster in the making—one potentially worse than the crisis of 2007–2009.

As this newest European crisis was building, on May 14, 2011, Dominique Strauss-Kahn, the managing director of the IMF, was arrested in New York City, accused of assaulting and attempting to rape a hotel maid. I was shocked. Many considered Strauss-Kahn the most likely successor to French president Nicolas Sarkozy. Brilliant and urbane, he had been a strong leader of the IMF. He was particularly clear-sighted about the need for the Europeans to act quickly and decisively to contain the crisis. No one could condone his alleged actions, but Strauss-Kahn's expulsion from international policymaking left a major gap at a critical moment. John Lipsky, an American economist who had been serving as Strauss-Kahn's deputy, filled in temporarily.

French finance minister Christine Lagarde, with the support of the U.S. government, succeeded Strauss-Kahn in July to become the first woman to head the IMF. The IMF's chief economist, Olivier Blanchard, a good friend of mine who had spent many years on the faculty at MIT, stayed on. Despite having just served in the French government, Christine, like Strauss-Kahn before her, showed no favoritism to European borrowers. Indeed, she would often criticize European governments' unwillingness to do more to foster economic growth. However, the Europeans, led by German finance minister Wolfgang Schäuble, showed little inclination to take advice, from the IMF, the Americans, or anyone else. On this, at least, they agreed.

MEANWHILE, IN THE United States, Congress appeared to be doing its best to roil the financial markets further. It was in a standoff with the Obama administration over raising the federal government's debt limit.

The debt ceiling law is a historical accident. Until World War I, when Congress approved spending, it routinely authorized any necessary issuance of government debt at the same time. In 1917, for administrative convenience, Congress passed a law that allowed the Treasury to issue debt as needed, so long as the total debt outstanding remained below a permitted amount. In effect, Congress separated its spending decisions from its borrowing decisions.

At some point, it dawned on legislators that approval of the debt ceiling could be used as a bargaining chip. Usually, these fights resembled Kabuki theater, with the party in power ensuring that the debt ceiling was raised (and taking the resulting political flak). Before 2011, the most serious battle had occurred in 1995, when a deadlock between President Clinton and the Republican Congress over the debt ceiling and spending bills led to two temporary shutdowns of the federal government. As political polarization in Washington increased, however, debt ceiling fights became less symbolic and, consequently, much more dangerous.

Many Americans believe that disputes about the debt ceiling concern how much the government should spend and tax. The debt limit is not about spending and taxing decisions themselves, however; rather, it is about whether the government will pay the bills for spending that has already occurred. Refusing to raise the debt limit is not analogous, as is sometimes claimed, to a family cutting up its credit cards. It is like a family running up large credit card bills and then refusing to pay.

One of the government's key commitments is paying interest on the national debt. Failure to make those payments on time would constitute default on U.S. Treasury securities—the world's most widely held and traded financial asset. At the time, about $10 trillion in U.S. government debt was held by individuals and institutions around the world. Even a short-lived default would likely have catastrophic financial consequences, while permanently damaging the credibility and creditworthiness of the U.S. government. A failure to make other government payments—to retirees, soldiers, hospitals, or contractors, for example—also would constitute an important breach of faith with serious financial and economic effects. Refusing to raise the debt limit takes the economic well-being of the country hostage. That ought to be unacceptable, no matter what the underlying issue being contested.

The fight over the debt limit in 2011 grew out of Republican efforts to cut government spending after the party's gains in the 2010 midterm elections. Various efforts to find a compromise, including a bipartisan commission headed by Alan Simpson, a former Republican senator from Wyoming, and Erskine Bowles, a White House chief of staff in the Clinton administration, had failed to produce results. In April, Tim had warned Congress that, without an increase in the debt ceiling, the government would run out of money around August 2. At the time of the warning, few thought that Congress would seriously consider default, and market reaction was muted.

The Federal Reserve serves as the fiscal agent for the Treasury, which means it processes most federal payments, including interest on Treasury securities. As the political debate went on, the Fed and Treasury discussed operational issues that could arise if Congress did not raise the debt ceiling on time. Fed supervisors and specialists in the plumbing of the financial system also talked to financial institutions about how they might deal with a delay in interest payments on Treasury securities. What we heard was disturbing: The computer systems used by banks and other financial institutions were almost completely unprepared to deal with even a short-lived default. The systems' designers had not contemplated the possibility.

On July 31, after months of brinkmanship, Congress finally came to a budget agreement that allowed the debt ceiling to be raised. The agreement was complex. Besides specifying spending cuts over the next ten years, it established a joint congressional committee, nicknamed the "super committee," to come up with additional reductions. If the committee failed to agree on sufficient cuts, it would trigger across-the-board cuts, known as "sequestration." I was relieved to see a resolution of the crisis, but I worried about whether the fragile economic recovery could withstand the austerity measures that Congress seemed intent on imposing.

There was a postscript: On August 5, the Standard & Poor's rating agency—citing, among other factors, the prospect of future budget brinkmanship—downgraded U.S. government debt to one notch below the top AAA rating. The rating agency had made an egregious error that caused it to overstate the estimated ten-year deficit by $2 trillion, which the Treasury quickly pointed out. S&P acknowledged the error but asserted that the mistake did not affect its judgment of the government's creditworthiness. I had the feeling that S&P wanted to show it was not intimidated. The episode highlighted the odd relationship between governments and rating agencies: Governments regulate the rating agencies, but the rating agencies have the power to downgrade governments' debt.

The downgrade added to the stress in financial markets, already skittish because of Europe. From July 25, the Monday after the Greek debt restructuring announcement and amid growing concern about the debt ceiling, the Dow fell about 1,800 points, or 14 percent, in four weeks. Ironically, over the same period, despite fears of a default on Treasury securities, investors snapped them up, pushing down the yield on ten-year Treasuries from about 3 percent to a little over 2 percent, a substantial move. The appeal of Treasuries as a safe port in a storm (together with concerns about Europe and the U.S. economy) evidently outweighed default fears.

HOUSING IN THE United States continued to be a key recovery headwind in 2011. With my encouragement, Board members Betsy Duke and Sarah Raskin constituted an ad hoc committee to think about how we might bring it back to life. Their efforts were supported by the work of David Wilcox, who became the Board's research director in July 2011 after Dave Stockton retired, and a team led by economist Karen Pence, a specialist in consumer finance. The committee focused on new foreclosures, which had declined from a peak of 2.1 million in 2009 but remained quite high at 1.25 million in 2011.

Monetary policy had helped bring down mortgage rates from about 6 percent in late November 2008, just before we announced the first round of mortgage-backed securities purchases, to about 4.5 percent at mid-2011. With mortgage rates lower, homeowners with good credit records and equity in their homes could refinance and reduce their monthly payments. Unfortunately, about a quarter of homeowners remained underwater in 2011, owing more than their homes were worth, and could not refinance. The early results of the Home Affordable Refinance Program, introduced by the Obama administration to help underwater borrowers whose mortgages were owned by Fannie or Freddie, had been disappointing. But the administration liberalized HARP's terms in October 2011, reducing fees and broadening eligibility, which greatly increased participation. Ultimately, the program facilitated about 3.2 million refinancings.

The administration's other main anti-foreclosure initiative, the Home Affordable Modification Program, offered servicing companies incentives to lower borrowers' payments—for example, by extending the repayment period for mortgages or lowering their interest rate. In practice, the program presented huge management challenges to the Treasury. Congress demanded close oversight of participating servicers and borrowers. That was understandable, but it led to operational demands on servicers that reduced their willingness to participate. And extensive documentation requirements dissuaded many borrowers from applying. In its first year, HAMP modified only 230,000 mortgages. As Treasury gained experience, it improved and expanded the program, allowing more mortgages to be modified.* But modifications did not always avoid foreclosures. Even with tight screening standards, 46 percent of the mortgages modified in 2009 re-defaulted, as did 38 percent of the 2010 modifications. The effects of the recession on jobs and family finances left many borrowers unable to make even moderate monthly payments.

Other than through our supervision of some lenders, housing fell largely outside the Fed's jurisdiction. Nevertheless, we saw it as a critical factor in the recovery and jumped into the debate. In a white paper released in January 2012, we offered suggestions for improving the administration's programs. We also analyzed alternative foreclosure-prevention strategies, such as onetime reductions in the amounts that borrowers owed, and we promoted alternatives to foreclosure such as short sales, in which lenders permit borrowers to discharge their debt by selling their homes for less than the loan amount. (A short sale is less costly than a foreclosure for both borrower and lender, and better for the surrounding neighborhood because the home doesn't sit vacant.)

Though we viewed our paper as constructive and even-handed, it drew strong criticism from several members of Congress. Senator Orrin Hatch of Utah, the senior Republican on the Senate Finance Committee, complained that we had intruded into fiscal policy. I don't regret putting out the paper. Not all foreclosures are avoidable, but many are, and reducing unnecessary foreclosures—as difficult as it can be—has many benefits, and not just for the borrowers and lenders themselves. The glut of foreclosed properties was an important rea-

* By late 2014, total modifications under HAMP would reach 1.4 million.

son for housing's slow recovery and, consequently, the economy's. But the reaction certainly showed that foreclosure prevention was as much politics as policy. Feelings ran strong, both among those who wanted more generous programs and those who believed the programs were already too generous.

In another chastening experience, we would learn firsthand the practical difficulties of addressing foreclosure problems. One of the appalling crisis-era mortgage practices involved "robo-signing," when servicing company employees signed millions of foreclosure documents (as if they were robots) without properly reviewing them. In 2011 and early 2012, the Fed and the Office of the Comptroller of the Currency ordered sixteen mortgage servicers, who together serviced more than two-thirds of all mortgages, to hire independent consultants to review every foreclosure initiated, pending, or completed in 2009 and 2010. Servicers would have to compensate borrowers who had been subjected to robo-signing and other unfair treatment. It soon became apparent, however, that the cost of reviewing millions of files would far outstrip the compensation paid to harmed borrowers. After many complaints from Congress and consumer advocacy groups, the Fed and the OCC stopped the process. A new system compensated borrowers based on relatively simple criteria. The goal was to achieve rough justice for borrowers without paying huge fees to consultants. Eventually, fifteen of the sixteen servicers agreed to pay $10 billion ($3.9 billion in cash and $6.1 billion in other forms of relief, including mortgage modifications). Direct payments were sent to 4.4 million borrowers.

THE RESURGENT FINANCIAL stresses emanating from Europe and the debt ceiling follies—along with long-standing headwinds such as housing—exacted an economic toll. By the end of the summer of 2011, the guarded optimism that I described at the April press conference had faded. Once again the economy looked to be approaching stall speed. We had ended QE2 at midyear as promised. I believed the program had helped create jobs and avert the deflation threat we saw in the fall of 2010. But now it was over, and FOMC participants were projecting only very slow progress toward full employment through 2013, with inflation remaining low. What else could we do?

We could start buying longer-term securities again, further expanding our balance sheet. But the FOMC's appetite for another round of full-blown quantitative easing seemed limited, at least for the moment. The criticisms of our policies were often exaggerated or unfair, particularly since we were receiving so little help from the rest of the government. But that didn't mean there weren't legitimate questions. Were our securities purchases effective? Our internal analyses suggested that they had been, but evidently not enough, on their own, to achieve an adequate pace of economic growth and job creation. Even if purchases had been effective in the past, with interest rates now so low, were we reaching the point of diminishing returns? Were credit market problems reducing the benefits of low rates?

Other questions concerned possible unwanted side effects. Besides inflation risks, FOMC participants were most concerned that additional purchases might threaten financial stability. Sheila Bair, after leaving the FDIC in July 2011, had warned that the Fed was creating a "bond bubble" by pushing down longer-term interest rates. She and others argued that artificially depressed bond yields might spike unexpectedly and send prices tumbling for existing bonds with yields that suddenly were sharply lower than yields on newly issued bonds. The resulting large and widespread losses might destabilize the financial system. We had in fact closely monitored the risks associated with a large jump in interest rates, particularly at banks and life insurance companies, both of which hold lots of bonds, and believed that they were manageable. But if the last few years had taught us anything, it was that we had to be humble about our ability to detect emerging threats to financial stability.

WITH SUBSTANTIAL NEW securities purchases and balance sheet expansion unlikely to win the Committee's support in the near term, it was once again time for blue-sky thinking. I had been discussing a wide range of monetary policy options internally since the previous summer. The conversations continued through 2011 and into 2012. I mentioned some ideas in public remarks, but many saw the light of day only in staff meetings and memos.

In my Jackson Hole speech in 2010, I had raised the possibility of reducing the interest paid on bank reserves from 1/4 percent to zero—or even slightly below zero. In effect, that would require banks to pay for the privilege of letting their liquid funds sit idle at the Fed rather than lending them out. But cutting the rate paid on reserves to zero likely would reduce market short-term interest rates by only a very small amount, perhaps between 0.10 percent and 0.15 percent. I had no strong objections to trying it; perhaps it would signal to the market that we were prepared to do whatever we could to aid the recovery. However, there were good arguments against the step. It could hurt money market funds and disrupt commercial paper and other financial markets, including the federal funds market. For example, if interest rates were lowered all the way to zero (or below zero), money market funds would have difficulty recovering management costs. If, as a result, the funds began to shut down, they would have to sell their commercial paper, closing an important channel of funding for that market.

I also considered pegging interest rates on securities with two-year maturities or less. We could do that by buying and selling those securities at the rates we chose to target. This step would powerfully signal our commitment to keep rates low for at least two years. However, to make this work we might be forced to buy enormous amounts of securities. Our balance sheet might balloon out of control, a risk we were not willing to take—at least not yet.

We looked at starting a "funding for lending" program that would provide cheap financing to banks that agreed to increase their lending to small and medium-sized businesses. The Bank of England and the British Treasury would adopt such a program in July 2012. The idea of jump-starting credit for smaller businesses was appealing. (Sarah

Raskin was a particularly strong proponent.) But U.S. banks had little interest in a funding-for-lending program. Unlike British banks, they had access to all the cheap funding they could use and saw few opportunities that they were not already pursuing to lend profitably to small businesses.

A more radical idea, supported by many academics, was called nominal GDP (gross domestic product) targeting. I had discussed it with Don Kohn, Janet Yellen, and Bill Dudley before launching QE2 in 2010.* Under nominal GDP targeting, the central bank no longer has a fixed inflation target. Instead, when growth is strong, it shoots for lower inflation. When growth is weak, it seeks higher inflation. In 2011, with growth quite slow, nominal GDP targeting would have suggested a temporary inflation goal of 3 or 4 percent or even more.

Fundamentally, nominal GDP targeting seeks to change public expectations of how the central bank will behave in the future and thereby affect asset prices and interest rates in the present. In 2011, for instance, the adoption of nominal GDP targeting would have implied that the Fed was committed to keeping short-term interest rates low for a very long time, and perhaps to undertaking additional asset purchases as well, even as inflation rose. If markets believed that commitment, they would bid down longer-term interest rates right away, thus supporting current economic growth.

The full FOMC would discuss nominal GDP targeting at its November 2011 meeting. We considered the theoretical benefits of the approach, but also whether it was desirable, or even feasible, to switch to a new framework at a time of great economic uncertainty. After a lengthy discussion, the Committee firmly rejected the idea. I had been intrigued by the approach at first but came to share my colleagues' reservations about introducing it at that time. Nominal GDP targeting is

---

* Nominal gross domestic product, or nominal GDP, is the dollar value, unadjusted for inflation, of the goods and services produced in the domestic economy. Growth in nominal GDP is the sum of output growth and inflation.

complicated and would be very difficult to communicate to the public (as well as to Congress, which would have to be consulted). Even if we did successfully explain it, other challenges remained. For nominal GDP targeting to work, it had to be credible. That is, people would have to be convinced that the Fed, after spending most of the 1980s and 1990s trying to quash inflation, had suddenly decided it was willing to tolerate higher inflation, possibly for many years. They'd have to be convinced that future Fed policymakers would continue the strategy, and that Congress would not act to block it.

But what if we succeeded in convincing people inflation was headed higher? That outcome, too, carried risks. Would people trust that future policymakers would have the courage and competence to quash inflation later, as the strategy dictated, even if doing so risked creating a recession? If not, nominal GDP targeting could increase fear and uncertainty about future inflation. Instead of spending and investing more, as hoped, households and businesses might become cautious and spend and invest less. Then the Fed could eventually find itself in a 1970s-style predicament—without credibility and with the economy suffering from both low growth and too-high inflation.

An idea related to nominal GDP targeting, but far easier to communicate, was simply increasing our inflation target to, say, 4 percent—without the commitment inherent in nominal GDP targeting to later bring inflation very low. People and businesses would spend more now, before prices went higher—or so the theory went. My former colleague at Princeton, Paul Krugman, would advocate that approach in an April 2012 *New York Times* piece with the headline "Earth to Ben Bernanke," accompanied by a drawing of me in a space helmet, looking clueless. (I was used to personal attacks by now, but I thought this one was more than a little unfair, since the Fed under my leadership had hardly been passive.) In my 2010 Jackson Hole speech, I had rejected a higher inflation target for many of the same reasons that would cause me to pull back from nominal GDP targeting. Whatever the benefits of higher expected inflation for growth—and they can be debated—raising people's inflation expectations substantially, using only talk, is easier in theory than in practice.

Although we ultimately rejected the specific approach of nominal GDP targeting, we did not reject the general principle that shaping expectations about future policy can influence current financial conditions. We had already tried to provide policy guidance, for example, by saying in March 2009 that we expected rates to remain "exceptionally low" (in other words, near zero) for an "extended period." As a next step, I pushed the Committee to replace the fuzzy "extended period" with a more specific phrase. At the August 2011 meeting, we said in our statement that we expected our federal funds rate target to remain low "at least through mid-2013"—that is, for at least two more years. The date was consistent with FOMC members' economic forecasts and model-based analyses of when increasing rates might become appropriate. Three FOMC members—Richard Fisher, Charlie Plosser, and Minneapolis Fed president Narayana Kocherlakota—dissented, in part because they didn't think the economy needed more monetary stimulus. Plosser also believed that using a specific date would suggest that we had flipped on the autopilot and would not change our target rate in response to countervailing economic developments.

I agreed that it would have been better to tie our policy plans more directly to conditions in the economy rather than setting a date. We make our policy decisions based on what's happening in the economy, and tying our guidance to economic conditions would have given markets more insight into our thinking. But it would take time to forge agreement within the Committee about how best to do that. In any case, the change in our language seemed to work. Investors pushed out their expectations of the first short-term rate increase, resulting in lower long-term interest rates. After a while, though, as the recovery continued to disappoint, one drawback of date-based guidance became evident. As our expectation for the first rate hike moved further into the future, we were compelled to adjust our statement. After the January 2012 FOMC meeting, we said we expected exceptionally low rates "at least through late 2014," and in September 2012 we would move the date out to mid-2015.

In the meantime, we had found a way to use our balance sheet to further depress long-term interest rates—without having to expand it. In September 2011, the Committee—with Fisher, Kocherlakota, and Plosser again dissenting—decided, by the end of June 2012, to purchase $400 billion of Treasury securities with maturities of six to thirty years. Instead of financing the purchases by creating bank reserves, however, we would sell an equal amount of Treasuries that we already owned, with maturities of three years and less.

We called it the Maturity Extension Program. The press, not quite accurately, nicknamed it "Operation Twist," after a Fed program of the same name during the early 1960s. Back then, under the leadership of William McChesney Martin, the Fed bought longer-term securities and sold shorter-term securities in an attempt to "twist the yield curve"—that is, lower long-term interest rates (to stimulate spending and investment) and raise short-term rates (to protect the value of the dollar, supposedly).* This time, our goal wasn't to move short-term and long-term rates in opposite directions but to bring long rates closer to rock-bottom short rates. With so many reserves already in the banking system and our promise to hold rates at zero at least through mid-2013, we saw little danger that selling short-term securities would lead to a significant rise in short-term rates. Thus, we expected our purchases under the Maturity Extension Program to have effects similar to those of our purchases under QE2.

THE POLITICAL REACTION to the Maturity Extension Program was muted, at least compared with the reaction to QE2. In part that's because the program involved no increase in bank reserves and was not

---

* The yield curve relates yields on a given type of security—say, Treasury debt—to the term of the security. Since longer-term rates generally exceed short-term rates, the yield curve normally slopes upward.

vulnerable to the "printing money" charge. Nevertheless, on the eve of our decision, the four top Republicans in Congress released another letter criticizing our interventions. House Speaker John Boehner and Senator Minority Leader Mitch McConnell—and their deputies, Representative Eric Cantor and Senator Jon Kyl—called on us to "resist further extraordinary intervention in the U.S. economy." I wondered who or what was behind the letter, since I had reasonably good relationships with all four of the authors and was always willing to discuss the economy and the Fed's policies with them. Boehner in particular had supported my reappointment and had told me in private meetings that he was glad I had been at the Fed during the crisis.

Although the public reaction to our latest program was relatively mild, the political environment in general remained poisonous, in large part because of the ongoing contest for the 2012 Republican presidential nomination. Pandering to voters' resentment and worry, the candidates tried to top one another in attacking the Fed and me personally. Former House Speaker Newt Gingrich said he'd fire me and called me "the most inflationary, dangerous, and power-centered chairman . . . in the history of the Fed." (More mildly, the eventual nominee, Mitt Romney, said he'd "be looking for someone new.") Texas governor Rick Perry won the Fed-bashing prize. In August 2011, at a campaign event in Iowa, he called our efforts to support economic growth "almost treasonous." He added, "If the guy prints more money between now and the election, I dunno what y'all would do to him in Iowa, but we would treat him pretty ugly down in Texas."

It was hard to ignore that kind of talk, and I worried that people would be misled by the absurd claims and charges (although when I heard what Governor Perry had said, I joked with staff members, echoing Revolutionary War firebrand Patrick Henry: "If this be treason, let us make the most of it"). The criticism wasn't just from the right. The left-wing movement Occupy Wall Street, which sprang up in major cities during the fall of 2011, lambasted Wall Street bailouts, income inequality, and the lack of jobs. Its protesters camped near Federal

Reserve Banks in Boston, Chicago, New York, and San Francisco. I told the Joint Economic Committee in October that I couldn't blame the protesters for being dissatisfied. "Certainly, 9 percent unemployment and very slow growth is not a good situation," I said. I worried that the criticism would affect morale within the Fed, so I met with employees to make sure they had the information they needed to respond to questions from friends and neighbors.

Our means of combating high unemployment—stimulating demand by pushing down both short-term and long-term interest rates—got us in hot water with another politically influential group: savers. In 2007, before the crisis, retirees and other savers had been able to earn more than 5 percent on, for example, a six-month certificate of deposit. For most of the period after mid-2009, they were lucky to find a CD yielding as much as 1/2 percent. As I tried to explain at every opportunity, the fundamental reason that interest rates were low was that a weak economy can't generate healthy returns on savings and investments. True, our policies pushed rates down even further, but we were doing that to promote economic recovery. Prematurely raising rates would only delay the time when the economy had strengthened enough to provide higher returns. And surely retirees would want a healthier job market as well, if only to prevent their twenty- and thirty-something children from moving back home.

Ironically, some of the same critics who said we were hurting savers also said that our policies were making rich people richer. (Since rich people save more than everyone else, apparently we were both hurting and helping these folks.) The critics based their argument on the fact that lower interest rates tend to raise prices for assets such as stocks and houses. Wealthy people own more stocks and real estate than the nonwealthy. However, this argument misses the fact that lower interest rates also reduce the returns that the wealthy earn on their assets. The better way to look at the distributional effect of monetary policy is to compare changes in the income flowing from capital investments with the income from labor. As it turns out, easier monetary policy tends to affect capital and labor incomes fairly similarly. Most importantly in a weak economy, it promotes job creation, which especially helps the middle class.

To get our story out and explain what we were doing and why, I continued to engage as much as possible with audiences outside of Washington and Wall Street, in venues rarely used by previous Fed chairmen. In November 2011, I visited Fort Bliss, in El Paso. On a frigid airfield at 4:00 a.m., I joined the base's commanding general, Dana Pittard, in greeting 250 soldiers returning from Iraq. I also met with a group of soldiers and their families, who asked many thoughtful questions. I had the same impression I'd had in many other meetings: People were worried, and they just wanted to understand better what was happening in the economy and how it would affect them. Despite Perry's prediction, I was not at all treated ugly in Texas. I returned home feeling renewed gratitude for the sacrifices of our troops.

In March 2012, I was invited to deliver a series of lectures on the Federal Reserve to undergraduates at nearby George Washington University. It felt good to be back in a classroom. I started my lectures with the founding of the Federal Reserve. I wanted the students to understand what a central bank does and that our actions during and after the crisis, though unusual in some respects, fit the historical purpose of the institution. I did an interview with ABC's Diane Sawyer in conjunction with the lectures. We also made the lectures broadly available, posting the videos and transcripts on the Board's website. The following year, Princeton University Press published them as a book.

Later in 2012, I received an indication, of a sort, that our outreach efforts were succeeding. I was invited to attend Washington Nationals batting practice on September 7. Joe Espada, third base coach for the Nats' opponent, the Miami Marlins, asked me to sign a ball, and Jayson Werth, the Nats' hirsute six-foot-five right fielder, asked me, "So what's the scoop on quantitative easing?" I was surprised but then I recalled that Werth was playing under a seven-year, $126 million contract, which gave him some interest in financial matters. (I kept the conversation on baseball.) Two days later, Richard Fisher received much the same question when after a concert he was introduced to cellist Yo-Yo Ma.

EUROPE'S FINANCES AND economy remained a mess through 2011 and into 2012, with effects spilling over into the U.S. and world economies. The staff of the Division of International Finance, now headed by Board veteran Steve Kamin, kept us well briefed. Kamin, an MIT-trained economist, had taken over from Nathan Sheets, another MIT grad, in August 2011. For me, one of the most important developments in Europe was a change in the leadership of the European Central Bank.

Jean-Claude's term as ECB president ended on October 31, 2011, after eight years. I had acknowledged his remarkable run and thanked him publicly in August at the Jackson Hole symposium. We had worked closely together and with other central bankers to arrest the crisis. I did not agree with his support of austerity and tight money in Europe. Jean-Claude, who was not an economist by training, seemed to me to be too willing to accept the moralistic approach to macroeconomic policy advocated by many northern Europeans and too dismissive of policies aimed at raising total demand in a deep economic slump. But he was shrewd, and he excelled at the diplomacy required of him by Europe's crisis. He was highly respected in Europe and around the world.

In the United States, the selection of a new Fed chairman is relatively straightforward. The president nominates; the Senate confirms. In Europe, however, ECB presidents emerge after a murky negotiation among the leaders of the major eurozone countries. Germany, the dominant economy, naturally expected to have a substantial say—even better, to be able to select a German national. However, the most plausible German candidate, Axel Weber, the head of the German central bank, had taken himself out of the running by resigning his post there in February. He was a staunch opponent of the ECB's bond-buying program. He saw it as inappropriate and perhaps illegal central bank financing of governments.

The next most obvious choice was Mario Draghi of Italy. Soft-spoken, bespectacled, and scholarly, Mario earned his doctorate in economics from MIT, graduating two years ahead of me. (We knew each other there only in passing.) He had academic experience (as a professor at the University of Florence), market experience (as a vice chairman of Goldman Sachs), and public-sector experience (as governor of the Bank of Italy, among other posts). He also had led the Financial Stability Board (the successor to the Financial Stability Forum), which helps coordinate financial regulation among countries.

Draghi's main problem was his nationality. Germany and other northern European countries might suspect that he would take the side of the debtor countries in making monetary policy or in fiscal disputes. But he smartly courted German media and public opinion, winning Chancellor Angela Merkel's endorsement and thus the ECB presidency. I was delighted. I both counted him as a friend and saw him as a dedicated and highly qualified public servant.

Like Jean-Claude, Mario understood the ECB's special role in the European power structure. And, within the ECB, he worked persistently to build alliances and to gain support for controversial measures. However, Mario—much more than Jean-Claude—was influenced by the New Keynesian framework that serves as the leading policy paradigm in the United States. That perspective made him more willing to push for expansionary policies to help the weak European economy. Indeed, one of Mario's first actions was to reverse Jean-Claude's interest rate increases of the summer. Europe nevertheless again lapsed into recession in the third quarter of 2011.

Draghi's greater activism included ensuring that European banks had access to essentially unlimited cheap funding and pushing his colleagues for additional interest rate cuts. And, famously, in a speech on July 26, 2012, Mario bolstered market confidence and reduced pressure on weaker euro-area countries with the simple declaration that the ECB would do "whatever it takes to preserve the euro." I took that to mean that, Bagehot-style, the ECB stood ready to backstop the debt of both countries and banks in the face of investor runs. Impressively, Mario's statement was viewed as so credible that Italian and Spanish bond yields fell by about 2 percentage points by the end of 2012, without the ECB actually having to make any bond purchases. It was a marvelous example of the power of communication in central banking.

All of Mario's steps went in the right direction, but, with fiscal policy creating even more powerful headwinds than in the United States, and stronger monetary measures (such as full-blown quantitative easing) facing stiff political resistance, European recovery remained elusive.

IN 2002, I had come to the Federal Reserve Board with the goal of increasing the Fed's transparency and accountability—and, in particular, of instituting a numerical target for inflation by which the Fed's performance could be judged. A little less than ten years later, in January 2012, I finally got my wish.

During that decade, the FOMC had debated inflation targeting many times. (Betsy Duke once quipped that she would gladly accept a target if only so she wouldn't have to talk about it anymore.) By now, most FOMC participants supported, or at least did not object to, the approach. For most, Greenspan's concern—that setting an inflation target would overly constrain policy decisions—had faded. In the difficult economic environment we confronted, clear communication was more important than flexibility. A numerical inflation target would signal both our strong resistance to deflation and our commitment to resisting too-high inflation.

However, since our mandate is set by law, moving forward required that we consult Congress and the administration. I had been doing that for some time. In January 2009, as the new administration was preparing to take office, Don Kohn and I had met with Tim Geithner, Larry Summers, and Christy Romer in my office to discuss our adopting a target. They didn't resist, but they saw the idea as a low political priority. Tim subsequently gave me a chance to explain it to President

Obama in a meeting in the Oval Office. The president listened care-fully and asked good questions. He told me that the Fed should do what it believed necessary.

But my well-rehearsed arguments failed to dent the skepticism of House Financial Services chairman Barney Frank. I had explained that an inflation target, if it increased businesses' and consumers' confidence in the Fed's commitment to low inflation, would permit us to more aggressively loosen policy in support of job creation. Barney understood my logic, but he also understood the importance of politi-cal "optics." He thought that the middle of a recession was the wrong time to risk giving the impression, by setting a target for inflation but not employment, that the Fed didn't care about jobs. He would not support the change. After I reported the results of my consultations to the FOMC, we decided once again to put off any major change in our policy framework. Instead, in February 2009, we inched closer by releasing the range of Committee members' individual projections under "appropriate monetary policy" for inflation, unemployment, and economic growth "over the longer run"—defined as roughly three to five years. That would give people a pretty good idea of where we were trying to steer the economy, without our explicitly adopting a target.

By early 2011, with the economy at least somewhat stronger, I thought the time had come to consider an inflation target once again. To emphasize the consistency of the approach with our dual mandate, I proposed that we introduce the target in the context of a broader statement that would make explicit our commitment to job creation as well as inflation control. Janet Yellen led a subcommittee, which included Charlie Plosser, Charlie Evans of the Chicago Fed, and Sarah Raskin. It developed a complete but succinct statement of our policy strategy. It set an explicit inflation target of 2 percent but emphasized that the Committee would take a "balanced approach" in pursuing both price stability and maximum employment.

The term "balanced approach" reflected the reality that the Fed's employment and inflation goals can come into conflict at times—for example, when inflation is too high (calling for tighter monetary policy) but unemployment is also too high (calling for easier policy). In the past, Fed officials had been reluctant to talk about that, preferring to emphasize that low inflation tends to promote a healthy economy and job market in the long run. The new policy statement acknowledged that the two objectives, while "generally complementary," could sometimes conflict in the short run, requiring policymakers to make a trade-off. For example, if inflation was modestly above target but unemployment was very high, the Committee might choose to risk higher inflation as the price of bringing unemployment down.

I met in my office with Barney Frank, now—with Republicans controlling the House—the ranking minority member on House Financial Services. I explained our proposal, including our clear recognition of both sides of our mandate. He still wasn't completely comfortable, but, based on our long working association, he was willing to go along. It didn't hurt that in the current environment no policy conflict existed: Both the low inflation and the high unemployment we were experiencing demanded easy monetary policy. I followed up my meeting with Barney with a dozen phone calls to congressional leaders. I knew from other consultations that Republicans would be okay with the statement. Many, like Congressman Paul Ryan of Wisconsin, had long supported an explicit inflation target.

The FOMC approved the policy statement and released it after the January 2012 meeting. Dan Tarullo abstained because he wanted more explicit language about the Committee's willingness to accept inflation temporarily above target if needed to bring down unemployment. Thanks to the groundwork we had laid, and our incremental approach toward adopting an inflation target, we heard little criticism from Capitol Hill.

At the end of 2011, Barney announced that he would retire from Congress the next year. Dan Tarullo and I invited him to the Fed for a farewell lunch. Barney had been a good friend to the Fed and an effective legislator—and he was uproariously funny. Once, when he and I disagreed on a legislative tactic, and of course he was proven right, he left a message with my secretary. "Some people like to say I told you so," it read. "Fortunately, I am not one of those people."

IN THE MOVIE *Groundhog Day*, the character played by Bill Murray lives the same day over and over again. By the spring of 2012 we were beginning to feel the same about the economy. As in the earlier two years, the job market improved over the previous fall and early winter but then stalled, with unemployment plateauing a little above 8 percent. Housing remained a drag on the recovery, and although Europe seemed a little calmer, financial market volatility was also impeding growth. The headwinds were still with us.

We had estimated the unemployment rate consistent with full employment at about 5.5 percent. Despite three years of recovery, we were still far from that goal, and we weren't optimistic about the prospects for faster progress. In June 2012, FOMC participants projected that unemployment, 8.2 percent at the time, would still be above 7 percent in the fourth quarter of 2014, more than two years later. Inflation, running slightly below 2 percent, was projected to remain below target in 2014.

At the press conference following the June meeting, reporters asked several times about the apparent contradiction between our policies and our expectation of glacially slow progress toward our employment and inflation goals. If we believed our own projections, shouldn't we be doing more? I responded that we had eased policy considerably already. At that very meeting, for example, we had extended the Maturity Extension Program through the end of the year, which would result in additional purchases of $267 billion in longer-term Treasury securities, matched by sales of shorter-term Treasuries. I also repeated a point I had frequently made, that our unconventional policy tools, such as quantitative easing, involved costs and risks as well as benefits. It made sense to use unconventional tools less aggressively than more conventional tools like interest rate cuts.

My answers were not illogical, and they reasonably captured the collective view of the Committee. But I was dissatisfied. Our projections clearly showed that, without further action, reaching our goals for the economy could take years. And we couldn't count on Congress for help. In fact, congressional gridlock presented a new problem. A "fiscal cliff" loomed at the end of the year. Without legislative agreement, the federal government would reach its borrowing limit, tax cuts enacted during the Bush administration would expire, and the sequestration (automatic, across-the-board spending cuts) would begin. I concluded we had to make faster progress toward our objectives and set about building a consensus among FOMC members for doing more.

I talked and emailed with voters and nonvoters alike. All had a voice at the FOMC table and could influence their colleagues. I had a particularly intensive ongoing email correspondence with Narayana Kocherlakota, a former University of Minnesota professor who succeeded Gary Stern at the Minneapolis Fed in October 2009. A nonvoter in 2012, Narayana had opposed additional monetary stimulus as a voter the year before. He had attributed much of the labor market's troubles to businesses' difficulty in finding workers with the right skills—a problem that required more education and training, not monetary policy stimulus. I didn't think the evidence supported his view. But my basic argument to him was the simple point that had convinced me: Our progress toward our goals was too slow. So long as we thought that our tools were effective and their risks could be managed, which I did, we should do more. Ultimately, after many discussions, Narayana deserted the hawks and joined the doves—a rare example of someone willing to change his mind when confronted with compelling facts and arguments.

THAT AUGUST, my father, Philip, died. After selling the family drugstore to a chain, he and my mother, Edna, had retired to Charlotte, North Carolina, where my mother grew up and where my brother, Seth, and his family lived. My parents lived in a small house before moving to a seniors' complex. My father fell ill and, after a months-long decline, died of heart failure on August 8 in the intensive care unit of the Presbyterian Medical Center. He was eighty-five. Seth and my sister, Sharon, had sat by his bedside, comforting him by singing the Hebrew prayers and songs he knew so well. Anna and I had visited him in the hospital, but I had to go back to Washington. He died before we were able to return for another visit. Instead, we returned for the funeral. He was a good man—ethical, kind, and gentle. I deeply appreciated the condolences from many friends, and an unexpected phone call from President Obama. But I was most surprised (and also touched) by a handwritten note of sympathy from Congressman Ron Paul.

BACK IN WASHINGTON, I continued working to build a consensus for additional monetary policy action. We had done a lot, and we had thought it would be enough, but the moribund job market showed otherwise. The unemployment rate, still far too high at 8.1 percent in August, understated its weakness. That month, 12.5 million people were unemployed (5 million of them had been out of work for more than six months). An additional 8 million were working part-time but preferred full-time work, and 2.6 million wanted to work but hadn't looked recently or had given up. At Jackson Hole on August 31, stepping up the rhetoric, I called the jobs situation "a grave concern." Firming up market expectations for a third round of securities purchases, I said we would "provide additional policy accommodation as needed to promote . . . sustained improvement in labor market conditions."

Two weeks later, at the September meeting, the Committee began what would become known as QE3. We couldn't further expand the Maturity Extension Program because we were running out of the short-term securities we sold to finance it. So, we would expand our balance sheet once again by creating bank reserves to purchase $40 billion a month of mortgage-backed securities guaranteed by Fannie, Freddie, and Ginnie in addition to the continuing $45 billion in monthly Treasury purchases under the Maturity Extension Program. Even more important, we said that if we did not see "substantial improvement in the outlook for the labor market," we would continue purchasing securities and employ other policy tools.

Like Mario Draghi, we were declaring we would do whatever it takes. Unlike QE1 and QE2, when we announced the expected purchase totals in advance, QE3 would be open-ended. It was risky. Either we reached our goal of substantial labor market improvement, or we would have to declare the program a failure and stop the purchases, a step sure to rattle confidence. But the advantage of open-ended purchases was that markets and the public would know that they could count on the Fed's support as long as necessary, which we hoped would promote confidence and keep longer-term rates low. No more start and stop.

At our December meeting, we expanded QE3 by committing to purchase $45 billion a month in longer-term Treasury securities after the end of the year, when the Maturity Extension Program finished. With the $40 billion in mortgage-backed securities purchases approved in September, our balance sheet would be growing at a rate of $85 billion a month. We also recast our forward guidance once again. Instead of saying that we expected our short-term rate target to remain exceptionally low through a particular date, we introduced what we called thresholds, an idea that Charlie Evans had been floating publicly and that both Janet Yellen and Bill Dudley had advocated internally. We said that we expected the target to stay low at least as long as unemployment remained above 6-1/2 percent and that our projections for inflation during the next one to two years remained at or less than 2-1/2 percent. Importantly, these numbers were *thresholds*, not *triggers*; we were not saying that we would raise rates when unemployment hit 6-1/2 percent, but rather that we would have to see unemployment at 6-1/2 percent before we would even consider raising rates. Once again, we were saying that we would do whatever it takes.

Richmond Fed president Jeff Lacker objected to both the additional

MBS purchases and the thresholds. He was the only FOMC member to dissent, but he wasn't the only one who was nervous. I thought that we would be able to begin phasing out the purchases at some point in mid-2013, but I knew that would depend on the data (and on factors outside our control, like fiscal policy). We might be buying securities for a long time. In poker terminology, we were all in.

CHAPTER 23

Taper Capers

The midwinter sun had set by the time my guests and I gathered in the chairman's dining room, overlooking the western end of the National Mall. The Martin Building, on that chilly Thursday evening, January 17, 2013, was otherwise deserted, except for the catering staff and several security agents idling in the hallway.

Inside the dining room, an oblong table was set for eight. Through floor-to-ceiling windows, we could see the illuminated Capitol, the Washington Monument, the Jefferson Memorial, the Lincoln Memorial, and, across the Potomac River, the Pentagon. Those whose attention strayed from the predinner conversation could observe at intervals the blinking lights of descending airliners following the river to Reagan National Airport.

The occasion for the dinner was the impending departure of Tim Geithner as secretary of the Treasury. In addition to Tim, my guests included three former Treasury secretaries, Robert Rubin, Larry Summers, and Hank Paulson; two former Fed chairmen, Paul Volcker and Alan Greenspan; and a former Fed vice chairman, Don Kohn—the same group that attended my farewell dinner for Hank four years earlier.

As we mingled before sitting down to eat, Hank and Larry animatedly discussed developments in China. Both had recently returned from trips there. Volcker and Rubin chatted quietly. Paul still carried considerable influence in policy circles, as evidenced by the adoption of the Volcker rule as part of the Dodd-Frank reforms. But now, at eighty-five and remarried three years earlier, he seemed mellower and more prone to unleash his booming laugh. Rubin, seventy-four, had fought crises in Asia, Latin America, and Russia as Treasury secretary under President Clinton. He had served as mentor to both Summers and Geithner before returning to Wall Street, where he had spent most of his career. He had witnessed the most recent crisis as a senior adviser at Citigroup.

I caught up with Tim and Don. Don seemed happy with his post-Fed activities, which included a position at the Brookings Institution (a nonprofit policy research organization in Washington) and membership on a committee at the Bank of England charged with preserving financial stability. Don had never headed an agency or cabinet department, but his presence raised no eyebrows. He had been in government longer than anyone else in the room and had been an indispensable adviser to both Greenspan and me.

Greenspan arrived late. He said he had been held up by appointments. At eighty-six, he shuffled rather than strode, but in other respects he had not slowed down. Along with his active social life and occasional tennis game, he continued to run his consulting business and was working on a new book.

Over steak and potatoes, we toasted Tim. The guest of honor was upbeat, telling stories and cracking jokes. I could never decide whether Tim's dry sense of humor was a defense mechanism or whether he was as truly immune as he seemed to the stress and criticism that came with his high-profile jobs. If his casual indifference was an act, it was convincing. Although he still looked remarkably youthful, Tim had been in public service since 1988, when he joined the international staff of the Treasury Department. After nearly four challenging years at the head of the department, he had been hinting none too subtly for months that he was ready to leave. President Obama had persuaded him to remain until the end of the first term, but Tim felt that it would be unfair to his family to stay into the second term, and Obama had acquiesced.

Despite the lively conversation, in some respects it was an awkward gathering, colored by complicated personal relationships, strong egos, differences in policy views—and a lot of history. Volcker and Rubin, and to a significant extent Greenspan, were uncomfortable with many of the policies that the Fed pursued during and after the financial crisis. (I remembered a tense lunch with Rubin in the same dining room, when he had tried to dissuade me from pursuing quantitative easing.) Larry had been critical of some of our actions as well, at least within the confines of the White House. But we shared a bond formed of common experience. Differences notwithstanding, we each had felt the satisfaction of being able at times to have a positive effect on the world.

Government policymaking at the highest levels involves long hours and near-constant stress, but it is exciting to feel part of history, to be doing things that matter. At the same time, we all knew the frustrations of struggling with extraordinarily complex problems under unrelenting public and political scrutiny. Rapidly changing communications technologies—first, twenty-four-hour cable television, then blogs and Twitter—seemed not only to have intensified the scrutiny but also to have favored the strident and uninformed over the calm and reasonable, the personal attack over the thoughtful analysis. In a world of spin and counterspin, we all knew what it was to become a symbol of a moment in economic history—to serve as an unwilling avatar of Americans' hopes and fears, to become a media-constructed caricature that no one who knew us would ever recognize.

But that's the baggage that comes with consequential policy jobs, as we all knew too well. The deepest frustration we shared, it soon became clear, was not with the baggage but with government dysfunction itself. The founders had designed a system to be deliberative; instead, it was paralyzed. Too often, the system promoted showboating, blind ideology, and malice. Nothing productive could be done, it seemed, until all the wrong approaches were tried first. Those around the table who had served in the 1980s and 1990s assured the rest of us that nasty politics and government gridlock were as old as the republic. Rubin talked about the debt ceiling and budget battles of his era. They bore a striking resemblance to recent fiscal fights.

As the dinner wound down, I joked that I would soon become the last of the group still drawing a government paycheck. Afterward, my security team and I dropped Larry Summers off at his hotel. He had left his White House position two years earlier and now his not-so-secret ambition was to be chairman of the Fed after my departure. In response to my questions, he said he supported current monetary policy, including the hundreds of billions of dollars of securities purchases we were making under QE3. I didn't know who would succeed me, but it was important to me that he or she continue our policies.

In a meeting in the Oval Office on February 5, I would repeat to the president what I had told him when he renominated me in 2009: I did not want to be considered for another term as chairman when my current term ended in January 2014. More than a decade in the Washington pressure cooker was enough. The president said that he understood. We talked briefly about possible replacements. He told me that his candidates were Summers, Janet Yellen, and Don Kohn, and he asked my opinion. I didn't want to influence his choice too much, since my support for any one candidate could easily be misrepresented as opposition to another. I told the president what I believed—that all three were very well qualified and would likely continue the Fed's current monetary policies.

GOVERNMENT DYSFUNCTION WAS on everyone's minds at Tim's farewell dinner because the federal government had, weeks earlier, teetered on the edge of the fiscal cliff—the nickname given a confluence of fiscal deadlines occurring at the end of 2012. (I was credited with inventing the phrase when I used it in congressional testimony a year earlier—but others had used it before in other contexts.) On December 31, absent action from Congress, the federal government would reach its borrowing limit, tax cuts enacted during the Bush administration would expire, and the sequestration would begin. Falling off the cliff would have dealt a huge blow to the recovery.

At the last moment, Congress and the administration managed to avert some of the worst outcomes. On January 2, President Obama signed legislation postponing the sequestration until March 1 and extending the Bush tax cuts for all but top earners. On the other hand, the temporary cut (2 percentage points) in the Social Security payroll tax that Americans had enjoyed for the past two years was allowed to expire. The debt ceiling was reached, but Treasury, as it had in past standoffs, employed accounting tricks to allow the government to keep paying its bills for a while longer.

Although the worst was avoided, the net effect of all the budget brinkmanship was a powerful increase in the strength of the fiscal headwind. The tax increases and spending cuts that did go into effect were likely to be a significant restraint on demand, and the uncertainty generated during the standoff (as well as the prospect of more brinkmanship) weighed on business and consumer confidence. The nonpartisan Congressional Budget Office would later estimate that fiscal measures in 2013 would lop 1.5 percentage points off economic growth in 2013—growth we could ill afford to lose.

Tim's last day as Treasury secretary was January 25. Legislation enacted on February 14 suspended the debt ceiling until May 18, giving Tim's successor, Jack Lew, a little breathing room to work out a longer-term deal with Congress. Jack, sworn in on February 28, was a bright, savvy attorney with long and varied experience inside and outside government. He had served in the Clinton administration as director of the Office of Management and Budget (among other roles) and in the Obama administration, again as OMB director and then as White House chief of staff. In between, he had worked as vice president for operations at New York University and as a senior executive at Citigroup. I would meet regularly with Jack over breakfast or lunch, as I had with his predecessors—John Snow, Hank, and Tim. Jack's reputation was as a fiscal expert, but he also knew a lot about financial markets and financial regulation. We quickly developed a good working relationship.

I DELIVERED THE Board's usual twice-a-year report to Congress at a Senate Banking Committee hearing on February 26. Monetary policy accommodation continued at full throttle, following our declaration in December that we would buy $85 billion in securities each month until the labor market outlook improved substantially. To me, the need for continuing with these purchases remained clear. Since bottoming out three years earlier, payrolls had grown by about 6 million jobs, but we were still more than 2 million jobs short of the level of employment before the crisis (a comparison that ignored subsequent population growth). The unemployment rate remained high—7.9 percent in January—and 12.3 million Americans were unable to find work. More than a third of them had been without a job for six months or more.

I felt a sense of urgency—the economy must make faster progress or many of the long-term jobless might never return to work—and I also felt frustrated that fiscal policymakers, far from helping the economy, appeared to be actively working to hinder it. "Monetary policy . . . cannot carry the entire burden," I told senators. True, Congress had made progress toward reducing the federal budget deficit—a positive development, all else equal. However, from my perspective they were looking at the problem the wrong way. As I had been arguing for some time, the most serious threats to fiscal sustainability were some years down the road, tied in large part to the aging of the population and rising health-care costs. We needed to improve the cost-effectiveness of American health care and ensure the solvency of key benefit programs, like Social Security. We also needed to increase productivity and economic growth, which would allow us to better afford the costs of an aging society. But lawmakers had avoided tackling those critical long-run issues in favor of near-term spending cuts and tax increases that weakened the already weak economy.

I didn't say it at the hearing, but I was also wondering how much longer the FOMC would support the ultra-accommodative monetary policy needed to offset the fiscal (and other) headwinds. The vote at the most recent meeting, on January 29–30, had been 11–1 in favor of continuing our policies, with Kansas City Fed president Esther George (taking up where her predecessor Tom Hoenig had left off) the only dissenter. But the vote didn't capture the extent of the concern and skepticism on the Committee. As everyone (including me) appreciated, the latest round of asset purchases was a gamble. I believed that the more open-ended approach of QE3 would prove more powerful at spurring growth and job creation than our previous efforts. But what if the economy stalled yet again, perhaps for reasons outside our control, such as fiscal stringency at home or a resurgence of the European crisis? We could find ourselves buying large quantities of securities for quite a while, a prospect that made many of my colleagues uneasy. I was particularly concerned that I could lose the support of three Board members: Jeremy Stein, Jay Powell, and Betsy Duke. Cleveland Fed president Sandra Pianalto, who was not a voter in 2013, also had concerns. Jeremy and Jay had joined the Board in May 2012 after the now standard confirmation delay in the Senate. Their swearing-in had brought the Board to full strength for the first time in six years.

I had been enthusiastic about their appointment. They would both help shore up the Board's financial expertise, which had been diminished by the departure of Kevin Warsh. Jeremy, a Harvard economist specializing in finance, had served as an adviser at both the Treasury and the White House during the early months of the Obama administration. I knew him and his work well. As the economics department chair at Princeton, I had tried to recruit him to the faculty. Jay, a Treasury undersecretary in the first Bush administration, had gone on to become a partner at the Carlyle Group investment firm. He was a Republican (the president had paired him with Stein, a Democrat, to increase the odds of Senate confirmation) but certainly no Tea Partyer. After leaving Carlyle he had joined the Washington-based Bipartisan Policy Center, where in 2011 he had worked effectively behind the scenes to educate legislators about the risks of failing to increase the debt ceiling. He had a reputation as a moderate and a consensus builder.

Jay and Jeremy, having arrived at the Board at the same time, spent a lot of time together, and I often met with them jointly. They both wanted to be supportive, but neither was entirely comfortable with our easy monetary policy and our growing balance sheet. Jeremy talked about his concerns in a series of speeches that received substantial media attention. He was particularly worried that our securities purchases could stoke excessive risk taking in financial markets. It was not a new argument, but Jeremy made it in more detail and in a particularly sophisticated way. He acknowledged the merit of my long-held view that the first and best line of defense against financial instability should be targeted regulatory and supervisory policies, not monetary policy. But he did not want to rely only on regulation and supervision. Financial risks could be hard to detect, he argued, and only higher interest rates could "get into all the cracks," as he put it, and reduce the incentives for excessive risk taking wherever it might occur. I agreed that higher interest rates could get into all the cracks, in the sense of their affecting a wide range of financial and economic decisions; it was for that very reason that using this tool to cure a perceived problem in financial markets risked creating ills for the broader economy.

Jay expressed his concerns mostly within the Fed, as did Betsy. Sandy, like Jeremy, spoke about her concerns in public remarks. The four were by no means hawks; they agreed that the recovery still needed substantial help from monetary policy. But they worried about the implications of our burgeoning balance sheet for financial stability, for our ability to exit our easy policies in the future, and for the political risks to the Fed if losses on our holdings meant that we couldn't pay remittances to the Treasury for a while.

The Fed is normally very profitable, since we typically earn a higher interest rate on our Treasury and mortgage-backed securities than we pay on the bank reserves that finance our holdings (1/4 percent at the time), and we pay nothing on the portion of liabilities represented by outstanding currency. After subtracting our operating expenses, we remit our profits to the Treasury, in turn reducing the federal deficit. Our remittances during and after the crisis were in fact exceptionally high—far higher than before the crisis—reflecting not only our larger securities holdings but also the profits we earned from our lending programs. But at some point a strengthening economy and rising inflation pressures would presumably force us to raise short-term interest rates. It was possible to end up temporarily paying more interest on banks' reserves than we earned on the securities we held, which in turn might lead to several years in which we had little or no profits to remit to the Treasury. We thought that outcome was unlikely, but we were up-front about the risk. I spoke about it in press conferences and congressional testimony, and we released a staff study that examined a range of scenarios for our remittances.

Of course, profit is not the point of monetary policy. When interest rates started rising, it likely would mean our policies were working and the economy finally was growing strongly and producing jobs. The public benefit of a stronger economy and more jobs would far outweigh any temporary effect of lower Fed profits on the federal budget. Moreover, as a side benefit, a stronger economy would improve the government's fiscal position—by increasing tax revenues, for example. That effect likely would more than offset any decline in our remittances. Still, despite these arguments, we knew we would have a political and public relations problem if our payments to the Treasury stopped for a time and we were still paying interest to banks, many of them foreign-owned. It was not a reason to make the wrong policy choices, but it was another source of concern.

Because they all had permanent votes on the FOMC, I couldn't afford to lose the support of the three Board members—the "three amigos," as Michelle Smith dubbed them. I needed to find a way to reassure them that our securities purchases would not continue indefinitely. As Jay told me, we needed an "off-ramp." There was already something of an off-ramp in the FOMC statement. It said we intended to take into account "the likely efficacy and costs" of the purchases. In other words, if we concluded that the program simply wasn't working, or if it was creating excessive risks, we would stop buying securities, even if we hadn't reached our goal of jump-starting the job market. Partly to accommodate the three amigos, I continued to highlight the potential risks of our unconventional policies, including in my Humphrey-Hawkins testimony on February 26. I made clear that I thought the benefits of our securities purchases had so far outweighed the risks. But, by drawing attention to the potential downsides of the program, I hoped to reassure the public as well as uneasy colleagues that we were not on autopilot and would throttle back if necessary.

I expected a thorough discussion of the efficacy, costs, and risks of continuing QE3 at the next FOMC meeting in March. As the meeting approached, I worked to keep everyone on board. I met with all the Board members. Unusually, I also gave Jay, Jeremy, and Betsy the opportunity to comment on the opening remarks I planned for the March news conference. I told them that while my view on securities purchases differed from theirs, I would do my best to accommodate their preferences. "My position as Chairman is untenable if I don't have the support of the Board," I told them. I said I expected that we would be able to slow our purchases by September, and possibly by June.

Meanwhile, journalists and traders speculated feverishly on when "tapering" would begin. That was the term the press had affixed to a strategy that involved gradual reductions in our securities purchases rather than a sudden stop. Though I had used it, I didn't particularly like it, and I tried to encourage others on the FOMC to use alternatives. "Tapering" implied that, once we had begun slowing purchases, we would reduce them along a predetermined glide path. Instead, I wanted to convey that the pace of purchases could vary, depending on the speed of progress toward our labor market objective and on whether the risks of the purchases were starting to outweigh the benefits. As usual, though, I had little influence on the terminology the press chose to use.

Whatever the strategy was called, communicating it clearly would be crucial. I very much wanted to avoid a repeat of the missteps made in preparing markets for a shift toward tighter monetary policy in 1994. Under Chairman Greenspan, the FOMC had cut the federal funds rate target sharply during and after the 1990–1991 recession. Then, after leaving the target unchanged for nearly a year and a half, policymakers began in February 1994 to nudge the rate higher amid early signs of overheating in the economy. Greenspan had tried to warn markets of the coming policy shift, but long-term rates reacted much more sharply than the Committee anticipated—with the yield on ten-year Treasury notes jumping from 5.6 percent in early January to 7.5 percent in early May. Evidently investors saw the Fed's February rate hike as the beginning of a much more rapid series of increases than the policymakers themselves envisioned. The FOMC at the time worried that the unexpected spike in long-term rates would slow the economy too much.

It worked out in the end. Greenspan achieved a soft landing that enabled the economy to continue growing, with low inflation. The 1990s turned out to be the longest expansion in U.S. history, and Alan, at least for a time, became the Maestro. But the ride had been bumpy. Now, nearly twenty years later, I hoped that the communication techniques we had developed—such as the unemployment and inflation thresholds for the first rate increase—would enable us to do better.

After the March meeting, between the statement approved by the Committee and my remarks at the press conference, the message I wanted to send seemed to get through—we were seriously discussing how to wind down our purchases, but we weren't ready to start. Or as the next day's *Wall Street Journal* headline put it: "Fed Not Ready to Tighten Policy—Yet." I knew that I had a delicate balancing act to perform. The center of the FOMC, including my three wavering Board members, was looking for a slowing of purchases sometime around midyear. Based on media reports and our surveys of securities firms, it appeared that many in the markets expected and hoped for a much later start. My job was to try to bring those differing expectations closer together, while continuing a policy that supported the recovery.

Our objective at the April 30–May 1 meeting was much the same as in March—to communicate that the economy wasn't quite ready for us to dial back our purchases but that the time was coming. The economy was growing moderately, helped by solid consumer spending (which in turn was helped by a decline in gasoline prices) and by rising housing construction. However, as we had feared, federal spending during the first three months of the year was already declining markedly, even before the full force of the sequestration hit. In our statement, we tried to convey our flexibility and reinforce the message that our future actions would depend on how the economy evolved. We said, "The Committee is prepared to *increase or reduce* [italics added] the pace of its purchases to maintain appropriate policy accommodation as the outlook for the labor market or inflation changes."

However, investors evidently heard only the "increase" part of the new phrase and inferred that the Committee was actively considering stepping up the pace of purchases. Stocks rallied moderately over the next three weeks. Market expectations for the future of QE3 were now less, rather than better, aligned with the expectations of most on the Committee.

I corrected the message, but sloppily, on May 22. In my opening statement to a Joint Economic Committee hearing that morning, I warned, "A premature tightening of monetary policy . . . would . . . carry a substantial risk of slowing or ending the economic recovery." I was pushing back against the views of hawks, inside and outside the Fed, who wanted to bring our securities purchases to a rapid conclusion. I wasn't trying to signal that we'd continue purchasing at the current pace forever. In fact, I didn't see a modest reduction in the rate of growth of our balance sheet as tightening; we'd still be easing monetary conditions, only less aggressively.

A short while after delivering my opening statement, in response to a question, I said, "We could in the next few meetings . . . take a step down in our pace of purchases." That afternoon, we released the minutes of the April 30–May 1 meeting. They revealed that some FOMC participants "expressed willingness to adjust the flow of purchases downward as early as the June meeting."

The market seesawed on what it perceived as mixed messages, though the statements, considered in their full context, were consistent. Stock prices rose on my prepared testimony, pared their gains on my comments during the question-and-answer session, and fell after the release of the minutes. The message that QE3 couldn't go on forever seemed, finally, to be sinking in. But the communications bumps reminded me of my rookie-season attempt to end a monetary tightening cycle in 2006 and renewed my appreciation of the difficulties encountered by Greenspan at the start of the 1994 tightening. They also reminded me of a story Dallas Fed president Richard Fisher included in one of his speeches about the early nineteenth-century French diplomat Talleyrand and his archrival, Prince Metternich of Austria. When Talleyrand died, Metternich was reported to have said, "I wonder what he meant by that?" It seemed that no matter what I said or how plainly I said it, the markets tried to divine some hidden meaning.

AFTER THE JOINT ECONOMIC COMMITTEE episode, I turned to a communications task I enjoyed far more than appearing at press conferences and congressional hearings. I traveled to two familiar places to deliver commencement remarks—Simon's Rock College and Princeton University. Our son, Joel, had graduated from Simon's Rock in 2006 and in 2013 was graduating from the Weill Cornell Medical College. Anna served on the Simon's Rock Board of Overseers.

I spoke there on May 18, a beautiful, sunny day, aware that, even though the recovery was now four years old, the graduates faced a tough job market. I tried to look ahead by decades rather than quarters, and to rebut economists who contended that the advanced economies were doomed to subpar growth for a long time. I told the graduates, "Both humanity's capacity to innovate and the incentives to innovate are greater today than at any other time in history." In short, I tried to convince them that New York Yankees Hall of Famer Yogi Berra was wrong when he said that the future ain't what it used to be. I had some fun with the Princeton remarks on June 2, offering the graduates ten suggestions in lieu of ten commandments. "Life is unpredictable," I told them, thinking of both my own career path and the economy and financial system's roller-coaster ride over the past seven and a half years. I also gave them a working definition of my chosen profession: "Economics is a highly sophisticated field of thought that is superb at explaining to policymakers precisely why the choices they made in the past were wrong. About the future, not so much."

Throughout my time as chairman, I was always happy to speak with teachers and students (whether privileged Ivy Leaguers, undergraduates at a historically black college, or adults returning to community college) and to affirm the importance of lifelong education. It wasn't just because Anna and I were both educators. Sound monetary policy, I knew, can support a healthy economy—but it can't create one. In the long run, the economy's ability to produce a rising standard of living for future generations depends on people having opportunities to acquire both economically valuable skills and the perspective that comes from a broad education. Nothing else matters as much.

ON JUNE 19, two and a half weeks after the Princeton baccalaureate ceremony, I sat in my office after my latest post-FOMC press conference. The elms along Constitution Avenue were in full summer leaf, but I wasn't looking out the window. Instead, I watched the sharp swings in the stock and bond markets playing out in jagged red lines on my Bloomberg terminal. In what became known as "the taper tantrum," ten-year Treasury yields and the dollar exchange rate were spiking, while the Dow was sinking. The possible economic consequences were troubling: If long-term interest rates continued to rise and stock prices continued to fall, it would damp investment and consumer demand, while a rising dollar would discourage export sales of U.S. goods.

At the just-concluded meeting, the FOMC had affirmed continuing securities purchases at the pace of $85 billion per month. But many around the table also wanted to lay the groundwork for our eventual exit from the program. To accommodate them, I described at the press conference a tentative, data-dependent path for winding down the purchases. We could moderate them "later this year," I said, if our forecasts predicted continuing improvement in labor markets and if inflation (running at about a 1 percent rate so far in 2013) was moving back toward our 2 percent target. After that, if all went well, we would continue to reduce our purchases in what I called "measured steps," ending around the middle of 2014. At that point, the unemployment rate, at 7.6 percent in May, would likely be around 7 percent, based on our projections. Unemployment of 7 percent, while not our ultimate goal, would represent a substantial improvement relative to the 8.1 percent rate in August 2012, when markets first started anticipating QE3. I thought it was important, if possible, that we end the purchases only when we could legitimately say they had achieved their purpose.

In an attempt to blunt any market overreaction to the prospect of moderating our purchases, I had stressed at the press conference a point that had been included in FOMC statements since December—that we expected to keep monetary policy very accommodative (in other words, keep the federal funds rate target near zero) for a "considerable time" after our securities purchases ended. Finally, to alleviate any market anxiety that we might be inclined, after completing our purchases, to quickly reverse course and shrink our balance sheet, I reported that a strong majority of the FOMC now expected we would hold on to our mortgage-backed securities until they matured, rather than selling them.

I had known that any discussion of reducing purchases would likely produce at least a mildly negative reaction in the markets, but I had thought—based on the New York Fed's surveys of securities firms—that the path I laid out was close to what markets expected. I even hoped that, by reducing uncertainty, we might produce a small positive reaction. Generally, I wasn't greatly concerned about short-term market fluctuations, but the movements on my Bloomberg screen after the press conference were not what I had expected. If the trends persisted, it would amount to an unintended tightening of monetary conditions.

What explained markets' strong reaction—and why did it surprise us? In retrospect, I think our view of market expectations was too dependent on our survey of securities dealers. Futures markets gave us a reliable read of where markets thought the federal funds rate was going—but not for our securities purchases. For that, economists at the New York Fed asked their counterparts at the securities firms, who paid careful attention to every nuance of Fed policymakers' public statements. In effect, our PhD economists surveyed their PhD economists. It was a little like looking in a mirror. It didn't tell us what the rank-and-file traders were thinking. Many traders, apparently, didn't pay much attention to their economists and were betting our purchases would continue more or less indefinitely. Some called it "QE-ternity" or "QE-infinity." Their assumption was unreasonable and entirely inconsistent with what we had been saying. Nevertheless, some investors had evidently established market positions based on it. Now, like Metternich, they looked at our statements about securities purchases and asked, "What do they mean by that?" Their conclusion, despite the plain meaning of what I said at the press conference, was that we were signaling an earlier increase in our federal funds rate target. They sold their Treasury securities and mortgage-backed securities, driving up long-term interest rates.

We mobilized to correct markets' mistaken impressions. I conferred with Jeremy Stein and Jay Powell by email and, on June 24, met with them over lunch. My next speech wasn't till July 10, but both Bill Dudley and Jay had public appearances scheduled on June 27 and Jeremy had a speech on June 28, so they could begin clarifying our policy plans. Ten-year Treasury yields and, more importantly, thirty-year mortgage rates had jumped around a half of a percentage point in the week since the meeting, a threat to home sales and construction. The Dow Jones industrial average had fallen nearly 4 percent, and the exchange value of the dollar had risen close to 3 percent. Emerging-market economies were also suffering as investors, anticipating they could earn higher interest rates in the United States, pulled their money out.

In their speeches, Bill and Jay stressed that we would not pare our securities purchases if we thought that would hurt the economy. "If the performance of the economy is weaker, the Committee may delay before moderating purchases or even increase them," Jay said. Bill explained that if labor market conditions fell short of the FOMC's outlook, "I would expect that asset purchases would continue at a higher pace for longer." Jeremy said that our policy stance hadn't fundamentally changed. In response to a question at my July 10 speech, in Boston, I stressed that any gradual downshift in securities purchases should not be confused with tighter monetary policy in the form of an increase in short-term rates. "The overall message is accommodation," I said. Our remarks helped. Mortgage rates and long-term Treasury rates eased a bit and stocks recovered somewhat. But markets remained jumpy.

UNFORTUNATELY, THE TAPER tantrum wasn't the only controversy that summer. At my June news conference, Ylan Mui of the *Washington Post* asked me about remarks made by President Obama, aired on PBS two days earlier. Obama had told interviewer Charlie Rose that "Ben Bernanke's done an outstanding job." He added, "He's already stayed a lot longer than he wanted or he was supposed to." This comment may have reflected the president's recollections of my mixed feelings at taking a second term and my determination to leave at the end of eight years. I ducked Ylan's question, as I had been ducking questions about my replacement since the previous summer, when Republican presidential candidates had tried to outdo each other in saying how quickly they would fire me. (For the record, unlike cabinet secretaries in the executive branch, the Fed chairman can't be removed from office without cause.)

I would have liked to answer Ylan's question, if only to avoid the false impression that I was being nudged from office. To the contrary, the president had given me no reason to think that he was dissatisfied or that his opinion of me now was any different from the one he had held when he reappointed me. Still, I avoided saying anything publicly about my plans on the advice of Michelle Smith and Dave Skidmore, who held to the tried-and-true practice that policymakers should avoid lame duck status as long as possible.

Speculation about who would succeed me reached fever pitch that summer. Most of the focus was on Larry and Janet. But others mentioned publicly included Don Kohn, Roger Ferguson, my Princeton colleague Alan Blinder, and my old thesis adviser at MIT, Stanley Fischer, who was finishing eight years as governor of Israel's central bank. I was unhappy with the White House's management of the process. The president and his advisers let speculation drag on week after week, to the point where I believed it threatened to damage the candidates' reputations and perhaps even create uncertainty about the course of monetary policy. For Janet, the circus was difficult and distracting, but she continued to focus on her work. Larry, despite his close relationship with the president and his acknowledged brilliance, had some important vulnerabilities, including a history of rubbing intellectual and political opponents the wrong way. As time passed without an announcement, it seemed to me that Janet was becoming the odds-on favorite. Larry's prospects suffered a fatal blow in late July when a third of the Senate's fifty-four Democrats, many in the party's liberal wing, signed a letter supporting Janet. Because the president could expect little Republican support for his nomination, he couldn't afford to lose Democrats.

The chairmanship wasn't the only impending personnel change at the Fed that summer. On July 11, Betsy Duke announced that she would resign from the Board at the end of August, after five eventful years. She mentioned that it had been her ambition to serve at the Federal Reserve long enough to see what normal times were like (she had joined the Board a little more than a month before Lehman), but that she had given up hope. Sarah Raskin, only the eighth woman to serve on the Board in its hundred-year history, on July 31 became the first woman nominated to serve as deputy Treasury secretary. Sandra Pianalto, president of the Cleveland Fed since 2003, announced on August 8 that she would retire early in 2014. I appreciated Sandy's constructive, low-ego approach through the years. She listened carefully—to her colleagues on the FOMC, and also to the businesspeople, bankers, and community leaders in her district. Like Jeremy, Jay, and Betsy, she had had reservations about large-scale asset purchases. But rather than making a splash by dissenting, she worked to persuade Committee members through thoughtful, low-key arguments. She expressed her views in speeches, but without the provocative rhetoric that Tom Hoenig had employed in 2010.

The central banking cast was changing internationally as well in 2013. Masaaki Shirakawa had stepped aside in March after five years as governor of the Bank of Japan. He had been a good colleague, cerebral and constructive. He had worked hard to help Japan's economy recover from the 2011 earthquake and tsunami. But he was also cautious and conservative, perhaps reflecting his long career at the Japanese central bank before becoming governor. His successor, Haruhiko Kuroda, the president of the Asian Development Bank and an outsider at the Bank of Japan, was seen as more in tune with the stimulative "Abenomics" policies of Prime Minister Shinzo Abe. According to press reports, he was expected to adopt more "Bernanke-like" tactics, including open-ended asset purchases and other vigorous efforts to bring Japanese inflation up to a 2 percent target.

On July 1, my old MIT colleague Mervyn King ended a decade as governor of the Bank of England. (Mervyn was knighted in 2011 and was made a life peer in 2013—making him a member of Great Britain's House of Lords—so I occasionally addressed him, tongue in cheek, as Lord Sir King.) I attended farewell ceremonies for Mervyn both in London and at a dinner at the British embassy in Washington. His successor was Mark Carney, the well-regarded head of the Bank of Canada. Carney, in turn, was succeeded by Stephen Poloz, a former research chief of the central bank and head of Canada's export promotion agency.

AFTER THE TAPER tantrum, monetary policy coasted into the summer. At the July 30–31 FOMC meeting, we made few changes in our statement. In my semiannual monetary policy testimony and in other venues, I continued to draw the important tactical distinction between our securities purchases and our interest rate policy. The main goal of our purchases had been to increase the economy's near-term momentum, I said, to bring it closer to self-sustaining growth. Near-zero short-term interest rates, in turn, would support economic growth for long after the purchases ended. The plan was akin to a multistage rocket, with booster rockets launching it into space and secondary engines keeping it moving after it reaches escape velocity.

The hearings before the House Financial Services and Senate Banking committees on July 17 and 18 marked my last appearances before Congress as chairman. Many of the legislators, including some who had sharply criticized our actions, went out of their way to thank or congratulate me, particularly for the Fed's actions during the crisis. Senator Corker, a Fed ally in much of the debate over the Dodd-Frank law but a bitter opponent of quantitative easing, said, "Thank you for your service, thank you for friendship, and whatever happens I wish you well." Five months earlier, at the previous monetary policy hearing, he had accused me of "throwing seniors under the bus" with policies that had the side effect of keeping rates on savings accounts and certificates of deposit very low. I liked and respected Corker, a capable legislator, but I could never get used to the Jekyll-and-Hyde nature of politicians. At least Senator Corker, unlike many of his colleagues, usually said the same things to me both in private and in public.

The hearings roughly coincided with the third anniversary of the passage of the Dodd-Frank Act, and I updated the lawmakers on our ongoing efforts to implement it. It had been a long and painstaking process. In writing the new rules, we had to coordinate not only with other U.S. regulators but—to achieve as much international consistency as possible—with our counterparts abroad as well. On July 2, we and the other U.S. bank regulatory agencies jointly adopted bank capital requirements tougher than even the higher standards established by Basel III. Since the Fed had led the first comprehensive stress tests in early 2009, the capital levels of the big U.S. banks had more than doubled. They were in a much better position to withstand economic downturns and financial turmoil and, as a result, keep lending to households and businesses. The week after we adopted the Basel III rules, the multiagency Financial Stability Oversight Council had designated the first two nonbank systemically important financial institutions—AIG and GE Capital, the financial services subsidiary of General Electric. The designations meant that they would be supervised by the Federal Reserve.

Jack Lew had been pressing the regulatory agencies, in public speeches and in private meetings at the Treasury, to pick up the pace of writing Dodd-Frank rules. On August 19, the president summoned us to the Roosevelt Room to apply a little more moral suasion. He was particularly anxious that by the end of the year we approve the Volcker rule, which banned banking companies from trading—for their own account—many securities, derivatives, and commodity futures and options. I appreciated the president's sense of urgency, but I also wanted to get the job done right. The five agencies tasked with writing the regulations to implement the Volcker rule found it extremely challenging to distinguish permissible from impermissible trading. But we met the president's deadline, adopting the final version on December 10.

Our constant concern, in writing regulations, was to preserve financial stability without constraining credit or economic growth any more than necessary. Two years earlier, JPMorgan CEO Jamie Dimon had asked me at a public forum whether we had calculated the cumulative economic effect of all the new rules we were putting into place. We did as a matter of course attempt to analyze the costs and benefits of individual rules, and even groups of related rules, but I told him that a comprehensive calculation wasn't practical. My answer wasn't very satisfying, and Jamie's willingness to challenge me in public on behalf of his fellow bankers made him a short-lived hero on Wall Street. A better answer would have been to point out to Jamie the immeasurable economic and human cost of failing to write adequately tough rules and permitting a repeat of the crisis we had recently endured.

THE JULY HEARINGS were my last public speaking event before the September 17–18 FOMC meeting. The long hiatus complicated the task of setting expectations for whether we would start reducing our securities purchases. Normally, I would have used my August speech at the Kansas City Fed's Jackson Hole conference to foreshadow any forthcoming policy shifts, but I had decided to play hooky. I had wanted to skip the conference the year before, too. My niece's bat mitvah was scheduled that weekend. But Esther shifted the date of the conference for me, and I agreed to attend. In retrospect, that was a good outcome. The media might have interpreted my absence as a slap at Esther in her first year hosting the conference—a message I definitely did not want to send. Still, my concerns about the conference were broader. It had become a media circus. Moreover, I thought it unfair that one Reserve Bank out of twelve should be the permanent host and agenda-setter of what had become the Fed's flagship conference.

Instead of Jackson Hole, Anna and I went on a five-day vacation, our first since I had been forced to cancel our trip to Myrtle Beach in August 2007. We visited family in Charlotte and went, just the two of us, to Asheville, North Carolina. We toured the Biltmore Estate, the largest privately owned house in the United States, and enjoyed the gardens designed by the famed Frederick Law Olmsted, the designer of New York's Central Park. We also took in some bluegrass music at a local dive in Asheville.

I was a little worried that skipping Jackson Hole would create a communications problem, but as it turned out the economic tea leaves were mixed and I wouldn't have been able to send a clear signal in any case. Despite the economic cross-currents, as the September meeting neared, market participants seemed increasingly to expect that we would, finally, start the proverbial taper. Two-thirds of the forty-seven economists surveyed by the *Wall Street Journal* during the week before the meeting predicted action.

On the eve of the meeting, I did not think the case was nearly that clear. The unemployment rate had edged down further in August, to 7.3 percent. But job growth looked to have weakened, with payroll increases averaging only 136,000 a month in July and August. I was also concerned that financial conditions were tightening too quickly. Thirty-year mortgage rates had leapt from less than 3.5 percent in May to a bit more than 4.5 percent. Other long-term interest rates had risen, too. Meanwhile, Congress and the president appeared headed for a showdown over legislation needed to raise the debt ceiling and fund government operations after the 2014 fiscal year began on October 1. I knew from our experience in 2011 that, at best, the brinkmanship would hurt confidence and, at worst, a default on Treasury securities could create tremendous financial upheaval.

The Committee split between members favoring a modest reduction in monthly purchases, say from $85 billion to $75 billion, and members who wanted to delay. Backed strongly by Bill Dudley and Janet Yellen, I recommended that we hold off in spite of market expectations for a reduction. I noted that, in June, I had never said that we would taper in September; I had only said "later this year." But more fundamentally, the economic outlook did not yet clearly justify reducing purchases. I wanted to send a strong message that our policy would depend on the outlook for the economy and the job market. After all, standing ready to do whatever it takes had been the whole point of open-ended securities purchases. The FOMC supported my recommendation, with only Esther George dissenting, as she had all year. Jeremy Stein joined the majority but said in a speech the next week that he would have been comfortable with starting to taper right away.

After years of trying to telegraph our moves, we surprised markets by doing nothing in September. The surprise eased the very financial conditions that had caused us to hesitate, making a step down in purchases more tenable. After our announcement, long-term interest rates fell while stocks rallied. The next day, the dovish *New York Times* editorial page said we were right to stay the course on securities purchases. That didn't persuade our critics, however. The headline on the *Wall Street Journal* editorial said, "Mr. Bernanke Blinks." It accused me of "a large failure of nerve." Echoing Rick Perry's remarks of 2012, a *Financial Times* columnist called me a "taper traitor." At this point in my tenure, I didn't care about the commentary, or about bond traders' anger at being wrong-footed. I just wanted us to do the right thing.

AS IT TURNED OUT, I wasn't sorry we held our fire. The Republican-majority House and the Democratic-majority Senate soon reached an impasse on the spending bills that keep the government operating. Republicans insisted on defunding the Affordable Care Act (known as Obamacare), and Democrats, not surprisingly, refused. The federal government "shut down" on October 1. (That's not the same as, or nearly as bad as, failing to raise the debt ceiling and defaulting on government debt.) An estimated 800,000 federal employees were told to stay home. However, 1.3 million civilian employees deemed "essential" reported for work, albeit without knowing when they would be paid, and 1.4 million military personnel and 500,000 postal workers also remained on the job. The Federal Reserve, funded by earnings on our securities portfolio, remained open.

In other words, many government functions continued, though a few places with high visibility, such as the national parks, closed. (On Sunday, October 13, an angry group of aging veterans and their supporters tore down National Park Service barricades blocking their access to the World War II Memorial on the National Mall. Good for them, I thought.) I was dismayed to learn that the Labor Department's report on September employment, due out October 4, would be delayed by the shutdown. Formulating effective monetary policy requires timely information. I telephoned Thomas Perez, secretary of labor, and asked whether he could provide the report on time if the Fed found a way to pay the cost. After checking with his lawyers, he got back to me to tell me that wasn't possible.

On September 25, just before the shutdown began, the Treasury Department announced that it would soon run out of accounting maneuvers to circumvent the debt ceiling and that a default would occur on October 17. Fortunately, on October 16, Congress—once again skating uncomfortably close to the edge—agreed to legislation to suspend the debt ceiling and fund the government for the next year. The president signed the bill shortly after midnight.

IN SOME GOOD news in the midst of the shutdown, the president announced his nomination of Janet Yellen to succeed me. Three weeks earlier, Larry Summers had withdrawn his name from consideration, saying in a letter that "any possible confirmation process for me would be acrimonious and would not serve the interest of the Federal Reserve, the Administration or, ultimately, the interests of the nation's ongoing economic recovery." I was happy for Janet but sorry that the process had been so difficult and contentious.

At 2:00 p.m. on October 9, I waited with Janet, her husband, George Akerlof, and other family members in the Roosevelt Room. Valerie Jarrett, the president's senior adviser, stopped by, introduced herself, and chatted with Janet. We were soon escorted to the State Dining Room. The president had asked me if I wanted to say a few words. I said no. It was Janet's day. She stood to the president's right and I at his left, my hands clasped in front of me, listening as he called me the "epitome of calm" and thanked me for displaying "tremendous courage and creativity" in taking "bold action that was needed to avert another Depression."

The president announced Janet's nomination, lauding her as a "proven leader . . . exceptionally well-qualified . . . [and] as vice chair

. . . a driving force of policies to help boost our economic recovery." In truth, she had far more experience in Fed policymaking than I had had on taking office. In her acceptance remarks, Janet emphasized her commitment to both aspects of the Fed's dual mandate—especially, given our circumstances, to putting people back to work. "The mandate of the Federal Reserve is to serve all the American people, and too many Americans still can't find a job and worry how they will pay their bills and provide for their families," she said. "The Federal Reserve can help, if it does its job effectively." From that point forward, my mission was to ensure a smooth transition.

The FOMC's next meeting was scheduled for October 29–30. This time, traders weren't expecting us to taper—and, this time, we met their expectations. The delayed employment report for September (released more than two weeks late, on October 22) had shown the unemployment rate ticking down to 7.2 percent, but employers had added a lackluster 148,000 jobs. Besides, we were still trying to sort out the economic effects of the government shutdown that had ended only two weeks earlier. Waiting seemed the wiser course.

By the December 17–18 meeting, the conditions were in place for taking the much-anticipated step of slowing our securities purchases. By then, we had the employment reports for October and November. The unemployment rate was now down to 7 percent—reaching that level much sooner than we had anticipated—and, with a revision to September's payroll figure, job growth had averaged nearly 200,000 over the previous three months. The FOMC approved a $10 billion reduction in the monthly pace, to $75 billion. Esther George joined the majority for the first time in her tenure on the FOMC.

However, Eric Rosengren of the Boston Fed dissented, arguing that slowing securities purchases was premature. He pointed out that inflation was still running well below our 2 percent objective. To accommodate his and other FOMC members' concerns, we adjusted our forward guidance for the liftoff of the federal funds rate. We said we likely would maintain the near-zero federal funds rate target "well past the time the unemployment rate declines below 6-1/2 percent, especially if projected inflation continues to run below the Committee's 2 percent longer-run goal." The addition of the phrase "well past the time" was a signal that we would be in no rush to raise short-term interest rates, even if we continued scaling back our securities purchases. Evidently our message was received: Markets accepted our decision calmly.

THE RESERVE BANK presidents had flown into Washington earlier than usual that week so that they could attend a ceremony, held on December 16, to commemorate the upcoming one hundredth anniversary of President Wilson's signing of the Federal Reserve Act on December 23, 1913. Two former chairmen (Volcker and Greenspan), the current chairman (me), and the soon-to-be chair (Janet)—representing thirty-four continuous years of Fed leadership—sat side by side at the Board table. Familiar faces at the event included former Board members Don Kohn, Roger Ferguson, Kevin Warsh, Randy Kroszner, Mark Olson, Sue Bies, and Betsy Duke. The oldest attendee, ninety-five-year-old Dewey Daane, had been nominated to the Board by President Kennedy. Nancy Teeters, eighty-three, also attended; a Carter appointee, she had become, in 1978, the first woman on the Board. All told, sixty-two current and former FOMC members assembled in the boardroom—the largest such gathering in the institution's history.

The event offered a fitting opportunity to sum up my thoughts about the Fed as my term wound down. I noted the values that had sustained the institution since its founding, as exemplified by the professional staff that serves it even as the top policymakers come and go—the commitment to dispassionate, objective, and fact-based analysis, and the dedication to public service. At least as important as any other value, I said, "has been the Federal Reserve's willingness, during its finest hours, to stand up to political pressure and make tough but necessary decisions."

My final month in office, January 2014, provided other opportunities to look back and look ahead. I had spent a lot of time thinking analytically about the crisis and its aftermath but, until an event at the Brookings Institution on January 16, very little about the emotions I had experienced. Historian Liaquat Ahamed (author of one of my favorite books, *Lords of Finance*, about the world's leading central bankers between the two world wars) asked me whether I had had sleepless nights. Of course I had. However, as events unfolded I repressed my fears and focused on solving problems. Looking back, though, it was like being in a car wreck. "You're mostly involved in trying to avoid going off the bridge; and then later on you say, 'Oh, my God!'" I told Liaquat.

My last week in office was a mix of the familiar routines of policymaking and the unfamiliar rituals of leave-taking. I had one last FOMC meeting to conduct, on January 28–29. Earlier in the month, the Labor Department had reported an unexpectedly large drop in the unemployment rate in December, to a five-year low of 6.7 percent. We saw little reason not to reduce our monthly securities purchases by another $10 billion, to $65 billion. No one dissented for the first time since June 2011.

The delicate task of normalizing monetary policy would fall to Janet and her colleagues. Dan Tarullo and Jay Powell would stay on. Sarah Raskin, confirmed as deputy Treasury secretary, would soon leave the Board. Jeremy Stein was expected to return to Harvard at the end of his two-year leave in the middle of the year. The president, on January 10, had announced Jay's nomination to a full term on the Board, along with two new nominees: Lael Brainard, who had served as Treasury undersecretary for international affairs through the worst of the European financial turmoil, and the venerable Stan Fischer, who would replace Janet as vice chairman. Demonstrating her self-confidence, Janet had pushed the administration to nominate Stan, a choice that I strongly supported. Not every new chair would be comfortable with such a strong number two. The press promptly dubbed them "the dream team."

My FOMC colleagues feted me on the evening of the first day of the

FOMC meeting. I had presided at similar events many times but wasn't used to being on the receiving end of so many kind remarks. Janet was extraordinarily gracious. "I believe the most remarkable aspect of your achievements of the last eight years has been your courage," she said. "You faced a constant cacophony of doubts and criticisms . . . and the understanding that if these criticisms were borne out, they might echo for all of history. I never saw this affect you. You remained determined, open-minded, and creative in your effort to do what was best for the country."

In return, I tried to do Janet a favor by urging the assembled FOMC members to be more constructive and less strident in their public remarks. Public airing of differences was understandable, and even beneficial, when developing new policy tools on the fly in unprecedented circumstances. "It's not surprising that the crew of a ship that sails into uncharted waters might find itself engaged in strenuous debate about how to sail the ship and, even, about where to sail the ship," I said. "Now, if not in sight of land, we are at least nearing known waters . . . [and] I urge you, in your public communication, to consider highlighting areas of common ground in addition to differences." It was a tough sell, I knew, but I owed it to Janet to try.

On the afternoon of January 30, hundreds of Board employees mobbed the ground floor of the Eccles Building atrium to say farewell. The theme of the event was baseball. We ate hot dogs, Cracker Jack, popcorn, and ice cream. But there was no beer. Monetary policy and banking regulation is a sober business. The staff distributed fake baseball cards with my career statistics: 86 FOMC meetings, 79 congressional testimonies, 226 speeches, and two *60 Minutes* interviews.

The next day, my last as chairman, I attended a retirement breakfast for my secretary, Rita Proctor. She had stayed on past her planned retirement date to keep my front office running smoothly. I joked that there should be a new measurement of efficiency called "the Rita." The majority of us could aspire, at most, to operate at a half Rita. I returned to my office and finished packing. Late that afternoon, a little earlier than usual, I walked out the office door—the cameras of assembled press photographers clicking as I walked down the long marble hallway to the wood-paneled elevator. I rode it down to the garage with security agent Bill McAfee and, one last time, was chauffeured home in the Board's heavily armored SUV.

The following Monday, February 3, Janet took the oath of office, administered by Dan Tarullo, now the longest-tenured Board member. That morning, I dressed in a polo shirt and blue jeans, ate breakfast, kissed Anna good-bye, and drove myself to the Brookings Institution, where I had been named Distinguished Fellow in Residence. Assisted by Dave Skidmore, on leave from the Board's Public Affairs Office, I started work on this book. My new office was smaller than the spacious quarters I had left on Friday, but the place had a familiar feel. My old friend Don Kohn was just down the hall.

Looking Back, Looking Forward

I am finishing work on this memoir a little more than a year after leaving the Federal Reserve. Anna and I still live in Washington. The program she founded for urban kids is flourishing. When not consulting or traveling to speak at meetings and conferences, I work on various projects at the Brookings Institution. As always, I follow the economy closely. But it's liberating to read about policy debates knowing that someone else will have to make and defend the tough decisions.

Janet Yellen has moved seamlessly into her new role. After the usual frustrating delays, Stan Fischer was confirmed as Board vice chairman and sworn in on May 28, 2014. He leads a committee that oversees the Fed's work on financial stability. Lael Brainard joined the Board on June 16, and Jay Powell was sworn in to another term the same day. Also in June, Loretta Mester, who had been research director at the Philadelphia Fed, succeeded Sandy Pianalto as president of the Cleveland Fed. In the fall, the three dissenters of 2011—Charlie Plosser, Richard Fisher, and Narayana Kocherlakota—announced their retirements. Charlie and Richard left in March 2015 and Narayana planned to step down in February 2016. Patrick Harker, president of the University of Delaware, was chosen to succeed Charlie. The long and staggered terms of governors and presidents ensure substantial policy continuity, as the Fed's founders intended.

During 2014, Janet continued the policies that she and I put in place. The securities purchases wound down smoothly, without significant financial disruptions or harm to the economy. When the purchases ended in October 2014, the Fed's balance sheet stood at nearly $4.5 trillion. That's a mind-numbingly large sum, but, relative to annual U.S. output of more than $17 trillion, it is similar to the central bank balance sheets of other major industrial countries.

The condition for ending QE3—substantial improvement in the outlook for the labor market—had undisputedly been met. In August 2012, when I foreshadowed QE3 at Jackson Hole, the unemployment rate was 8.1 percent. In October 2014, as the purchases were ending, the unemployment rate was 5.7 percent and headed lower. The economy added nearly 3 million jobs in 2014, the largest annual increase since 1999. Those gains capped a cumulative increase of nearly 10.7 million jobs over the five years from 2010 through 2014.

The Fed's securities purchases and lending programs turned a large profit for the government. The Fed sent almost $100 billion to the Treasury in 2014, another record, bringing remittances during the six years from 2009 on to nearly $470 billion—more than triple the remittances during the six years before the crisis (2001–2006) and nearly $1,500 for each man, woman, and child in the United States.

Short-term interest rates remained at rock bottom early in 2015, consistent with the FOMC policy guidance of the past few years, though markets expected the Committee would finally be able to raise rates from near zero sometime later in the year. Of course, how far and how fast rates would rise depended on the economy. Despite falling unemployment, wages grew slowly in 2014, an indication that the demand for labor was not yet outstripping supply. Consequently, the Fed appeared to have room to keep policy easy, supporting further job growth without risking too-high inflation.

Slow growth of the global economy, together with a stronger dollar, crimped U.S. exports early in 2015, contributing to a first-quarter slowdown in the overall economy. Still, in the United States, positive economic signs abounded. American consumers, whose spending accounts for roughly two-thirds of the economy, were in their best shape in years. Households had reduced their debt, their interest payments were low, and the value of their homes was higher, as was the value of most retirement accounts. A sharp drop in oil prices, from $100 a barrel in July 2014 to around $50 in early 2015, though a problem for U.S. energy producers, provided what amounted to a large tax cut to consumers in the form of lower gasoline and heating oil prices. Consumer confidence, as measured by surveys, had rebounded. Housing, though still weak, had picked up significantly since the recession. And, on average, the fiscal policies of the federal, state, and local governments had moved from restrictive to about neutral, neither supporting nor restraining growth. Inflation remained quite low—below the Fed's 2 percent target, even excluding declining energy and food prices—and seemed likely to remain so for a while. It will be important for the Fed's credibility to show that it is serious about keeping inflation near its 2 percent target. As the world has learned, too little inflation is just as bad as too much inflation.

WE CAN'T KNOW exactly how much of the U.S. recovery can be attributed to monetary policy, since we can only conjecture what might have happened if the Fed had not taken the steps it did. But most evidence, including research inside and outside central banks, finds that unconventional monetary policies—including both quantitative easing and communication about policy plans—promoted economic growth and job creation and reduced the risk of deflation.

One reason to believe that the Fed's policies were effective is that, when compared to the experience of other industrial countries, the recovery in the United States looks particularly good (Figure 4). At the end of 2014, U.S. output of goods and services was more than 8 percent higher than at the end of 2007, the pre-crisis peak. That's not great— only 8 percent total economic growth over seven years (a period including the crisis and the recession). But output in the eurozone at the end of 2014 was still about 1-1/2 percent below its peak. German output, which is about one-third of total eurozone output, was 4 percent above its peak, implying that the rest of the eurozone has done exceptionally

FIGURE 4: Aggressive Monetary Policy Helped the U.S. Economy Recover Faster Than Other Industrial Economies

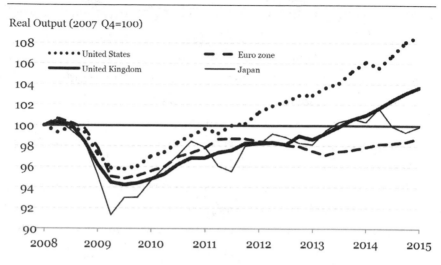

Real Output (2007 Q4=100)

At the end of 2014, U.S. output was more than 8 percent higher than at the end of 2007, the pre-crisis peak. Output in the eurozone was about 1.5 percent below its peak, British output was a bit more than 3 percent above peak, and Japanese output remained slightly below its pre-recession highs. The data begin in 2007 Q4 and continue through the end of 2014. Sources: U.S. Bureau of Economic Analysis, Statistical Office of the European Communities, UK Office of National Statistics, and the Cabinet Office of Japan

poorly. British output was a bit more than 3 percent above peak, and Japanese output remained slightly below its pre-recession highs.

Some of the international variation in the pace of recovery reflects longer-term factors, like differences among countries in labor force growth. But differences in economic policy appear to explain a significant portion of the variation. Though it was the epicenter of the 2007–2009 crisis, the United States has had the strongest recovery because the Fed eased monetary policy more aggressively than did other major central banks, and because U.S. fiscal policy, although a headwind during most of the recovery, was less restrictive than elsewhere. Our 2009 bank stress tests also deserve some credit, since they helped set the U.S. banking system on a path to better health relatively early in the recovery.

The eurozone's poor performance, including an inflation rate well below the European Central Bank's objective, resulted partly from monetary and fiscal policies that were much tighter than demanded by economic conditions. Markets also saw the early rounds of European bank stress tests as less credible than the American stress tests. European policy choices reflected special circumstances, including the debt crises in Greece and other countries, as well as the structural defects of the eurozone, most importantly the lack of coordinated national fiscal policies. But faulty macroeconomic analysis also led to Europe's problems. As Tim Geithner and I had warned, Germany and its allies within the eurozone pushed too hard and too soon for fiscal austerity in countries (including Germany) that did not have near-term fiscal problems, while at the same time resisting unconventional monetary actions (like quantitative easing). The European Central Bank, under Mario Draghi's leadership, finally did implement a large quantitative easing program, but it did not begin until early 2015, almost six years after similar programs were initiated in the United States and the United Kingdom.

Without economic growth, Europe's unemployment worsened. The divergence from the United States is striking. In 2009, at the end of the financial crisis, unemployment was about 10 percent in both the United States and the euro area. But by the end of 2014, eurozone unemployment had risen to about 11-1/4 percent, compared with a decline to less than 6 percent in the United States. And, much more so than in the United States, European unemployment has been concentrated among the young, denying them the opportunity to develop their skills through work experience. A less experienced and less skilled labor force in turn may worsen Europe's longer-term growth prospects.

The United Kingdom and Japan are the intermediate cases. In the United Kingdom, the Bank of England under Mervyn King and Mark Carney generally pursued monetary policies similar to Federal Reserve policies, helping to produce a moderate recovery. That the

United Kingdom did not perform quite as well as the United States likely reflects tighter fiscal policies put in place by Prime Minister David Cameron's Conservative government and the country's close trade ties to the eurozone.

Japan, although better off than Europe, had essentially zero growth from 2007 into 2015, even though the crisis hit Japan's financial sector with less force than it did other industrial countries. Japan's ongoing problems with deflation and poor fundamentals (such as a shrinking labor force) help explain its disappointing performance. However, under Prime Minister Shinzo Abe and central bank governor Haruhiko Kuroda, Japan in 2013 adopted more expansionary policies, including a quantitative easing program that is much bigger, relative to the size of Japan's economy, than anything undertaken by the Federal Reserve. By 2015, the results suggested that Japan had made progress against deflation. To achieve a broader revival, Japan must definitively end its deflation, as well as reform government regulations that protect entrenched interests and block competition in domestic industries such as services, construction, and agriculture.

Emerging-market economies, including China, India, Brazil, Russia, and Mexico, now account for about half the world's output. Emerging markets were also hurt by the crisis, in large part because global trade collapsed. Since the crisis their performance has varied, depending on policy choices and on other factors such as whether the country is an oil exporter. China, for example, recovered relatively quickly from the crisis, in part because of a large fiscal stimulus program in 2009, and is now again focused on longer-term economic reforms. For continued success, China must reduce its dependence on exports and reorient its economy toward producing goods and services for its own people. China also urgently needs to clean up its environment, strengthen its social safety net, improve financial regulation, and reduce corruption. As China's economy matures, its population ages, and it catches up technologically with the West, its growth will slow from its breakneck pace of recent decades, though it should remain high compared with developed countries.

Importantly, after the taper tantrum in 2013, policy changes by the Fed and other major central banks had not stressed the financial systems or economies of emerging markets, at least as of early 2015. And, as we predicted, they were benefiting from the rebound in the U.S. economy as Americans imported more.

THE FEDERAL RESERVE changed substantially during my time as chairman. We became more transparent and more focused on financial stability. At the same time, new threats emerged that could hamper future Fed policymakers' ability to act forcefully to preserve financial stability and support the economy. Our inability to foresee or prevent the crisis, and some of our responses, especially our rescues of AIG and Bear Stearns, hurt the Fed politically and created new risks to its independence.

With Republicans in control of both the House and the Senate after the 2014 elections, three proposals particularly concerned me. Senator Rand Paul of Kentucky had taken up his father's cause and was pushing so-called audit-the-Fed legislation that would give members of Congress the power to order reviews by the Government Accountability Office of the Federal Reserve's monetary policy decisions. If that authority had been in place in the years following the crisis, opponents of our policies could have used GAO investigations as instruments of intimidation and possibly prevented many of the steps we took to help the economy.

Second, a proposal emerged in the House in 2014 that would require Fed policymakers to follow a formula for setting interest rates, such as the one devised by John Taylor of Stanford, rather than independently exercising their judgment. As with audit-the-Fed, the subtext of the bill is the desire of some in Congress to exercise more control over monetary policy. Of course it is Congress's right and responsibility to set the broad goals for monetary policy and to hold the Fed accountable for achieving them. To be truly accountable, however, the FOMC must also be given the flexibility to pursue its mandated goals free of short-term political pressures.

A third proposal, under development in early 2015 by conservative Republican senator David Vitter of Louisiana and liberal Democratic senator Elizabeth Warren of Massachusetts, would place new restrictions on the broad-based Federal Reserve emergency lending facilities that contributed so greatly to arresting the crisis. Significant restrictions were already put on the crisis-fighting powers of the Fed, the FDIC, and the Treasury as part of Dodd-Frank, on the presumption that the FDIC's new authority for winding down failing systemic firms would reduce the need for those powers. However, still further restrictions on the Fed's ability to create broad-based lending programs and to serve as lender of last resort could prove extremely costly in a future crisis.

I hope that the Fed's increased transparency will help it maintain its independence, even as it remains democratically accountable. The Fed now fashions monetary policy within a formal framework that includes a 2 percent inflation objective and a commitment to take a balanced approach whenever its inflation and employment goals conflict. The chair's press conferences, the expanded economic and interest rate projections by FOMC participants, and the lively debate evident in Fed policymakers' speeches continue to provide the Congress, the public, and the markets with considerable information about the Fed's strategy and its rationale. The days of secretive central banking are long gone. Today, the Federal Reserve is not only one of the world's most transparent central banks, it is also one of the most transparent government agencies in Washington.

Transparency matters for markets and for monetary policy, but it also matters in other ways. As chairman, I expanded the Fed's communication with Main Street Americans by appearing on TV shows like *60 Minutes*, by giving a series of university lectures, and by leaving Washington to meet with people from many walks of life. Janet

Yellen—who was raised in a middle-class family in Brooklyn, and who focused her academic studies on the unemployed—has continued this outreach. For example, at her instruction, the Fed created a new advisory council of consumer and community development experts who will make sure that Board members are well informed about Main Street concerns.

Besides leading the Fed to be more transparent, the crisis drove it to restore the preservation of financial stability as a central part of its mission. Maintaining stability requires attention to both the "trees" and the "forest" of the financial system. At the level of the trees, we rethought and strengthened our traditional supervision of banks, using powerful new supervisory tools, such as the annual stress tests of large banks. At the level of the forest, we greatly increased our attention to the stability of the financial system as a whole. Staff members now regularly monitor shadow banking and other parts of the financial system outside the Fed's primary jurisdiction. This more holistic perspective should allow the Fed to identify vulnerabilities and risks that an institution-by-institution approach might miss.

The Fed's understanding and conduct of monetary policy itself changed considerably during my chairmanship. The Fed and other central banks demonstrated that monetary policy can still support economic growth even after short-term rates fall close to zero. The tools we developed, including large-scale securities purchases and communication about the expected path of monetary policy, likely will go back on the shelf when the economy returns to normal. I expect monetary policy once again will consist mostly of changing short-term interest rates and that the Fed's balance sheet will shrink gradually as its securities mature. Still, the unconventional policy tools we developed can be revived if needed.

IN EARLY 2015, the reforms begun with the 2010 Dodd-Frank law and the international Basel III negotiations were well on their way toward full implementation. Taken together, the new rules should create a financial system that is significantly safer. Nevertheless, future financial shocks are inevitable—unless we are prepared to regulate risk taking out of existence and suffer the consequent decline in economic dynamism and growth. The most important post-crisis reforms seek not to eliminate shocks entirely but to increase the financial system's ability to withstand them. These reforms include increased capital and liquidity requirements, especially at the largest banks; elimination of regulatory gaps that left major institutions like AIG effectively unsupervised; more transparent and safer derivatives trading; improved consumer protection; and new authorities that will allow the government to close failing financial firms with less risk to the financial system.

Still, as of early 2015, much remained to be done on the regulatory front. The FDIC, working with the Fed, had made substantial progress in implementing its authority to safely wind down failing, systemically important financial firms. The largest firms have submitted living wills, describing how they could be dismantled if they reached the brink of failure. However, closing a large international financial institution without significant disruption will be a hugely complex task. More work is needed to improve firms' living wills and to coordinate with foreign officials on plans for winding down multinational financial companies.

Runs on short-term funding were a major contributor to the severity of the crisis. Regulators have reduced the risk of runs by requiring banks to hold considerably higher levels of easily sold (liquid) assets. Additionally, bank regulators are considering imposing higher capital requirements on large banks that rely more than their peers on short-term funding. Still, the risk of short-term funding runs has not been eliminated, particularly the risk of runs on nonbank institutions not subject to the new liquidity rules. The Fed and other regulators in early 2015 were considering requiring higher collateral levels for all short-term loans made through the repo market. That would make borrowing in repo markets more costly, but it could also make the loans safer and reduce the risk of runs, no matter who the borrower.

What about the too-big-to-fail problem? Regulators are implementing the basic approach adopted in Dodd-Frank. Large financial firms now face higher capital requirements and more stringent supervision. As a result, managers and shareholders of large firms must decide whether the economic benefits of their size compensate for the extra regulatory burden. General Electric, in April 2015, announced plans to sell off most of its financial division over the next several years. If realized, the restructuring would represent a successful example of tougher regulation encouraging a systemically important firm to break itself up. Additionally, the very existence of the orderly liquidation authority puts the creditors of big financial institutions on notice that they could lose money. That should reduce the ability of supposedly too-big-to-fail institutions to borrow more cheaply than their not-too-big-to-fail rivals. Over time, Congress and regulators should become increasingly comfortable that the largest firms can operate safely, and, if they do fail, that they can be shut down without destabilizing the financial system. If regulators cannot attain that assurance, they should use their authority under existing law to break up or simplify the largest firms.

Although thoroughgoing reform of financial regulation was essential, experience will surely show that not all the new rules offer enough benefits to justify their added regulatory burden. Congress and the regulatory agencies must protect the core reforms. Nevertheless, both should be willing, over time, to modify laws and rules that have proven to be unworkable or that impose heavy burdens with little or no benefit. Regulators will also need to watch for instances of tighter bank regulation driving risky activities into less regulated parts of the financial system.

WE CAN'T SAY exactly when, but eventually the U.S. economy will be growing more normally, with unemployment at its sustainable level and inflation near the Fed's target. Taking into account yet another of Yogi Berra's insights—it's tough to make predictions, especially about the future—what can be said about our country's long-term economic prospects?

Doubtless the U.S. economy faces major challenges. We pay a lot more for education and for health care than most other industrial countries, with results that are not meaningfully better and are often worse. The average age of our population is increasing, which means the proportion of retirees to working people is growing. That increases fiscal pressure on the federal government, which provides Social Security and Medicare to the retired. Political gridlock and dysfunction in turn block sensible spending and tax measures as well as other steps to strengthen growth, such as regulatory reforms, improved education and training, and productivity-improving public investment in infrastructure and technology.

We are not living up to our cherished vision of the United States as a land of opportunity. In part because of deficiencies in education for kindergarten through high school, many Americans lack the skills they need to succeed in a globalized, high-tech economy. Inadequate education and skills are certainly one of the principal reasons for the long-term trends of increasing inequality and the "hollowing out" of our middle class. These trends help explain why many Americans believed, years into the recovery, that the economy remained in recession. Whatever the data said, it still felt like a recession to those unable to benefit from the expanding economy. The Fed can support overall job growth during an economic recovery, but it has no power to address the quality of education, the pace of technological innovation, and other factors that determine if the jobs being created are good jobs with high wages. That's why I often said that monetary policy was not a panacea—we needed Congress to do its part. After the crisis calmed, that help was not forthcoming. When the recovery predictably failed to lift all boats, the Fed often, I believe unfairly, took the criticism.

Despite undeniable problems, I see the United States as one of the most attractive places to live, work, and invest over the next few decades. I'll mention three, of many, reasons for my optimism.

First, our aging society notwithstanding, U.S. demographics look significantly better than in most other industrial countries and even many emerging markets (such as China, which is feeling the effects of its decades-long one-child policy). Our fertility rates are relatively high and, importantly, we welcome more immigrants than other countries. A younger, growing population fuels a more rapid expansion of our workforce and increases economic dynamism, for example, by creating a larger market for high-tech products. I would also guess that the United States, with its relatively flexible labor markets, will prove more successful than many other countries in accommodating older people who want to continue to work.

Second, the United States has maintained its lead in technological innovation, which has become ever more important for economic growth. Most of the world's best research universities are in the United States, and we have become much more adept at commercializing technological advances. Other countries must envy the many high-tech companies that have sprung up near leading universities in areas like Silicon Valley, Kendall Square in Cambridge, Massachusetts, and the Research Triangle in North Carolina. Innovation is not limited to web companies, software apps, and electronic devices like smartphones. For example, new drilling technologies created an oil and gas boom that propelled the United States to the top ranks of energy producers.

Finally, our tradition of entrepreneurship and the dynamism of our markets have proved consistently successful in creating new industries and new products, a pattern that is likely to continue. The size and diversity of the United States leave room for upstarts to challenge existing businesses that have become complacent. Indeed, areas of the country that once lagged economically—my native South, for example—have become vibrant in recent decades, even as some older Rust Belt cities have found ways to revitalize.

These three factors and others make me optimistic. Success is hardly inevitable, however. Good policies are essential. We need, for example, rational immigration policies that are open-handed but also do not discriminate against the most skilled workers, as we do now. Governments must continue to invest—in basic technology, in education, and in infrastructure. Critically, we need to be more flexible in how we help people acquire job skills. Improving education from kindergarten through high school is important, but it is hardly the only way to raise skill levels. We should take a closer look at early childhood education, technical schools, apprenticeship programs, community colleges, adult retraining, and other ways to foster lifelong education. For example, as chairman, I visited an innovative retraining program in Richmond. It was cosponsored by private employers, the state of Virginia, and two community colleges. The colleges trained workers for specific job openings at participating employers, with the employers paying part of the cost. We also must ensure that the decade-old slowdown in the growth of health-care costs continues. And the federal tax code has not been thoroughly overhauled since 1986, and it shows.

REALIZING OUR POTENTIAL as a nation will require a new approach to leadership. Our politicians, and even some of our technocrats, it seems to me, focus too much on defeating ideological opponents and scoring debating points. They focus too little on forging consensus and finding ways for everyone to win by making progress, even imperfect progress, toward shared goals.

I arrived in Washington as a quiet, reserved professor—with a research background that proved to be quite useful in the financial crisis. But I quickly learned that, in both the public and private spheres, how you lead is as important as what you know. I tried to lead in a way that was consistent with my personality and strengths but also appropriate for the situation. As a former academic, I valued collegiality, creativity, and cooperation. I emphasized that policy decisions should be based on open-minded discussion, not the views of only one individual. I tried to foster debate in our meetings and I encouraged creativity—blue-sky thinking. Despite complaints of cacophony, I did not try to prevent Fed policymakers from expressing dissenting views publicly.

The collegial approach had many advantages. Blue-sky thinking led to new ideas; careful discussion winnowed and tested those ideas. Involving everyone from FOMC policymakers to staff members in blue-sky thinking gave each person a stake in making the resulting policies work. Encouraging public debate reassured people outside the Fed that we were considering a wide range of views. The collegial approach built goodwill and trust, which proved vital when events forced me to take action without much or any consultation.

Those times, though, were exceptions rather than the rule. At central banks, credibility—confidence that policymakers will back up their words with deeds—is crucial to effective policymaking. A strong consensus, carefully constructed and patiently sustained, helps build credibility. It usually results in better decisions, based on an assessment of fact that is as objective as possible. That's what I learned about leadership during my time at the Federal Reserve.

These principles should be more broadly applied in Washington. Not all progress is based on collegiality and compromise, of course. Sometimes it's necessary to stand on principle. But it's hard to avoid the conclusion that today we need more cooperation and less confrontation in Washington. If government is to play its vital role in creating a successful economy, we must restore comity, compromise, and openness to evidence. Without that, the American economy will fall tragically short of its extraordinary potential.

ACKNOWLEDGMENTS

This book would not have been possible without the superb editing, writing, and research of Dave Skidmore of the Federal Reserve Board's Office of Public Affairs. Dave, a former Associated Press reporter, took a year's leave from the Board to assist me. His work at the Fed, where he oversaw the preparation of my public remarks and provided sound advice, covered the entire period described in these pages. His dedication to our book project went above and beyond the call of duty. I am very grateful for his hard work and careful attention to every page of the manuscript. I relied on his eye, as a former journalist, for the telling anecdote and the evocative quote. He helped me translate technical economic concepts into terms accessible to a broader readership. He made the book much, much better.

Ever resourceful and always cheerful, Pari Sastry assisted us with outstanding research. After finishing a two-and-a-half-year stint as a research assistant at the Federal Reserve Bank of New York, she delayed her matriculation at law school to work with us. I appreciated her enthusiasm and dedication to building an accurate historical record of the pre-crisis period, the crisis itself, and its aftermath.

For providing a congenial working environment and research support, I would like to thank the Brookings Institution, particularly its president, Strobe Talbott; David Wessel, the director of the Hutchins Center on Fiscal and Monetary Policy; and Ted Gayer, director of the Economic Studies program. David convened a Brookings reading group—including himself, Ted, Liaquat Ahamed, Don Kohn, Louise

Sheiner, and Justin Wolfers—whose members offered many helpful comments. Sarah Holmes, also of the Brookings Institution, provided excellent administrative assistance.

Other friends and colleagues read all or part of the manuscript, and their comments made the book better and more accurate: Tobias Adrian, Scott Alvarez, Bob Barnett, Jeremy Bulow, Bill Dudley, Norman Eisen, Bill English, Gary Gorton, Anil Kashyap, Rick Mishkin, Ananda Rose, and Lars Svensson. I thank each of them without implicating them.

I also appreciate the generosity of former colleagues in sharing their recollections, including Don Kohn, former Board members Sue Bies and Kevin Warsh, Board communications director Michelle Smith, Board congressional relations director Linda Robertson, Tim Clark of the Board's banking supervision division, and former Board consumer affairs director Sandy Braunstein. Board photographer Britt Leckman contributed excellent photos for the book.

Bob Barnett and Michael O'Connor gave me the benefit of their extensive experience in the roles of legal advisers and literary agents. They provided copious advice and support throughout the writing and publishing process.

I am grateful to W. W. Norton, our publisher, and to Norton president Drake McFeely and senior editor Brendan Curry, for comments on the manuscript and for shepherding the project through development and publication. Associate editor Jeff Shreve helped us compile the photos for this book and Rachel Salzman led the publicity efforts. Janet Byrne provided meticulous copyediting. Others at Norton making great contributions behind the scenes included Meredith McGinnis, Bill Rusin, Jeannie Luciano, Louise Brockett, Devon Zahn, and Nancy Palmquist. Thanks also to freelancer Cynthia Colonna for promptly providing interview transcripts.

The essential encouragement and support provided by my family, especially my wife, Anna, will have been evident in these pages. I would like to thank her once more, as well as our adult children, Joel and Alyssa, who—despite busy lives of their own—always find time to call and ask how I am doing.

Finally, to end where the book began, I would like to express my deep appreciation for the work and commitment of my former colleagues at the Federal Reserve. The Board allowed me access to emails and other materials that helped refresh my recollection of the events recounted in this book. More importantly, at a time when many despair of Washington, the Fed continues to demonstrate that economic policy can be made in a manner that is thoughtful, transparent, and collegial as well as in the interest of all Americans.

A NOTE ON SOURCES

This book draws on many sources, including previously unused primary sources (emails, memoranda, and interviews); the author's recollections; contemporaneous public documents, such as speeches, reports, and congressional hearing transcripts; contemporaneous news accounts; published books and articles; and economic data. To conserve space, I have made chapter-by-chapter notes and a selected bibliography available only online; please see www.couragetoactbook.com/. Below I describe some general sources used frequently in the preparation of this book.

Federal Reserve documents

The Federal Reserve's website, www.federalreserve.gov, provides extensive historical information as well as information on current policy.

- For information about the Federal Open Market Committee, minutes of policy meetings, and postmeeting statements, see www.federalreserve.gov/monetarypolicy/fomccalendars.htm. Economic projections by FOMC members appear quarterly as an appendix to the minutes of the meeting for which they are submitted.
- Transcripts of FOMC meetings and supporting materials are released with a five-year lag. Transcripts and other historical materials can be found at www.federalreserve.gov/monetarypolicy/fomc_historical.htm.
- Federal Reserve press releases, including, for example, authorizations of emergency facilities and FOMC statements, can be found at www.federalreserve.gov/newsevents/press/all/2015all.htm.
- Speeches by members of the Board of Governors are at www.federalreserve.gov/newsevents/speech/2015speech.htm. For congressional testimony by Board members, see www.federalreserve.gov/newsevents/testimony/2015testimony.htm.
- The Federal Reserve Board's Monetary Policy Report, available at www.federalreserve.gov/monetarypolicy/mpr_default.htm, is released twice each

year in conjunction with the chairman's testimony to Congress. It reviews economic, financial, and policy developments.

Other public documents

- Transcripts of Senate and House hearings can be found at www.gpo.gov/ fdsys/browse/collection.action?collectionCode=CHRG.
- Material made available by the Financial Crisis Inquiry Commission, including archived interviews and documents, is available at fcic.law.stanford.edu/ report.

Data sources

Unless otherwise stated, data mentioned in the text are as known to policymakers in real time, rather than the finally revised data. Important data sources for this book include:

- The Real Time Data Center of the Federal Reserve Bank of Philadelphia (see www.phil.frb.org/research-and-data/real-time-center). The center compiles initial data releases and subsequent data revisions on key macroeconomic variables such as output, inflation, consumer spending, and employment. Original sources for most macroeconomic data are the Bureau of Economic Analysis (www.bea .gov) and the Bureau of Labor Statistics (www.bls.gov).
- The FRED database, maintained by the Federal Reserve Bank of St. Louis and accessible at research.stlouisfed.org/fred2, provides extensive economic and financial data for the United States and other countries. It also provides users flexible tools for graphing or manipulating data series.
- The Board of Governors provides data on key interest rates in its H.15 release; see www.federalreserve.gov/releases/h15/data.htm. Data about the Fed's balance sheet are provided weekly by the H.4.1 release at www.federalreserve.gov/ releases/h41. Data on commercial paper rates and amounts outstanding come from www.federalreserve.gov/releases/cp. Data on the assets and liabilities of each sector of the U.S. economy come from the Federal Reserve's Financial Accounts of the United States database; see www.federalreserve.gov/releases/ z1. The Federal Reserve's National Information Center is a repository of information on banks' assets and liabilities. For example, assets held by the top fifty bank holding companies can be found at www.ffiec.gov/nicpubweb/nicweb/ top50form.aspx. The Monetary Policy Report to Congress, mentioned above, is also a useful source of data.

- EDGAR, the SEC's database of company accounting reports, includes firm-level data on earnings, capital, assets, and liabilities. See www.sec.gov/edgar .shtml.
- Bloomberg L.P. provides prices of financial assets, including intraday highs and lows for individual stocks, government securities, and other money market instruments.

SELECTED BIBLIOGRAPHY

For a more extensive bibliography, see www.couragetoactbook.com/.

Some key books and articles referenced in the text are listed below:

Ahamed, Liaquat. *Lords of Finance: The Bankers Who Broke the World*. New York: Penguin Press, 2009.

Bagehot, Walter. *Lombard Street: A Description of the Money Market*. New York: Scribner, Armstrong & Co., 1873.

Bair, Sheila. *Bull by the Horns: Fighting to Save Main Street from Wall Street and Wall Street from Itself*. New York: Free Press, 2012.

Bernanke, Ben S. *Essays on the Great Depression*. Princeton, NJ: Princeton University Press, 2000.

———. *The Federal Reserve and the Financial Crisis*. Princeton, NJ, and Oxford: Princeton University Press, 2013.

Cassidy, John. "Anatomy of a Meltdown: Ben Bernanke and the Financial Crisis." *The New Yorker*, December 1, 2008, pp. 48–63.

Financial Crisis Inquiry Commission. *The Financial Crisis Inquiry Report*. Washington, DC: Government Printing Office, 2011.

Friedman, Milton, and Anna J. Schwartz. *A Monetary History of the United States, 1867–1960*. Princeton, NJ: Princeton University Press for the National Bureau of Economic Research, 1963.

Geithner, Timothy F. *Stress Test: Reflections on Financial Crises*. New York: Crown Publishers, 2014.

Gramlich, Edward M. *Subprime Mortgages: America's Latest Boom and Bust*. Washington, DC: Urban Institute Press, 2007.

Greenspan, Alan. *The Age of Turbulence: Adventure in a New World*. New York: Penguin Press, 2008.

Irwin, Neil. *The Alchemists: Three Central Bankers and a World on Fire*. New York: Penguin Press, 2013.

Kaiser, Robert. *Act of Congress: How America's Essential Institution Works, and How It Doesn't*. New York: Knopf, 2013.

Paulson, Henry M., Jr. *On the Brink: Inside the Race to Stop the Collapse of the Global Financial System*. New York: Business Plus, 2010.

Sorkin, Andrew Ross. *Too Big to Fail: The Inside Story of How Wall Street and Washington Fought to Save the Financial System—and Themselves*. New York: Penguin Press, 2010.

Shiller, Robert J. *Irrational Exuberance*. 2nd ed. Princeton, NJ: Princeton University Press, 2005.

Wessel, David. *In Fed We Trust: Ben Bernanke's War on the Great Panic*. New York: Crown Business, 2009.

INDEX